Later Writings
of the Swiss Anabaptists
1529–1592

Anabaptist Texts in Translation

Classics of the Radical Reformation

Dedicated to

Werner O. Packull:

scholar, teacher, colleague, and friend

ANABAPTIST TEXTS IN TRANSLATION

Anabaptist Texts in Translation is a publication series sponsored by the Institute of Anabaptist and Mennonite Studies (IAMS) at Conrad Grebel University College, Waterloo, Ontario, and published in cooperation with Pandora Press. The aim of the series is to provide English-speaking readers with reliable translations of significant Anabaptist texts.

1. *Later Writings by Pilgram Marpeck and his Circle. Volume 1: The Exposé, A Dialogue*, and Marpeck's *Response to Caspar Schwenckfeld*. Trans. Walter Klaassen, Werner Packull, and John Rempel, 1999.

2. *Biblical Concordance of the Swiss Brethren, 1540.* Trans. Gilbert Fast and Galen A. Peters; introduction Joe Springer, ed. C. Arnold Snyder, 2001.

3. *The Earliest Hymns of the* Ausbund: *Some Beautiful Christian Songs Composed and Sung in the Prison at Passau, Published in 1564.* Trans. with introduction by Robert A. Riall, ed. Galen A. Peters, 2003.

4. *Later Writings of the Swiss Anabaptists, 1529-1592.* Trans. H. S. Bender, C. J. Dyck, Abraham Friesen, Leonard Gross, Sydney Penner, Walter Klaassen, C. Arnold Snyder, and J. C. Wenger, ed. C. Arnold Snyder, 2017.

Classics of the Radical Reformation

Classics of the Radical Reformation is an English-language series of Anabaptist and Free Church documents translated and annotated under the direction of the Institute of Mennonite Studies, which is the research agency of the Anabaptist Mennonite Biblical Seminaries, and published by Plough Publishing House.

1. *The Legacy of Michael Sattler.* Trans., ed. John Howard Yoder.
2. *The Writings of Pilgram Marpeck.* Trans., ed. William Klassen and Walter Klaassen.
3. *Anabaptism in Outline: Selected Primary Sources.* Trans., ed. Walter Klaassen.
4. *The Sources of Swiss Anabaptism: The Grebel Letters and Related Documents.* Ed. Leland Harder.
5. *Balthasar Hubmaier: Theologian of Anabaptism.* Ed. H. Wayne Pipkin and John Howard Yoder.
6. *The Writings of Dirk Philips.* Ed. Cornelius J. Dyck, William E. Keeney, and Alvin J. Beachy.
7. *The Anabaptist Writings of David Joris: 1535–1543.* Ed. Gary K. Waite.
8. *The Essential Carlstadt: Fifteen Tracts by Andreas Bodenstein.* Trans., ed. E. J. Furcha.
9. *Peter Riedemann's Hutterite Confession of Faith.* Ed. John J. Friesen.
10. Sources of South German/Austrian Anabaptism. Ed. C. Arnold Snyder, trans. Walter Klaassen, Frank Friesen, and Werner O. Packull.
11. *Confessions of Faith in the Anabaptist Tradition: 1527–1660.* Ed. Karl Koop.
12. *Jörg Maler's Kunstbuch: Writings of the Pilgram Marpeck Circle.* Ed. John D. Rempel.
13. *Later Writings of the Swiss Anabaptists: 1529–1592.* Ed. C. Arnold Snyder.

Later Writings of the Swiss Anabaptists
1529–1592

TRANSLATED BY
Harold S. Bender, C. J. Dyck, Abraham Friesen,
Leonard Gross, Walter Klaassen, Sydney Penner,
C. Arnold Snyder, and J. C. Wenger

EDITED BY
C. Arnold Snyder

PLOUGH PUBLISHING HOUSE

Published by Plough Publishing House
Walden, New York
Robertsbridge, England
Elsmore, Australia
www.plough.com

Plough produces books, a quarterly magazine, and Plough.com to encourage people and help them put their faith into action. We believe Jesus can transform the world and that his teachings and example apply to all aspects of life. At the same time, we seek common ground with all people regardless of their creed.

Plough is the publishing house of the Bruderhof, an international community of families and singles seeking to follow Jesus together. Members of the Bruderhof are committed to a way of radical discipleship in the spirit of the Sermon on the Mount. Inspired by the first church in Jerusalem (Acts 2 and 4), they renounce private property and share everything in common in a life of nonviolence, justice, and service to neighbors near and far. To learn more about the Bruderhof's faith, history, and daily life, see Bruderhof.com. (Views expressed by Plough authors are their own and do not necessarily reflect the position of the Bruderhof.)

Copyright © 2019 by Plough Publishing House
All rights reserved.

ISBN: 978-0-874-86281-2

Library of Congress Cataloging-in-Publication Data

Names: Bender, Harold Stauffer, 1897-1962, translator. | Snyder, C. Arnold, 1946- editor, translator.
Title: Later writings of the Swiss Anabaptists, 1529-1592 / translated by Harold S. Bender, C. J. Dyck, Abraham Friesen, Leonard Gross, Walter Klaassen, Syndey Penner, C. Arnold Snyder and J. C. Wenger. ; edited by C. Arnold Snyder.
Description: Walden, New York : Plough Publishing House, 2019. | Series: Classics of the radical Reformation ; 13 | Originally published: Kitchener, Ontario : Pandora Press, 2017. | Includes bibliographical references and index. | Summary: "Primary sources reveal that despite severe persecution and expulsion, an underground Anabaptist movement continued to flourish in its birthplace, Switzerland"-- Provided by publisher.
Identifiers: LCCN 2019044935 (print) | LCCN 2019044936 (ebook) | ISBN 9780874862812 (paperback) | ISBN 9780874862829 (ebook)
Subjects: LCSH: Anabaptists--Doctrines--Early works to 1800. | Reformation--Switzerland--Sources. | Switzerland--Church history--16th century--Sources.
Classification: LCC BX4933.S9 L38 2019 (print) | LCC BX4933.S9 (ebook) | DDC 230/.43--dc23
LC record available at https://lccn.loc.gov/2019044935
LC ebook record available at https://lccn.loc.gov/2019044936

Table of Contents

Preface ix
List of Illustrations and Abbreviations xi

Introduction
    C. Arnold Snyder 1

I   Martin Weninger, Regarding Church Attendance and Separation
    (before 1535) 16

II Two Writings by Wilhelm Reublin 27
    Confession of Faith, J. Kautz and W. Reublin (1529) 41
    Strasbourg Preachers' Reply 45
    Letter from W. Reublin to Pilgram Marpeck (1531) 48

III Hans Fischer Responds to Questioning (1548) 57

IV Interrogation of Jakob Maler (1553) 68

V Agreement Made by the Brothers and Elders at Strasbourg,
    Assembled because of the Question of
    the Origin of the Flesh of Christ (1555) 76

VI Letter of Zylis and Lemke to Menno Simons,
    Concerning Avoidance [Shunning] (1557) 84

VII The Strasbourg Discipline (1568) 92

VIII [Thomas Meyer], Concerning the Christian Ban
    (before 1575) 100

IX Prefaces to Three "Swiss Brethren" Hymnals 118
    Ein außbundt Schöner geistlicher Lieder (ca. 1555) 130
    Etliche schöne Christliche Geseng (1564) 132
    The *Ausbund* (1583) 135

X Letter to the Magistrates in Bern (1585)	139
XI Introduction to *Codex 628, Berner Burgerbibliothek*	153
XII A Short, Simple Confession	170
XIII Concerning Separation	446
XIV Anabaptist Supplication to the Zurich Magistrates (1589), Andreas Gut	532
Concerning the Anabaptist Supplication, [Johann Rudolf Stumpf]	543
XV Answer from the Swiss Brethren to the Polish [Brethren] (1592)	549
Appendix: Authors and Works Cited and Copied in *Codex 628*	564
Scripture Index	575
Name and Subject Index	589
Translators	608

Preface

The project that led to the *Later Writings of the Swiss Anabaptists* was conceived more than two decades ago, when a sabbatical leave from Conrad Grebel University College in 1993/1994 allowed me to explore some of the historical treasures located in the Staatsarchiv in Zurich. The discovery that Swiss Anabaptist communities in the later decades of the sixteenth century were actively writing, copying and circulating manuscripts of surprising length and sophistication led to the decision to transcribe, translate, and publish some of these little-known and under-studied sources.

Initial encouragement to pursue publication came from Karl Koop and then John Rempel, successive directors of the Classics of Radical Reformation series. The members of the editorial advisory group connected with CRR publications in those days, especially John D. Roth and Gerald Mast, immediately engaged with the project and provided welcome support and very helpful feedback as this proposed translation volume took shape and then ground on, year after year. Likewise, Barb Gingerich and Mary Schertz, dedicated members of the Institute of Mennonite Studies, continued to encourage the completion of the translation project. After all these years of delays and changes, I am very pleased that this volume can be included in the CRR series, now under the leadership of Jamie Pitts of Anabaptist Mennonite Biblical Seminary. Sincere thanks to all involved.

It was clear from the start that completing this volume would require a team of dedicated translators. The task of translating the massive *Codex 628* was taken on by Leonard Gross, Abraham Friesen, Walter Klaassen, and the present writer. This work was completed in fairly timely fashion, but some years would pass before the whole could be annotated, edited and provided with appropriate introductions. Early in the project Sydney Penner, then a young student on his way to graduate work at Oxford and an academic career, collaborated with me on translating some smaller pieces, as part of his summer work at Pandora Press. Most recently, he contributed his expertise in Latin by translating some epigrams that were found (somewhat incongruously) in the 1575 Anabaptist writing on the ban (chapter VIII below). In the late stages of preparation, the translation of the Swiss Brethren answer to the Polish Brethren (chapter XV below) was skillfully emended by Willem de Bakker. There were, in addition, pieces already translated and published that we decided should be updated and re-published as part of this collection. These pieces were translated originally by Harold S. Bender, C. J. Dyck, and J. C. Wenger. Their work is here posthumously and gratefully acknowledged, with added thanks to the *Mennonite Quarterly Review* for allowing the editing and re-publication of these documents.

In the later stages of preparation, as the historical introductions and notations were being prepared, good colleagues and friends James Stayer, John D. Roth, Martin Rothkegel, Karl Koop, and David Neufeld generously read many drafts, most of them far too long, and provided thorough and thoughtful responses, suggestions and corrections. I owe them all more than a simple thank-you can express.

This project has been supported financially along the way. Thanks to the Heritage Historical Library, Aylmer, Ontario, for its financial support in 2003, which allowed the work to move forward. More recently, funds in support of the final publication were generously granted by the Schafer-Friesen Research Fellowship, located at Goshen College, Goshen, Indiana. Thanks are due to Laureen Harder-Gissing, director of the Institute of Anabaptist and Mennonite Studies, Conrad Grebel University College, for her collaboration and support for the inclusion of this volume in the Anabaptist Texts in Translation series. Christian Snyder and Beth MacIntosh of Pandora Press also helped this project through to completion, and Stephen Jones greatly improved the final product with expert editing.

At the beginning of this project two decades ago Werner O. Packull, my departmental colleague at Conrad Grebel University College, was at the peak of his productive years, publishing his monumental *Hutterite Beginnings* in 1995. I learned very much, and continue to learn, from his published work, including the book on Peter Riedemann that he completed with Karin Packull's collaboration in 2007 and published with Pandora Press. Werner was unfailingly generous with his time and expertise, and helped me with this project and others in countless ways. I learned a great deal from the personal conversations and exchanges we enjoyed and took for granted in our days as teaching colleagues. I particularly came to cherish Werner's quiet humor and gentle, irenic spirit. We miss his cheery *Grüss Gott!*, his customary greeting and blessing to us.

This book is dedicated to Werner Packull with the greatest of affection, respect and gratitude. *Gott sei mit dir.*

Arnold Snyder, March 16, 2017

Illustrations and Abbreviations

Illustrations

Codex 628 (1590)	154
The "Simple Confession" (1590)	178
Textual Borrowing in the "Frankenthal" Strand of Manuscripts	180
Textual Relationship between the Simple Confession, Codex 628 (1590) and the Zurich "Simple Confession" (1588)	184
Growth of Marpeck's "Two Swords" Argument for Religious Toleration	188
Concerning Separation: Why We Do Not Attend Their Churches	450

Abbreviations

ARG   *Archiv für Reformationsgeschichte*

CWMS   *The Complete Writings of Menno Simons* (Scottdale, PA: Herald Press, 1956).

Franck, *Chronica*
    Sebastian Franck, *Chronica, Zeitbuch unnd Geschichtsbibel* (Strasbourg, 1531). References will be to the edition published in Ulm, 1536 (photo-reprint, Darmstadt: Wissenschaftliche Buchgesellschaft, 1969).

Frankenthal *Protocoll*
    Protocoll. Das ist / Alle Handlung des Gesprechs zu Franckenthal inn der Churfürstlichen Pfaltz / mit denen so man Widertäuffer nennet / Auff den 28. May angefangen / und den 19 Junij dises 1571 jars geendet.

Hutterite *Chronicle*
    The Chronicle of the Hutterian Brethren, I (Rifton, NY: Plough Publishing House, 1987).

Jecker, *Ketzer-Rebellen-Heilige*
    Hanspeter Jecker, *Ketzer-Rebellen-Heilige. Das Basler Täufertum von 1580-1700* (Liestal: Verlag des Kantons Basel-Landschaft, 1998).

Klaasen and Klassen, *Writings*
> Walter Klaassen and William Klassen, eds., *The Writings of Pilgram Marpeck* (Scottdale, PA: Herald Press, 1978).

Leu and Scheidegger, *Zürcher Täufer*
> Urs B. Leu and Christian Scheidegger, eds., *Die Zürcher Täufer, 1525-1700* (Zurich: Theologischer Verlag, 2007).

LW   *Luther's Works,* American Edition (55 vols.; ed. Jaroslav Pelikan and Helmut T. Lehmann; Philadelphia: Muehlenberg and Fortress, and St. Louis: Concordia, 1955-86).

ME   *Mennonite Encyclopedia*
MGBl   *Mennonitische Geschichtsblätter*
MH   *Mennonitica Helvetica*
MQR   *Mennonite Quarterly Review*

Ottius, *Annales*   Joh. Heinrico Ottius, *Annales Anabaptistici*, (Basel, 1672).

Pipkin and Yoder, *Hubmaier*
> H. Wayne Pipkin and John H. Yoder, eds., *Balthasar Hubmaier* (Scottdale, PA: Herald Press, 1989).

QGT IV   Manfred Krebs, ed., *Quellen zur Geschichte der Täufer, IV, Baden und Pfaltz* (Gütersloh: Bertelsmann Verlag, 1951).

QGT VII   *Quellen zur Geschichte der Täufer, VII Band, Elsass, I. Teil*, eds. M. Krebs and H. G. Rott (Gütersloh: Gütersloher Verlag, 1959).

QGT VIII   *Quellen zur Geschichte der Täufer, VIII Band, Elsass, II. Teil*, eds. M. Krebs and H. G. Rott (Gütersloh: Gütersloher Verlag, 1960).

QGTS I   *Quellen zur Geschichte der Täufer in der Schweiz, I, Zurich*, ed. L. von Muralt and W. Schmid (Zurich: Theologischer Verlag, 1952).

QGTS II   *Quellen zur Geschichte der Täufer in der Schweiz, II, Ostschweiz*, ed. Heinold Fast (Zurich: Theologischer Verlag, 1973).

QGTS III   *Quellen zur Geschichte der Täufer in der Schweiz, III, Aargau, Bern, Solothurn*, ed. Martin Haas (Zurich: Theologischer Verlag, 2008).

QGTS IV   *Quellen zur Geschichte der Täufer in der Schweiz, IV, Drei Täufergespräche in Bern und im Aargau*, ed. Martin Haas (Zurich: Theologischer Verlag, 1974).

Rempel, *Kunstbuch*
> John D. Rempel, ed., *Jörg Maler's Kunstbuch. Writings of the Marpeck Circle* (Kitchener, ON: Pandora Press, 2010).

Roth and Stayer, *Companion*
> John D. Roth and James M. Stayer, eds., *A Companion to Anabaptism and Spiritualism, 1521-1700* (Leiden, Boston: Brill, 2007).

STAZ   Staatsarchiv Zürich

Wolkan, *Lieder*   Rudolf Wolkan, *Die Lieder der Wiedertäufer* (Berlin, 1903; reprint: Nieuwkoop: B. de Graaf, 1965).

Introduction

C. Arnold Snyder

A full century ago, the historian Cornelius Bergmann observed that when the Swiss Anabaptists were faced with renewed attacks in 1585—attacks spearheaded by the Bernese magistrates and supported by Zurich and Basel—they no longer were the relatively helpless and "simple" people they had been sixty years earlier. By 1585 the Anabaptists in Switzerland were employing a wider array of intellectual tools in their defense.[1] Bergmann, who studied the Anabaptist movement in Zurich from its beginnings up to 1660, could make such an observation because he had the benefit of a long-range historical view. Historians of Swiss Anabaptism since Bergmann have, with few exceptions,[2] truncated the investigation of Anabaptism in Switzerland, focusing instead on Swiss Anabaptist *origins* in Zurich and the first five to ten years of its existence.[3] This discussion was initiated by

---

1 "... sie 1585 nicht mehr so hilflos und 'einfältig' vor der Tatsache der Aarauer Beschlüsse standen wie in der ersten Zeit nach den Reformationsjahren." Cornelius Bergmann, *Die Täuferbewegung im Kanton Zürich bis 1660* (Leipzig: Nachfolger, 1916), 61. Bergmann's work has retained its value as one of the few studies of Anabaptism in Switzerland (primarily Zurich) ranging from the beginnings of the movement, into the seventeenth century.

2 One exception is John D. Roth, whose study of Swiss Brethren development carried into the seventeenth century, but did not focus only on Switzerland. "By the end of the century, the Swiss Brethren were not writing systematic theology. But their experience with the disputations had forced them to respond to a series of difficult theological questions—especially those related to the authority of the Old Testament, church discipline, the relationship between faith and works, nonresistance, and the role of the Christian magistrate so that their understandings of these topics were clearly more nuanced than they had been a half-century earlier." John D. Roth, "Marpeck and the Later Swiss Brethren, 1540-1700," in John D. Roth and James M. Stayer, eds., *A Companion to Anabaptism and Spiritualism, 1521-1700* (Leiden: Brill, 2007), 356.

3 Most recently, see Andrea Strübind, "Anabaptism in Switzerland," in Amy Nelson Burnett and Emidio Campi, eds., *A Companion to the Swiss Reformation* (Leiden: Koninklijke Brill, 2016), 389-443. Although the title is promising, the chapter itself is a demonstration of the truncated view of Swiss Anabaptism that has come

Mennonite historians who identified Swiss "founders" of the Anabaptist movement,[1] then dominated in the 1970s by the monogenesis/polygenesis debate[2] and a social-historical reading,[3] and more recently by debate about whether early Swiss Anabaptism should be characterized as a "religious" or a "social" movement, or both.[4]

After detailing the Schleitheim Articles of 1527, most historians of Anabaptism in Switzerland writing in the past century have found less and less to say, particularly about Anabaptist spiritual or religious thought past the 1530s.[5] Robert Friedmann, for example, concluded that the *Ausbund* (the Swiss Brethren hymnal), the *Confessio Thomas von Imbroich*,

---

to dominate the general historical narrative. The story of Anabaptist beginnings in Zurich is told again in copious detail; the historical, theological, and spiritual development of Anabaptism in the Swiss Confederation over the latter part of the century remains unexamined.

1   As, for example, Harold S. Bender, *Conrad Grebel, c. 1498-1526. The Founder of the Swiss Brethren Sometimes Called Anabaptists* (Scottdale, PA: Herald Press, 1950).

2   James Stayer, Klaus Deppermann, and Werner Packull, "From Monogenesis to Polygenesis: The Historical Discussion of Anabaptist Origins," MQR 49 (April 1975), 83-121; Martin Haas, "Der Weg der Täufer in die Absonderung," in Hans-Jürgen Goertz, ed., *Umstrittenes Täufertum, 1525-1975. Neue Forschungen* (Göttingen: Vandenhoeck & Ruprecht, 1977), 50-78.

3   As in Hans-Jürgen Goertz, *The Anabaptists* (London: Routledge, 1996).

4   I am one of the historians guilty of spilling excessive ink on Anabaptist beginnings in Switzerland, arguing that early Swiss Anabaptism must be seen as both a religious and a social movement. See Arnold Snyder, "The Birth and Evolution of Swiss Anabaptism (1520-1530)," MQR 80 (October 2006), 501-645, and the more abbreviated "Swiss Anabaptism: The Beginnings, 1523-1525," in Roth and Stayer, *Companion*, 45-82. My reassessment of the early Swiss Anabaptist story was, in part, in response to the work of Andrea Strübind, *Eifriger als Zwingli: Die frühe Täuferbewegung in der Schweiz* (Berlin: Duncker & Humblot, 2003). See the review of Strübind's work by James M. Stayer, and Strübind's response, in MQR 78 (April 2004), 297-313.

5   This point was already being made in 1959. Hans J. Hillerbrand noted then that "... the time *post* 1533 is the most neglected in sixteenth century Anabaptist history and needs further study.... There has been a tendency to lump together testimonies and Anabaptist confessions from various periods of the sixteenth century." See "Remarkable Interdependencies between Certain Anabaptist Doctrinal Writings," MQR 33 (January 1959), 73. For an example of a truncated description of Swiss Anabaptism, see C. Henry Smith, *The Story of the Mennonites*, fifth edition, revised and enlarged by Cornelius Krahn (Newton, KS: Faith and Life Press, 1981), 3-18.

Introduction 3

the *Dordrecht Confession* of Anabaptists in the Netherlands, and the *Froschauer* Bible were the books that "constituted the spiritual equipment of the brotherhood in Switzerland as far as the records go."[6] Archival findings have allowed modifications to Friedmann's conclusion at this point, particularly since they reveal that Swiss Anabaptists communicated extensively by circulating handwritten writings rather than by circulating printed books.[7] Surviving manuscripts demonstrate that Anabaptists in Switzerland, although lacking "outstanding leaders" as Friedmann said, nevertheless had at their disposal more "spiritual equipment" than was previously thought.

A narrative that describes a Swiss Anabaptism crystallized into final shape in 1527 by the Schleitheim Articles—while partially justified—does not adequately describe the dynamic negotiations and changes in different Anabaptist communities in Switzerland as the decades of the sixteenth century unfolded, and as these communities responded to the changing social, political, and religious realities that surrounded them. Swiss Anabaptism was born and grew within the particular and peculiar contexts provided by the Swiss Reformation as it developed in the various states and territories of the Confederation.

When the Reformation emerged in Swiss lands, it came perilously close to ripping the Confederation apart along confessional lines. It soon came to war, but after the Second Kappel War in 1531, at which Zwingli lost his life, a workable stalemate was negotiated and the Confederation managed to survive. The Protestant states (Zurich, Bern, Basel, Schaffhausen, St. Gallen, Appenzell, and Graubünden [Grisons]) remained, but the expansion of Protestantism ceased; the Catholic states regained some lost ground, but otherwise also had to be content with the status quo. Although the Protestant states all moved to institutionalize a recognizably

---

6 Robert Friedmann, *Mennonite Piety Through the Centuries* (Goshen, IN: Mennonite Historical Society, 1949), 35-36. Friedmann does point out that "it is evident from the hymns which have been preserved, that the inner life of the Swiss brotherhood was much richer than might be supposed on the basis of the above books." Ibid., 36.

7 Even in the earliest period, Hubmaier aside, Swiss Anabaptists did not rely on print to spread their message, but rather relied on personal contacts and the circulation of handwritten sources. See Alejandro Zorzin, "Die Verbreitung Täuferischer Botschaft in der Anfangzeit der Schweizer Brüder," in MH 31 (2008), 11-25.

"Swiss" version of reform by the next century, as independent states each progressed along this path at its own speed and with its own emphases.

The Confederate states continued to meet together to resolve internal and external issues. One of the internal issues on which all the states agreed, regardless of confession, was that the Anabaptist movement was a threat to the political and religious order, and should be prosecuted as such. The rate and intensity of persecution and prosecution varied with the state in question,[8] but thanks to their outlaw status in Switzerland the Anabaptists "never thrived numerically" there.[9] Anabaptism's opportunity for greater political influence had come and gone, it could be argued, with the brief rise and fall of the peasants' resistance in 1525. From that point on, Anabaptists played the role of dissenting religious and social nonconformists, living a semi-underground existence in villages and rural areas, viewed with continual suspicion by the magistrates as possible disturbers of the peace.

That the Anabaptists were virtually all peaceful and pious people, serious about living holy lives in harmony with the biblical witness, was something almost everyone agreed upon. That their religious dissent placed them outside of legal social and political boundaries was not the result of inherently revolutionary impulses, but rather a consequence of the way the Swiss Reformation defined society and the state as a theocracy: necessarily united under one official confession. Religious nonconformity was, by this definition, sedition—that is, a threat to the unified social order.

The process of "confessionalization"—the state's co-optation of the church and its use of the church as an agent of the state—began in earnest in the Protestant Swiss states after 1531 and proceeded to full

---

[8] The Catholic states executed fewer Anabaptists, but then Anabaptists tended not to seek refuge there, with the exception of Solothurn, since prosecution and execution tended to be swift and decisive in those states. According to Claus-Peter Clasen, of the 73 known and probable executions of Anabaptists in Switzerland, "Sixty-one of these 73 executions, or 83%, took place between 1525 and 1539." Close to eighty percent of the recorded Anabaptist executions in Switzerland took place in the Protestant states, with the Catholic states executing only 16 Anabaptists from 1525 to 1618. See Claus-Peter Clasen, "Executions of Anabaptists, 1525-1618. A Research Report," MQR 47 (April 1973), 115-56, *passim*.

[9] J. C. Wenger, *Glimpses of Mennonite History and Doctrine* (Scottdale, PA: Herald Press, 1959), 37.

Introduction

implementation in the next century.[10] In light of the compartmentalization of Protestant and Catholic confessions to their respective states, the baptizing movement proved to be one of the significant impediments to the establishment of religious unity and practice in the Swiss evangelical states, offering a grassroots alternative to official Reformed theology and centralized church reform "from above," and stubbornly refusing to disappear. The confessionalization process followed its own pattern of development within each evangelical state, and so offered different opportunities and limitations to the baptizing communities at different times. There were also different power dynamics between countryside and city in the individual evangelical states. In some territories and states the villages resisted centralized control. In these areas the Anabaptists could survive, protected by family and kinship networks (their *Freundschaft*) that often included local officials charged with policing functions. Anabaptism played a small role within the larger Reformation process, throwing sand in the gears of the church/state machine, but it did play a role—even if that role was primarily contrarian, both theologically and socially.

The conversations (or debates) that took place between the Reformed and the Anabaptists were from the start biblical ones, matters of interpretation and application. As opponents of the move to confessionalization, Anabaptists were called on to justify their resistance to assimilation. Their persistence in presenting biblical arguments over the century did demand and produce responses and biblical arguments in return. The Anabaptist insistence that discipline should be seriously applied in the church pressured the Reformed to continually revisit their decision to lodge social discipline in the hands of the state. Continued Anabaptist criticism of clerical shortcomings prompted the Reformed states to respond with better training and stronger discipline of their clergy. Anabaptist opposition to reading the Old and New Testaments together as

---

10 As noted in Leu and Scheidegger, *Zürcher Täufer*, 99. John D. Roth offers the following definition, after surveying the literature: "the term 'confessionalization' identifies a pattern in early modern Europe in which representatives of the territorial state sought to assert greater control over the daily lives and habits of their subjects by co-opting established forms of religious discipline (confessions, catechisms, visitations, church ordinances, etc.) and by bringing local clergy and religious practices under the authority of a central consistory." John D. Roth, "The Limits of Confessionalization: Social Discipline, the Ban and Political Resistance Among Swiss Anabaptists, 1550-1770," MQR 89 (October 2015), 518, and n. 4.

one unitary covenant attacked the very heart of Reformed theocracy, and formed the basis for Anabaptist refusal to accept baptism as equivalent to circumcision, to taking up arms, or to swearing oaths. In the latter part of the century, sophisticated Anabaptist pleas for freedom of conscience and religion were grounded in a reading of the Testaments as progressively revelatory, and an insistence that Christian conduct should be ruled by the words and life of Jesus, not by "Moses." The story of Anabaptism in Switzerland over the course of the sixteenth century is one of stubborn, principled biblical engagement with larger reforming forces that were moving inexorably towards confessional uniformity.

The primary historical sources relating to later Swiss Anabaptism have remained largely unpublished, and therefore relatively inaccessible.[11] Thankfully, the Anabaptist archival trove in Switzerland is being mined by more and more historians working in individual regions. Hanspeter Jecker has painstakingly documented the story of Anabaptism in Basel into the seventeenth century;[12] Urs Leu and Christian Scheidegger have done the same for Zurich, in somewhat less detail;[13] Martin Haas and Hans Rudolf Lavater have done much the same for Bern.[14] All these historians have been accessing local archives and summarizing their findings on later Swiss Anabaptism in numerous publications. In fact, there are substantial published records

---

11 For an impressive listing of archival sources documenting Anabaptism just in Zurich, see Hans Rudolf Lavater, "'... von mir Hans Müller der Arm, das sich Gott über unß alli erbarm!' Zürcher Täuferakten des 17. Jahrhunderts in der Bayerischen Staatsbibliothek München (Cgm 6083)," MH 32/33 (2009/10), 109-10, especially 110, notes 5 and 6. As Lavater points out, the actual archival deposit relating to Anabaptism in Zurich—particularly for the seventeenth century—goes far beyond what I noted in a preliminary report published in 1995, following a few months of work in the Staatsarchiv, Zürich. See Arnold Snyder, "Research Note: Sources Documenting Anabaptism in Zürich, 1533-1660," MQR 69 (January 1995), 93-99.

12 Hanspeter Jecker, *Ketzer-Rebellen-Heilige. Das Basler Täufertum von 1580-1700* (Liestal: Verlag des Kantons Basel-Landschaft, 1998), is an impressive example of the kind of archival source work that is needed elsewhere.

13 Leu and Scheidegger, *Zürcher Täufer*.

14 See Martin Haas, "Die Berner Täufer in ihrem Schweizerischen Umfeld I: Gesellschaft und Herrschaft," and Hans Rudolf Lavater, "Die Berner Täufer in ihrem schweizerischen Umfeld II," both in Rudolf Dellsperger und Hans Rudolf Lavater, eds., *Die Wahrheit ist untödlich: Berner Täufer in Geschichte und Gegenwart* (Bern: Simowa Verlag, 2007).

Introduction 7

documenting Anabaptism in Schaffhausen, territories around St. Gallen and the Graubünden, Bern, the Aargau and Solothurn, extending the story well beyond the Zurich beginnings and past the 1530s into the 1560s.[15] Sources beyond 1560 usually are available only in local archives.

This present volume of translated Anabaptist sources contains a selection of writings circulating in Swiss Anabaptist communities in the "hidden years," from 1529 to 1592. Although this collection features some interrogations and some short documents that have been translated before, the bulk of the translations published here are of Anabaptist writings for which critical editions or publications in the original German do not exist. In these cases translations were done from transcripts prepared by the present writer from manuscripts (or in some cases, copies of manuscripts) preserved in the archives of Bern and Zurich, where they have remained in relative obscurity.[16] The text that dominates the collection published here, both in terms of length and complexity, is the massive 466-page *Codex 628*, copied in 1590 and containing a wide sampling of material that was circulating in Swiss Brethren circles at the end of the century (Chapters XI, XII, and XIII). Readers of this volume thus have an opportunity to peruse, in translation, some significant archival holdings that document the development of Swiss Anabaptism over the length of the sixteenth century.

The first chapter in this collection contains a small tract written by Martin Weninger, former colleague of Michael Sattler and promoter of separatist Anabaptist teachings in the Schaffhausen, Bern, and Solothurn regions. Although he eventually recanted, his "Regarding Church Attendance and Separation" (ca. 1535) is a lucid defense of Swiss Brethren separatist convictions. This writing was first published many years ago in the *Mennonite Quarterly Review*. The translation by J. C. Wenger has been re-worked and is used here with permission.[17] Chapter

---

15 The four volumes of the *Quellen zur Geschichte der Täufer in der Schweiz* (QGTS) are indispensable. Of course, these published sources still need to be augmented with work in local archives for a full accounting, since the published materials represent just a fraction of relevant documentation.

16 The author prepared transcriptions of the archival originals translated in chapters III, VIII, X, XII, XIII, and XIV. These transcriptions have not been published.

17 Original in QGTS, II, #141, 108-13. English translation by J. C. Wenger, "Martin Weninger's vindication of Anabaptism, 1535," MQR 22 (July 1948), 180-87; edited with permission.

II contains two writings by Wilhelm Reublin, one of the original baptizing leaders joining forces with Conrad Grebel, Felix Mantz, and Michael Sattler. Reublin baptized Balthasar Hubmaier and also worked closely with Pilgram Marpeck in Strasbourg. Although these writings date from an earlier time (1529 and 1531, respectively), they nevertheless provide insight into baptizing currents inside and outside the Swiss Brethren. In a joint confession of faith written in the Strasbourg prison in 1529, Reublin and the spiritualist Jacob Kautz show surprising unanimity of opinion, focusing their criticism on the state church preachers.[18] Such criticism is a noted recurring theme in sixteenth-century Anabaptist writings. By 1531, however, the spiritualist and Swiss Brethren streams had formed separate currents in the Anabaptist stream. In Reublin's letter of 1531 to Pilgram Marpeck, translated by J. C. Wenger and previously published in the *Mennonite Quarterly Review*, we get a rare view, though not a favorable one, of the Austerlitz Brethren, the first of the communal groups that had emerged and begun to flourish in Moravia three years earlier, in 1528.[19] The relationship between the later Marpeck Covenanters, heirs of the Austerlitz Brethren, and the Swiss Brethren becomes important as the sixteenth century progresses. Reublin's letter indicates important beginnings of that relationship.

Chapters III, IV, V, and VI all date from mid-century, a period for which documentation is relatively scarce for the baptizers in Swiss territories and for the Swiss Brethren generally. Chapter III contains a translation of the interrogation and confession of Hans Fischer (1548). His testimony sheds light on the baptizing movement north of Zurich, more than twenty years after the first baptism in that city.[20] Because information for the Zurich region of this period is scarce, Fischer's testimony opens a valuable window into the underground Anabaptist

---

18   Original in QGT VII, #168, 197-99. Translation by the author.
19   Original in C. A. Cornelius: *Geschichte des Münsterischen Aufruhrs. Zweites Buch.* (Leipzig, 1860), 253-59. Published in English as "A Letter from Wilhelm Reublin to Pilgram Marpeck, 1531," translated by J. C. Wenger, MQR 23 (April 1949), 67-75. This translation has been slightly revised and updated, with permission of the publisher.
20   Hans Fischer, Nov. 21, 1548. Interrogation and Confession. Found in STAZ EI 7-2, #94. Transcription by Arnold Snyder; translation by Sydney Penner and Arnold Snyder. Most of this document has since been published in QGTS III, #290, 125-26.

Introduction

world of the Zurich *Unterland*, revealing a little of how it functioned and what beliefs were being defended at mid-century. In 1553, in Toggenburg county, a land ruled by the Abbot of St. Gallen, an uneducated Anabaptist leader named Jakob Maler was arrested and interrogated at some length. This previously untranslated document, found in Chapter IV, provides a small window through which we can observe a "simple" rural Anabaptist leader defend his beliefs.[21]

Chapters V, VI, VII, and XV stem from meetings of Swiss Brethren in the city of Strasbourg in 1555, 1557, 1568, and 1592, respectively. There were six known conferences of Swiss Brethren leaders held in Strasbourg from 1554 to 1607; this volume reproduces the conclusions of four of those six.[22] Although no comprehensive list of participants exists, it is very probable that Swiss Brethren leaders from Switzerland were represented at all of these conferences; they are explicitly named as being present at several of the meetings. The topics and conclusions addressed by these conferences of Swiss Brethren shed light on how the developing supra-regional tradition was dealing with divisive theological issues, and also re-organizing its church practices.

Chapters V and VI address theological and ecclesiological differences between the Swiss Brethren and the Mennonites to the north. The "Agreement" found in Chapter V is an attempt by the Swiss Brethren to come to a position concerning the incarnation of Christ.[23] It is a response to, and a mild rejection of, the "divine flesh" position held by Menno Simons and other followers of Melchior Hoffman in the north. Chapter VI addresses the question of whether persons—especially spouses—who have been banned (disciplined) should also be shunned (avoided altogether)

---

21 A critical edition of this document is found in QGTS II, #391, 309-14 (after June 1, 1553). Translation by Sydney Penner and Arnold Snyder.
22 See John S. Oyer, "The Strasbourg Conferences of the Anabaptists, 1554-1607," MQR 58 (July 1984), 217-29. As Oyer notes, we know of the 1554 conference only because a city scribe claimed it happened; no minutes have survived. The 1607 conference essentially reaffirmed the findings of the 1568 conference. Ibid., 218-19.
23 "Verdragh ghemaeckt by de Broederen en Ousten tot Straesborgh, vergadert van wegen de wetenschap van de herkomst des vlees Christi" (1555), in S. Cramer and F. Pijper, eds., *Bibliotheca Reformatoria Neerlandica* ('s-Gravenhage: Martinus Nijhoff, 1910), 226-28. Translated by the author.

until their full repentance and re-acceptance into the community.[24] The strict practice was defended and promoted by Leenaert Bouwens, Dirk Philips, and Menno Simons in the north. In the letter Zylis and Lemke wrote to Menno, they argued that married persons should not be subjected to shunning, even if one of them has been disciplined with the ban. Menno rejected this milder view and excommunicated all of the Anabaptists who held it.

Chapter VII contains a document from 1568, previously translated by Harold S. Bender. It is interesting for the light it sheds on the development and change in church polity among the Swiss Brethren.[25] Among other things, it is striking how important an authoritative leadership structure has become among the Swiss Brethren of this time, particularly in light of the more egalitarian positions associated with this confessional stream in earlier decades. Chapter XV, chronologically at the end of the collection, stands in line with earlier meetings of Swiss Brethren leaders in Strasbourg.[26] It contains a letter of reply by these leaders to a Socinian (Polish Brethren) overture for union. The only reason we know of this conference is that the "Reply" was translated into Dutch and preserved in a later printed collection of documents. The Swiss Brethren assembled in 1592 make their position on the Trinity and the Incarnation clear, vis-à-vis the Socinian confession presented to them.[27] An increasing sophistication

---

24 Original in Abraham Hulshof, *Gescheidnis van de Doopsgezinden te Straatsburg van 1525-1527* (Amsterdam: J. Clausen, 1905), 226-31. Translated by the author with reference to an unpublished translation by C. J. Dyck, 2005, generously shared by John D. Roth, Goshen College.

25 H. S. Bender, ed., "The Discipline Adopted by the Strasburg Conference of 1568," MQR 1 (January 1927), 57-66. The original document does not carry a title but is simply called an "agreement." It was Bender who gave the name "Discipline" to this document. When the writers refer to it, they call it an *Ordnungsbrief*, or "Letter of Regulations." Slightly edited and published here with permission.

26 "Copye ende Seecker Antwoordt van de Switser broeders ofte Hooghduytschen, alsoo genoemt; Over-gegeven aende Poolsche, betreffende het punct der Menschwordinghe ende der Godheydt Jesu Christi, in *Handelinghe der Vereenigde Vlaemse en Duytsche Doopsgesinde Gemeynten, gehouden tot Haerlem anno 1649 ... met de dry confessien aldaer geapprobeert* (Vlissinghe: Geleyn Jansz, 1666), 74-81. Translated by Cornelius Dyck, with editorial emendations by Willem de Bakker.

27 The Polish Brethren confession to which the Swiss Brethren responded is found in Theodor Wotschke, "Ein dogmatisches Sendschreiben des Unitariers Ostorodt," ARG 12 (1915), 137-54.

Introduction

in the way the Swiss Brethren dealt with Incarnational issues is evident as the conferences progress.

One of the original marks of Anabaptist ecclesiology was the ban or "fraternal admonition." The practice was based on Jesus' words as recorded in Matthew 18. The manner of practicing the ban remained an issue within Anabaptist communities, but the ban itself continued to be a central pillar of Anabaptist church practice. The lack of such a practice was a consistently stated reason for Anabaptist separation from what they called an "undisciplined" state church. Chapter VIII translates a small book "Concerning the Christian Ban" that was written before 1575 and was circulating in handwritten copies, of which three have survived.[28] It appears that this booklet was never printed and is published here for the first time. Swiss Anabaptists clearly continued thinking about the ban and reprising its importance in the last quarter of the sixteenth century.

All Anabaptists composed hymns or, more accurately, they composed texts that they sang to the tunes of common folk songs. These hymns were transmitted orally and in manuscript copies, and eventually made their way into print collections. The Swiss Brethren tradition claims the *Ausbund* (1583), justly famous as the oldest hymnal in continuous use in Christendom; the Old Order Amish still sing selections from the *Ausbund* in their worship services.[29] Although the *Ausbund* and its printed predecessor, "Some Beautiful Christian Songs Composed and Sung in the Prison at Passau" (1564),[30] both say that their hymns were written by "the Swiss" (meaning the Swiss Brethren), that is in fact not strictly true. The core of 50 hymns that were incorporated from "Some Beautiful Christian Songs" into the *Ausbund* were composed around 1536 in the dungeon prison in Passau by communal Philippites fleeing Moravia, not by Swiss

---

28 All three versions of "Vonn dem Christen Ban unnd ußschluß der unghorsammen und bösen menschen von den frummen und glöübigen in der gmein gottes, wie unnd warumb er sölle brucht werdenn" are found in STAZ, sig. EII, 444. They were transcribed and collated by the author; translation by Sydney Penner and Arnold Snyder.

29 The earliest known edition, dated 1583, carries the title *Auβund / Etlicher schöner / Christlicher Geseng....* This first edition contained 131 songs.

30 *Etliche schöne Christliche Geseng* (1564), facsimile print, Mennonite Songbooks, German Series, Vol. 1, general editor Irvin B. Horst (Amsterdam: Frits Knuf, n.d.). In English translation, *The Earliest Hymns of the* Ausbund (Kitchener, ON: Pandora Press, 2003).

Brethren as such. The larger *Ausbund* collection of 1583 incorporated these hymns as well as others from diverse sources, including some non-Anabaptist ones and many from non-Swiss Brethren Anabaptist writers.

The question of who might have put together the eclectic *Ausbund* collection has remained open, but the prefaces to various hymnals contain valuable clues. The printed "Some Beautiful Christian Songs" collection of 1564 has a preface that differs substantially from the preface to the *Ausbund* collection printed some 19 years later. And to complicate the picture, the earliest Anabaptist hymnal to use the word *Ausbund* in its title (ca. 1555) features a third distinct preface.[31] In chapter IX all three prefaces are translated for the first time, so that readers may note differences and similarities in tone and content. It is striking how similar in tone the later *Ausbund* preface is, in its open and nonpartisan approach, to the tolerance-promoting literature circulating among the Swiss Brethren in the 1580s and 1590s. This may provide an important clue to the provenance of the *Ausbund* collection.

The year 1585 marked a turn to more severe action against the Anabaptists in Zurich, Bern, and Basel, with new mandates marking renewed magisterial resolve to stamp out the baptizing movement. Chapter X translates the reply of anonymous Anabaptists to the 1585 Bernese mandate.[32] The letter is directed to the magistrates of that city and argues the case for toleration of Anabaptists as loyal subjects who simply understand Scripture differently. It is a moving apology, although in the end it did not succeed in swaying the magistrates to a milder position.

Chapters XI, XII, and XIII deal with *Codex 628*, a bound manuscript copied in 1590, covering 466 handwritten pages.[33] The Codex is found in the

---

31 "Ein außbundt, Schöner geistlicher Lieder auß dem Alten vnd Newen Testament zu samen getragen, Zu trost den Christgleubigen, mit nothwendigen Concordantzen, Für die einfeltigen einem yeglichen geseng nach zu suchen, Zeugnuß der schrifft" (Cologne, ca. 1555). Thanks to Martin Rothkegel for generously forwarding the basic information and an image of the title page of this book. Also noted in R. Wolkan, *Die Lieder der Wiedertäufer* (Nieuwkoop: de Graaf, 1965), 118, n. 1.

32 Original document in STAZ, EII, 443, 105-110: "Abschrifft der Teüfferen brieff an ein Herschafft zu Bern gesendt den 18. Decemb. Anno 1585." Transcription by Arnold Snyder; translation by Walter Klaassen and Arnold Snyder.

33 "Ein kurtze einfaltige erkanntnuß uff die dryzehen artickell so verlouffens 1572 (sic) Jars zu Franckenthal in der Pfaltz disputiert worden, allen der warheitt begierigen Gottsgeliepten / on fleysch partheyischen hertzen ze erwegen und

Introduction

Burgerbibliothek at Bern; it was transcribed by the author and translated by a team consisting of Leonard Gross, Abraham Friesen, Walter Klaassen, and the author. Chapter XI is introductory, providing an overview of the Codex as a whole in some detail. Chapter XII contains a translation of the first of the two discrete writings that make up the Codex, a writing called "A Short, Simple Confession," of which a much shorter, edited version was submitted to the Zurich authorities in 1588.[34] The "Simple Confession" is a detailed defense of Anabaptist beliefs structured around the 13 points argued at the Frankenthal Disputation of 1571 in the Palatinate.[35]

Chapter XIII is a translation of the second discrete writing contained in *Codex 628*. It is called "Concerning Separation. Why we do not attend preaching at the papal, Lutheran and Zwinglian churches."[36] The only previously known version of this writing is a copy published by Heinrich Bullinger in 1560, as part of his anti-Anabaptist polemic *Der Widertöufferen ursprung*. Bullinger reproduced a tract that appears to have been composed around 1546.[37] The 1590 copy translated in this present collection more than doubles the length of Bullinger's print in an apparent expansion of the original. Our translation identifies the shared and unshared parts of these

---

urtheyllen heimgestellt...," found in *Codex 628* of the Berner Burgerbibliothek. Microfilm copy in the Mennonite Historical Library, Goshen College, Goshen, Indiana, microfilm #203.

34 The "Short, Simple Confession" covers the first 366 pages of *Codex 628*, transcribed by the author. The first half of this writing was translated by Leonard Gross; the second half was translated by Abraham Friesen. A printed edition of the redacted Zurich version of the "Simple Confession" is found in Leu and Scheidegger, *Zürcher Täufer*, 335-402.

35 The Protocol of the Frankenthal debate was published as *Protocoll. Das ist / Alle Handlung des Gesprechs zu Franckenthal inn der Churfürstlichen Pfaltz / mit denen so man Widertäuffer nennet / Auff den 28. May angefangen / und den 19 Junij dises 1571 jars geendet* (Frankenthal, 1571).

36 *Codex 628*, 369-466; transcribed by Arnold Snyder; translated by Arnold Snyder and Walter Klaassen.

37 Heinrich Bullinger, *Der Widertöufferen ursprung/fürgang/Secten...etc.* (Zurich: Christoffel Froschower, 1561; photo-reprint, Leipzig, 1975), 214r-231r. Critical edition in Heinold Fast, ed., QGTS, II, Ostschweiz, 141-65. An English translation of Bullinger's much shorter text was published as "Answer of Some who are called (Ana)Baptists, why they do not attend the Churches," Shem Peachey and Paul Peachey, trans. and ed., MQR 45 (January 1971), 5-32. A new translation of the 1590 copy was prepared.

prints, making it possible to see what the later Anabaptist copyists saw fit to emphasize and highlight some fifty years after the composition of the original tract.

The penultimate writing in the collection is a "Supplication" written in 1589 by the long-time Anabaptist Andreas Gut, presented in chapter XIV.[38] He appealed for toleration yet one more time from the Zurich magistrates. Coming as it does on the heels of the 1588 submission of a shortened version of the "Simple Confession" to the Zurich authorities, and sounding many of the same themes, it appeared that Gut might have had something to do with the 1588 writing.[39] It has now been established, on the basis of an analysis of Gut's handwriting, that he did not personally copy or edit the Zurich version of the "Simple Confession."[40] Its origins have not yet been established. As a kind of footnote to Gut's appeal to the Zurich magistrates, we have appended some notes for a reply from the hand of Johann Rudolf Stumpf, the head of the Zurich church. In those notes the influence of Heinrich Bullinger's line of anti-Anabaptist reasoning can be seen quite clearly.

This collection of writings from Swiss Anabaptists will provide attentive readers new perspectives on the baptizing movement in Switzerland in the last half of the sixteenth century. Obviously there was much more going on among the baptizers in Switzerland than simply repeated defenses of the Schleitheim Articles, although Schleitheim's emphatic separatism is stoutly defended repeatedly in writings throughout the century. At the same time, the documents reveal a separatism increasingly tempered by an evident desire to integrate further with the surrounding world. The appeals to authorities that they tolerate the baptizers as "dissenting loyal subjects" demonstrate a different mentality than do earlier stark calls for abandoning all that does not stand within "the perfection of Christ." The writings published here add more depth and further nuance to the story of

---

38   Found in STAZ, EII, 443, 110v-114. Transcribed and translated by the author.
39   This was Bergmann's mistaken conclusion and my own. Cf. Bergmann, *Täuferbewegung*, 61; Arnold Snyder, "The (Not-so) 'Simple Confession' of the Later Swiss Brethren," MQR 73 (October 1999), 678; 683.
40   See Leu and Scheidegger, *Zürcher Täufer*, 336.

Introduction

the Swiss baptizers of the later sixteenth century, even if they do not begin to answer all the questions one might have.[41]

---

[41] It is my intention to publish a succinct history of Anabaptism in the Swiss territories in the near future, God willing. This work is already well underway, but not yet ready for publication. It will serve as a companion volume to this present collection of sources.

I
Martin Weninger, Regarding Church Attendance and Separation
(Before 1535)[1]

Introduction

Martin Weninger (also known as Ling, Lingky, or Lincki) first appears in the Anabaptist record in a document dated November 18, 1525. The entry reads: "Marthy Ling from Schaffhausen and Michael Sattler from Staufen in the Breisgau are to be released upon the swearing of an oath of loyalty and the payment of costs."[2] This link between Sattler and Weninger remained over the next decade, as Weninger taught and promoted Sattler's Schleitheim ecclesiology in eastern Swiss territories until 1535.

The event that appears to have brought Martin Weninger and Michael Sattler to Zurich was the second public disputation on baptism, held in Zurich from November 6 to 8, 1525.[3] That disputation was declared to have been won by the Zurich preachers. The Zurich authorities declared that those who were baptizing adults, and refusing to have children baptized, were to desist.[4] Those who refused to conform and swear obedience to the authorities were sentenced to an indefinite term in the tower. Conrad Grebel, Felix Mantz, and George Blaurock, who had argued the Anabaptist case publically at the disputation, were sentenced to imprisonment on November 18; Margret Hottinger was also to be placed in prison if she

---

1   Original in QGTS, II, #141, 108-13; English translation by J. C. Wenger, "Martin Weninger's vindication of Anabaptism, 1535," MQR 22 (July 1948), 180-87; edited with permission.
2   QGTS, I, #133, 136.
3   For the following, see C. Arnold Snyder, *The Life and Thought of Michael Sattler* (Scottdale, PA: Herald Press, 1984), 79-83.
4   Testimonies by those concerned in QGTS, I, #120-#124, 120-28.

refused to obey milords. She refused, and was also imprisoned in the tower.⁵

Following these notices of sentencing and imprisonment of the Zurich citizens, the same Zurich court record notes the expulsion and swearing out of the non-citizens Ulrich Teck, Martin Weninger, and Michael Sattler. Of the three, only Teck had a record of previous Anabaptist activity; Weninger and Sattler appear to have been interested and involved bystanders at this point in their lives—but clearly, in the eyes of the authorities, they were interested enough in the movement that it warranted arrest and an expulsion order requiring an oath. Although neither Sattler nor Weninger was prepared to defend the Anabaptist position in November 1525, both would become leaders in the early Swiss Anabaptist movement, with Sattler eventually demonstrating the ultimate commitment of martyrdom as witness to his beliefs—something Weninger would not be able to do.

Michael Sattler, the former Benedictine prior of St. Peter's of the Black Forest, was responsible for framing the Schleitheim Articles in 1527, which gave a strong ethical, pacifist, non-swearing, and separatist direction to the fledgling baptizing movement.⁶ On the verge of emerging as an important leader among the Swiss Anabaptists, he was arrested soon after the Schleitheim gathering (by March 18, 1527⁷), tried, savagely tortured, and executed by fire by the Austrian authorities on May 20, 1527; his wife Margaretha was drowned two days later.⁸

Martin Weninger was a weaver from the Swiss village of Thayngen in the Schaffhausen region of northern Switzerland. He became an Anabaptist and a leader sometime after his November recantation and departure from Zurich in 1525.⁹ He was active in the regions bounded by Basel,¹⁰ Strasbourg, Bern, and Solothurn.¹¹ Given his home territory in the Schaffhausen region,

---

5   QGTS, I, #136, 136.
6   Translation in John H. Yoder, *The Legacy of Michael Sattler* (Scottdale, PA: Herald Press, 1973), 34-43.
7   Snyder, *Life and Thought*, 100.
8   For these events, see Snyder, *Life and Thought*, 100-104.
9   Biographical information from Heinold Fast, QGTS, II, #33, n. 1, 41.
10 QGTS, II, 575, n. 16 places Weninger in Basel in 1529 and 1530.
11 At the time of Weninger's arrest in Schaffhausen, November 1535, the Solothurn authorities reported by letter that he had been in their territory "for a long time" (*ein gutte zytte in unser landtschafftte hin und wider gewandlett...*), QGTS, II,

and his expulsion with Michael Sattler, he was a likely participant at the Schleitheim gathering in 1527; his own Anabaptism certainly was shaped by Schleitheim, as is evident in his later public statements and writings.

In 1532 Weninger emerged as the leading Anabaptist spokesperson at the Zofingen disputation,[12] along with Hans Hotz.[13] As the transcript of the disputation makes clear, Weninger defended an Anabaptist position informed by the Schleitheim Articles, in virtually all of its details, but particularly in his understanding of the separated nature of the "true church."[14] Sometime before 1535 he composed his "Vindication" (*Rechenschaft*) of Anabaptist separation, the document translated below.

In early November 1535, Weninger was arrested with other Anabaptists in Schaffhausen, and was brought to recantation. In his testimony he revealed that he had not been allowed to preach or teach by his community because he had sworn an oath in Baden some two years earlier, that is, around 1533.[15] As part of his sentence he was to publically recant in both Schaffhausen churches, as well as in the church at Schleitheim; the recantations of his fellow imprisoned Anabaptists followed quickly.[16]

Although Weninger did eventually recant, his "Vindication" of separation remains an excellent example of how Schleitheim separatism was shaping Swiss Anabaptist ecclesiology in the mid-1530s. In fact, when the "Vindication" and the Preface to *Etliche schöne Geseng* (1564) are read together, it is evident that they are cut from identical cloth, even down to the sequence of the biblical positions and arguments presented. Weninger's writing, then, provides us with a reference point for a Schleitheim-

---

#152, 120; for his activity in Solothurn, including an arrest in December 1530, and banishment in January 1531, see QGTS, III, #871, #892, #895, #908.

12 For the transcript of the Zofingen disputation, see QGTS, IV, 69-256; short summary in Yoder, *Anabaptism and Reformation*, 102-106; a more detailed description in Snyder, "The Birth and Evolution of Swiss Anabaptism," 501-645, on Zofingen and Weninger in particular, 610-14.

13 For a biographical sketch of Hans Hotz, noting sources, see Snyder, "Birth and Evolution," 611, n. 446.

14 Details reviewed in Snyder, "Birth and Evolution," 612-14.

15 QGTS II, 116.

16 On Weninger's arrest, testimony, and trial, see QGTS, II, 114-20; 123-25, *passim*. His recantation on December 5, 1535 is reported in ibid., #159 and #160, 124-25. See subsequent numbers for recantation reports.

Regarding Church Attendance and Separation 19

influenced, separatist Swiss Anabaptism, against which we can measure changes and modifications in the coming decades. What is outlined by Weninger sometime around 1534 is clearly a "Swiss Brethren" position, as a comparison with later confessions makes clear.

Regarding Church Attendance and Separation[17] (Before November 1535)[18]

I, Martin Weninger, called Lingky, wish the knowledge of and obedience to the will of God, the righteousness which comes from faith in Christ and results in works (Philippians 1[:29ff?], 3[:5-14], Titus 3[:1ff], Hebrews 11[:1ff], James 2[:22]) to all who seek to worship God in the spirit, with their hearts in the truth, and to serve Him with words and works, to His praise in Christ. Amen. (Colossians 3[:16ff], 1 Corinthians 10[:31?]).

Brother Galle Hafner has admonished me to provide an account concerning the church attendance of the children of this world, who walk in the uncleanness of impure lusts just like other heathen (1 Thessalonians 4[:5], 1 Peter 1[:14] and 4[:2ff]). I am inclined to do this in order to show everyone the foundation of the hope that is within me [1 Peter 3:15].

Christ calls us to guard ourselves from the mixed teaching of the Pharisees and the perverted Scripture teachers[19] who wish to be masters of Scripture but don't know what they are setting forth or saying (Matthew 16[:6], 1 Timothy 1[:7]), and teach things that are useless—just as the pastors teach useless things for shameful earnings (Titus 1[:11ff]): lazy bellies, not able to work, all with deceitful minds, just like our [state church] pastors.[20] David says: They teach only sin and glory in their pride and speak vain contradictions (Psalm 59[:13]), just as our [state church] pastors do now, teaching sins and strengthening [people] in sins with their frivolous teaching, as it says in Ezekiel 13[:3], Jeremiah 23[:1ff]. They minimize the harm of the wantonness of the people's life of sin (Jeremiah 8[:11], 6[:14], 2 Peter 2[:1ff]), saying peace where there is no peace and promising freedom to those who blaspheme God with their actions and walk according to the

---

17 Original translation by J.C. Wenger in MQR 22 (July 1948), 180-87; used with permission, and modified for publication here.
18 See QGTS II, 108, n. 1.
19 *Schrifftverkeerten*, recalling the common saying "Die Gelehrten—die Verkehrten" (The learned ones—the perverted [or "screwed up"] ones).
20 We translate *pfaffen* as "[state church] pastors." Wenger chose to translate the term "priests," but the persons Weninger was referring to were Reformed pastors in Swiss Protestant territories, not Catholic priests. "Clerics" or "parsons" would also be possible translations of the term.

lust and desire of their evil hearts (Jeremiah 23[:1ff], 2 Peter 2[:18ff]), and they themselves are servants of corruption and sin (Romans 6[:16ff], John 8[:34]). Those who walk in darkness and have no fellowship with the light of Christ (1 John 1[:6]) are called Christians—even pious Christians and brothers. The apostle of God calls them "children of the Devil" when he says: Whoever does what is right, is of God and has the new birth of the Spirit, but whoever does not do what is right, but commits sin, is of the Devil and not of God, because sin is not of God. Such a one has never known God and also will not see God (1 John 3[:3ff], 3[:6ff], 5[:18ff?] and 3 John 1[:10]). Those who transgress the teaching of Christ have no God (2 John 1[:9]), and all their piety will be worth nothing (Ezekiel 18; 33[:12ff], James 2[:14ff]).

Through such evident witness it is now clear that the teaching of the [state church] pastors is not of God, and does not correspond to the teaching of Christ and the apostles. It is also no wonder that such false apostles and deceptive workers pose as the apostles of Christ. For the Devil, the god and prince of the world himself (2 Corinthians 4[:3ff], John 12[:31], 14[:30], Ephesians 2[:2ff]), poses as an angel of light. It is no wonder that his servants, who draw the wanton people to themselves (2 Peter 2[:14], Jeremiah 23[:1ff]) and strengthen them in their sins so that they are less and less disposed to repent and live (Ezekiel 13[:3ff]), also pose as preachers of righteousness. Their end will be according to their works (2 Corinthians 11[:15]).

Now when such hirelings and shepherds paid a set wage see the wolf coming, they flee and do not lay down their lives for their sheep (John 10[:12]). The little sheep of Christ will not listen to such shepherds [John 10:3]. The foolishness of such shepherds, who come as if from Christ—whether or not He sent them—will be manifested to many in the Free Territories [of Aargau], moved as these shepherds are by the seditious, blood-thirsty spirit which brought destruction in the rebellion of Korah, etc. Also many Zwinglian pastors have returned to the pope in Thurgau,[21] ignoring how it went with those to whom they had promised their lives,

---

21 The common territory of Thurgau, which had undergone Zwinglian reform, began a process of re-Catholicization after the Second Kappel War (1531) between the Protestant and Catholic cantons. Zwingli lost his life in battle during this conflict. QGTS II, 109, n. 11.

and so were found to be liars (Revelation 2[:2]). Those who had not wished to recognize this must now see that it is true.

[The state preachers] teach contrary to Paul (Romans 6[:1ff]) that one cannot be free of sin and live in righteousness. [They say] that one must sin until the grave, and no one is able to keep God's commandments (1 John 3[:3ff], 5[:18]), which is not true. The apostle of God testifies that Christ bore our sins on His back so that we might be without sin and live in righteousness. How can and dare the [state church] pastors say that no one can do what is right and live without sin (John 1[:12ff], 1 Peter 2[:24], 3[:18])? Christ took away our sin and undid the work of the Devil. The work of the Devil that Christ undid is sin, the sin unto death, the death of damnation, as Paul also testifies in Hebrews 2[:14ff] that Christ took the power of eternal death away from the Devil, so that He might deliver us from sin—we who all our lives had been in fear of death and in bondage to sin. As it stands written in Titus 2[:14], He has delivered us from all kinds of unrighteousness. How would He have delivered us from the power and imprisonment of the Devil if we continued to live in sin of the Devil and had not received power, grace for grace, to oppose the Devil with a firm faith in Christ? If we who seek to be righteous through Him were still found to be living in sin, what then would we have received from Christ (Galatians 2[:17])? For He broke the bond and made captivity captive and gave gifts to all humanity, and we have been set free (Psalm 124[:7], 2 Timothy 2[:26], Ephesians 4[:8]). Sinners will not stand in the judgment of God nor remain in the congregation of the righteous (Psalm 1[:5], 5[:5-7]). Sinners will be destroyed together and be wiped out (Psalm 37[:2, 9, 20, 28], 1 Corinthians 6[:9ff], 2 Peter 2[:3ff], Matthew 7[:19], 13[:40-43, 49ff], Luke 13[:5], etc.).

Therefore, woe to the fickle and the sinners, who walk on two streets (Ecclesiastes 2, Luke 16[:13]), and woe to the one bound by and entangled in sin, for in the end such a one will be taken and burned in the fire (4 Esdras 16[:78], John 15[:6]). Now observe how the poor [state church] pastors weaken the passion of Christ and employ it for lasciviousness and a cloak of wickedness (1 Peter 2[:16], Jude 1[:2?]). Peter says: As those who are free, and yet not like those who use freedom to do evil [1 Peter 2:16]. As Paul also admonishes (Galatians 5[:1]): Stand fast in your freedom and do not cast it from you, for its reward is great (Hebrews 10[:35]), for as Jesus Christ has set you free, do not allow yourselves to be joined to the servile

Regarding Church Attendance and Separation

yoke. For where the Spirit of Christ is, there is freedom, and the body is dead for the sake of sin (Romans 8[:10], 2 Corinthians 3[:17]). Whoever does not have the Spirit is not of Christ (Romans 8[:9]). For those who are Christ's have crucified their flesh and destroyed their evil desires by desisting from the lusts of error (Galatians 5[:24], Ephesians 4[:22]). Therefore, since the kingdom of Christ is internal (Luke 7[:21]), firmly within us, we have the grace to do God's will and serve Him, to please Him with discipline and fear (Hebrews 12[:28], Ezekiel 36[: 26ff], 1 John 5).

Since, therefore, we are under grace, sin cannot rule in our mortal bodies (Romans 6[:12]). For this reason did Christ die for all, that all who live should not live unto themselves, nor for their desires, but rather live for Him who died for us and rose from the dead (1 Corinthians 6[:14, 17?], 2 Corinthians 5[:15], 1 Thessalonians 5[:9ff]). We do not shun the light. For whoever is of God, hears God's Word (John 8[:47], 18[:37], 1 John 4[:6]). The [state church] pastors walk and are not in the light, for their works are evil (John 3[:19ff], 7[:7], 8[:12?]). For there is no darkness in light (2 Corinthians 6[:14]). It has no fellowship with darkness. Those who teach others and do not act on it themselves will soon experience the wrath of God (Romans 2[:13, 21ff], Matthew 7[:21], Luke 6[:46ff], Psalm 50[:16-21]). "Lord, we have preached..." But He will say to them: "I know you not. You have done evil (Matthew 7[:22ff]). Depart from me." Christ calls those His brethren who hear God's word and do the will of His Father [Matthew 12:50].

Dear one,[22] how many today are brothers and sisters of Christ, and do God's will? Therefore your fellowship (*gemeinschafft*) is not a brother- and sisterhood (*bruderschafft*) of Christ, for you accept as brothers and sisters adulterers, drunkards, blasphemers, misers, usurers, dancers, carnival masqueraders (*fassnechter*), alley ruffians—all without a ban to distinguish between those who do good or evil. Dear one, why is it so? For this reason: Because the [state church] pastors, who should be disciplining the people, are exactly like the people [they are to discipline] (Hosea 4[:9ff]). Therefore Paul teaches and admonishes us that we should purify ourselves from such people (2 Timothy 2[:21]), for we are not to be in fellowship with the Devil (1 Corinthians 10[:20]). The Devil has fellowship with those who obey him in sin. But he flees from those who

---

22 Reference to the recipient of the writing, probably the state church clergyman Galle Hafner. So John C. Wenger, MQR 22 (July 1948), 184, n. 29.

resist him (James 4[:7], 1 Peter 5[:8ff]). David says: I do not dwell with wanton people, nor have fellowship with hypocrites; I hate the assembly of the wicked (Psalm 26[:4ff]).

Now since they do not preach the teaching of Christ, and do not agree with the saving words of the doctrine of godliness, Paul teaches us that we are to shun them (1 Timothy 6[:3-5], Romans 16[:17]). For it is possible for them to turn many away from the faith, such as Philetus and Hymeneus, of whom Paul teaches us to keep clear (2 Timothy 2[:17]). Do not receive anyone into your house, nor greet anyone, who does not bring the teaching of Christ (2 John 1[:10ff]). Whoever greets such a person has fellowship with that person's evil works. How should I follow him into a temple or to other places when, if he were to follow me, I should have nothing to do with him so as not to have part in his evil works? A teacher should be an example to his flock in love, faith, purity and good works, and care for the sheep (John 10[:4], 1 Timothy 4[:12], 3[:2ff], 2 Timothy 1[:13], Titus 2[:7], 1 Peter 5[:3], Matthew 5[:20?]). This is completely lacking among them, as the Scriptures testify. Who should regard such people as God's apostles, when they lack the witness of an apostle? Now it is evident that the [state church] pastors have neither the doctrine nor the manner of life of apostles, and yet they say they are apostles and that the Lord is with them.

They say that the Gospel is a burden that no one is able to bear, contrary to the words of Jeremiah 23[:38]: You shall not call my Word a burden. For Christ says (Matthew 11[:30]): My yoke is sweet; my burden is light. John testifies: His commandments are not heavy (1 John 5[:3]). And we keep His commandments, and do what is pleasing before Him (1 John 3[:33]). He is the one who has made us acceptable, and who works in us both the willing and the doing (2 Corinthians 5[:5, 18], 3[:5], Philippians 2[:13], Ezekiel 36). He has created and prepared us for good works, so that we may walk in them (Ephesians 2[:10]). Therefore the power and all the glory belong to God alone (2 Corinthians 4[:7]), Daniel 9. Christ teaches us to beware of the deceivers of this world, for if it were possible they would mislead even the elect (Matthew 24[:4], 2 Peter 3[:17]). Paul [was] an apostle of Jesus Christ, sent of God alone, not from men or through men (Galatians 1[:1]). The rulers of the world have elected the [state church] pastors and sent them out for a specific wage. Therefore they are of the world, and the world listens to them (1 John 4[:5]). In this way what Paul prophesied is fulfilled (2 Timothy 4[:3ff]): They will choose teachers for themselves who will tickle their ears, and they will not hear the truth, the saving teaching of Christ, as also now the sect of the Nazarenes is spoken against everywhere (Acts24[:14], 28[:22]). John says [1 John 1:6]: Those who say that they have fellowship with Christ and still walk in darkness, that is, in sin (Ephesians 5[:8ff]), lie and do not speak the truth. Therefore the [state church] pastors tickle their ears with lies in that they attribute to them the name and fellowship of Christ while they nevertheless still walk in darkness. And Paul testifies that He is the cause of salvation for those who obey His will in His death or suffering (Hebrews 5, 1 Thessalonians 5).

Those who hold fast to the beginning of the nature of Christ (as He has imparted His nature in the things of those who are God's, from their youth until the end of their lives)—they are the ones who become a part of Christ (Hebrews 3[:14]). Therefore Christ says: Those who endure to the end (Matthew 10[:22]) will be saved. But not with wrongdoing, rather with doing good, as it says in Ezekiel 18. But those who persist in wrongdoing until the end Christ calls false Christians and false apostles who mislead many (Matthew 24[:4ff]). Paul also testifies: Evil people and seducers will go from bad to worse, misleading others and allowing themselves to be misled (2 Timothy 3[:13]). It is true that they say they know God, and yet they are disobedient and an abomination before God, unfit for all good works (Titus 1[:16], 1 John 1[:6ff], 2[:4]). They are the ones who love the sensual pleasures of the temporal life more than God, have no love of the good, and give the appearance of a godly manner of life, but deny its power (2 Timothy 3[:4ff]). Paul admonishes us to turn away from such a painted-on faith.

Concerning separation read: 2 Corinthians 6[:14ff], Revelation 18[:4], Acts 19[:9], Ephesians 5[:11], 2 Timothy 2[:19ff], 1 Peter 4[:4], John 15[:18ff]. One is to separate oneself from their evil works, and not from the world, insofar as one may keep oneself from being soiled by them (1 Corinthians 5[:10], James 2[:21, 27], 2 Peter 1; 4, Ephesians 4[:17ff]). The preaching of the [state church] pastors, when they testify from the pulpit, is also an unfruitful work. No preaching helps; the more time passes, the worse things get; no one improves. The testimony, that the wrong is getting the upper hand, is also true of the [state church] pastors (Matthew 24[:12]). Just as the Lord said of the time of Lot and Noah, so it is in this land [Luke 17:26-30]; may He come when He will.

Now you have the testimony that the [state church] pastors and Christ and His apostles do not share one teaching. For the pastors speak vain contradictions, as has been noted and adequately proven on the basis of the truth. Paul teaches us to judge spiritual things spiritually, and not according to their appearance (1 Corinthians 2[:12]) and not as the Jews did (John 7[:1]). Those who live and are minded in a carnal way cannot apprehend God's ways or the things of the Spirit. Such things are foolishness and riddles to carnal people; they cannot know them, for they are things that must be judged spiritually. Therefore let all persons see to it that they not judge what is not given to them to judge, and blaspheme (1 Peter 2[:1]) what they do not understand, to their own condemnation and the reward that unrighteousness brings with it.

If something is from God, all humankind cannot bring it down; but if it is not from God, it will disappear of its own accord (Acts 5[:38ff], Matthew 15[:13]). Those of Zurich[23] did not wish to be lords, and it cost them their land. They had to be torn up by the roots; also those from Basel. But look, it is turning green again in their land first. If the Lord had not been with us they would have swallowed us alive, Psalm 124[:2ff], and our bones would be no more. Our shield and protector is God [Psalm 129, 144]. We overcome our enemies through the faith and patience of Christ, following the example of Christ. All glory and honor be to God alone in His congregation (*gemeind*) in Christ Jesus. Amen.

God's seal: 2 Timothy 2[:19].

To do the right thing out of fear of God is pleasing to God (Acts 10[:35] etc.).

---

23 Both Wenger and Fast agree that this reference and the sentences following refer to the nonresistant Swiss Anabaptists, and the persecution they had endured in Swiss territories. Cf. MQR 22 (July 1948), 187, n. 53 and QGTS II, 113, n. 20.

II
Two Writings by Wilhelm Reublin
Confession of Faith by Jacob Kautz
and Wilhelm Reublin (1529);
Letter of Wilhelm Reublin
to Pilgram Marpeck (1531)[1]

INTRODUCTION

Wilhelm Reublin was born around 1480 in Rottenburg on the Neckar.[2] He studied at the University of Freiburg and, for a time, at Tübingen, and began a career as an ordained priest in the parish of Griessen (between Schaffhausen and Waldshut), a post he resigned in 1510. He next appears in the record in 1521, as people's priest of St. Alban's church in Basel, carrying the title of *magister*. In Basel he preached reform to enthusiastic crowds said to number in the thousands. He favored the authority of Scripture and opposed Roman Catholic masses, fasting, and the church hierarchy. By June 1522 the local bishop was successful in having him expelled from the city.[3]

Reublin made his way to the Zurich area and came to reside in the village of Witikon. The residents there (one suspects, at his urging) soon called him as their pastor in December 1522, even though the post was not theirs to fill. The tithe in Witikon was collected by the Great Minster chapter of Zurich; the chapter appointed and paid the Witikon cleric with that local tithe.[4] The Reublin matter, which raised

---

1   C. A. Cornelius, *Geschichte des Münsterischen Aufruhrs. Zweites Buch* (Leipzig, 1860), 253-59. Published in English as "A Letter from Wilhelm Reublin to Pilgram Marpeck, 1531," trans. J. C. Wenger, MQR 23 (April 1949), 67-75. Wenger's translation has been slightly revised and updated with permission, with reference to the original text as printed in C. A. Cornelius.
2   Basic biography in ME, IV, 304-307. More recent and detailed is Peter Bührer, "Wilhelm Reublin: Radikaler Prediger und Täufer," MGBl 65 (2008), 181-232.
3   Many more details on the Basel period in Bührer, "Wilhelm Reublin," 184-87.
4   For this and the following, see Arnold Snyder, "Swiss Anabaptism: The beginnings, 1523-1525," in Roth and Stayer, *Companion*, 51-53.

the question of whether local communities had the right to elect their own pastors, was referred to the Zurich council, and in March 1523, the council allowed Reublin to remain as parish priest in Witikon, as long as the tithe continued to be paid to the Great Minster and Reublin was supported by separate funds raised by the parish. Soon there was resistance in several other rural villages to paying the tithe. The movement was clearly led by Reublin, for he continued to preach against the misuse of the tithe by the wealthy, "stinking," and high-living clergy.[5]

Already early in his path as a reformer, we see some character traits that seem to mark Reublin throughout his life: he was resolutely anti-authoritarian, a persuasive orator, an instigator, something of a rabble-rouser, and quite capable of eliciting immediate popular support—at least for a time. In Witikon, he continued fomenting unrest, next encouraging acts of iconoclasm, all of which contributed to the Council calling a public disputation on the matter of images and the mass.[6] When the Council reserved the decision as to when and how to implement change, Reublin continued to push for radical biblical reform from his pulpit in Witikon, instructing his parishioners that the baptism of infants was not biblical. When several Witikon families refused to bring their newborn children for baptism in the summer of 1524, and Reublin's role in the matter surfaced, he was imprisoned and questioned, and the infants were ordered to be baptized.[7]

Throughout his brief career as the elected pastor of Witikon, Wilhelm Reublin remained at the center of radical biblical agitation for reform, against the established political and religious powers. The themes of his radical preaching, namely local election of pastors by congregations, the un-biblical nature of the tithe, and the idolatrous nature of images, would be echoed in the Peasants' War of 1525, an event in which he would play a small role later, in the village of Hallau. More immediately, his opposition to infant baptism placed him alongside his new friends Conrad Grebel

---

5 See James Stayer, "Reublin and Brötli: The Revolutionary Beginnings of Swiss Anabaptism," in *The Origins and Characteristics of Anabaptism*, Marc Lienhard, ed. (The Hague: Nijhoff, 1977), 83-102.
6 Snyder, "Birth and Evolution," 509-13.
7 QGTS, I, #11, #12, 10-11; Snyder, "Birth and Evolution," 524.

and Felix Mantz, in the middle of an emerging struggle in Zurich and its neighboring towns.

In the fall of 1524, Zwingli held talks concerning infant baptism with Conrad Grebel and Felix Mantz, his former supporters in reform, but they could not come to agreement.[8] A disputation before the Council was called to decide the question, and was held on January 17, 1525. Reublin, Grebel, and Mantz spoke against infant baptism. The result was predictable: Zwingli's defense of infant baptism was declared the winner, and the Council decreed that the Zurich citizens, Grebel and Mantz, were not allowed to agitate further concerning baptism; Wilhelm Reublin and other non-citizens were given eight days to leave the city.[9]

A few days later, probably on the evening of January 21, 1525, the first adult baptisms took place, in defiance of the city's mandates. Although Reublin is not named as a participant (only Grebel, Mantz, and George Blaurock are identified by name in surviving records), it seems inconceivable that he would not have been present and received baptism at this time. He was, in any case, present and a participant in the explosion of adult baptism that began the following day, on January 22, in and around the village of Zollikon, although most of the baptizing was done by Mantz, Blaurock, and Johannes Brötli.[10]

On January 26, a contingent of baptizing leaders moved from Zollikon towards the Schaffhausen region, where peasant unrest was nascent. Reublin and Brötli traveled to the village of Hallau, where they would settle for a time and emerge as village pastors; Grebel would spend the next two months in neighboring Schaffhausen. More importantly, on January 29 Reublin arrived for a two-day stay in Waldshut to continue contacts (already cultivated by Grebel) with Balthasar Hubmaier, reformer of that city.[11] That contact and others bore fruit on April 15, 1525, when Reublin baptized Hubmaier and 60 more persons in Waldshut, with Hubmaier then

---

8   Details in Snyder, "Birth and Evolution," 531-34.
9   Snyder, *Life and Thought*, 69-70; Werner O. Packull, *Hutterite Beginnings* (Baltimore, MD: Johns Hopkins University Press, 1995), 20-22.
10 On events in Zollikon, see Fritz Blanke, *Brothers in Christ*, trans. J. Nordenhaug (Scottdale, PA: Herald Press, 1961).
11 Snyder, "Birth and Evolution," 550-51; "Reublin erntete, was Grebel gesät hatte." Bührer, "Wilhelm Reublin," 197.

baptizing around 300 more people that same Easter season, including most of the city's governing councillors.[12]

By this time Reublin and Brötli had been acclaimed as the pastors of the village of Hallau, where they took over the local church. They would remain in their posts for seven months, during the height of the Peasants' War, until the war turned against the peasants and they were forced to flee. In the meantime, they preached against the "unbiblical" tithe and proceeded to baptize adults in the parish church. Many of the baptized went on to participate in the armed hostilities. In August 1525, the city of Schaffhausen sent troops to arrest the Hallau pastors, but the soldiers were turned back by villagers who faced them down, "weapons in hand."[13]

Following the collapse of the Peasants' War, the baptizing movement changed its mind about two of Reublin's earlier radical biblical themes, and he appears to have modified his position as well. Concerning the tithe, the Anabaptist position remained that *collecting* the tithe was not biblical, but *paying* the tithe to governments who demanded it was what good Christians were bound to do.[14] Anabaptists were law-abiding, tax-paying subjects, not rebels or insurrectionists. In the matter of bearing the sword and engaging in political action, a point on which Reublin's pastoral actions in Hallau and Waldshut spoke volumes,[15] Reublin would soon be associating with the uncompromising pacifist baptizer and separatist, Michael Sattler, and apparently supporting the separatist Schleitheim program. Reublin left no writings from this period that would place him in a resolutely Schleitheimian camp on all points.

Reublin's activities now shifted away from the Schaffhausen, Hallau, Waldshut area to a region bounded by Strasbourg in the west, Esslingen in

---

12 Snyder, "Birth and Evolution," 550-51. According to Hubmaier's later testimony, it was Reublin who was "the instigator of baptism," who came to him repeatedly and eventually convinced him and baptized him. See H. Wayne Pipkin and John H. Yoder, eds., *Balthasar Hubmaier* (Scottdale, PA: Herald Press, 1989), 153. The editors note that Reublin was the first Anabaptist leader to baptize outside the canton of Zurich. Ibid., 153, n. 8.
13 James Stayer, "Reublin and Brötli," 93-98; Snyder, "Swiss Anabaptism: The Beginnings," 69; on the Hallau period, Bührer, "Wilhelm Reublin," 198-200.
14 Snyder, *Life and Thought*, 75.
15 "Reublin and Brötli's actions at Hallau indicate an open, flexible approach to government and the sword in 1525." Snyder, "Swiss Anabaptism: The Beginnings," 69.

the north, and Ulm to the east.[16] By March 1526, Reublin was in Strasbourg, baptizing new members—apparently the first to begin baptizing in that city.[17] He debated baptism with the reformer Wolfgang Capito, who in a letter to Zwingli described him as pious and honorable, but somewhat undependable. Reublin avoided repeated invitations to a public disputation on the subject of baptism and left the city, apparently having started a rumor that "the preachers had yielded to him and accepted Anabaptist doctrine."[18] He soon surfaced in his hometown of Rottenburg and neighboring Horb, establishing Anabaptist congregations in the region.[19]

On February 24, 1527 a gathering led by Michael Sattler took place in the village of Schleitheim which resulted in the adoption of seven articles sometimes called the "Brotherly Union" or the "Schleitheim Articles." Other participants are not known definitively, but Wilhelm Reublin was almost certainly a participant and close to Sattler, because less than a month after the gathering (before March 18) Sattler was arrested in the town of Horb, where he appears to have accepted the pastoral leadership of the congregation which had been founded by Reublin.[20] It is virtually certain that Reublin persuaded Sattler to work in that area. Arrested at Horb along with Sattler were his wife Margaretha, but also Reublin's wife Adelheit and young son, as well as several others. Somehow, Reublin himself managed to "slip away" and escape arrest, while Michael and Margaretha Sattler died martyrs' deaths a few months later at the hands of a Habsburg court, an event recorded and publicized by Reublin himself in a circular letter.[21]

---

16   Bührer, "Wilhelm Reublin," 200ff.
17   So Klaus Deppermann, *Melchior Hoffman: Soziale Unruhen und apokalyptische Visionen im Zeitalter der Reformation* (Goettingen: Vandenhoeck & Ruprecht, 1979), 158. Also Snyder, "Birth and Evolution," 629-30.
18   ME, IV, 395.
19   In a letter to the Strasbourg authorities, Count Joachim von Zollern of Hohenberg reported in 1528 that Reublin was an evil, insurrectionist, deceitful person who had brought and begun Anabaptism in Rottenburg and Horb. *Quellen zur Geschichte der Täufer, VII Band, Elsass, I. Teil*, ed. M. Krebs and H. G. Rott (Gütersloh: Gütersloher Verlag, 1959), #160, 191. Hereafter QGT VII.
20   There is no evidence to support the theory that Reublin was "co-author" of the Schleitheim Articles, as suggested by Bührer, "Wilhelm Reublin," 202.
21   See Snyder, *Life and Thought*, 98; 100-102. Reublin's wife, Adelheit Lemenni, was a citizen of Zurich, for whom Zurich appealed in a letter to Horb, June 19, 1527. QGTS, I, #221, 249. How long she and her infant son were imprisoned is not clear from the record. An archival note, dated after July 17, 1527, says that she and her

Adelheit Reublin appears to have recanted some months later in order to be released from prison.

After the disastrous events in Rottenburg and Horb, Wilhelm Reublin travelled next to Ulm, where he stayed for a time, until in fall 1527 he surfaced in Esslingen, where his sister lived. He was successful in introducing Anabaptism to Esslingen and remained active in the area until 1528, leaving behind a congregation of about 200 members.[22] In his definitive study of Anabaptism in Esslingen, John Oyer says that "Reublin's influence on the new congregation was undoubtedly more formative than that of any other Anabaptist minister."[23] One might expect, then, given Reublin's proximity to Michael Sattler and Schleitheim, that he would champion the Schleitheim Articles as an ecclesiological model, much as Martin Weninger would do in eastern Switzerland. But beyond the common Anabaptist teachings on baptism, the ban, and the Lord's Supper, Reublin does not seem to have stamped his churches with Schleitheim's emphatic separatism. In Esslingen he worked closely with Christoph Freisleben, a follower of Hans Hut, and Hans Leupold, a south German Anabaptist leader, with no evident friction. In practice, Esslingen Anabaptists were flexible about swearing oaths; they often attended public preaching while meeting secretly with other Anabaptist believers, and even did guard duty on the city walls, some carrying weapons.[24] Judging from the practice of his followers, it appears that Reublin's Anabaptism was pragmatic, acquiring specific shape according to circumstances.

---

one-and-a-half year old son were still in prison, and had been there since early March, although Reublin's letter reporting the events of Sattler's trial (after July 17, 1527) notes a general recantation that could include his wife. QGTS, I, #224, 250-53.

22   Bührer, "Wilhelm Reublin," 203-204.
23   John S. Oyer, "Anabaptists in Esslingen: A Viable Congregation under Periodic Siege," in John S. Oyer, *"They Harry the Good People out of the Land." Essays on the Persecution, Survival and Flourishing of Anabaptists and Mennonites*, ed. John D. Roth (Goshen, IN: Mennonite Historical Society, 2000), 191-321; citation, 198-99. For the reformation in Esslingen, see ibid., 195-96. Events in Esslingen are summarized in Snyder, "Birth and Evolution," 620-23; Packull, *Hutterite Beginnings*, 80; 345, n. 26.
24   Snyder, "Birth and Evolution," 620-23.

Reublin's time in Esslingen came to an end in February 1528, when he was flogged out of the city by the authorities.[25] He emerged in Strasbourg again, where now he worked with Jakob Kautz and Hans Bünderlin, both spiritualistically inclined Anabaptists. His ongoing interest in economic justice is visible in Strasbourg as well: the group of Anabaptists he led there met regularly for services and had appointed deacons who collected and distributed goods to the needy. On October 22, 1528, a meeting was interrupted by the police, and Reublin, Kautz, and Fridolin Meyger (Meier) were captured and imprisoned, as was Pilgram Marpeck, who had arrived in Strasbourg in September 1528.[26] Meyger was released on swearing an oath; Marpeck was released, with no comment in the record.[27] Reublin and Kautz remained in the tower, requesting a disputation with the city preachers, a request that was never granted.

On January 15, 1529, Reublin and Kautz presented a joint confession of faith to the authorities.[28] Their confession, translated below, illustrates some basic points of agreement, as of January 1529, between the "Swiss" Anabaptism of Reublin and the "Denkian" Anabaptism of Kautz.[29] Two years earlier, Kautz had posted seven theses on the cathedral door at Worms, an action that eventually got him banned from the city. Some of those articles point to a strong spiritualism underlying his Anabaptism. It was perhaps on some of these points that Reublin disagreed with Kautz, but any points of disagreement were never named. Unfortunately, a longer confessional writing that Kautz and Reublin submitted to the preachers is no longer extant, although a lengthy refutation of that longer writings

---

25 Bührer, "Wilhelm Reublin," 205.
26 QGT VII, #153, 184-86 documents the arrest. Ibid., #155, 188-89 for more on Kautz and Reublin, who were still in the tower on October 26, 1528.
27 Martin Rothkegel concludes that Marpeck had united with the Anabaptist group in Strasbourg that included Kautz and Reublin. Martin Rothkegel, "Pilgram Marpeck and the Fellows of the Covenant: The Short and Fragmentary History of the Rise and Decline of an Anabaptist Denominational Network," MQR 85 (January 2011), 16. Reublin later joined the Austerlitz group that had sent Marpeck to Strasbourg, with disastrous consequences, as his letter to Marpeck (below) reveals.
28 ME, IV, 305-306.
29 Snyder, "Birth and Evolution," 638-39. Reublin stated that he was not in agreement with Kautz "in all points," but the document doesn't clarify what exactly those points were. QGT VII, #167, 195.

still exists.³⁰ Below we will translate some extracts from the preachers' refutation that shed some further light on the positions being held by Kautz and Reublin in 1529.

Sometime before March 16, 1529, Reublin was released from the Strasbourg tower, "sick and lame" and "eternally banished" from the city;³¹ Kautz was expelled a few months later, on November 29, 1529.³² Reublin appears to have gone next to the Zurich area, for a witness reported that he "read and preached" at an inn at Weiningen sometime before April 27, 1529.³³ Kautz eventually ended up in Moravia, where from 1534 to 1542 he served as rector of the Latin schools in Iglau and Olmütz, no longer publicly associating with Anabaptists.³⁴

In the last few months of 1530, Reublin appeared in the Austerlitz community in Moravia, by his own report, still in ill health. According to the Hutterite *Chronicle* (not a friendly source), he was not permitted to teach.³⁵ In the absence of Kilian [Auerbacher],³⁶ one of the community's preachers, Reublin began instructing members of that community in after-dinner Scripture readings. He soon ran into opposition from the community leaders, particularly "old Jacob Wiedemann," who had founded the community. The letter Reublin wrote to Pilgram Marpeck, translated below, gives his side of the story of the events that transpired, as he once again entered into conflict over matters of truth and Scripture, as he saw it.³⁷ The Hutterite *Chronicle*, which considers all participants in the division to have been illegitimate leaders, presents a more hostile view of the events.³⁸ The upshot was a leadership split in

---

30   QGT VII, #170, 200, n. 3 notes the missing long confession; #171, 201-18 contains the refutation.
31   QGT VII, #170, 200, n. 6; #174, 226-227.
32   QGT VII, #196, 250.
33   QGTS, I, #281, 296, n. 3; Bührer, "Wilhelm Reublin," 209.
34   See Martin Rothkegel, "Täufer, Spiritualist, Antitrinitarier und Nikodemit. Jakob Kautz als Schulmeister in Mähren," MGBl 57 (2000), 51-88; Geoffrey Dipple, "The Spiritualist Anabaptists," in Roth and Stayer, *Companion*, 277.
35   Hutterite *Chronicle*, 86.
36   So identified, QGT VII, #240, 300.
37   Rothkegel suggests that with this letter Reublin "tried to win over Marpeck, then a commissioned messenger of the original Austerlitz congregation, to the new group in Auspitz." Martin Rothkegel, "Anabaptism in Moravia and Silesia," in Roth and Stayer, *Companion*, 183.
38   Hutterite *Chronicle*, 87-89.

the community, with Reublin and some three hundred members of the Austerlitz congregation departing to re-settle eventually in the village of Starlitz.

Unfortunately, this was not the beginning of a positive new chapter for Wilhelm Reublin. According to the only account left to us, from the Hutterite *Chronicle*, he was shown to be an unfit teacher, a liar, and "an unfaithful, malicious Ananias." According to the *Chronicle*, a church member visiting from Swabia could not agree with Reublin on an unnamed point of doctrine. Reublin denied that he had said what he was accused of saying, but then was shown to be lying by witnesses. Then he became very ill, and it came to light that he had hidden money of his own for his own use. According to the *Chronicle*, it was at this point that he was expelled from the community he had led.[39]

This expulsion appears to mark the end of Reublin's active involvement as an Anabaptist. After a brief stay in the Horb-Esslingen area in the summer of 1531, he settled in the Moravian village of Znaim, where there was a non-communal Anabaptist presence numbering around 50 persons in 1535.[40] Reublin apparently played no role with the Anabaptists in Znaim; at least, no involvement is documented. Sporatic records from diverse sources give a cloudy picture of his life and religious connections after 1531.[41] He made repeated attempts to return to Switzerland, apparently with no success. In Znaim, Reublin rented a room in the Kaplanhof, administered by the city to provide housing for the minor clergy of the St. Nikolaus parish church. The fact that he paid rent meant he wasn't among the minor clergy. Reublin made his living as a letter courier, and was paid occasionally for writing assignments.[42] In August 1535 he wrote to ask Heinrich Bullinger for help in getting back some of his wife's inheritance (more than 100 pounds) from Zurich.[43] This coincided with Reublin's documented activity as a letter

---

39 Ibid., 90-91.
40 Details which follow are from Martin Rothkegel, "Täufer und ehemalige Täufer in Znaim. Leonhard Freisleben, Wilhelm Reublin und die 'Schweizer' Gemeinde des Tischlers Balthasar," MGBl 58 (2001), 37-70; esp. 50-54.
41 Records in Znaim are available only after 1546, when Reublin would have been at least 62 years old. Rothekegel, "Täufer in Znaim," 50.
42 Ibid.
43 Bührer, "Wilhelm Reublin," 214.

courier between Znaim, Ulm, and Zurich in 1535/36.[44] It is not known if his appeal to Bullinger was successful.

In 1546 Reublin delivered a letter from the Znaim municipal authorities addressed to the Zurich Council, offering religious freedom and six years free of taxes for immigrants. There is no record of a reaction from Zurich to his offer.[45] Martin Rothkegel has unearthed a copy of a letter written in 1547 by Reublin to the government of Zurich.[46] The occasion for the letter was the end of the Schmalkaldic war, which had pitted the forces of the Holy Roman Emperor Charles V against the Protestant Schmalkaldic League. The short war (1546/47) had ended with the defeat of the Protestant forces in April 1547 at the Battle of Mühlberg. In August 1547 Reublin wrote to Zurich, warning the city that he had information that imperial forces were planning to wage a war to bring down the Protestant Swiss cantons. This seemed to be passing on a potentially useful political tip. However, the letter soon turned into a sermon. Reublin called Zurich to repent and advised setting hope on the risen Lord. Then his tone became more stridently anticlerical, recalling the martyred and persecuted prophets and pastors who had once been active in Zurich. The new Reformed clergy were no better than the old Catholic clergy. As Rothkegel notes, the letter demonstrates that although Reublin was in personal contact with Bullinger and others, he had not altered his fundamental assessment of early Reformation events in Zurich; some of his early reforming fire was still present.

In 1554 Reublin applied to live in Basel, offering to do useful work in the hospital, but his appeal was turned down. He also made an attempt to receive his paternal inheritance in Rottenburg in 1559, and even travelled to Augsburg to petition Ferdinand I. Ferdinand—surely unaware of Reublin's true identity—granted the petition in February 1559.[47] By this point Holy Roman Emperor, Ferdinand was the very man who had sought death for Michael and Margaretha Sattler and who had ardently pursued Reublin himself as an arch-heretic in the 1520s and incarcerated his wife and child.

---

44 Rothekegel, "Täufer in Znaim," 51-52 for details.
45 Leu and Scheidegger, *Zürcher Täufer,* 132.
46 A transcript of the letter is reproduced in ibid., 61-64.
47 Packull, *Hutterite Beginnings,* 221, n. 32; Bührer, "Wilhelm Reublin," 219.

Reublin died at an unknown date, apparently of natural causes, close to the age of eighty.[48]

Wilhelm Reublin was an omnipresent figure in early Swiss Anabaptism. The list of his one-time associates reads like an early Anabaptist who's who: Conrad Grebel, Felix Mantz, Balthasar Hubmaier, Michael and Margaretha Sattler, Jacob Kautz, and Pilgram Marpeck, to name just some of his more prominent colleagues. The record shows that Reublin was a peripatetic leader who baptized many and founded a number of important Anabaptist communities. In his letter to Pilgram Marpeck he described himself as having been "commissioned" to "proclaim the Word of God," and in his Anabaptist years he seems to have functioned mostly as an evangelist and church-planter, ready to move on when the situation demanded it. Nevertheless, his leadership promise never seemed to mature or bear the kind of fruit one might have expected.

The historical record and his few writings present a man who was passionate about the evils of social and economic inequality, always ready to engage the weapon of the "word of truth" against those whom he saw as oppressors. He was a persuasive orator, but the outcome was often divisive. One receives the impression of a person who was somewhat abrasive and vehemently sure of the righteousness of his cause, something that led him into repeated conflicts. But the historical record also outlines a man who not only picked his public battles with some care, but developed a talent for living in the shadows and staying out of jail.[49]

During his Anabaptist years, Reublin was passionately committed to adult baptism as the only proper biblical baptism and was also a relentless opponent and critic of the state church preachers. On many other issues that were proving divisive among the Swiss Anabaptists, however, he seems to have been flexible and pragmatic, rather than doctrinaire. On the question of nonresistance, he appears initially not to have tied such a

---

48 Packull, *Hutterite Beginnings*, 220-21.
49 A report from Schaffhausen to Strasbourg, written November 4, 1528 when Reublin was imprisoned in Strasbourg and in response to a query from that city, gives an impression of Reublin's elusiveness. Schaffhausen authorities were well informed of Reublin's widespread activities of preaching and baptizing in and around Hallau, and outline their own efforts to capture him, "dead or alive." They report that in spite of concerted efforts, they were never able to apprehend him. Manfred Krebs, ed., QGT, IV, #406, 417.

position to baptism, for he baptized the non-pacifist Balthasar Hubmaier in 1525 and in the same year was defended by citizens-at-arms when he was pastor at nearby Hallau. Nevertheless, by 1527 he was closely associated with Michael Sattler, the author of the Schleitheim Articles. Sattler insisted on nonresistance, the absolute non-swearing of oaths, and a principled separation from the world for those who had accepted baptism as adults.

The communities subsequently led by Reublin, however, did not follow a strict separatist Schleitheim model, as the practice of the pragmatic Esslingen Anabaptist community demonstrates. Reublin also seemed to personally bridge the growing gap between baptizers and spiritualists that came to an open breach in the 1530s, as his work in Strasbourg and joint confession with Jacob Kautz demonstrates, and in the pre-Jacob Hutter years, he also moved easily between those who retained private property and the Moravian communities who voluntarily shared their goods in common.

Wilhelm Reublin was an Anabaptist leader who never did put down deep roots in one congregation or compose significant writings. Unlike virtually all of his early Anabaptist colleagues, he lived a long life and died a natural death, at the end no longer involved in the Anabaptism he was instrumental in shaping and promoting.

The Writings

The first of the writings translated here, the so-called "confession" by Reublin and Kautz, is not really a full-fledged confession of faith. It deals with only two issues: baptism and the nature of the true church. According to preliminary comments, the authorities had requested a short and pointed writing dealing with just these two issues. Reublin and Kautz first argue against infant baptism and in favor of the baptism of those who have repented, been spiritually reborn, and publically professed faith in Jesus Christ. The second major topic addressed is really a justification for an all-out attack on the state church pastors and preachers for not establishing Christ's church on the basis of adult baptism, or the "right planting" as they say. In the end, the writers say that time is too short to list all the ways in which the state church pastors have failed. There is no mention of time being too short to discuss other theological or ecclesiological issues, such as the Lord's Supper, the ban, the oath, the sword, and so forth. In other words, what has survived from their pen is a very limited "confession of faith."

Reublin and Kautz also wrote a longer defense of their beliefs. It is, unfortunately, no longer extant, but a lengthy refutation by the Strasbourg preachers has survived. Here and there it purports to quote what the co-authors had written. In some cases what the preachers report goes beyond what Reublin and Kautz say in the short written document that we have. As a brief addendum to the translation of the "confession," we will reproduce some of what the Strasbourg preachers report Reublin and Kautz saying in the lost writing.

Perhaps the most interesting addendum is the report that the authors hold that there are two churches, one invisible and the other visible. The "inner" nature of the church continues to appear as a Reublin/Kautz theme throughout the preachers' refutation, as in the "inner" calling of true shepherds. This "inner" emphasis probably reflects Kautz's influence more than Reublin's, but such spiritualist notes are not absent in Reublin's documented writings. The preachers also note that Reublin and Kautz maintain that the church must be sustained by preaching (admonition), the Lord's Supper, and the ban.[50] Finally, the preachers' writing draws out the implications of the Reublin/Kautz description of the true church, saying that if what they say were true, Christians would exist only in Anabaptist gatherings—a conclusion they emphatically reject.

The second writing translated below, Wilhelm Reublin's letter of complaint to Pilgram Marpeck, is a fascinating glimpse into the group dynamics of the Austerlitz community in Moravia that was instituting an early (pre-Hutterite) experiment in communal living. It was this community that had sent out Pilgram Marpeck as a representative to Strasbourg. It is clear that Reublin had grown close to Marpeck in Strasbourg and that he felt at home in this Moravian community—at least among its rank and file—but it is equally clear that he was marching to the beat of his own drummer. The evidence points to a strong authoritarian leadership at Austerlitz. Reublin's resistance to authority surfaced here again, this time bridling at the limitations imposed by an Anabaptist leadership. His listing of the failings of the Austerlitz leadership is fascinating, but one is not sure how to read between the lines or how exactly to interpret the accusations.

---

50 Exactly matching the three *notae ecclesiae* emphasized by Balthasar Hubmaier in Nikolsburg. Rothkegel, "Anabaptism in Moravia and Silesia," 170.

This letter provides an intimate glimpse into how forceful personalities leading Anabaptist groups could and did break those groups apart, always ostensibly because of disagreements over biblical principles.[51] Sadly, this historical circumstance would repeat itself countless times in the history of Anabaptist descendants.

---

51 Werner Packull's detailing of the Moravian schisms is definitive. See *Hutterite Beginnings*, chapter 9.

A Brief, Written Confession of Faith of Jakob Kautz and Wilhelm Reublin, Submitted to the Strasbourg Council[52]
(January 15, 1529)

Greeting, etc. On January fifth of the year 1529 your graces informed us at length, through the noble and wise lord, squire Johann Sturm and lord Francis, druggist, that we should let your graces understand in writing, in the briefest way possible, but in its essentials, first, what we believe concerning rebaptism, as you call it, for which reason we are imprisoned; secondly, what has moved us to compare your graces' preachers to incapable, unskilled builders, who only know how to tear things down but not how to build things up, etc. With the following, gracious lords, you have our answer.

What we have taught and believe concerning the baptism of believers (and we know of no other baptism) we are now and have long since been ready to bring to the light to many, with holy Scripture. But until this day it has not been possible to find the light or the truth, either because we are not the ones through whom God, the Lord of the world, will make the truth known, or because the world, as a despiser of light and truth, is not worthy of it.

But, gracious lords, our undertaking will not excuse or blame anyone, for the following reasons. First, because we are aware that we are somewhat lacking and, because of the dangers connected with all judgments, we would like very much to be excused. Second, because we are in darkness, you are in the light; we are imprisoned, you are free; we are falsely slandered and despised, you are imperfect and, as one sees, powerful. Therefore, we insignificant and pious ones must suffer for our accusation, although [our accusation] is true. For the bitter truth, through no fault of its own, always brings hate to bear on one's back. Third, that following the command of our eternal master Christ, we wish to free those from whom we earlier had made requests in vain, insofar as it is not against God. So it is our humble request that we be released from this matter for the indicated reasons. But since your graces will have it this way and no other way, we

---

52 Original in QGT VII, #168, 197-99.

have demonstrated our obedience by giving our answer in two points, as briefly as possible.

In the first place, we freely and openly confess before God and the entire world, that for a long time we did not honor God, as if He lay unrevealed, and we led a heathenish life along with other heathens. But by the mercy of God, out of grace through his sent Word, we were called away from the Devil, whose servants we were, to Him, and away from the darkness in which we lived, to His wondrous light. We did not fail to have faith in the heavenly message, but rather we made a covenant with God in our hearts, to serve him henceforth in holiness all the days of our lives, by his power, and to disclose what we had received [in the spirit] to our covenant partners [*bundtsgenossen*].[53]

By the reception of water baptism, we also allowed ourselves to become members of the body of which Christ is the head, as the Scriptures say [Colossians 1:18]. And the power of baptism in water follows immediately, for as soon as we begin to admonish the unrighteousness of the world, out of love, and also when we draw away from the abominations of the world by the power of baptism, we are despised by the world along with our head, Christ (as can be clearly seen today), and are hunted down from one city to the next. Where the holy cross has driven us, like the wind drives a ship on the sea, we have helped others as much as possible, as is the nature of love, which is disposed that way. And when it comes, the goodness of God falls upon us out of grace and also proclaims the way to salvation through Christ, which is true yieldedness [*gelasenheit*]. And we baptize those who have given themselves to God in the same measure as we have, on their request, and not on our own [authority], but rather on the basis of Christ's strong command, which says: "Go forth, teach all peoples, baptizing them in the name of the Father, the Son, etc., teaching them to keep what I have commanded," etc. [Matthew 28: 19-20].

---

53 According to Martin Rothkegel, this is the first known appearance of what would become a term of self-identification for members of the Marpeck group and the Austerlitz Brethren. He notes that "Kautz and Reublin then belonged to the group of Strasbourg Anabaptists with whom Marpeck had achieved spiritual unity." Martin Rothkegel, "Pilgram Marpeck and the Fellows of the Covenant: The Short and Fragmentary History of the Rise and Decline of an Anabaptist Denominational Network," MQR 85 (January 2011), 16.

From these words it can be amply ascertained what we maintain about water baptism, namely that it is an inscribing of believers into the outer community of God. Also [we learn] who should be included by baptism at their own request and not excluded, namely those who have heard the word of repentance and have accepted it in their hearts. In such a way Peter baptized those who gladly accepted his word; Philip first proclaimed the faith to the circumcised, and afterwards baptized them. For a confessed faith is the wine from which baptism always follows, as the hoop or sign in front of the inn [*keller*] gives notice of the wine inside; [the sign] never precedes, but always follows. For how would it be if someone erected a hoop while the grapes still stood on the staves, and could just as easily spoil as be bottled?

From this it is clear that infant baptism is not the command of Christ, for it is not known who among [the children] is an Esau or a Jacob, a believer or an unbeliever, concerning which a true servant of Christ should question [someone coming for baptism] as much and thoroughly as possible, as did Peter, Philip and Paul. Otherwise one is not following the command of the Lord, who commanded that believers be baptized: Matthew 28[:19], Mark 16[:16]. Whoever requires more evidence concerning this, let him read the sixth chapter of Romans 6[:3ff.]; if he takes it to hand, he will see that we have spoken the truth. Also Acts 2[:38], 8[:12f.], 9[:18f.], 10[:47f.], 16[:31ff.], 18[:8], 19[:2ff.], 22[:12ff.] etc. In the Acts of the Apostles it is clear that in the time of the Apostles newborn infants were not baptized as they are today, but rather only the instructed believers, for the command of Christ sufficed. So much concerning baptism, which we have brought to the light for those who demanded that we give a further accounting, with a refutation of the opponent's argument with which they are disposed to defend the groundless infant baptism.

In the second place you should know, gracious lords, that it is our daily experience that your gracious lords' preachers can justly be compared to incapable, unskilled builders, able only to destroy much and build up nothing. For as is known, only five or six years ago they broke away from the pope's community together with the signs of their duty, namely baptism and the Supper—and not unjustly—but until this day they have not gathered together a community according to Christ's ordering, much less built one up. In observing the right planting of baptism and the Supper, we see that they are misused in the same way [by the preachers] as they were by the pope.

It is therefore no wonder that we suspect that [your preachers'] calling is not heavenly, from God, but rather earthly, from men. We had much more to point out about their failings (truly not for our sake), but the brevity of your request and our carrying it out did not allow it. Therefore it will have to wait until its appointed time. God will do as He wishes. That [the preachers] together with all people be converted to Him, to an eternal, unsurmountable reward, is something we desire from the heart. Amen.

In conclusion, gracious lords, if anyone thinks that we have treated him unfairly [*thuen im zu kurtz*], let him punish us by demonstrating the truth and doing it, and not only with words, as is the custom. If that were to happen we would be ready to recant to him. Would to God that we were punished with an eye on the truth, as with a similar mind we wish to confess that they have done us an injustice! But unfortunately, it is all in vain. We have gone to a lot of trouble for such things to have befallen us, etc.

Given in the tower, the 15th of January, 1529, the 86th day of our captivity.

Jacob Kutz [Kautz] and Wilhelm Rebly [Reublin], bound by Jesus Christ and according to the flesh because of your graces.[54]

---

54 The apparent meaning is "bound by obedience to Christ's will, and physically imprisoned because of you, the magistrates."

The Strasbourg Preachers to the Council.[55] Reply to the Second Writing that Jakob Kautz and Wilhelm Reublin Directed against Them
[No Longer Extant]
(January 23, 1529)

Excerpts

On the inner, invisible church and the outer, visible church[56]

In the first place, the afore-mentioned Kautz and Reublin claim that Scripture gives notice of two communities or churches, the one an inner and invisible [church], which is bound to no city, time, or person, gathered together with no human intervention, concerning which Christ has commanded nothing to his own. And the other an outer, visible [church] whose dimension, manner and ordering has been taught by Christ and put into practice by the apostles, and how they are both to be gathered and maintained.[57]

---

55 "[1529] Januar 23. Die Straßburger Prädikanten an den Rat. Entgegnung auf die von Jakob Kautz und Wilhelm Reublin gegen sie eingereichte zweite Schrift." QGT VII, #171, 201-18.

56 These are themes that resonate strongly with several of Kautz's seven theses posted in Worms in 1527. "1. The word that we speak externally with the mouth, hear with human ears, write and print with human hands, is not the life-giving, true or eternally abiding Word of God, but rather only a testimony or indication of the inner, with which the outer sufficiently corresponds. 2. Nothing external, be it word or sign, sacrament or promise, is the [actual] power that is able to insure, comfort and assure the inner person.... 7. Just as Adam's outer bite into the forbidden fruit harmed neither him nor those who descended from him, as long as the inner acceptance [of that bite] remained unfulfilled, so also is the physical suffering of Jesus Christ not the true Satisfaction or Atonement to the Father without inner obedience and the highest desire to obey the eternal will of God. No one should judge these articles except that one alone who speaks and testifies in all human hearts, as the Scripture says. The reason: No human being is commanded by God to judge the truth, rather only to give witness to the truth." Original in Christian Hege, *Die Täufer in der Kurpfalz: ein Beitrag zur badischpfälzischen Reformationsgeschichte* (Frankfurt am Main: Kommissionsverlag von Hermann Minjon, 1908), 35-37, *passim*; translation by the author.

57 Ibid., 201.

[The preachers appear to cite, verbatim, a passage that they say they cannot understand. The passage appears to be a condensed spiritualist argument against coercion in matters of faith: since the "outer" church only serves to point to the inner movement of God's Spirit in the true, spiritual church, coercion in outer things accomplishes nothing.]

The words which we cannot understand are these: "In the second place, Scripture speaks of a second, outer, sensory [*entpfintliche*] and visible church, the first material object [*gegenwurff*] that God wishes to have, both Jews and gentiles, when they don't pay heed to the movement of the spirit in their hearts. It is exactly the way in which an outer guide or sign first brings knowledge of themselves, and then afterwards inwardly, to a knowledge of His eternal goodness and will. For this reason, coercion is against the church's nature and property." Thus far Kautz and Reublin's words.[58]

How the church of Christ is to be gathered together

Now Kautz and his people maintain that in order to gather together a church, the following is necessary: first, a shepherd whose call is heavenly, from God, and not earthly, from men; who also is bound to no city or person or element; who goes into all the world to gather together the scattered sheep from among both Jews and Gentiles. After which he will preach the Gospel and afterwards [administer] outward baptism to those who have heard and accepted [the Gospel]. To maintain the church they say there must be admonition [i.e., preaching of the Word], breaking of bread, and the ban.[59]

In the third place, Kautz and his people make baptism so necessary to the gathering together of the church—baptism following the heard and accepted preaching of the Gospel—that wherever that exact order is not accepted and respected as correct, the gathering together of the church is completely hindered, Christ is made a liar and the apostles seducers, Scripture is falsified, the commands of Christ torn apart, which public falsehoods we are said to present in order to escape from the cross. This is a summary of Kautz's and Reublin's words.[60]

---

58 Ibid., 202.
59 Ibid., 203-204.
60 Ibid., 205.

How the church is to be maintained
Now since Kautz and Reublin . . . esteem the baptism of Christ so highly, and cast aside infant baptism, they say that we truly did tear down the pope's building, in part, but that to this day we have not begun or actually constructed a true Christian community, and even less have we maintained one in its essentials. . . . For in their opinion, there are no Christians in Strasbourg outside the Anabaptists; for they say that we have not even begun to construct God's house.[61]

Summary of Kautz's teaching
Christ has ordered that one should only baptize those who have accepted the Gospel. Therefore where baptism is used in any other way and infants are baptized, there the house of God, which is a Christian community and church, has never begun. In good German, this is to say that there is no Christian in Strasbourg, and there will also be none as long as infants are baptized, until only those are baptized who have first heard the Gospel and after that given themselves over to Christ.[62]

---

61 Ibid., 214.
62 Ibid., 217.

A Letter that Wilhelm Reublin Sent to Pilgram (Marpeck), Concerning the Articles that He Publicly Testified Against the Brothers from Austerlitz
(January 26, 1531)

Grace, peace and mercy from God, and the true knowledge of Jesus Christ be multiplied among you through the clarity of the eternal Word in the power of the Holy Spirit to do the unchangeable will of our Father in heaven, so that His holy name may be praised and blessed in and through you and us, now and forever, Amen.

Dearly beloved Brother in the Lord, I am constrained by heartfelt and divine love, with which I have ever loved you,[63] to inform you about our situation and life, and what has transpired in the meantime between us and those of Austerlitz.[64] Know therefore that I, as I wrote to my brother-in-law Caspar Schueler, have been badly deceived concerning the congregation (*die gmein*) because of certain articles—as he also saw himself; and I have discovered the elders themselves to be false deceivers, and untrue in doctrine, life, and work in each and every point: so that I have often wished that, if offense were to have arisen from my first writing, I had during that time held my hand in a burning fire. Therefore, dearly beloved brother, do not be angry and or regard me as guilty, for it was they who deceived me with clear and learned words. It is unspeakable how they have repaid the just God, and the marvelous deeds done and accomplished through us.[65] You with us will freely from the heart now and in eternity thank the Eternal Father in Christ Jesus, Amen.

As soon as my brother Caspar departed from Austerlitz the elders themselves discussed many points from the Scripture with me for three days that week, in which points I always found them unsound and untrue

---

63 Reublin here indicates a fairly long and intimate friendship with Marpeck.
64 The events in the Austerlitz community, narrated here by Reublin, are told from the Hutterite perspective in the Hutterite *Chronicle*, 89-92. In the Hutterian view, both Jacob Wiedemann and Wilhelm Reublin were unfaithful leaders, although the *Chronicle* concludes that Wiedemann was more at fault, and had acted unfairly against Reublin and the group that left with him from Austerlitz.
65 The final break between Reublin's group and those at Austerlitz had taken place only eighteen days before this writing, hence the sharp tone of the letter.

in doctrine, and I overcame them always with the truth so that they had to give way and after many disputes they often gave me the kiss of peace. But in their hearts they were not true, as was demonstrated later by their actions. It so happened that I took Kilian's place[66] in preaching during his absence. When, in the course of instructions, I prayed the Lord's Prayer several times with the members of Christ, the elders brought about discontent, strife and great rumors in the members, so that I was obliged to hold another discussion with the elders. Although they withstood me vigorously, the truth nevertheless prevailed and overcame their error. To God be praise eternally, Amen.

After this it happened that following an evening meal I wished in God's freedom to proclaim the Word of God to which I have been commissioned, so that I might give to others and to myself joy, comfort and edification according to the gift of the Holy Spirit. So I began to speak with a clear voice that which the Spirit showed me from the open book of the Holy Scripture of 1 Peter 1. The following evening the hearers entreated me to continue further, which I did. But when the elders saw the earnestness of the people, a larger group having assembled on the benches because of their thirst to hear the Word of God, on the third night they sent the people out of the room. They went into another room which was called "the school." I followed them there and taught them with a full voice, and the size of the group increased. At the first only eight or nine persons had been present.

At that time Old Jacob,[67] one of the elders, wished to leave the congregation and having called the people together made a very long address on the marvelous works and wonders he and his brethren at Nikolsburg and Austerlitz had accomplished. Finally he called out the names of those brethren who were to be the only ones permitted to teach, and no one else; neither was anyone to listen to the preaching of anyone else. This speech grieved and saddened me, for I knew well what the outcome would be. I comforted myself much with the Lord's grace and Spirit, and regarded the

---

66 Probably Kilian Volckhamer, one of the leaders at Austerlitz. Packull, *Hutterite Beginnings*, 215.

67 According to the Hutterite *Chronicle*, 86-89, Jacob Wiedemann was the leader of the struggle with Reublin. Wiedemann died as a martyr in Vienna, 1536. But it was Jacob Hutter who expelled Reublin for not turning over to the Brotherhood all his money (Ibid., 91).

Lord's command more highly than that of men. He would certainly speak to me, and I to Him, in His own time. But for the sake of greater charity and peace with the crafty I said to George Zaunriden[68] and to George Prentl, the appointed elders of the Congregation, along with Thomas Lindner[69] of Schwatz: "May I now no longer speak, and comfort neither myself nor others with God's words, and is the Spirit bound as far as I am concerned?" They replied that I might speak, but that without their permission I could not extend the hand of improvement to others with the grace and gifts of God. Thereupon I proceeded with more teachings.

When Kilian, Frantz, and the other elders heard of this they hurriedly sent messengers to Old Jacob with written messages.[70] He came, summoned me before the elders, and inquired why I was teaching without their command and authorization. I asked them again whether I was not teaching the truth. They replied that it was indeed the truth but they wanted to know why I was teaching. I answered: "Ask the people—they are the reason—or go with me before the people who are being taught and I will indicate to you how and why I teach. For I have taught openly, and I wish to show the reason openly, and I will not settle this with you in corners any more." Then they were angry and full of wrath against me, and counseled day and night how they might expel me.

When therefore the people assembled after the evening meal, Old Jacob entered the room and cried out saying: "What is this? We did not give a command to this effect, and it is also contrary to our regulation for a person to teach here. Therefore depart and go to your homes." The brethren, however, spoke up and said: "If you were a true servant of Christ you would not forbid us to hear the Word of God"—and with many other words. And so I taught what the Lord gave me.

Early the next morning the elders held yet another council, called in about sixty men and severely accused me in my absence that I taught at the wrong times and against their orders, that the people were running after me, and that I was a false prophet. Then George Zaunridt, my dear brother, said: "You cannot bring that upon Wilhelm in all eternity." Old Jacob answered and said to George: "I observe that when one probes Wilhelm's

---

68 Called "Zaunridt" below; "Zaunring" in the Hutterite *Chronicle*.
69 Thomas Lindl in the Hutterite *Chronicle*.
70 The Hutterite *Chronicle*, 87, also reports the dispatching of messengers to fetch Jacob Wiedemann, the founder of the Austerlitz community.

wounds, you also cry out." After many words he requested that when my case was being discussed George Zaunriden should keep silent—so that they could the more easily expel me. Then George said, "It is not God's will that I should remain silent where I see that decisions are not made in a righteous manner." Old Jacob replied again: "If you then do not wish to keep silent you shall depart from us so that we may more simply dispose of Wilhelm's case." To that, however, George replied, speaking as much as was consonant with love. He also asked whether I had not preached the truth. The elders replied that they were not objecting to the teaching, and they stated further that they knew well that I was teaching God's commandments and truth, but at an improper time and contrary to their regulation; for they have three appointed days in which to teach; and at any rate, said Kilian an elder, we wish to stay by our regulation, come what will.

Thereupon many of the brethren who had heard me were called before the elders and plied with cunning and sharp questions as to whether they did not wish to remain obedient to their elders, as they had begun at Austerlitz. Whereupon one, to satisfy them, answered and asked why they wanted to expel me on account of the word of God, and now forbid, bar, and obstruct God's word in their house. They also did the same to many sisters, attacking and scolding them, saying that my teaching was of the devil, when they themselves had formerly praised it and pronounced that it was of God. The more they employed cunning, deceit, and untruths the more their roguery became evident.

On New Year's Day about three [o'clock] the elders and many of their followers took counsel how they might find authorization to ban and condemn me. When day broke they called together the whole community of about six hundred persons, men and women, and accused me sharply and severely before all the people as a disturber and a trouble-maker, defaming me with many words. Then Old Jacob related how he had built the house and had led the people from Nikolsburg, and requested those who regarded him and his colleagues as pious, righteous, and true ministers to follow him to one place. Those who stayed with me and supported me were George Zaunridt, David a Bohemian brother, Burckhart von Offen, and many of the people, both of men and women. As we therefore stood there the other party sent six persons to us inquiring why the people with me did not join them. Thereupon I and all the people replied: Since I have been accused, I have requested to make a reply, as would be right and in accordance with imperial and divine law. But I was not permitted to proceed that day although we sat out in the cold from morning until evening; I was not able to proceed. All they wished to do was to take the people away from me, but the people were well able to understand the matter.

On the Monday following New Year's day, the elders took counsel with some of their men, and on Tuesday they demanded of me, George, and Burckhardt, that since we had labeled their elders as false teachers and prophets we should now prove this before them. We replied: Since we have been accused before all the people we wish to make our reply before all the people, answering with the truth and with Holy Scripture which will bear witness and overcome what has been said about us. We requested only to appear before the people and the congregation. Therefore the congregation was summoned. On Wednesday I stood with my brothers George, David, and Burckhart before the congregation in the courtyard (*im hof*) and stated that Jacob, Kilian, and Franz together with their elders were false teachers and prophets, unfaithful to God and His children, and that I would prove this by the truth of Scripture and from living men.

First I said that they were not a Christian Congregation believing in one God and having one baptism, as they boasted against me and all the world, the proof of which was that they did not manifest in truth the fruit of the Holy Church of God, but even hindered and delayed others in this, and falsely accused me—which they could not deny.

In the second place, they have grieved the Christian community, which has its being, work, and power in the Holy Spirit, and have rejected, diverted and ruined the springs of divine grace and mercy which should flow in the Spirit to the children of God. For they have robbed, extirpated, and removed the power of the grace of God from teachers and the hearers.[71]

In the third place, they treated the community falsely and with great deceit concerning temporal and physical goods, and not as they at the first had stated and promised to me. They practiced "respect of persons," granting to the rich their own little dwelling, Franz and his wife maintaining their manner of life just like the nobility. As to food the common brother must reckon peas and cabbage as good, but the elders and their wives dine on roast meat, fish, fowl and good wine, for I have never seen any of their

---

71 This appears to be a reference to 1 Corinthians 14, a text commonly used to argue against the church state preachers' monopoly of the spoken word in church. Packull, *Hutterite Beginnings*, 216.

wives at a common table. Another person may not even have shoes or a smock, but they have made good trousers, coats, and furs in profusion.

Fourth, they taught that water baptism is a work of righteousness, whereas it is a work of faith. I have heard this from their own mouths, from the elder Jacob, for which I also reproved him for in the presence of his brethren at the time, for he said that all his comfort and salvation rested in the water.

Fifth, they say that those who have received the Holy [Spirit], who have recognized the will of God and have transformed their lives by the power of the Holy Spirit, such persons may teach and are truly sent by God. But they did not wish to recognize me as such, contrary to their own word and work.

Sixth, they condemn the children to hell contrary to all truth and Scripture, which in response to our request they have asserted.

Seventh, they have set aside the Lord's Prayer without any foundation in truth, which by God's grace I reproved with the truth, also contrary to their will.

Eighth, they never wanted to pay [the Emperor] Charles [V] the blood-money and tax when he was at war, which my Caspar also certainly heard, and the Lord of Austerlitz himself, with great animosity, paid money to the state for the brethren. But as soon as Caspar arrived they became willing to pay this blood-money, apart from any necessity. Concerning this brother David also spoke openly against them, but they also acted against him falsely, thereby proving themselves to be great liars.

Ninth, the young women are bound in marriage to the young men without the knowledge and consent of their heart, with much pressure and compulsion, by God's command. In the beginning they denied this and would not admit it until in the work I learned of four sisters who left their husbands, of whom three are still among us.

Tenth, the young children suffer from a lack of milk and are ruined by solid food; more than twenty are wasting away and have been ruined: even a stone would feel pity for them. Many donated fifty florins to the congregation, only to see their children suffering hunger. By this one can easily see that their project rests only on money and purse, for they also took away my money. But God would not have it.

These articles I testified against them and revealed the truth before all the people, bringing it all to the light by the grace of God. Therefore I said: Since this is true and undeniable I will withdraw from you as impure, false, misleading prophets and liars, together with all those who fear God out of a pure heart, and who love Him, according to the command of God our Lord. And I said to them further: Since in the space of four weeks you have received four hundred gold pieces from two purses, you should make clear what you have dispensed to my brethren and sisters from the money which they submitted to you. The treasurers replied that they did not have one cent, and that they had spent twenty florins for grain. That was all the account they could give for that large sum of money.

Early the next morning I went to the Jews with certain brethren. The Jews told me that they had received from them the day before a large handful of ducats to exchange; and so it was that they did not have any coins. This also I reported openly before them in the community, but no one replied. They gave neither farthing nor cent to the brothers and sisters, yea, not a roll of bread; they even tore the sheets and covers from the beds of the brothers and sisters.

Therefore trusting in God and His grace, and for the sake of the truth, we left Austerlitz on the eighth day of January, departing from the false brethren and shaking the dust off our shoes against them [Matthew 10:14]. Oh how richly and powerfully God manifested His power to the blind, the lame, the lepers, and the cripples, and showed Himself faithful. They held up their heads to testify to God's truth as they departed with us. We numbered two hundred and fifty,[72] not counting the children, as we departed on a single day. Jews and heathen were moved to pity and sympathy by this sight at Austerlitz. We had to leave behind approximately forty sick persons in a small cottage because they could not follow us, but we provided them with servants and supplies according to their need.

Let everyone think for himself how delightful such a journey was in such poverty, with little money and many children, in wintertime. But the grace and mercy of God and the love of Jesus Christ is still greater among His people, for they were all happy and in good spirits and courageous in heart, comforted by the Spirit of God and having good assurance. No one asked: What will we eat or drink? Or where will we find shelter? But the dear Father who has never forsaken the children who trust in Him stretched out His mighty arms over us and led His people marvelously through the enemy to a rich and precious island in the sea, in the interior of

---

72 The Hutterite *Chronicle* puts the number at one hundred and fifty.

Moravia among the Bohemians, where wine, grain, fish, meat, and all kinds of food are found in greater abundance than in all of Germany.

Through a noble lady in the market at Auspitz God provided for us a place of freedom on which to settle, without any compulsion in matters of faith, to work at hand trades, to plant crops, to build, to purchase houses and to possess them, in a village called Starlitz, a parish-estate, where we now have fifty brethren and sisters. Our hearts, however, are not turned toward this but toward the kingdom of God, for one cannot strive to receive the precious pearls without the cross. Therefore he who wishes to join us must take up his cross and follow us, for apart from suffering and the cross one cannot be saved.

Blessed be God who by His Spirit in the midst of extreme danger has armed us with His strength against this false spirit and has permitted us to triumph. May His holy name be blessed eternally through Christ Jesus, Amen.

Here therefore you now have a brief account of what has happened to us in the past. And do not estrange yourself from me because God led me as a sick man from Strasbourg to Moravia. I would prefer peace but arrived in the midst of unrest. May God be praised forever and eternally, Amen.

Dearly beloved Brother Pilgram, I entreat you to show my letter quickly to all the dear saints and brethren for the sake of Christ and His holy righteousness, so that no one be deceived through the false brethren at Austerlitz and through their messengers and, as we have indicated to you, be led astray. So keep watch and take care of yourselves and of the people of God that you not be deceived. The locksmith to whom you gave the letter addressed to us was corrupted by the false brethren so that he did not wish to come to us although he was spoken to by our brethren. On the Friday after Paul's Conversion,[73] brother Sebastian Thaurer and Hans Eschlperger together with other brethren arrived here with us, also Hans Zuck of Altorf. These greet you heartily and wish you well in the Lord. They say that the roads are open and not unsafe . . . . Those with us are one in the Lord and at peace. That which is of further urgency the brother who is the bearer of this letter will report to you orally, for he resided at Austerlitz longer than we.

Be then commended to the Lord. The Christian church at Auspitz sends greetings to you and to all the brethren scattered here and there in

---

73   The celebration of Paul's conversion is held on January 25.

your community, and requests that you pray for us in the Lord. We will do the same for you. Greet for me Martin Leopolden, Anderlin, Peter and Wolffen von Landaw, and all those who love us. The grace of God keep you and us from all evil, Amen.

Written in Auspitz in Moravia on January 26, 1531. We have indeed sent other letters to you but believe that they have been delayed by the merchants. If possible, arrange to send a copy of this letter to Erhard Rosenstock outside the city of Zurich so that he may send it on to others.

III
Hans Fischer Responds to Questioning
November 21, 1548[1]

INTRODUCTION

Virtually nothing more is known about Hans Fischer beyond the little we can glean from this record of his interrogation and eventual recantation. From the locations that he identifies and the persons that he knew, it is clear that he was part of the stubborn Anabaptist communities that survived underground in the area north of Zurich, roughly within an area bounded to the east by Winterthur, to the north by Schaffhausen, and to the west by Waldshut. His testimony gives witness to clandestine meetings in local woods where baptisms and marriages took place.[2]

The information eventually given by Fischer provides many interesting glimpses into Anabaptist life in Switzerland around mid-century, a period of time for which there are very few extant sources. At one point Fischer testifies that he was won for Anabaptism by a "Mathis" who had lived in Bremgarten (about 15 kilometers west of Zurich), but who had since moved to Moravia. He says that he was not baptized by Mathis, but by Hanns Bechi of Kimenhof around 1539. This would place his conversion by Mathis Wiser at some undertermined earlier time.

The man who baptized Fischer, Hans Bechi (or Bächi) of Kimenhof, near Bülach, makes few appearances in the historical record, but his presence in the baptizing movement goes back to the first generation of Anabaptists in the region north of Zurich. He was arrested in early 1528, and at his hearing in January of that year, he named as his teachers

---

1   Document located at STAZ, signature E I, 7.2, #94. Transcription by Arnold Snyder; translation by Sydney Penner and Arnold Snyder. Most of the document has since been published in QGTS III, #290, 125-26.

2   See the references to this document in Leu and Scheidegger, *Zürcher Täufer*, 103, 111ff., 117, 119, 121, 124ff., and Christian Scheidegger, "Bullinger und das Verhör des Täufers Hans Fischer," in *Der Nachfolger, Heinrich Bullinger (1504-1575)*. Katalog zur Ausstellung im Grossmünster Zürich, ed. Emidio Campi (Zurich, 2004), 18-22.

Carli Brennwald, Michael Sattler, Mumprat of Constance, and Conrad Winckler—a who's who of early Swiss separatist baptizers who set the direction for what later Anabaptists called the "Swiss Brethren" branch.[3] At his 1528 hearing Bechi testified that he had been instructed by Scripture and by his teachers that infant baptism was a mistake and adult baptism was the correct practice. He professed obedience to milords in all that did not oppose his conscience, and said he was willing to be instructed. The record does not say what happened next, but by 1538 or 1539, Bechi was clearly active as an itinerant baptizer in the same area, for that is when, in a clandestine ritual in a forest, he baptized Hans Fischer into a local Swiss Brethren community. Finally, according to Fischer's testimony, Bechi had performed a marriage in a forest sometime around April, 1548. We thus have two decades of documented Anabaptist activity for the elusive Hans Bechi, with a decade of apparently uninterrupted clandestine Anabaptist leadership, including baptisms and marriages, from 1538 to 1548.

Not much is known about Mathis Wiser of Bremgarten, the man who converted Hans Fischer, but he also appears occasionally in the historical record for about a decade, from 1538 to 1548. Surprisingly, Wiser first appears in the record as one of the primary "foreign" spokesmen, along with Hans Hotz, Heinrich Weninger, and Georg Träffer, at the Bern Disputation, which took place from March 11 to 17, 1538.[4] Wiser spoke often and at length on the subjects of the "calling" and "sending" of preachers (Art. 2), the nature of the church (Art. 3), Baptism (Art. 4), the Oath (Art. 5), Civil Authority (Art. 6), and the Ban (Art. 7).

Clearly Mathis Wiser was well versed in Anabaptist teachings and appears to have been an Anabaptist leader for some time. Not only was he trusted to speak for the entire group, but his answers have a practiced homiletic tone, undergirded firmly with relevant Scripture references. His contributions to the debate reveal a stubborn grasp of his basic positions, which he was not afraid to repeat again and sometimes refine with further biblical examples and references. His critique of the Reformed pastors and their church was prominent and unrelenting. On reading his interventions

---

3   QGTS I, nr. 246, 270-71.
4   Transcript of the Bern Disputation, March 11-17, 1538 in QGTS IV, 257-467. The index on 475 notes 63 instances of Wiser speaking at the Disputation.

at the Disputation, one has no trouble imagining him convincing Fischer to accept the Anabaptist way.

Fischer testified in 1548 that Wiser had left the Zurich area and moved to Moravia. We can be sure that this was so because in a letter written by Cornelius Veh from Austerlitz, Moravia in 1543, he greets Wiser as a beloved brother and "co-worker" and sends greetings as well to the church of Christ "in and around Zurich."[5] Clearly, sometime between 1538 and 1543, Wiser was in Moravia and apparently became a part of the Marpeck "Covenanters" led at Austerlitz by Cornelius Veh. Furthermore, by 1543 he had returned to the Zurich area, where he was a recipient of Veh's greetings; it is possible that between 1543 and 1548, he had returned again to Moravia.

In any case, the information found in Cornelius Veh's letter poses a conundrum. Wiser's contributions at the Bern Disputation show him strongly defending Swiss Brethren positions such as an unwavering separation between the church and the world, a refusal to recognize magistrates as Christian, and a resolute denial of oath-taking in any form. Wiser strongly defended a life that would be visibly different and separated from "the world" around. On all these matters the Marpeck Covenanters were far more flexible than the Swiss Brethren.

In the same letter in which he called Mathis Wiser his "beloved brother," Cornelius Veh called both the "Swiss" and the Hutterites "dangerous and destructive sects" because of their emphasis on external obedience and observances.[6] Clearly, he did not consider his "beloved brother" Mathis to be a member of the Swiss Brethren in 1543, even though Wiser had publicly defended explicitly Swiss Brethren positions five years earlier, in 1538. Perhaps Wiser converted from strict Swiss Brethren separatism to the more moderate and pragmatic position of the Marpeck Covenanters sometime after 1538 and before 1543. If Wiser was considered a "co-worker" of the Pilgramite Covenanter, Cornelius Veh, by 1543, this means that some members of the Marpeck Covenanter network were working among the Swiss in the Zurich area, possibly still recruiting believers

---

5   Heinold Fast identifies "Mathis Wiser" as the "Mathis" that Hans Fischer names in his testimony. QGTS, II, #305, 227-28, nn. 1 and 3; also QGTS III, 125, n. 5. Veh's letter is found in John D. Rempel, ed., *Jörg Maler's Kunstbuch. Writings of the Marpeck Circle* (Kitchener, ON: Pandora Press, 2010), nr. 24, 455-71.

6   Rempel, *Kunstbuch*, 465.

around mid-century. The movement of a prominent Swiss Brethren spokesman to the more moderate Marpeck Covenanters is evidence of active communication and movement between these two baptizing groups at that time.

Nothing more has thus far appeared in the historical record about Mathis Wiser, Hans Bechi, or Hans Fischer, following Fischer's confession of faith and eventual recantation in 1548, documented below.

Text

When the ordained authorities, together with Heinrich Bullinger,[7] M. Rudolf Walter,[8] M. Joder Buchman, and M. Otto Werdmüller,[9] further questioned Hans Fischer, the Anabaptist from Pfungen,[10] regarding his previously-written articles, he offered this answer. (*Margin*: Once again, at you my lords' instructions.)

First, concerning the proclamation and preaching of the Word of God he holds to the following answer: [The Word of God] is not being proclaimed according to the command and Rule of Christ and the holy apostles, and especially [not according to] the establishment and instructions of the holy apostle Paul in the Epistle to the Corinthians.[11] Namely, any believer may preach following anyone else, giving a heartfelt and comforting exhortation

---

7   Heinrich Bullinger (1504-1575) joined the evangelical movement in 1522. He was the evangelical pastor in Bremgarten, 1529-1531, when he was elected to replace Ulrich Zwingli as Antistes, or head of the Zurich church. He remained in that post until his death. He was a tireless correspondent, staying in touch with evangelicals internationally, from England to Poland. Some 12,000 letters written by Bullinger have survived. He also published sermons, and exegetical and polemical works. See Rudolf Pfister, "Bullinger, Johann Heinrich," in: *Neue Deutsche Biographie* 3 (1957), 12. Accessed online: http://www.deutsche-biographie.de/pnd118517384.html, Sept. 24, 2014.

8   Rudolf Walter or Walther or Gwalther (1519-1586) was a Reformed Protestant pastor who was educated in Heinrich Bullinger's home. He distinguished himself as a scholar and clergyman. He married Ulrich Zwingli's daughter and became Antistes of the Zurich church in 1575, succeeding Bullinger. He was a popular preacher whose homilies covered virtually all books of the Bible. His five sermons on the "Antichrist," based on Matthew 24 and directed against the papacy (Zurich, 1546), received wide circulation. See "Gwalther, Rudolf," in *Neue Deutsche Biographie*, VII Band, 360-61. Accessed online, March 11, 2014: http://daten.digitale-sammlungen.de/~db/0001/bsb00016325/images/index.html?id=00016325&nativeno=360.

9   Otto Werdmüller was Archdeacon at the Zurich Grossmünster.

10 Pfungen is a small village in the district of Winterthur, in the canton of Zurich.

11 The paraphrase that follows makes it clear that Fischer is referring to 1 Corinthians 14:26-33, where Paul counsels all who come to worship to share the revelation each has received. The exclusive right of state church pastors to speak in worship services was taken as evidence that their worship services were not being conducted according to the New Testament order. This argument is developed at

to the people, or if he can proclaim [the Word of God] better than the preachers, then he may speak, so that it may serve for the betterment of the congregation. [A believer] should announce and reveal [the Word of God] in this way which, however, is no longer practiced in our churches.[12]

Regarding holy baptism, he gave the following reply: [Baptism] should be practiced in the churches according to the rule and command of Christ. Only those should be baptized who are born into the good and true faith, and also have come to an understanding and repentance of their sins, and have given themselves to God. [These should be baptized into the community] as a covenant sign (*ein pundt zeichen*) and seal of their faith, for baptism, as Scripture says, is a burial of the old man, [meant] for one who turns from sin and rises again into a new life [Romans 6:3-4].

Since infants have no conscience and know neither good nor evil, it follows therefore that one should not baptize them in their infancy. He gave as evidence the Gospel of Mark in chapter 18 [sic] which says: And Jesus said to his disciples, go into all the world and preach the Gospel to all creatures, that whoever believes and is baptized, will be saved. But whoever does not believe will be condemned [Mark 16:15-16]. For here belief is prior and baptism should follow from it. Anyone can well understand, then, that baptism should be given only to those who are mature in the faith and have a knowledge of good and evil. But by this the children have not been excluded from the kingdom of God, for they are God's. Their salvation is [not] hindered, if they have not yet been baptized. But if the learned ones can give him a single reason from Scripture that infants should be baptized, as he and his brothers have clearly indicated that no one but those who believe are to be baptized, he will gladly hear it.

Concerning the Supper or the Lord's breaking of bread, it is found clearly described in the holy Gospels, why it was established and how we should keep it. But now in our churches it is handled directly contrary to what the Holy Scripture clearly teaches, [which is] that all sinners such

---

length in the 1590 copying of "Why we do not attend their Churches," *Codex 628*, beginning at manuscript page 368. Such pages identified hereafter as, e.g., <368>.

12   The scribe identifies with the state churches and uses the first person as referring to the prosecuting position, not Hans Fischer's position. In the preceding, "our churches" means "our state churches."

Hans Fischer Responds to Questioning

as blasphemers, harlots, adulterers, the malicious, drunkards, the quick-tempered, the envious, and other such sinners, who have not shown visible improvement and repented of their sins and have not yielded themselves to God, are to be excluded from [the Lord's Supper]. There is no Christian unity apparent among us, even though such unity was commanded primarily in the celebrating of communion.[13]

But if it is said: Judas was also a sinner, and a grave one at that, since he betrayed our Savior Jesus Christ, and yet Christ did not exclude him from the Last Supper even though he knew what Judas would do, but rather, on the basis of [Judas's] faith and trust, let Judas eat with him. Therefore, since in the institution and celebration of that first Lord's Supper sinners were present, it follows that one should exclude no sinners from Communion, but rather accept everyone as partakers on the basis of the faith and trust they should have in God. To this [Hans Fischer] said that just because it had been prophesied of Judas that he should betray Christ, and therefore Scripture had to be fulfilled through and in him, it does not therefore follow that [the Supper] must include every sinner today. Rather, it is far more important that we keep the command of Christ and the apostles.

The ban is also not kept according to the command and Rule of Christ and the apostles in the [state] churches, as is to be understood in his first answer, for the [responsibility] for the punishment and chastisement of sins is not given exclusively to them, the state preachers and the jurors, but rather, it is permitted to every Christian to uncover [sins] and render judgment in the churches.[14]

How the preachers and servants of God should be and live [or "be conformed": *gestaltet syn solten*] is sufficiently reported in Paul's epistles to Titus [1:6-9] and 1 Timothy [3:1-13]. Especially in the epistle to Timothy,

---

13 It is interesting that the focus of the Supper discussion is not the "real presence" or what "happens" in the Supper, but rather the Supper is subsumed into a discussion of proper ecclesiology: the Lord's Supper is a celebration of the unity of the Body. This unity is the "primary reason" for the commandment to celebrate. That commanded unity demands the participation of pure members. The Supper and the ban are thus closely integrated.

14 Clearly the preachers argued that the ban was also used in their churches. The argument on the Anabaptist side was that the ban belonged in the hands of all church members, not only the designated clergy.

the life and walk of the preachers is to be blameless before the congregation, and in the fear and love of God they are to take and have a good wife. But he finds the contrary with you, for many of you learned [preachers] are encumbered with and addicted to the same sins and vices that Paul clearly forbade. Since there is no evidence of any good fruit of the Gospel either with the congregation or with you—and one can know by the fruit whether his tree is good or evil—and since those who preach do not practice what they teach, it therefore follows that no one hears them and that they do not proclaim the truth, for the Word and Gospel of God are never proclaimed and preached without fruit, as Christ himself bore witness.

Concerning the political authorities, he considers them to have been instituted and ordained by God for the protection of the righteous and punishment of the wicked, to maintain justice and the law, protect and shield widows and orphans, and foster peace and unity. What one owes through taxes, tithes, and duty, which are rightfully to be paid, should be paid dutifully, without expressing a single excuse in opposition. But those who are Christian may not judge with the sword and may not shed an evildoer's blood.[15]

And lastly, concerning the swearing of oaths that God swore to himself, as ordained and commanded in the Old Testament, he lets it stand as it is. Things that have already happened do not need oaths to attest to them. But to swear an oath that things in the future will come to pass and be true, is against the Holy Scripture, for with people who carry the name of Christian, yes should be yes, and no should be no.[16]

As to whether he, Hans Fischer, will refrain from his resolve against every article of the ordained authorities and also the preachers and learned, especially with Holy Scripture, against the Gospel and Christian love, discipline, and unity—rather than being continually contrary through his own reason, misunderstanding, and conviction—and lastly [whether he]

---

15 The reported answer appears to be abbreviated. The implication of the final sentence seems to be that Hans Fischer is denying the possibility that magistrates may also be members of the church, i.e., Christians, although there may have been more nuance in his answer than the scribal notes indicate.

16 Another scribal hand begins here.

Hans Fischer Responds to Questioning

will, through the teaching of God, go to the Christian church for the good of his salvation, separating from his evil resolve and rebaptism, concerning which he has been defeated with Holy Scripture, knowing the truth and simple Word of God, being obedient to my gracious lords' Christian mandates, he stays with his previous answer, persisting strongly therein.

And when he was asked further when he married his wife and whether she also joined the Anabaptists with him, he said that he was recently married and that she went with him to the Anabaptists. She is also from Wülflingen.[17]

And whether he would finally say in earnest who had baptized him, and also where he gathered together with his Anabaptist brethren, he will simply tell no one.[18]

But after the ordained authorities, at my gracious lords' request, returned again to Hans Fischer and admonished him in utmost seriousness to report the gatherings and other Anabaptists, also the leaders [*vorstender*] and teachers of the same, also who baptized him and who persuaded him to be rebaptized, he named the following locations and persons.

First, one called Mathis, who lived in Bremgarten but has moved to Moravia, had secretly taught him about rebaptism and persuaded him.

Then Hans Bechi from Kümenhofen in the Embrach district had baptized him in the Siglistorfer woods near Kaiserstul nine years ago, but who else had been there he could no longer say, as he had been young then and had paid no attention to anyone.

Then these were the places where they, the Anabaptists, had gathered and come together. First, in the Kleckgow [Klettgau] in the Kütal, at which gathering Georg Sattler from Oberhallow had been their teacher and leader [*vorstender*]. Also in Siglistorf, on the main street, and around Weiningen in the county of Baden, where their teacher was Hans Guntelmeiger from

---

17   Wülflingen was a small village about two kilometers east of Pfungen, towards Winterthur, now a suburb of Winterthur.
18   Another scribal hand begins here.

Bern, but who had since died. Also, in the woods below Glattfelden and Kaiserstul, and also in the Bülach woods.

Then he gave the names of the following people:
Heinsi Müller from Endingen, who formerly was imprisoned in Baden because of baptism and who promised the bailiff to stay away from [the Anabaptists] but had returned to them again.

Stefan from Heglingen. His father was tried before the court in Kußenburg because of baptism. Andli Studer from Bülach.

Also one called Barteli who lives in the county of Baden.

Adelheit Kin from Embrach, with two daughters.

Hans Zobeli from Rorbis. Müller's wife from Glattfelden.

Berchtold and blonde Hans from Tschipfen.

Adelheit Spilman and her mother, and also Adelheit Spilman from Tellikon.[19]

Anli, an old woman from Glattfelden.

Henß Nesper and his mother from Höri.

These persons went to both the gatherings in Glattfelden and in the county of Baden.

Hans Flam in Kleckgow [Klettgau] and Heinrich Wininger[20] from Schleiten [Schleitheim] went to the congregation in Kelckgow [Klettgau] in Kutal.

Concerning marriages and weddings, so recently carried out by them, he gave this reply. When the Anabaptists had a gathering in Weiningen approximately four weeks ago, the above-mentioned Hans Bechi married [two people]: Fridli, a blacksmith's helper from the Bernese area who at that time worked in Dietikon, and a young woman from Utlikon near Würenloß, since they both desired this.

---

19 For a brief biography of Adelheit, see C. A. Snyder and L. H. Hecht, eds., *Profiles of Anabaptist Women* (Waterloo, ON: Wilfrid Laurier University Press, 1996), 38-42.
20 Heinrich Weninger from Schleitheim also appears as a "foreign" spokesman at the Bern Disputation of 1538, along with Mathis Wiser. In the protocol he is said to be from Schaffhausen. QGTS IV, 265; QGTS III, 384.

Hans Fischer Responds to Questioning

After my lords, the ordained authorities again asked Hans Fischer whether he wished to recant all the above articles, and wished to keep my gracious lords' church regulations that are practiced in milords' city and country according to the evangelical teachings, and whether he wanted to separate himself completely from Anabaptism; he promised to do so, with the additional statement that he wants to keep and carry out milords' city laws. He further humbly requested that he be freed from his severe, interminable imprisonment.

IV
Interrogation of Jakob Maler
June 1553[1]

INTRODUCTION

What we know about Jakob Maler is limited to events that took place in 1552 and 1553. According to his testimony, Jakob Maler and his wife were baptized in Lucerne during Lent 1552 by a blacksmith named Fridlin from the lower Thurgau. On September 19, 1552 Maler was arrested in Luzern, but released on October 12 following a recantation and an oath. In his testimony he said he knew of an Anabaptist in Toggenburg, a weaver with a black beard, and although he also knew of many other Anabaptists, he didn't know them well enough to name them.[2] Apparently he re-settled in the county of Toggenburg, which was under the rule of the Abbot of St. Gallen.

Enforcement of the mandates forbidding Anabaptism in Toggenburg appear to have been lax, judging from complaints by neighboring Confederate states.[3] This changed in 1553. Sometime before June 1 a mass arrest took place in Toggenburg. Among the clergy sent to question the imprisoned Anabaptists was Jakob Stössel, pastor at Wil, who had some experience debating with Anabaptists. In the group of eleven people arrested was their apparent leader, the recently baptized Jakob Maler, and detailed questioning focused on him. He confessed that he had been a "reader" for the group, although he denied being a leader or a teacher. He also confessed that his reading skills were rudimentary.

The document translated here is Stössel's report to the St. Gallen Abbot of his interrogation of Maler, which took place shortly after June 1, 1553. It

---

1   A critical edition of this document is found in QGTS II, #391, 309-14 (after June 1, 1553). Translation by Sydney Penner and Arnold Snyder. For the sake of clarity, the translation introduces paragraph breaks not present in the original.
2   QGTS II, #391, 309, n. 4.
3   See QGTS II, #388, 306 (before June 8, 1551) for a complaint lodged at the Confederate Diet in Baden concerning lax enforcement in Toggenburg.

Interrogation of Jakob Maler

is a relatively long and detailed interrogation of a rank and file Anabaptist reader and leader. This makes it a rarity for the document-starved mid-sixteenth century. We have unusual access here to the thought world of a leader of a rural Anabaptist community in the Swiss mountains, somewhat limited by the narrow set of questions reported by the pastor, but valuable nevertheless for what it does reveal.

We see that the commitment to adult baptism was strongly defended as the proper biblical baptism, and that such a baptism and the living of a good and moral life were closely linked together. The preachers were criticized strongly for not living as they preached. The strong moral and ethical emphasis on living a reformed life is on evidence here, as a continuing mark of Swiss Brethren conviction. The oath did not come up for discussion, nor did other typical Anabaptist confessional points, since the questioner did not raise them.

There is no notice of Jakob Maler's execution; he appears to have been exiled from the territory, for his property was confiscated by the Abbot's officials. There is no further information in the record about him or his wife.

Jakob Stössel[4] to Abbot Diethelm.[5]
Report of the Interrogation of Jakob Maler and Other Anabaptists in the Lütisberg Castle[6]

At the request of lord Jochannss, governor of Wil, also lord Hoffaman who is chancellor there. They asked that I, for God's sake and to comfort and help poor souls, would consent to go to the Anabaptists they imprisoned in Lütisberg, and hold a Christian discussion with them so that if God were to bestow grace and they were to be corrected with biblical writings, they might thereby turn from their erroneous, ungodly, unchristian faithlessness. I consented [to this] and rode there with Hoffaman in the night of the first day of June to hold a discussion with the eleven. Jacobus Stösell writing.

Initially the bailiff [*Vogt*] spoke with him [Jakob Maler] and asked him, if he had not thought better of it and whether he would not be willing to desist from his erroneous, false and evil, obstinate position, and if he was still of the opinion that he had expressed today to the men who had talked with him and asked him questions.[7] He [should] want to do the right thing, to examine himself and be obedient to the authorities, not to disdain them with preaching and teaching all over the place. For he [should] understand that in such matters a ruler [*ein oberkeyt*] will not permit something which is against the will of God.

To this he answered that he was not against the word of God, [especially] the teaching that one should act rightly and keep the Ten Commandments (with many words). That is why he is no longer a soldier, or a blasphemer,

---

4 Jakob Stössel had been the pastor in Wil since 1551. As a result he was well acquainted with Anabaptists. He mentions debating with Konrad Wick from Wil (Wick was executed in 1550); in 1556 Stössel was involved in questioning Poley Muntprat in Wil. See QGTS II, #373, 291, n. 3.

5 Abbot Diethelm Blarer, Abbot of St. Gallen monastery from 1530 to 1564. QGTS II, #371, n. 3.

6 Lütisberg is a municipality located between Wil and Lichtensteig, in the district of Toggenburg, St. Gallen state.

7 Heinold Fast concludes that these men were Catholic priests. At this time there were only four Catholic parishes in Toggenburg. See QGTS II, #389, 307, n. 11.

etc. But he is neither a teacher nor a leader [*forstender*], and no one can or should refer to him as such.

The bailiff, at the request of Hoffaman [asked]: Why then did you teach and read in the nooks [*in den wincklen*] and where you gathered?

Answer: When there was no one among them who was able to read, he had been asked [to read], and he had done so. He cannot read well, but they were satisfied with what he had done.

Bailiff: People everywhere have a priest or preachers, who preach and teach.[8] You should go to them and be obedient like others, and attend the churches, etc.

Answer: If he is allowed to keep reading, he will happily be obedient and not avoid the churches, and will read freely and for free and take no pay for it, willingly laboring and working. He has now learned to work at the spinning wheel. For the Lord says, you have received freely, freely should you give, Matthew 10[:8]. The clergy, whether priests serving mass or the preachers, require salaries and that people give them a lot, but he wishes to do it for no pay.

Bailiff: You said before that you were not a teacher and have never taught, but you yourself admit that you have read when people let you read; at the same time you also say that you want to attend the churches and be obedient. You contradict yourself and show yourself to be lying. It is said [in Scripture] that they who serve at the altar should take their sustenance there [1 Corinthians 9:13] and that the day laborer is worthy of his wages [Luke 10:7].

Answer: He indicated, with many words, how they deal with their leaders and teachers.

---

8 The reference to both priests and preachers recognizes the unique situation in Toggenburg at this time of the co-existence of Catholic and Reformed parishes. Both were legitimized by law; Anabaptist preachers were forbidden.

And when we had understood his confused, wandering speech,[9] I [Jakob Stössel] spoke with him myself: I have understood the words of the bailiff and your own, and I am happy to hear that you desire to be devout and saved. I ask you, why would you let yourself be baptized another time, in order to be good? Where is this found in Scripture?

Answer: The Lord says: "Whoever believes and is baptized, will be saved" [Mark 16:16].

Question: Were you not baptized as an infant?

Answer: It is all the same, whether he was baptized as an infant or not.[10]

Question: Do you not hold your infant baptism to be good and effectual, that it is able to remove the sin that we inherit from our parents? And that the [baptized] child is then sufficiently prepared for salvation, even if the child does not yet believe and is still immature?

Answer: He considers infant baptism to be neither good nor evil; and I had to force the answer out of him, as he constantly tried to make me look foolish with the article on good words and good works [James 2]; for he simply held that if he did not keep the commandments of God, then baptism is of no use even if he lets himself be baptised a thousand and another thousand times.

Question: Whether he considers the baptism of John, or the baptism of Christ, which the apostles used, to be the better or more effective baptism, or whether they are of the same value.

He resisted mightily to answering this question, not wanting to give an answer even up to ten times, always making excuses. Eventually he gave the answer that the two baptisms are the same, one as good as the other, one as effective as the other. But before this answer he said he did not know which one was better.

---

9   Original: *vertzug*. Editor: *"das Drumherumreden."* QGTS II, 311, n. 42.
10 Editor: *"es bleibe sich gleich, ob er als Kind getauft sei oder nicht."* QGTS II, 311, n. 46.

Interrogation of Jakob Maler

To that I [Jakob Stössel] said: Shame on you! You wish to read and teach in the assembly but do not know the difference between the baptisms of John and Christ? But if one is supposed to be like the other, I asked him, then why did Saint Paul baptize those persons at Ephesus again, who had already been baptized with John's baptism, according to Acts 19[:1-6]? It must follow, that one was not as good as the other. He gave no answer at all to this, and no more could be gotten from him. He pressed this chapter urgently, however, determined therewith to support his own view.[11]

He also gave his first answer, that it was too lofty for him and that he was not educated and well read. He did not want to engage in disputation.

Answer [Jakob Stössel]: He should be ashamed of himself, that he teaches and does not know the difference; why does he not let those educated and trained in Scripture correct him, since he does not have better knowledge.[12]

Question: Though you give me no answer to it, I ask you again:" whether you have never read that man is conceived and born in sin, Psalm 50[:7], and that man, though not a day old, does not stand before God without sin? "For we have all sinned and are in need of the glory of God [Romans 3:23], and whoever then says that he is without sin is deceived [1 John 1:8].

Answer: He has read the Psalm frequently and cannot deny it.

Question: Why not let the baptism of infants hold? For it was given in Christ as a remedy for original sin, and so much depends on it. Whoever is not baptized will not be saved. Unless you are born again for the second time of water and the Holy Spirit, you may not enter into the kingdom of heaven [John 3:5]. And were you Anabaptists "born again, for a second time?" Baptize them in the name of the Father, Son, and the Holy Spirit [Matthew 28:19]. For the child that is not baptized is robbed of salvation."

Answer: No, for the Lord says: Let the children come to me, for of such is the kingdom of heaven [Matthew 19:14].

---

11 The meaning is not clear. Did Maler continue to cite James 2?
12 These comments were inserted in the margin of the manuscript.

Question: So then are the children without sin, that they need not be baptized?

Answer: Yes. How can they sin in their mother's womb or share in or pay for their parents' sin?

Question: Surely you know from your previous testimony, that the child is conceived and born in sin, and there is the verse given by the Lord in John 3[:5], referred to above. For he excludes neither the children nor the old people, but rather announces that it is necessary for all. Unless, one—*quis*—whoever that may be, etc.[13] I must ask you again: What is the cause, that we all have to die as said in the verse by Saint Paul [Romans 5:12]? Is it not because of sin?

Answer: Yes, it is the cause.

[Jakob Stössel]: Therefore, if the child does not sin and is [born] without sin as you testified earlier, it follows that God deals more harshly with the blameless children than he does with those who are evil and old, [in that] God lets [the sinless children] die. Perhaps you do not know what the sin of children is. It is this, that we all inherit sin from Adam and Eve, because they broke God's command. Because of this original sin God made a covenant with the Israelites, with Abraham, and gave him the circumcision. Whoever did not have it, had their name removed from the book of life. In the same way, whoever does not have the sign of the covenant, holy baptism, will not see the kingdom of God. I had thought that I had worked more fruitfully, but you persist in your mindset and your views and demand to be corrected from Scripture; but when we give you Scripture, you do not accept it. I beg you that you pray to God for grace, that you might come to an understanding of your sin and become again a child of the churches of God.

[Jakob Stössel]: His belief and view is that faith should come before baptism and that they [infants] would be children of God without baptism. He says that baptism is only a sign that he, the believer, has made a personal

---

13   Stössel refers to the Vulgate version of John 3:5: "... dico tibi, nisi quis renatus fuerit ex aqua, et Spiritu sancto, non potest introire in regnum Dei." His point is that "quis" refers to any and all persons, young or old.

Interrogation of Jakob Maler

commitment, that from now on he wants to refrain from sin. He refuses to recognize that the baptism removes the sin that he committed both before and after he reached understanding. Do not corrupt those who are righteous.[14] I did not question him regarding the swearing of oaths.

[Jakob Stössel]: The other persons who lie in chains also hold his views, especially [in saying] that they do not want to listen to the preachers. Their preachers are not good, for they do not practice their own teachings.[15] A bishop should live a blameless life and be holy [1 Timothy 3:2].

Earlier I spoke much in Wil with the baptizer Wygeren [Konrad Wick from Weiern], etc.[16] It is useless, as they stick to their views even when they trap themselves in their own words.

Likewise when disputing with the one from Lucerne [Jakob Maler]. For even though he lacks reasonable grounds and makes himself look ridiculous, he is crafty. And when those who lack understanding and are uneducated hear him, it is no wonder that they follow him. And yet, when one puts an article before him and stays with it, he is at an end immediately and comes up with other [positions], to avoid facing the question.

His wife[17] is also stiff-necked [stubborn]. I fear she is as guilty as any man. She gives no further reply or answer, other than that she had believed and had let herself be baptized. She gives no answer concerning infant baptism.

May your Noble Grace accept this from me as a willing and obedient subject, [as a] brother in your Noble Grace's convent. For I shall be willing to serve your Noble Grace in such matters to the best of my ability.

Written by Jacobus Stössel, in haste.

---

14 The exact meaning is not clear.
15 The original German sentence contains two double negatives; both cases have been translated as actually meaning negatives.
16 See QGTS II, #371, #372. Konrad Wick was interrogated in December 1549 and sentenced to death by drowning in July 1550.
17 She is unnamed, but it is noted that she was baptized with her husband in Lucerne during Lent 1552. QGTS II, #391, 309, n. 4.

V

Agreement Made by the Brothers and Elders at Strasbourg, Assembled because of the Question of the Origin of the Flesh of Christ[1]

1555

INTRODUCTION

Located on the Rhine river and functioning for centuries as an important location for transportation, trade and commerce, the city of Strasbourg was also an early center of baptizing activity. The city's location and tolerant attitude towards religious dissenters virtually guaranteed the presence of Anabaptists there.[2] Although the city's preachers increasingly opposed Anabaptism, and the city passed a mandate against the baptizers already in 1527, Anabaptists in Strasbourg met with relatively mild treatment, facing no more than imprisonment, attempts at persuasion and, as a last resort, banishment. This attitude changed with a series of civil mandates beginning in 1534; by 1540 the Strasbourg Council would threaten corporal punishment, loss of property, and loss of life in a mandate directed against the Anabaptists. Even after the Münster fiasco, however, Strasbourg remained a surprisingly tolerant city in practice, home to a small number of Anabaptists in the 1540s and beyond. John Oyer has noted that in the second half of the sixteenth century, the city authorities still did not practice capital punishment, but continued to rely on banishment to control the

---

1   "Verdragh ghemaeckt by de Broederen en Ousten tot Straesborgh, vergadert van wegen de wetenschap van de herkomst des vlees Christi" (1555), in S. Cramer and F. Pijper, eds., *Bibliotheca Reformatoria Neerlandica*, VII ('s-Gravenhage: Martinus Nijhoff, 1910), 226-28.
2   See the article "Strasbourg," ME IV, 639-642; C. Arnold Snyder, "The Strasbourg Context," in *Anabaptist History and Theology: An Introduction* (Kitchener, ON: Pandora Press, 1995), 129-41.

Anabaptist movement.[3] The contemporary saying that "He who would be hanged anywhere else is simply driven from Strassburg by flogging" seems to have held true throughout the sixteenth century.[4]

All major Anabaptist groups and persuasions were present in Strasbourg in the decade after the first baptisms in Zurich in 1525. Wilhelm Reublin, a representative of the earliest Swiss baptizers, is one of the first recorded Anabaptist leaders in the city, present in 1526.[5] The South German spiritualist stream of baptizers arrived most visibly in November 1526 with the presence of Hans Denck, who was followed in short succession by other Anabaptist leaders such as Ludwig Hätzer, Jakob Groβ, and Michael Sattler.

The divisions and tensions between different Anabaptist groups became increasingly visible from 1527 to 1533. Refugees had arrived from Balthasar Hubmaier's Waldshut and increasingly from South German locations such as Augsburg, where followers of Hans Hut were numerous. In September 1528 another strand of South German/Moravian Anabaptism arrived with Pilgram Marpeck, who became a citizen, an employee of the city, and active in relief for the poor and for refugee Anabaptists. In 1529, the "spiritualizing" Anabaptists Hans Bünderlin and Christian Entfelder arrived in Strasbourg, militating and writing against the "external" practices of water baptism and the Lord's Supper, advocating an inner, spiritual church and church practices. Their spiritualizing tendencies were reinforced by Caspar Schwenckfeld and Sebastian Franck, two non-Anabaptist spiritualist dissidents also resident in Strasbourg at this time. This provoked a visible division among the baptizers in the city and led to Marpeck's written defense of external church practices in 1531.[6] Finally, into this mix came Melchior Hoffman in the summer of 1529. He led a separate visionary, apocalyptic group of Anabaptists from whom would

---

3 John Oyer, "The Strasbourg Conferences of the Anabaptists, 1554-1607," MQR 58 (July 1984), 218-29.

4 Cited in George H. Williams, *The Radical Reformation*, third rev. ed. (Kirksville, MO: Sixteenth Century Journal Publishers, 1992), 363.

5 Klaus Deppermann, *Melchior Hoffman: Soziale Unruhen und apokalyptische Visionen im Zeitalter der Reformation* (Goettingen: Vandenhoeck & Ruprecht, 1979), 158.

6 Marpeck's *A Clear Refutation* and *A Clear and Useful Instruction*, in Walter Klaassen and William Klassen, eds., *The Writings of Pilgram Marpeck* (Scottdale, PA: Herald Press, 1978), 43-106.

originate all Anabaptism in North Germany and the Netherlands, most spectacularly, the militant Anabaptism of Münster and subsequently and more permanently, the peaceful, separated Anabaptism of Menno Simons and Dirk Philips.

By 1533 there were visible boundaries dividing the Anabaptist groups in Strasbourg. An Anabaptist who lived there from 1529 to 1534 described those in Strasbourg as divided into three main groups: following Hoffman, Kautz, and Reublin respectively, with the Hoffman and Kautz groups "a little mixed together."[7] These leaders represent the visionary, apocalyptic strand of Anabaptism (Hoffman), the spiritualist strand (Kautz), and the separatist Swiss strand (Reublin). From an estimated 2,000 Anabaptists in Strasbourg in 1534 the numbers dropped steadily, most dramatically after Martin Bucer won over the Melchiorite leaders Peter Tasch and Georg Schnabel and most of their followers in 1538 and 1539.[8] Although he was banished in 1532, Marpeck continued correspondence with Anabaptists in and around Strasbourg into the 1540s, and small numbers of Swiss Brethren remained in the city and the area. It is virtually impossible to know with accuracy what Anabaptists remained in Strasbourg, particularly when they avoided detection and arrest. There are some second-hand reports. A local school teacher, not an Anabaptist, identified five baptizing groups in 1555: Hutterites, Hofmannites, Swiss, Pilgrammites, and Zabites.[9] A court testimony dated 1561 identified three Anabaptist groups around Strasbourg: Pilgramites, Gabrielites (?), and Sattlerites.[10]

As the sixteenth century progressed, Swiss and South German Anabaptists moved northward along the river into the Palatinate and regions of the lower Rhine, and met Dutch and North German Anabaptists who were spreading southward. The Swiss and South German Anabaptists were generally identified as "High Germans" in their encounters with the Dutch and North German Anabaptists. In these encounters theological differences became apparent, particularly concerning the doctrine of the incarnation and in the application of the ban. In the second half of the

---

7   Testimony of Hans Frisch, QGT VII, 288-89.
8   Werner Packull, "The Melchiorites and the Ziegenhain Order of Discipline, 1538-39," in Walter Klaassen, ed., *Anabaptism Revisited* (Scottdale, PA: Herald Press, 1982), 11-28. On the estimated numbers, see ME, IV, 641.
9   To whom the "Zabites" refers is unknown.
10 See ME, IV, 642-43.

sixteenth century, Strasbourg became more important as an occasional strategic meeting place for Anabaptist representatives from far-away places than for its local Anabaptist congregations.

There were five known meetings in Strasbourg in the later sixteenth century: in 1554, 1555, 1557, 1568, and 1592, with a sixth in 1607. The 1554 meeting is reported in an archival note but left no extant documents. Three of the remaining meetings dealt with issues of contention that had arisen between the Mennonites in the north and the Anabaptist groups further south. The 1555 meeting produced a letter, translated in this chapter, in which the groups came to an apparent agreement about language concerning the incarnation, or how Christ assumed human flesh. The Mennonites had adopted Melchior Hoffman's heterodox "celestial flesh" teaching; this the southern Anabaptists rejected, remaining with orthodox statements stating that Jesus had taken flesh from Mary.

The second divisive issue that had arisen between the northern and southern groups had to do with banning and shunning. The Strasbourg conference of 1557 attempted to deal with this issue, and mitigate the harsh application of the ban that Menno Simons and Leenaert Bouwens were urging. The letter by Zylis and Lemke, written to Menno Simons on behalf of the conference participants, is translated in chapter VI, below. It failed to achieve its objective of reconciliation, for in 1559 Menno rejected a moderate approach to the ban, and Dutch elders eventually pronounced the ban on the "High Germans" who refused to comply with a strict position on the ban.[11]

The 1568 meeting was a gathering of Swiss Brethren who met to adopt a "discipline" meant to govern congregational life. Chapter VII below contains a translation of the resulting "Discipline." The 1592 conference was a meeting of "High German" Anabaptists responding to Socinians (Polish Brethren) concerning the Trinity and the question of the incarnation of Christ. It is found in translation in Chapter XV below. The original letter was composed by Rauff Bisch, the primary spokesman at the Frankenthal Disputation of 1571.[12]

In the context of meetings between the Mennonites and the so-called High Germans of the south, it should be mentioned that the

---

11 ME, IV, 642-43; Cornelius Krahn, *Dutch Anabaptism* (The Hague: Nijhoff, 1968), 237, nn. 70 and 76.
12 ME, IV, 643-44.

excommunication of the High Germans by the Dutch took place after a "long and furious" debate at a conference further down the Rhine which took place in Cologne. High German and Frisian representatives held a return conference in 1591 in Cologne and adopted a conciliatory confession, called the "Concept of Cologne." This healed the breach concerning the ban for a time, and came to include the more liberal baptizers, the Waterlanders, as well, but Leenaerdt Clock, who led the way to framing the Concept of Cologne, eventually abandoned it and formed a separate group in 1613. He was concerned that church discipline was now becoming too lax, especially among the Waterlanders. The "Concept of Cologne" can be read in continuation with the writings concerning the ban published here, as part of the same dialogue process. It has recently been translated and published by Karl Koop in *Confessions of Faith in the Anabaptist Tradition, 1527-1660* (Kitchener, ON: Pandora Press, 2006), Chapter 7, pages 115-22.

Agreement Made by the Brothers and Elders at Strasbourg, Assembled because of the Question of the Origin of the Flesh of Christ

Since we brothers and elders many times are forced and often and in many ways and forms are driven, time and again, to speak concerning the incarnation (birth) of Christ; (and) just as we have always been bound and ready (and still are) to give an account to everyone who demands to know the ground of our faith, and the hope of faith that is ours, so we servants and elders were invited again by the brothers that are called Hofmanites, and by the brothers in the Netherlands, and have gathered together in Strasbourg from many places. And when we earnestly considered this article, we discovered by God's grace, that through a misunderstanding on both sides, the birth of Christ was pushed too high, or too low. Because of this, peace and fraternal unity has disappeared. Therefore we justly measured our ignorance, and called to the Lord; and so we have seen our lack, guided above all by the Scriptures in the fear of God, which we rightly should believe above all, and which we should in no way change, overturn and falsify.

For it is true that the Scripture in many places seems to indicate that Christ brought his flesh from heaven,[13] John 1[:14], 3[:13, 31], 6, 7[:29], 8[:42], 14, 16[:28], 17[:18]; 1 Corinthians 15[38-49]; Hebrews 1[:3], 7[:15-17], 13; Revelation 1. But likewise the Scripture also seems to indicate that Christ took flesh and received it from Mary, Genesis 3, 22; Deuteronomy 18[:15-22]; 2 Samuel 7[:12-17]; Isaiah 11; Psalm 131[Psalm 132:11-12?]; Acts 2[:29-30]; Romans 1[:2-4]; Philippians 2[:7-8]; Hebrews 2[:9-18]; Revelation 5.

---

13   The original text gives only Bible books and chapters. The verse numbers have been added by the editor. In some cases, such as John 1:14, the indication is clear, but the Gospel of John contains many verses pointing to Jesus' divine origin that could have been interpreted in a "heavenly flesh" manner. In most cases, the editor has provided verses that appear to be the ones indicated but remain inferences; in cases where no verses are noted, either the entire chapter is relevant, or no obvious verses were found.

But not this alone, for (Scripture also says) that Christ is the Father, Isaiah 9[:6], John 14[:1-11]; and God himself, Micah 5[:2-4]; Baruch 3[:35-37]; John 1[:1-14], 20[:28]; Romans 9; 2 Corinthians 5[:18-21]; 2 Timothy 3; 1 John 5.

Therefore it happened for us just as for those who wished to build the useless tower (of Babel): in the same way the Lord confused our speech, so that no one could understand the other. Perhaps this occurred because we tried to know more than one ought to know, Romans 12 [Romans 11:33-36?], and because we did not pay enough attention to the Scripture which says: don't inquire after things that are too difficult for you, and don't attempt to investigate what is too great for you. But strive for what lies before you here, for you cannot grasp hidden things, Ecclesiasticus 3[:21-23].

Therefore we confess that from now on we should and will, by God's grace, keep his commandments, John 13, 14, 15 and his ordinances, Matthew 18, and to keep the same in a given-over life [*een afgesturven leven*], with a pure and yielded heart, in order to walk in true righteousness, for therein is found salvation, and it is the knowledge of God and Jesus Christ, John 17[:3]. Therefore it is written, to know you is the perfection of righteousness, Wisdom [of Solomon] 15[:3], and, "In this way we confess that we have known him, if we keep his commandments. Whoever says 'I know him' and does not keep his commandments, such a one is a liar, and there is no truth in such a one. But whoever obeys his Word, in such a one truly is the Love of God perfected," 1 John 2[:4-5].

In this we must give him honor, that we believe his Word above all, and confess it to be true: (that we) confess and declare in our inmost persons that Christ is truly God, Ephesians 2. And since no one is able to tell of his birth, Acts 8, so we believe and confess with Peter, Martha and the Ethiopian eunuch (*de Besnedene*), he is a Son of the living Father, Matthew 16[:16], John 11[:27]; Acts 8[:27-39]. And in our simplicity we wish to remain with the Scripture, which declares and confesses: "The word became Flesh, and dwelled among us," John 1[:14].

Now since it is not only dangerous but also condemnable, not to fulfill the Word, Deuteronomy 4[:2-4], Proverbs 30[:6], Revelation 22[:7], therefore we wish to make our consciences captive under the obedience of Christ, and confess him in all places, according to the Scripture: also that a godless life and evil appearance be opposed more by a Christian and godly walk, than with the mouth. And that from now on we will not speak, outside of the clear Scripture, about how far or near, high or low, Christ became man, and we will give a faithful warning to any that we hear speaking concerning this, outside of what Scripture says.

As you have also confessed and wished to confirm such a thing with us, to wit:[14]

>Philips van Dankelsz
>Lourens van Mundelsz
>Quirijn van Nachalden
>Veltijn van Bethen
>Martijn Snyder

Taken from the copy, accurately translated from High German, into the Netherlandish tongue, by I.H.V.P.N. In Amsterdam, Anno 1610, the second of September.[15]

---

14 Heinold Fast observes that in spite of the "Dutch" sounding names, none of the signatories were from the Netherlands. The Agreement was drafted and signed by High Germans who had received only verbal assurances from Dutch leaders. This sentence expresses the hope that leaders in the north will also "sign on" to the Agreement. In fact, the Agreement was emphatically rejected by both Menno and Dirk. See Heinold Fast, "Wie sind die oberdeutschen Täufer 'Mennoniten' geworden?" MGBl (1986/87), 86-88.

15 The meaning of the initials is not clear, but they were used by Carel van Ghent of the Flemish Anabaptists. See S. Cramer, ed., *Bibliotheca Reformatoria Neerlandica* VII ('s-Gravenhage: Nijhoff, 1910), 491-92.

VI
Letter of Zylis and Lemke to Menno Simons, Concerning Avoidance (Shunning)[1]
1557

INTRODUCTION

Zylis Jacobs and Lemke Cramer were two "High German" ministers who functioned as spokespersons and intermediaries. They wrote to Menno Simons and other Dutch and North German Anabaptist leaders concerning the conclusions reached at a conference in Strasbourg in 1557.[2] Their letter provides further information about the meeting of some fifty ministers and elders who had gathered from "Moravia, Swabia, Switzerland, Württemberg, Breisgau and Alsace and from many places one hundred and fifty miles away." The representatives had come together initially because of a conflict about original sin that had erupted between a pastor from Worms and another from Kreuznach. The dispute had divided the Anabaptists of the region, but it was resolved at the Strasbourg conference of 1557.

A second topic came up for discussion at this meeting in Strasbourg, namely concerning church discipline. The issue was whether persons who had been banned but who remained unrepentant should also be shunned. This issue had a troubled history in which Zylis, Lemke, and Menno were all involved.

In 1555 "five brethren" from the congregation in Franeker, Friesland, had written to Menno Simons asking for his help in solving a disagreement

---

1   Abraham Hulshof, *Gescheidnis van de Doopsgezinden te Straatsburg van 1525-1527* (Amsterdam: J. Clausen, 1905), 226-31. Translated by Arnold Snyder with reference to an unpublished translation by C. J. Dyck, 2005, generously shared by John D. Roth, Goshen College.
2   ME, IV, "Strasbourg Conferences," 642-43.

concerning church discipline.[3] Menno's letter of reply did not resolve the various issues.[4] At about the same time a member in Leenaert Bouwens's church in Emden had been excommunicated and his wife, Swaen Rutgers, was now expected to shun her husband. When she refused to do so, she was threatened with excommunication herself. Menno wrote a letter in November 1556 in which he suggested that if the person in question "is permitted in all matters to keep the faith, and is moreover bound in conscience so that he [she] dared not leave such a mate," such a person should be allowed to remain with his or her marriage partner.[5] Menno initially was disposed to moderation and flexibility in applying disciplinary rules.

Leenaert Bouwens and Dirk Philips, however, had arrived at more stringent conclusions. Menno was summoned to a meeting in Harlingen with Bouwens and Philips, where Menno argued the more moderate case. But the younger elders would not be dissuaded, and eventually succeeded in winning Menno's agreement: henceforth banned members were to be avoided (shunned), even by their marriage partners.

In April 1556 the question of church discipline brought Lemke Cramer, Zylis Jacobs, Heinrich Krufft, and others to see Menno at his home in Wüstenfeld. Lemke Cramer had been an Anabaptist leader since 1550 and had hosted Menno in his home in Illikhoven around 1553. Zylis Jacobs (or Zilis, Zielis, Sielis, Zelis) was a Mennonite elder, active in Cologne and along the Rhine as far as Strasbourg, and a strong leader in the church.[6] Heinrich Krufft, about whom little is known, was preacher in the Anabaptist congregation in Cologne.[7] This group of "High German" leaders met with Menno for two days, discussing the issue of church discipline. It appears, given what Menno would write later, that he expected the stricter practice to be introduced in Cologne and further south.

Some scholars state that Bouwens and Menno called a meeting of Dutch and High German leaders at Cologne in the spring of 1557, but very

---

3   On these events, see Krahn, *Dutch Anabaptism*, 230-37; idem., *Menno Simons* (Karlsruhe: H. Schneider, 1936), 94-97.
4   Text of Menno's letter in CWMS, 1043-45.
5   Cited in Krahn, *Dutch Anabaptism*, 232. Text of Menno's letter in CWMS, 1050-51.
6   ME, IV, "Zelis," 1022-23.
7   ME, III, "Krufft, Heinrich," 250.

few High Germans came. Menno himself does not mention this meeting; historian Cornelius Krahn doubts that the meeting ever happened.[8] Even in the absence of such a meeting, however, there is good evidence of Menno's attempt to win over the High Germans to the stronger position on banning and shunning.

The letter from Zylis and Lemke, summarizing the results of the meeting of Swiss Brethren leaders in Strasbourg, should be read as a studied reply to the strict position being adopted in the North by Bouwens, Philips, and Menno. It is a conciliatory letter that nevertheless rejects Menno's position, and hopes that things will not come to schism. Specifically naming Menno, the writers of the letter admonish him not to go to extremes in banning and shunning. That hope, as noted above, did not materialize.

Dirk Philips responded first with a tract called "The Ban"; Menno composed a longer treatise in response titled "Instruction on Excommunication." Both were published in 1558 and both reiterated the strong position on banning and shunning.[9] It appears that the next step was taken by Zylis and Lemke, who responded in 1559 with a pamphlet directly attacking Menno. Although that pamphlet has not survived, we can surmise some of the content and tone by Menno's aggrieved reaction, characterizing the pamphlet as "gross falsehood and slander."[10] In particular, it appears that Zylis and Lemke had characterized Menno as an "unstable weathercock" who changed his mind on the banning and shunning issue.

In January 1560, Menno composed his last known writing—certainly not his best—his "Reply to Zylis and Lemke."[11] Towards the end of this vexed reply, in which he again asserts the necessity of strict shunning, even of marriage partners, he recalls his conversations with Zylis and Lemke. As Menno tells it, Lemke had departed the conversations in 1556 in openly-stated agreement with Menno. Although Menno granted that Lemke remained a little uneasy about marital shunning, he insisted that the latter had spoken about introducing Menno's practice in his own church. And now Lemke, said Menno, did not want this repeated anywhere

---

8   Krahn, *Dutch Anabaptism*, 235.
9   Dirk Philips, "The Ban," in C. J. Dyck, W. E. Keeney and A. J. Beachy, eds., *The Writings of Dirk Philips* (Scottdale, PA: Herald Press, 1992), 238-53; Menno Simons, "Instruction on Excommunication," in CWMS, 959-98.
10 CWMS, 1011.
11 CWMS, 999-1015.

near Cologne or its whereabouts. So, concludes Menno, who then is the "unstable weathercock?"[12]

Menno ended the letter by acknowledging the reply from the "Overlanders," who had urged that shunning not be pushed to extremes, and then launched into attacks on those who take such a position: "You lie, vituperate, backbite, slander, and call heretical me and my beloved brethren without any truth. . . . . You beget many defamers, liars, profaners, and ranters." He then concluded that since the High Germans had not submitted to God's Word and were not obedient to it, then neither he nor his fellow members may "be your brethren"—in the absence of further confession and repentance by the High Germans.[13]

Menno Simons seems to have already excommunicated the High Germans at the time of this writing, shortly before his death. Some sources say that Dirk Philips and Leenaert Bouwens continued discussions the High Germans in the Cologne area, with no success. They are said to have excommunicated the High Germans sometime around 1560 for not upholding strict banning and shunning.[14] With this came a definitive separation between the North German/Dutch Anabaptists and the Anabaptists further south, as well as continued strife between the "moderate" and "strict" parties in the Netherlands and Northern Germany.

---

12   Ibid., 1013.
13   Ibid., 1014-15, *passim*.
14   Krahn reviews the evidence in *Dutch Anabaptism*, 237, nn. 70 and 76.

Letter of Zylis and Lemke

We wish you grace, peace, and mercy from God the Father; also true steadfastness in the faith and perseverance in all temptation and tribulation, in the name of our Lord Jesus Christ, through the power and working of the Holy Spirit. Amen.

Dearly beloved brothers and members in the Lord, we should fittingly and continuously thank God for His inexpressible grace and mercy and great love, that He has chosen us before the world [was created] and called us into his heavenly kingdom out of the shadow and darkness of this world, made us who were His enemies into friends, and revealed to us the mystery of His divine will; and all this through Jesus Christ, through whom we have redemption through His blood, namely the forgiveness of our sins; to whom be all honor, praise and majesty eternally. Amen.

Further, beloved brothers in the Lord, since our hope and expectation is in God, that He has gathered us together with you in the same faith of the knowledge of Jesus Christ, to serve Him in this faith for eternity, our request and admonition to you all is that you will remember the beginning of your calling and the affirmation to which you testified in baptism, to which our word in the Lord is "yes" and "amen." We desire and ask God that He will grant us His grace in Jesus Christ, for of ourselves we can do nothing, that we think of His ends with our words and works, and that our entire lives be righteous, according to his godly will and pleasure, to His eternal praise and our life eternal. Amen.

Dear brothers, we hope that you will not hold the preceding admonition against us, for we expect and believe that you have already been taught of God, for our God wishes to grant us that his commandments truly be written in our hearts. Amen.

Further, dear brothers, concerning the articles (because of which the brothers came to us), about which we met together in Strasbourg with all the elders; we desire an answer from our dear brothers, whether they are satisfied with the decisions which our elders from many lands together have drafted in the fear of God, as follows.

First, concerning craftsmen and merchants, one should proceed according to the custom in a given land, as need requires, neither irritating nor hindering, paying careful attention to God's word in Holy Scripture concerning what it permits and supports.

In the second place,[15] concerning shunning of brothers and sisters who have fallen away we should act as follows. First, the nature of the sin ought to be considered, and that any action be compatible with the Word of Christ and his apostles. We must make determined efforts for the purity and preservation of the congregation, and that the fallen brother and sister be prepared for repentance. This must be done with moderation according to the witness of Scripture, with aid, mercy, and helpfulness to them when necessary. Therefore, dear brothers, it is our fervent prayer and request to you that, for the sake of God's honor and praise, you will be satisfied and content with this solution. Thus we may finally be one people, at unity and peace with each other. Then we may with one voice praise God, through Jesus Christ. Amen.

With this we commend you to God and the word of His grace that will keep us in his eternal peace. Amen.

This is the conclusion of the High German brothers. It is their heartfelt desire that this not be received as a command but as a brotherly admonition. Also, that all pious Christians, who are minded as Christ is, will leave their possessions in order to praise and glorify God here on earth. That these persons, for the Lord's sake, forsake as much as possible all unnecessary work, which only leads to wickedness or ostentation, boasting or great pride, and pursue that which is useful and honest.[16]

We also fervently desire that the brothers in the Netherlands do not counsel husband and wife to separate because of the ban. Damage and vice will follow from it rather than God's praise and the welfare of souls. The commandment regarding marriage far outweighs the one regarding shunning.

Their heartfelt desire also is, according to their limited understanding and gift received from God, that they encourage the Netherlanders with all their heart, to seek justice, peace, love, and unity with the hope that, in the Lord, the Netherlanders will be of the same mind towards them, and that they not prevent our unity and peace, since the God of peace and love has called us into peace and unity. Therefore we hope in the Lord, who has

---

15 The translation of the following paragraph is based on Walter Klaassen, ed., *Anabaptism in Outline* (Scottdale, PA: Herald Press, 1981), 231.
16 The following paragraph in Klaassen, ibid.

accepted us as His children, that we be minded as He is. May the almighty, eternal God grant us true unity of the Spirit and His eternal peace so that we may reach and receive the highest possible peace in both flesh and spirit. May the eternal God help us to this end through Jesus Christ our savior and redeemer. Amen.[17]

Also, our dear brothers, I cannot hide the fact that some fifty elders and ministers came together at Strasbourg from Moravia, Swabia, Switzerland, Württemberg, Breisgau, and Alsace and from many places one hundred and fifty miles away. And a teacher was with us from Michael Sattler's time, and the agreement of Michael Sattler[18] was drawn up in his house; he has been in the faith more than thirty years. There also was a brother there who had been tortured eleven times and maintained the faith. Since that time persecution has ceased, but earlier more than four hundred persons were put to death in Bernese territory in Switzerland.

These brothers all came together because of the disagreement at Worms, where two leaders were asked to resign. This disagreement concerned original sin and whether the sin was of the soul or the flesh. This needless argument has been resolved, an unnecessary issue and human invention. We all give God thanks that it had been set aside, for it extended ten or eleven miles wide and fourteen or fifteen hundred people who were believers were led astray. Well, the Lord be praised that they dropped the matter and willingly gave themselves over to discipline.

Now, our brothers, I cannot hide from you that they told us of fifty communities from the Eyfelt[19] to Moravia, some with a membership of five to six hundred brothers and sisters, and that these communities all stand with us in the faith, confessing God and His Son our Lord Jesus Christ. May the eternal, almighty heavenly Father strengthen us all in this true faith, granting us perseverance in our faith to the end of our lives. Amen.

---

17 This wish for peace is the end of the official document, but the elders added some closing comments to it, from which it appears that Zylis and Lemke were not the only ones participating in the gathering, but that a large number of elders united with them in full agreement with the writers in one voice, wishing heartily that full unity might be preserved, adding the following to the writers' letter to Menno. As noted by C. J. Dyck.
18 An apparent reference to the Schleitheim Articles.
19 This may be a reference to the Eifel region southwest of Bonn, or perhaps Eyfeld near Bern, Switzerland.

Letter of Zylis and Lemke to Menno Simons

The ministers and elders who have been with us wish all ministers and elders in the Netherlands much grace and mercy and also perseverance in the faith and in all temptation and affliction to persevere in patience to the end and so be faithful in their ministry. We also wish with all our heart that all brothers and sisters be mindful of their calling. May the almighty God make it so, powerfully and in fact in all of you and in us. Amen.

Now it is our heartfelt and friendly prayer and desire, namely Zylis and Lemke and also all the brothers and sisters who are here with us, that our dear brother Menno together with all ministers and elders in the Netherlands who serve the congregations of God, put forth every effort and diligently seek peace, love, and unity, that we may all serve our almighty God in one spirit through the bond of peace. We also hope, as much as is possible for us, to work diligently on this. We pray that you may be content with this our simple confession, and not push the matter to extremes, which would break or delay our unity, sadden many pious hearts, and we too, who would lose so much of our labor and expenses we have had, which are not to be ignored if we long to achieve peace and unity, as well as the more than one hundred miles we have traveled. God grant us his peace and praise that the unity of all the congregations of God may have been achieved. Amen.

Dear brother Menno, do not be troubled by our comment that you "not push the matter to extremes." This means that no one should work so sharply against us that [our unity breaks], but rather proceed with prudence and humility. With this we commend you to God together with all brothers and sisters, that the word of His grace may rule in all our hearts. Amen.

VII
The Strasbourg Discipline[1]
1568

Introduction

Among the hand-written copies preserved by Amish immigrants to North America is a collection of church ordinances adopted by Swiss Brethren pastors and representatives in Strasbourg in 1568, and reconfirmed by a later conference in that city in 1607. A further appendix of four more regulations was drawn up by Swiss Brethren in Switzerland in 1630 and is attached to some copies of the 1568 document. The lineage of the present copies appears to run from Strasbourg into Alsace, the Palatinate, Switzerland, and Hesse. With the migration of Amish groups, the "Discipline" made its way to Pennsylvania, Ohio, Indiana, and Iowa, and is reported to be in the possession of Anabaptist descendants in the Emmental and the Jura.[2]

The 1568 "Understanding" or "Agreement" (*Abred*) of the ministers and elders was practical in nature, establishing some rules and guidelines for the congregations that identified with the Swiss Brethren. As such, it is a valuable snapshot of issues considered important in these congregations at this time in history. Several developments can be observed.

It is notable that the authoritative role of bishops or elders (*Aelteste*) has clearly emerged and is now emphatically underscored. Article 7 makes clear that bishops are ordained to visit congregations and that it is their

---

1   See H. S. Bender, ed., "The Discipline Adopted by the Strasburg Conference of 1568," MQR 1 (January 1927), 57-66. The original document does not carry a title, but is simply called an "agreement." It was Bender who gave the name "Discipline" to this document. When the writers refer to it, they call it an *Ordnungsbrief*, or "Letter of Regulations."

2   Ibid., 58-59. This agreement remained known in Europe as well, as the copying history at the end of the document makes clear. In 1895, Ernst Müller reported on its contents. See Ernst Müller, *Geschichte der Bernischen Täufer* (Nieuwkoop: B. de Graaf, 1972; reprint of 1895 edition), 50-52. Müller cites as his source a manuscript held by the Emmental and Jura Mennonites (*Taufgesinnten*).

The Strasbourg Discipline

role to fill any ministerial vacancies: they are to ordain ministers and other bishops by the laying on of hands. In other words, there is now a tangible, ordained line of authoritative pastoral succession at work in these communities. The ordained bishops are to travel to congregations with the ministers (article 2), in order to instruct incoming bishops in how to manage things (*in der Haushaltung ... unterwiesen*). Ministers and bishops are also to give counsel (permission) to those wishing to be married (article 12) and are to be consulted before the undertaking of any significant business dealings (article 16). Ordained ministers and bishops are not to be opposed by any members, and any member who does so is to be silenced by the bishops (articles 17 and 18). Perhaps the difficulty of finding enough ordained bishops to be present in all scattered congregations led to the adoption, in 1630, of the provision that in the absence of an ordained bishop, any member in good standing who had the confidence of the congregation could be in charge of communion, baptism, marrying, and discipline.

In highlighting the authoritative role of bishops, the Strasbourg Discipline documents a rather dramatic shift among the Swiss in church polity concerning leadership. The Schleitheim Articles (1527), by contrast, are far more "congregational" in polity, specifying that congregations are to choose their own ministers from among their members and also allowed for ministers to be disciplined by members, if the need arose. What was formerly the rule has, a century later, become the exception.

The articles concerning the care of traveling ministers and their families point to the real dangers faced by the leaders of these communities. Articles 3–6 outline guidelines for the care of the imprisoned and the children and orphans of persecuted leaders. Several articles shed light on practices of the time, such as how communion was practiced (article 8) and the public kneeling of those who were repenting of sin (article 9). The inclusion of this latter article suggests that such public repentance was common enough to warrant mention. It is interesting as well that water baptism was to be dispensed with if, on examination, the aspiring member had been baptised already following repentance and profession of faith (article 15).

It is equally notable that separation from the world is underlined by the mention of such practices as not hunting game (article 19), wearing simple dress (article 20), avoiding economic entanglements (articles 21, 22), and not using weapons to harm anyone. On the question of nonresistance, the

Strasbourg Discipline has only one article, allowing members to stand watch, or to hire someone in their place, but forbidding them to do harm to anyone (article 23). To these separatist provisions the 1630 discipline adds that no one should bring matters to a government court (article 3).

In the context of the subject matter of the preceding Strasbourg meetings of 1555 and 1557, it is interesting to note how the document of 1568 deals with the issues that had come up before, in discussions with the Dutch. Article 14 of the Discipline deals with the incarnation, and reaffirms the orthodox position concerning the two natures of Christ, "a Son of God after the Spirit, and a Son of David after the flesh," clearly not accepting the Christology promoted by Menno and Dirk. The article reiterates the hope expressed in 1555 that disputes concerning this matter should be avoided, but it also definitely rejects any docetically-tinged Christology.

On the question of banning and shunning, article 10 of the Discipline speaks only to shunning (*die Meydung*) and supports the practice in general for those who have "fallen away." There is no mention at all of whether banned marriage partners are to be shunned as well (the "strong" Mennonite position in the North) or whether the marriage vow supersedes the demand to shun a banned member (the position argued by Zylis and Lemke). In other words, the "moderate" position assumed by the Strasbourg conference in 1557 is not reiterated here, but is met with silence. What this indicates about the practice in these Swiss Brethren congregations is therefore not clear.

The translation below follows closely the 1927 translation by Harold S. Bender, with only minor changes. The text of the 1630 discipline is also translated, as are the concluding notices of various copies appended to the manuscript used by Bender as his manuscript source. The translation is reproduced with permission from the *Mennonite Quarterly Review*.

Agreement of the Ministers and Elders [or Bishops: *Aeltesten*] of Many Localities, in Conference at Strasbourg in the Year 1568; Reaffirmed at the Strasbourg Conference in 1607

First: to warn against leaving the meeting; to earnestly admonish those who leave the meeting without godly causes, and not to permit it.

2. The ministers shall visit the neighboring congregations [or communities: *Gemeinden*] and provide for all their needs, and comfort the members with beneficial teaching. Ordained [*bestätigte*] bishops should travel with them, by whom the prospective bishops may be instructed in how to manage things.

3. The ministers and bishops should visit, provide for, and comfort the wives and children of those ministers who travel in danger or who are in prison, so that these ministers may be comforted and gladdened by brotherly love and care, whether they are in prison or absent for other reasons.

4. All who are sent out for this purpose are to be provided and furnished with all necessities, etc.

5. Orphans shall be remembered and taken in before other servants, and shall be disciplined as children.

6. The poor, untrained children and orphans of members [*Brüdern*] and bishops shall be brought up from the goods of the community, as opportunity affords; the children of the wealthy, however, shall be brought up with a proper sum from their own goods.

7. Ordained bishops should visit the congregations, fill all offices, and where there are no ministers or bishops, ordain them by the laying on of hands.

8. There shall be no fixed rule concerning the breaking of bread, as to whether the minister breaks it and gives it or whether each one breaks it. Only that everyone is to be admonished so that in blameless hearts and consciences and in unity with Christ there may be one bread and one breaking. No one is to be forced into another usage, and everyone should [break bread] in their own community.

9. The humbling and kneeling of those who have sinned and return with penitent hearts must take place in the heart before God. But the [physical] act of kneeling should not be done away with because of this.

10. Shunning [*die Meydung*] shall be practiced with those who forsake the truth of the Gospel and the fellowship [*Brüderschaft*], who may have caused harm to the name of God and the fellowship. Therefore we desire that [members] withdraw from all who have fallen away, with all propriety and humility, following the teaching of the apostles.

11. A brother shall greet a brother and a sister greet a sister with the kiss of the Lord; those who have not been received [into the fellowship] are not to be welcomed by a brother or a sister with a kiss, but rather with the words "may the Lord come to help you."

12. Those who wish to enter the state of matrimony shall do so with the knowledge and counsel of the ministers and bishops. It shall be undertaken in the fear of God, and it is fitting that it be done with the knowledge and notification of the parents.

13. If believers are persecuted and driven away by unbelieving spouses, they are admonished to continue in fervent prayer and to stand fast by the Lord in patience until the Lord provides a way out. In order to avoid such danger, believers shall marry only in the Lord, and not in unbelief, be they maidens, youth, or widows.

14. Concerning the incarnation of Christ, one should abide by the Holy Scripture as Paul testifies concerning him: a Son of God according to the Spirit and a Son of David according to the flesh, and as Peter confesses,

The Strasbourg Discipline

a Son of the living God. And as far as is possible, all disputing should be avoided and excluded.

15. All those who wish to unite with us but who have been baptized by others should be diligently examined, whether repentance has been born in them and they have believed in Christ and been baptized on this basis. Such are not to be baptized again.

16. No brother shall engage in buying, or constructing, or in other unnecessary business dealings without the counsel, knowledge, and consent of the brothers and bishops.

17. If one or more brothers rise up with invective[3] or rebellion against the ministers and bishops and foment unrest, such shall be reprimanded and punished according to the manner of the Gospel. Such wandering[4] and back biting will be tolerated from no one, nor will such slander be accepted by any brother or sister, whether from strangers or those at home. Rather, such matters shall be dealt with according to the regulations [*auf die Ordnung gewiesen*].

18. Furthermore, if anyone in the congregation were to rebel against the ministers and bishops, such a one shall be silenced by the bishops and admonished privately, so that they [the bishops] not lose heart [*damit sie nicht kleinmuehtig werden*].

19. Those members who wish to trap or shoot game shall be reprimanded according to the order of the Lord. If they are disobedient, they are to be punished with the ban and excluded, unless it is done in free territory.

20. Tailors and seamstresses shall hold to the plain and simple style and make absolutely nothing for pride's sake.

---

3   The German text has "Anfahung (?)." Bender, "Strasburg Discipline," 62. Reference to Grimm's *Deutsches Wörterbuch* suggests a copying error, and that what was meant was "Anfahrung" or "invective."

4   "Ummenlaufen," or perambulate. Thanks to David Neufeld for locating the definition of this word.

20.[5] Brothers and sisters shall remain with the present form of our regulation [*Ordnung*] concerning apparel and have nothing made for the sake of pride.

21. If a brother or a sister has money or valuables and wishes to entrust them to someone, they ought to give such things to brothers or sisters, and not trust them to the world.

22. If a brother or a sister has debts with the world, such a one may let the authorities demand it, and set a date [for payment], but thereafter allow nothing to be mortgaged.

23. If a brother is supposed to stand watch or guard in a village, field, woods or forest, he may hire someone, if it is for the best, or he himself may stand guard, as long as no one is harmed, and also if he does not carry weapons such as a spear and the like.

Another Letter of Regulation. Agreement Made on the 10th day of October 1630.

The Swiss Brethren of Switzerland were together near Hoffingen, in Finstertüelen[6] and together discussed, counseled, and agreed to better observe the regulation of the Gospel [*Ordnung des Evangeliums*] in the community of God, following the confession and statement of the old brethren, to keep to it and to take care where something may have been neglected.

---

5   The original text has two items listed as "20."
6   The original has: "in der finstern Thuellen." Finstertüelen is a rural settlement about 3 kilometers northeast of Zofingen, Canton Aarau. Thanks to David Neufeld for locating and sharing this information. The settlement is close to Oftringen. Perhaps the reference to "near Hoffingen" was meant to say "near Oftringen." See: http://elexikon.ch/FINSTERTH%C3%9CELEN/42_0125.

The Strasbourg Discipline

1. If a brother or a sister has committed a public sin, from which may God protect us, such a one will be publicly punished.

2. If someone wishes to move away because of suffering, they will not be allowed to do it without godly cause.

3. No one shall allow himself to be brought before the government court, nor shall anyone else be prosecuted because of financial debt.

4. That an appointed minister [servant: *Diener*] who has a good testimony and is trusted by the people, may well take charge of the breaking of bread [communion], baptizing, giving in matrimony, punishing and excluding, in the case of no ordained minister being available, who may have been prevented [from being present] for any reason.

Copied—1733, 1774, by Christian Guengerich of Hüninghausen, March 1, 1789, April 14, 1800, [and] 1820. I received this Letter of Regulation [*Ordnungsbrief*] from Friedrich Hagi at Martinscreek, Ohio, in the year 1860, and returned it to his son in Iowa.
Copied by me, Jacob Schwarzendruber.

The copyist of this manuscript, Jacob Schwarzendruber, was born in 1800 in Mengeringhausen, about an hour from Hüninghausen in Waldeck in Germany,[7] and died in the year 1868 on the 5th of June in Johnson County, Iowa.
Friedrich Schwarzendruber

---

7 Meringhausen was a village, now a municipal district in Bad Arolsen, Waldeck-Franckenberg, Hesse.

VIII
[Thomas Meyer], Concerning the Christian Ban
(Before 1575)

INTRODUCTION

The ban—or the form of church discipline the Anabaptists also called "fraternal admonition"—emerged as one of the original marks of Anabaptist ecclesiology, based as it was on Jesus' words as recorded in Matthew 18. The ban remained an issue within Anabaptist communities as they struggled with its practical application and implications, as has been made clear in the preceding documents. But the ban also was a continuing point of contention between Anabaptists and the Protestant preachers and authorities, and a stated reason for Anabaptist separation from an "undisciplined" state church. Swiss Anabaptists continued thinking about the ban and reprising its importance in the last quarter of the sixteenth century.

In this connection, it is noteworthy that three handwritten copies of a small book on the ban have survived in the Zurich archives. "Concerning the Christian Ban" was written sometime before 1575 and clearly was circulating in Zurich territory in manuscript copies; no printed copy has been found. It appears to have been written by one Thomas Meyer of Rätterschen, "not far from Lindow by Lake Constance." The Staatsarchiv Zurich possesses three different manuscript versions of the book.[1] We do not know if this little book also circulated in other areas of Switzerland or beyond, but its existence in multiple confiscated hand-written copies

---

1   All three versions of "Vonn dem Christen Ban unnd ußschluß der unghorsammen und bösen menschen von den frummen und glöübigen in der gmein gottes, wie unnd warumb er sölle brucht werden" are found in STAZ, sig. EII, 444. The relationship of the extant copies is the following: a) a copy of the manuscript dated 1575 (142ff.); b) an undated copy, written in an early 17th century hand (227ff.); c) a dated copy, copied 1634 (242ff.). The transcription and translation is based on the 1575 copy: STAZ, EII 444: 142-63, collated and compared with the later manuscripts for corrections, emendations, etc.

argues for a wide circulation at least in the Zurich area. Beyond these few facts, we know virtually nothing more about the author or this writing.

On the surface one could say that there is nothing very surprising about the the book's contents. In some ways it simply repeats generally accepted Anabaptist views concerning the ban. Nevertheless, it is also a unique writing, reflecting a context of discussion that speaks to the last quarter of the sixteenth century. The practice of the ban is argued in a theocentric way, with copious references to the Old Testament, and the practice of the ban is referenced to the issue of religious toleration. In its conclusion the writer makes reference to early Reformers and their writings on the ban, of which he approves as being biblically sound, but concludes that those early teachings were not followed, and so separation from the state churches is necessary. In these ways, this later Swiss writing on the ban shows that at least some Swiss Brethren in the latter quarter of the century were reflecting on the ban in new ways.

Comparison with Balthasar Hubmaier's early writings on the ban reveals some immediate differences. In his earliest Anabaptist writings Hubmaier connected the practice of the ban to the water baptism that incorporated believers into the church. With the water, Hubmaier wrote in July 1525, one also "submits and surrenders to brotherly discipline according to the order of Christ, Matthew 18:15ff."[2] Two years later Hubmaier wrote an entire tract on the ban which again cemented the connection between the baptism of believers and fraternal admonition, underlining now the necessity for discipline, given the human propensity to sin.[3] Hubmaier's target in this writing, however, is what he describes as the false evangelical position of wanting to be saved by faith and grace alone, apart from the deeds of a good life. Truly reforming the church, he insists, means controlling the new Adam's rebellion with fraternal admonition.[4]

---

2   Balthasar Hubmaier, "Summa of the Entire Christian Life," in Pipkin and Yoder, *Hubmaier*, 85-86.
3   Balthasar Hubmaier, "On Fraternal Admonition," in Pipkin and Yoder, *Hubmaier*, 372-85; see 374 for the argument in favor of the "wholesome medication" of the ban. In his "Christian Catechism" of 1526, Hubmaier places discipline first under the rubric of water baptism: "And if he should trespass herein he will accept brotherly admonition, according to Christ's order, Matthew 18:15ff." Ibid., 349. Fraternal admonition is elaborated at more length, ibid., 352-54.
4   Ibid., 375-77.

Speaking to the early Reformation discussions, Hubmaier insists that it is in this way, and no other, that the church will truly be reformed.

Fifty years later, Thomas Meyer's tract on the ban strikes different notes. Of course, Matthew 18 still provides the central New Testament "ordering" for fraternal admonition, and it is assumed that adult baptism means acceptance of the fraternal discipline. But Meyer's tract seems designed, rather, to convince fellow Christians to institute the ban, and to this end the tract presents three reasons why the ban should be practiced.

The first is that God desires his people to be pure and undefiled. In arguing for a pure and disciplined church, Meyer makes broad use of Old Testament passages which exhort Israel to purity. This theocentric argument is not found in Hubmaier, who relies on New Testament passages to argue for the practice. It is notable that, fifty years later, Swiss Brethren are arguing from the Old Testament and the New that God's historical will concerning his people has not changed, an argument more usually associated with Reformed opponents of Anabaptism, such as the Reformed theologians who argued such a position at the Frankenthal disputation in 1571 with regard to government and the sword.

In this tract Meyer argues that God has always desired a pure and disciplined people, and has supported the exclusion of the disobedient. There is an echo here of Menno Simons's second writing on excommunication, with its reference to Deuteronomy and Joshua,[5] or Dirk Philips's appeal to both Testaments in his writing on "The Ban."[6] Although there is no obvious sign of textual borrowing by Meyer from either Menno or Dirk, in appealing to the Old Testament in favor of a pure church, he is echoing a position already argued by Anabaptists in the Netherlands.

Although Meyer does not repeat Hubmaier's connection of baptism and the ban, he does revisit the necessity for discipline in connection with the celebration of the Lord's Supper. The point is the necessity of maintaining a church without spot or wrinkle: the people of God must maintain purity, especially in their spiritual practices. The criticism of churches that do not practice such discipline is evident.

---

5   See CWMS, "A Clear Account of Excommunication" (1550), 462-63.
6   See "The Ban" (1558) in Dyck, Keeney, and Beachy, eds., *The Writings of Dirk Philips*, 242-48. For example: "... both the Old and the New Testament place these previously mentioned and similar transgressors outside the congregation of God...." Ibid., 245.

The second argument put forward by Meyer is that diseased members contaminate the body as a whole. This argument was used by Hubmaier, in passing, but is elaborated at more length by Meyer, citing not only biblical proof texts, but also Latin epigrams on the subject. Here again one is reminded not of Hubmaier, but of Menno, who wrote in 1550 that "It is a common saying, One scabby sheep mars the whole flock. The lepers were not allowed among the healthy in Israel; they had to stay in segregated places until cured."[7] Menno's images also appear in Meyer, even though there seems to be no direct textual borrowing.

The third and most important reason for the ban, says Meyer, is that it serves to bring about the conversion and salvation of those who had been destined for damnation. The point of the ban is not exclusion, but rather the spiritual well-being of those who are on the path to eternal disaster. In concluding this point, Meyer contrasts the ban with the capital punishment used by Christians of his day. The person who is killed as a form of punishment can no longer amend or be converted to a new life. The ban, by contrast, is an invitation to improvement and salvation. Furthermore, Christ commanded his followers not to root out the weeds from among the wheat, but to allow them to grow until the harvest. Killing dissenters thus violates Christ's will and order, which is spiritual discipline, not the physical destruction of the disobedient.[8]

And finally, Meyer mentions in passing the early Reformers, namely "Zwingli, Oecolampadius, Luther, Bucer, and other learned people," whose writings rightly supported the biblical practice of fraternal admonition. The practice of the ban, however, was never instituted in their churches. For this reason, says Meyer, we separate from the mainline churches.

Meyer's writing thus shows itself to be of the same cloth as many of the other writings circulating at this time in manuscript form in Swiss Anabaptist congregations, and found in this present collection. The call to admonition rather than physical punishment or execution, the call for toleration, and the pointing to early reformation writings and Reformers as examples of what was once taught, but not carried out in the later Reformation, ring the same notes as other Anabaptist writings of this last

---

7   CWMS, "Account of Excommunication," 471.
8   Cf. Menno's comments, "But now the Holy Spirit does not teach us to destroy the wicked, as did Israel, but that we should sorrowfully expel them from the church...." Ibid.

quarter of the sixteenth century, as these Anabaptist groups attempted to address the confessionalizing trends of their day.

We do not know why this book was composed at this time or for what specific audience. Perhaps the people for whom the book was composed lacked access to previously-composed Anabaptist writings on the ban. Perhaps the author wished to strengthen the disciplinary boundaries of Swiss Anabaptist communities, as confessionalization pressures increased. Or perhaps, as John D. Roth has suggested, the writing was intended to win over Reformed laity to a disciplined and committed Anabaptist faith.[9] Whatever the case, the book was composed, copied, and circulated, and formed part of the literary inheritance for at least some Swiss Anabaptists in the latter half of the sixteenth century and into the seventeenth.

---

9 My thanks to John D. Roth for generously sharing with me two unpublished papers in which he analyzes the Meyer tract in the context of confessionalization trends in Switzerland in the sixteenth and seventeenth centuries. John D. Roth, "Thomas Meyer's *On the Christian Ban*: Social Discipline, Group Identity and Understandings of the Ban among the Swiss Brethren, 1550-1700," read at the Sixteen Century Studies Conference, Cleveland, Ohio, November 3, 2000 and "Social Discipline, Group Identity and Understandings of the Ban Among the Swiss Anabaptists, 1550-1770," paper read at "The Power of Religion in Social Life" conference, Calvin College, January 24, 2003. Roth finds Meyer's tract noteworthy "because the author consciously targeted his rhetorical appeal to a lay Reformed audience." Roth, "Social Discipline," 13.

Concerning the Christian Ban and Exclusion of Disobedient and Evil People from the Devout and Faithful Believers in the Congregation of God; How and Why it Should be Used[10]

It is necessary that in the worldly order, in the guilds of the craftspeople and in all other trades and worldly or earthly dealings and matters, a strong and proper rule is kept and used, through which dishonest and disobedient people are overcome and punished to their own disgrace, but serving as an example to others. Likewise Christ has decreed that in his churches and believing congregations, the unfaithful and wicked people not only be brought to their own shame, their sins being punished through the exclusion of the ban and binding to repentance, but also that this be a warning to others, to instil horror and fear. In this way God has also commanded in the Old Testament and spoken to his people[11]: You are to remove and purge the evil from among you, so that all Israel hears, and will fear God, and will never again resolve to do such evil things.[12] The index to the Zurich Bible says concerning the ban that believers should ban and exclude all those who are a stumbling block in their teaching or life.[13] On this matter, consult the Scripture: Matthew 18; 1 Corinthians 5; 2 Corinthians 6; 2 Thessalonians 3; 1 Timothy 1; Romans 16; Ephesians 5; etc.[14]

---

10   Translation by Sydney Penner and Arnold Snyder.
11   *Margin*: Deuteronomy 13; 19; 21.
12   Appears to be a collated paraphrase of Deuteronomy 19:19-20 and 21:21.
13   Beginning in 1536, the Zurich printer Froschauer added a thematic concordance (*Zeyger*) to the prefatory material of his printing of the Bible. One of the topics treated in this index was the "Ban of the Faithful." An edited version of Froschauer's index was added, in 1567, to the *Biblical Concordance* published and used by the Swiss Anabaptists beginning around 1540. See G. Fast and G. A. Peters, trans., *Biblical Concordance of the Swiss Brethren, 1540* (Kitchener, ON: Pandora Press, 2001), especially the "Bibliographical Introduction" by Joe A. Springer, xxiii-xxxix, xxix-xxxi, and 125.
14   These Scripture references, with the exception of Romans 16, can be found listed and in some cases cited directly, in the Swiss Brethren *Biblical Concordance*. See

Therefore the ban is to be used in Christian churches and congregations of God. When a Christian believer falls into grave sin and publically offensive vice, as is described in 1 Corinthians 6 and Galatians 5,[15] they should be separated and excluded from Christian fellowship and from all believers. Paul admonishes the believers and says: "Remove the one who is wicked from among you" [1 Corinthians 5:13].[16] However, such a one should first be warned and admonished according to the Rule of Christ [Matthew 18:15-18], even if the sin is serious, public, and scandalous.

Exclusion is not considered a terrible[17] or bad punishment when done by believers. But when one is removed from his position and office by the world, or had one's honor removed or is punished in another way—this is greatly noticed. But [in fact] it is much greater and more serious to be removed from the congregation of God, for it is not the body, but the soul, heart, and mind that are affected. When a person is banned according to the command of Christ, he should not only be disgraced before the people, but also separated from all fellowship of believers here on earth.

But what is much more serious, such a person is to have no part in the kingdom of God, for that belongs only to believers, from whom he has been excluded. Take note, these are Peter's keys of which Matthew speaks in chapter sixteen [Matthew 16:19]. The Lord Christ himself teaches with clear words in Matthew 18, where he pronounces his judgement over the excluded and says: "Truly I say to you that what you bind on earth, will also be bound in heaven, and what you loose on earth, will also be loosed in heaven" [Matthew 18:18].

We clearly note here, that what the believers do by Christ's power and instruction on earth shall also hold good in heaven and be done before God himself. Therefore, what the faithful ban according to the Rule of Christ shall also be separated from God and his kingdom.

Now, everyone with understanding can well grasp what kind of anguish and pain would be brought to the conscience of a person when he is excluded from the kingdom of God and stands in Satan's power.

---

ibid., under "Separation" and "Brotherly Rebuke," 56-60; 63-64.
15   Cf. 1 Corinthians 6:9-10; Galatians 5:19-21.
16   *Margin*: 1 Corinthians 5
17   The variant readings of "grimme" are "gringe" (Ms. b) and "gmeine" (Ms. c), either of which would change the meaning of this sentence. We have translated the word "grimme," found in the oldest extant version.

Concerning the Christian Ban

What greater or more painful punishment could befall a reasonable and understanding person? Therefore whoever does not fear this punishment and is not horror-stricken, reveals clearly enough that he [or she] is not a Christian but an unbeliever and a crazy person, not worthy of Christ's name; let alone that such a one be among Christians and believers, being a part of their community. There is less understanding and fear of God with such people than among Jews and pagans. They will be dishonored when they are separated from God and must go into Satan's power.

Therefore the learned scribes do not understand the ban and its punishment of sin. They are the ones who in our time teach against the ban and say, if we were to use the ban, nothing good would follow and come of it. For if one were to exclude from the churches evil people and children of the world with loose morals, it would be no punishment to them. Rather, they would be glad for it, since they do not have much desire to go to church anyway. If church were forbidden to them, they would have a good reason not to come to church, but [instead] go to the pubs and other places.

This is foolish, ignorant, and mindless talk, but one which the learned in our time present without shame, only revealing their foolishness and ignorance of spiritual matters, as every intelligent person before and after them can easily recognize. For how could it be a minor punishment to one who wants to be a Christian, to be separated from all fellowship of believers and from the kingdom of God, as has been heard?

Yes, they say further, the common man and the ignorant do not understand. They do not know what effect the ban and its punishment have.

Answer: We have the learned ones to thank for that, for why do they not teach the people and the folk better and not otherwise? Should not those who are foolish and ignorant in the law and word of God be faithfully and thoroughly instructed? Or why do they consider such people to be believing Christians, people who have less understanding and fear of God in them than pagans do naturally, and who despise all discipline and mastery? Do they not know that Christ teaches that such people are to be treated as pagans, Matthew 18[:17]? Or have they not read in Paul, that one is not to drink or eat with such people, that is, one is to have no fellowship with them?[18]

---

18 *Margin*: 1 Corinthians 5

If then the learned have no knowledge, how then should the unlearned know? If the eyes cannot see, how should the ears and other members of the body be able to see? And if the shepherd himself has gone astray, how then will it go with the poor sheep?

Here we see what is meant when God says through the prophet Isaiah: "Oh my people, those that lead you, lead you astray" [Isaiah 3:13].[19] For "those who deal in the law," says God in another place, "do not know me" [Jeremiah 2[:8].[20] That is why the blind have to lead one another and together fall into the pit, as Christ teaches, Matthew 15[:14].

In order to advance with my intention [in this writing], however, I must say more about the ban and its ordinances and thoroughly show what its benefit and end is; namely, why and for what purpose someone who previously belonged to the Christian fellowship is excluded and handed over to Satan, for the destruction of his flesh, as Paul says.[21]

This certainly takes place not simply to shame someone before others, or to remove such persons from God and his people so that they remain in Satan's power and tyranny. Surely not. It certainly does not take place for such an end as this, but rather for the sake of other, better reasons. There are three, above all, as we will hear.

Reason for the ban and the separation of those who are evil from those who are righteous

First, the church of God is to be holy, pure, and unspotted, separated and cleansed from all offensive sins and vices. Regarding this, consult the Scripture: Isaiah 52; 60; 61; Colossians 1; and Ephesians 5.

Wherever one finds people who are publicly depraved and filled with vice in the congregations of God, they should be removed. As Paul says: "Remove the one who is wicked from among you," 1 Corinthians 5[:13]. In order that the people of God not be impure but remain holy and blameless, God has commanded all his people that they should root out evil from among them, and be holy as he is holy.[22] It has happened that an entire people has been severely punished by God because of one

---

19 *Margin*: Isaiah 3
20 *Margin*: Jeremiah 2
21 *Margin*: 1 Corinthians 5[:5]
22 *Margin*: Deuteronomy 13; 19; 21; Leviticus 34; Genesis 34; 1 Samuel 34; Joshua 7

Concerning the Christian Ban

evil person or because a lesser evil has not been rooted out [Joshua 7; 22:20]. For a single overlooked and unpunished sin will be accounted to an entire people and a single sinful, evil person disgraces and defiles an entire congregation, if such a one is not banned and rooted out.[23]

What is one to say, then, of a people in whom are found so many public sins and sinners, that is stained and soiled with so many offensive vices and godless people? How is God able to be present with his grace, Spirit, and gifts with such a people, when in an earlier time he left his people because of just one man's sin and disobedience? Concerning that which is not public, and is unknown to everyone [but God], see Joshua chapter seven. How then will it go, when one knows of such misdeeds and still does not punish them, which is what happens in our time?

That is why every congregation of God must root out that which is evil according to his Word and command, and separate from it through the ban. For if even a single person is not punished according to the order (and Word) of God, and not disciplined according to his Word, that person's unpunished, open and public sin will be accounted to the entire congregation, including even the most devout. The reason for this is that they are slovenly, careless, and disobedient in not punishing and rooting out evil according to the Word of God, but rather sparing it and looking the other way.[24]

Where it is like this, where the evildoer and thief, the traitor and murderer,[25] or in sum whoever does evil is passively left unpunished, with people peering through their fingers, God must punish and root all of them out, of which you have clear examples in Holy Scripture. Especially see in this regard how the priest Eli was too lenient towards the sins of his sons;[26] similarly, King Saul, who did not eradicate the Amalekites following God's command [1 Samuel 15].[27] Likewise, note how it went with Hamor, the ruler, and his entire people, because of the whoring that Shechem did in the city but that was not punished.[28]

---

23 *Margin*: Joshua 2[22?]; 2 Corinthians 7
24 Original: *durch die finger gsächen*: literally, "peeking through the fingers," or pretending not to see something obvious.
25 The English translation is distinctly more clumsy than the rhythmic German: *der häler und stäler, der verräter und thätter*.
26 *Margin*: 1 Samuel 3-4
27 *Margin*: 1 Sam. 34 [sic]
28 *Margin*: Genesis 34

For God hates not only those who sin and do unrighteousness and evil, but also those who do not punish the sin and the transgression, as is written in Proverbs 17[:15]. That is why devout and believing people should punish those who are unbelieving and disobedient to God and his Word and remove them from their midst, so that they may remain a pure and blameless congregation of Christ. Or where this cannot be done, the devout and obedient sheep of Christ should go out from among the antagonistic goats and wicked people, shun them, and have nothing to do with them, so that they not partake of their sins, and not become soiled through fellowship with them. This is what the Scripture teaches and commands. Concerning this, consult 1 Corinthians 5; 2 Corinthians 6[:14-18]; 2 Thessalonians 3[:6-15]; Leviticus 16; Revelation 18[:4-8]; and Matthew 18[:15-20].

This should especially be followed in the Lord's Supper, from which all unbelieving and impure people should be excluded, for all who join with one another in partaking in the Supper should be one body of Christ; they are to be fellow members of Christ's body, and hold one another to be such. For how can it be right that the body and members of Christ have fellowship with the body and members of Satan, contrary to what Paul teaches?[29] Or should unbelieving and unrepentant usurers, gamblers, harlots, winebibbers, and others of their kind have fellowship with believers in Christ? May that be far from us, for believers cannot consider such people as members of Christ and cannot have fellowship with them.

Believers cannot have, should not have, nor should they attempt any fellowship in matters of God and the faith with those who are not in Christ, but who are servants and members of Satan, excluded from the kingdom of God by Scripture because of their sins.[30] For [accepting] such would not only be contrary to the nature and essence of the faith and believers, it would also be contrary to all Scripture that testifies and speaks: "The righteous detest the wicked, but the wicked detest the righteous";[31] "The righteous have joy when justice is done, but the wicked

---

29 *Margin*: 2 Corinthians 6[:14-18]; 2 Corinthians 10 [sic]
30 *Margin*: 1 Corinthians 6[:9-10]; Galatians 5[:19-21]
31 *Margin*: Proverbs 29[:27]

Concerning the Christian Ban

detest it."³² That is why the devout and godless stand together as a sheep and wolf,³³ the unbelievers and believers as Belial and Christ.³⁴

Take note then that since all who come to the Lord's Supper are one body of Christ and also are to have fellowship with one another as members in Christ, as brothers and sisters, it is not only proper but also necessary that all harlots and rogues and other vice-filled people be separated from the pure body of Christ and the holy fellowship of his believers, so that the entire body of Christ and the whole congregation not become impure and stained.³⁵ For we know well that only one ill member makes the whole body and all members weak and ill, and that only a little leaven sours the whole dough. Likewise, one person harms and stains a whole congregation, as has already been heard.³⁶

If that is how the believers are commanded in the Word of God regarding mere outward and physical things, [namely] to have no fellowship with the godless, then how much less will this be permitted to them in the Supper. Christ has instructed that one is not to give what is holy to the dogs and should not throw pearls before swine, Matthew 7[:6].

But where does such a thing happen more often than precisely in the Lord's Supper, where such a deep mystery, the spiritual bread of heaven that belongs only to believers, is given without distinction, contrary to Scripture, to every drunkard, gambler, whore, blasphemer, usurer, and, all in all, to every rough, indulgent person and loose child of the world? These are people who not only understand nothing about [the Supper], but who also despise all spiritual things and also the word of God, and consider [the Supper] less than a full feast for the stomach, which would enthuse them more and please them better. For the esteemed sacrament of the body and blood of Christ should properly be held with great honour and respect, so that it is not wantonly given to the unworthy, to whom it is of no benefit,

---

32   *Margin*: Proverbs 21[:15]
33   *Margin*: Ecclesiasticus. 13[:17]
34   *Margin*: 2 Corinthians 6[:15]
35   *Margin*: 1 Corinthians 5[:6]; Galatians 5[:9]
36   *Margin*: *Argten a minori.* Deuteronomy 12; Exodus 23; 1 Corinthians 5; Leviticus 18

but rather only serves to their harm and judgement, 1 Corinthians 11[:27-34].³⁷

I affirm this, that man makes himself partaker of others' sins against Scripture, in giving the Supper to them and having fellowship with those who should be banned and shunned according to Holy Scripture.

Thus is indicated the first reason why evil should be separated from the devout and the believers;³⁸ namely, because believers are to be a holy temple of God, a holy congregation of God, yes, a pure body of Christ.³⁹ In order to have fellowship with Christ your head, all godless and vile people should be removed and separated from the body and fellowship of Christ and his believers, so that the body of Christ, that is, his congregation, not have spots, wrinkles, or other such things, but rather be holy and blameless, Ephesians 5[:27]; Titus 3[:10-11]; 1 Peter 3; Colossians 1[:18]).⁴⁰

In the second place, those who are evil should be distinguished from the righteous, so that [the righteous] not also become corrupted and contaminated.⁴¹ For many a person knows well that the company and presence of evil eats at him, like a cancer, and runs free just as water or a strong river runs over the lindens and sandy ground or soil. Likewise, as yeast or leaven spreads through an entire, large dough, 1 Corinthians. 5[:7]. Also, as a fire goes at a pile of wood or straw and does not let up until it is all consumed and burned, so also if one does not fight [evil] and put it out at the beginning and in time.⁴²

This image applies to sin which, although it starts small and seems insignificant, ceaselessly increases, eats at you, goes from one to the next, until it can no longer be resisted, just as a fire that reaches and burns from one house to the next in a city or village. *Ita mali venenum serpit et quo latius eo desperatius* ["Thus the poison of evil creeps along; the more it spreads, the more hopeless matters become"].⁴³ As soon as one does not

---

37 *Margin*: 1 Tim. 5; Num. 15
38 *Margin*: 1 Corinthians. 3; Col. 1
39 *Margin*: Eph. 15 [sic]
40 *Margin*: The evil are separated from the good
41 *Margin*: Note: Parables
42 *Margin*: How sin and evil eats at you
43 This saying may have origins in Bernard's thirty-third sermon on the Song of Songs, where he says "Serpit hodie putida tabes per omne corpus ecclesiae, et quo latius eo desperatius" ("A fetid pestilence is creeping through the whole body of

Concerning the Christian Ban

punish the sin and simply overlooks it, immediately it comes again, a third and a fourth time and finally so far that it can no longer be rooted out.[44] That is why it is most necessary that sin always be resisted from the beginning, and that evil be separated from good, so that the good is not also corrupted.

In the congregations of God it takes place now and should continue to take place, that whores, the malicious, the drunkards, and in sum all those who teach and live offensively be banned and excluded, so that such vices do not become common with everyone, and also corrupt the good. One sees how it is with people in general, that they readily make reasons and excuses to sin and be unrighteous, since they are depraved by nature and inclined to evil rather than to good.[45] For everyone thinks that what another has should also be given to him, and what is not sin to another should therefore not be punished in him either. *Nil. u. deterius corrumptorum hominum. Exemplis quibus et obtimique qui inficiuntur pulfertim cum natura ad malum omnes simus propensi.*[46] That is why this should be handled as with a body that has lazy members, and as one would with a herd of sheep among which there are some that are ill and scabby. Likewise, as one treats someone with a mark of leprosy in a house or among a people. One must burn, cauterize, cut off, and separate, removing the healthy and the evil from each other, so that the new members and healthy people or sheep will not be damaged by the sick.

Christ also teaches in this way in Matthew 5[:29-30] and Matthew 18[:8-9] and in Mark 9[:43-48], where he says to pluck out the offensive eyes and cut off the offensive hand and foot and throw them away. This should be understood to apply to [offensive] people also, even if they are beneficial

---

the church. The more it spreads, the more hopeless"). Thanks to Sydney Penner for this notation and translation, and for the Latin translations that follow.

44 *Margin: Iuvenal prinsipiis obsta, nam frustra medicina parati mali, dum per longum convaluere usum* appears to be a version of the saying attributed to Ovid: *principiis obsta; sero medicina paratur, cum mala per longas convaluere moras* ["Block the beginnings, for medicine is prepared in vain when the illness has gained strength through long delay"].

45 *Margin: Licentia omnes etiam optimi, fuint deteriores* ["Even all the best would be made worse by unrestrained freedom"].

46 *Margin:* Parable. ["Of the things that corrupt people nothing is worse. In these cases even the best ones are corrupted, especially since by nature we are all disposed to evil"]. The translation is a conjecture; the text is extremely obscure.

to us, helpful and faithful; likewise father and mother, wife and child, or good friends.⁴⁷ Believers should remove such from among themselves and from the body, that is, exclude them from the congregation of Christ with the ban, since they want to be offensive and a hindrance to the kingdom of God. Consult Deuteronomy 13[:6-11] concerning this.⁴⁸ For it is preferable and better, as Christ himself teaches, that the body lose some members, than that the whole body with all its members be thrown into hell.

It is preferable and better for every person, that he come without his teacher, without his father and mother, without wife and child, and without all his friends and go to heaven in everlasting joy, than that together with them, all go into hell and everlasting suffering and pain.

The second reason for the ban is made clear and revealed by all this, namely, how and why good and evil should be separated from each other. This is so that man, as is commonly said, not be corrupted by evil company, and a little leaven not ruin the entire dough, 1 Corinthians 5[:6]; Galatians 5[:9].⁴⁹

In the third place, the real reason and final fruit and benefit of the ban follows, for which reason the foregoing has been said about the excluded one, and toward which everything should be directed. Namely, not that the excluded person should be eternally excluded from the church of God and be condemned, but rather much more, so that the excluded sinner be brought to shame and disgrace by his sins, so that he recognizes and acknowledges them with weeping and sorrowful repentance, which had not yet been done. Yes, that the sinner turn his life around with change and improvement, and in the future, better guard against sin.

As soon as such appears and is revealed in the banned person,⁵⁰ believers should graciously accept such a one into their fellowship and consider [the repentant person] a fellow member according to the Rule of Christ and the instructions of Paul. All this alerts and warns not only the excluded sinner, but also all the others who hear of it, so that they take

---

47 *Margin*: Mark 9; Deuteronomy 13
48 *Margin*: Take note
49 *Margin*: Version in Ms. (b) seems least corrupted: *Finis excommunicationis: est enim datio vitae et reversion peccatoris* ["For the end of excommunication is the giving of life and the turning back of the sinner"].
50 *Margin*: Matthew 18[:15-35]; 2 Corinthians 2[:6-8]

Concerning the Christian Ban

better care, guard themselves from sin and instill a fear of doing evil, so that it not fail them.

It is for this reason that God sternly commanded the people of old many times.[51] You should remove and root out the evil from among you, he says, so that all the people hear of it and fear him and are no longer stained, and no longer set out to do such evil things among you.

See, devout reader, how Christ has given and commanded a beneficial and healthy punishment and discipline to his church, out of the eternal wisdom of the Father, who well knows, without doubt, what is beneficial and necessary for his congregations. Likewise, how and with what they must be disciplined, built up, and maintained in Christian order and uprightness.

It is also noteworthy and worth knowing that such punishment and ordering of the ban is much more beneficial and necessary for the churches of God than when they kill and root out those who are evil. For Christ also forbade such bodily punishment to his followers in the parable of the good seeds and weeds, Matthew 13[:24-30], and allowed that it was not to be used in his congregations among the believers. For the soul and salvation are endangered by such bodily punishment.

Therefore, the ban of the congregations of Christ is much more useful and beneficial since it leads to repentance and grace, so that they may come to forgiveness of their sins.

But those who use the sword to cut away all [possibility of] repentance and improvement, lead the majority [of their victims] to die without proper repentance and forgiveness of their sins. That is why Christ[52] has forbidden believers in his congregations to do such weeding and rooting out,[53] for he did not come to condemn anyone [John 3:17; 12:47], but rather to save souls and to seek what was lost.[54] For with the punishment of the ban, every person is given time, place and means for repentance, change, and conversion. This is not sought by the death and destruction of the sinner and evildoer, but rather what is sought is only the sinner's improvement and life.

---

51 *Margin*: Deuteronomy 13; 19; 21
52 *Margin*: Matthew 13[:24-30]
53 *Margin*: Luke 9[:51-56]
54 *Margin*: Luke 19[:10]

For through the ban many are chastised for their sins and are shamed before the people, so that they desist, repent, and also are converted and live.

But a person who is not dealt with in this manner never properly perceives his sin. Much less, I say, does such a one repent, but instead becomes hardened more in evil and unrighteous feelings until he has the rope around his neck, at which point no repentance and improvement can help anymore.

For when one has rejected the grace of God in his healthy days and in good times, all remorse and repentance is in vain when God's judgement approaches.[55] About which it is written: "Today, today, if you hear his voice, do not harden your hearts" [Hebrews 3:15], "but exhort one another all day as long as it is called today" [Hebrews 3:13]. Likewise, "do not tarry in turning to the Lord and do not put it off from day to day."[56]

So much is written about the ban of the believers which is grounded not only in Holy Scripture, but also in the books of Zwingli, Oecolampadius, Luther, Bucer, and other learned people, who also like us now have taught and written about the ban, to which their own books give clear and manifold witness to the present day.

But because they not only do not use the ban but, contrary to Holy Scripture and their own books and teachings, berate and discard it, we have no fellowship with them as people who have abandoned the commandments of the Lord and have left his way.

May God have mercy on his people and give us the spirit of understanding and discernment to recognize evil and to choose the good. Amen.

---

55 *Margin*: Hebrews 3[:12-15]; 13 [sic]
56 *Margin*: Ecclesiasticus 5[:7]

Thomas Meyer[57] from Rätterschen in the flesh, not far from Lindow on Lake Constance.[58]

This book belongs to the honorable and modest Jagli Hürliman from Bürg.[59] 1575.

---

57   Thomas Meyer is the apparent author of the text. See STAZ, EII, 444, 159 and 257v, respectively. Text c has on a separate page "Hans Herman Zydler of Herisow uf dem Eggen copied this book in the year 1634." The STAZ EI/EII catalogue states incorrectly that he was the author of the book. Copy a) establishes a copying date of 1575. Zydler therefore was a copyist, not the author of the book. Cf. STAZ, EII, 444, 259.
58   Rätterschen, presumably a small village, has not been located. Lindau is located on the eastern shore of Lake Constance.
59   Although further references to Thomas Meyer have not been found, John D. Roth documents that Jagli Hürliman was an Anabaptist, citing J. P. Zwicky von Gauen, ed. *Schweizerisches Familienbuch* 3 (Zurich, 1949), 204, 238, 241. Thanks to John D. Roth for sharing his unpublished paper, "Thomas Meyer's *On the Christian Ban*: Social Discipline, Group Identity and Understandings of the Ban among the Swiss Brethren, 1550-1700," read at the Sixteenth Century Studies Conference, Cleveland, Ohio, November 3, 2000. The reference above is found on page 2, note 4 of Roth's paper.

IX
Prefaces to Three "Swiss Brethren" Hymnals

Ein außbundt Schöner geistlicher Lieder (ca. 1555), *Etliche schöne Christliche Geseng* (1564), and the *Ausbund* (1583)

Introduction

Anabaptists began composing hymns very soon after the first baptisms in 1525, adapting the tavern pastime of composing alternate lyrics sung to popular tunes of the day (an activity called *contrafacta*). By the end of the sixteenth century many hundreds of such folk hymns had been composed, memorized, sung, and circulated in manuscript copies.[1] These hymns recounted individual martyrdoms, versified Scripture passages and Psalms, and repeated doctrinal and biblical teachings central to the Anabaptist faith. Quite a large number of these hymns also were brought to print. These Anabaptist hymns are in fact one of the central theological deposits of the sixteenth-century baptizing communities, examples of "community hermeneutics" and "communal theology" in action. Even their compilers expected them to be read as well as sung.

The *Ausbund* hymn collection is the benchmark "Swiss Brethren" hymnal, having remained in continuous (though no longer universal) use by Swiss Brethren descendants from 1583 until the present day; the Old

---

1   On Anabaptist hymnody, see Helen Martens, *Hutterite Songs* (Kitchener, ON: Pandora Press, 2002); Rosella Reimer Duerksen, "Anabaptist Hymnody of the Sixteenth Century," Music doctoral dissertation, Union Theological Seminary, 1956. The indispensable works remain Philip Wackernagel, *Das deutsche Kirchenlied*, vol. III (Leipzig: Teubner, 1870) and Rudolf Wolkan, *Die Lieder der Wiedertäufer* (Berlin, 1903; reprint Nieuwkoop: B. de Graaf, 1965). Most recently, see Ursula Lieseberg, *Studien zum Märtyrerlied der Täufer im 16. Jahrhundert* (Frankfurt: Peter Lang, 1991).

Prefaces to Three "Swiss Brethren" Hymnals 119

Order Amish have continued to sing selected hymns and stanzas from the original compilation into the twenty-first century. Of all the writings of the later Swiss Brethren, the *Ausbund* is undoubtedly the most historically important and influential, given its continuous presence within Swiss Brethren communities.[2]

Surprisingly, there exists no serious study and systematic analysis of the biblical theology expressed in Anabaptist hymns generally, or of the *Ausbund* in particular. One assumption historians have made (usually unspoken) is that the contents of the *Ausbund* reflect "Swiss Brethren" teachings, given that the 1583 hymnal identifies some of its hymns as having been composed by the "Swiss," and that the Swiss Brethren tradition used the hymnal as its own subsequently. By saying this was a "Swiss Brethren" hymnal, the default conclusion seems to have been that the *Ausbund* could be read seamlessly with the Schleitheim Articles, the presumed benchmark for Swiss Brethren everywhere and at all times.[3]

The assumption of seamless continuity leaves unexplored the nature of theological development that occurred in this confessional tradition in the fifty years separating the birth of Anabaptism in Zurich and the printing of the 1583 *Ausbund* collection. Who compiled the *Ausbund*, and what kind of theological currents and influences were reflected in the hymns chosen and assembled? What theological influences did the Swiss Brethren absorb when they claimed the *Ausbund* as their own?

By the latter half of the sixteenth century, the Swiss Brethren were increasingly incorporating new material into their theological and literary

---

2   There is now a full translation into English of hymns contained in modern editions of the *Ausbund*. A selection of 69 hymns appears in *Songs of the Ausbund, volume I* (Millersburg, OH: Ohio Amish Library, 1998); the remaining hymns appear in *Songs of the Ausbund, volume II* (2011). The preface is not translated in either volume. One hymn included in the 1583 Ausbund edition was omitted from editions beginning in 1622, and is not found in the above translations. The omitted hymn, *Freuwt euch jr Christen alle*, #38 in the *Etliche schöne christliche Geseng*, can be found in *The Earliest Hymns of the Ausbund* (Kitchener, ON: Pandora Press, 2003), 333-39. Thanks to Joe Springer, Mennonite Historical Library, Goshen, Indiana, for his help in sorting out bibliographical and historical details for this introduction.

3   The questions of "Swiss Brethren" nomenclature and identity remain contested issues at present. See Arnold Snyder, "In Search of the Swiss Brethren," MQR 90 (October 2016), 421-515.

corpus. When the *Ausbund* is considered in light of the emerging group of writings circulating in Swiss Brethren circles, some significant questions arise.

The core of hymns making up the *Ausbund* are 51 (of an original 53) which were composed and sung in 1535-1537 by prisoners held in the dungeon of the castle at Passau, at the confluence of the Danube, Inn, and Ilz rivers. These 53 hymns from the Passau dungeon were printed in Frankfurt in 1564.[4] This collection carried the title "Some Beautiful Christian Songs Composed and Sung in the Prison at Passau" (*Etliche schöne Christliche Geseng*).[5] The Preface to the collection, translated below, explicitly names the authors of the hymns as the "Swiss Brethren." But we now know that most of the prisoners at Passau were Philippites, followers of Philip Plenner, who had lived communally in Moravia and had been arrested attempting to flee to their homelands in German territories.[6] By 1540 some of the prisoners and their hymns had made their way out of prison and back to German lands. There many of them joined (or perhaps re-joined) Swiss Brethren congregations to whom "they bequeathed their legacy of song."[7]

The 1564 print does not carry the word *Ausbund* anywhere in its title, although seven years later at the Frankenthal Disputation (1571), the Reformed theologian Dathenus referred to the errors contained in the Anabaptist songbook called the *Ausbund* which he felt advocated works righteousness.[8] Some historians, including the present author, suspected that there may have been a non-extant precursor to the 1583 *Ausbund*

---

4 Ulrich Kopp of Wolfenbüttel has established Georg Rab of Frankfurt as the printer. Thanks to Martin Rothkegel for kindly sharing this information, prior to his publishing it. E-mail, December 27, 2016.

5 *Etliche schöne Christliche Geseng / wie sie in der Gefengkniß zu Passaw im Schloß von den Schweitzer Brüdern durch Gottes gnad getict und gesungen worden*, (1564), facsimile print, Mennonite Songbooks, German Series, Vol. 1, general editor Irvin B. Horst (Amsterdam: Frits Knuf, n.d.). In English translation, *The Earliest Hymns of the* Ausbund (Kitchener, ON: Pandora Press, 2003).

6 See Packull, *Hutterite Beginnings*, 89-98; 284-89.

7 Ibid., 286.

8 Dathenus gave this warning: "Dann in dem außbund / oder geistlichem Liederbuch seind gar vil gefehrlicher reden / dardurch die einfeltigen auff dem Wohn und Opinion von der gerechtmachung der Werck / leichtlich köndten geführet werden...." Frankenthal *Protocoll*, 504.

circulating by 1571, and this remains a possibility. However, Martin Rothkegel has located a print of hymns from ca. 1555, apparently printed in Cologne and now preserved in the Vatican library, with the word *Ausbund* in its title. It may be that the 1571 Frankenthal reference to the "Ausbund" hymnal may have been referring to that collection.[9] We will consider the "Vatican Ausbund" collection presently.

To return to the Passau hymn collection, the adoption of so many Philippite hymns by Swiss Brethren communities indicates an interesting shift in emphasis for the Swiss Brethren, for the Passau hymns are decidedly more spiritualistic in tone and content than were Swiss Brethren writings of the 1520s and '30s. Nevertheless, the Preface to the 1564 collection fits very well with the separatist, ethically serious "two kingdoms" theology one associates with the Schleitheim Articles and the early Swiss.[10] There is a strong concern with false teaching, false prophets, and growing social decadence in "these last dangerous times." An emphatic ethical theme runs throughout, with the repeated lament that people do not wish to repent and amend their lives. The primary cause of this sorry state of affairs is attributed to the Protestant preachers, or "servants of Mammon," who appease easy-living sinners for cash, preaching an easy reliance on Christ's atonement and satisfaction for all sins. The result, says the writer of the 1564 Preface, will be damnation in hell fire. For this reason the songs have been brought to print, in the hope that they might be an instrument for repentance and a turning toward God. The Preface to "Some Beautiful Christians Songs," at least, sounds very "Swiss Brethren" notes.

---

9   Claude Baecher notes that the literal meaning of the word *Ausbund* is "selection." Claude Baecher, "L'Ausbund ou Chant des Prisons. Introduction, Analyse et traduction des avantpropos du recueil de chants des anabaptistes," MH 15/16 (1992/93), 173-74. Most recently, "paragon" or "model of excellence" have been noted as sixteenth-century meanings. See Ervin Beck's observations in *Pennsylvania Mennonite Heritage* (October 2016). The first use of *Ausbund* in the Vatican print suggests the meaning of "collection," or perhaps "selection from the best." Thanks to Joe Springer and Martin Rothkegel for their help in unravelling the etymology of the word.

10 Werner Packull narrows the gap between Philippites and early Swiss Brethren, noting that "Philippite teaching and practice appear to have been akin to those of early Swiss Anabaptism as reflected in the *Swiss Order*.... Given these positions, Philipite transformation into Swiss Brethren...would seem less surprising." Packull, *Hutterite Beginnings*, 98.

It is evident that many Philippites had little trouble integrating with the Swiss Brethren once they had returned to the Rhineland, the Palatinate, and Württemberg. The 1564 Preface to the Passau hymns, with its strong concern for right living, certainly sounded notes that harmonized nicely with early Swiss Brethren concerns. But conversely, one wonders how well the Swiss absorbed some of the more spiritualist themes that run through the Passau hymns themselves. Hymn 29 of *Etliche schöne Geseng* (Hymn 107 in the *Ausbund*), for example, uses some exalted divinization imagery in its 23rd stanza, common in the mystical tradition but less so in early Swiss Brethren writings:

> If God the Lord gives you his Spirit and you no longer hang onto creatures, then you will also be a dwelling place of the pure divinity, of his manner and nature. In your heart will you taste his goodness and his very great power, for which you will keep yourself naked and faceless.[11]

The enabling of an obedient life by means of a spiritual regeneration and an attitude of *Gelassenheit* before God is a more typically South German Anabaptist theme—one thinks of the writings of Hans Hut, Hans Denck, Leonhard Schiemer, Hans Schlaffer, and Pilgram Marpeck, for example. This spiritualist strand is found in many of the Passau hymns, undergirding a strong emphasis on a new life and right living. This same strand is also present in the writings of the Marpeck Covenanters, giving evidence of Marpeck's grounding in early South German Anabaptism. As is evident with the case of *Codex 628*, Marpeckite writings also began to circulate in Swiss Brethren circles in Switzerland in the last half of the sixteenth century, apparently becoming "Swiss" writings as they were copied, re-copied, and circulated in Swiss Brethren communities (see chapter XI below).

The hymn collection preserved in the Vatican carries the title "A selection (*Ein außbundt*) of beautiful spiritual songs brought together out of the Old and New Testament, for the comfort of believers in Christ, with a useful concordance for the simple, so that the testimony of Scripture

---

11   Translation from *The Earliest Hymns of the* Ausbund (Kitchener, ON: Pandora Press, 2003), 254.

can be sought out for every song."[12] This appears to be the first edition (ca. 1555) of a hymn collection that would be published numerous times. However, the copy found in the Vatican is the only one in that series that has the word *Ausbund* in its title. The apparent second edition of this hymnal carries the slightly different but still-recognizable title, "A beautiful little songbook (*Gesangbüchlein*) of spiritual songs brought together out of the Old and New Testament by devout Christians and lovers of God."[13] We will refer to this strand of hymns, published in successive editions, as the Vatican *Ausbund/Gesangbüchlein* group of hymns.[14]

Ulrich Kopp, an expert in typography in Wolfenbüttel, has established that the Vatican edition of the "Ausbund of beautiful songs" was printed in Cologne by Anton Kaiser; the subsequent *Gesangbüchlein* now found in Trier ("Beautiful little song book") and the 1583 *Ausbund* may also have been printed in Cologne, although the printers have not yet been identified; several more "Swiss Brethren" texts were printed there in the last third of the sixteenth century.[15] It is apparent that there was a center of printing activity in Cologne or in the Rhineland in the last half of the century and that one or two printers published a significant number of titles by and for

---

12   *Ein außbundt, Schöner geistlicher Lieder auß dem Alten vnd Newen Testament zu samen getragen, Zu trost den Christgleubigen, mit nothwendigen Concordantzen, Für die einfeltigen einem yeglichen gesang nach zu suchen, Zeugnuß der schrifft* [Cologne: Anton Kaiser, ca. 1555]. The printer was identified by printing expert Wolfgang Kopp of Wolfenbüttel. Thanks to Martin Rothkegel for generously forwarding the basic information and an electronic copy of this book. Also noted in Wolkan, *Lieder*, 118, n. 1. Wolkan, however, had not actually seen the book.

13   *Ein Schon gesangbüchlein Geistlicher lieder zusamen getragen/Auß dem Alten und Newen Testament/Durch frome Christen und liebhaber Gottes*. A print exists at Trier, dated ca. 1563-1565. Available online: http://www.dilibri.de/stbtrdfg/content/titleinfo/831025. In comparing the two titles, it is apparent that the word *gesangbüchlein* has replaced the phrase *Ein außbundt* of the earlier title, perhaps pointing to the intended meaning of the word *Ausbund*, namely "a selection" or "selected collection."

14   Martin Rothkegel has established the connection between these editions, information he kindly shared with me in e-mails between October and December 2016. Joe Springer notes that this book is currently part of the Vatican's "Bibliotheca Palatina," a collection originally housed in Heidelberg, taken to the Vatican in 1622 as spoils of war. E-mail, January 5, 2017.

15   Thanks again to Martin Rothkegel for this information, shared in several e-mails.

"Swiss Brethren" so-called. A closer look at the provenance and the content of the three hymnals associated with the Swiss Brethren, however, soon illustrates how complicated the picture can become.

The provenance of the Passau hymns poses the least trouble, the main points of obscurity being the questions of how these Philippite hymns managed to leave the Passau prison and how they were preserved and used in the intervening three decades before their publication as "Swiss Brethren" hymns in Frankfurt in 1564. The ethically rigorous and separatist preface to this hymnal, if not all the hymns themselves, recalls Swiss Brethren spiritual emphases.

The Vatican *Ausbund/Gesangbüchlein* hymnal presents a more complex story, evident when we consider its title, preface, and contents. The Vatican *Ausbund* has close ties to a Dutch collection of hymns called the *Veelderhande Liedekens / gemaect wt den Ouden ende Nieuwen Testaments* ("Various Songs composed from the Old and New Testament," first edition ca. 1552-1554). The shared reference to the "Old and New Testament" in this Dutch title and the Vatican *Ausbund* title indicate textual borrowing, and indeed the Prefaces to both hymnals are virtually identical. The Vatican *Ausbund/Gesangbüchlein* Preface (translated below) is none other than a German translation of the Dutch preface found in the earliest editions of the *Veelderhande Liedekens* (ca. 1552-1554). Furthermore, the Vatican *Ausbund/Gesangbüchlein* incorporates two songs from that Dutch songbook (with more added in subsequent editions). As Rudolf Wolkan notes, the textual roots of the entire collection seem to lie in the Netherlands, with a significant majority of the songs apparently translated into German from Dutch.[16]

The apocalyptic call heard in the preface to this hymnal, the call to learn the art of "spiritual singing" in order to join the 144,000 elect before God's throne at the end of time, sounds a theme that clearly reflects Dutch Anabaptist spiritual currents. All the same, the Vatican *Ausbund/Gesangbüchlein* also contains one song also found in the Passau hymn

---

16 Wolkan, *Lieder*, 96-99, has more detailed information. He notes that "der grössere Teil des Liederbuchs auf niederländische Lieder zurückführt." Ibid., 102; see also Duerksen, "Anabaptist Hymnody," 53.

collection, indicating borrowing from that tradition of hymnody,[17] as well as many hymns freely borrowed from elsewhere.[18]

If this summary description of theological crosscurrents were not complex enough, the story becomes even more entangled when we approach the 1583 *Ausbund*.[19] In the roughly two decades separating the printing of *Etliche schöne Geseng* (1564), the Vatican *Ausbund/ Gesangbüchlein* (ca. 1555), and the first-known printing of the *Ausbund* in 1583, an anonymous editor or editors gathered together a larger collection of hymns (131 in all), integrating hymns from an even wider range of sources and brought that collection to print. The 1583 *Ausbund* collection begins with a "first part" of 80 hymns from various sources, and then turns to the Passau hymns. With *Ausbund* hymn 81, the *Etliche schöne Geseng* (Passau hymns) were reproduced essentially as they had appeared in the 1564 print.[20]

The expanded *Ausbund* collection featured a new title and a new Preface (translated below) that indicated new hopes and concerns for the expanded volume.[21] The title reads: "Selection (*Ausbund*) of some beautiful Christian songs that were composed in the castle prison at Passau by the Swiss, and also by other true-believing Christians here and there. To be used in a non-partisan (*unparteilich*) and completely helpful way by each and every Christian, regardless of religious affiliation."

The *Ausbund* title sounded explicitly ecumenical notes that were not heard in the 1564 title, and the new preface continues the theme. The *Ausbund* preface explains that the hymns were gathered and published at the request of "good-hearted people" who were "not of a single religious

---

17 The shared hymn is "Merkt auf, ihr Völker all gemein," composed by Michel Schneider in the Passau dungeon, ca. 1536. See Wolkan, *Lieder*, 36; 94; Vatican *Ausbund*, fol. 83, verso and *Geseng*, p. 8. By the fourth edition of the *Gesangbüchlein*, ten hymns found in the Geseng had been incorporated.
18 See Wolkan, *Lieder*, 94-96.
19 *Außbund / Etlicher Schöner Christlicher Geseng, wie die / in der Gefengnuß zu Passaw im / Schloß von den Schweitzern, und / auch von andern rechtgläubigen / Christen hin und her ge- / dicht worden. // Allen und jeden Christen, / welcher Religion sie auch seyen, unparteilich und fast nützlich / zu brauchen.* 1583. Following Wolkan, *Lieder*, 118.
20 Two hymns from the *Etliche schöne Geseng* were not reproduced, numbers 3 and 17. The rest of the order remained unchanged.
21 See Baecher, "L'Ausbund," MH 15/16 (1992/93), 171-87.

affiliation" (apparently not at the request of "Swiss Brethren" alone). The hymn writers represent various religious points of view, and their hymns have been left unchanged. As if to demonstrate the fact, the first hymn in the subsequent collection was written not by an Anabaptist, but by the spiritualist Sebastian Franck (although he is not mentioned by name); the second hymn is a versification of the universal statement of faith, the Apostles' Creed; the third hymn then turns to the more typically Anabaptist theme of martyrdom, and the suffering of all the faithful throughout history. The Anabaptist hymns comprising the first part of the new book are representative of a wide spectrum of Anabaptist and non-Anabaptist groups, pointing to the inclusive and "ecumenical" tendencies of the compiler(s).

A numerical compilation of non-Swiss Brethren hymns published in the 1583 *Ausbund* reveals that 94 of the 131 hymns originated outside the denominational and confessional stream we may identify as "Swiss Brethren." The tally is as follows: 51 hymns (the "second part" from hymn 81 to hymn 131) originated with the Philippites and were composed between 1535 and 1537. Of the 80 hymns of the first part, 11 were taken over and translated from the Dutch publication *Het Offer des Heeren*; 11 more can be found in the Vatican *Ausbund/Gesangbüchlein*, although Wolkan demonstrates that these eleven hymns (originally Dutch) were freshly translated for the *Ausbund* edition; 10 new hymns are attributed to writers with demonstrated connections to the Marpeck Covenanter network;[22] 5 hymns were borrowed from Weisse's Bohemian Brethren hymnal of 1531; and there are a few more borrowed from Lutheran sources and even one converted Roman Catholic hymn. Indeed, this is a surpassingly odd "Swiss Brethren" collection of hymns, regardless of the nod to the "Swiss" hymns (which were actually Philippite hymns) in the title.

The theological reason for the inclusive approach is immediately made evident in the preface to the 1583 *Ausbund*. True faith, the preface states, is not the result of human striving or human coercion, but is a gift of God. Or, as the preface notes further along, God's children are those who are driven by God's Spirit. The songs collected in the *Ausbund* are thus "spirit speaking to spirit," and are sent out by those who have been "drawn by

---

[22] Hans Bichel composed five hymns; Sigmund Bosch composed three; one each is attributed to Leupold Scharnschlager and Walpurga von Pappenheim, respectively, although the actual authorship of these latter two is doubtful.

God" to others who have been similarly "drawn." No singers of these hymns will be forced to believe anything that does not correspond with their understanding of Scripture.

The free faith of those drawn by God and taught by the Holy Spirit is immediately contrasted with the situation "in the present day," where subjects are coerced, with sword, prison, and fines, into hypocritically "confessing" that they believe exactly what their overlords believe. The extended appeal for religious toleration is sounded here and is developed by analyzing the proper role of the magistrates in keeping order, and the role of religious teachers and leaders as instructors of the magistrates.

The establishment of political authority directly from God is affirmed (Romans 13), with some caveats: magistrates are appointed to keep *civil* order, and the final authority remains God, who has granted them their political office and the power to execute it. But political authorities have not been granted the power to extend their legislation and coercion into matters of faith, for these are matters of the Spirit, not questions of civil order. When coercion happens in these matters, magistrates have overstepped the bounds of their biblical mandate from God.

The blame for the misuse of political power in matters of faith, however, is laid at the door of the false religious teachers, who in their ignorance of spiritual things sow their seed among thistles. When their misguided sowing bears no good fruit, they try to reap results forcibly with violence and the sword, inciting the authorities to punish those who will not conform to their false teachings. The entire enterprise is misguided, says the preface, for no human being can bring about faith, by any means. Faith is always a spiritual gift from God. Physical punishment and coercion have no place in the spiritual realm. Only the spiritual "punishment" of admonition and the ban may be used among Christians and in matters of faith.

The *Ausbund* preface ends with a strong challenge to the priests, preachers, and teachers—those who incite magistrates to violence against those who will not submit to their false teaching. Such people should consider their condemnable role in shedding the blood of the innocent and should note that "Christians don't persecute; they are persecuted."

The theme of the faithful having suffered persecution at the hands of the unrighteous throughout history returns in conclusion.

Whoever wrote the *Ausbund* preface very likely had a hand in organizing and preparing this eclectic hymn collection for publication. Who might this have been? Noting the characteristics we have mentioned, Amos Hoover suggested that the 1583 *Ausbund* was not published by Swiss Brethren at all, but rather by "half-Anabaptist" friends of theirs, as a plea for toleration.[23] Claude Baecher proposed the thesis that the preface and the collection may have been done by "an author belonging to the large family of spiritualists," and not necessarily by an Anabaptist, and put forward the name of Daniel Sudermann, a Schwenckfelder who passed through an "Anabaptist" phase on his way to a more eclectic spiritualism.[24] An earlier analysis of the *Codex 628* manuscript strand suggested a third thesis, namely a possible Marpeck-Covenanter connection.

If the manuscript borrowing and copying that was taking place in Switzerland from 1571 on points to growing Covenanter/Swiss Brethren interaction, and if the well-documented Covenanter argumentation for religious toleration re-appears in the *Ausbund*, it is not unreasonable to suggest the thesis that the *Ausbund* collection may represent a concrete expression of Covenanter ideals, perhaps in coordination with "Swiss Brethren" who had grown less militantly separatist. The eclectic nature of the Covenanter network and its predilection for "borrowing" ideas and texts fits well with the diverse collection of hymns brought together in the 1583 *Ausbund* edition.[25] Certainly the collection as a whole looks more comfortably Marpeck/Covenanter than separatist Swiss.

At the same time, the printing history that points to Cologne as a center of "High German/Swiss Brethren" publication in the later sixteenth

---

23 Amos Hoover, "Who Edited and Published the First Ausbund?" *The Diary* 6 (1972), 114; summarized in Baecher, "L'Ausbund," 179, n. 41.

24 Baecher, "L'Ausbund," 184, n. 71. Referring to the sentence in the 1583 preface, that "although the authors are not of the same religious beliefs, yet the song of each is herein left untampered," Baecher notes: "Cette phrase peut même signifier que la publication et le travail de compilation aient pu être faits par un auteur appartenant à la grande famille des spiritualistes, exaltant la liberté de culte, et pas nécessairement par une plume anabaptiste." "L'Ausbund," 179.

25 C. Arnold Snyder, "The (not-so) 'Simple Confession' of the later Swiss Brethren. Part I: Manuscripts and Marpeckites in an Age of Print," MQR 73 (October 1999), 677-722.

Prefaces to Three "Swiss Brethren" Hymnals 129

century, and the free borrowing of hymns from the Dutch and "High German" traditions may point to more ecumenically-minded Anabaptists in the north as possible compilers of the collection that became the quintessential "Swiss Brethren" hymnal.[26]

None of these theses about the editor and compiler of the *Ausbund* has yet been demonstrated with any finality. The evidence represented by the three very different and unique "Swiss Brethren" hymnal prefaces, translated below, provides a glimpse into the lively world of Anabaptist hymnody in the late sixteenth century, as it was unfolding in the lower Rhine regions towards the end of the century, incorporating diverse theological currents and emphases. By extension, we can glimpse the blending of a variety of Anabaptist currents as North and South met and interacted. At present, this churning reality poses more questions than it furnishes answers.

---

26 Martin Rothkegel is currently investigating these questions and will shortly bring the results of his research into print.

Preface
Ein außbund Schöner geistlicher Lieder (ca. 1555)

A selection of beautiful spiritual songs brought together out of the Old and New Testament, for the comfort of believers in Christ, with a useful concordance for the simple, so that the testimony of Scripture can be sought out for every song

Revelation 19[:5]
Praise our God all his servants, small and great.

Psalm 150[:6]
Let all that lives praise the Lord.

To the Christian Singer

You have here, Christian singer, some songs that were brought together to God's honor and praise by several students of the Gospel. We wish to admonish every person that they not be upset by the fact that the praiseworthy Psalms and other beautiful spiritual songs have been omitted. This was done only because of the expense.

Everyone should be sure that they use the songs to the highest praise of God, and not flippantly. Rather, [sing] exactly like the children of Israel did when God freed them from the Pharaoh's hand. They praised the Lord and exulted and said, "I will sing to the Lord for he has done great things. He threw horses and wagons into the sea."[27]

Since he also has rescued us from the power of the Devil with his blood,[28] it is right that we thank and praise him for that with our whole hearts,[29] as it stands written, "Sing and raise psalms to the Lord in your hearts, and let everyone give thanks at all times to God and the Father, in the name of our Lord Jesus Christ."[30] As the wise man said, "Bloom like a

---

27 *Margin*: Exodus 15
28 *Margin*: Revelation 1[:5-6]
29 *Margin*: Psalm 97 [perhaps Psalm 98?]
30 *Margin*: Ephesians 5[:19-20]

rose garden, sing a song of praise, praise God for all works, give the Lord glory and honor, strengthen his praise with your lips."[31]

Therefore every Christian should, when he sings spiritual songs or Psalms, always sing more with the heart than with the mouth, so that the words that are sung have also been eagerly absorbed by the heart. For if someone praises God with the mouth, and not with the heart, that praise is not pleasing [to God].[32] But all Christians should diligently learn to sing here, so that they might learn to sing the new song with all the elect, [the song] the hundred and forty-four thousand have learned before the throne of God.[33]

To this end may we be helped by God the Father through Jesus Christ our Lord and Savior.

AMEN

    Love the Christian song at all times
    Happily let all the worldly songs go idle
    And so, with a little work, you will learn wisely and well
    And with desire and joy for God your heart will be converted
    All who are to sing or read these songs
    I ask you not to be lazy or quarelsome
    Understand and learn from the heart
    And a devout walk[34] will be the result.

---

31 *Margin*: Ecclesiasticus 39[:13-14]
32 *Margin*: Ecclesiasticus 15[:9]
33 *Margin*: Revelation 14[:1-5]
34 Or "pious way of life": *einen frommen wandel.*

Preface
Etliche schöne Christliche Geseng (1564)

Some Beautiful Christians Songs Composed and Sung by the grace of God in the Prison at Passau by the Swiss Brethren

Psalm 139 [140:5-6]

The proud have laid a trap for me, wanting to snare me with cords; they have laid traps for me where I needed to go. Therefore I said to the Lord: You are my God, etc.

It is the case that in this present world, dear friendly reader, the times have become so dangerous and troublesome in matters of faith that the common man hardly knows where to go, as Christ prophesied. For human beings have been kept from the truth for a long time through the establishment of false ceremonies and false freedoms, and many false prophets and apostles in these last days have exalted themselves fraudulently under the appearance of the truth. So[35] it is hardly remarkable that where the situation was right, [even] the elect were tricked into error. For love has grown cold in many people, unrighteousness has gained the upper hand, and many are scandalized by Christ. Thus is Esdras's saying truly fulfilled today in our land, when he said: "A land will ask another, and say, 'Dear one, has righteousness made its way through you?' and it will answer, 'no.' Up to now, human beings live in hope, but do not attain it," etc., all of which we have taken to heart.[36] Thus we see that the way of truth is hidden to many, the land is unfaithful, and often the truth is weakened [*geschwecht*] by ignorance and malice.

Not the least reason for all this is the above-mentioned servants of Mammon, who in their error drink up Balaam's wages, and seek the Gospel more out of shameful profit than out of a disposed mind. They teach that the truth may be held in wrong-doing and give comfort to frivolous consciences, whom they should rather terrify and give a reason for improvement. Thus

---

35   *Margin*: Matthew 24[:3ff]
36   *Margin*: 4 Esdras 5[:11-12]

is the entire land now filled with iniquity and misdeeds such that almost no one today recognizes that they have a conscience given by God[37] that regrets doing evil, which says: Why have I done this? Instead we wish to push it off onto the old inherited sin of Adam, and say: "We are all poor sinners, born in sin. But truly Christ paid the debt and opened the door to paradise through his death, and has done away with the glittering sword of our consciences through his blood. And thus from now on we have free access to the true tree of life, as long as we remain in the freedom that Christ has won for us."

But just as Esau carelessly sold his birthright,[38] so also the human children of today place little value on Christ's atonement and his shedding of blood, and with the lost son[39] no longer seek their father's house, preferring to go to ruin in hunger, and narrow down the time for improvement to the very last minute. They should take care that they not end up next to Esau[40] and be robbed of their future goods and blessings, which the righteous God truly will demand with interest from all persons' hands. They don't notice that God truly warns us daily, as a true father, with famine, destructive storms, and pestilence. Still the world will not come to its senses and be sorry for its sins[41] and do penance. Therefore the plagues will afflict them one day, in death, suffering, hunger and they will be burned with fire. For God the Lord who will judge them is strong, for their sins have risen up to heaven, and the Lord[42] has considered their iniquity. The smoke of their suffering will rise up from eternity to eternity, and they will have no rest, night or day. Therefore Scripture says, Blessed is the one who watches, and remains clothed so that he does not wander naked, so that no one may see his shame [Revelation 16:15].

All of which gives us good reason to bring these spiritual songs into print, of which only some were printed earlier. Perhaps through these songs

---

37 *Margin*: Jeremiah 5[:24]
38 *Margin*: Genesis 25[:29-34]
39 *Margin*: Luke 15[:11ff]
40 *Margin*: Hebrews 12[:16-17]
41 *Margin*: Revelation 18[:8]
42 *Margin*: Revelation 14[:11]

someone will be struck by God's word to turn from evil, and will win a love for God, and will be seized in the heart not by the affliction in these songs, which is everyone's true test of being Christian, but rather by the true promise of God for those who patiently persevere to the end. This is what distinguished these brothers (who are called the Swiss) in all their bondage. They did not rejoice in the shadows of Jonah's shelter [Jonah 4:5], but rather accepted Christ's heat with joy. They valued the shame of Christ higher than the treasure of the entire world, something we desire for all our friends and foes. May they better their lives, to the honor of God, because of this little book. To this end may we here in this time, in good conscience with the Lord, find peace, and beyond in eternity. Amen.

Preface
The Ausbund (1583)

A selection of some beautiful Christian songs that were composed in the castle prison at Passau by the Swiss, and also [songs composed] by other true-believing Christians here and there. To be used in a non-partisan and completely helpful way by each and every Christian, regardless of religious affiliation

You will find in this book, dear reader and singer, truly lovely songs which have been collected at the request of good-hearted people. And although these people are not of a single religious affiliation, nevertheless in this book the songs of each are left unchanged with the hope that none of Christ's little sheep will be torn from his Father's hand by songs or any other means. Furthermore, it is not for everyone to have faith in Christ, for faith is not a result of human custom, or coercion, or willing, or doing, but rather it is a gift of God's mercy, yes, a spiritual gift of God, sent down from above. It is not something that comes from flesh and blood, like the Jewish seed of those who were under the first testament or covenant. Rather, it is an inscription of the Spirit of Christ on the minds and hearts of those who have entered into the new covenant made by God, under which covenant the Lord will be recognized through the forgiveness of the sins of the smallest to the greatest.

Therefore it is our hope that all those who are taught and drawn by God will find nothing harmful herein. For no one will be forced to believe anything, other than what seems to correspond with Scripture, unlike what one sees with many today, against (the teachings) of Scripture. As it unfortunately occurs today, what the Overlord believes, so must the majority of his subjects also believe. Many confess through coercion, or hypocrisy, or to attain favor, and are also held to that by the penalties of sword, prison and money by people of no understanding. This happens with the papists, and also with others who, because of their rejection of papal teaching and their oral confession pride themselves on being better Christians and closer to the teaching of the Apostles.

In these difficult and important things, in all cases the teachers and preachers of these orders—who consider and pride themselves with being servants of peace or leaders—(should) admonish the authorities to remain in their office of keeping order in civil matters by punishing evil, through which office the good and honorable will be protected, and not to overreach beyond the commanded order. They should remind them that anyone in civil authority is ordained a magistrate over the darkness of this world, that is, to punish evil and unrighteousness. The godless heathen Nero was commanded to establish such an office (for the magisterial office makes no one a Christian), for which reason Paul admonishes Christians in Romans 13 to give the authorities obedience, as God's servants, and to pay the taxes due to them. Therefore God called the heathen king Nebucadnezar his servant, Jeremiah 23 and 24 [Jeremiah 25:9], for political authorities are called a rod of his wrath, Isaiah 10[:5].

But [the magistrates] should see to it that they not be incited to misuse their office, for since the office of all magistrates is ordained of God (as Christ's word to Pilate makes clear: if it were not given to you from above [Luke 19:11]), it behooves every magistrate to consider Daniel's words, that the Most High has power over human kingdoms, and gives power to those whom he wills. Therefore human beings are more bound to give obedience to God [Acts 5:29], the giver of political authority, than to him who has received it from God. Here all caretakers or those appointed by the magistrates should take care that they not afflict the innocent, and try to escape responsibility [by saying]: It is my gracious Lord's command; I must do it. Everyone should know that Pilate's servants, who struck and crucified Christ, will not be considered blameless before God on that day because of the command of their overlord. Whoever has ears to hear should note this, understanding its meaning.

But many people think that such things originate mostly at the incitement of the teachers, because they see them sowing their seed in thistles, and their teaching returns no fruit. They plant through the punishment of sword, prison and money. But the Lord speaks to them, Malachi 1[:13]. because man takes what belongs to God's office, namely, that which is driven by [God's] Spirit and should be accepted with willing hearts, is forced onto people by fleshly coercion. For truly it is in no man's power to grant faith, Romans 10, or to punish the lack of faith. The punishment [for lack of faith] is eternal damnation, which is in Christ's hands. Will things not go poorly with such an unscriptural undertaking?

It would therefore be a good thing for people to remove the blindfolds from their eyes, and not give themselves such honor; rather let Paul's words come to the fore: those who are driven by God's Spirit are God's children.

With this all human driving is excluded, except for the way the Apostles established the Christian church through the power of the Holy Spirit, by means of the ban. They expelled those who were evil, but certainly did not drive them from the land, or accept the erring among them. Many today do the opposite: what the Apostles did through the power of God and the means of the ban, they do by means of mandates of the magistrates, and so wish to force faith onto people by external force. No matter how earnestly they pursue it, certainly no godly testimony of improvement or new birth results from it. Let every Christian judge for himself whether the Lord Christ, who will remain with his church until the end of the world, is to be found among such thoughtless people.

When one places the Apostles next to the teaching and the actions of some of today's teachers, let everyone freely decide how well (today's teachers) measure up to Paul's saying in Philippians 3[:17] where he says: "Follow after me. Look to those who walk according to our example." With this the office of the magistrate, who is to punish evil in civil matters, is not nullified; only in matters of faith. For a magistrate is ordained to punish visibly evil works, and not [to punish] deficient faith. For lack of faith is an invisible thing, just as true faith is the acceptance of things not seen [Hebrews 11:1]. So it is also the nature of the case that the punishment and recompense [in matters of faith] belongs to God alone, who sees all secret things. Therefore everyone must give a personal account before God concerning what has been done, be it good or evil. For no human being can see into secret things, or judge in such matters before the time of the Lord comes, when the judgments of the Lord will be revealed.

Therefore the church of Christ recognizes another judgment in this, namely the ban as it was commanded and used by Christ and the Apostles. Therefore those who incite the magistrates should reconsider their harsh judgment, that their eventual condemnation not be made more severe by the shedding of innocent blood. For it belongs to Christians, who follow their master and teacher, not to persecute, but to be persecuted. But what about all those who wish to know what daylight is, even though it is not nighttime or dark? And when such persecution in the name of Christ (by which they mean to serve God) fails to happen, [they wonder] how will Scripture be fulfilled?

May the God-fearing reader with a non-partisan mind judge all these things. Here we leave, in the place of a warning, in the briefest Christian meaning, with due consideration, [the following]: that in all such things, one should try to bring about, not fleshly or earthly praise, but rather much more a crown of thorns with Christ.

X
Letter to the Magistrates in Bern
(December 18, 1585)

Introduction

Sixteenth-century Bernese territories were home to a significant number of Anabaptist adherents, as well as the scene of concerted efforts by the city magistrates to eradicate the movement. The arrest, expulsion, and execution of Anabaptists from Bern and its territories, however, was not constant. After ferocious persecution in the 1530s, Bernese policy shifted to a milder approach in the 1540s, the magistrates of the time apparently content to allow a certain level of underground Anabaptist activity to take place. Harassment, arrest, and banishment did not disappear, but were greatly diminished.

This milder approach changed again in 1566, when the magistrates adopted a harder line. The new mandate essentially insisted on strict adherence to the earlier mandate of 1538, which had not been enforced with any rigor, and concluded by calling again for the execution of recalcitrant Anabaptist backsliders.[1] The immediate result of the 1566 mandate was the execution of two Anabaptist leaders: Wälti Gerber was beheaded in 1566 and Hans Haslibacher, the last Anabaptist to be put to death in Bern, was executed in 1571.[2] Both men had been identified as Anabaptists already in the 1530s, and lived and worked in Bernese territory for decades prior to their final arrest and execution.

---

1 More details in Hanspeter Jecker, "'Biss das gantze Land von disem Unkraut bereinigt sein wird.' Repression und Verfolgung des Täufertums in Bern—ein kurzer Überblick zu einigen Fakten und Hintergründen," in Rudolf Dellsperger and Hans Rudolf Lavater, eds., *Die Wahrheit ist untödlich: Berner Täufer in Geschichte und Gegenwart* (Bern: Simowa Verlag, 2007), 97-131; for events in 1566, 104.
2 On Gerber, QGTS III, #1057; on Haslibacher, #1058ff.

Increased repression by the Bernese authorities coincided with increased activity from Hutterite missionaries, who arrived regularly each spring and encouraged people to flee to Moravia to join their colonies there. Significant numbers of Anabaptists from Bern did leave the territory for Moravia, prompting Bern to call a meeting of the Swiss evangelical states to discuss what might be done to combat the "Anabaptist problem." In the summer of 1585, at Bern's initiative, representatives from Bern, Zurich, Schaffhausen, and Basel met in Aarau. A joint report from that meeting (*Gutachten*) was accepted by those states. Each state was free to apply the recommendations according to its own lights. Zurich subsequently published a new mandate against the Anabaptists in August 1585, and Bern followed suit in September of that year.[3]

After noting that Anabaptists were increasing in the territory, in spite of all efforts, the Bernese mandate explicitly blamed the preachers and the evil lives of the secular leaders for the problem.[4]

> Especially among the preachers and clergy, some are completely lax in preaching and housekeeping, given over to dissolute lives, with drunkenness, gluttony, and other excesses and bawdiness. And the same vices, unfortunately, are also to be seen in the secular order: adultery, miserliness, deception, usury, arrogance, maledictions, swearing, and staggering drunkenness. These are the primary reasons that many pious, God-fearing people, who seek Christ from the heart, are scandalized and leave and separate themselves from our church.[5]

As will be seen below, the Anabaptist writers who responded to the 1585 Mandate were quick to reinforce the point that the preachers were at

---

3   Jecker, "Biss das gantze Land," 105-106.
4   A copy of the Basel Mandate is found in Joh. Henrico Ottius, *Annales Anabaptistici* (Basel, 1672), under the year 1585, 172-77.
5   "Besonders under üch Predicanten und Kilchendieneren / etliche gar unflyssig im Predigen und Hußhalten / dem liederlichen Läben / Truncknheit und Füllerey / ouch anderen Uppigkeiten und Unzuchten ergäben / Und by dem weltlichen Stand derglychen Laster leyder ouch vorhanden sind / daß Eebruch / Gyt / Betriegen / Wucher / Hoffart / Flucken / Schweeren / und die Truncknheit im schwanck / wölches die fürnemste ursach / daß vil frommer Gottsförchtiger Lütten / so Christum von Hertzen suchend / sich ergerend / von unseren Kilchen trönnend und absünderend." Bernese Mandate, 1585, as copied in Ottius, *Annales*, 173.

the heart of the problem, particularly because they counseled kings (and magistrates) to persecute and silence the prophets of God.

But of course, the solution to the "Anabaptist problem" as set out in the Mandate was not to extend toleration to the baptizers, but rather to urge Bernese subjects, preachers in particular, to obey the civil mandates with reformed, moral lives and to persuade the Anabaptists to become part of the state church. Those Anabaptists who could be convinced were to be re-accepted into the state church; but those who stubbornly refused to obey and renounce their Anabaptism with an oath were to be led to the border and expelled, warned that if they returned they would be punished "in body and goods" as "disobedient, backsliding, perjuring people."[6] Punishment was ordered for those who fed, housed or sheltered Anabaptists. In Bruce Gordon's summary, the mandate

> required all people to take the oath of obedience to the state, to attend church on Sundays, to bring their newborn child to church for baptism within eight to fourteen days, to attend the Lord's Supper, and to avoid all Anabaptist meetings. Those who returned to the Anabaptists were threatened with torture and death. Leaders of the Anabaptist movement were to be executed, and those who attended meetings of the sect were to be fined one hundred pounds.[7]

In conclusion, the Mandate reminded preachers and officials of their sworn duty to uphold the ordered provisions, and preachers in particular were ordered to clean up their lives and provide a good example to the "common people." Finally, the preachers were ordered to read the Mandate from the pulpits of their churches.[8]

By the 18th of December 1585 an Anabaptist reply to the new Bernese Mandate was in the hands of the bailiff of Aarburg, and two days later was read before the city council of Bern. The authors of the letter, in the end,

---

6 "... sy als ungehorsame / abtrünnige / meyneyde Lut / an Lyb und Läben zestraffen." Ibid., 174.
7 Bruce Gordon, *The Swiss Reformation* (Manchester: Manchester University Press, 2002), 210.
8 Ottius, *Annales*, 176. As Gordon summarizes it, "The mandate concluded with an expression of the magistrates' contempt for the indolent clergy of the Reformed church whose pathetic performance in the parishes was the principal cause for the nourishing of the Anabaptists."

argued that the Bernese magistrates should tolerate them as good, devout and obedient subjects, who obeyed the morals mandates far better than most, even though their earnest reading of Scripture had led them to a different profession of the Christian faith than the one held in the territory.

It was a heartfelt and moving request for freedom of faith and conscience, but in the end it proved to demand more "toleration" than the Bernese magistrates could bring themselves to allow.

Copy of the Anabaptist Letter Sent to the Magistrates in Bern, December 18, 1585.[9]

Our reply to the honored, steadfast, princely wise lords, Mayor and the Small and Great Councils of the city of Bern, our dear lords and superiors.

To the highly honored, steadfast, princely wise lords, Mayor and the Small and Great Councils of the city of Bern, our dear lords and superiors, we wish our friendly greeting and offer our willing service as your subjects, rendering obedience to the honorable magistrate in all things that we are able to understand through the Word of God.

Since, dear lords, we have received a harsh mandate from you, in which we have noted and understood that you have taken a position towards us as if we did not wish to be obedient or subject to God's Word, which is the reason you decided to issue such a mandate.

Therefore it is our friendly, obedient request to you, dear lords, that you examine this our brief and simple response (concerning your mandate) with patience and forbearance, since in the first place our bodies and lives and our possessions are endangered by you. In the second place [the mandate] goes against the Spirit and judgement of God and threatens our consciences, for which reason we must earnestly consider and give attention to this matter. Therefore we ask you, dear lords, that you read this our letter without prejudice or respect of persons and measure it on the scale of the Holy Spirit whom we desire above all to be the judge in this matter, since both you and we must await the judgement and sentence of God. For you are judged not by men, but rather by God, etc., Paralipomenon 19 [2 Chronicles 19:6-7], who judges without regard to the person. Therefore we fervently desire to submit our cause to the wisdom of God which is to be emphatically distinguished from the wise of this world, as Paul in 1 Corinthians 2 and 3 clearly writes. Among other things he says concerning this godly wisdom, that none of the rulers of this world had known it, for

---

9   Translation by Walter Klaassen and Arnold Snyder. The translation was prepared from a transcription of the document found in STAZ, EII, 443, 105-110: "Abschrifft der Teüfferen brieff an ein Herschafft zu Bern gesendet den 18. Decemb. Anno 1585." Transcription by Arnold Snyder.

if they had, they would not have crucified the Lord of glory. Concerning this James says in chapter 3: The wisdom from above is first pure, then peaceful, friendly and tractable, willing to be persuaded, full of mercy and good fruits, etc.[10] Wise Solomon also says in the book of Wisdom in the first chapter [Wisdom of Solomon 1:1, 4]: Diligently seek wisdom, you who rule the land, keep to the Lord in goodness, and seek him in the simplicity of your hearts. For an evil mind will not attain wisdom, and wisdom will not live in those who are bound to sin, etc.

Dear lords, we are sending you this letter not because we think you do not know these things (and more) without our writing to you, but rather because a truly clear vision and a pious understanding and God-fearing heart must make correct judgements concerning God's Word, and distinguish from one another what is clear and what is obscure.

Now God the Lord, who sees and knows all human hearts, whose eyes are sharper than flames of fire, knows that we desire from the heart to be obedient and submissive to God and his Word, so far as we may understand by his grace. Therefore Christ Jesus, true, gentle King and Lord, so kindly calls and invites us to his Holy Gospel, [saying] that we should come to him, and he would grant rest to our souls. For he said: Take my yoke upon you, and learn from me, for I am meek and humble of heart, and you will find rest for your souls. For my yoke is easy and my burden is light [Matthew 11:29-30]. We do not wish to disregard his grace-filled voice, for it enlivens our hearts. We desire from our hearts to be taught by him. Your mandate also requires that we should allow ourselves to be instructed by God's Word.

Now we know that we are not guilty in any way of clinging to any error or baseless judgement by God's Word, the teaching of Christ and the Apostles and the Holy Gospel. For our faith is in one God, the Father, in his Son Jesus Christ, and in the Holy Spirit, and also in all the other things that are affirmed in the general articles of the Christian faith [i.e., the Apostles' Creed], as Christ and his Apostles have taught. We also desire to believe this, to live according to it through God's grace and power, and [according to] all institutions, commandments, and example of Christ and his Apostles, in baptism, the ban, the Supper and in all things that they have given and taught us. Therefore, we do not wish to accept anything that is taught or practiced otherwise. We have and desire to have nothing

---

10   James 3[:17].

Letter to the Magistrates in Bern

to do, either in part or in general, with those in error, be they Münsterites or others, who are not grounded in the Word of God and the Holy Gospel, or to participate in their faith. Therefore our faith should not be called a misguided sect, unless they wish to blame us for being of the sect of the Nazarene, as the Scripture scholars called Paul, Acts 24[:5, 14]; we reject any other designation.

Further, dear lords, we wish to let you know that we desire to be your good and obedient subjects, in interests, tolls, tariffs, and all the rest of your laws and commands that are not against God, as befits true subjects, insofar as our loving God gives us grace, and insofar as we can obey the same without damage to our consciences. We need to let you know, dear lords, that your mandate and the mandate of Christ (namely the New Testament), which is sealed with his innocent blood, contradict each other in their intention. In our simplicity, we cannot comprehend how they agree. Rather, in the Lord's word in Matthew 5 and the works of mercy, Matthew 25 and in other places, the Holy Gospel teaches us differently than what we understand your mandate to say. We beg you, dear lords, do not be angry with us, for it is not as if we simple and unlearned ones are wishing to instruct and teach you in your wisdom. Rather, it is a case of opening our hearts to you, concerning what burdens our consciences, and what is irreconcilable in your mandate and the teaching of Christ. Therefore we beg you for patience and forbearance.

In the first place, your mandate wishes to drive us from the faith. We are firm in our conviction and also that the mandate is not grounded in Christ's teaching. We regard it as too strict and overwhelming that you intend to proceed against us so severely. With us you call on the same Christ we do. Nowhere in his teaching and his life, nor in the entire Gospel do we find that we should coerce someone else. For Christ said, Matthew 5 [:43-44]: You have heard that it was said, you shall love your neighbour and hate your enemy. But I say to you, love your enemy, bless those who curse you, do good to those who hate you, pray for those who harm and persecute you, etc. Just before that he says: You should not oppose evil [Matthew 5:39]

Now, we do not wish to offend or hate you. Rather, we heartily pray for you. And so we believe, dear lords, following the Gospel in our simplicity, that you should be minded towards us in the same way, since even the law does not allow one to hate those who do one good. We believe that the New

Testament allows it even less, since the Lord tells us to love our enemies. For what Christ taught us, he lived out for us in his own life, and asked us to follow him. This we earnestly wish to do. Although this simple, truthful teaching of Christ is explained and interpreted differently by many as repeatedly happens, for our part, in our simplicity, we cannot accept those interpretations which make the Lord's word incomprehensible. Therefore we rejoice to remain based on the Lord's words and hope that we will not go astray. For the Lord clearly distinguished his peaceful kingdom and the kingdom of this world before the judge Pilate and said: My kingdom is not of this world. If my kingdom were of this world my servants would be fighting to keep me from being handed over to the enemy, John 18[:36].

From Christ's words we can make the distinction that his servants here, in this time, will not fight and struggle for his kingdom with physical, fleshly swords, since his kingdom is not of this world. Likewise, in Luke 9[:52-56] we also see that when the Samaritans did not wish to accept Jesus' saving teaching, he did not force faith on them, although he was the Lord himself who had all things in his power. And when the disciples asked whether they should call fire down from heaven to destroy the Samaritans, as Elijah had done, he made a clear distinction and said: Do you not know which spirit's children you are? For the Son of Man has not come to destroy the souls of human beings, but to save them.

Thus we find this king to be peaceful in all his life and doings, and a prince of peace who carried his kingdom on his shoulders and said to his disciples, John 14[:27]: My peace I give to you, my peace I leave with you, not as the world gives. And in chapter [John 15:18-19] he says: If the world hates you, know that it hated me before it hated you. If you were of this world, the world would love you, but you are not of this world. I have chosen you out of this world and therefore the world hates you. And in John 16[:33] he says: I have said these things to you so that you have peace in me. In the world you are afraid, but be comforted: I have overcome the world.

And therefore, dear lords, the teaching of this spotless Lamb does not correspond with your mandate. And that is where the problem lies: we cannot accept both at the same time without harming our consciences. Therefore we beg you, dear lords, do not force us against our consciences in matters of faith. For the Gospel does not allow bringing anyone to faith by force. For Christ says: Whoever will follow me, let him take up his cross [Matthew 16:24]. He did not say, whoever must follow me. He said further in

Letter to the Magistrates in Bern

Matthew 10[:14]: Wherever people will not accept your teaching, shake the dust from your feet and leave that house or town, etc.[11] He did not say: force them to it. He said further: I am sending you like sheep among the wolves, etc. [Matthew 10:16]. It is not in the nature of sheep to act as wolves, or to persecute or coerce anyone. For Paul says in Galatians 4[:29]: But just as at the time he who was born of the flesh persecuted him who was born of the Spirit, so it is now also. And Rudolf Walter, preacher in Zurich, wrote in his five sermons against the Pope, called *The Antichrist:* Christ coerced no one to believe in him and his teaching with force, but rather he taught and preached in a friendly way, etc. Paul said in 2 Thessalonians 3[:2] that not everyone has faith. Rather, it is a gift from God. If it is a gift, it cannot be forced with any human power or sword;[12] rather it must be obtained through grace and power from above, etc. Also the householder does not want the weeds uprooted as long as the time of harvest is not at hand. For when the servants said to the lord, Matthew 13[:29-30]: Do you want us to go out and uproot [the weeds], the lord said: No. In doing so you will also pull up the wheat along with the weeds. Let them grow together until the harvest. Here we see, bright and clear, that it is not the Lord's will to uproot the weeds with human hands (insofar as this relates to the gift of faith as noted above). And even if our faith were like weeds, who can accuse us? We understand here from the Lord's word, that this [uprooting] is the duty of the angels, and not of the office of the magistrates. Otherwise we could not accept the office of magistrates as written about by Peter and Paul, Romans 13, 1 Peter 2.

Therefore my noble, wise lords, you know well whether or not your scholars induced you to produce such a hard mandate.[13] Above all, the

---

11 *Margin*: Luke 9; Matthew 16; Mark 8
12 *Margin*: James 1
13 Perhaps the writers of this letter knew that the Bernese preachers had prepared a memorandum for the magistrates earlier in 1585 concerning Anabaptist policy in Bern. In fact, the preachers' analysis of the "Anabaptist problem" in that memorandum was to place the blame on the civil authorities for their lax enforcement of the law: since the penalties against returning Anabaptist preachers were no longer being strictly enforced, they were returning in great numbers. The Bernese preachers recommended arrest and a sentence of service as galley slaves. See QGTS III, #1065; Martin Haas, "Die Berner Täufer in ihrem Schweizerischen Umfeld I: Gesellschaft und Herrschaft," in Dellsperger and Lavater, eds., *Die Wahrheit ist untödlich*, 26.

Most High, who sees into the secrets of human hearts knows it. But we know, and you yourselves know that the Scripture scholars and the highly educated of this world, in the New and Old Testaments, have always been disposed to lead the magistrates to suppress the simple truth and to establish persecution. That was also the excuse of the kings of Israel and Judah, who were led to persecute and kill the true prophets sent by God. For this reason the prophet Jeremiah denounced the house of Judah and Jerusalem for their sin and unrighteousness, and proclaimed God's wrath against them. Then they said: Let us go quickly and plot against Jeremiah, we pastors who have been entrusted with the law, the magistrates in their wisdom, and the prophets who never lack God's word. Come, they said, let us cut out his tongue so that we do not have to listen to his words any more, Jeremiah 18[:18]. Likewise Amaziah, the idolatrous priest, denounced the prophet Amos to king Jeroboam, and said: Amos is setting the house of Israel against you; the land is not able to bear all that he has said, Amos 7[:10]. And Zechariah said to the house of Judah: So says the Lord, why do you transgress the laws of the Lord so that you cannot prosper, for you have forsaken the Lord, and he will also forsake you. Then they made a covenant against him and stoned him to death, following the king's command, between the temple and the altar, 2 Chronicles 24[:20-21], Matthew 23[:35]. And there are still many more examples like this which we leave aside for the sake of brevity.

Likewise in the New Testament Christ and his apostles together had to suffer the greatest opposition from the learned ones, denounced by them as seducers and revolutionaries. Christ was given over to the cross by them; Stephen was denounced and stoned to death; Paul was denounced in Philippi and Thessalonica as if he had acted against the order and laws of the Roman Empire in a seditious way, Acts 16 and 17.

Therefore, dear lords, it is a completely dangerous and slippery policy to deal in such things, for the judgement of God and the judgement of man are completely unlike, and human beings many times bless what is not blessed by God. On the other hand, what is blessed by God they will often anathematize, etc. As the prophet Hosea says (Hosea 9[:7]), they could consider the prophets fools and spiritual persons as numbskulls, so thoroughly have the sins of hate and senselessness gained the upper hand. And since Jerusalem held to such an abominable judgement concerning true righteousness, and shed so much innocent blood, she had to repay

Letter to the Magistrates in Bern

it with great fear as the prophets testify in the Scriptures and especially in the Lamentations of Jeremiah (Jeremiah 4[:12]) where he says: Neither the kings of the earth nor all the inhabitants of the land believed that the enemy and adversaries would enter the gates of the city of Jerusalem, but it took place because of the sins of their prophets and the evil of their priests, who shed the blood of the innocent [in the city] so that the blind stumble on the streets and soil themselves with blood even though they had not touched any bloody garment. Therefore all who do as Jerusalem did can expect nothing better. For David says in Psalm 115[116:15], precious in the eyes of the Lord is the death of his holy ones, and in Zechariah 2[:8], whoever wrongs the Lord's own touches the apple of his eye.

Further, dear lords, there is an obstacle in your mandate which we cannot understand. We beg you to hear us and act towards us with patience. For Christ the Lord, to whom is given all power in heaven and on earth, Matthew 28[:18], taught against all unkindness. He went before us, as was said above, and summarized love and said: As you wish others to do to you, so do also to them. That is the law and the prophets [Matthew 7:12]. Therefore, dear lords, since we wish to be obedient to you from the heart (in all things not contrary to God) we beg you, do not coerce us against our hearts and consciences in matters of faith.

You should consider and weigh in your hearts what it would be like if someone coerced you to another faith against your hearts and consciences, which you could not recognize or accept in your hearts. If then you were not obedient, your property and possessions would be taken, and you would be expelled from the land and forbidden to return on pain of death, the words of Esdras would be fulfilled for you, when he says, 4 Esdras [2 Esdras 16:71-73]: they will steal from and plunder all those who fear God; they will take their goods and expel them from their houses. Then it will be seen who my elect are, who are tested as gold in the fire. Likewise, if you fulfilled what Isaiah says in chapter 59 (Isaiah 59[:15]), the truth is imprisoned and whoever turns from evil must be despoiled. Likewise, if it were to happen to you as David says in Psalm 82 [Psalm 83:4-5]: They say, come let us root them out, so that they will be a people no more, etc. For they conspire together in their hearts. If you think to deal with God [in this way], we ask you to truly consider in your hearts and allow the Most High to judge, whose judgement will not fail.

This, my dear lords, is our brief and simple letter and answer to your mandate, against coercion in matters of faith. But we beg you, dear lords, that you will consider our simplicity with grace and accept it and understand it for the best. And if you wish and have the time, you can read in Ulrich Zwingli's *Article Book* in the 36th article; likewise Martin Luther's little book that he wrote in the 23rd year (1523) concerning the Worldly Authority, how far its power should extend, in which he demonstrates profusely with testimonies from the Old and New Testaments that no one should coerce anyone to faith.

Therefore, dear lords, our other articles of the faith, baptism, ban, Supper, and other ordinances, if we had written about them to you also, we would have feared to bore your wisdoms. Nevertheless, we were willing and are still disposed to do so. For we can say "Yes" and "Amen" to all that was said in the Frankenthal Disputation. After the preachers had considered it extensively, it came quickly to us little people. Therefore we simply asked someone else to help us. Since none of us from Switzerland were there, we are pleased to speak a little to those articles about which things are said publicly contrary to what we believe.

As far as baptism is concerned, we are unfairly accused of saying that infant baptism is nothing. Much has been written concerning our real reasons. Indeed, we baptize following the usage and teaching of Christ and his apostles, Matthew 28, Mark 16, Acts 2, 8, 10, 19, etc. The Supper of the Lord we celebrate as a remembrance of the Lord's generosity and his death, Matthew 5, 26, Mark 14, Luke 22, 1 Corinthians 11, and for the awakening of true fraternal love. We are unjustly slandered by those who say otherwise about us. We use the ban according to the command of Christ and the apostles, Matthew 18, 1 Corinthians 5, 2 Thessalonians 2, etc. We hold marriage to be between a man and a woman, following God's ordering, Genesis 2, Matthew 19, 1 Corinthians 7, 1 Timothy 3, Titus 1. We believe with Paul as he said to the Hebrews, that marriage should be honourable and the marriage bed unsullied. But the fornicators and the adulterers will be judged by God, Hebrews 13. Therefore, we are unjustly slandered when it is said (as is said about us) that we fornicate with one another, as some say, because it is the Father's will. Truly, with the Lord's help we will neither take part nor form a community with those who are stained with such abominations.

Letter to the Magistrates in Bern

We are also accused of wishing to be saved by our own works, thus making Christ's sacrifice vain and useless, to which we say a complete "No." For everything good that we can do and accomplish we consider a debt, Matthew 7, John 15, James 2, and the fruit of true faith. For James says: What good is it, dear brothers, if someone says he has faith but does not have works? For just as the body is dead without the spirit, so also is faith dead without works, James 2[:14, 17]. We know well enough that in eternity no other answer for our sins can be found in heaven or on earth, neither cross nor suffering, or any means other than the pure red blood of the Easter Lamb Christ, which was poured out and shed once out of pure grace, mercy and love for the forgiveness of all our sins, Isaiah 53, Matthew 26, Luke 22, Romans 3, Colossians 1, 1 Thessalonians 1, 1 John, Revelation 1, 7. Therefore we are unjustly accused of wishing to be saved by our own works and suffering.

Now, dear lords, insofar as you might think that we cannot be depended upon to fight the enemy or to protect the fatherland, we say that we simply do not believe that war or any other hard punishment will befall you or come over the land because of those who fear God from the heart, but rather only because of the many sins that are neither recognized or atoned for. All the histories of the Bible attest to this. Do not fear to lose your land because of us. For the Jews had the same fear in the time of Christ that if they allowed him to continue, everyone would believe in him and the Romans would come and take the land and the people. You should truly consider that if Christ's teaching had been able to help protect the promised land, their fear would have been stilled and destruction avoided. But since they did not believe [Christ's] teaching and life, they considered him and his messengers to be enemies, and executed them. Then fear and concern, and the power of the Romans struck and overwhelmed them. It was pitiable, as the Lord had prophesied.

Therefore, dear lords, you should not be concerned about us, for there are so few of us, and then we even offer the left cheek for the right; it is pathetic. You can certainly find enough soldiers if large numbers would help. But if God sends his punishment, no number of people will be able to help.

In conclusion, dear lords and superiors, we beg you as subjects that you, in your magisterial office, which has been ungracious towards us, will receive our simple letter with mercy and grace, and also that you will not be offended if we have not recognized someone's worthiness and station appropriately. Our simple request to you is that you consider our suffering along with us. For God, from whose eyes nothing is hid, knows that from our hearts we wish you well. So if you were to accept our letter in grace, we would receive that with great thankfulness from God and you. But if this were not to happen, and you would not consider our plea, this would still not stop us (so far as God gives grace) to pray to the Lord for you from the heart, that he not destroy you on our account, and that we might bear the cross with patience. For we cannot be separated from our simple confession as stated above; instead, with God's help and patience, we will strive unto death. Amen. With this we commit all things and you yourselves to the Most High. May he graciously have mercy on us all.

Dated December 18 in the 85th year (1585)

[Scribal note]

On the 20th of December this letter was delivered to the lord mayor of Wattenwyl, by J. David Michel, bailiff at Aarburg (unkown to him, it was delivered to his mother's house), and it was read in the morning before the council, after which it was sent to H. Fedminger to keep.

XI
Introduction to *Codex 628*
Berner Burgerbibliothek

Codex 628 is a handwritten, bound book of diverse Anabaptist material that spans 466 pages. It came to reside in the Burgerbibliothek at Bern at an unknown date. It is a complex production, as will be noted in some detail in the introductions to the two chapters that follow, but at its simplest level *Codex 628* is composed of two discrete writings. The first is *A Short, Simple Confession* (ms. pages 1-366), which the copyist notes was begun on January 6, 1590 and completed Monday, January 29, 1590; the second is *Concerning Separation, why we do not attend preaching at the papal, Lutheran and Zwinglian churches* (ms. pages 369-466), the copying of which was completed on February 8, 1590.[1] As the graphic on the following page illustrates, the writings occupy their own space in the manuscript, as separate books, but the copyist's hand is the same for both and they are copied sequentially into the codex. In other words, *Codex 628* (1590) was copied/edited by one person.[2] Each of the two writings making up the codex will receive its own introduction, but the codex as a whole merits some comment.

Codex 628 is a virtual encyclopedia of Anabaptist beliefs and positions, repeating convictions about the Christian life inherited from the past, but also speaking creatively to contemporary issues. The *Simple Confession*, the first writing in the codex, is constructed around a detailed response to the official published *Protocol* of the Frankenthal

---

1   Original manuscript pages will be identified as <pages>. Much of the information here was previously published in Snyder, "The (not so) 'Simple Confession' of the Later Swiss Brethren. Part I: Manuscripts and Marpeckites in an Age of Print," 677-722; and Arnold Snyder, "The (not so) 'Simple Confession' of the Later Swiss Brethren. Part II: The Evolution of Separatist Anabaptism," 87-122. In that earlier analysis, emphasis fell on the "Simple Confession," the first of the two writings contained in *Codex 628*. The second writing, "Concerning Separation," received virtually no analysis. That omission is corrected below.

2   There are seven pages of the manuscript that were copied by someone else, namely pages <217-24>. See Snyder, "The (not so) 'Simple Confession,' Part I," 714-15.

153

Codex 628
(1590)

Simple Confession (pages 1 to 366)

Preface
Introduction

1. OT/NT
2. Believers in the OT/NT
3. Sword/Government
4. Oath
5. Trinity
6. Incarnation
7. Original Sin
8. Faith/Works: Atonement
9. Divorce
10. Community of goods
11. Resurrection
12. Baptism
13. Lord's Supper

Conclusion (End Times)

Concerning Separation (pages 367 to 466)

1. 1 Cor. 14:26-34 not followed
2. They coerce faith and conscience
3. They are not a people of peace
4. They demonstrate lack of the Holy Spirit
5. They do not use the ban in their churches
6. No discipline means no true Lord's Supper
7. They don't teach first, then baptize
8. They abolish the cross of Christ (suffering)

Disputation that was published in 1571, the year of the disputation itself.³ Although the brethren had the opportunity to make corrections to the disputation notes, the authorities were pleased with the results of their public relations exercise, and generally considered the debate to have been a triumph for their side.⁴

Some Anabaptists evidently were not satisfied either with the answers given in debate or with the published protocol, because sometime after the debate a point-by-point review of the thirteen questions raised at Frankenthal was composed and began to circulate in manuscript form. In that writing, which we have named Q1, the anonymous author went beyond a merely defensive posture and argued a Marpeckian Covenanter Anabaptist position energetically and at length. An analysis of *Codex 628* reveals an expansion of Q1 by a copyist/editor, perhaps partially aided by others. Whether that copyist/editor was the 1590 copyist is impossible to ascertain. But in any case, the *Codex 628* version of the *Simple Confession* (1590 copy) must be seen as an edited and expanded version of a previously-composed response to the *Protocol* from Frankenthal. We will identify the expanded version of the Q1 response to the Frankenthal *Protocol* as Q3.

In the case of *Concerning Separation*, the second item making up *Codex 628*, the core writing is a manuscript that has survived in two known versions: the first is a version published as part of a book written by Heinrich Bullinger in 1561, and the second an expanded version found

---

3 *Protocoll. Das ist / Alle Handlung des Gesprechs zu Franckenthal inn der Churfürstlichen Pfaltz / mit denen so man Widertäuffer nennet / Auff den 28. May angefangen / und den 19 Junij dises 1571 jars geendet* (Frankenthal, 1571). The best treatment of the debate, in English, is by Jesse Yoder, "A Critical Study of the Debate Between the Reformed and the Anabaptists, Held at Frankenthal, Germany in 1571," unpublished PhD dissertation, Northwestern University, Evanston, Illinois, 1962. See also the two-part article by Jesse Yoder, "The Frankenthal Debate with the Anabaptists in 1571: Purpose, Procedure, Participants," MQR 36 (January 1962), 14-35; "The Frankenthal Disputation: Part II. Outcome, Issues, Debating Methods," MQR 36 (April, 1962), 116-46; and Heinold Fast, "Die Täuferbewegung im Lichte des Frankenthaler Gesprächs, 1571," MGBl, N.F. 23 (1971), 723.

4 As late as 1585 the Basel authorities considered the Frankenthal disputation to have been a successful blow against the Anabaptists. See Jecker, *Ketzer-Rebellen-Heilige*, 84.

in *Codex 628*, apparently expanded by the same 1590 copyist/editor (or a precursor) who had re-worked the response to the Frankenthal *Protocol*.

Codex 628 is an overly large, patchwork quilt of copied and redacted material, with anonymous additions, which taken together are of varying quality. As will be noted below, in the respective introductions to the *Simple Confession* (Chapter XII) and *Concerning Separation* (Chapter XIII), careful attention to copying patterns provides insights into how the Swiss Brethren community in the late sixteenth century addressed the issues they considered important in their time by circulating handwritten texts such as this Codex. We can identify portions of text included in the Codex that appear in verbatim renderings in different late sixteenth-century apologetic submissions to Swiss authorities, for example. The evidence suggests that several smaller documents speaking to particular themes were in existence outside the larger collection bounded by *Codex 628*. But the latter also includes copied excerpts from previously-printed books. In editing *Codex 628* for publication we have done our best to identify copied and paraphrased material, recognizing that there will be copied material that will have eluded our best efforts at identification.

Of course, we would like to know who might have put together such a large and comprehensive document as *Codex 628*. The best answer seems to be that it was a community effort, regardless of the identity of the 1590 copyist. Nevertheless, *Codex 628* does provide a few clues about this copyist and editor, although not enough to determine his actual identity. Near the end of the copying of the *Simple Confession*, at page 365 of the Codex, the copyist lets us know that he was not the sole writer of the text:

> *Finally, my reader, beloved in God, you should know that this small work is not mine alone; for before I came to it, another God-enlightened person—as is my hope—put his talent to work in the fear of God and, through his industry and seriousness of purpose, extended his hand to me. Thus, wherever it appeared to me that he had properly dealt with the matter, I allowed his work to remain unchanged, accepting his industry and work with thanks and placed it here as it was. Others also helped me in this work. But where I have shortened the material, and in some other instances extended it, I hope—that when his and my small*

work again falls into his hands—he and every God-fearing person will readily understand from the text why I was moved, and what caused me, to do this.

Armed with this information we know for certain that the editor who wrote these words (perhaps the 1590 copyist) was working from previously composed works—the core of which appear to be Q1 (the original response to the Frankenthal *Protocol*) and *Concerning Separation* (earliest copy ca. 1546)—that he added to and subtracted from those writings wherever he felt it was necessary to do so, that "others" also "helped" with his work and, as he notes further along, that he himself composed a lengthy preface and conclusion to the Q1 document. With this information in hand we can identify the boundaries of the "added" preface and conclusion to Q1 fairly easily. Several interpolations into the *Simple Confession* text are also readily visible upon careful reading,[5] as will be examined in the respective introductions to those texts below.

The full text of *Codex 628* as it has come down to us, although it is written in one hand, is nevertheless a blending of writings by several authors, as a careful reading of the text makes clear. The 1590 copyist/editor adds these further clarifications:

I would nevertheless sincerely desire that someone else with more understanding and wisdom would come to the aid of us both, especially in those places where we have been too simple for such an exalted work. Should anyone wonder why I wrote such a lengthy preface and conclusion, he should consider their purposes and what is treated in the work. [Those who do this] will the more readily be able to understand the other articles.[6]

In sending out the copied and edited work into the community, the copyist invites the continuation of the editorial process of correction and amendment from any who may have "more understanding and wisdom" and who see places that need improvement. *Codex 628* thus provides an example of how a "community hermeneutics" functioned in the circulating manuscripts being used by Anabaptist communities. We can read the resulting manuscript as a freeze-frame of what was in fact a dynamic

---

5   See Snyder, "The (not so) 'Simple Confession,' Part I," 690-99, and the illustration below on page 178.
6   *Codex 628*, 365-66.

process of theological discussion and discernment in the Swiss Anabaptist community, put into concrete form in the copied and edited texts that this community modified and circulated.

There is evidence that the copyist/editor of *Codex 628*, while content in some places to copy information from writers like Balthasar Hubmaier, the anonymous respondent to the Frankenthal *Protocol*, and the original author(s) of *Concerning Separation*, nevertheless also went to some trouble to consult sources directly, especially when citing the writings of early reformers. One comment in particular is worth noting. Reference had been made to Martin Luther and his early statements regarding faith and baptism. On pages <218-220> of the codex, the copyist/editor cites a published sermon by Luther, noting folio and page, and asserts that he has "faithfully copied" Luther's words. He then admits that an earlier reference to Luther had been copied from a trusted source but Luther's publication itself had not been consulted:

> But what [Luther] wrote in his sermon on the mass, where he noted, in some 17 articles—as we remarked above—that signs like baptism and communion signified nothing without a preceding faith, for they were like a sheath without a knife, like a case without a gem, like a winepress without wine, etc., I have taken from a printed booklet that in turn took it from [Luther's] writings. That is why I have not been able to determine in which year it was printed or on what page it is to be found. But I have no doubt [of its veracity], for the person who made the booklet bore witness to his faith with his blood in Vienna, Austria. (<220-221>)

In fact the copyist/editor had cited the (unnamed) *Old and New Teachers on Believers Baptism* written by Balthasar Hubmaier and published in 1526. It was the unnamed Hubmaier who testified to his faith by martyrdom in Vienna. This passing remark alerts us to the fact that the *Codex 628* copyist/editor was taking some pains to ensure accuracy in his copying of Reformation authors. The identification of folio and page is a good indicator that the copyist/editor is at work.

The cumulative evidence points to the conclusion that the copyist/editor was a relatively well-educated person, fluently familiar with the Bible and having access to a reasonable collection of Reformation and church history sources. For example, in the preface to the *Simple Confession*—a part of the Codex for which he claims authorship—in a section that begins with Jesus' saying that he is sending his followers out as sheep among wolves (Matthew 10:16), the copyist/editor cited a variety of Scripture passages, most of which can be found under the topic of "persecution" in the widely-used *Concordance und Zeyger* (<22>).[7] Then followed several pages describing the suffering of the prophets, with biblical sources supplemented here and there with material from Pseudo-Epiphanius's *Lives of the Prophets* (<25> and following). Beginning with the account of the martyrdom of the apostle Peter, the writer then referred to unnamed extra-biblical sources, repeatedly referring to "the histories" or "the historians" (<28> and following). Here the copyist/editor relied on Sebastian Franck's *Chronica, Zeitbuch unnd Geschichtsbibel* (Strasbourg, 1531), copying verbatim from the third Chronicle that Franck had titled "From Peter to Clement 7th." The copyist/editor appears to have used other historical sources as well— the account of Peter's martyrdom does not match what Franck says, for example—but it has not yet been possible to identify those sources. But an analysis of these few pages indicates that the *Codex 628* copyist/editor had a wider literature in his reach, and that he was referring to it, citing it, and editing it for an Anabaptist purpose.

Toward the end of the preface, the copyist/editor cites Erasmus's German-language commentary, "Evangelical and apostolic writings of the New Testament," to the effect that "true theologians" are those who are humble, renounce the world and are moved by Christ's Spirit (<71>). It is the kind of citation that would appeal to the copyist/editor, who was obviously a person comfortable with books and a fairly sophisticated level of reading but also mistrusted the pride of the "learned ones."

A biting anti-intellectualism runs through the copyist/editor's prose, as when he notes that the children of Satan are experts in words *about* Christ, apishly reciting books by heart, but that the content of many of their books is "thoroughly rapacious and impure" (<21>). One has the sense that the world of scholarship is one that the copyist/editor knows

---

7   *Concordantz und Zeiger der namhafftigsten Sprüch aller Biblischen Bücher alts und news Testaments / auffs kürtzest verfasset und zusamen gebracht* (n.p., n.d., ca. 1540). Translated as *Biblical Concordance of the Swiss Brethren, 1540* (Kitchener, ON: Pandora Press, 2001).

at close quarters and has emphatically rejected. Of course, all the while he utilizes the tools such a world has afforded: literacy, libraries, and critical reading and writing skills.

In the concluding paragraphs of the *Simple Confession*, the copyist/editor again acknowledges "another God-enlightened person" whose work he has copied and amended. He then clarifies that his own work is not to be confused with the books of the "learned scribes" and that he wrote in a simple manner by intention, suggesting by this that he could well have done otherwise:

> Now I have intentionally not sought to write this book with the skill of the highly educated, worldly-wise university professors and scribes. Rather [I have sought to write] in accordance with simplicity and the clear and pure truth which has been sealed with the precious and innocent blood of Jesus Christ, and which has been testified to, even unto death, by his holy apostles and martyrs. May the merciful God lead me in simplicity, humility and the true fear of God, and in a genuine, pure brotherly love, keeping me steadfast to the end. Amen.
>
> And even though this booklet is issued without the name of any author—to make apparent that no carnal honor or praise is sought—I nevertheless feel more liberated and at peace in my heart for having excused myself and spoken of my assistant. For the Christian's glory is not vain honor. Therefore Paul himself says, Galatians 6[:14]: Far be it from me that I should boast, except in the cross of our Lord Jesus Christ, through whom the world has been crucified to me, and I to the world. End (<366>).

Towards the end of the manuscript, after appealing to God's grace for completion of the book, the copyist/editor returns to the matter of authorship, and makes the following observations:

> ... in and of myself, I am too weak and small, and I confess freely that were I to want to acquire any praise or honor I would be practicing the art of the false prophets who suck and steal their art from one another out of books, and then embellish that very thievery with their own names, as if they were themselves such wise, fine learned gentlemen. May my Lord and God protect me

> *from such spiritual pride. My worthiness truly deserves ignominy and dishonor as befits a useless servant—albeit one who is hungry and thirsty for righteousness, if I may speak happily from the heart.*
>
> *But all the glory, praise and honor belongs to the Lord God. . . . . I can report to you, my beloved reader, that I am truly free in my heart, for I know the cunning serpent rather well, how it can flatter the flesh at different places. That is how I set out to invest my small, limited gift. It would give me the greatest joy if, when my Lord Jesus takes souls into his kingdom, I could bring something on that day with the Lord's help—and so return my little gift and pound with interest. To this end may dear God grant grace, blessing and benediction. Amen.* <417-418>

The copyist/editor is aware that his scholarly "gifts," although perhaps limited as he humbly suggests, nevertheless could have rebounded to his praise if he had identified himself by name. One senses a hint of temptation in the thought, and the suggestion that he has known such temptation before, when his "flesh was flattered." The reader is left with the impression, both from the nature of the work and from the autobiographical asides, that the copyist/editor is someone who has known a life of scholarship but has taken some deliberate pains to turn away from it.

The copyist/editor clearly identifies with the Marpeck Covenanters. In an interpolated section of the *Simple Confession* he makes reference to "**our** *Bundzeugnuss*" (<289>, emphasis mine). The book with which he personally identifies here is Pilgram Marpeck's *Vermanung* (Admonition) of 1542, which was also commonly called "*das Buch der Bundesbezeugung*," or the book of witness to the covenant.[8] The copyist/editor's own theological emphases indeed line up perfectly with

---

[8] For the text of this book, see Klassen and Klaassen, *Writings*, 159ff. In a letter Pilgram Marpeck wrote to congregations in Moravia he notes that he is also sending "twenty testimonies of the covenant," or *Bundtzeugknussen*, a reference to Marpeck's *Admonition* of 1542. The letter is found in Rempel, *Jörg Maler's Kunstbuch*, 371-78; ref. on 377. See especially Martin Rothkegel, "Pilgram Marpeck and the Fellows of the Covenant: The Short History of the Rise and Decline of an Anabaptist Denominational Network," MQR 85 (January 2011), 7-36.

the theology expressed in the *Vermanung* and also with the Marpeckite views of the author of Q1.

What were the issues that concerned the Anabaptists in Swiss and South German territories in the last quarter of the sixteenth century, and what significant changes are visible in the later writings circulating among the Swiss Anabaptists? On the evidence of *Codex 628* we can say that the issues of baptism, the ban, the Lord's Supper, the oath, and the sword remained defining matters that continued to require biblical defense and explanation. Nevertheless, the political and religious circumstances had changed, and the heightened concerns that run through the codex for clarification of the relationship of church to state and the appeal for toleration reflect those changed circumstances. The process of confessionalization had advanced in many places, and the state church preachers and theologians had become the primary proponents of religious uniformity, urging active and coercive political action to achieve the end of a unified and enforced confession for their states and territories, as demonstrated by the recommendations of the Zurich church leader, Johann Rudolf Stumpf, to the Zurich magistrates (see chapter XIV, below). Religious toleration, increasingly promoted by Anabaptists and other nonconformists, ran counter to the confessionalizing currents of the day.

Toleration and the "church/world" duality

A primary concern voiced by the 1590 copyist/editor is the establishment by the civic magistrates of a policy of toleration of Anabaptists as loyal but religiously dissenting citizens. This is a central theme that runs the length of *Codex 628*. The copyist/editor concludes his preface addressing the "dear Lords" with these words:

> *Therefore, dear Lords, you who are spurred on and incited by the learned of this world to persecute and abuse people on account of their faith, consider the matter carefully. For as surely as the Lord is living, you are fighting not against flesh and blood, but against the One who has eyes flaming like fire, who judges and fights with righteousness.* . . . <74>

The church-state agreements concluded at the Bern Synod of 1532 come in for direct criticism in the codex, particularly in the second copied book, *Concerning Separation*, where a discrete piece of writing

Introduction to Codex 628

addresses the Synod and criticizes the consequences of the conclusions taken there. One has the impression that the material on these pages was written close to the time of the events criticized; the material sits within the codex occupying its own place with a separate title and conclusion.[9] The recommendations by theologians at the Worms Colloquy of 1557, that the magistrates should punish Anabaptist dissidents with force,[10] while not directly mentioned in the codex, was indirectly noted and opposed every time the codex writers focused on the issue of the preachers and the magistrates. In Anabaptist eyes, the state-supported theologians and preachers were the primary "instigators" urging the magistrates to employ coercion and violence against them.[11]

The Peace of Augsburg (1555) achieved a partial political/religious compromise by legalizing either Roman Catholicism or Lutheranism

---

9 In the codex, pages <401-17>. The writing begins with its own title, "*Concerning the Bern Synod: Its result of severe persecution and the spilling of much believing Christian blood, with which the Bernese have been stained, sullied and marked,*" and ends with a resounding "*Amen.*"

10 Shortly after the Pfeddersheim debate, Lutheran theologians met in Worms and in November 1557 published the *Prozess wie es sol gehalten werden mit den wiedertäufern durch etliche gelehrten, so zu Worms versamelt gestellt* (Worms: Köpflein, 1557).

11 Although John Oyer notes that there was no direct connection between the Pfeddersheim disputation and the subsequent *Prozess*, it didn't appear this way to contemporary Anabaptists. Diebold Winter and Hans Bichel, both leading spokesmen at Frankenthal, connected the two events, and decried the actions of the Lutheran clergy. Winter stated at Frankenthal, "... since the Pfeddersheim Disputation is indicated [in the Palatine mandate], I thank God that we can return to it once again. I was there. We discussed five articles. And thereafter things were published about us which we had never thought, let alone would have ever talked about. Also to our dismay a very sharp mandate was issued against us. If we were such people as are represented in the *Prozess*, we would not be worthy to stand before your eyes. We want to record this as a protest: this is our complaint and protest, that we were treated too briefly [unfairly] at Pfeddersheim." Translation from John S. Oyer, "The Pfeddersheim Disputation, 1557," in J.-G. Rott and S. L. Verheus, eds., *Anabaptistes et dissidentes au XVIe siècle* (Baden-Baden: Valentin Koerner, 1987), 462. For his part, Hans Bichel wrote a hymn published in the *Ausbund* decrying the *Prozess*: *Ausbund* hymn 46, "Ein gfare zeit vor nie erhört, seit Gott erschuf Himmel und Erd." The Hutterites also protested. See W. Wiswedel and R. Friedmann, "The Anabaptists Answer Melanchthon," MQR 29 (July 1955), 212-31.

in imperial territories. All non-Catholic or non-Lutheran Christians, however—meaning all Reformed, Anabaptists, Schwenckfelders, or other "sectarians"—were thereby outlawed in the empire.

Anabaptists must have realized that they had little hope of toleration by way of imperial mandate. They had far better chances of being tolerated at the local level, looking to local princes and magistrates in whose power it lay to apply (or ignore) the imperial mandates. The Anabaptists set out to convince local authorities that they were no threat to the social order, and so should be tolerated as benign non-conformists. There is an upsurge of such directed Anabaptist apologetic writing in the 1580s and '90s, of which the Preface to the *Ausbund* (1583), the *Anabaptist Letter to Bern* (1585), the *Simple Confession* submitted to the Zurich authorities in 1588, Andreas Gut's "Supplication" to the Zurich authorities in 1589 (Chapter XIV below), and *Codex 628* provide examples.[12]

In order to persuade authorities to grant them toleration, Anabaptist apologists argued biblically and historically, a practice begun by Balthasar Hubmaier,[13] Pilgram Marpeck,[14] and Leupold Scharnschlager,[15] citing early

---

12   The Preface to the *Ausbund* is explicit in its appeal to those appointed by the magistrates: "all caretakers or those appointed by the magistrates should take care that they not afflict the innocent, and try to escape responsibility [by saying]: it is my gracious Lord's command; I must do it. Everyone should know that Pilate's servants, who struck and crucified Christ, will not be considered blameless before God on that day because of the command of their overlord." See above, page 136.

13   Hubmaier's subject was baptism, not toleration, but his historical approach was followed by others. Balthasar Hubmaier, *Old and New Teachers on Believers Baptism* (printed in Nikolsburg in 1526). Critical edition in Gunnar Westin and Torsten Bergsten, eds., *Balthasar Hubmaier Schriften* (Gütersloh: Gerd Mohn, 1962), 227-55; translation in Pipkin and Yoder, *Hubmaier*, 245-74.

14   "Where the governmental authority is used, as it was in the Old Testament, to root out the false prophets, Christ's Word and Spirit are weakened, and are turned into a servile spirit designed to uphold insufficient and weak laws. For the Word of God is the sharp, two-edged sword, separating and chastising false and true, good and evil." From Pilgram Marpeck's "Confession" of 1532 to the Strasbourg authorities, Klaassen and Klassen, *Writings*, 150. See also [Pilgram Marpeck], "Exposé of the Babylonian Whore," *Later Writings by Pilgram Marpeck and his Circle* (Kitchener, ON: Pandora Press, 1999), 24-48.

15   See Scharnschlager's plea for toleration, ca. June 16, 1546, written to the Strasbourg authorities, in which he repeatedly appeals to the early writings of Luther and Zwingli, and pointedly notes how their teachings have changed. In Zwingli's case,

church fathers as well as the reformers' own early writings on baptism and in favor of toleration, freedom of conscience and belief. *Codex 628* contains one such collection calling for toleration which we have identified as Q2 (see the introduction to Chapter XII, below, for a fuller discussion). This material, composed at an unknown time by anonymous writers, would continue to be copied and utilized into the next century by the Swiss Brethren. Its apologetic utility was obvious, putting state church theologians in the uncomfortable position of having to explain why, if Luther and Zwingli had earlier opposed religious coercion and the execution of so-called heretics, their theological heirs were now supporting and recommending those very actions.

OLD TESTAMENT AND NEW TESTAMENT:
A HERMENEUTICAL SHIFT

By the last quarter of the sixteenth century, Reformed and Lutheran theologians had gained decades of experience debating Anabaptists and had developed effective strategies. Mainline theologians paid particular attention to the Anabaptist understanding of the relationship between the Old and New Testaments, a point on which subsequent biblical arguments (particularly ethical ones) would stand or fall. The Reformed theologians at Frankenthal pursued the tactic, promoted early on by Bullinger, of urging an early agreement on the *equivalence* between the Testaments, in order to argue against the absolutizing of Jesus' ethical commands.[16] The Anabaptist debaters at Frankenthal did their best, but struggled with the question.

---

his taking of the worldly sword to defend the Gospel ended badly indeed. "Sehet, wie dem Zwingl und den seinigen mit jrem glauben und lere ist gangenn, wie schrecklich enndt er hat genomen mit den seinen, die er hat gelert, den glauben mit weltlichem swerdt furdern, schutzen und meren!" QGT VIII, #576, 346-53; citation 349.

16 See H. Fast and J. H. Yoder, "How to Deal with Anabaptists: An Unpublished Letter of Heinrich Bullinger," MQR 33 (April 1959), 83-95. As summarized by Claus-Peter Clasen, "Prior to the Zofingen disputation in 1532, Heinrich Bullinger advised Berchtold Haller that the Anabaptists should first be urged to accept two basic hermeneutic principles: that all disputed questions should be decided on the basis of both the Old and the New Testaments; and that passages in the Scriptures should be interpreted according to other clear statements in the Scriptures, in a nonliteral manner, and with faith and love as guidelines." Claus-Peter Clasen, *Anabaptism: A Social History* (Ithaca, NY: Cornell University Press, 1972), 396-97.

The reply contained in *Codex 628* (Q1) to the question of the relationship between the Testaments provides a more nuanced Marpeckite response to the hermeneutical questions posed by the Frankenthal theologians.[17]

Rebirth and Discipleship

One of the explicit points of contention in the 1530s between Pilgram Marpeck and the Swiss Brethren was what Marpeck perceived to be an overly rigorous Swiss zeal for church discipline. The approach in the Marpeck nework, if Marpeck's letter of criticism can be believed, was a more patient one, waiting for the fruit rather than rushing to cut off the flower, as he put it. The Swiss Brethren leaned in a legalistic and literalistic direction in ethical matters, reading Jesus' "commands" as ethical absolutes to be obeyed.

By the last quarter of the sixteenth century, the Marpeckite approach to ethics instead emphasized spiritual rebirth as the true foundation for ethics. The result was a less rigorous and literalistic application of church discipline. A focus on spiritual rebirth, so evident in *Codex 628*, provided for a more nuanced definition of the nature and way of life of the spiritually reborn children of God (a life marked by love), to be contrasted with the lives of the "children of this world" who manifest envy, hate, and the desire to control and coerce consciences. In good Marpeckite fashion, the anonymous Q1 respondent to Frankenthal tied the Old Testament/New Testament distinction neatly together with rebirth and ethics:

> Moses, given his charge, was not able to do more than to communicate the consequences of sins, or that the transgressor would be punished. Christ, on the other hand, takes this further for his own, making it possible to avoid and eliminate one's inner fleshly cravings, carnal desires, and passions of the heart (2 Timothy 2[:20-26]). <100>

What makes Christians and the Christian life unique is not simply that Christians "obey" Jesus' commands such as loving enemies, but more, that the resurrected Christ spiritually enables or "makes possible" the living of a new life for those who become reborn children of God.

---

17   See the detailed discussion in Snyder, "The (Not So) 'Simple Confession': Part II," 89-100.

Interestingly enough, the more mystical concentration on a fundamental spiritual change that necessarily transforms one's outer life, also runs through the hymns composed in the Passau dungeon by captive Philippites, hymns that were subsequently appropriated by the Swiss Brethren in the *Ausbund*.[18] The South German mystical influence thus seems to have reached the Swiss Brethren through Philippite hymnody as well as through Marpeck Covenanter leaders and writings. If the wider Covenanter network was influential in bringing together the *Ausbund* and then passing it on to the Swiss Brethren, its members also were responsible for re-emphasizing the centrality of spiritual rebirth and bequeathing it to the Swiss as a hymnological inheritance.

Two Swords and Two Kingdoms

Anabaptist appeals to the authorities for toleration of their dissenting religious views stumbled on a common obstacle, not present for Luther or Protestant apologists who also spoke of the "two kingdoms" of this world and of the spirit. The "two kingdoms" of Schleitheim, unlike Protestant understandings, specified a chasm between the "perfection of Christ" (the church) and "the world" outside the "perfection of Christ." The civil authorities, said Schleitheim, while ordained by God to maintain civil order, nevertheless could not at the same time be part of the "perfection of Christ"—that is, magistrates could, by definition, never be considered Christians while exercising their office. Several decades later, appealing for Christian toleration to authorities that were being labelled automatically as non-Christian proved more than a little uncomfortable for Anabaptists. As the Reformed theologians put it, when debating the Swiss Anabaptists at Frankenthal in 1571, "It is terrible for a Christian to say that government is necessary, wanting its protection, yet not granting it the power to enforce evil and protect the right."[19]

The Schleitheim Articles had been composed in 1527, in the expectation that Christ would soon return. The document reflected scant concern for extended life "in this world" or for those who govern

---

18 See *The Earliest Hymns of the* Ausbund: *Some Beautiful Christian Songs Composed and Sung in the Prison at Passau, Published in 1564*, trans. with an introduction by Robert A. Riall, ed. Galen A. Peters (Kitchener, ON: Pandora Press, 2003).

19 Snyder, "The (Not So) 'Simple Confession': Part II," 102. See the full discussion in Snyder, ibid., 101-107.

in "the world," and little thought was given to what the "perfection of Christ" might look like over an extended period of time. The assumption was that time itself would soon come to an end. By the last quarter of the sixteenth century, however, Schleitheim's polarity was increasingly problematic, particularly in the absence of the second coming of Christ. Anabaptist groups were in the world, for good or ill; they needed places of safety and refuge, and they appreciated good government and wished to be treated as loyal, law-abiding, peaceful subjects. The position that dismissed civil authority as essentially non-Christian, part of Satan's worldly kingdom, was increasingly difficult to maintain—especially since toleration of loyal Christian dissenters was being recommended to those same magistrates.

In *Codex 628* we find an innovative attempt to speak to the dilemma, with a position proposed that showed more latitude than the Schleitheim Articles had allowed. The central distinction made by the Q1 writer is that there are different *kinds* of Christians, not an absolute distinction between Christians (true church) and non-Christians (world). The author of Q1 writes: "It is very difficult for one person to manage" being a true Christian and a ruler, but "this is not to say that a ruler is of the devil, as we are accused of saying by our detractors; they [the magistrates] should remain in their office as is ordained and commanded by God."[20] The attempt to resolve the "two kingdoms" dilemma found in *Codex 628* merits attention, even if there is little evidence that the proposed Marpeckian-colored church/state "solution" left a permanent impression on the subsequent tradition.

CHURCH AND WORLD

At the same time that the Swiss Anabaptists were intensifying their appeal to the political authorities for political space and religious toleration, they were simultaneously attacking the legitimacy of the state clergy— often with a copious listing of the faults and deficiencies of the "learned ones"—and with a staunch refusal to participate in state church services. The expanded version of *Concerning Separation* found in *Codex 628* demonstrates how simple earlier critiques of the clergy—particularly of Protestant state clergy—had grown, flourished, and even luxuriated into a

---

20 Cited in ibid., 104. The wording here is virtually identical to the positions taken by Denck and Marpeck some decades earlier. See ibid., 105, n. 67.

Introduction to Codex 628

fairly sophisticated catalogue or encyclopedia of complaints and grievances by the end of the sixteenth century.

These comments must suffice as a brief introduction to *Codex 628*. The collection is rich and multi-textured, providing some surprising insights into the intellectual world of the Swiss Brethren in the last decades of the sixteenth century. Careful readers will be able to chart the growth and development of the basic Swiss Brethren convictions and expressions of the Schleitheim Articles. Likewise, the Codex can provide a late-century baseline against which to measure developments to come in the following century.

XII
A Short, Simple Confession[1]
[As found in *Codex 628*, 1-366]

INTRODUCTION

The first discrete writing presented in *Codex 628* is *A Short, Simple Confession*, taking up the first 366 pages of the 466-page manuscript. The version found in *Codex 628* (1590), translated below, is the most complete extant version of the writing. The second extant copy of this text is a redacted version submitted to the Zurich authorities two years earlier, in 1588. It was called "A Simple Confession. To the mayor and council of the city of Zurich, concerning the reason for the great division and disagreement among all who boast of Christ and the Holy Gospel."[2] Given that the *Codex 628* version post-dates the edited Zurich one by two years, we can safely posit the existence of a third copy, no longer extant, that predated both the edited Zurich version and the more complete version found in *Codex 628*.

In fact, the *Simple Confession* in its two extant versions points to a significant "family" of related documents that were circulating in Swiss Anabaptist circles in the last quarter of the sixteenth century. In this

---

1   "Ein kurtze einfaltige erkanntnuß uff die dryzehen artickell so verlouffens 1572 (sic) Jars zu Franckenthal in der Pfaltz disputiert worden, allen der warheitt begierigen Gottsgeliepten / on fleysch partheyischen hertzen ze erwegen und urtheyllen heimgestellt...," found in *Codex 628* of the Berner Burgerbibliothek. Microfilm copy in the Mennonite Historical Library, Goshen College, Goshen, Indiana, microfilm #203. A translation of the current German word *Erkenntnis* would render "Discourse." We have chosen to interpret the word as meaning *Bekenntnis* (Confession) not only because the document is in fact a confession of Anabaptist faith, but also because the copyist of the codex explicitly identifies this first document as "our confession" (... *wie wir dann oben im dritten artickell unserer bekantnuss bewyssen*..., Codex 628, <384>), as does an independent copyist/editor in Zurich.

2   A printed edition of the redacted Zurich version of the "Simple Confession" is found in Leu and Scheidegger, *Zürcher Täufer*, 335-402.

A Short, Simple Confession

introduction we will summarize what has been discovered so far about the complex relationships within this family of manuscripts.

The manuscript strand described here emerged against the background of a debate between Swiss Brethren and Reformed theologians at Frankenthal in the Palatinate in 1571, noted earlier in our present volume.[3] Because that debate was sponsored by the civil authorities of the Palatinate and was structured by Reformed theologians, the agenda consisted of points considered particularly relevant by the Reformed. Nevertheless, the points debated did correspond to central Anabaptist concerns generally, although the Reformed interlocutors were not entirely clear on the differences in belief among the Swiss Brethren, Hutterite, and Mennonite groups. A detailed and lengthy record of the disputation, the *Frankenthal Protocol*, was published subsequently. In the "Simple Confession" response to the Protocol that began to circulate in manuscript form in Swiss Brethren circles, the author (an anonymous Anabaptist) went beyond a merely defensive posture, and pushed the Anabaptist point of view energetically and at length. Other Anabaptist copyist/editors added to the original.

Surviving documents in the Swiss archives demonstrate that parts of this lengthy manuscript were put to use in other contexts: it was freely copied, excerpted, edited, and borrowed from. Parts of the larger manuscript were incorporated into apologies directed to the governments of Bern and Zurich, in 1585 and 1588 respectively, and one section was brought to print in 1618.

AN OVERVIEW OF THE FRANKENTHAL MANUSCRIPT STRAND

1. *The Protocol of the Frankenthal Disputation.* The Frankenthal Disputation lasted from May 28 to June 19, 1571.[4] The nineteen days of

---

[3] Robert Friedmann, who was not aware of the manuscript tradition we will be describing, noted that the Frankenthal Disputation "has scarcely anything to do with the brethren in Switzerland proper." Friedmann, *Mennonite Piety*, 35. One Bernese manuscript, dated 1585, claims that no brethren from Switzerland were actually present at the Frankenthal debate. Nevertheless, as we will see, the intellectual currents and written material set in motion by Frankenthal are very much in evidence in Anabaptist circles within Switzerland itself.

[4] For scholarship on the Frankenthal Disputation, see above in this present volume page 155, note 3.

debate featured 37 separate half-day debating sessions.[5] There were three official scribes recording the proceedings in great detail, and after the disputation ended two copies were made for each side. The brethren had the opportunity to make corrections at that point, and then the results were printed and published in the *Frankenthal Protocol*. Standing behind the *Simple Confession* and all the other manuscripts we are examining here is the printed account of the disputation: *Protocoll. Das ist / Alle Handlung des Gesprechs zu Franckenthal inn der Churfürstlichen Pfaltz / mit denen so man Widertäuffer nennet / Auff den 28. May angefangen / und den 19 Junij dises 1571 jars geendet*. The *Protocol* runs to 710 pages of printed text.

The disputation itself featured a good bit of intellectual browbeating of the untrained Anabaptists by the Reformed theologians.[6] There was a good deal of talking past one another, as the Anabaptist participants warily tried to figure out linguistic and disputational conventions, and the Reformed spokesmen (especially the theologian and pastor Dathenus) insisted that the Anabaptists were being evasive, or if not that, at least were simply incompetent. The unfamiliar pressure of a disputation context, along with the fact that the published protocol proceeded to fill its margins with anti-Anabaptist commentary throughout, was probably reason enough for at least some Anabaptist leaders to wish to clarify their own positions, in their own way, on all of the questions debated. Given official satisfaction with the outcome of Frankenthal, it would appear that the Swiss Brethren did not fare very well in public opinion either in the debate or in the subsequent publication.[7]

2. The *Short Simple Confession* in *Codex 628*, 1-366. The most complete extant Anabaptist reply to the *Frankenthal Protocol* is titled *Ein kurtze einfaltige erkanntnuß uff die dryzehen artickell so verlouffens 1572 (sic)*

---

5   Yoder, "Frankenthal Debate," 23.
6   Well documented by Jesse Yoder, "Frankenthal Disputation: Part II," 131-44, and in more detail in Jesse Yoder, "A Critical Study," chapter IV, *passim*.
7   Religious disputations were significant public relations exercises, intended to win the hearts and minds of the populace. A chance comment in a document from 1585 reveals that at this late date, the authorities in Basel, at least, considered the Frankenthal disputation to have been a successful strike against the Anabaptists. See Jecker, *Ketzer-Rebellen-Heilige*, 84.

Jars zu Franckenthal in der Pfaltz disputiert worden . . . . ["A short, simple understanding [or confession] concerning the thirteen articles as they were disputed in this past year of 1572 (sic) at Frankenthal in the Palatinate . . . ."]. The title seems to suggest a composition date of ca. 1573; in any case, the disputation seems to have been a recent and fresh event for the author of the original reply to the Frankenthal *Protocol*.[8] The most complete copy of the *Simple Confession* takes up the first 366 pages of the 466-page *Codex 628*, but it is an expanded copy of an original response to the *Protocol*. We have identified an original reply to Frankenthal, which we are calling **Q1**. That original writing was subsequently edited and considerably expanded by an unnamed author/editor. We are calling the most complete, expanded version of the *Simple Confession* **Q3**. The copying of *Codex 628* (namely, the first 366 pages) was begun, we read on the first page, on the 6th day of January 1590; the entire copying process of **Q3** took 23 days and then continued with the copying of an expanded version of the tract *Concerning Separation*. It is evident that *Codex 628* is a copy, not an

---

8   This reply to the events in Frankenthal currently resides in the Berner Burgerbibliothek (hereafter BBB). For several years this manuscript was known to me only as microfilm #203 at the Mennonite Historical Library, Goshen, Indiana, from which I prepared a transcription. I was unaware of some earlier research notes published in the MQR relating to this codex. The original manuscript has since been located and identified as Codex 628 of the Berner Burgerbibliothek. My thanks to Mark Furner for his help in this regard. See the brief notice of the encounter with this codex in "Research Notes," MQR 30 (January 1956), 77 and the interesting parallels traced by Hans J. Hillerbrand in "Remarkable Interdependencies," pp. 73-76. A note by Delbert Gratz in MQR 31 (October 1957), 295, states that the *Kunstbuch* and "other Anabaptist source material in the Stadt und Universitätsbibliothek Bern was microfilmed for the Mennonite Historical Library, Bluffton College." This may have included Codex 628, but nothing further was made known in print. Jesse Yoder was aware of the existence of the codex, but apparently made no use of it. See Yoder, "The Frankenthal Disputation: Part II. Outcome, Issues, Debating Methods," MQR 36 (April 1962), 146, n. 54. After the flury of activity relating to this codex in the late 1950s and early 1960s, nothing further (to my knowledge) has appeared in print until the recent book by Hanspeter Jecker, *Ketzer-Rebellen-Heilige*. The derivative "Simple Confession" submitted to the Zurich authorities is reproduced in the appendix to Leu and Scheidegger, *Zürcher Täufer*, 335-402.

original autograph.[9] When we refer to the entire Bernese manuscript we will refer to its archival number, *Codex 628*. The *Simple Confession* (**Q3**) which is embedded in the first part of that codex has a more complex structure that will be elaborated below.

3. Hypothetical Manuscript Q1. Internal evidence in *Codex 628* points not only to an earlier complete manuscript (**Q3**) of which the *Simple Confession* in *Codex 628* is a copy, but also to an even earlier original writing which has to have predated **Q3**, and which the author/editor of **Q3** copied, edited, and expanded with the addition of a lengthy Preface and Conclusion. We must posit the existence of **Q1**, an earlier manuscript (no longer extant) which was the original written response to the issues that were debated at Frankenthal, and which makes up the core of the expanded *Simple Confession* found in *Codex 628*.

The primary evidence concerning the pre-existence of **Q1**, and the subsequent construction of document **Q3**, comes from the writer/editor of **Q3**, who in his concluding comments kindly took the time to explain (to future readers who might wonder), that he himself had added the lengthy preface and concluding section to deal more fully with certain matters not taken up in the other articles.[10] There were, then, two primary "authors" of **Q3**, the second of whom was responsible for an enlarged edition.[11] This enlarged edition (including the preface and the conclusion) was then used by the copyist of *Codex 628* and also abridged and partially copied in the abbreviated Zurich version of the *Simple*

---

9   Zuschreiben angefangen Sambstag den 6. tag Jenners deß Newen Calenders Im 1590 Jar. Codex 628, p. 1. The copyist makes the following note, following the conclusive *Ende* of the material: *Beschriben unnd vollendett Montag den 29 tag Jenners deß Newen Calenders im 1590 Jare*. Ibid., 366. Hillerbrand, "Remarkable Interdependencies," assumes that this copy is the autograph and that this answer to Frankenthal was composed some twenty years after the disputation, a conclusion which must be corrected.

10 "Wa aber yemandt beduncke / warum ich so ein lange vorred und beschluß gemacht / der welle erwegen wohin dise vorred und beschluß hin lendett / und was daselbst gehandlett / sich fugklicher dahär dann in die anderen artickell schicken wellen." *Codex 628*, <365-66>.

11 The author of **Q3**, after describing how he has enlarged a previous work, says: "But above all I would with all my heart happily see someone with more understanding and wisdom *help us both* [my italics], where we have been too simple for such a high work." *Codex 628*, < 365>.

Confession.[12] Furthermore, since by his own report the author/editor of **Q3** also inserted material from other sources into an original **Q1** text, we are alerted to be on the lookout for signs of such interpolations within the text of *Codex 628*.

Following the lead of the concluding comments made by the author/editor of **Q3**, we do find a preface that takes up the first 79 pages of the *Simple Confession* in *Codex 628*. Following these pages of prefatory material there is then a natural break in the manuscript, and an explicit turn to the Frankenthal articles. Likewise at the conclusion of the discussion of article 13 on the Lord's Supper (p. 342 in *Codex 628*) there is a 24-page concluding section which does not fit the pattern of **Q1**. These two additions by the editor/author of **Q3** are readily identifiable in *Codex 628*.

When we take away the 79-page preface and the 24-page conclusion, added by the author of **Q3**, we are left with a manuscript that begins dealing systematically with the 13 articles of Frankenthal, but also is interrupted here and there by fairly obvious interpolations. These, we can assume, were the work of the editor/author of **Q3** or a closely-related precursor. The nature of the interpolations fits the concluding comments of the writer of **Q3**, for they are copies of previous writings that were simply inserted at more-or-less appropriate places in the **Q1** text and argument.

On page 79 of the *Simple Confession* (*Codex 628*) a heading appears that reads *Warumb diß schryben beschehenn* ["Why this writing was done"]. It is apparent that the **Q1** document begins here. Immediately following the heading, the author of **Q1** gives us some clues about his own relationship to the debate at Frankenthal:

> We read in the third book of Esdras [by current reckoning, 1 Esdras] that the young men who looked after the king's person competed with each other, to see who among them could bring forth the cleverest and wisest speech. This pleased the king and his officials so much, that they granted Zerubbabel, who surpassed the others, his wish, that the city of Jerusalem and the Temple itself be rebuilt at their cost, even though they themselves [i.e., the king and his officials] had not ordered such a contest to be carried out.

---

12 The Zurich version of the *Simple Confession* includes large parts of the preface, and so stands in the line of **Q3** rather than **Q1**.

> *In the same way that the work of this young man (who had carried out what they had not ordered him to do) pleased this powerful king and his officials, we also hope that no one who understands God's Word will be vexed that some, be they who they may be, make known their understanding concerning the thirteen articles that were debated at Frankenthal, out of love of the truth. Out of such a hope we have put forward what we, by the grace of God, believed concerning each of these articles, as briefly as we were able....[13]*

The scriptural reference to this text in Esdras is a fitting parallel to the Frankenthal disputation on a number of counts. In both cases there are "disputants" vying before a ruler and his court, each trying to demonstrate greater cleverness and wisdom. The winner of the biblical contest, Zerubbabel, prevailed by arguing that the truth is the most powerful force in the created world. The truth is no "respecter of persons," either rich or poor, mighty or simple. Zerubbabel concluded his speech by saying "Blessed be the God of truth," and was rewarded by king Darius with the granting of his wish that Jerusalem and the Temple be rebuilt.

The author of **Q1** wished to place his response to Frankenthal within the framework of an intellectual contest in which the truth would have the final word. This is, so to speak, the subtext provided by the biblical account. What the powerful and mighty may claim is of no account, before the truth and the God of truth, who is no respecter of persons. But the explicit lesson the writer wishes to extract from the tale points to his own "uninvited" task as a writer (whoever he may be) and his own distance from the debate itself: just as Zerubbabel was rewarded even though he was not *assigned* the task he took on, so also the writer hopes that none of the faithful will be upset that he has taken up a task to which he was not assigned. He is writing simply "out of love of the truth."

This interesting bit of exegesis suggests strongly that the writer of **Q1** was someone who was not present at the debate itself, and who stood somewhat at the margins of the previous discussions. This would fit well if the author of **Q1** was a member of the Marpeck Covenanter network who had taken an interest in the Swiss Brethren "conversation" at Frankenthal, and was now joining that conversation, uninvited.

---

13   *Codex 628*, <79>.

The **Q1** material has three particular linguistic and thematic characteristics. It is, first of all, directly concerned with Frankenthal, and responds closely to the logic and argumentation we read in the *Frankenthal Protocol*. In the second place, the author of **Q1** consistently applies a sophisticated "figurative" exegetical method, closely parallel to the approach of the Marpeck Covenanters, which is based on a distinction between the divine law given to Moses at Sinai, and the spiritual law of Zion revealed by Jesus Christ, often described as the distinction between "shadow" and "light," or "yesterday" and "today." Thirdly, the author of **Q1** explicitly emphasized the centrality of spiritual rebirth for the children of God who follow the spiritual "law of Zion." The latter two emphases, with a more explicitly spiritualist tone than was seen among the followers of Schleitheim in the early decades of the century, suggest that the author of **Q1** was most likely a member of the Marpeck Covenanters. Finally, the material in **Q1** is notable for the clarity of its organization and the natural, logical progression of its lines of argument. One has the impression that the author of **Q1** was accustomed to linear, textual argumentation.

As the graphic outline on the following page illustrates, when the additions and interpolations of **Q3** are set to one side, the **Q1** response to Frankenthal takes shape as a coherently organized text that covers approximately 160 pages of *Codex 628*. By contrast, taken as a whole that includes additions and interpolations, the *Simple Confession* that survives as the first 366 pages of *Codex 628* is a patchwork quilt of authors, ideas, and arguments, made all the more confusing by the lack of explicit attribution of authorship. Usually the author/editor of **Q3** will simply begin copying material from another author and book with no sign to the reader that a different source is now speaking, and of course, only rarely are the sources being used identified for the reader.

4. ***Hypothetical Manuscript Q3.*** Since the Zurich version of the *Simple Confession* (submitted 1588) predates the copying of *Codex 628* by two years (copied in 1590), and the Zurich version of the *Simple Confession* represents an edited form of material found in more complete form in *Codex 628*, we must posit the existence of at least one manuscript copy (and possibly more than one) that predates both the *Simple Confession* in *Codex 628* and the abridged Zurich version. This copy (or a related copy or

The Simple Confession

(Q1 core ca. 1573; copied and expanded, 1590)

	Preface [Codex 628 copyist/editor]		*5-79*
Q1	Why this writing was done	79-80	
	Reason for the division	80-88	
	1. OT/NT	89-110	
	2. Believers in OT/NT	110-12	
	3. Sword/Government	112-33	
	Document Q2: Luther, Zwingli etc. on Toleration		*133-51*
	Anticlerical insertion		*152-58*
Q1	4. Oath	158-63	
	5. Trinity	163-69	
	6. Incarnation	169-80	
	7. Original Sin	180-82	
	8. Faith/Works; Atonement	182-91	
	9. Divorce	191-94	
	10. Community of Goods	194-97	
	11. Resurrection	197-99	
	12. Baptism	199-200	
	Insertion: Hubmaier, Old and New Teachers		*200-13*
Q1	12. Baptism (cont.)	213-24	
	i) argument/answer	224-29	
	ii) argument/answer	229-38	
	iii) argument/answer	238-54	
	Insertion: Circumcision: "How Scripture" paraphrased		*254-59*
Q1	12. Baptism (cont.)		
	iv) argument/answer	259-70	
	v) argument/answer	270-72	
	vi) argument/answer	272-75	
	Insertion: Seb. Franck: "Kriegbuchlin"		*275-87*
	Other themes		*287-89*
	Hubmaier: "Dialogue with Zwingli"		*289-316*
	"How Scripture" verbatim		*316-32*
Q1	13. Lord's Supper	332-42	
	Conclusion; End Times [Codex 628 copyist/editor]		*342-66*

two) was available to the authors/editors of both *Codex 628* and the Zurich *Simple Confession*, and must have contained virtually all of the *Simple Confession* and the bulk of the expanded material found in the first 366 pages of *Codex 628*. Hereafter we will identify this precursor to both *Codex 628* and Zurich's *Simple Confession* as manuscript **Q3**.

Since no copy of this manuscript is known to have survived, we cannot say how much more or less material it contained than the *Simple Confession* version of *Codex 628*. For graphic purposes, the boundaries of the *Simple Confession* material in *Codex 628* and **Q3** are identical. To our knowledge, the boundary of **Q3** does not include *Concerning Separation*, the second writing included in *Codex 628*. It is important to note the existence of a logically necessary manuscript **Q3**, however, for it demonstrates the fact that multiple copies of this large manuscript were in circulation among the Swiss Anabaptists in Switzerland sometime between 1571 and 1590.

Since the material added to an original response to the Frankenthal Protocol is readily visible, we are able to identify the concerns of this later author/editor (or editors). The material composed by (not copied by) the author/editor of **Q3**—material that expands the original text of **Q1**—tends to repetition and generally gives the impression of a writer lacking advanced training or practice in the conventions of literary argumentation. Besides the heavy verbatim copying of other texts, three themes predominate in the material added by the author/editor of **Q3**: an explicit argument for religious toleration, an End Times theme not evident in **Q1**, and a strong anticlerical sentiment that occasionally reveals a deep reservoir of anger directed against the state clergy.[14] A favorite rhetorical technique of the **Q3** author is to list (repeatedly) the sins and vices displayed by the state clergy: drunkenness, gluttony, whoring, etc.

The general themes visible in **Q3** all make perfect sense in the context of the social and political situation of Swiss Anabaptists living in the territories of Zurich, Bern, and Basel in the 1580s and '90s. For the author/

---

14   In the search for Anabaptist leaders who might have had a hand in composing and editing the Frankenthal strand of manuscripts, it is worth noting that a strong anticlericalism and an emphasis on the End Times are important themes in the *Ausbund* hymns composed by Hans Bichel. Likewise, Hans Jakob Boll is directly connected to several documents in the Frankenthal strand, as well as having once possessed the Covenanter collection of writings, the *Kunstbuch*.

Textual Borrowing
in the "Frankenthal" Strand of Manuscripts

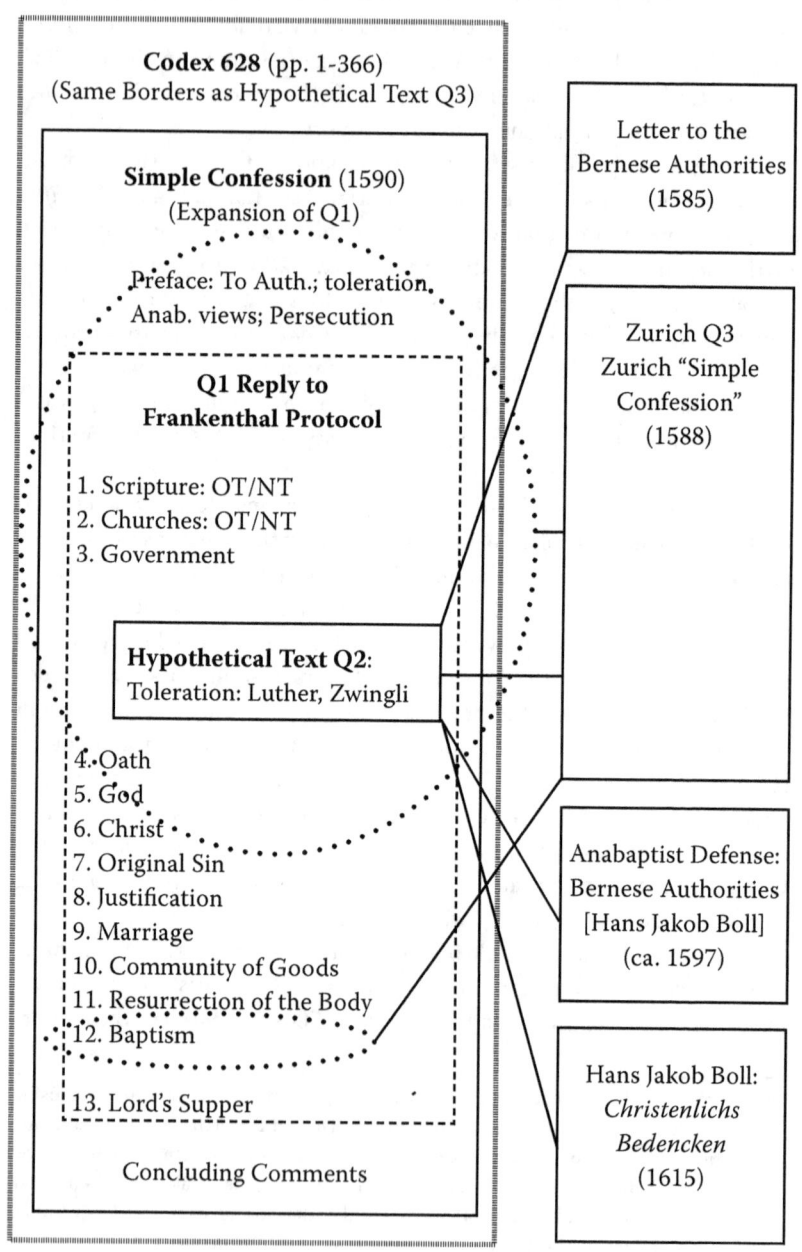

editor of **Q3**, the logical and theological details of the Frankenthal debate were less pressing than the fact of state pressure and persecution, and the continuing "slander" directed against the Swiss Anabaptists by the state clergy. The power struggle in which the Swiss Anabaptists were involved in the 1580s and '90s saw them pitted against the state clergy, with the Anabaptists vying for influence with the Swiss authorities. The Anabaptists accused the clergy of moral failure in reform and pleaded for toleration; the state clergy accused the Anabaptists of stubborn sedition and urged the authorities to take punitive action against them. The 1590 copy of *Codex 628* emerged in this context and is, in part, an Anabaptist literary effort to make the case to the magistrates that the Anabaptists should be considered benign government subjects who happen to disagree with the clergy on some scriptural matters.

The addition of previously published writings to the **Q1** text is a mark of the **Q3** editor/author. Some of the writings copied into (or closely paraphrased in) **Q3** are known to us in previously printed versions. The list of such copied authors and writings identified so far is impressive and is without a doubt only partial, limited by our ability to identify the originals. The identified references and titles are gathered in an Appendix, below.

Among the most significant of the Anabaptist writings that were copied into the *Simple Confession* are two works by Balthasar Hubmaier. Hubmaier's *Old and New Teachers on Believers Baptism* (Nikolsburg, 1526)[15] appears on pages <200-13> of *Codex 628*. Most of Hubmaier's *Dialogue with Zwingli's Baptism Book*, printed originally in Nikolsburg in 1526, is copied verbatim in *Codex 628*.[16] Since Hubmaier's original work cited numerous authorities on the question of baptism, from Origen, Jerome, and Church Councils, as well as contemporaries such as Zwingli, Luther, and Capito, the lack of attribution made it appear to the reader of *Codex 628* that the author of **Q3**/*Codex 628* had consulted and was citing numerous authors and texts. In fact, the copyist of *Codex 628* had

---

15 Gunnar Westin and Torsten Bergsten, eds., *Balthasar Hubmaier Schriften* (Gütersloh: Gerd Mohn, 1962), 227-55; translation in Pipkin and Yoder, *Hubmaier*, 245-74.

16 *Codex 628*, <289-316>. Text of Hubmaier's original in Westin and Bergsten, *Balthasar Hubmaier Schriften*, 164-214; translation in Pipkin and Yoder, *Hubmaier*, 166-233.

simply copied Hubmaier's work—or, better said, had copied a *previous copy* of Hubmaier's work—and has in this way added an impressive list of "authorities" and texts to a discussion of baptism.[17] There is no explicit attribution of authorship to Hubmaier anywhere in the codex, the closest being a reference to him as an unnamed martyr who died at the stake in Vienna.

The anonymous *How Scripture Should be Discerningly Exposited* (n.p., n.d.; now attributed to Pilgram Marpeck and Leupold Scharnschlager) also makes an appearance in the codex.[18] This interesting little tract on hermeneutics has been incorrectly attributed to Michael Sattler for decades; a translation into English was included in John H. Yoder, *The Legacy of Michael Sattler*.[19] The evidence now points decisively away from Sattler to a later composition date (post 1530), and to Marpeck and Scharnschlager as the most probable authors of the tract, pointing again to strong Marpeck Covenanter links.[20]

This discussion could be virtually endless, pointing to inserted citations written originally by people as various as Martin Bucer, Epiphanius, Erasmus, Sebastian Franck, Balthasar Hubmaier, Martin Luther, Pilgram Marpeck, Rudolf Walter, and Ulrich Zwingli, not to mention the numerous secondary references to other authors and authorities that entered *Codex 628* because they were cited in copied writings. Interested readers may wish to turn to the Appendix for a thorough listing—which is to say, as thorough as this editor was able to compile, and most certainly not the definitive list.

---

17 There is evidence that both *Codex 628* and Zurich's *Simple Confession* copied from a previously edited copy of Hubmaier. At one point both versions faithfully copy a reference to Zwingli's Baptism Book of 1525 which a previous copyist/editor had interpolated into the Hubmaier original. Whether this was the work of the author of **Q3** or of another editor is not clear. The parallel interpolation of the Zwingli reference appears in *Codex 628*, <209>, in Zurich's *Simple Confession*, 174.
18 *Codex 628*, <316-32>.
19 John H. Yoder, *The Legacy of Michael Sattler* (Scottdale, PA: Herald Press, 1973), 150-77.
20 See Werner O. Packull, "Pilgram Marpeck: *Uncovering of the Babylonian Whore* and other anonymous Anabaptists tracts," MQR 67 (July 1993), 351-55. Yoder's statement that "there seems to be no record of sixteenth or seventeenth-century awareness of the tract" must now be revised, since most of the tract is copied into the **Q3**/*Codex 628* manuscript.

5. **The Zurich Version of the Simple Confession (Zurich Q3).** The next most complete copy of the *Simple Confession* known to survive is the already mentioned *Einfaltig bekanntnus. An Burgermeister und Ratth der Statt Zurich was die ursach des grossen zwyspalts und zwytrachts sye under allen die sich Christy und des H. Evangeliums rümend.*[21] ["A Simple Confession. To the mayor and council of the city of Zurich, concerning the reason for the great division and disagreement among all who boast of Christ and the Holy Gospel."] This writing is found in the Staatsarchiv, Zurich, under the EII signature. As the title makes clear, the purpose of the writing was apologetic. It was directed explicitly to the mayor and city council of Zurich, and set out to make the Anabaptist case for toleration of the baptizers as loyal citizens, even if nonconforming in some religious matters.

In earlier publications I mistakenly associated this manuscript with the name of Andreas Gut, an Anabaptist leader residing at Affoltern am Albis, near Zurich. A careful comparison of manuscripts and hands by Christian Scheidegger has concluded that the Zurich version of the *Simple Confession* was produced and submitted by anonymous Anabaptists, independently of Gut.[22] Independent evidence dates the submission of the Zurich *Einfaltig bekanntnus* in 1588.[23] Hereafter we will identify this Zurich version of the *Simple Confession* as **Zurich Q3**. Approximately 85 percent of this *Simple Confession* is a verbatim duplication of material found in more complete form in *Codex 628*, but the Zurich version of the *Simple Confession* (1588) is a much abridged version of material found only in *Codex 628* (1590). In an apparently related effort to move the Zurich authorities toward toleration of Anabaptism in their territories, Andreas Gut submitted a five-page, signed "Supplication" to the authorities in April of 1589. Chapter XIV,

---

21   It is found in STAZ, signature EII, 443, 121-97.
22   Leu and Scheidegger, *Zürcher Täufer*, 336: "Das vorliegende Bekenntnis hat nichts, wie in der Literatur behaptet worden ist, mit Andreas Gut zu thun." See 336, note 13.
23   Joh. Henrico Ottius, *Annales Anabaptistici* (Basel, 1672), notes the submission of the "prolixam et satis elaboratam" writing of the Anabaptists to the Senate of the city of Zurich in the year 1588. There can be no doubt about the identity of the writing. Ottius gives the title as the "Einfaltig Bekanntunuß," and correctly lists the section headings, and notes further that much of what is written there is old (*ex antiquitate*) but that its arrangement is unique. See 179 (anno 1588).

Textual Relationship between the Simple Confession, Codex 628 (1590) and the Zurich "Simple Confession" (1588)

Simple Confession (1590)

Codex 628: Preface	5-79
Q1: Why this writing	79-89
Reason for division	80-88
1. OT/NT	89-110
2. Believers in OT/NT	110-12
3. Sword/Government	112-33
Codex 628: doc. Q2 on toleration	133-51
Anticlerical	152-58
Q1: 4. Oath	158-63
5. Trinity	163-69
6. Incarnation	169-80
7. Original Sin	180-82
8. Faith/Works;	
Atonement	182-91
9. Divorce	191-94
10. Community of	
Goods	194-97
11. Resurrection	197-99
12. Baptism	199-200
Codex 628: Hubmaier: Old/New	
Teachers on Baptism	200-13
Q1: 12. Baptism (cont)	213-24
i) argument/ans.	224-29
ii) argument/ans.	229-38
iii) argument/ans.	238-54
Codex 628: "How Scripture"	254-59
Q1: 12. Baptism (cont.)	
iv) argument/ans.	259-70
v) argument/ans.	270-72
vi) argument/ans.	272-75
Codex 628: Anti-Christ; S. Franck	275-87
Other themes	287-89
Hubmaier: "Dialogue"	289-316
"How Scripture"	316-32
Q1: 13. Lord's Supper	332-42
Codex 628: Conclusion	
(End times)	342-66

Zurich "Confession" (1588)

Copied	Omitted
7-24	25-32
33-46	47-48
49-52	53-71
72-74	75-77
78	79
80-87	88
89-97	98-99
100-105	
106	
107-112	113
114-120	
121-130	
131-133	
134-140	141-42
143-150	151-58
159	160-63
	164-88
188-190	191-92
193-194	
	195-200
201-213	
213-217	218-24
225-233	234-36
237-238	
	239-54
255-258	259
	259-70
270-272	
	273-366

184

A Short, Simple Confession

below, contains this "Supplication" as well as some internal responses by the Zurich clergy to his attempt to influence the magistrates in the direction of toleration.

6. *The 1585 Letter to Bern*. In the Staatsarchiv, Zurich is a copy of a letter written by Swiss Anabaptists in 1585 to the authorities in Bern, under the title *Abschrifft der Teüfferen brieff an ein Herschafft zu Bern gesendt den 18. Decemb. Anno 1585* ["Copy of a letter the Anabaptists sent to the authorities in Bern, December 18, 1585"].[24] This appeal for toleration contains some text that parallels and paraphrases material in *Codex 628* and the Zurich *Simple Confession*, as well as some verbatim material found in both *Codex 628* and Zurich's *Simple Confession*.[25] One example is worth citing. Commenting on a favorite Anabaptist verse, the writer notes: "For Christ said: Whoever *wishes* to follow after me, let him take up his cross. He did not say, Whoever is *forced* to follow after me...."[26]

7. *The Anabaptist Defense to Bern*. Included in a manuscript collection brought together by Adolf Fluri, now residing in the Burgerbibliothek in Bern, is a copy of an undated Anabaptist apology directed to the Bernese authorities. The title reads: *Apologia der widertheüffern an ein g. oberkheit der statt, das man sÿ ihrer sect halb unantastet lasse*.[27] ["Defense of the Anabaptists directed to the honorable authorities of

---

24 STAZ, EII, 443, 105-10. See Joh. Henrico Ottius, *Annales Anabaptistici*, 172-76, for the text of the 1585 edict which elicited this reply.
25 Cf. especially STAZ, EII, 443 (the *1585 Letter to Bern*, chapter X above), 107a-108a with *Codex 628*. There is also a later direct reference to the material collected in Q2, when this summary sentence appears: "Und so ir lust hetten, und uff bemuyen möchten in Ulriich Zwinglis Articul buch den 36 articul läsen, Item Martin Lauters buchly das er im 23 jar an die Wältlich Oberkeit gschriben, wie wyt sich irer gwalt erstecke dorinnen er wytlouffig mit zügnissen des Alten und Nüwen Testaments bewärt, das man zum glouben niemant mit gwalt zwingen sölle." The *1585 Letter to Bern*, 109b. The 1585 Letter to Bern also contains a reference to the Frankenthal Disputation.
26 "Dann Christus sprichyt: Wer mir nachvolgen wil, der nemme syn crüz uff sich. Er spricht nit, wer mir nachvolgen muss." The *1585 Letter to Bern*, 107b. Emphasis mine.
27 Miss.Hist.Helv.XXX.188, Burgerbibliothek Bern. My thanks to Mark Furner for bringing this manuscript to my attention, and to Pastor Paul Hostettler for making his transcription available to me.

the city, that they be left alone on account of their sect"]. The title of the extant copy clearly was added by a third party—the brethren never referred to themselves as "Anabaptists" or "sectarians," which were sixteenth-century euphemisms for heretics. Although it is much shorter (only 16 folio pages) than either *Codex 628* or Zurich's *Simple Confession*, it contains a substantial core of material (approximately 50 percent) that duplicates, verbatim, material found in *Codex 628* and Zurich Q3 and that would appear in printed form as Hans Jakob Boll's *Christenlichs Bedencken* in 1615. The dating of this short document remains uncertain, but it may well come from the year 1597, in response to an anti-Anabaptist edict republished in that year in Bern.[28] We will identify this "Apologia" as the *Anabaptist Defense to Bern*.

8. Hypothetical Manuscript Q2. An analysis of *Codex 628* and some of the common material copied by the Zurich *Simple Confession*, the *1585 Letter to Bern*, the *Anabaptist Defense to Bern*, and Boll's *Christenlichs Bedencken* of 1615 leads us to posit the existence of a discrete document which advocated freedom of conscience in matters of faith. This readily-identifiable discrete piece of writing appears in *Codex 628*, interpolated by **Q3** into **Q1**'s reply to Frankenthal's discussion of the sword.[29] This writing, not known to have been printed anywhere in the sixteenth century, is a sophisticated argument for religious toleration following a pattern of argumentation first outlined in the 1530s in Strasbourg by Pilgram Marpeck and his co-worker, Leupold Scharnschlager. The writer of this piece (to all appearances **not** the author/editor of **Q3**) collected and collated writings from earlier writers and reformers, notably from Martin Luther and Ulrich Zwingli, on the theme of religious toleration. We will call this document **Q2**.

On page 133 of *Codex 628* the following sentence appears, marking the beginning of this extraordinary bit of writing:

---

28 Ottius, *Annales Anabaptistici*, 172-76, reproduces the text of the 1585 edict, which was republished again in 1597. For an account of Bern's reaction to the Swiss Brethren in these years, see Ernst Müller, *Geschichte der bernischen Täufer* (Frauenfeld, 1895; reprint edition, Nieuwkoop: B. de Graaf, 1972), 84-92.

29 *Codex 628*, <133-51>.

> But that the authorities with their worldly sword do not belong in the church and the community of God, thereby mastering, grieving, and persecuting consciences, is not something that is just now being demonstrated and proven by us out of Holy Scripture. Rather, Martin Luther and other learned ones before us also clearly wrote about it, and proved and demonstrated it with Holy, Godly Scripture....

The unique structure and approach of the material that follows is strongly reminiscent of Hubmaier's argumentation in his booklet *Old and New Teachers Concerning Baptism*. In the **Q2** collection, the writings of Ulrich Zwingli, Martin Luther, Rudolf Walter, and others are cited in order to demonstrate that early in their careers, these Reformation luminaries argued that faith could not be coerced by external means but was rather a gift of God's grace. It is evident that the **Q2** collection also was copied and used numerous times by Swiss Anabaptists in the last quarter of the sixteenth century.

The *Anabaptist Defense to Bern* (which is unfortunately undated) contains the most extensive citations of Reformation authors, as the illustration demonstrates. Of the manuscripts currently known to us, the *Anabaptist Defense to Bern* may well stand the closest to the most complete compilation of what appears in **Q2**.

The line of argumentation in **Q2** is already evident in writings by Marpeck and Scharnschlager published in the 1530s. There are no parallel efforts that we know of from Swiss Brethren, Hutterite, or Dutch Anabaptist circles, although there is one close parallel from a Schwenckfeldian writer in the 1550s. The basic structure and approach of the argument in **Q2** was set by Marpeck himself, in a tract he published in the early 1530s (anonymously) called *Exposé of the Babylonian Whore*.[30] As Neal Blough has convincingly argued, in composing the *Exposé* Marpeck borrowed arguments from earlier writings of Luther (especially from *Temporal Authority: to what extent it should be obeyed*, 1523), and directed those arguments back to him and other reformers who were beginning to link church reform to political power.

---

30 For an English translation of this text, see Walter Klaassen, Werner Packull, and John Rempel, eds. and trans., *Later Writings of Pilgram Marpeck and His Circle* (Kitchener: Pandora Press, 1999), 24-48. For the literature establishing attribution to Marpeck, see ibid., 22-23.

Growth of Marpeck's "Two Swords" Argument for Religious Toleration

	Simple Confession Codex 628 (1590)	**Zurich Q3 (1588)**	**Defense of Anabaptists to Bernese Authorities [Boll, n.d]**	**Boll's *Christenlich Bedencken* (1615)**
P. Marpeck, *Exposé of the Babylonian Whore* (ca. 1532).	(Titles in bold also in Zurich Q3)	Copied from Simple Confession, Codex 628: Numbers 3, 4, 5, 6, 7, 9, 11, 12 and 13.	1. Zwingli, *36 Articles* (1536)	1. Boll's "Foreword", 3-6
L. Scharnschlager, "Letter to the Strasbourg Authorities" (1534).	1. Luther, *Temporal Authority* (1523)		2. Zwingli, *Article Book* (1523)	2. Verbatim match, 7-9
Both rely on M. Luther, *Temporal Authority* (1523).	2. Zwingli, *Article Book* (1523)		3. Zwingli, *Divine and Human Righteousness* (1524)	3. 1532 Bern in Codex 628, in Boll, 10.
	3. Zwingli, *Divine and Human Righteousness* (1524)		4. Luther, [*The 17th Psalm*]	4. Verbatim in Boll, 11
	4. Luther, *Temporal Authority* (1523)		5. Luther, [*Seines elteren Postil*] (1531)	5. Almost verbatim in Boll, 11-16
	5. Luther, *Peter's Epistle* (1524)		6. Luther, [*Gospel*, 4th Sunday after Trinity]	6. Boll continues citing Walther, 16-18. Verbatim, Codex 628, <142-43>
	6. Luther, *The 17th Psalm*		7. Luther, *Peter's Epistle* (1524)	7. Boll continues citing Walther, 18-19. Verbatim, Codex 628, <149-50>
	7. Walther, *Anti-Christ* (1546)		8. Luther, *Temporal Authority* (1523)	8. Boll cites Strasbourg reformers. (no match), 20-23.
	8. Walther, *Incarnation of Christ* (1571)	**Letter to Bern (1585)**	9. Walther, *Incarnation of Christ* (1571)	9. Boll, 24-27, from Def. of Anabaptists, 3-4; 9.
	9. Zwingli, *36 Articles* (1536)	From Simple Confession, Codex 628: Walther, *Anti-Christ* (1546)	10. Luther, *Temporal Authority* (1523).	10. Verbatim in Boll, 27-35; continues with Luther, 31-33
	10. Franck, *Chronica*		11. Booklet re. the *Bern Synod* (1532)	11. Boll's conclusion, 35-40 (ref. to Franck's *Chronica*, 36)
	11. Booklet re. the *Bern Synod* (1532)		12. Luther, [*Seines elteren Postil*] (1531)	
	12. Walther, *Incarnation of Christ* (1571)		13. Booklet re. the *Bern Synod* (1532)	
	13. Hubmaier, *Old/New Teachers* (1526)		14. Walther, *Anti-Christ* (1546)	
			15. Hubmaier, *Old/New Teachers* (1526)	
			16. Luther's "obgemelten postil"	

Marpeck argued (as had Luther in 1523) for the existence of two swords and two kingdoms, neither of which should infringe on the legitimate territory of the other. Christians are bound to obey the temporal authorities in all outer things. But conversely, governments cannot be given power over spiritual matters of faith and conscience.[31] In short, the basic structure of the arguments we see elaborated in **Q2** are already present in Marpeck's nod to Luther's *Temporal Authority: to what extent it should be obeyed* in his *Exposé* and were further developed by Marpeck's long-time associate Scharnschlager.

In 1534 Scharnschlager wrote a letter to the Strasbourg authorities in which he specifically made an argument for toleration on the basis of the early writings of Luther and Zwingli.[32] He asked the authorities to note the "turning" that had taken place among Lutherans and Zwinglians, namely "what one finds in the earlier writings of such preachers, and what is said and written today."[33] The distinction Luther and Zwingli had made earlier, that was being ignored in 1534, was the distinction between the spiritual and the worldly swords. Each has its office and its function, and should not be mixed together, argued Scharnschlager. In particular, it is not part of the duty of the worldly sword of government "to rule in faith and in matters of the spirit, nor to persecute or banish on that basis."[34] The parallels of method and argumentation between Marpeck's *Exposé*, Scharnschlager's letter, and the material in **Q2** are obvious.

Scharnschlager died in 1563. It is *possible* that he composed the bulk of the detailed argumentation of document **Q2** which was then copied and passed on, but the evidence at the moment is too slight to suggest a conclusive answer. One hypothesis that is suggested, however, given what we know of how the Marpeck Covenanter network collaborated in composition and writing, is that one or more writers in that network further developed Marpeck and Scharnschlager's observations concerning Luther

---

31   See Neal Blough, "*The Uncovering of the Babylonian Whore*: confessionalization and politics seen from the underside," MQR 75 (January 2001), 37-55.
32   On Scharnschlager and Marpeck, see ME, IV, 443-46; the letter to the Strasbourg authorities is found in QGT VIII, 346-53; English translation by William Klassen, trans. and ed., "Leupold Scharnschlager's Farewell to the Strasbourg Council," MQR 42 (July 1968), 211-18.
33   QGT VIII, 349.
34   Ibid., 351.

and Zwingli, and that this writing then began circulating widely among Covenanter and Swiss Brethren leaders in the latter part of the century. An internal reference in the most widely shared **Q2** material to one of Rudolf Walter's writings, published in 1571, would suggest a *terminus a quo* of that date, seeming to exclude Scharnschlager from consideration. The problem is that given the communal and progressive nature of the "authorship" of Covenanter writings, a later copyist/editor could easily have inserted the Walter material into a previously existing document. Certainly most of the writings cited in **Q2** (the notable exceptions are the later writings from Walter) date from the 1520s, '30s, and '40s.

In any case, with Marpeck's *Exposé* and the Scharnschlager letter we have clear evidence that the Marpeck Covenanters were re-working earlier Lutheran and Zwinglian statements concerning toleration and coercion in matters of conscience and faith, and turning them into systematic arguments for the separation of the two swords and the two kingdoms. Furthermore, evidently these earlier Protestant materials were being used in apologetic fashion by the Marpeck network as early as 1532. A preliminary conclusion that offers itself for further testing is that document **Q2** is a product of the Marpeck Covenanter network, taken up and used for apologetic purposes by the later Swiss Brethren. It is significant, further, that these same arguments for toleration surface again in the 1584 preface to the Swiss Brethren hymnal, the *Ausbund* (see Chapter IX). Two hymns in the Ausbund, numbers 46 and 66, both associated with the former Marpeck follower Hans Bichel, continue the call for religious toleration and the "two swords/two kingdoms" argument.[35]

Interestingly, there are parallels to the pro-toleration writing we are calling **Q2** outside Anabaptist circles, many echoing the same biblical themes and pursuing similar lines of argumentation to those seen in the **Q2** collection. Perhaps the **Q2** collection drew on non-Anabaptist writings promoting religious toleration, but our exploration (admittedly incomplete) failed to uncover such a direct, verbatim source. In the absence of a demonstrated precursor, the **Q2** collection may well be considered an

---

35 Bichel is listed as the author of hymn 46, which decries the attempt to make Christians "with the sword." Hymn 66, which addresses the distinction between the two swords (*von dem Underscheid der beyden Schwerdter, nämlich des Schwerdts der Rach, und des Geistes*), is to be sung "in the same melody as Hans Büchel's song."

Anabaptist variant of this genre of literature, a genre which is interesting in its own right.

A notable instance of the pro-toleration genre as a whole is Sebastian Castellio's *De haereticis* (*Concerning Heretics. Whether they are to be persecuted and how they are to be treated. A collection of the opinions of learned men both ancient and modern*), published in 1554.[36] Castellio cited carefully-chosen selections from church fathers such as Augustine, Chrysostom, and Jerome, a task already done by Sebastian Franck in his *Chronica, Zeitbuch unnd Geschichtsbibel* (Strasbourg, 1531), a work from which Castellio borrows and copies extensively. Anabaptist writings, including *Codex 628*, also make frequent reference to Franck's *Chronica*, as well as citing the writings of the Reformers and occasionally also citing patristic writings in a selective way. The method in these later Anabaptist writings mirrors what Franck, Castellio, and others were doing. Anabaptist copyists would not have had to look too far to find well-organized citations that suited their purposes.

Among the contemporary writings reproduced by Castellio in favor of religious toleration were Luther's *Von weltlicher Obrigkeit* (*Temporal Authority: to what extent it should be obeyed*) of 1523; Johannes Brenz's 1528 response to the brutal execution of Michael Sattler[37]; a variety of excerpts from Erasmus's writings; selections from Caspar Hedio's writings; and even carefully chosen pro-toleration snippets from such unlikely sources as Urbanus Rhegius and John Calvin.[38] The Schwenckfeldian response to the

---

36 English translation and excellent bibliographical essay in Roland Bainton, *Concerning Heretics. Whether they are to be persecuted and how they are to be treated. A collection of the opinions of learned men both ancient and modern* (Columbia University Press, 1935; New York: Octagon Books, 1965).

37 J. Brenz, *Ob ein Weltliche Obrigkeit mit Göttlichen und billichen Rechten möge die Widertäuffer durch Fewer oder Schwerdt vom Leben zu dem tode richten lassen* (1528). Critical edition in M. Brecht, G. Schäfer, F. Wolf, eds., *Johannes Brenz. Früschriften, Teil 2* (Tübingen: Mohr, 1974), 480-98.

38 Bainton notes, "To discover anything in the writings of Urbanus Rhegius suitable for inclusion in the *De haereticis* was a positive achievement." Bainton, *Concerning Heretics*, 66. For one of Rhegius' appeals for the arrest and execution of Anabaptists, see C. A. Snyder, ed., *Sources of South German/Austrian Anabaptism* (Kitchener, ON: Pandora Press, 2001), "Justification for the Prosecution of Anabaptists" (1536), 213-27. Concerning Calvin, Bainton quips "If Calvin ever wrote anything in favor of religious liberty it was a typographical error." Bainton, *Concerning Heretics*, 74.

Peace of Augsburg (1555) by Theophilus Agricola, published in Augsburg in 1558, also follows the "old and new teachers" pattern, citing patristic authors and early Reformation writings in favor of toleration in religious matters.[39]

Luther's *Temporal Authority: to what extent it should be obeyed* (1523), with its positing of temporal and spiritual kingdoms, remained a favorite reference in this genre of literature. It provided a useful theoretical framework, followed by several later writers. The *Codex 628* copyist refers to this writing of Luther and then summarizes:

> *Concerning the soul, God can and will not allow anyone to rule over it, except himself alone. Therefore, when the worldly powers interfere by enacting laws regarding the soul, they are attacking the reign of God, and only corrupting and ruining the soul.* (<77>).

This conclusion, built on Luther's two-kingdoms/two swords foundation, and utilized early in Marpeck and Scharnschlager's Anabaptist defense of toleration, is repeated in numerous contemporary pro-toleration writings.[40]

In addition to common appeals to the writings of the early Reformers in favor of uncoerced consciences, other shared themes appear in slightly different guises across the spectrum of pro-toleration writings. To name just a few: being persecuted is a sign of Christ and the apostolic church; persecuting others is not a sign of Christ; Jesus' parable of the tares and the wheat (Matthew 13) explicitly calls for toleration or forbearance of the

---

39 Theophilus Agricola [i.e., Georg Mayer of Leder], *Ein Bedencken von dem Geschrey und gemeiner Red, dass man nyemandts solle lyden und dulden, der nit inn allem Bäpstlich oder der Augspurgischen confession anhängig ist* (Augsburg, 1558), in *Corpus Schwenckfeldianorum*, vol. 16 (Pennsburg, PA: Schwenckfelder Church, 1959), 282-345. The editors describe the book as "a superb and convicting symposium of the early statements of Luther and other reformers, historians and church fathers opposing compulsion in religious matters." Ibid., 283.

40 "... der unglaub und die ketzerey, so lang sie bloß on andern anhang bleiben, alleyn dem word Gottes zu straffen zugehörig seyen." Brenz, *Ob ein Weltliche Obrigkeit*, 485. Basil Montfort (pseud. for S. Castellio), wrote: "The magistrate has no more right to perform the office of the minister than has the minister to assume that of the magistrate." Ibid., 235; [Pilgram Marpeck], "Exposé of the Babylonian Whore:" "All external things including life and limb are subjected to external authority. But no one may coerce or compel true faith in Christ, for it is concerned not with temporal but eternal life." *Later Writings by Pilgram Marpeck and his Circle*, 27.

A Short, Simple Confession

erring, not their execution;[41] the true Christian church uses the ban, not the sword, to discipline those in error.[42] Occasionally Jesus' call in Matthew 5 to love enemies and turn the other cheek will also make an appearance in this wider literature.[43] When Anabaptists repeat these themes they are not "lone voices" crying in the wilderness. They had allies in the wider world of toleration-favoring, dissenting sixteenth-century Christians. In their calls for toleration in Zurich in 1588 and 1589, the Anabaptists were joined by a small circle of Schwenckfeldian nonconformists who pleaded for the same response.[44]

9. *Hans Jakob Boll's* **Christenlichs Bedencken** *(1615).* There is one further, spectacular instance of the continuing influence of the two swords/two kingdoms argument for toleration as seen in the **Q2** strand of documents, which are in turn, embedded in the expanded **Q3** version of the *Simple Confession*. In 1615 Hans Jakob Boll, a former Anabaptist reader and budding proto-Pietist living near Bern, published the **Q2** material, with an added preface and conclusion, as an extended argument for religious toleration.[45] Hanspeter Jecker's initial work in identifying Boll has since

---

41   This is the recurring, central biblical theme in Castellio's *De haereticis* and also found in Brenz, *Ob ein Weltliche Obrigkeit*.
42   Argued already in 1528 by Brenz, *Ob ein Weltliche Obrigkeit*, where he points to Matthew 18 and says that the spiritual way of Christ is not to kill false prophets, as in the Old Testament, but to "avoid" them: "Und das geistlich verlassen oder meyden ist durch das leiblich erwürgen der falschen Propheten im Gesetz bedeutet und angezeygt." Ibid., 486.
43   E.g., Franck, *Chronica,* "Die drit Chronica" (Ulm, 1536), cxxxvi, recto to cxxxviii, recto, notes that Christ himself suffered violence and did not inflict any. Later in the church, the "spiritual persons" (clergy) are forbidden vengeance and the sword. Although the Roman Catholic clergy have arrogated the name "spiritual" to themselves, it should apply to all Christians: "Nun was seind die recht geystlichen / dann die Christen / an deren statt sich die geystlichen gesetzt haben...." cxxxvi, verso. The Roman church, however, condemns as heretics, lay Christians who claim Christ's teaching.
44   See Christian Scheidegger, "Wahrheit und Subjektivität. Warum schwenckfeldische Nonkonformisten in Zürich 1588 gegen Glaubenszwang protestierten," in MH 31 (2008), 91-111; also Leu and Scheidegger, *Zürcher Täufer*, 144ff.
45   *Christenlichs Bedencken. Ob einem Evangelischen Christen gebure jemanden umb dess Glaubens willen zu verfolgen* (n.p., 1615). My thanks to Hanspeter Jecker for sending me a copy of the print found in the Schweizerische Landesbibliothek Bern, sig. L theol. 789^{14}.

been expanded and modified by the archival work of Roland Senn.[46] We now know that Hans Jacob Boll, the author, evidently was a miller. He had a younger brother named Jacob Boll, who was a healer (*Bruchschneider*) specializing in hernias. Both were from Stein am Rhein, born perhaps a year or two apart. Unfortunately, the historical records sometimes confuse matters by interchanging their names. Hans Jacob Boll was an Anabaptist for about 30 years, from ca. 1580 to 1609. His brother Jacob became an Anabaptist around 1588 but left the movement by 1599. Hans Jacob moved in unspecified Anabaptist circles. Jecker assumes they were Swiss Brethren on the basis of later contacts. Boll was described as having read and commented on texts by a Zofingen Anabaptist in testimony given in Bern in 1617.[47]

The immediate occasion for Boll's publication in 1615 was the highly publicized, and unpopular, beheading of the Anabaptist Hans Landis by the Zurich authorities in 1614—Landis was to be the last Anabaptist to be put to death by the Zurich magistrates. Boll was hoping not only to pressure Swiss governments to stop persecution of religious dissidents, but to also promote a renewed religious and moral reform in Swiss territories.[48] The Bernese authorities got wind of the publication almost immediately, and were successful in locating and destroying most of Boll's prints before they could be circulated. They also brought Boll to a final recantation in 1616, although in his testimony he clarified that he had already left the Anabaptists around 1609. His pro-toleration publication, although it pleaded that a distinction should be made by the authorities between pious and harmless Anabaptists on the one hand and blasphemers and evil doers on the other, nevertheless was written

---

46   Roland Senn, "Wer war (Hans) Jacob Boll? Die Geschichte zweier Täufer aus Stein am Rhein," MH 37 (2015), 11-44.
47   Jecker, *Ketzer-Rebellen-Heilige*, 307, and n. 77, where an Anabaptist witness from Zofingen testified to Boll's functioning in this capacity.
48   In his conclusion, Boll urges readers to ask God in heaven "to ignite our hearts with the fire of His love," that each one look after personal repentance and with God's help, improve personal shortcomings and failures. He hoped that readers would be found to have "a correct, true, living Christian faith and that, in the manner of a true, living, saving faith" they would help one another "in a new, born again life, following the example of Christ." [Hans Jacob Boll], *Christenlichs Bedencken*, 39.

A Short, Simple Confession

by someone who now worshipped in the Reformed tradition and publicly subscribed to the second Helvetic confession.[49]

The body of Boll's 1615 forty-page printed text very closely matches the "Defense of the Anabaptists to the Bernese Authorities," with lengthy verbatim citations.[50] This is not surprising, since the "Defense" (or "Apology") that survives in the Bernese archives is written in Boll's hand, and in January 1616 he confessed to having written it "some years ago."[51] Interestingly, at several points where the "Defense" terminates a copied passage, Boll's print follows the more complete version extant only in *Codex 628* and the Zurich version of the *Simple Confession*. Boll is evidently reproducing previously composed and edited material for most of his 1615 text (we can identify verbatim antecedents for about 60 percent of Boll's print). It appears that he stitched together a text that suited his particular purposes in 1615. Access to previously written material would have been easy for him since he had personal access to *Codex 628* and the "Apologia" of ca. 1597. *Codex 628*, copied in 1590, contains a small section copied in Boll's own handwriting, and a later recipient of the manuscript noted on the front page that it had been given to him by Hans Jacob Boll "my close friend."[52]

Although it is plausible that Boll himself wrote the preface and the conclusion to the published booklet of 1615 (as he himself admitted), was he the original author of its contents? Was Boll himself, as he asserted to the authorities, the one who selected the texts from the works of Zwingli, Luther, Walter, and others, and arranged them in the form of an extended

---

49 Senn, "Wer war...?", 33.
50 See Hanspeter Jecker, "'Zum ersten vor unser Thüren wüschen.' Hans Jakob Bolls Mahnschrift von 1615 wider die Täuferverfolgungen," in M. Erbe, H. Füglister, et al., eds., *Querdenken. Dissens und Toleranz im Wandel der Geschichte. Festschrift zum 65. Geburtstag von Hans R. Guggisberg* (Mannheim: Palatium Verlag, 1996), 347-62. An updated and comprehensive treatment is now available in Jecker, *Ketzer-Rebellen-Heilige*, ch. 12, 270-334, which must be read together with Roland Senn, "Wer war (Hans) Jacob Boll?, 11-44.
51 "... bestätigte Boll, die "Apologia" vor Jahren verfasst zu haben..." Senn, "Wer war....?", 31; that the "Apologia" is in Hans Jakob Boll's hand has now been established. See ibid., 36-37.
52 Senn, "Wer war...?", 40, n. 154; Jecker, *Ketzer-Rebellen-Heilige*, 324ff.

argument for religious toleration?[53] If we assume that Boll was the sole author of the *Christenlichs Bedenken* of 1615, what then are we to make of the textual connections and disconnections between that print, and earlier surviving manuscripts?[54]

In terms of the manuscript text line we have been following, one question posed by Jecker is central: Was the compiler of *Codex 628* (copied in 1590) the same man as the author of the *Christenlichs Bedenken* of 1615, and was Hans Jacob Boll that man?[55] In the end Jecker draws no firm conclusion, and Roland Senn's extensive work, although it clarified many biographical details, also could not offer definitive evidence to answer this question. Hans Jacob Boll appears to have had in his possession many Anabaptist writings, and he functioned as an Anabaptist teacher at one time, but it is still unclear whether he was the primary author of any of these earlier writings, a co-author, or primarily a copyist/editor.

One interesting fact, however, is that the literature that passed through Hans Jacob Boll's hands had close connections to the Marpeck Covenanter network. The *Christenlichs Bedenken* of 1615 and "Apologia" of ca. 1597 continue the Covenanter theme of promoting toleration in matters of faith, a theme appearing in more complete form in *Codex 628* (1590), which was once in Boll's possession. The content of *Codex 628* also reveals strong Covenanter themes. Finally, Boll was once in possession of the *Kunstbuch*, a collection of Marpeck-related writings compiled by the Covenanter Jörg Maler and a key source of knowledge about the Covenanters. We know this because Boll wrote an abbreviated family chronicle on the back pages of the *Kunstbuch*; the entries date from 1579 to 1594.[56] Although Boll seems to have consorted with Swiss Brethren Anabaptists, it appears that he represents an important link between the Covenanter and Swiss Brethren traditions.

---

53 See Boll's repeated claims to authorship in Jecker, *Ketzer-Rebellen-Heilige*, 302; 308.
54 For a detailed and extended discussion of the issues at play, see Snyder, "The (Not So) 'Simple Confession': Part I," 713-19. The discussion here is an abbreviated version of the details to be found there.
55 Jecker, *Ketzer-Rebellen-Heilige*, 326.
56 Senn, "Wer war...?", 35.

The hypothesis I have suggested, that the **Q2** document on toleration was originally a Marpeck Covenanter production, still suffers from critical missing links in that no persons, manuscripts, or prints have yet come to light that would connect the Marpeck/Scharnschlager argument and approach in the 1530s with the full-blown manuscripts which appear in the late 1580s (see the illustration on page 188 of this volume). More research may well lead to the conclusion that it was Hans Jacob Boll who picked up promising beginnings and turned them into a coherent argument for toleration, and that his **Q2** document was copied subsequently into the manuscript strand we have been tracing—although at present I find this conclusion not entirely convincing, in light of Boll's biography and the manuscript evidence. The question of the precise extent of Boll's contribution to the Frankenthal manuscript stream will have to remain open until more research is done.

Jecker's research has uncovered the remarkable fact that Hans Jacob Boll cultivated a far-flung network of Anabaptist relationships, maintained friendly relationships with Swiss Anabaptist leaders, was in possession of important Covenanter literature, and continued to promote pro-Anabaptist ideas "behind the scenes," even after he had left the Anabaptists.[57] The case of Hans Jakob Boll, and the kind of detailed source studies carried out by Jecker and Senn, shed important light on the way in which Anabaptists texts and ideas exerted an influence far beyond the immediate circle of church members.

Jecker's studies re-open the question of whether Anabaptist thinking had any influence on the proto-Pietist movement. Jecker's research shows that there were members of the Reformed church in Switzerland (including active pastors) who were interested in Anabaptist reform ideas and literature.[58] These reform-minded people were inspired by the "free church" idea— although not as much by the emphatically separatist Schleitheim form, as by the more flexible "two swords" articulation of Marpeck and the Covenanter

---

57 After his arrest, Boll confessed to having put on the appearance of a good, Reformed church-goer, all the while remaining a hidden Anabaptist. Jecker, *Ketzer-Rebellen-Heilige*, 308.

58 See Jecker, *Ketzer-Rebellen-Heilige*, and *idem.*, "'Prüfet Alles Das Gute Behaltet.' Oder: Wie Menno einen reformierten Pfarrer von Murten nach Mähren reisen lässt," MH 20 (1997); in English, "'Test Everything; Hold Fast to What is Good': How Menno Caused a Reformed Pastor to Travel from Murten to Moravia," MQR 74 (January 2000), 7-26.

network. These same people also were inspired by the emphasis on rebirth and new life found in Anabaptist writings. Hans Jakob Boll, for instance, was not so much interested in remaining a part of a visibly separatist Anabaptist conventicle as in a wider Christian renewal and reform. To that end he not only copied and published Marpeckite literature, he also bought and read the writings of the proto-pietist Lutheran Johann Arndt.

It is illustrative of the potential offered by the Anabaptist manuscript tradition, that material that had been circulating in manuscript form for decades among the Anabaptists could be, and was, copied and circulated among Reformed Christians, and would exert its influence in that milieu. That such copying and circulation actually took place suggests it is not far-fetched to attribute a long-term influence (of a "proto-pietist" kind) on Protestantism by the "radical reform" ideas of the Anabaptists.

10. *Seventeenth-Century Continuations.* It should at least be mentioned that in 1645, during the increased persecutions of the Swiss Brethren by the Zurich authorities, the brethren from that area composed a lengthy apologetic writing that picked up many of the themes found in the "Frankenthal family" but re-worked those themes in a new way. The reading and analysis of this material, however, lies outside the scope of this book.[59]

Conclusion

From an analysis of the surviving texts we can trace the rudimentary outlines of the transmission (or "publication") process of this "Frankenthal family" of manuscripts among Swiss Anabaptists in the late sixteenth century. A text written in response to the Frankenthal debate was composed and subsequently circulated and copied. This text (**Q1**), which appears to have been written by someone in the Marpeck Covenanter network of influence, provided the skeletal structure of a manuscript which then grew by the addition of editorial comment, and by the addition of material considered relevant by a later copyist or copyists (**Q3**). This larger writing

---

59 The *Christenliche und kurtze verantwortung der brüdern, dieneren und eltisten in dem Zürich gebiedt über das büchlein oder manifest so außgangen in der statt und landtschafft Zürich anno 1639*, (1645) is found in P. Wälchi, U. Leu, C. Scheidegger, and J. D. Roth, eds., *Täufer und Reformierte im Disput* (Zug: Achius Verlag, 2010), 177-212.

A Short, Simple Confession

also circulated and was copied in its turn. In some cases, the larger writing appears to have been copied intact (hence *Codex 628*); but there are also instances where the larger text was contracted by the selective copying of only portions of the available manuscript (hence the Zurich version of the *Simple Confession* [Zurich Q3], the *1585 Letter to Bern*, and the *Anabaptist Defense to Bern*, the latter of which we now know was written by Hans Jacob Boll). Both editorial processes—addition and subtraction—were at work in the transmission process within this one manuscript strand over a period of some twenty years.

In contrast to the static form offered by printed texts, the anonymous hand copying of manuscript texts by Anabaptist leaders provided a very plastic medium for the transmission of Anabaptist ideas—with a closer affinity (in its plasticity) to the oral/aural medium than to the "fixed text" of print. The manuscript medium made possible a form of *Gemeindetheologie*: successive Anabaptist copyists did not feel bound to parrot and faithfully transmit a fixed, "canonical" text. Rather, the community itself shaped texts that came into their hands by actively editing them as they copied—primarily by omission and addition of material.

When previously printed texts were copied into the more plastic manuscript medium, they were then subjected to further rounds of "copy editing" by later Anabaptist copyist/editors. Since manuscript copies of prints seem to have been far more available than the original printed texts themselves, the re-edited and handcopied texts of former prints took on a new life in the manuscript medium. The manuscript copies were copied in their turn—and thus subjected to even further revisions by later copyists.

As one notable example of this process, a portion of Hubmaier's pamphlet *Old and New Teachers on Believers Baptism* (printed in Nikolsburg in 1526) entered the Frankenthal manuscript strand, and was copied successively into the next century—with no attribution of authorship.[60] Hubmaier's words simply were blended anonymously into the general Swiss Brethren manuscript literature that continued circulating and being copied. In this way a selection from Hubmaier's book finally was

---

60   Of the two editions of this text, it was the second, longer edition that was copied in *Codex 628*. Critical edition in Westin and Bergsten, eds. *Balthasar Hubmaier Schriften*, 227-55; translation in Pipkin and Yoder, *Hubmaier*, 245-74. The sections copied into *Codex 628* appear on pages <200-13> of the manuscript.

copied into a large apologetic manuscript written by Swiss Brethren in 1645, which was then sent to the Anabaptist brethren in the Netherlands. Once there, Hubmaier's bit of text was translated into Dutch, and was then printed in the *Martyrs Mirror*, identified only as part of a letter received from Swiss Brethren in Zurich—Hubmaier's original authorship having long since been forgotten.[61]

It is a significant fact that the links in the communication chain that connected Hubmaier's original printed words of 1526 with their reprinting in Dutch in the *Martyrs Mirror*, some 144 years later, were links forged exclusively by quill pens, paper, ink, individual Swiss Brethren copyists, and clandestine manuscripts. The printed word not only was mediated by oral/aural means—by being read aloud to listeners—printed texts in the Swiss Brethren tradition also were mediated, preserved, and circulated by hand-copied manuscript versions. Likewise, some original works that never were printed nevertheless circulated in manuscript form and exerted their underground influence in this manner. Thomas Meyer's book concerning the ban (Chapter VIII above) is one such example.

If we wish to know more about the development of Swiss Brethren thought in Switzerland during these years, we will have to pay special attention to the use of the manuscript medium, rather than relying on an analysis of the sparse number of prints the brethren managed to produce. The *Simple Confession*, translated below, provides an opportunity to peruse a complex and influential copied book that circulated widely in Swiss Anabaptist circles in the last quarter of the sixteenth century.

In the translation that follows, italicized portions represent text that is shared, virtually verbatim, by *Codex 628* and Zurich Q3.

---

61 See Thieleman J. van Braght, *The Bloody Theater or Martyrs Mirror*, trans. Joseph F. Sohm (Scottdale, PA: Herald Press, 1972), 1115-18.

A Short, Simple Confession on the Thirteen Articles Which Were Debated in 1571[62] at Frankenthal in the Palatinate

A short, simple Confession on the thirteen articles which were debated in 1571 at Frankenthal in the Palatinate, composed for all those to consider and pass judgment on, who, beloved by God, desire the truth and want to be without human bias; also written as a justifiable warning, founded upon God's Word, to all magistrates who claim for themselves the Gospel and the name, Christian, yet who attempt at the same time through coercion to force and compel people against their wills into faith.[63]

Wisdom of Solomon 18[:4][64]

"It is appropriate that those who are deprived of light, and are cast into the darkness of prison by those who, O Lord, are keeping your devout and faithful children imprisoned, through whom the incorruptible splendor of the law is to be proclaimed to the world." Of such, however, the world is not worthy. Hebrews 11[:38]

This writing was begun on Saturday, the sixth day of January of the new calendar, in the year 1590. <1>[65]

---

62 Original manuscript has 1572.
63 Sections of this document are found in a slightly different arrangement, but almost verbatim, in the Zurich version of "Einfaltig Bekanntnus." This latter document will be identified hereafter as "Zurich Q3," and verbatim portions will appear in italic in the text.
64 Biblical references in the manuscript are to book and chapter; they do not note verse numbers. Wherever possible, these have been identified, and are noted within square brackets. Where specific verses are not identified in this text, they either were too obscure for the editor to identify, or the chapter itself is relevant to the subject matter in question. The numerous Scripture references in the margins are noted in footnotes; Scripture references within the text remain there, as they were in the original.
65 Numbers marked in this manner <1> indicate that the preceding page bears this number in the original codex. In the codex the numbers appear at the top of the page.

John 15[:18-19]

"If the world hates you, know that those of the world hated me before hating you. If you were of the world, the world would love you; but you are not of the world. I have instead chosen you out of the world, therefore the world hates you."

James 4[:4]

"You adulterers and adulteresses, do you not know that friendship with the world is enmity with God? Whoever desires to be a friend of the world will be God's enemy."

Galatians 1[:10]

Paul says, "If I were still pleasing humans, I would not be a servant of Christ."

Wisdom of Solomon 5[:4]

"They are the ones whom we had earlier held in contempt, with whom we carried on with our ridicule and words of scorn. Oh, how very foolish we were in assuming their lives to be irrational, and their end without honor," etc.

1 Corinthians 1[:26-27]

"Not many wise according to the flesh, not many powerful, not many from the nobility are chosen; instead, God has chosen those who are considered to be foolish by the world, that he might shame the wise," etc. <2>

Matthew 13[:9]; Revelation 22[:17]

"Whoever has ears to hear, may he or she hear."

Matthew 19[:12]

"Whoever is able to fathom it, may he or she fathom it."

1 Corinthians 2[:6-8]

"That, however, about which we speak is perfect wisdom, and not the wisdom of this world, nor the wisdom of the magistrates of this world, who ultimately must needs cease. Rather, we speak of the divine wisdom which is found in mystery, lying hidden, which God, before the world was created, ordained for our glory, which none of the magistrates of this world had perceived. For if they had perceived this glory, they would not have crucified the Lord of glory."

A Table of Contents of What is Dealt With in this Booklet

1) First, a Preface to all magistrates who claim for themselves the Gospel and the name, Christian.

2) The reason for the schism among those people and groups who together departed from the Papal church. And in addition where, in these last times, the temple of God and of the High Priest may be sought and found. <3>

List of the Thirteen Articles

1) First, whether the writings of the Old Testament are as valid for Christians as those of the New.

2) Whether the believers in the New Testament formed one community and people of God with the believers in the Old Testament.

3) Whether a Christian may be a magistrate who punishes those who are evil with the sword.

4) Whether a Christian may swear under oath, namely, calling upon the name of God as a witness.

5) Whether God the Father, God the Son, and God the Holy Spirit are uniquely one in their divine essence.

6) Whether Christ received the essence of his flesh from the substance of the virgin Mary, or from somewhere else.

7) Whether children are conceived and born possessing original sin, resulting in their being by nature children of wrath, and standing under eternal damnation.

8) Whether the perfect obedience of Christ, entered into through the true faith, is the unique and only sufficient payment for our sins and the source of our salvation; or, on the other hand, whether we are saved in part through faith in Christ through grace, and in part through the cross and good works. <4>

9) Whether the ban and unbelief permit one to divorce.

10) Whether Christians are allowed to purchase and own their own possessions.

11) Whether the essence of this human body will rise again at the Last Judgment, or rather, whether another body will be created by God.

12) Whether the children of Christians should or may be baptized.

13) Whether Holy Communion is merely an empty sign and admonition to practice patience and love, or whether it is also a mighty sealing of the saved community which all believers have with Christ unto eternal life.

What follows is the Preface to all magistrates who claim for themselves the Gospel and the name, Christian. <5>

<6 -- blank page>

Preface

To all magistrates who claim for themselves the Gospel and the name, Christian, who also attempt to force and coerce people into accepting faith through imprisonment and through death by drowning, fire and the sword: we, nonresistant lambs of Christ, wish you God's grace, the illumination of the Holy Spirit, and a clear and open countenance which is able with open, pure, and impartial judgment to differentiate between what is clear and muddy, pure and impure, light and darkness, and Christ and Belial, to the end that you no longer oppose the strength from On High, and so avoid needing to experience with sorrow, in the Lord's time, who you really have been persecuting.

We know very well, O highly-regarded lords and princes who reign in the worldly sectors, *that you (instigated by your scholars) accuse us of being a rebellious sect of heretics and judge our whole religion and faith through the eyes of the evil enemy and impure spirit—which also happened to Christ and his holy apostles before us*[66]*and, as the Lord Christ foretold, would also be our lot.* [Zurich Q3, 123] You also proclaim in your public mandates that you have just cause to persecute us since we are not willing to submit and be obedient to the divine word.

But God the Lord, who sees and knows all human hearts, whose eyes are also sharper than fiery flames, <7> *knows that we desire from our hearts to be obedient and subject to God and his word, so far as we are able by his grace. Therefore we have not separated or cut ourselves off from the Apostolic church (which is in Christ Jesus), nor have we established a rebellious sect outside that church. Rather we have drawn much closer to it and have given ourselves over to it entirely and pledged ourselves to serve God and Christ in it with a pure, unsullied conscience.*[67]

But what the divine word is, to which we are to be obedient if we want to be saved, may the almighty God grant us (and also you, dear lords and magistrates), to recognize,[68] *in his son Jesus Christ.*

Now all understanding, enlightened, devout hearts who are loved by God, know that Holy Scripture (Old and New Testaments) testifies loud and

---

66 *Margin*: Matthew 10, 12; Mark 3; Luke 11, 12; Acts 24, 28
67 Zurich Q3 adds: *in all the ordinances and commandments of Christ and his holy apostles, as far as God grants us grace and mercy.*
68 Zurich Q3 adds: *and also to all those who desire it from the heart.*

clear that Christ Jesus, the blessed and highly-praised Son of God, is the only saving Word, and that it is not possible to be saved by any other means, manner or way than through the name of Jesus Christ, as Peter states, Acts 4:[12], [and Paul:] "For through him everything in heaven and on earth is reconciled" Colossians 1[:20].

Therefore Paul the apostle states to the Philippians, 2:[9-11] that "God has raised him up and given him a name that is above all names, so that in the name of Jesus every knee that is in heaven and on earth and under the earth shall bow, and every tongue shall confess, <8> that Jesus Christ is the Lord, to the praise of God the Father." For he alone (as he himself says) is the way, the door and shepherd of the sheepfold [John 10:1-16], to whom Moses and all the prophets pointed, and as Moses said:[69] "Whoever will not hear him will be destroyed," Acts 3:[23]. Therefore all who preceded him, who indicated another way other than through this one Word that was made flesh, John 1[:14], namely, Jesus Christ, are thieves and murderers, John 10[:8].

Now one hears from virtually all nations and parties who wish to be Christian, that they also confess him verbally (although some among them adulterate it, not wanting to accept its true worth), for which reason there is little disagreement between us (concerning a confession of faith). But this is not the whole thing. What the great conflict and discord is among all of us concerning the Word of God—since we clearly confess that He alone is the Word as noted above—may the almighty God grant us to know the following: what the great conflict actually is, but also among whom, where it originated, and how it developed, etc.

Therefore we confess, for our part, that not all who recognize Him as the Word are [actually] in Him, for if all of them were in Him there would be no division among them. Christ Himself, the word of life, says: "My peace I give unto you; my peace I leave for you <9> and I give it to you not as the world gives. Let not your hearts be troubled and do not be afraid" [John 14:27],[70] that is, "Do not turn away from me and forsake my peace on account of worldly tyranny and persecution, otherwise you will not be in me and I in you."

And in the fifteenth chapter of John he says, "I am the true vine and my father the vine dresser. Each branch of mine which produces no fruit he

---

69   Zurich Q3 adds: *according to Peter's testimony.*
70   Zurich Q3 adds (*Margin*): *John 14.*

will cut off, and each which produces fruit he will purify, so that it bears more fruit." [John 15:1-2] And he says further, "You are now pure because of the word that I have spoken to you. Abide in me, and I in you. Just as the branch cannot bring forth fruit by itself unless it remains on the vine, so also you cannot, unless you abide in me. I am the vine, you are the branches. Whoever abides in me, and I in him or her, will bring forth much fruit, for without me you are able to do nothing. Whoever does not abide in me will be cast away like shoots which wither, are gathered and thrown into the fire and burned," etc.[John 15:3-6]

"Persevere in my love. If you keep my commandment, then persevere in my love. [John 15:9-10]*This is my commandment, that you love one another just as I have loved you."* And John states in John 13[:34-35], "By this all will recognize that you are my disciples, if you love one another."

Now since you, dear lords, confess <10> with us that Christ is the Savior, the word, the way, door and shepherd of eternal life, to whom has been handed over everything in heaven and on earth, and furthermore that the great king and shepherd gave himself for the whole world,[71] to instruct and to teach, so that they might be able truly to receive him, namely, his word and peace, and abide in his love, as he says many times in John in the 13th chapter[72] in the presence of his disciples, where he also gives them such a fine parable about a true vine, thereby noting his goodness in all things concerning his teaching and life toward all people; and since he is teaching them here the true and pure, unfeigned love, repentance and mending of life, laying aside the old person who is conformed to this world, and in its stead, putting on the new person who is created and conformed to Christ Jesus, so that all people may now perceive and experience the great love and faithfulness of our Lord and Savior Jesus Christ—therefore for his sake all conflict ought to cease among us, and should be far away from us all, and we therefore ought to be a unified, peaceable people in Christ Jesus, just as he and his disciples were.

And whoever wishes to testify to this <11> and truly recognize it— namely that deep, humble, holy, peaceable life and teaching of Christ, which will be visible in all his disciples, according to the measure of the gifts of his Spirit—may such a person yield in true obedience to his teaching, to the mandate and testament of the most powerful and highly praised king,

---

71 Zurich Q3 adds: *with his great faithfulness and love for us.*
72 *Margin:* John 13; 14; 15

Christ Jesus, which he sealed with his holy, innocent blood, and received it from (the Father's) hand in order to swallow and digest it, so that the book itself might be conformed to his nature, and that he might come to resemble the book, Revelation 10[:9-10], Ezekiel 2[:8-10]. Such a person [wishing to testify to this] will then truly perceive the nature of the conflict between us concerning the Word of God, for the book is the Word of God, and Christ is the Word, John 1[:1-5]. "I am," says Christ, "the one who is speaking with you," John 8.

Therefore it is now obvious and known to all believing and enlightened, elected hearts how Christ completed his teaching and life, and proved his testament, and declared so often that nothing other than the beautiful fruit (of a devout Christian life) may appear on this true vine, which will be visible on its branches like good grapes on a branch which has been grafted onto the vine. Otherwise there will be no grapes. Everyone ought to know that just as the vine does not continue to produce grapes except <12> through the branches, and not on the vine itself, so also Christ, through his disciples and followers: "If you abide in me," he says, "you will bring forth much fruit" [John 15:5].

So by now the Christian life should be clearly visible to all Christians: all Christ's teaching is the Christian's teaching; his love, our love; his mercy, our mercy; his patience, our patience; his peace, our peace; his suffering, our suffering; his death, our death; his resurrection, our resurrection; his ascension, our ascension. For no one goes to heaven[73] *unless one has come from heaven, says the Lord; and unless one is born anew, one cannot see the kingdom of God, John 3[:5], for through the new birth*[74] *a person is grafted into the vine, planted and given grace.*

Therefore, whoever surrenders to such a Christian life may be baptized in the name of Christ, and partake of the Holy Supper with all true Christians and children of God, which then feeds and refreshes and quickens the soul unto eternal life. It does no good in any other form, but rather only serves to harm a person seriously, for the name of Jesus is holy; but whoever lives an unholy life in sin and vice will <13> have no part with him. Such must first of all surrender to Christ in faith and trust, allow themselves to be purified by [Christ],[75] *and surrender unto His true obedience, on the basis of which*

---

73 Zurich Q3 adds (*Margin*): *John 3.*
74 Zurich Q3 adds: *which comes down from heaven.*
75 Zurich Q3 adds: *as noted above, John 15.*

they may be baptized properly in the name of the Father, the Son, and the Holy Spirit, as is documented below in greater detail in the Twelfth Article on the basis of the Divine Word, and—in the spirit of true, unvarnished love—partake of the Holy Supper with all the children of God, without any falsity, deceit or hypocrisy.

Therefore no one who uses an old wineskin as a container[76] or [who is wearing] an old, dirty garment, should go through the gates in the Temple and the House of the Lord and give orders and join the guests at his table, for no one is worthy of this except one who previously has been renewed through the Spirit of God. The old wineskin is not able to contain the good, noble wine, nor is the dirty garment fitting for the Lord's Supper. Therefore no one may sneak in, for the Lord of the Supper, Christ Jesus, moves about, looking at his wedding guests, and says to the one with the dirty garment: "How did you enter, not wearing a wedding garment?" And he will say to his servants: "Bind him hand and foot, and throw him <14> into the outer darkness, where there will be weeping and gnashing of teeth," Matthew 22[:13].

For this reason the Apostle Paul states in 1 Corinthians 5[:7-8][77]: "Cleanse out the old leaven that you may be a new lump, as if you were unleavened. For Christ, our paschal lamb, has been sacrificed. Let us, therefore, celebrate the festival, not with the old leaven, the leaven of malice and evil, but with the unleavened bread of sincerity and truth." In this manner the children of God are to be prepared for the Supper of the Lord.

Therefore we should put on the proper, true, wedding garments for the Lord Jesus Christ, and guard against and purify ourselves from all sin and unrighteousness—not that we of ourselves would be able to be pure and without sin, but rather through our Lord Jesus Christ. As long as we are and remain twigs and branches in him, the true vine, the heavenly sap and good fruit from the vine will flow into the branches. For the mouth of eternal truth, which cannot lie, says in John 14[:12] "Truly, truly I say to you, whoever believes in me will also do the works that I do, and will do greater works than these." For this reason Paul states: "You are his handiwork, created through Jesus Christ." [Ephesians 2:10].

Since we then are <15> only the tools, and the Lord completes his work through us, we have absolutely nothing about which to boast, since in our own strength we are able to create nothing good; rather it is the Lord God

---

76   *Margin*: Matthew 9[:17]
77   *Margin*: 1 Corinthians 5

who produces the good through his own, to whom belongs all praise and honor eternally. Paul states further, Galatians 2[:17-20], *"If, in our endeavor to be justified in Christ, we ourselves were found to be sinners, is Christ then an agent of sin? Certainly not! But if I build up again those things which I once tore down, then I prove myself a transgressor. For through the law I died to the law, that I might live to God. I have been crucified with Christ; it is no longer I who live, but Christ who lives in me."*

And again, he says to the Romans in the 5th chapter [Romans 5:20]: *"The law has come so that sin might gain the upper hand; but where sin has gained the upper hand, there grace increases all the more."* He says, immediately following in the 6th chapter [Romans 6:1-2, 16-23]: *"What are we to say now; should we persist in sin so that grace may prevail? May that be far from us, etc. .... Don't you know to whom you are giving yourselves as servants in obedience, and that you are the servants of the one to whom you give obedience, be it to sin unto death, or to the obedience of righteousness? But God be praised, that you were servants of sin, but now you have become obedient* <16> *from the heart to the example of the teaching to which you were made subject,* for only by becoming free from sin do you become servants of righteousness. For just as you once yielded your members to the service of impurity and evil, to ever greater iniquity, so now yield your members to the service of righteousness, that they may be saved. *For the wages of sin is death, but the gift of God is eternal life* in Christ Jesus our Lord."

Therefore, as noted above, whoever remains in Christ, and Christ in him, will produce much fruit.[78] But whoever does not remain in him will not produce fruit, but will be cut off like a non-producing shoot and cast into the fire, John 15[:6]. Therefore St. John states in 1 John 3[:8-9]: "Whoever remains in him does not sin; whoever sins has neither seen nor experienced him." And again: "Whoever commits sin is from the devil, for the devil sinned from the beginning."

Because of this the Son of God appeared that he might undo the work of the devil. Whoever is born of God does not sin, for his seed remains with him and such a one dare not sin. In this way one can recognize, says John, who are the children of God, and who are the children of the devil. Whoever does not live rightly is not from God, for everything which is born of God, he says in the 5th Chapter [John 5:28-29], overcomes the

---

78 *Margin*: Matthew 3[:10]; 7[:19]; Luke 3[:9]; Jeremiah 11[:16]

world, and our faith is the victory which has overcome the world. <17> For this reason *Peter writes, 2 Peter 1[:4], "If we flee from the fleeting desires of the world, we will become partakers of the divine nature."*

Therefore, whoever has become a participant in the divine nature, and is of the divine nature as Paul says in Acts 17[:28?], such a one truly has the son of God in him, and also has life in him, and brings forth good fruit, as noted above. But whoever is not truly in him or lives in him, such a one does not have life, and cannot bring forth good fruit. For the word of the Lord is firm and unmovable, when he says, as has been noted above, John 15[:4-5], *"Just as the branch cannot bring forth fruit by itself unless it remains joined to the vine, so also you cannot bring forth fruit unless you remain in me. I am the vine, you are the branches; whoever abides in me and I in him will bring forth much fruit."*

Therefore John says: "Whoever is born of God does not sin, rather, the [new] birth from God preserves him." For it is true that a person who believes in Christ truly receives a living and active Jesus Christ in the flesh; yes, his living water, rich in grace, wells up in him to become a living fountain leading to eternal life.

But any spirit, says John, that does not confess that Jesus Christ came in the flesh, is not from God, 1 John 4[:3]—that is to say, any spirit that denies <18> and claims that it is impossible, and does not confess that Jesus Christ performs and carries out his works in his elect believers. As Paul says, 2 Corinthians 6[:16], "You are the temple of the living God; as God said, 'I want to dwell in them and walk in them.'" Likewise, 1 Corinthians 3[:16-17]: "The temple of God is holy, and you are that temple. Do you not know that you are God's temple, and that the Spirit of God lives in you?" Likewise 1 Corinthians 6[:19]: "Your body is a temple of the Holy Spirit, which you have from God, and you are not your own." Likewise, Ephesians 2[:10]: "You are his handiwork, created in Christ Jesus unto good works."

Any spirit that does not confess this, and presumes that what Christ promised to his own is impossible, and all that Christ achieves through his own [is impossible], such a one is not from God, 1 John 4[:2-3]. For the Lord says further, "Those who love me will keep my word, and my Father will love them, and we will come to them and make our dwelling with them. But those who do not love me do not keep my word." Therefore, where the dwelling of God and Christ is, there also His commandments are kept, for God does not dwell in an impure temple in which his word is not kept but rather is brazenly violated.

Therefore John says, 2 John 1[:7-10]: "Whoever transgresses, and does not remain in the teaching of Christ has no God; but whoever abides <19> in the teaching of Christ has both the Father and the Son. If someone comes to you and does not bring this teaching, do not welcome him into your house, and do not greet him"—namely, with the greeting of the peace of Christ, in order to be able to acknowledge the believers, and so receive one another in the house of God. "For whoever greets [one who does not bring Christ's teaching]," says John [2 John 1:11], "has fellowship with his evil work."

But now the would-be Christians, *who have been crying out for a long time: "Here is the temple of the Lord, here is the Christian church," and who then [go on to] coerce and force people into [that church] by means of prison, torture, martyrdom, and the shedding of blood*[79]—*how can they thus be planted in Christ,*[80] *born again from above by the Spirit of God, living not in accord with the flesh but rather with the spirit*[81] *and manifesting that form of love toward one another which Christ taught and commanded? Unfortunately one can see in their daily lives what kind of fruit they bear and bring forth*, as we want to substantiate below with documentation and in truth.

For although Satan is quite able to manifest himself as an angel of light in his members, who regard Christ highly in words, speaking and singing and knowing a great deal about him, and in this manner, following him apishly, and who give great energy to reciting books by heart—we still see clearly that true Christians are recognized only by genuine, pure love (since [the devil] cannot, and may not have pure love) <20>, as the Lord himself says.

In the same manner, the content of [many] books is thoroughly rapacious and impure. And because [the devil] wants to appear to be the sole bride of the Lamb and groom of Christ, with his Anti-Christ and child of perdition and his followers, and wants no one else alongside him to be considered legitimate, he therefore sets himself against the true Christians with great seriousness, against those who cherish pure love. For

---

79   Zurich Q3 adds: *and lack of mercy.*
80   Zurich Q3 adds: *John 15.*
81   Zurich Q3 adds: *Romans 8.*

A Short, Simple Confession

his approach does not rest upon a pure love and the truly active, newly reborn life of Christ, but is only an apish imitation of the same: the reciting of books and parchments by heart, and an outward pretense through which he can pry into the affairs of his members under the pretense of Christ. He falls short, however, of life-creating love, at which point he and his members give up, not desiring to continue to follow [Christ] closely. For they do not possess [this love], which does not become [the devil's] kingdom—a love, however, which is the sole entrance into the kingdom of Christ, which in turn is not of this world.

Therefore we truly know, and we are not surprised, that in this world—since Satan is the prince of the world—the pure praiseworthy truth, rich in love, and the members who are born of this truth, must take second place to fleshly reason and human wisdom, as Christ himself <21> *earlier said to his own, Matthew 10[:16]:* "Behold, I am sending you as sheep among the wolves," *etc.* "You will be made to answer before their courts [Matthew 24:9], and you will be scourged [Mark 13:9] in their assemblies [Luke 21:12], and you will be led before princes [John 16:1] and kings for my name's sake, as a testimony against them and against the heathen.[82] Brother will give over brother unto death,[83] and a father his son, and children[84] will rise up against their parents and send them to their deaths; and you will be hated by everyone for my name's sake."

Likewise, "The disciple is not above his master, nor the servant above his lord. It is enough for the disciple to be like his master and the servant like his lord. If they have called the master of the house Beelzebub, how much more will they malign those of his household?" [Matthew 10:24-25]

Likewise, Matthew 24[:9]: "They will give you over to tribulation, and kill you; and you will have to be hated by everyone for my name's sake; at that time there will be many disputes, with much betrayal."

And Christ says, John 16[:2-4]: "They will place you in the ban. The time is coming when whoever kills you will think he is doing God a service thereby.[85] And they will carry this out for the reason that they have known neither my father <22> nor me. But this I have spoken to you, so that when the time comes, you will remember what I have told you."

---

82 *Margin*: Matthew 24; Mark 13; Luke 21; John 16
83 Zurich Q3 adds: *Luke 21.*
84 Zurich Q3 adds: *John 16.*
85 *Margin*: John 15

Therefore Paul states, Acts 14[:22]: "We must pass through much tribulation to enter the kingdom of God," and 2 Timothy 2 [2 Timothy 3:12], "All who want to live a godly life must suffer persecution. *The prophet Esdras says the same thing, 4 Esdras 16[:70-73]: "All places will become one place, and a great attack will take place against all those who fear God. They will be like maniacs, sparing no one, plundering and slaughtering all who fear God. They will take their goods from them, and throw them out of their houses. Then it will be known who my elect are, and they will be tried like gold in the fire." Isaiah likewise says in Chapter 59 [Isaiah 59:15], "The truth will be imprisoned, and whoever protects himself from the evil ones must be despoiled."*

The holy David also speaks concerning the enemies of Christ and their followers, Psalm 83[:4]: "They say, 'truly we will root them out so that they will no longer be a people,' for they have conspired together in their hearts." Likewise his son, Solomon, also says, Wisdom 2[:12-20] how the ungodly will rise up against the devout, <23> *namely: "Let us trap the devout person, for he is useless to us and opposes our deeds. He rebukes us as having sinned against the law, and accuses us as transgressors of all decency. We cannot stand to see him, for his life is not like our life, and his ways are completely different. He treats us like liars, and he avoids our ways as if they stem from an impure thing. Let us overwhelm and torture him to see how honorably, discreetly and patiently he will behave. Let us bring him to a most shameful death."*

Likewise the prophet Hosea 9[:7]: "They consider the prophet to be a fool and the spiritual one a ninny"—to such a degree has sin, hate and nonsense gained the upper hand. Likewise the holy Job says [Job 12:4-6?] that whoever calls upon God and whom God hears, is an insult to his neighbor; whoever is devout and blameless becomes a laughing stock; the light and torch of devotion is despised by the godless and the rich; truly they lead astray those who wish to walk firmly and surely. Likewise Proverbs 13[:19]: "A desire fulfilled is sweet to the soul; but to turn away from evil is an abomination to fools."

Consider Jeremiah in the 18th Chapter, where the prophet Jeremiah punished the house <24> of Judah and Jerusalem on account of their sins and unrighteousness. By way of response they said [Jeremiah 18:18] "Come, let us plot against Jeremiah, for the law shall not perish from the priest, nor counsel from the wise, nor the word from the prophet. Come,

A Short, Simple Confession

let us cut out his tongue, so we need not have to keep hearing his words." And earlier in the eleventh Chapter [Jeremiah 11:19]: "'Let us destroy the tree with its fruit, let us cut him off from the land of the living, so that his name will no longer be remembered.'" Therefore they say, "You shall not prophesy in the name of the Lord, or you will die by our hand" [Jeremiah 11:21]. This actually took place later when they stoned him to death, as Epiphanius, Isidorus, and others testify.

Likewise the prophet Isaiah, when he truly warned and admonished them about their sins, abominations and idolatries, finally, through the command of the godless King Manasseh (if the actual event took place as written) was murdered, having been sawed to death with a wooden saw, and terribly tortured by another person.[86]

In this regard Zechariah of the house of Judah says, 2 Chronicles 24[:20-21], "Thus says the Lord: 'Why do you transgress the commandments of the Lord, so that you cannot prosper? Because <25> you have forsaken the Lord, he has also forsaken you.' But they conspired against him, and by command of the king they stoned him to death in the court of the house of the Lord." Ahab rebuked the prophet Elijah for having disrupted all of Israel, who with his godless Jezebel persecuted and expelled him [1 Kings 19:1].

Micaiah [Micah] the prophet,[87] after having prophesied to King Ahab and Jehoshaphat against the four hundred false prophets, was hit by the false prophet Zedekiah on the cheeks and placed in prison upon the command of King Ahab, and fed with bread and water in tribulation. The old historians report that they finally pushed him off a cliff.[88]

Amaziah, the priest of idols, reproved the prophet Amos[89] that he was preaching such [a message] that the land was not able to bear all his words, and denounced him to King Jeroboam, saying "Amos has conspired against you in the very center of the house of Israel; the land is not able to bear all his words," and Amos was expelled by him and the

---

86 The anonymous author of this part of the text inserts some details that originate with *De Vitis Prophetarum* [*The Lives of the Prophets*] attributed to Pseudo-Epiphanius (*Patrologia Latina*, XLIII). Isaiah being sawed to death is one such detail.
87 *Margin*: 2 Chronicles 18[:12ff]
88 As reported in *The Lives of the Prophets*.
89 *Margin*: Amos 7[:10-11]

king. Epiphanius, in the book which he wrote on the life and death of the prophets, reports that the prophet Amos was severely struck by the priest of Bethel, Amaziah, and suffered much slander and verbal abuse at his hand <26> along with much evil, secret hypocrisy, and deception. Finally he was beaten and murdered in his sleep by [Amaziah's] son with a bludgeon.[90] Likewise, Shadrach, Meshach, and Abednego were thrown into the fiery furnace because they did not want to worship the idolatrous image of King Nebuchadnezzar.

The prophet Daniel[91] was imprisoned twice, although innocent, and thrown into the lions' den, and there fed by God and protected and saved from the lions because he had served his God firmly, without hypocrisy, remaining faithful without wavering because of fear. Eleazar, the old, courageous hero who loved the Law of God,[92] after painful torture, was sentenced to death because he would not stoop to hypocrisy.

The same happened to the mother with the seven sons, who were instructed to eat pork, contrary to the Law of God, whereby they would have sinned.[93] They instead had their tongues cut out, their hair and skin skinned from their heads, their hands and feet cut off, and then were slowly fried and roasted alive in hot boilers and cauldrons.

Likewise in the New Testament, Christ and his holy apostles and disciples were sentenced to death, after being tortured with all sorts of torment, having been forced to suffer the great opposition of the scribes, condemned by them as being seducers, <27> heretics, and rabble-rousers. Christ was captured by them in their vengeance, bound with rope, led into their false assembly wherein they testified about him with false evidence, deriding and damning him. Their servants, with the knowledge and will of their lords, hit him with fists, spit in his holy face, whereupon he was delivered to Pilate through the council of religious leaders and scribes as a blasphemer and seducer.

John the Baptist was sentenced to death by the sword by Herod the tetrarch[94] because he rebuked him on account of adultery, through the instigation of Herodias, his brother's wife, who had been staying with him,

---

90   As reported in *The Lives of the Prophets*.
91   *Margin*: Daniel 6; 12 in the *History*
92   *Margin*: 2 Macc 6[:18-20]
93   *Margin*: 2 Maccabees 7[:1-41]
94   *Margin*: John the Baptist

A Short, Simple Confession

committing incest which had become known. Saint Stephen was accused through false witnesses[95] and stoned to death as a revolutionary. James the apostle,[96] brother of John the Evangelist, was executed with the sword on account of his witness about Jesus Christ.

Likewise the holy apostle Peter was crucified, as the histories[97] document, as his Master, John 21[:18-19] had prophesied and portended, with which death he would glorify God. Yet he requested that his feet be placed above, and his head below, for he did not consider himself worthy of being crucified like his Lord and Master.[98]

Andrew the apostle, a brother to Simon Peter in flesh and <28> spirit[99]—and in both, a comrade of the cross—preached the Gospel of Christ, through the urging of the Holy Spirit, in Achaia, the Asian land. And while he was converting many people to faith in Christ he was thrown into prison by Regio, the provincial ruler at Patrae in Achaia because, among other things, he had converted the ruler's wife and brother from heathen idolatry to the Christian faith. He was then beaten by his captors and constables, and bound with ropes onto a cross which was then set up. In approaching the cross he greeted it with the following words: "Greetings to you, O holy cross, soaked with the blood of my Lord. For you are adorned with his limbs, in a manner equal to that of the most precious gem." He is said to have lived on the cross for two days.

Philip the apostle, it is reported[100] was crucified at Hieropolis in Asia, and was stoned while on the cross.

---

95 *Margin*: St Stephen
96 *Margin*: St James
97 *Margin*: St Peter
98 At this point the copyist begins listing information that matches what is found in Sebastian Franck, *Chronica, Zeitbuch unnd Geschichtsbibel* (Strasbourg, 1531). References will be to the edition published in Ulm, 1536 (photo-reprint, Darmstadt: Wissenschafliche Buchgesellschaft, 1969). One of the "histories" to which the copyist refers is Sebastian Franck's *Chronica*.
99 *Margin*: St Andrew. See Franck, *Chronica*, III Chronica, xiiii, recto, under "Andreas der Achaisch Apostel."
100 *Margin*: St Philip. See Franck, *Chronica*, III Chronica, xiii, verso, under "Philippus der Scitisch Apostel."

Bartholomew the apostle is reported in historical accounts[101] to have been flayed by his enemies, and then beheaded.

James the Lesser, an apostle and teacher of the congregation and church in Jerusalem[102] was placed high up on the rooftop of the temple, and admonished by the Pharisees and scribes <29> to renounce his Lord Jesus, and to disband his people. When he countered them, however, witnessing to and confessing Christ as the true, living Son of God, who was sitting in heaven to the right of his Father, they climbed up to him and had him hurled down from the heights of the Temple, saying to the people: Let us stone James, the one who is considered righteous. They immediately began to stone him. And while he was still breathing, lifting his half-dead hands toward heaven, and praying for his enemies, he was stoned to death, hit by a boulder which was hurled at him by a soldier from a rampart launcher.

Regarding the apostle Thomas[103] the historians write that after he preached the Gospel to the Parthians, Medes, Persians, Hyrcanians, and Brahmans, and converting many people to Christ in upper and lower India, he was stabbed in his side by a lance or spear, in this way coming to the one whose side he had also touched and felt.

Matthew the apostle from Bethlehem, born of the tribe of Judah[104] and well trained in the Law, full of the Holy Spirit, pure in body, and with clarity of speech, witnessed to and mightily proclaimed the Lord Jesus. <30> For this reason the Jews brought a formal action against him, accusing him of blasphemy against God and the Law. And when absolutely nothing could turn him from Christ, not even menacing threats, but rather he remained steadfast in the confession of and witness to Jesus Christ, the high priest pronounced the following judgment upon him, telling him: "Your words have spoken against you; your blood is upon your own head." Soon thereafter he is said to have been tortured and stoned, and thereafter beheaded with an executioner's sword, in this manner giving up his spirit to God with upraised hands.

---

101 *Margin*: St Bartholomew. See Franck, *Chronica*, III Chronica, xiiii, recto, under "Bartholomeus der Apostel in Lycaonia / India / und Armenia."

102 *Margin*: St James the Lesser. Basic story in Franck, *Chronica*, III Chronica, xi, verso, under "Jacobus der Apostel zu Hierusalem."

103 *Margin*: St Thomas. See Franck, *Chronica*, III Chronica, xiiii, recto, under "Thomas der Apostel Asie."

104 *Margin*: St Matthew. This account does not match what Franck writes in *Chronica*, III Chronica, xiiii, verso, under "Mattheus ein Apostel Judae und Ethiopie."

A Short, Simple Confession

Simon the Apostle was chosen to preach in Egypt.[105] He also suffered greatly for the sake of Christ, witnessing in Egypt, but with few conversions. After the martyrdom of James he went to Jerusalem to lead and feed the church of God. There again he was charged by his enemies, taken before Attilus, who had been placed as governor over Judah, after which he was tortured long and hard. There he is said to have ended his life as a martyr, so that everyone who was present, including the judge himself had to marvel that this one-hundred-and-twenty-year-old man had suffered to such a degree the severe martyrdom of the cross. <31>

The apostle Judas Thaddaeus,[106] a brother of Simon and James the lesser, preached Christ in Pontus and Mesopotamia, transforming the wild, untamed people with the Gospel and the teaching of Christ, after which he traveled with Simon his brother to Persia, entering the city of Edessa and meeting with King Abgarus, who had been struck down with a physical affliction, healing him and converting him to Christ.[107] And after a long period of witness to Christ, he is said also to have received the crown of martyrdom.

In summary, the histories and the historians witness clearly that all the holy apostles ended their lives through the cross and suffering, being persecuted by their enemies on account of their witness concerning Jesus Christ and then, with severe torture, sentenced to death and executed—except for John the Evangelist and the beloved disciple of Christ,[108] the brother of James the greater. He alone, from among the twelve apostles, is said to have died a natural death. Yet he too is said to have been bound and captured in Asia, and taken to Emperor Domitian in Rome and there, as Tertullian reports, placed in hot and fatty oil. And since God protected him from death, he was sent to the isle of Patmos, where the Son of God shone, revealing to him many mysteries, <32> how events were to take place up to the end of the world—as may be found throughout the Book of Revelation.

---

105 *Margin*: St Simon, 120 years old. See Franck, *Chronica*, III Chronica, xiiii, verso, under "Simon der Apostel in Egypten."

106 *Margin*: St Judas. See Franck, *Chronica*, III Chronica, xv, recto, under "Judas Thadeus ein Apostel in Mesopotamia."

107 *Margin*: The historians report how this king had wanted Christ to heal him in his illness, imploring Christ, after his Ascension, to send one of his disciples

108 *Margin*: St John the Evangelist. See Franck, *Chronica*, III Chronica, xv, recto, under "Johannes Apostolus der letst."

Paul, the chosen apostle,[109] was called from high heaven by the Son of God Himself, and sent out to proclaim the Gospel, through which he suffered many types of danger, cross and tribulation (Acts 9, 13, 14, 16, 17, 18, 19, 21, 23, 24, 25, 27 and 28). At Philippi and Thessalonica[110] he was reviled for acting in a revolutionary manner against the Roman Empire's laws and decrees; at Athens he was reproached by the worldly-wise as being a babbler and proclaimer of foreign deities. [Acts 17:18]

Likewise *at Caesarea*[111] *the high priest Ananias of Jerusalem and Tertullus, along with the elders of the governor Felix, judged Paul to be dangerous, that he was inciting all the Jews in the world to revolt, and was a leader of the sect of Nazarenes.*[112] To list the many and various tribulations, dangers, cross and suffering of the holy apostle Paul which he suffered at the hands of the Jews and Gentiles on account of his witness to Jesus Christ would take up a great deal of space. In short, however, Paul himself speaks against his enemies, the false apostles (2 Corinthians 11[:23-27]), saying: "I have labored far more intensely than they, experienced far more imprisonments, <33> and was more often near death. Five times I have received from the Jews the forty lashes minus one. Three times I was beaten with rods. Once I received a stoning. Three times I was shipwrecked; for a night and a day I was adrift at sea; on frequent journeys, in danger from rivers, danger from bandits, danger from my own people, the Jews; in danger from Gentiles, danger in the city, danger in the wilderness, danger at sea, danger from false brothers and sisters; in toil and hardship, through many a sleepless night, hungry and thirsty, often without food, cold and naked," etc. And finally, after protracted and horrible suffering and tribulation, Paul was executed by the sword under Emperor Nero, certainly not as a holy man and messenger of God the Lord, but instead as a sectarian, rabble rouser and revolutionary.[113]

This shows how impure the judgment of the world is: What God blesses and hallows the world curses and maligns, exemplified by what happened

---

109 *Margin*: St Paul
110 *Margin*: Acts 16; 17
111 *Margin*: Acts 24[:1-5]
112 *Margin*: Christians are still being called sectarians today. This point was much-used and elaborated upon by Franck in his "heretics" section of the *Chronicle*.
113 For some of the content in the paragraphs on the Apostle Paul, see the lengthy treatment in Franck, *Chronica*, III Chronica, xi, verso-xiii, verso, beginning under "Paulus eyn Apostel der Heyden."

A Short, Simple Confession 221

to Christ and to the chosen martyrs, as manifestly documented historically, and which will be documented until the end of the world—namely, that the devout will come up short against the ungodly and against human reason, as Paul says, Galatians 4[:29] "the one born according to the flesh persecuted the one born according to the Spirit."

This is still occurring today, and will so continue, according to the written <34> content of the holy scripture of the Old and New Testaments *until the time when the page will be turned again*, and such persecutors and tyrants will be dumbfounded, and testify *as did the wise King Solomon wrote in the book of Wisdom, 5[:4-13]:* "See, there are the ones whom we once ridiculed, whom we expelled, mocking and insulting them, thinking that their life was madness and their end dishonorable. Look how they now are being counted among the children of God and have a place among the godly. We have strayed far from the way of truth, the light of devoutness has not shone on us. What use is our arrogance to us now, and of what use is the splendor of our parliaments? All these things have passed away like a shadow, like a freighter that sails hither and yon, leaving no sign of virtue behind us, and consequently being consumed in our wickedness." *These and other similar words will be spoken in hell by those who have sinned, etc.*

But the godly will abide in eternity. The prophet Ezekiel, Ezekiel 32[:20ff] also states how God wreaked vengeance on such godless tyrants—on the Egyptians and the Assyrians with all their hordes, likewise on Elam and all its people, likewise on the land of Edom with its kings and princes, also on all the <35> northern princes together with the Sidonians, on Meshech and Tubal and all their people who at one time brought terror into the land of the living and who scourged, persecuted, and tortured the devout who lived in God, and how God plunged them into hell.

As the prophet says, He has cast them down into the land of those who live outside; the more beautiful you are (he says) the further you will be cast down to the uncircumcised, to those who have been slain with the sword: "Its company is all around its grave, all of them killed, fallen by the sword, who spread terror in the land of the living."[114]

Therefore they carry their disgrace together with the others who have gone to hell, those who laid their swords under their heads, whose misdeeds are on their corpses since they, as heroes, had brought terror into the land of the living, and had terrorized the devout who lived in

---

114 [Ezekiel 32:23.]

God. Therefore they lie in hell, with their graves all around, and their swords under their heads.

But now someone may say, these were uncircumcised and unbelieving heathen (of whom Ezekiel speaks) who acted in an ungodly way, also fighting against the people of God. We, to the contrary, are Christians, the people of God; we hold to the Christian faith and holy Gospel; therefore, the uncircumcised <36> who are led to hell have nothing to do with us.

To this we answer: It is even worse to boast of a lord, yet to act contrary to that lord's will and command. For Christ coerced no one with force to follow him and his teaching.[115] Neither did he command his disciples and believers to persecute and tyrannize, as we desire to prove below in the Third Article, on the basis of divine authority and even upon the actual writings of the Reformed theologians themselves. He foretold to his own disciples how for his own name's sake they would be hated and persecuted,[116] exhorting them to triumph and overcome under the cross, with patience, and to force no one into faith through coercion but instead to shake the dust from their shoes and depart from those who had no desire to accept his teaching.[117]

Now, how the scribes, kings and senators at Jerusalem treated the prophets, our redeemer and savior Jesus Christ, and his holy apostles, this we have by now come to understand very well from the above, regarding those who clearly wanted to be the people of God, and who pointed to and made manifest the Son of God and his servants.

For although [the rulers] were commanded in the Old Testament[118] to put the false prophets to death, one finds nowhere in Holy Scripture that they killed a false <37> prophet, but instead, in every case, they invoked a perverse, impure judgment against the true prophets and chosen people of God; indeed, against the Son of God himself. Therefore they did not err any less than did the uncircumcised heathen; in fact they deserve a harder sentence since the unbelieving heathen did not know as much as they did,

---

115 Zurich Q3 adds: *as [Rudolf] Walter himself wrote as is reported many times concerning this law-giver from Zion and Jerusalem.* On Rudolf Walter (also called Walther or Gwalther), see above, page 61, note 8 in this volume.
116 Zurich Q3 adds: *Likewise he sent them like sheep among wolves*
117 *Margin*: Matthew 10, Mark 6; Luke 9, 10. Cf. Franck, *Chronica*, III, cxxxvi, recto.
118 *Margin*: Deuteronomy13; Jeremiah 14; Zechariah 13

and did not consider themselves to be a special people of God, to which point the Lord himself speaks when he said to the Pharisees and Scribes, John 9[:41], "If you were blind you would have no sin; but since you say, 'We see,' your sin remains."

Therefore he says, Matthew 23[:29-38], "Woe to you, scribes and Pharisees, you who build the tombs of the prophets and decorate the graves of the righteous, saying, 'Had we lived during the times of our ancestors, we would not have taken part with them in shedding the blood of the prophets.' In this manner you are actually testifying against yourselves, implying that you are the children of those who had killed the prophets. Go on and complete your ancestors' work. You snakes, you brood of vipers; how will you avoid condemnation to hell? Therefore behold, I send you prophets, sages and scribes, some of whom you will kill and crucify, and <38> some whom you will whip in your synagogues, persecuting them from town to town, so that upon you will fall all the blood of the righteous that has been shed on earth, from the blood of Abel the righteous, to the blood of Zechariah the son of Berachiah, whom you murdered between the temple and the altar. Truly I say to you, all this will come upon this generation. 'Jerusalem, Jerusalem! You who kill the prophets and stone those who are sent to you. How often have I desired to gather your children as a hen gathers her young under her wings, and you were not willing. Behold, your house will be left in desolation.'"

Therefore, as is written in Luke, Chapter 19 [Luke 19:41-44], "He looked upon the city of Jerusalem and cried over it, and said, 'If you only knew the things that make for peace, you would be thankful on this very day. But now they are hidden from your eyes. Indeed, the time will come upon you when your enemies will surround you and the children among you, and lay siege, hemming you in on every side and crushing you to the ground, leaving no stone standing upon another, since you did not recognize the time of your visitation.'"

Therefore Saint Stephen said to them (this followed the time that they had made bold in carrying out their malice against the Lord Jesus, and with derision had delivered <39> him to the cross and had attacked his holy apostles through persecution): "You stiff-necked people, uncircumcised in heart and ears, you forever oppose the Holy Spirit, just as your ancestors did. Which of the prophets did your ancestors not persecute? They killed those who foretold the coming of the Righteous

One, and now you have become his betrayers and murderers" [Acts 7: 51-52].

Therefore all those who have ever held to such an unclean judgment against true righteousness, and who have shed so much innocent blood, have needed to pay dearly enough for it with overwhelming dread, with eternal dread and agony, and also in this world, as is recorded throughout the writings of the prophets, and especially in the lamentation of Jeremiah, Lamentations 4[:12-14] where the Prophet says: "The kings of the earth did not believe, nor did any of the inhabitants of the world, that foe or enemy could enter the gates of Jerusalem. It was for the sins of her prophets and the iniquities of her priests, who shed the blood of the righteous in the midst of her. Blindly they wandered through the streets, so defiled with blood that no one was able to touch their garments."

Likewise in Lamentations 2[:21]: "The young and the old are lying on the ground in the streets; my young women and my young men have fallen by the sword; in the day of your anger you have killed them, slaughtering without mercy." <40> *And further on in Chapter 4 [Lamentations 4:5-11]:* "Those who feasted on delicacies now perish in the streets; those who were brought up in purple and scarlet now adorn themselves with dung. Their transgressions were greater than the transgressions of Sodom, which was overthrown in a moment, though no hand was laid on it. Her Nazarites were whiter than snow," says the prophet, yea, "whiter than milk; their color was ruddy like the agate in which a precious stone is set, their beauty and smoothness like a sapphire. Now their visage is absolutely black, so that you cannot recognize them. Their skin, shriveled up on their bones, is as dry and stiff as wood. Those who were killed by the sword are more comely than those who died of starvation. Women, who certainly are compassionate by nature, boiled their own children for food with their own hands during this time of such wretched depravity. And the Lord vented his grim wrath upon them."

That all this was fulfilled concerning Jerusalem, as Christ the Son of God *and his prophets prophesied about her, is obviously known to the entire world. And since those who had a command to expel and kill the false prophets*[119] *had to suffer and endure such great hardship, with great dread and distress, yet in their judgments were so wickedly deceitful*

---

119 *Margin*: Deuteronomy 13.

A Short, Simple Confession 225

and corrupt, so perverse and deluded, how do today's persecutors wish <41> to vindicate themselves, those who boast so highly and gloriously of Christ?

Or does today's world think—a world which according to the words of the Lord Jesus himself is becoming more evil the longer it exists, and is growing and increasing in unrighteousness, wantonness, envy, hate, materialism, usury, drunkenness, gluttony, fornication, adultery, impurity, arrogance, *condescension, haughtiness,* foul language, cursing, etc., *as they among themselves confess*—that they can improve upon the old, pious golden world?

Will not the scribes of the Old Testament stand next to today's scribes on the day of judgment and say, Oh we misjudged. Our court judgments deceived us. Since we were commanded to execute false prophets we took action, based upon our legal opinions. We executed them because their precepts and life were different from ours. We were unwilling to tolerate them. Oh, how blind we were, and how miserably have our verdicts deceived us and missed their mark.

But you have absolutely no alibi or excuse, since Christ, the eternal Son of God did not command, but forbade anyone to force others to believe through coercion, or to kill and persecute [for reasons of faith].

Therefore all who act as Jerusalem acted may expect no better, as the prophet Esdras notes, 4 Esdras 15[:21]: "Just as they have done to my elect until this day, says the Lord, so God will do to you, and let harm come over you." <42> *The Son of God said truly to Saint John, in Revelation, chapter 2 [Revelation 2:10], "The devil will throw some of you into prison" (that is, men will do it, through whom the devil rules and carries out his work* [Ephesians 2:1-2], *putting you to the test,* namely, as Peter confirms at various places that faith is valued as being much more precious than gold[120] which, though perishable, is tested by fire), *"and for ten days you will have affliction. Be faithful until death, and I will give you the crown of life."*

But it follows in chapter 13 [Revelation 13:10], that whoever puts another into prison will himself go to prison; and whoever kills with the sword must be killed by the sword. And in chapter 16 [Revelation 16:5-6] the angel of God says, "Lord, you are just in your pronouncements, for they

---

120 *Margin*: 1 Peter 1; Wisdom [Ecclesiasticus] 1; Revelation 2

have shed the blood of the saints and the prophets, and you have given them blood to drink, of which they are worthy." The royal prophet [David] also speaks to this in Psalm 37[:14-15]: "The ungodly draw the sword and draw their bows in order to do away with the righteous, but their bows will be broken and their swords will pierce their own hearts."

Since Christ has foretold the way of cross, suffering and sorrow for us, which is at the same time the true path and way to the kingdom of God and to eternal life, he therefore also says in John's Revelation,[121] "Whoever triumphs will inherit everything. I <43> will be his God, and he will be my son." Likewise[122] "to the one who triumphs I will give to eat from the tree of life that stands in the middle of God's paradise." And further on he says, "those who triumph will be dressed in white clothes, and I will not remove their names from the book of life, and I will confess their names before my father and his angels" [Revelation 3:5].

The wise king *Solomon* also says, Wisdom 3[:1-4], "The souls of the righteous are in the hand of God, and no agony of death will ever touch them. In the eyes of the foolish they seemed to have died, and their departure and death was thought to be a disaster; yet they are at peace. For though in the sight of others they suffered some pain, their hope is on immortal things. Having been disciplined a little, they will receive great good, because God tested them and found them worthy of himself; like gold in the furnace he tried them, and like a sacrificial burnt offering he accepted them."

The Lord also says, Matthew 10[:32-33], "Whoever confesses me before the people I will also confess before my father in heaven; whoever denies me before the people I will deny before my father in heaven." He says, further, "Do not fear those who kill the body but cannot kill the soul; rather fear him who can destroy both <44> soul and body in hell."[123]

Therefore Jesus, son of Sirach, says in Chapter 4 [Ecclesiasticus 4:27-28]: "Do not . . . show partiality to a ruler. Fight to the death for the truth, and God will fight for you." Likewise the Lord spoke through the prophet Isaiah in Chapter 51 [Isaiah 51:12-13], "Why then are you afraid of a mere mortal

---

121 *Margin*: Revelation 21[:7]
122 *Margin*: Revelation 2[:7]
123 Zurich Q3 adds: *Whoever wishes to, may read Fourth Esdras chapter 2; likewise Revelation chapter 7, concerning what the distressed and suffering servants of Christ may await, and how the page will be turned*

who must die, a human being who fades like grass? You have forgotten the Lord, your Maker, . . . You fear continually all day long because of the fury of the oppressor, who is bent on destruction." And earlier in Chapter 43 [Isaiah 43:1-2] he says: "Do not fear, for I have redeemed you; I have called you by name, you are mine. When you pass through the waters, I will be with you; and through the rivers, they shall not overwhelm you; when you walk through fire you shall not be burned, and the flame shall not consume you."

The holy David also says in Psalm 46[:1-3]: "God is our refuge and our strength, a help in the greatest needs that befall us. Therefore we will not fear, though the earth should sink, though the mountains disappear into the heart of the sea; though the waters of the sea roar and foam, though the mountains tremble with its tumult. Selah."

For these reasons we, upon putting our hand to the plow, are never more to look back, for we have a faithful Lord King and Captain who will fight and do battle for us, if <45> we truly submit ourselves with our whole heart. For a greater one is with us than is with them, as the devout King Hezekiah said, 2 Chronicles 32[:8]: "With them is an arm of flesh; but with us is the Lord our God, to help us and to fight our battles."

Truly *it is only for a short time that we will need to suffer the encounter of heat, affliction, fear, grief, vexation, robbery, persecution, prison, execution by fire, water and sword, and every sort of torture and martyrdom. The messenger is already at the door who will say to us, Come, you beloved, and enter into the joy of our Lord. For then this short time of ours will be transformed into eternal laughter, and our fleeting pain into unending exultation.*

The tyrants with their bloody mandates[124] will no longer exist, and the time will be over for all our persecutors, avengers, hangmen, and torturers. We will follow the Lamb, with great joy and honor. Esdras speaks to this, 4 Esdras 2[:36-38, 42-47]: "Flee the shadows of this world, receive the joy of your glory . . . giving joyful thanks to him who has called you to the celestial kingdom. Arise, stand erect and see the number of those who have been sealed at the feast of the Lord. . . . I, Ezra, saw on Mount Zion a great multitude that I could not number, <46> and they all were praising the Lord with songs. In their midst was a young man of great stature, taller than any of the others, and on the head of each of them he placed a crown, but he

---

124 Zurich Q3 adds: *which are applied more strongly in some parts of the German nation than in others.*

was more exalted than they. And I was held spellbound. Then I asked an angel, 'Who are these, my lord?' He answered and said to me, 'These are they who have put off mortal clothing and have put on the immortal, and have confessed the name of God. Now they are being crowned, and receive palms.' Then I said to the angel, 'Who is that young man who is placing crowns on them and putting palms in their hands?' He answered and said to me, 'He is the Son of God, whom they confessed in the world.'"

Saint John also writes in his Revelation chapter 7 [Revelation 7:9-17; 21:4], witnessing there to Ezra's vision by saying: "After this I looked, and there was a great multitude that no one could count, from every nation, from all tribes and peoples and languages, standing before the throne and before the Lamb, robed in white, with palm branches in their hands. . . . Then one of the elders addressed me, saying, 'Who are these, robed in white, and where have they come from?' I said to him, 'Lord, you are the one that knows.' Then he said to me, 'These are they who have come out of the great ordeal; they have washed their robes and made them <47> white in the blood of the Lamb. For this reason they are before the throne of God, and worship him day and night in his temple, and the one who is seated on the throne will shelter them. They will hunger no more, and thirst no more; the sun will not strike them, nor any scorching heat; for the Lamb at the center of the throne will watch over them, and he will guide them to springs of the water of life, and God will wipe away every tear from their eyes.' . . . Death will be no more; mourning and crying and pain will be no more. . . .'"

Therefore, although the elected believers may be led away by their enemies like a scattered flock, as God says through the prophet Baruch, [Baruch 4:25-26], "My children will need to endure rough roads," Paul also says in Romans 8[:36-37], quoting Psalm 44[:11], "'For your sake we are being killed all day long; we are accounted as sheep to be slaughtered.' No, in all these things we are more than conquerors through him who loved us." The prophet Isaiah also says, Isaiah 25[:8-9], "The Lord God will wipe away the tears from all faces, and will remove the disgrace of his people from all the earth, for the Lord has spoken. It will be said on that day, Lo, He is our God in whom we have trusted, and he has saved us. This is the Lord for whom we have waited; let us be glad and rejoice in his salvation."

A Short, Simple Confession

David also speaks to this, Psalm 126[:6]: "Those who go out weeping, <48> bearing the seed for sowing, shall come home with shouts of joy, carrying their sheaves." Thus Christ our Lord and Master went before us, through cross, suffering and tribulation, and through this entered into his glory. And he also prophesied this to us, that if we want to be heirs of his kingdom and glory, we shall also likewise need to follow this path and none other, since the servant is not to be esteemed more highly than his lord.

For this reason Christ admonishes us to enter through the narrow door[125] *for the door is wide and the way is broad which leads to damnation, and there are many who pass through it. But on the other hand, the door is small and the way narrow which leads to life, and few there are who find it. [Matthew 7:13-14].*[126] *The prophet Esdras also says*[127]*: "'There is a city built and set on a plain, and it is full of all good things; but the entrance to it is narrow and set in a precipitous place, so that there is fire on the right hand and deep water on the left. There is only one path lying between them, that is, between the fire and the water, so that only one person can walk on the path. If now the city is given to someone as an inheritance, how will the heir receive the inheritance unless by passing through the appointed danger?' . . . The righteous, therefore, must endure difficult circumstances while hoping for easier ones."* <49>

And therefore, since this narrow and small way to life is marked by the cross and tribulation, as Paul says, 2 Timothy 3[:12], all who wish to live in a godly manner in Christ Jesus must suffer persecution, and as is said in the Acts of the Apostles [Acts 14:22], "It is through many persecutions that we must enter the kingdom of God." Likewise, as the Lord says, Matthew 5[:44], "Love your enemies; bless those who curse you, do good to those who hate you."[128]

---

125 Zurich Q3 adds: *for this truly is a narrow way for flesh and blood, namely to be harmed and robbed in body and possessions for Jesus Christ's sake.*

126 Zurich Q3 adds: *Likewise in another place he says [Matthew 21, 22], There are many called, but few are chosen. All people are called to the heavenly kingdom and eternal glory, but the seed is scanty, and few indeed are able or wish to walk through this small door and onto this narrow way. But all who wish to be saved must go through these—this narrow, cramped path and through this small door—or remain outside eternally.*

127 *Margin*: 4 Esdras 7[:6-9; 18]

128 *Margin*: Matthew 16[:24-25]; Mark 8[:34-35]; Luke 9[:58-62]; 14[:26-27]

Likewise, we are to deny ourselves, take up our cross, and renounce all that we have: father and mother, wife and child, brother and sister, house, farm, field, meadow, silver, gold and our own lives,[129] *repenting, and becoming like children,*[130] *being born anew from above.*[131] *And as the Apostle says further, crucify the flesh with its lusts and desires,*[132] *not living according to the flesh*[133] *but according to the Spirit,*[134] *putting off the old person and putting on the new, who is created in the manner of God in true righteousness and holiness,*[135] *not to judge, but leaving vengeance to God, and giving food and drink to our enemies,*[136] *in this manner following our Lord Jesus, our predecessor.*[137] *But this is far too narrow a path for the whole world and for all would-be Christians,*[138] *for whom the cup of the cross and tribulation, which our Lord Jesus drank before we did, is far too bitter to drink.*

Christ prepared the far-too-narrow path, leading the way, he who truly is King of kings, Prince <50> of princes, and the highly praised and blessed Son of God, to whom has been given all power in heaven and on earth[139] *who, although he was truly in the form of God and an agent of the almighty glory and divine majesty, nevertheless he emptied himself, taking the form of a servant, being born in human likeness. And being found in human form, he humbled himself for our sake and became obedient to the point of death—even death on the cross [Philippians 2:6-8], and was not ashamed to walk this narrow, small, despised path, upon which he brought eternal richness to our souls.*

---

129 *Margin*: Matthew 18[:3]; John 3[:3]
130 Zurich Q3 adds: *Matthew 10; 1 Peter 2*
131 Zurich Q3 adds: *Christ said plainly and clearly, one who does not renounce what one has cannot be my disciple, Luke 14.*
132 *Margin*: Galatians 5[:16ff]; Romans 8[:1-27]; Ephesians 4[:4;17-32]; Colossians 3[:1-17]
133 Zurich Q3 adds: *2 Corinthians 6; 1 Thessalonians 5, 1 Peter 1, 4, 5*
134 Zurich Q3 adds: *Romans 8*
135 Zurich Q3 adds: *Ephesians 4; Colossians 3*
136 Zurich Q3 adds: *Romans 12*
137 Zurich Q3 adds: *and so seek what is above, where Christ sits at the right hand of God, and to think on what is above and what is earthly, as Paul says in Colossians 3.*
138 Zurich Q3 replaces "would-be Christians" with *for all unrepentant children of the squire Adam.*
139 Zurich Q3 adds: *Matthew 28*

A Short, Simple Confession

Every proud, arrogant, intelligent, natural, worldly-wise, educated person must marvel at this narrow and small path, which is so contrary and loathsome to flesh and blood, for this narrow and small way absolutely is not prepared according to their understanding and human reason, and education.

Indeed, the Lord Jesus established something completely abhorrent here for all worldly-wise, educated, and arrogant pretenders to wisdom, and according to their reasoning, something unquestionably crazy, when he prepared a lowly path of affliction as the way to the kingdom of heaven, with the Lord Jesus, the great Prince and King, himself having proceeded down this same path.

Had he come, however, as an almighty <51> king and prince, having lived according to the flesh, and wielding his scepter according to worldly wisdom in pride, haughtiness, arrogance, greed, guzzling, gluttony, envy, hate, cursing, blasphemy, etc., as well as in persecuting, expelling, banishing, and torturing those who fear God through warring and the shedding of blood as is the custom of the whole world and the would-be Christians,[140] which is the very nature of the broad and wide path leading to damnation—then the whole *world and would-be Christians*[141] *might well consider following him freely, and not be so utterly ashamed of his aggrieved discipleship, despised as it is by the world.*

Since he, however, forbids every sort of vengeance for all those who wish to be his disciples, who want to travel the narrow way which leads to the kingdom of God, where he commands us to love our enemy, to bless those who curse us, to disown everything we have, to take up the cross, deny ourselves and follow him, and to shun every sin and unrighteousness—through which we lose the kingdom of God and earn the punishment of eternal damnation—consequently the path for them is simply too narrow and small, and few there are who thus walk on it.

That few will be saved is also testified to in the fourth book of Esdras in the 8th chapter [4 Esdras 8:1-3] and Matthew 20[:14-15?] and 22[:14]. That they on the other hand are walking down the broad, well-traveled, wide path leading to damnation may be seen in the life and walk of the whole world, <52> about which Holy Scripture teaches, pronouncing a sentence upon the learned and unlearned, upon the noble and the lowly, upon all

---

140 Zurich Q3 adds: *unrepentant children of Adam*
141 Zurich Q3 adds: *Matthew 7*

those who commit transgressions, who have not been renewed through the Spirit of God and ruled by the Spirit.

Moses says clearly, Deuteronomy 32[:15ff], that the perverse and insane ways ruined them, and they are not his children, on account of their scars and rabble. Christ also says this to Abraham's ungodly sons, John 8[:42, 44]: "If God were your Father, you would love me. . . . You are from your father the devil, and you choose to do your father's desires." "Whoever loves me," he says, John 14[:23ff], "will keep my word"; but on the Last Day the word shall judge such a one who has heard, yet who has not lived accordingly.

The apostle Paul also says, that whoever lives according to the flesh,[142] will have to die. The wages of sin is death,[143] and the works of flesh are obvious, such as fornication, adultery, impurity,[144] lewdness, sexual gratification, defilers of boys, worshipping images, magic, enmity, conflict, jealousy, anger, quarreling, dissension, schism, hate, murder, drunkenness, gluttony, arrogance, miserliness, betrayers, those who shed the blood of the innocent, thieves, murderers, gossipers, perjurers, magicians, liars, the unmerciful, and all forms of disobedience to God and his word: if such do not mend their ways, <53> they will not possess God's kingdom. Read in Romans 1, 1 Corinthians 6, Galatians 5, Ephesians 5, and Revelation 21-22 what all ungodly, unrepentant individuals may expect.

Why should we then desire to be yoked to the world—and to all would-be, carnal Christians—cultivating their unrepentant, sinful lives and thereby wounding our souls along with them eternally, being thus robbed of the crown of eternal life? We would be far better off had we never been born than that we should neglect and so lose the eternal inheritance with sins and carnal lusts. And even if the devil himself with great seriousness opposes us with all his servants and persecutors, and even if the foolish people say to us, "You will have absolutely no place or home if you do not do as other people; then where will you go? The world will not tolerate this. Who is able to resist the beast, Daniel 7, 8; Revelation 13, 14? You must also accept his faith, his worship services, and memorials."

---

142 *Margin*: Romans 8[:6, 13]
143 *Margin*: Romans 6
144 *Margin*: Galatians 5; Genesis 38; 1 Corinthians 6; Romans 1; Revelation 21, 22

A Short, Simple Confession

Look how the whole world worships the beast, and becomes a part of it. How, specifically, do you want to respond, if you cannot extol it? For if you do not so respond, power has been given to the beast to strive against the devout, in order to overcome them in body and life. Here, then, is the patience of the saints, the only means to victory in times of need. <54> This patience depends solely upon God's strength, according to divine counsel and wisdom, in the fear of God, Psalm 2[:11]; Psalm 27, granted that one cannot harm a hair on your head before your time, and that the world, with its prince and god, cannot extend itself further than what the great eternal God decrees and sets as the goal, Matthew 10; Job 1, 12; 21; 1 Corinthians 10.

Why would we then desire to accept his mark, about which the blessed John writes, Revelation 13[:16], that the names of all those who dwell upon the earth, who worship the beast, are not written in the living book of the Lamb? Whoever, then, defiles himself, resulting in his being outside the book of the Lamb and of Life, such a one has no part in the kingdom of God.

Why should we then desire, for such a short time, to play the hypocrite with this beast, stroking and protecting our flesh, and remain outside the Book of Life, in this manner enacting a foolish exchange, interchanging the eternal good for a temporal mess of pottage and a life of financial gain?

It is many, many thousand times better, more useful and preferable to burn up and melt away temporal financial and material gain, all of which I must allow to pass away: hat and hair, possessions and blood—indeed, all that might get in the way of the Eternal, and keep me outside the Book of Life, where I have no part in the Lamb of God. For Christ says loud and clear, Mark 8[:35-37], "Whoever would save his life will lose it; and whoever loses his life for my sake and the Gospel's <55> will save it. For what does it profit a person to gain the whole world and forfeit his life? For what can one give in return for one's life?"

Also consider Psalm 49, my dear reader, showing that it costs too much to ransom one's soul from death, that one therefore will need to allow the consequences to stand forever. All of the world's material possessions, silver and gold, pearls and precious stones, and all the pomp and circumstance of the kingdoms of this world are too little to effect a ransom.

For this reason we do well to remain awake, along with the five wise virgins [Matthew 25:1-13], preparing our lamps with the true, pure oil, so that we may be worthy wedding guests and true witnesses to the Truth. For Christ also says, Whoever is ashamed of me and my words in this adulterous and sinful generation, such will the Son of Man also be ashamed of when he comes in the majesty of his Father with the holy angels.

To this the angel of God from heaven also says, Revelation 14[:9-11]: "If any one worships the beast and his image, and receives the mark on his forehead or on his hand, he also shall drink the wine of God's wrath, poured unmixed into the cup of his anger, and he shall be tormented with fire and sulfur. . . . And the smoke of their torment goes up for ever and ever; and they have no rest, day or night, these worshipers of the beast and his image, and whoever has accepted <56> his mark."

Therefore the voice from heaven warns us, Revelation 18[:4], saying: "Come out of her, my people, lest you take part in her sins, lest you share in her plagues." Likewise the prophet Isaiah in the 52nd chapter [Isaiah 52:11] says: "Depart, depart, go out thence, touch no unclean thing; go out from the midst of her, purify yourselves, you who bear the vessels of the Lord." And thus the Prophet Jeremiah says as well, in chapter 51 [Jeremiah 51:6], "Flee from Babylon, let every man save his life! Be not cut off in her punishment. . . ."

And again, Paul the apostle says, 2 Corinthians 6[:14-18]: "Do not be unequally yoked with unbelievers. For what partnership have righteousness and iniquity? Or what fellowship has light with darkness? What accord has Christ with Belial? Or what does faith have in common with unbelief? What agreement has the temple of God with idols? For we are the temple of the living God; as God said, 'I will live in them and move among them, and I will be their God, and they shall be my people. Therefore come out from them and be separate from them, says the Lord, and touch nothing unclean; then I will welcome you and I will be your father, and you shall be my sons and daughters. . . .'" <57>

This is the true wisdom and fear of God, to separate oneself, in accordance with Holy Scripture, from the world, having nothing in common with their abominations and hypocritical sanctities, or accepting or taking on their religious symbols through which we would defile ourselves, even if because of this they may storm and rage against us all the more, as John says, Revelation 13[:15-18], "caus[ing] those who would not worship the

A Short, Simple Confession

image of the beast to be slain. All, both small and great, both rich and poor, both free and slave, are to be marked on the right hand or the forehead, so that no one can buy or sell without the mark, that is, the name of the beast or the number of its name. This calls for wisdom," says John.

To be sure, it truly is wisdom to protect oneself from this beast and his flock, so that one may escape their punishment and misery by not taking part, and hence not subjugating one's self to this anti-Christian harlotry and seduction in this last, dangerous era and last call to the Supper of God, during which time the Antichrist and haughty one, whom this beast symbolically prefigures and means, and as has been prophesied—established in the Temple of God with force and great power in order to master and rule the consciences and hearts of men and women.

This we must prevent, for the Temple of God is found in the hearts of believers, 1 Corinthians 3[:16-17], 2 Corinthians 6[:19-20]; 2 Corinthians 6[:16-18], hearts which this man of sin and child of depraved perversity, <58> who bypasses everything which God names and honors, desires to rule and bind with his precepts and laws. He wishes to have a kingdom of this world, and thus for a long time he has been fighting with coercion and with horrible tyranny and inhuman shedding of blood.

But Christ says, "My kingdom is not of this world;[145] if my kingdom were of this world, my servants would fight, that I might not be handed over to the Jews; but my kingdom is not from here." And to his disciples he says: "If you were of the world,[146] the world would love its own; but you are not of the world; I chose you out of the world, therefore the world hates you," John 15[:19].

Here we have the word of the Lord loud and clear, and the pure, untwisted judgment from the mouth of God, as to who the true disciples and messengers of God are, namely, not those who are exalted and honored by the world, who become highly trained thanks to large endowments and great places of higher learning, but rather those whom they hate,[147] persecute, expel from the land, revile, torture, and kill, and must be treated as "the refuse of the world and the offscouring of all things," 1 Corinthians 4[:13].

---

145 *Margin*: John 18[:36]
146 *Margin*: John 15
147 *Margin*: Matthew 10, 24; John 16

For this reason the blessed John says, 1 John 3[:1], "See what great love the Father has given us, that we should be called children of God; ... that is why the world does not know us. ..." The blessed James also says,[148] <59> "You adulterers! Do you not know that friendship with the world is enmity with God? Therefore whoever wishes to be a friend of the world makes himself an enemy of God." And Luke 6[:26], where the Lord Christ says: "Woe to you, when all men speak well of you, for so their fathers did to the false prophets," who will tickle their ears with flattering words[149] preaching what they like to hear, 1 Kings 22; Isaiah 5, 28; Jeremiah 8, 14, 23, 28; Ezekiel 13, 22; Micah 3. And the holy apostle Paul says, "If I were pleasing to people, I then would not be Christ's servant." [Galatians 1:20]

Now, however, this sinful person is, along with his prophets and followers, acceptable and pleasing to the world, to the fleshly, non-reborn people, who then show [the false prophets] great honor and reverence, and of course grant and reward such a one and his servants and scribes with temporal goods, great endowments and benefices, and with the most beautiful sought-after pleasures of this world.

The devil showed to the Son of God all the kingdoms of the world and their splendor and said all of it would be his (for he, the devil, is called a prince of the world); if [Jesus] honored and worshipped him, he would give [Jesus] everything. The Son of God refused him this, not wanting to accept anything from him, for his kingdom is not of this world, as noted above [Matthew 4:8-10]. Therefore he banished the crafty serpent, which is able to snare the flesh with lovely carnal caresses, flattery, and all sorts of snares pleasing to flesh and blood. <60>

This same flesh and blood, however, received from the devil all the fleshly desires and lusts of this world, caressing and fondling their flesh in all the fleshly desires—pride, arrogance, lewdness, fornication, adultery, petulance, drunkenness, gluttony, and every sort of sin and vice in which and through which they serve the devil, honoring him in this manner day and night, and carrying out his every wish. And in this regard, all those who do not desire to serve the devil, as well as those not wanting to play the hypocrite with them in their religious services, who [as a consequence], as already mentioned, are persecuted even unto death, until the time when the page [of history], along with [the devil] will also be reversed and

---

148 *Margin*: James 4[:4]
149 *Margin*: 2 Timothy 4[:3]

A Short, Simple Confession

turned back, and his foolishness leading to eternal destruction will become apparent, as Paul says, "the Lord Jesus will slay him with the breath of his mouth and destroy him by his appearing and his coming," 2 Thessalonians 2[:8].

This courageous appearing will happen after the time when the devil has played out his works, with all sorts of deceitful signs and wonders being carried out, and with all sorts of seducing temptations leading to unrighteousness among those who will be lost. Since they have not taken on the love of truth which leads to salvation, therefore their God will [judge] them mightily for going astray by believing liars and the lying spirits, namely, the enemies of the cross of Christ,[150] the end of which will be damnation. <61>

These do not serve the Lord Christ, but serve their bellies, for the belly is a god. They mislead innocent hearts with fondling and flattery, drunk with wine as the prophet Isaiah says,[151] filled with strong drink, and therefore they watch people erring, and fail in their judgments. Therefore, says he, they are blind watchmen who have no knowledge, dumb dogs who cannot bark, but instead turn to riches and drunkenness, going about with false lies,[152] for from the least to the highest, they all are motivated by shameful earthly gain.[153] From prophet to priest they go about filled with lies. Their tongues,[154] like sharp spears, speak treacherously. Publicly they speak in a friendly and peaceable way with their neighbors; covertly, however, they deceive them, just like secretive, conniving cats, who first of all entice, and then claw, giving the death stroke.[155] They bring grief to the righteous heart with their lies—to whom, however, the Lord does not bring grief. They embitter, and turn such a one away from upright living, but strengthen the hand of the godless so that such a one departs from the evil path all the less.[156]

Imperial diets and worldly goods take possession of their whole beings, and they can make no distinction between holy and unholy, with

---

150 *Margin*: Romans 16; Philippians 3
151 *Margin*: Isaiah 28[:7-8]
152 *Margin*: Isaiah 56[:10-12]
153 *Margin*: Jeremiah 6[:13]
154 *Margin*: Jeremiah 9[:3]
155 *Margin*: Ezekiel 13[:18ff?]
156 *Margin*: Ezekiel 22[:26ff?]

no ability to distinguish between the pure and impure. Those who want to become pure <62> by separating themselves from this abominable filth and impurity, and are determined not to walk with them on their old smooth [wooden: *holtzweg*] paths, must be dirtied, hated and scorned by them.

The priests who[157] should have reproached injustice, yet who instead imparted impurity and injustice, are exactly like the people, for which reason their teaching returns without fruits, and no blessing or benediction is behind it. For this reason the prophet Hosea has given them this title, saying,[158] "The crowd of priests is just like a nest of robbers, and their arms are like those of murderers and villains, for they bring every villany to pass." Their judgment is soiled with sins, lewdness and unrighteousness, and their eyes are darkened so that they hold the person who is rich in spirit to be insane, and the true prophets[159] end up being their fools. For this reason the Lord speaks against such false watchmen and self-appointed shepherds, who are driven by their soft god, the belly.[160] At the same time that they are gnawing into their people with their teeth, and grinding them to bits, they were also preaching peace, and declaring war against any who do not throw something into their mouths. Therefore their revelation will be like the night and their prophecy like darkness. Their judges speak the law swayed by bribes and gifts; their priests teach for the sake of financial gain; and their preachers proclaim only for the money. Yet they want <63> to be seen as the only ones who keep to God's way, stating that "the Lord is certainly among us, so that no misfortune may come upon us."

The holy apostle Paul also saw in his day such false watchmen and prophets in the spirit, whether in the New Testament or in the Old, and prophesied that they would not remain outside,[161] but after his departure would come in among them, but also from among themselves (among those who once embodied the apostolic churches), who would not spare the flock, but who would speak perverse things, and draw the disciples to their ways,[162] exemplifying a fine appearance of a holy way of life, but denying its

---

157 *Margin*: Hosea 4[:4-9]
158 *Margin*: Hosea 6[:9]
159 *Margin*: Hosea 9[:7]
160 *Margin*: Micah 3[:5; 11]
161 *Margin*: Acts 20[:29]
162 *Margin*: 2 Timothy 3[:1-9]

A Short, Simple Confession

strength,[163] for he says, such false apostles and deceitful workmen disguise themselves as apostles of Christ, and that is also no wonder, for even the devil himself disguises himself as an angel of light.

So it is not strange that although the devil's servants pretend to preach righteousness, [Paul] says that even if they continue to teach until their end, they will not come to a knowledge of truth since they love human desire more than God. For just as Jannes and Jambres opposed Moses [2 Timothy 3:8], so also these men oppose and blaspheme the truth.

Peter also writes[164] that in their reviling in matters of which they are ignorant, they will be destroyed, bringing the reward of wrongdoing upon themselves, for it is their great pleasure to revel daily. They are blots and blemishes, reveling <64> in their deception. They have eyes full of adultery, insatiable for sin. They entice unsteady souls. They have hearts trained in greed. Thus they are accursed children who have forsaken the right way, who in their error are following the way of Balaam who also loved the wages of unrighteousness, for which he received his punishment. They utter loud, empty boasts of folly; they entice with licentious passions of the flesh those who were inclining to the right way, and now walk in error; they pervert the grace of God with licentiousness,[165] and promise them freedom, but they themselves are slaves of corruption, for whatever overcomes a person, it is to that that one is enslaved.

Therefore, since the Holy Spirit has placed before our eyes something of a reflection and pattern of the false prophets, our eyes should now also be open to see where the false prophets hover and reside, namely those who emulate this pattern, who with no integrity and no pouring out of the heavenly dew, stamp people's hearts with their false impressions, and imprint and display the sign of the beast and, under the semblance of the holy Gospel, corral [people] and fence them in <65> with their false shepherd's crook or staff. They mix in their leaven and human religiosity, utilizing it in a perverse manner unto their own corruption, as is the custom of such false, self-proclaimed religious enthusiasts, who have been such progenitors of deception from the beginning[166] being cast about like a dreadful wind at noon or in the dead of night; as a people without water; as

---

163 *Margin*: 2 Corinthians 11[:12-15]
164 *Margin*: 2 Peter 2[:12-19]
165 *Margin*: Jude 1[:4]
166 *Margin*: 2 Peter 2; Jude 1[:12ff]

bare, fruitless trees, twice dead and uprooted; as wandering stars and wild waves of the sea which boast of, and cast up the foam of, their own shame when they are drunk and mad, singing lewd and knavish songs as is most certainly customarily known, heard and seen.

It is true that some are better able to keep secret and cover over their filth and abomination than others, for which reason our dear Lord and Savior Jesus Christ has faithfully warned us about them when he says, Matthew 7[:15-20], "Beware of the false prophets, who come to you in sheep's clothing but inwardly are ravenous wolves. You will know them by their fruits. Are grapes gathered from thorns, or figs from thistles? So, every sound tree bears good fruit, but the bad tree bears evil fruit. A sound tree cannot bear evil fruit, nor can a bad tree bear good fruit. Every tree that does not bear good fruit is cut down and thrown into the fire. Thus you will know them by their fruits," says Jesus Christ.

This difference, however, and recognition <66> of the false prophets who have been deceiving us for a long time already, hardly occurs in the Christendom of today. We might also succumb to such deception [ourselves], if we did not take note of what today's prophets in would-be Christendom are bearing and bringing in by way of fruit.

All of us together boast, to be sure, of Christ and his holy Gospel as being precious and lifted up, and also reproach the false prophets everywhere who have opposed and persecuted Christ and his holy apostles, those who were defiled by their above-mentioned wickedness. At the same time we could do otherwise with our critical eyes, which at present are turned outward rather than inward, searching our own hearts—whereby we are nicely taking the speck out of the eyes of others without recognizing at the same time the log in our own eyes[167]—forgetting thereby that no one desires to live under the number and lineage of the false prophets.

One group wants to ascribe all this to the Pope and to all those who[168] wish to follow and hobnob with his group, [claiming] that he is the true Antichrist, he and all his priest-ridden councils, cardinals, bishops, monks, pastors, and the whole adulterated and oil-anointed crowd—the real deceivers, money mongers, book-preachers, whorish priests, false watchmen, and prophets. On the other hand, the Pope accuses the

---

167 *Margin*: Matthew 7[:3-5]
168 Q3 has: *nitt* ("do not"), which seems extraneous to the intended point being made and seems to be an error on the part of the original copyist.

Lutherans and Zwinglians and others who have separated themselves from his abominations and idolatry, <67> that they are the false prophets and dividers of the Christian church. Thus on both sides they get into each other's hair, blaspheming, slandering, reproaching, defaming, warring, shedding blood, robbing, burning, etc., and each party claims to be innocent, attributing this title [of being false prophets] to the other side, and stuffing them into this same hole.

If one analyzes such persecutors, how they compare to the image of Christ, of his apostles, and to the members of the old Christian, apostolic churches—none of whom persecuted anyone for the sake of faith, as will be substantiated adequately in the first and third articles below—if one measures their life and walk against this image of the prophets, Christ and his holy apostles, then it will become evident how the lewd and deceitful false prophets in sheep's clothing are themselves exemplifying and living out these very accusations mentioned above.

And what they reproachingly damn and curse concerning the above-mentioned false prophets, they themselves are doing, stuck in the same rotten heap of rubbish, entangled therein over their ears. A devout God-fearing person may well marvel concerning God's just judgment, that He can have such fine unfaithful watchmen and false prophets that they thus utter pronouncements of judgment against themselves. They must prophecy that in His given time God can let a short sentence fall upon them, namely: you cunning <68> and twisted, false wolves and foxes and poisonous snakes and brood of vipers, you who have broken into my vineyard and sheepfold with your tricks, poisoning, defiling, laying waste, and violating the noble branch; biting, chewing and swallowing my lambs with your bloodthirsty throats that lie under your rebellious hats and hair. I pass sentence upon you on the basis of your own statements, since you are committing exactly that which you scolded and condemned others for having done.

For this reason we are to separate from such twisted, false prophets, and shun and flee from them in accordance with the teaching of Christ and his holy apostles, so that we are not injured in our souls and corrupted by them, whereby we would become refuse as they are, eternally.

But whoever persists in such pollution, in spite of all sincere warning, keeping company with such false prophets—they will promise such a one comfort and security, with their lying prophesies—they all together will thereby go astray, groping about in darkness, since they then will find no light, but rather will stagger about just like the drunkards. Since they did not want to accept the love of truth, God poured into them a stubborn, lazy spirit, closed their eyes, and allowed such lying spirits to come to them, as <69> the [true] prophets describe so well, such as Jeremiah says, Jeremiah 5[:31]: The [false] prophets and priests teach falsely, which pleases my people. For one finds ungodly people who secretly lay snares, waiting for people and lusting after children, intending to pounce upon and kill them. And like a nest full of little birds,[169] so also are your houses full of what they have won with deceit and cunning. That is the source of your great empire and riches, and the reason why they are so obese.

Thus says the Lord:[170] "Woe to you who sew magic bands upon all wrists, and make veils for the heads of persons of every stature, in the hunt for souls! Will you hunt down souls belonging to my people, and keep other souls alive for your profit? You have profaned me among my people for handfuls of barley and for pieces of bread, putting to death persons who should not die and keeping alive persons who should not live" [Ezekiel 13:18-19]. Furthermore, that which is good you call evil, and evil, good.[171] Darkness you make into light and light into darkness. This you acquire with your lies[172] (and perverted scribblings) among my people who listen to your lies. But the present world also will have no lack of such shrewd flatterers. Paul long ago prophesied regarding such false prophets and their followers, saying, "the time will come that they will not tolerate sound teaching, <70> but having itching ears they will accumulate for themselves teachers to suit their own liking, and will turn away from listening to the truth and wander into myths."[173] All those will go down in judgment who have not believed the truth, but who have held onto lies and injustice.

Our intention is not to write these things for the highly educated, worldly-wise and cross-fleeing scribes, nor for the haughty sophists and arrogant tyrants who have little to do with our writings, and who are not prone to being struck with fear by God's Word. Rather, we are writing for all those who believe in Christ, those who have not drowned in the

---

169 *Margin*: Ezekiel 22; 34; Micah 3
170 *Margin*: Ezekiel 13[:18-19]
171 *Margin*: Isaiah 5[:20]
172 *Margin*: Ezekiel 15
173 *Margin*: 2 Timothy 4[:3-4]

A Short, Simple Confession

sophisticated learning of their own wisdom—as may be found in this ungodly society in general—but rather to those who are humble, who are standing in tribulation under the cross, and who have studied in the school of Christ at the feet of the Lord.

Such individuals Erasmus (in the Preface of his *Postilla*, printed in Zurich) considers to be the true theologians.[174] Whether such a person be a farmer or a weaver, he is still a great teacher if he disdains the world and its riches, both in desire and demeanor—indeed, with his whole life. One finds no sign of being puffed up in such a one, but only Christian patience, humility, and a new, born-again life.[175]

We also do not want to forget all good-hearted people, both governing authorities and subjects. We would like to put our writing, taken from God's Word, into their hands [but also] the Reformed theologians' own writings—however slippery they may be, <71> forcing themselves into matters of faith. For Divine judgment and human judgment are quite unequal, and a clear perspective and a judicious, devout, pious heart in God is needed to interpret God's Word without prejudice, also in deciding between what is clear and what is muddy.

We have remained patiently silent for a long time up to now, responding little in our own defense, suffering patiently, and accepting all that has been done to us. The reason for our silence is that the[176] *scribes of this world, out of irritation, would have misinterpreted our responses, construing our writings as saying something other than what they truly mean to us.*

---

174 The reference is to Desiderius Erasmus, *Paraphrasis oder postilla teütsch, das ist, Klare Ausslegung aller evangelischen und apostolischen Schrifften des Neüwen Testaments...*, trans. Leo Jud (Zurich: Froschauer, ca. 1552). PDF copy read online from www.e-rara.ch/zuz/content/pageview/967556.

175 Erasmus' text reads, in part: "Theologus heißt einer der von Gott und göttlichen dingen redt/under jnen aber findt man die mer von irrdischen dann von göttlichen dingen reden.... Das wär mir ein rechter Theologus der nit mit gwundenen künstlichen argumenten/sonder mit lauterer begird/mit dem gesicht/mit den augen und allen geberden/ja mit seinen gantzen läben/die welt und reychthumm leert verachten. Der mit ernst leert daß man sich diser welt nichts halten noch trösten sölle/sonder ein Christ sölle gantz und gar an Gott hangen.... Welcher ja dieses und der gleychen auß dem geist Christi bewegt leert und prediget ... den halt ich für ein Theologus/ob er gleych ein bauwr oder wäber ware. Und welcher nach diser leer sein gantz läben und sitten/thun und lassen anrichtet und gstaltet/ der ist ein grosser leerer." Ibid., 8.

176 Zurich Q3 adds: *"highly-esteemed"*

Another reason [why they misinterpret us] is that *in their writings they mix us in with the false sects such as the Münsterites, among others, who in the guise of evangelical truth and Christian community had their wives in common, just like the fallen and apostate Nicolaitans, serving the abominable, impure, dissolute vice of adultery and immorality.* We desire no fellowship here or there with the likes of either group, any more than the holy apostles desired to have fellowship with those false apostles who had posed as genuine and true apostles.

The fact that even the devil is capable of appearing in the guise of a true apostle is exemplified in Judas, and at various places in the Acts of the Apostles and in the Epistles, how the holy apostles suffered on account of the false prophets, prophesying what would happen to them, Acts 20[:22ff]; Romans 16[:17-20]; 2 Corinthians 11[:13-15]; 1 Timothy 4[:1-3]; 2 Peter 2[:1-3]; 1 John 2[:18-26], 4[:1]; 2 John 1[:7-11]; Jude 1[:17-19].<72>

For this reason we have Holy Scripture, as already noted above, [that tells us] to separate from such depraved, stained people, and to depart from them, and where it becomes evident to us that such a person arises among us, we discipline such with the ban and Rule of Christ and his apostles, Matthew 18[:15-17], Luke 17[:3-4], 1 Corinthians 5[:1-13], 2 Thessalonians 3[:6; 14-15], whereby [he or she] absolutely may not partake with us of the holy sacraments.

Therefore we can rejoice when the learned of this world proclaim all sorts of ugly, deceitful things against us, in this manner unjustly misrepresenting us by speaking falsehoods about us.

If we, however, in turn wanted to pay them back with equivalent compensation, not lying about them but rather only wanting to point to the truth, then we would need to bring them to recognize and consider what manner of great books we would need to write if we wanted to describe and point out all their impurities, wranglings and conflicts, as well as all their shameful acts and vices—fornication, adultery, drunkenness, gluttony, and other abominations which they practice. Indeed, we would need to produce a far greater book than that which has been written against us, with falsehoods—about which the Impartial Judge will [someday] testify on our behalf.

Therefore it is not we, the suffering and persecuted lambs of Christ who <73> desire to have peace with all people, but they—those envious of us—who are the ones muddying the healing and clear water of the grace of

A Short, Simple Confession

God. For it is as clear as day that they have been standing upstream in the brook, roughing up the bottom of the brook with their feet and so muddying the water, while accusing us who are situated downstream, when it is they who have dislodged all sorts of intrigue, smut and petulance which we have permitted in patience to run over us.

But the Righteous and Impartial Judge will help the fearful and unlettered, in His own time and according to His own sense of justice, the [Righteous Judge] who is able to differentiate between the guilty and the innocent, the persecutor and the persecuted, and the one living according to the Spirit and the one living according to the flesh.[177]

Therefore, dear lords, you who are spurred on and incited by the learned of this world to persecute and abuse people on account of their faith, consider the matter carefully. For as surely as the Lord is living, you are fighting not against flesh and blood, but against the One who has eyes flaming like fire, who judges and fights with righteousness, who is crowned with many crowns, whose Name nobody knows except He himself, who is clad in a robe spattered with blood. His name[178] is The Word of God who rules the Gentiles with a rod of iron, who treads the wine presses of the fury and wrath of Almighty God, who has a name written on his robe and on <74> his thigh, "King of all kings" and "Lord of all lords."

Therefore, consider carefully, for all persecutors are contending against this very One in such things, with their instruments of torture and death. Consider what God the Lord says through the prophet Zechariah[179] about his chosen people of faith, who are here despised and persecuted: Whoever touches you touches the apple of my eye. The death of the saints, says David,[180] is precious in the sight of the Lord. The Lord Jesus from heaven says to Paul, who was persecuting his believers,[181] Saul, Saul, why do you persecute me? It will hurt you to kick against the goads.

Therefore, dear lords, it is Jesus of Nazareth whom you are persecuting, and not only us. Therefore, wake up and consider carefully what you in God's time will need to account for, and what will befall you. For we and all of you shall be called before a Judge where neither power nor prestige,

---

177 *Margin*: Matthew. 10[:26], 24[:36]; Mark 13[:32]; Luke 21; John 16; Galatians 4
178 *Margin*: Revelation 19[:11-16]
179 *Margin*: Zechariah 2[:8]
180 *Margin*: Psalm 116[:15]
181 *Margin*: Acts 9[:4; 26:14]

neither speaking eloquently nor holding high office will be of any avail, when justice will be meted out upon all flesh, impartially, and without respect of persons. At that time the destitute refugee will have his day in court, and the murdered Christ, in his otherworldly [being] freed from the power of death and the hands of tyrants, will enter into his promised inheritance, kingdom and majesty.

Therefore, dear lords, who have been placed as heads and regents over the people, in all you do, be fearful of <75> God. For God the Lord shall reign over all people in heaven and in his kingdom, including human thoughts and consciences. He will allow no one to take his place in his otherworldly temple, 1 Corinthians 3[:18ff]; 6[:19-20]; 2 Corinthians 6[:16], desiring His Majesty's reign alone to prevail.

Dear lords, accept this in love, and do not be provoked by [what we write], for the truth must be confessed. And even if the stones were to talk, you should still look to Christ and his Word, and you will find the truth. The omnipotent, eternal Father, through his eternal Wisdom, Christ Jesus, has so ordered and commanded everything for you, according to his Divine counsel, will and providence, concerning his church: in doctrine, sacraments and in life.

Why, then, do the worldly wise and learned scholars want to be so arrogant and bring you to alter all of this, and to decree such through your mandates, as if the almighty, eternal Word has to be bent crooked under your command and power, and the Divinely-blessed ordering of the Son of God—regarding baptism, the Lord's Supper, and the ban—concerning which there are at hand, crystal-clear and pure writings from Christ, the eternal son of God, as also practiced by his holy apostles.

Currently all this is being transformed by your learned scholars, through human wisdom, into a more convenient form and "improved" set of customs, without one iota of a clear, express, command of God, as we want to show below, bright <76> and clear, on the basis of pure, holy, Divine Scripture, but also from your own books, what [your scholars] wrote about these things at the outset [of the Reformation], and correctly so, concerning the Gospel.

It is always high arrogance and foolishness when the earth and its ashes try to rise above Christ Jesus, the very one who established each of you as princes and judges. Heaven belongs to the Lord, says David, but he gave the earth to the human race.

It is clear to us that when someone rebels against the emperor or king, desiring to take over the kingdom and government, that such is not to be tolerated, and would not happen without punishment. How much less so will it remain unpunished, when a miserable, guilty, earthly being rises up against the all-powerful Emperor and King, Christ Jesus, attacking his kingdom, and so desiring to push [Christ] off the throne of his Divine Majesty—as Martin Luther himself wrote in his booklet *Concerning Temporal Authority*, in 1523, in signature D, leaf 1: Concerning the soul, God can and will not allow anyone to rule over it, except himself alone. Therefore, when the worldly powers interfere by enacting laws regarding the soul, they are attacking the reign of God, and only corrupting and ruining the soul.[182]

Ulrich Zwingli also contends, in his *Article Book*, in the 36th article <77> which he writes against the Pope: "As long as you emphasize outward weaponry, it is obvious to all of us that you are neither a follower of Christ, nor of Peter, but are of the devil and the true Antichrist."[183] *Furthermore, in his booklet* Concerning Human and Divine Righteousness, *published in 1524, signature E, leaf 3, he writes regarding the office of the magistracy:* "reigning over human souls and consciences does not stand within the magistrates' jurisdiction, in obedience to their oath. They are not competent to do this. As little as they can know what dwells in the human heart, so little are they able to rule the human heart in their attempt to make it devout or evil, believing or unbelieving."[184] *Furthermore, in signature H, leaf 3, in the same booklet it states that no magistrate dare ever punish what pertains solely to the conscience of the inner person.*[185]

---

182 "Temporal Authority: to what extent is should be obeyed," in *Luther's Works*, vol. 45, ed. Walther I. Brandt (Philadelphia: Muhlenberg Press, 1962), 81-129; citation on 105. (*Luther's Works* cited hereafter as LW.)

183 "Auslegen und Begründen der Schlußreden," in *Zwingli, der Verteidiger des Glaubens*, II. Teil (Zurich: Zwingli-Verlag, 1952), commentary on the 36th Article, 95-6. English translation in E. J. Furcha, trans., *Huldrych Zwingli Writings, vol. 1: The Defense of the Reformed Faith* (Allison Park, PA: Pickwick, 1984), 250.

184 "Divine and Human Righteousness," trans. by E. J. Furcha, in Furcha, *Huldrych Zwingli Writings*, 25.

185 "They [the authorities] should not punish anything that pertains to the conscience of the inner being alone, for to judge that is in God's hand alone." Furcha, *Huldrych Zwingli Writings*, 39.

But to what degree Zwingli later held true to his own teaching[186] will follow below in the third and twelfth articles. *[This will also include Zwingli's spiritual] descendants, living at present, who oppose the devout Christians who have never harmed them. For [devout Christians], in accord with their intelligence and reason, and their conscience, by no means wish to participate with them in their worship services, life and walk.*[187] *All this is readily seen in the light of day,* and will be referred to in greater breadth in the third article, from the writings of Martin Luther and other scholars.

Therefore magistrates need to be content to remain within the power of their office, up to the limits placed upon it in God's Word, <78> and not usurp God in his temple, 1 Corinthians 3[:16-17]; 2 Corinthians 6[?]. Thus our desire is to be subject and obedient to magistrates in all just and legitimate things, as will follow in the third article in far greater detail. For we are willing and ready to give to Caesar what is Caesar's, and to God what is God's.

---

186 Zurich Q3 adds: *this, God in his heaven knows.*
187 Zurich Q3 adds: *thereby inciting the magistracy and opening themselves to persecution.*

Why This Writing was Undertaken

We read in the third book of Esdras [3 Esdras 3:1-4:63] that the young men who kept guard over the person of the king devised a contest among themselves as to which of them could come up with the most intelligent and wisest statement. This pleased the king and his officials so greatly that as a reward they permitted Zerubbabel, who had won out over the other two[188] young men, to build Jerusalem and the Temple, at the king's expense, even though they had not authorized the contest.

Just as the efforts of this young man pleased the powerful king and also his officials, even though his actions were unauthorized, in the same way we, too, hope that no one knowledgeable in God's Word will be aroused to anger, when several individuals—whoever they may be—out of love for the truth have made known their response to the thirteen articles disputed at Frankenthal.

On the basis of such hope and out of God's grace we have undertaken to state our position regarding each of these articles, writing as succinctly as we could, desiring to point everyone to the truth, in love, and not to the detriment of anyone, <79> but solely out of heartfelt compassion and admonition, for in these difficult and adverse times we are seeing the foolish and the impure opinions and understandings in divine matters in which the most intelligent and very wisest of this world are mired.

THE REASON FOR THE SCHISM AMONG THOSE PEOPLE WHO TOGETHER DEPARTED FROM THE PAPAL CHURCH

Although all parties of so-called Christendom esteem the light, Gospel, and the Christian name highly, and with enough reverence, even so the great majority of the populace is still mired in the middle of darkness, and thus in our view they have not yet emerged victorious, even though all of us have left the papacy. For just as the children of Israel did not immediately enter the Promised Land even though they had been freed from Egypt and expelled by the Pharaoh himself, to such a small degree are we in the promised kingdom of heaven for having been freed from the Pope's yoke and fetters.

---

188 Ms. has *three*.

For just as the children of Israel first and foremost had the Pharaoh with his army behind them as a mighty foe, and the Red Sea before them, so also all those who have now gone out from this spiritual Egypt still have a common foe behind them who, without distinction, persecutes them with sword, spear, and bow, and with water and fire. But before them, instead of the Red Sea, stands a glassy sea <80> mixed with fire, as is written in Revelation 15[:2].

This is the letter of Scripture of the Old and New Testaments which, together with many and various human laws, is commanded and forbidden through coercion and oppression,[189] *with punishment of life and limb, but also in taking away land and possessions. All this, taken from old and lingering origins, is woven together and hardened and fused like glass, with the result that no human ingenuity, reasoning or wisdom makes it possible for one to be able to crawl, wade, swim or pass through it.*

And here we should be thinking how we might escape from such dangers which encompass us, front and rear, and how we should depend upon Christ our Commander-in-Chief, just as the former did upon Moses, yielding in the same way to Christ's counsel and will, in obedience to him. And if Moses, through God's power, was able to part the Red Sea, making a path through it for Israel and was able to bring down and fell the Pharaoh, their enemy in pursuit, why could not Christ, the Son of God, who is greater than Moses, do it as well?

Now if we really were going around with certain thoughts, such as desiring to slay our enemies with earthly weapons out of our own strength, and passing through and fathoming the glassy sea with human wisdom and, what is even much more evil, in the middle of our exodus from Egypt even hating, <81> banishing and at times killing[190] *one another—the greater the evil, the better it is*[191]*—by such action we would be pleasing the Pharaoh but would be vexing Christ our Commander-in-Chief so that he might withdraw the hand with which he had led us out, and take it from us, and leave us mired as a wild, contentious people, somewhere between beast and angel,*

---

189 *Margin*: Human commands are considered to be higher than all the commands of God—see the 12th Article.
190 Zurich Q3 has: *persecuting* instead of "killing."
191 Zurich Q3 adds: *As Paul says (Galatians 4), "Just as in the past the one born according to the flesh persecuted the one born according to the spirit, so does it also occur today,"* he says.

A Short, Simple Confession

as one says. In other words, we would be strengthening the Pharaoh who opposes us, and making the glassy sea all the more unseemly, so that those who have the love and desire for fighting would be able truly to assuage their wants and cravings.

In the light of such blindness in which we truly have been mired, and still are mired up to our ears, we want to present our views concerning the above-mentioned articles on the basis of the simple grace which is in us, not holding the opinion that we alone hope to win the prize, as did the wise Zerubbabel, but that we may give others, who have more grace and Spirit than we, just cause to win it. Even though we do not immediately obtain the precious jewel lying at the end, we still want to rejoice with those who reach it, and by no means, as Cain did to his brother Abel, hate or envy them as is the common practice today. We hope the Lord may be patient with our modest gifts and the simple grace in us, but also recognize the good will that is in us.

But now we believe that it is necessary for us to probe to the utmost what is the most central reason for the division between the people who jointly departed from the papacy. <82> For if we could establish this, then we would have a good understanding of the way to peace. *In our view, the most important or greatest reason is the fact that in these last days, we do not recognize what and where our Temple is, or who our High Priest is,*[192] *or what the customs and laws are of this same Temple and High Priest, and to what degree the same may be compared, or not compared, to the Law of Moses. Therefore, we first want to present our exposition, point by point, on the basis of prophetic and apostolic writings.*[193]

The prophet Isaiah says in the Second Chapter [Isaiah 2:2-4], and Micah, in the Fourth [Micah 4:1-3]: "In the days to come—that is, in the last days—the mountain of the Lord's house shall be established as the highest of the mountains, and shall be raised above the hills and all the nations shall stream to it. Many peoples shall come, admonishing one another, 'Come, let us go up to the mountain of the Lord, to the house of the God of Jacob; that he may teach us his ways and that we may walk in his footsteps.' For out of Zion shall go forth instruction, and the word of the Lord from Jerusalem. He shall judge between the nations, and shall arbitrate for many peoples; they shall forge their swords into plowshares, and their spearheads or pikes into

---

192 Zurich Q3 adds: *whether or not we already confess it in words, as noted above.*
193 Zurich Q3 adds: *doing this, in our simplicity, out of the light of truth*

pruning hooks, sickles and saws; one people shall not lift up weapons against another people, neither shall they learn war any more."

And this has <83> now been revealed, has taken place, and has been proclaimed much more broadly and clearly through Christ, the eternal Son of God, through his teaching and example, to all his chosen people and believers, even to the end of the world, as will be amply shown in the first article below. *In these words of both prophets, however, we are able, through God's grace, to locate with exactitude the mountain, the Temple, the High Priest, the customs of the Temple and High Priest—all of which have been promised to us in these last days. For the mountain which is higher than all other mountains, and exalted above all hills, is not Mount Horeb or Sinai, or Bethlehem, or any other mountain on earth, but heaven itself, in which in these last days the Temple, or the Tabernacle of the Testimony,[194] has been built, not by human, but by God's hands.*

For since they repeatedly defiled His Temple, which He had ordered to be built, setting the thresholds of their kings and princes by His threshold, and their doorposts beside His doorpost, and leading people uncircumcised in heart and flesh into His Sanctuary,[195] He wished to exalt, place, and build his Temple out of sight of such carnal and mundane people, on a mountain which is higher than all other mountains and hills. We may learn of this not only from Isaiah and Micah, but also from the prophet Ezekiel at many places.

This Temple is closed to all arrogant, unrepentant sinners,[196] as Saint John in his <84> *Revelation*, and the holy apostle Paul testify, 1 Corinthians 6[:9-10]; Galatians 5[:19-21]; Ephesians 5[:3-13]; Revelation 21[:8-9]; 22[:15],[197] as noted above. *It is open, however, to all who repent, and are of contrite spirit and heart. Therefore the Lord says through the prophet,* "Heaven is my throne and the earth is my footstool; what is the house that you would build for me, and what is my resting place? All these things my hand has made. . . . But this is the one to whom I will look, to the humble and contrite in spirit, who trembles at my word."[198]

---

194 [See, e.g., Revelation 15:5]
195 *Margin*: Ezekiel 43[:7-8]; 44[:7]
196 *Margin*: Revelation 22
197 *Margin*: these are the dogs, sorcerers, fornicators, murderers, hypocrites
198 *Margin*: Isaiah 66[:1-3]

A Short, Simple Confession

In this same fashion Saint John also says, "Blessed are those who do his commandments, so that they will have the right to the tree of life and may enter the city by the gates,"[199] *which is the New Jerusalem. This means, in short, whoever fears God and walks on his paths is on the holy mountain of God and in his Temple, no matter where he may have spent his years on earth. Yet whoever forsakes his fear of God, and walks according to the vanity of his own heart, is already in outer darkness, even if he were in the very middle of paradise, and were to cry out a thousand times: "Here is the temple of the Lord! Here is the temple of the Lord! Here is the temple of the Lord! Here is the Christian church!"*[200]

And since the kings and high priests, established and ordained according to the law of human commandments, did not wish to do good <85>—detaining this or that person who had stumbled a bit, even though the person was blameless—for this reason God, out of the strength of never-ending Life, established Christ his only-begotten Son as king and high priest in this temple, as Paul writes to the Hebrews.[201]

Paul also continues this theme elsewhere in the same epistle, saying: "We have such a high priest, one who is seated at the right hand of the throne of the Majesty in the heavens, a minister in the sanctuary and the true tent that the Lord, and not any mortal, has set up."[202] *Further, "Christ did not enter a sanctuary made by human hands, a mere copy of the true one, but he entered into heaven itself, now to appear in the presence of God."*[203] *[And still further:] "For it was fitting that we should have such a high priest, holy, blameless, undefiled, separated from sinners, and exalted above the heavens. Unlike the other high priests, he has no need to offer sacrifices day after day, first for his own sins, and then for those of the people; this he did once for all when he offered himself. For the law appoints as high priests those who are subject to weakness, but the word of the oath, which came later than the law, appoints a Son who has been made perfect forever."*[204]

---

199 *Margin*: Revelation 22[:14]
200 *Margin*: Jeremiah 7[:4]
201 The book of Hebrews was long thought by many to have been written by Paul, although most scholars today would question this assumption.
202 *Margin*: Hebrews 8[:1-2]
203 *Margin*: Hebrews 9[:24]
204 *Margin*: Hebrews 7[:26-28]

Since in these last days we have another temple and another high priest, therefore we also have another law. For all those who want to do battle under the banner of this king and high priest <86> are no longer under the law that came from Mount Sinai, which taught them to conquer the Promised Land of Canaan, wiping out its inhabitants with sword, bow and spear. Instead, it is the Law and the Word of the Lord which proceeded from Jerusalem and Zion through Christ himself, the heavenly King and High Priest, which teaches peace to the people, breaks the bows of war, sends the horses and wagons away from Jerusalem, beats swords into plowshares, and spearheads into pruning hooks, sickles, and saws, leading to a holy life upon which one may stand steadfastly and fearlessly on Judgment Day before the face of God and the holy angels.[205]

If in the past we had recognized the whereabouts of the temple—the temple itself with its high priest and his way of life, as we earlier should have been able to understand from Scripture—then there would have been less quarreling and wrangling among all those who want to be Christians than has unfortunately been the case up to now.

For since we have no correct knowledge of these things, one person imagining Rome to be the mountain upon which the House of the Lord is situated; another person, Wittenberg; the third, Switzerland; the fourth, some other country—each person, in turn, seeing [the Mountain of the Lord] in a specific country according to individual human desire. This results in each person also inventing a high priest, permitting that own person's teachings and life to prevail, and slowly but surely it all grows and is established within, <87> so that even the teachings and life of Christ and his apostles must give way. Indeed, when somebody would come to a fighting host from time to time with spiritual and earthly weapons, and one wished to bring the reason for the conflict into the light, virtually no one would agree, concluding therefore that a Christian was born to fight.

Therefore if we want to emerge victorious over our enemies, who lie ahead and behind us, and sing the song of the Lamb and of Moses the servant of God, then we must let go of all forms of conflict, and begin all over again, forgetting about earthly locations—whether Rome, Wittenberg, Switzerland, or any other place—and even remove from our sight the Pope, Luther, Zwingli, and all other individuals, no matter how holy they appear to be, and instead search out the true and ancient paths which lead to the

---

205 *Margin*: Zechariah 9; Psalm 46[:9]; 76; Isaiah 2[:1-4]; Micah 4[:1-4]

Mountain and House of the God of Jacob. To be sure, it is true that every human being, including the Pope himself, has something of the Light within. Indeed, Caiaphas could not have been without gifts, since he was high priest, so how could these [aforementioned leaders] be completely without the Light? But there is no person who is the Light itself. Where we do not acknowledge this fact, we will not only fail to reconcile the present divisions, we will produce even more difficult and damaging consequences in the future.

For each will continue trying to force the other into the church of Christ, and exclude, condemn, and accuse as a heretic the one who is not yet inside, and who does not know what or where the church of Christ is. <88> The First Article now follows.

[The First Article]

Whether the writings of the Old Testament are as valid for Christians as those of the New[206]

It is not fitting to say yes or no to this question unless one specifies of which part of the Old Testament scriptures one is speaking.[207] *For it is clear to all parties that the Old Testament is not a single entity, but rather is divided into three parts. One part teaches how a person should act towards God and humankind—as is taught in particular through the Ten Commandments. This is without doubt the part which the Lord himself referred to, when he said that he had not come to annul the law, but rather to fulfill it. Therefore he sharpened the law in Matthew 5, as we will hear in due course, desiring to have it written in the hearts of human beings rather than only on stone tablets, and furthermore, written not by pressure and coercion, but through*

---

206 Concerning this and the following article, see Snyder, "The (Not So) 'Simple Confession': Part II," 91-100, for an analysis of how the Swiss Brethren approach to the Old and New Testaments at Frankenthal was expanded by the Marpeckite/Covenanter author of the "Short Simple Confession."

207 The theologians at the Frankenthal debate had insisted on a "yes or no" answer. The Q1 respondent evades the logical trap.

the power of his Holy Spirit, and that this is called a new law.[208] This is not to say that the law was not present earlier, but that the Lord would teach the law in a different manner from the way in which Moses, Samuel and all the prophets and high priests were accustomed to teaching it in their time.

The second part of the law, then, would be the segment which teaches that priests and Levites from given families, and also civil judges and authorities, chosen from among their own people, were to be established. They taught the law, enforcing it with force and the sword—to all of Abraham's seed, and also to the others who wished to live among them—punishing the transgressors not only with words, but also with the sword. <89> This is without a doubt that part of the law about which the Lord said, that "the law and the prophets prophesied until John [the Baptist] came," [Matthew 11:13] when the kingdom of God would be proclaimed anew through the Gospel. With these words the Lord without a doubt wishes to say, that although the harshness of the law and the prophets demanded the stoning of the idolater, the transgressor of the Sabbath, the adulterer, the disobedient son, and all who do and promote evil—eye for an eye, hand for a hand—that in His church and community this must cease. For the kingdom of God is proclaimed, from the time of John [the Baptist] and thereafter, through the Gospel, namely, in a different, happier, and less-severe manner, as noted above.

Therefore John the Baptist opened the door of the kingdom and community of God to the harlots and open sinners (which the law would have stoned), if they confessed their sin and repented—people who otherwise, according to the law, would not have been able to enter even into the third generation.[209] The Lord himself says to the Pharisees that "the tax collectors and the prostitutes are going into the kingdom of God ahead of you," [Matthew 21:31] that is, if they mend their lives in true repentance.

The Lord has more to say in the New Testament, Matthew 5[:38] about the annulment of this part of the law by his church which is gathered together by the Holy Spirit: "You have heard that it was said, 'An eye for an eye and a hand for a hand.' But I say to you, <90> Do not resist evil,"—even though up to now you have interpreted the law as including [the resisting of evil], and carrying this out in practice.

---

208 *Margin*: The prophets did not teach this as applying to their time, but foretold and prophesied these things, to find their fulfillment in our time

209 [See, e.g., Exodus 20:5]

That you should be acting and teaching otherwise is indicated by the prophets Isaiah and Micah, as noted above, where they say, He will teach the nations peace, and that on his holy mountain no more will one person harm or abuse another. Zechariah also speaks to this, Zechariah 9[:9-10]: "Rejoice greatly, O daughter Zion! Shout aloud, O daughter Jerusalem! Lo, your king comes to you; triumphant and victorious is he, humble and riding on a donkey, on a colt, the foal of a donkey. He will cut off the chariot from Ephraim and the war horse from Jerusalem; and the battle bow shall be cut off, and he shall command peace to the nations."

And the royal prophet David is also in agreement with this, Psalm 46[:8-9] when he speaks through the Spirit of God as follows: "Come, behold the works of the Lord; see what desolations he has brought on the earth. He makes wars cease to the end of the earth; he breaks the bow, and shatters the spear; he burns the wagons with fire." Likewise, Psalm 76[:2-3]: "His abode has been established in Salem, his dwelling place in Zion. There he broke the flashing arrows, the shield, the sword, and the weapons of war, Selah."

Now if in the last days, Zion, Jerusalem and <91> Ephraim signify [Christ's] church and community, as is clearly noted here, then we certainly are hearing with what weapons and armor those who truly wish to participate therein are to clad themselves.

The third part of the law included circumcision, the paschal lamb, many and various food sacrifices, sacrifices of drink and incense, together with their feasts and holy days, through which, when they sinned, they believed themselves to be purified and made righteous. As long as they had or knew nothing better and they used these as they were supposed to, then such worship was acceptable, about which the Lord afterwards gave witness many times from heaven, lighting the sacrifice and turning it to ashes. When they did not use them properly, however, they also were often clearly punished for it, as were especially the sons of Aaron [Leviticus 10:1-3]. Now and then, [the Lord] "looked through his fingers" at them, as the saying goes, patiently enduring them for a time. Finally when they, even after a long period of warning and admonishing, did not correct themselves and instead despised the Lord and his prophets, the Lord kicked out the bottom of the bucket[210] and allowed his wrath and punishment to fall upon them, burning the only place and temple where they were allowed to sacrifice and to celebrate feast and holy days. He thereby indicated to them to what degree

---

210 Zurich Q3 adds: *as they say.*

he valued their sacrifices and ceremonies when they outwardly conformed to the letter [of the law] yet did not purify themselves within, from the heart, <92> nor set things right with their neighbors before they had offered their gift on the altar.

Since this part of the law is predominantly tied to a specific place, a specific race, and to a specific era, the Lord annulled it—or as it is said, fulfilled it—since he wanted, in these last days, to call out to the very ends of the world, offering himself to all races to be their God. For since it was impossible to remove sin through the blood of oxen, calves, and goats, as the Epistle to the Hebrews clearly testifies, he himself became the blood sacrifice and through this, brought to an end this part of the law [Hebrews 9:11-14].

Therefore as much of each part of the law and writings of the Old Testament Christ and his apostles regard as binding, the exact same is what God-fearing Christians will also regard as binding. But whatever he rejects and annuls, they are not to establish on their own authority, for they should recognize that if Christ is Lord of the Sabbath, as he indeed does call himself, then he is also Lord of the law.

The fact that [Christ] annulled and established the law in the manner just described, however, is also additionally testified to by the prophet Jeremiah in the thirty-first chapter where he says, Behold, "the days are surely coming, says the Lord, when I will make a new covenant with the house of Israel and the house of Judah. It will not be like the covenant that I made with their ancestors <93> when I took them by the hand to bring them out of the land of Egypt—a covenant that they broke, for which I punished them, says the Lord. But this is the covenant that I will make with the house of Israel after those days, says the Lord: I will plant my law within them, and I will write it on their hearts; and I will be their God, and they shall be my people. No longer shall they teach one another, or say to each other, 'Know the Lord,' for they shall all know me, from the least of them to the greatest, says the Lord" [Jeremiah 31[:31-34].

Paul speaks to this in the epistle to the Hebrews, in the eighth chapter, where he says "In speaking of a 'new covenant,' he has made the first one obsolete. And what is obsolete and growing old will soon disappear" [Hebrews 8:13]. Likewise he says in the same chapter, "But Jesus has now obtained a more excellent ministry, and to that degree he is the mediator of a better covenant, which has been enacted through better promises. For if

A Short, Simple Confession

that first covenant had been faultless, there would have been no need to look for a second one" [Hebrews 8:6-8].

Therefore, although the New Testament is grounded in the Old, and the New must and ought to be proven through the Old, we still read that the temple, the priesthood, the way of life and law of the heavenly temple, as well as the promise, turned out to be entirely different, with much of the old needing to come to an end and something new needing to be established [in its place]. If, therefore, certain things have ended and something better has been established, <94> how then can the writings of the Old Testament be binding for the Christian in the same manner as those of the New? For since a person's most recent will and testament, in the law of the land, preempts the validity of an earlier version, who then will not be led to believe that the Old must give way to the New, and that the Old must be judged according to the New, but not the New according to the Old?

Some ask, however: If one does not accept all those things as valid and good for a Christian, which according to the Old Testament were good and blameless, does this mean that the Holy Spirit has changed? To this we say no. [The Holy Spirit has not changed;] the times, however, have changed. The time for those in the Old [Covenant] was morning; for us, however, the time is afternoon; in their time the world was beginning and growing green, but in our time it is drying up and wearing out. And just as a wise and intelligent father will overlook many things in his child because of its youth, yet punishing that child for the very same things when he becomes older, in the same way God, the Holy Spirit, dealt in a special way with the world when it was still in its best age, and deals in a special way [with the world] now that it has fallen into the pit. Just as the above-mentioned father—who deals with his young child differently than he does when it becomes older—remains unchanged, so also the Holy Spirit is by no means to be blamed, lectured, or sent back to school by human cleverness and sophistry, even though [the Spirit] did allow certain things in the Old Testament <95> which it now forbids, or forbade then what it now allows.

It is no wonder that not everyone can reconcile these changes and differences, for it also vexed the Jews, and was a great stumbling block to them. Therefore the Lord himself said he had come into this world for judgment so that the blind would see, and that those who could see would become blind. The prophets also said the same about him: he was the stone one strikes against a stone one stumbles over, leading to the fall and resurrection of many in Israel [Isaiah 8:14-15; 1 Peter 2:8].

If now the writings of the Old and New Testaments were held to be equal, so that [both parts] were equally binding for Christians, then the Lord Christ himself would not have borne witness to such a change, and likewise the prophets, prophesying and foretelling the same—which the Son of God himself then established, as has already been noted above and will be verified below with bright and clear words.

But if the Lord Jesus had come, utilizing such ingenious and sophisticated reasoning as did Moses, King David, Solomon, or Elijah, and living according to their ways, sanctions, and prohibitions, and had he enjoyed great prestige and splendor which worldly human reason esteems so highly—if he had established [his kingdom] in the manner of the worldly kings and powerful princes, then people would have been more disposed to believing in him and his signs and wonders than was actually the case.

But since [Jesus] <96> crucified no one, and instead allowed himself to be crucified, suffered in the flesh, and left us an example as Peter says [1 Peter 4:1], therefore such a Christ, with his teaching and his life, became the downfall of the Jews and a resurrection for the believing Gentiles. May it please God not to treat the would-be Christians of today the way he treated the Jews back then.

Examples of the disparity [between the Old and New Testaments], however, are easy to find.[211] Jacob took two sisters as his wives, something Moses had forbidden before the time of Christ, although Moses permitted two and even more wives, and a letter of divorce. Christ forbade all this for those who wish to be his disciples. Moses killed an Egyptian; Samuel [killed] Agag the king; Elijah [killed] the priests of Baal [Exodus 2:12; 1 Samuel 15:33; 1 Kings 19:1]. Christ would not extinguish the glowing wick, or break the bent reed. He also would not grant the disciples' request that they command fire to fall down upon those who would not receive them, as Elijah had done. He restored the ear of his enemy and adversary after Peter had cut it off; he also prayed for his enemies on the cross, and taught us in his Word and Holy Gospel that we should be his followers [Isaiah

---

211 From this point through codex page <107> the original manuscript alternates marginal notes indicating "Old Testament" and "New Testament." They have been omitted here.

A Short, Simple Confession

42:3; 2 Kings 1:10, 12; Luke 9:54; John 18:10; Luke 23:34; Matthew 10:38; John12:26].

In the Old Testament, the people of God are likened to a small daughter that God the Father in his mercy has taken into his house, educating her properly and decently until she has reached marriageable age, <97> at which time he gave her his own Son as bridegroom.

The people in the New Testament are married to Christ through faith, have entered into a covenant with and are a bride of Christ, and will share in all his goods and gifts. God the Father sends out an invitation regarding this Son's wedding to all peoples within the whole circle of the earth.

Up to the time of Christ, the people in the Old Testament were preserved under the law, which played the role of a taskmaster. They had outward ceremonies and worship practices, and were given the promise of temporal and earthly goods and gifts, of a land flowing with milk and honey.

The New, however, holds forth something much better, namely, spiritual and heavenly goods and an eternal kingdom. It has a spiritual, divine law, the perfect, inalienable law proceeding out of Zion, converting and bringing back the soul. It is established and revealed through the Son of God himself, to those whom the Father has established as heirs of all things.

The Old Testament kingdom and priesthood was <98> imperfect, pompous, leaned on someone [other than God] for security, and relied on retribution.

The New Testament kingdom and priesthood is perfect, lacks nothing, is not pompous, and forsakes the old as unnecessary for the sake of something better—in this manner making sure that [the new] does not lapse. For in it all physical cravings and needs become superfluous.

The Old Testament kingdom and priesthood was only a shadow, a figure, temporal, and coming to an end.

The New Testament kingdom and priesthood is heavenly, eternal, and without end, a clear light and torch held high for ever and ever.

The Old Testament manifests a harsh and severe spirit, the spirit of coercion and fear and the crossbow, leading to a heavy and uncertain conscience, and fear of death, the devil and hell.

The New, however, manifests a meek and a good, gracious and peaceable spirit; the filial, child-parent spirit; the power of joy and love, including a joyous, confident conscience, that hopes in eternal life.

The Old Testament has an external, physical people and an external sign and covenant, namely, circumcision, through which one may know its people outwardly.

The New, however, has an inner, spiritual people and an inner mark, namely, the sealing of the Holy Spirit, and one cannot correctly single out this people from everyone else solely through external means, for their life is hidden with Christ in God.

The Old Testament affirms an outer, coerced form of worship, Sabbath, customs and ceremonies, with which the conscience was burdened, being bound to place, time and person.

The New, on the other hand, affirms a new, inner, free, <99> and personally chosen form of worship, found in believing and reborn hearts.

This is not to say that after the coming of Christ the outer word, sacraments or ceremonies were consequently rejected or canceled in the light of the practices of the New Testament, [which they were not,] as long as they were used in accord with their true spiritual meaning, namely that through them the believing conscience is directed beyond itself directly to God through Christ; for without the true, real, indwelling power of the Holy Spirit, all external sacraments and ceremonies are not useful, but rather are harmful to people's souls.

The power of the Old and first Testament was found solely in works: in holding to the letter of the law, in human holiness, in worldly piety and an appearance of outer righteousness, seen as irreprochable by the people—see Hebrews 9[:1-10], Romans 10[:5] and Philippians 3[:9].

The power and fulfillment of the New and last Testament, on the other hand, is found in faith and the true acknowledgment of Jesus Christ. It is found in spiritual holiness, in divine love, in heartfelt piety and inner righteousness which is valid before the face of God, Matthew 5[:1-48]; Romans 3[:21-31]; Philippians 3[:7-21].

Moses, given his charge, was not able to do more than to communicate the consequences of sins, or that the transgressor would be punished.

Christ, on the other hand, takes this further for his own, making it possible to avoid and eliminate one's inner fleshly cravings, carnal desires, and passions of the heart, 2 Timothy 2[:20-26]. <100>

The Old had an outer, human mediator, namely, Moses; it had an outer priesthood, outer unction, an outer kingdom, an outer sword, law, and judgment.

The New has an inner, spiritual mediator, namely, the person of Jesus Christ. It has an inner kingdom and priesthood, the kingdom of our Lord Jesus Christ which he establishes in the newly reborn person, in righteousness, peace, and joy in the Holy Spirit, Romans 14[:17]. It has an inner sword that cuts away evil desires from the heart, that divides and separates all that leads away from God, namely, the sword of the Spirit which is the Word of God, Ephesians 6[:17]; Hebrews 4[:12].

In the Old Testament a physical, figurative political authority was established that belonged to God's testament, that looked after and enforced the law of Moses and all that pertained to it, and served the figurative matters of God with the sword and other such things.

In the New Testament there is a spiritual political authority,[212] *namely, our Lord Jesus Christ, who says, John18[:36]*[213] *"My kingdom is not of this world"—[the one] whom God the Father placed over all things as head of his church, Ephesians 1[:22]. [Jesus Christ] reigns, defends, protects and represents his people and his teaching, which is the word of the cross and the Gospel of the grace of God in the Holy Spirit—not the* brac[c]hium seculare *(the secular arm), or the* <101> *calling up of worldly power, but rather the patience of the saints, the ministration of Christ, and the dispensing of the mystery of the kingdom of God, 1 Corinthians 4[:1]. For the weapons of our knighthood, says Paul, are not physical, but mighty before God to destroy*

---

212 *"ein geistliche obrikheit"* is the striking phrase in the original.
213 *Margin*: My kingdom is not of this world, John 18

the fortifications, with which we overcome all attacks and all the forces that rise up against the acknowledgment of Christ, 2 Corinthians 10[:3-6].

In the Old Testament it was decreed, an eye for an eye, a tooth for a tooth, hand for hand, foot for foot, burn for burn, ox for ox [Exodus 21:24-32]. Likewise, you should love your neighbor and hate your enemy [Matthew 5:43]. Therefore also the Jews, as a figurative illustration, fought against the Hittites, Amorites, and other Gentiles, and expelled and eradicated them as their enemies, since they were to have no fellowship with them, to make no covenant with them, or to show them any favor, Deuteronomy 7[:1-2].

In the New Testament Christ says, "Resist not evil; rather, if someone strikes you on the right cheek, offer your other as well, and if someone takes your coat, offer him your cloak as well." Likewise, "love your enemies and bless those who speak evil of you,"[214] *and do good to those who hate you: "Repay no one evil for evil. . . . Beloved, never avenge yourselves."*[215] *Here the church is not fighting in a physical way, but in a spiritual way against sin, death, hell, Satan, and against all evil desires. And since the Apostle knew this, as a field marshall in such a war,* <102> *he gave a command to the knights of Christ, saying: Put on the armor of God, so that you may be able to withstand the cunning attacks of the devil [Ephesians 6:11].*

Nevertheless, some individuals spitefully reproach us for our views, saying that since Moses also commanded the love of enemies, Exodus 23[:4-5], therefore Moses' teaching and Christ's teaching in Matthew 5 are one and the same.[216] *Given this pretext, they mix Moses and Christ together, through which the true spiritual meaning and understanding remains hidden behind the curtain and under cover, so that the Mosaic power and sword may be maintained and defended in the church and community of God.*

To this we answer, whoever desires to jest and toy with Holy Scripture, distorting and interpreting it according to his or her own understanding,[217]

---

214 *Margin*: Matthew 5[:39-40, 44]; Luke 6[:29]
215 Zurich Q3 adds (*Margin*): Romans 12[:17, 19]
216 Here the author is responding directly to an argument made at the Frankenthal disputation and published in the *Protocol* of the proceedings. See *Protocoll*, 475-76. This interchange is summarized in Yoder, "A Critical Study of the Debate Between the Reformed and the Anabaptists," 160-61.
217 Zurich Q3 adds: *and to paint on another color.*

A Short, Simple Confession

such we must sadly allow to happen. However, that Christ's teaching, Matthew 5[:43-45], and Moses' teaching, Exodus 23[:4-5] are one and the same teaching cannot be concluded if one simply allows Holy Scripture to remain in its clear meaning. For the loving of enemies as commanded by Moses was to be observed only among the Israelites themselves—those living next to each other—and concerned oxen and asses. Therefore this had to do solely with their own, and not with the asses or oxen of the Gentiles, who were their enemies. Just as the law, Leviticus 19[:17-18] says, you are not to avenge or hold a grudge against the children of your people, <103> the meaning here is—as has also just been noted in Exodus 23[:4-5]—only for and among the children of Israel. King Solomon also taught doing good to the enemy in this way, Proverbs 25[:21-22]. For if this were to be understood as being between Israel and the Gentiles, how could God have been able to bring them to abandon their vengeance and hatred against the Gentiles, their enemies? Therefore, since [this Mosaic love of enemy] is to be understood as applying only among the Israelites, it is therefore contrary to the teaching of Christ, Matthew 5[:43-44]; Luke 6[:27-31], 9[:52-55], 23[:34] which speaks [equally] to the Jews and Gentiles and to all peoples on earth.[218] Therefore [the Mosaic love, and the teaching of Christ] cannot be interpreted as being one and the same.

The Old Testament has to do with children according to the flesh, stemming from the first birth.

The New Testament, however, has to do with children according to the Spirit: children of rebirth and of the promise, to whom God the Father reveals his mysteries, which also has to do with the kingdom of heaven, Romans 9[:22-26]; John 3[:3]; Matthew 18[:1-6].

The first (children) persecute the second,[219] Galatians 4[:29], as did Cain to Abel, Ishmael to Isaac, Esau to Jacob, and as the Pharisees did to Christ.[220]

---

218 *Margin*: Matthew 28[:19]
219 Zurich Q3 adds: *those born according to the flesh [persecute] those born according to the Spirit*
220 Zurich Q3 adds to this phrase: *as the Pharisees did to the prophet and Christ and his apostles*

But the (children of the Spirit) persecute and hate no one, rather the faith and patience of the saints reigns among them, Revelation 14[:12] and also the love of God and the patience of Christ, 2 Thessalonians 3[:13], as it does with those who truly know that they, following their Lord Christ, must enter the kingdom of God by much suffering and tribulation, 2 Timothy 3[:12].

In the Old Testament certain food and drink were specified as being the only ones the people were permitted to partake of, and when <104> they ate or enjoyed other foods, they were considered unclean.
In the New Testament Christ teaches that what enters the mouth does not make a person unclean, but instead, what proceeds from the mouth.

In the Old Testament it was taught that a transgressor was to be stoned, Deuteronomy 18, 22[Note: probably Deut 13:10, 21:21]; some were to be burned, Leviticus 20[:14]; some were to be beaten with rods, Deuteronomy 25[:1-2]; some to be punished by taking their possessions; some were to be exiled from the community, Leviticus 18[:28-29].
In the New Testament, on the other hand, Christ teaches us to avoid and depart from those who do not wish to accept the teaching of the Gospel, and as a testimony against them even shaking off any of their dust that clings to our shoes, Matthew 10[:14]; Luke 10[:10-11]. Furthermore, regarding those who have accepted the Gospel, yet do not live and walk according to the same, one should admonish them on the basis of the Word, a first, and then a second and [even a] third time. Where such admonition does not help, one is to separate from them and treat them as Gentiles, Matthew 18[:15-17]; 1 Corinthians 5[:1-13]; 2 Thesslonians 3[:6, 14-15].[221]

The Old Testament taught the righteousness of the law regarding the conquering and taking possession of the Promised Land. If, however, the righteousness of this law had been permanent, "there would have been no need to look for a second one," Hebrews 8[:7].
The New Testament teaches the righteousness which enters the kingdom of heaven as being better than the righteousness of the law, about which Paul speaks regarding the Son <105> of God, the true lawgiver from

---

221 Zurich Q3 adds: *In the Old Testament it is said, You are not to swear false oaths, but are to carry out the oaths you have made before God, Matthew 5*

A Short, Simple Confession

Zion, saying, "But Jesus has now obtained a more excellent ministry, and to that degree he is the mediator of a better covenant, which has been enacted through better promises. For if that first covenant had been faultless, there would have been no need to look for a second one," Hebrews 8[:6-7].

The Old Testament teaches that those who acknowledge their sins, and suffer regret because of them, need to offer all sorts of sacrifices of food, drink and incense, with which they believe themselves to be cleansed. Paul also speaks about this when he says, "Since the law contains but a shadow of the good things to come and not the essence of these realities, it can never perfect those who approach with the same sacrifices that are continually offered year after year. Otherwise, they would have ceased being offered, since the worshippers, cleansed once for all, would no longer have any consciousness of sin. But in these sacrifices there is a reminder of sin year after year. For it is impossible for the blood of bulls and goats to take away sins," Hebrews 10[:1-4] for this cleansing was too limited.

The New Testament teaches that those who acknowledge their sins, and are sorry for them, place their hope and comfort in the merit of Christ, the unspotted Lamb, as Paul states, Hebrews 10, a sacrifice offered for sin which is valid eternally. It fortifies the hearts of his faithful ones with the renewal of his Holy Spirit and not with food and drink, as was the case with Moses. <106>

The Old Testament served the sons of Abraham alone, and those who submitted under them to circumcision and the acceptance of their practices.

The New Testament serves all peoples on earth, and yet at the same time, only the new person who submits with good will to the obedience of Christ.

Even if this simple and true teaching of Christ and his holy apostles, which differentiates between the Old and New Testaments, might well be interpreted and exegeted by many in a different way than what has emerged here as the interpretation of a number of us—God knows, with what diligence—still for our part, in our simplicity we cannot take up a highly sophisticated, human, learned philosophy, which only darkens the Word of the Lord. Therefore, our greatest certainty is to remain with the words of the Lord Jesus and his holy apostles, through which we have before our eyes a crystal-clear differentiation between the Old and New Testaments as has already been shown adequately and at length, with Holy Scripture.

Saint John also says this in Chapter One, that the law was given through Moses; grace and truth has come through Jesus Christ. From this it may clearly be noted that just as the law embodied the spirit of justice and revenge in rooting out sins,[222] unrighteousness, and the transgressor of the law alike, so also has Christ reversed all this in his grace.

Therefore, in this era, rich in grace, the spirit of [Old Testament] righteousness does not continue in its severity and vengeance, as was the case under the law. This transformation the Lord <107> also communicated to his disciples,[223] when they wanted to call down fire upon the Samaritans, as Elijah had done, when the Samaritans did not want to accept the Lord with his healing teachings. There he differentiated for them, on the one hand, the spirit of the law[224] of vengeance and also of justice, which on Judgment Day will punish the world,[225] and on the other hand, the spirit of the era of grace and peace, and of the one who prayed for his enemies on the cross, when he said, "Do you not know to which spiritual children you belong? The Son of Man has not come to destroy the human soul, but to preserve it" [Luke 9:56].

Now, whoever wishes to discredit the Son of God and send the Wisdom of God back to school could ask whether, then, there are two Holy Spirits since he said, "Do you not know to which spiritual children you belong?" Here, at least for a moment, there would be room for jesting, but very soon we would become like them in our foolishness.

For our part, we have confessed above that there is only one Holy Spirit. But through the Savior, the Prince of Peace and the King of heaven and earth, the Spirit's harshness has been transformed and tempered by way of grace and mercy, through the eternal providence of the unchangeable God—Father, Son, and Holy Spirit—who established it from eternity. This is incontrovertible. [To understand it otherwise] would turn the Lord's own words upside down, interpreting and exegeting them contrary to their meaning.

---

222 *Margin*: Deuteronomy 7[:1-5]
223 Zurich Q3 adds (*Margin*): Luke 9[:54-55]
224 Zurich Q3 adds (*Margin*): Luke 23 *(Probably an incorrect reference).*
225 Zurich Q3 adds (*Margin*): Acts 7 *(Probably an incorrect reference).*

A Short, Simple Confession

Therefore in this time, rich in grace, the severe and vengeful spirit of justice is not applicable or carried out, as was the case under the law,[226] and this will continue until the end of the world. <108> When this time of grace comes to an end, then this one Spirit of the Father and the Son will punish the world's evil.

For God did not send his Son into the world in order to judge the world,[227] but that the world might be saved through him, since he is the Savior. For when they brought the adulterous woman to him, who according to the preciseness of the law had earned the death sentence, he did not condemn her or wound her further according to the dictates of the law, but rather offered her his grace and healing medicine, since he had come to heal, saying, "Go and sin no more" [John 8:11].

That the Lord says, however, John 5[:22], "The Father judges no one, but has given all judgment to the Son," from this we must note carefully who it is who through sin and vice is wasting this time of rich grace, and who does not want to accept this Savior and King with a sincere heart. When this time of rich grace—during which time Christ is sitting in judgment of no person, who instead is a mediator between God and humanity—[when this time] is over and comes to its end, such a person, when the world comes to an end, will be punished for all his or her wickedness and lack of repentance by the aforementioned one Spirit of the Father and the Son, when the Son of Man will stand in judgment. For Christ says, Matthew 16[:27]:[228] "It will come to pass that the Son of Man will come in the glory of his Father and his angels, and then he will repay each according to his works." <109>

We have now, in our small way, placed before the eyes of the God-fearing reader the distinction between the Old and New Testaments. We also desire to remain with and accept this incontrovertible and valid distinction, to the same degree that Christ and his holy apostles remained with and accepted it, as incontrovertible and valid. For this we have been unjustly and unfairly maligned by the mendacious pens of the scribes, who state that we indiscriminately reject the Old Testament and do not honor its validity.

---

226 Zurich Q3 adds: *out of the eternal providence and pleasure of the Father, Son, and Holy Spirit, as mentioned above*
227 *Margin*: John 3[:17]
228 Ms. has: John 16, but cites Matthew 16.

For although the two testaments are not the same through the ages, as has been verified above repeatedly at various places, the Spirit of God as the figure and the truth certainly knows how to make them both equal following the time and revelation of the eternal, unchangeable will of God in Christ Jesus. Only the Spirit of God, and a spiritual person taught by God, knows how to seek out the Old Testament witness concerning Christ and his kingdom and, utilizing a spiritual judgment, how to draw the truth from the figurative symbols, and apply this to Christ.

The Second Article

Whether the believers in the New Testament formed one community and people of God with the believers in the Old Testament

Answer: *Holy Scripture testifies that God is not only the God of the Jews, <110> but also of the Gentiles, and that he handed over to Christ his Son all the kingdoms of this world to all the extremities of the earth so that all tongues—all Gentiles and peoples—shall fall down at his feet, bow down and worship him, both the from the past and the coming world, for there is but one flock and one shepherd who guides and leads all those who are to be his into one sheep stable* [Revelation 15:4, 4:8-11; John 10:16].

However, just because the Lord ruled those who lived before Moses without the law, solely through enlightenment and the power of his Holy Spirit, and that he ruled those who lived in Moses' time and following through the coercion and force of the law, and is ruling those who have lived since the time of Christ through the Gospel—it does not follow from this that therefore the reign during these three epochs was one and the same, or that the Holy Spirit of God changed, or that there is not, or will not be, one community of God, all of which has been adequately explained in the preceding article[229] concerning the writings of the Old and New Testaments.

Much has already been laid out above, but there is more to be said about these contrasting eras of [God's] reign: the one before Moses, without the law; the second, under the law; but also the current one, our final era

---

229 *Margin:* The Holy Spirit is immutable and unshakable

of grace in which the true and genuine believers are ruled through the Gospel. *In this regard the Lord God is not desirous of justifying himself for permitting something in one given era, while forbidding the same in another era.* For us to request this from him is as poorly justified as it is for those who complained to him, believing it to be unjust that he equalized the day's wages so that those who had just arrived at the eleventh or last hour in his vineyard <111> received the same wage as those who had arrived in early morn and had to suffer the scorching heat all day long. For, as he says in the same passage, he has the power to do what and how he wishes, with what belongs to him [Matthew 20:1-16].

For he has so decreed, deciding to rule the earth in this manner, in his eternal election, through his eternal boundless wisdom by which he had already scrutinized and searched through everything in all of eternity, before the foundation of the world was laid, in such a manner as noted above. Therefore he is the eternal, almighty, immutable, unshakable God,[230] yesterday as he is today and in all eternity. However, times do change, as has been sufficiently noted.[231] If the Father has not changed, then the Holy Spirit also has not changed.

Now the scholars and the highly learned challenge us further:

The Third Article

Whether a Christian may be a Magistrate and Punish those who are Evil with the Sword

Answer: In order to answer this question one must first of all take note of and review what and who a Christian is, and also what and who a magistrate is. Indeed, describing a genuine Christian is a relatively simple and attainable matter when contrasted with describing a magistrate who wields the worldly sword—which is a highly intricate and perplexing matter.

The holy apostle Peter was a Christian when he told the Lord, You are the Son of the living God. He was also <112> a Christian when he said to the Lord that he should spare his own—at the time the Lord began to mention his intention of going to Jerusalem. He was also a Christian when he said

---

230 Zurich Q3 adds: *in his Son Jesus Christ and the Holy Spirit*
231 Zurich Q3 adds: *and said*

to the Lord that he wanted to go with him to his death, but then went on to deny him three times, after which he fell into great distress, weeping bitterly from the bottom of his heart. He only became a true Christian, however, when he, as is written in Acts[232] was flogged, and then left the presence of the council rejoicing that he was worthy to suffer dishonor for sake of the name of Christ. Likewise when he said, "Since therefore Christ suffered in the flesh, arm yourselves also with the same intention" [1 Peter 4:1].

Thus the disciples of the Lord were Christians when they still held on to their own possessions, lived with father and mother, wife and children, in their own homes, and carried on with their crafts and businesses. They were, however, much better Christians when they forsook all for the sake of the name of Jesus Christ, following the Lord in the time of affliction, for which the Lord not only praised his apostles, but also comforted and rewarded them, saying, "Truly I tell you, when the Son of Man is seated on the throne of his glory, you who have followed me in the rebirth will also sit on twelve thrones, and judge the twelve tribes of Israel."[233] To be sure, the Lord was not speaking of the changes they were then making, but of those which the Lord <113> knew they would be making after the sending of the Holy Spirit.

Therefore, concerning the question of whether a Christian may be a magistrate and punish with the sword those who are evil, it is good to ask at the outset exactly what one means by the term "Christian" for, as noted above, there are various types of Christians, as seen in our consideration of the apostles themselves. What is fitting and proper for one is not proper for another. We at times also accept something today in good faith as "Christian," of which we ourselves are ashamed tomorrow.

For a true Christian is already a citizen of the kingdom of heaven, and one with the saints, as such forgetting what is here below on earth, such as his father's house, friendship, country, children—as Abraham did when the Lord called him—reaching toward what is above, where Jesus sits at the right hand of God. (The true Christian) forges his earthly weapons into plowshares, pruning hooks, sickles, and saws as mentioned above in the first article.[234] He does not oppose evil by wreaking vengeance on his enemies, nor

---

232 *Margin*: Acts 5[:40-41]
233 *Margin*: Matthew 19:[28]
234 *Margin*: Matthew. 5[:43-48]; Romans 12[:14-21]

A Short, Simple Confession

does he avenge himself, but rather leaves vengeance to God,[235] mastering his soul in patience. He walks according to the law that comes out of Zion, and according to the Lord's word which comes from Jerusalem and is written in his heart through the Holy Spirit. He punishes the sinner and the ungodly with the sword which proceeds from the mouth of the Lord.

In contrast, a magistrate is an earthly lord who, just as a Christian is rooted above, dwells here on the <114> earth. Because of his office he shall consider and create that which serves to increase his kingdom and honor. He must acknowledge and act according to the law that was given on Mount Sinai, and which also grows in the human heart: eye for eye, hand for hand, protecting the devout and punishing the evildoer according to his crime—and this not only with words, but also with worldly coercion and might. Therefore, to be a true Christian, as mentioned above, and to be a magistrate who wields the worldly sword, are so notably opposed one to the other, that it is difficult for one person to manage both at one and the same time.

This is not to say, however, that a magistrate is of the devil, as we are accused of saying by our detractors; we want magistrates to remain in their office, as ordained and established by God.

For Noah's ark, but also the tents of the presence and the temple of Solomon, are figurative prototypes for the church of Christ, as may be learned in the Epistle to the Hebrews. But Noah's ark had three different floors or chambers:[236] one for the impure beasts, the second for the pure, the third for the people, all of whom were to be saved from the flood.

Thus, too, the tents of the presence were distinguished according to rooms: one for the children of Korah who were commanded to look after <115> external things, but not to enter or they would die; another room below the door of the tent which was called holy, in which the priests sacrificed daily; and yet another room further inside called the holy of holies, into which no one dared enter except for the high priest once a year. And the temple was made according to this same plan, and had these same customs and rights.

But since the children of Korah wished to be pure, and were not satisfied being the servants of the Lord in rendering external service, they were swallowed up and consumed by the wrath of the Lord. Saul was cast out of

---

235 *Margin*: Isaiah 2[:4]; Micah 4[:3]
236 Zurich Q3 adds: *as is believed*

the kingdom for the same offense. Usa, who thoughtlessly laid his hands on the treasures of God, was struck dead by the Lord. When Nadab and Abihu, the sons of Aaron, brought unholy fire into the sanctuary of the Lord, which he had not commanded them to do, fire came out from the presence of the Lord and consumed them.[237]

Therefore these things, which are not part of the church of Christ itself but only a pre-figuring of the same, have their separate places where each and every person properly belongs, insofar as they are made of a piece of the old Adam. But when a person orders and establishes these things himself, other than how they ought to be ordered and established according to the Word of the Lord, then that person must also experience God's wrath, as noted above.

Who will not also believe <116> that the church of Christ, which is the very essence [and not merely the figure], so proclaimed by many, does not also have its own places into which each and every person may properly enter, according to that person's life and walk? And when one goes further in this regard than is appropriate, is such a one not more of an abomination to the Lord in the holy city than he is an accepted servant?

But in saying all this, we do not mean to deprecate a magistrate of the people who is called a Christian, or to give cause for the removal of the same, may our Lord[238] protect us from this. We recognize and maintain that magistrates are needed among the children of men who do not desire to be ruled by the illumination of the Holy Spirit, in order that they may be maintained in decency and fear. Instead, we wish to show the magistrates the path[239] through which they may rather obtain God's blessing than his wrath, and upon which their government without a doubt will be able to flourish in hope and expectation, and so long continue its rule.

For we see that the scepter of our enemy and opponent[240] is flourishing and increasing, whereas ours is withering and declining. The Turk wants to be God's servant, and yet is neither inside nor outside the church of Christ. We, on the other hand, desire to be in the sanctuary not only outwardly, but also inwardly, handing over to other builders <117> our earthly power and

---

237 *Margin:* Leviticus 10[:1-2]
238 Zurich Q3 adds: *and God*
239 Zurich Q3 replaces "the path" with: *in this article what our confession is*
240 Zurich Q3 adds: *the Turk*

A Short, Simple Confession 275

the worldly sword.²⁴¹ *Therefore as Christians we ought to reflect upon the cause of their increase and of our decline.*

The Holy Spirit of God lamented and cried out through the prophet Ezekiel in chapter 43²⁴² to the children of Israel saying, *You from [the house] of Israel have gone too far with your abominations. You bring people with uncircumcised heart and flesh into my sanctuary, through which you desecrate my house, etc. There shall be no foreigner in my sanctuary whose heart and flesh is uncircumcised. Likewise, in addition your kings set their thresholds and my threshold, their doorposts and my doorposts next to one another, with only a wall between theirs and mine [Ezekiel 43:7-9].*

We contend that the same is also to be lamented in today's would-be Christendom.²⁴³ For we also bring people with uncircumcised hearts and flesh into God's sanctuary when we acknowledge as good Christians people those who are mired in open sins and vices, such as people who are arrogant, pretentious, conceited, shrewd, fornicators, adulterers, greedy, usurers, guzzlers, gluttons, etc., upon whom Paul has already proclaimed judgment—unless such people mend their ways in true repentance, 1 Corinthians 6[:9-11], Galatians 5[:19-21], Ephesians 5[:3-5]. Yet a person who is currently stained by filthy lucre, or by his own quarreling wantonness or who for some other reason turns against a neighbor who never wronged him—with strangling, thievery, and every conceivable crime and brutality²⁴⁴—such an individual may still reside within today's would-be Christendom and, he believes, partake of the holy sacraments in the Lord's <118> sanctuary, although everyone is aware that he is completely drunk with greed and the licentiousness of the flesh, and extols such a lack of virtue as if he were holding up a praiseworthy work.

Likewise, we set the Lord's²⁴⁵ threshold and the king's threshold too close together when we bring magistrates with their worldly swords into the sanctuary of the Lord, and admonish and urge them to punish with the worldly sword individuals whom we should punish with the Word of God and the sword of the spirit. Such a sword a magistrate is entitled

---

241 Zurich Q3 adds: *and scepter*
242 Zurich Q3 adds: *and 44*
243 Zurich Q3 replaces "would-be Christendom" with: *people who consider themselves Christians*
244 Zurich Q3 omits some of the foregoing, but adds: *stained with such vices*
245 Zurich Q3 adds: *sanctuary and*

to wield and use outside the church against mother and father slayers, thieves, murderers,[246] etc., and where the healing teachings of the Gospel are contravened but which are to be punished outside the church of God.

But to use such coercion in the church or sanctuary of the Lord is as much of an abomination to the Lord as when the priests in the Old Testament brought in foreign fire, and lit their offerings with it; when, on account of their uncleanness, the holy fire would not burn.

From this it is clear to each and every one who has knowledge of God, that being a true Christian is of such condition and character that flesh and blood finds it uncongenial. For the path into Christianity is so small and narrow that one must deny oneself many times. Father, mother, wife and children, and everything one has—body, possessions, and blood—<119> one must leave behind, if a person wishes to walk the path that lies ahead, and not go backwards.[247]

But being a magistrate is so congenial to flesh and blood that often a person does not wait until he is called to the office or until such an office is handed over to him, but rather takes the office himself in both proper and improper ways. For although a person is, and ought to be, a servant of God in such an office, he often holds his Lord's command and bidding in the least regard, and often acts with greater regard for his own desires and fancies.

Therefore to be a true Christian, and at the same time to be a magistrate is impossible, humanly speaking. However, through God it is possible, who is able to grant grace so that, according to the words of the prophet Isaiah, even bears, lions, and leopards will live together with the lambs and will eat their food [Isaiah 11:6-7]. This means that a magistrate, of whatever rank, is to lay down at the Lord's threshold the sword and staff which he has for punishing the above-mentioned acts of wickedness, and go to the place where Christian teachings, demeanor, and discipline ought to be and indeed are being taught and lived—going, not as a magistrate, but as a child—and like a child, submitting to being taught and edified.

The reason for this is that one should accept the kingdom of God as a child, and not as a great lord, according to the Lord's own words. And on his holy mountain, that is, in the Christian church, no longer will one person harm or offend another,[248] but show only the charity of a Christian spirit

---

246 Zurich Q3 adds: *and against other wrongdoers*
247 Zurich Q3 adds: *as already stated*
248 Zurich Q3 adds (*Margin*): Isaiah 2; Micah 4

A Short, Simple Confession

where subjecting a person to the requisite punishment of the Mosaic spirit is impossible for human cleverness.

But we want to <120> listen yet further to the witness of Holy Scripture: Jacob the Patriarch prophesied that the scepter shall not depart from Judah until the hero comes [Genesis 49:10]. Since the Jewish kingdom, which at that time was God's people, came to an end in Christ and was taken away from them, it is clear that Christ desires to rule with his spiritual sword alone, among his newly-born people.

We also have, in this regard, one of his mysteries and prototypes within the house of Gideon, in the Book of the Judges chapter 8 [Judges 8:23-9:18], where Gideon spoke to Israel: "I will not rule over you, and my son will not rule over you." But Abimelech, the son of his slave woman, went and became king. There Jotham spoke to them in a parable how the olive tree, upon being asked by the trees to reign over them, did not want to be king. Nor did the fig tree. But the bramble accepted this gladly, etc., from which we see and learn that even more so a Christian, who often is compared to the olive tree, fig tree, grapevine, and other equally fine trees, may wield no worldly sword, but instead is to live out his Christian fruits of peace, gentleness, and humility.

Conversely, concerning the world's brawling and fighting, wrangling and quarreling—as the bramble is accustomed to doing—such is not to be found among Christians. Instead, their life and walk is to be lived out in the manner noted above, so that the prophecy of Isaiah may be fulfilled: "Instead of the thorn <121> shall come up the cypress; instead of the brier shall come up the myrtle" [Isaiah 55:13].

God speaks through the prophet in Hosea 13[:11]: "I gave you a king in my anger, and I took him away in my wrath." That which here had been given in anger does not harmonize with Christ's blessing and grace. Nor can the child of blessing and grace be the servant of vengeance and wrath.

Christ says, Blessed are the meek, blessed are the merciful, blessed are the peacemakers, blessed are those who are persecuted for righteousness' sake. All this opposes the office of the sword and coercion, as has been explained above in the first article contrasting the differences between the Old and New Testaments.

Christ teaches his own to pray: Forgive us our debts. Thus, Christians dare never exercise revenge. For whoever requites injustice and evil with vengeance and the sword, with capital punishment and imprisonment, the same would in effect be saying, in praying the Lord's Prayer: "As I have done to my brother and neighbor, so, God, do also to me."

Christ says to his disciples, I am sending you as sheep into the midst of wolves, and points them to the depths of the cross, suffering and tribulation that they will need to suffer from the wolf-like people, Matthew 10[:18-19], 24[:9]; Mark 13[:9]; Luke 21[:12]; Daniel 11[:33-35], who will persecute them even unto death, believing at the same time they are therewith performing a pleasing service for God, John 16 [:2]. Thus it is not in keeping with their nature that the lambs of Christ act in a wolf-like way, for Paul says, Galatians 4[:29]: "The child who was born according to the flesh persecuted <122> the child who was born according to the Spirit. So it is now also."

Christ says to his disciples further, Matthew 20[:25-26], when the two sons of Zebedee desired to reign through worldly means, still understanding Christ's kingdom to be a worldly kingdom and dominion, "You know that the worldly rulers lord it over the people, and the high officials command with coercion. It will not be so among you; but whoever wishes to be great among you must be your servant, and whoever wishes to be first among you must be your servant."[249]

See, Christ broaches here the theme of the magistracy and the lords of the world, and speaks with clear words, "it will not be so among you." Here he is not only speaking to the twelve, but to each and every Christian and member of his church, for he says, Mark 13[:37], "What I am telling you, I am telling everyone."

Likewise, when he had fallen into his enemies' hands, and Peter wanted to defend and protect his Lord, cutting off the ear of the high priest's slave with his sword, the Lord reprimanded him for doing this and said, "Put your sword back into its place, for all who take the sword will perish by the sword" [Matthew 26:52].

With these words the Lord completely proscribed the worldly sword before his death, and desired that his own and also those who were not supposed to have the sword and mete out vengeance, lay the sword down. For the spiritual sword, and the worldly sword each has its separate sheath: the spiritual belongs in the church <123> of Christ, the worldly, within the world, in order to punish the wicked, as explained above.

---

249 *Margin*: Matthew 20; Mark 10; Luke 21

A Short, Simple Confession

Nowhere can one find that Peter or another apostle thereafter took out or wielded a sword, but kept it in its place. This is why the holy apostle Paul says [2 Corinthians 10:4-5], "the weapons we fight with are not physical, but spiritual and powerful before God, destroying everything that rises up against the knowledge of God."

The Lord, to be sure, said to his disciples that they were to buy swords, and allowed this to happen so that they had two swords with them. He did this, however, for the sole reason that he desired to have them come to understand later, on the Mount of Olives, how his final testament was to be carried out. For since he wanted to abolish the old law with his death, to the degree that it incorporated legalistic and figurative elements, and wished to abrogate Mosaic coercion, he consequently wanted the two aforementioned swords to be carried to the Mount of Olives to show his disciples there, just before his death, how his own people were to regard the physical and worldly sword from then on—namely, that we are to leave it in its place. For whoever takes the sword will perish by the sword. Furthermore, when [the Lord] retorted to Peter [John 18:11], ["Put your sword back into its sheath.] Am I not to drink the cup that the Father has given me?" the Lord gave him to understand that if he contended against this, he would be contending against the will of God.

Therefore we should also learn thereby, that since Christ promised the cross, tribulation, and persecution to the elect believers, if they desire to enter the narrow path to <124> life they will need to suffer considerable persecution brought on by the children of the world. And if they wanted to contend and fight against such persecution, they would be contending and fighting against their own salvation. From this it follows that if we were to grasp the sword, we would perish by the sword.

Some people also think that since the apostles still numbered eleven, and each did not have a sword, that the two swords consequently signify the spiritual and the worldly swords [respectively]—the spiritual belonging within the church and fellowship of Christ, Ephesians 6[:11-17]; Hebrews 4[:12], about which the prophets prophesied, Isaiah 2[:4]; Micah 4[:3]; Zechariah 9; Psalm 46 and 76, the worldly sword belonging in the world to punish those who are evil, Ecclesiasticus 17[:17]; Matthew 22[:15-21]; Romans 13[:1-7]; 1 Timothy 1[:8-10]; Colossians 2[:16-17?].

However, since the Lord Christ reproached the Apostle Peter, who could not yet sort out these matters well enough, thinking he was doing the Lord a favor—who had permitted his disciples to carry two swords to the Mount of Olives, finally abolishing thereby the vengeance of the sword among his own—but Peter was not aware of this, but instead had set his hope on saving his dear Lord and Master with the sword. How much more will those be reproached who have now heard long enough that Christ and his holy Apostles have forbidden every form of vengeance for Christians, Matthew 5; Luke 6[:20-38]; Romans 12[:9-21], yet who powerfully execute vengeance with all their <125> might, thereby alienating themselves from every form of the cross and tribulation which the Lord had prophesied for his own[250] Matthew 10[:16-39]; Luke 10[:3], 21[:12-19]; John 15[:18-20], 16[:2; 33]? They act not according to the nature of peaceful lambs, but following the nature of wolves, thereby forcing and compelling individuals into accepting their faith, in contradiction to the teaching of Christ.

The Lord says to his disciples, "Whenever someone does not welcome you or listen to what you say, go out from that house or place." He does not say, "coerce them into accepting your words,"[251] but says instead: "Shake the dust from your feet as a witness, and tell them that they should know that the kingdom of God has come near to them. I tell you, on that day it will be more tolerable for Sodom and Gomorrah than for that town."[252]

The Lord said further in John 16[:8-11] that the Holy Spirit would come and punish the world for its sins, etc. Thus human coercion against unbelievers is now subject to the Holy Spirit, since all things belong to the Holy Spirit—not to speak of their punishing the true Christian apostolic faith—persecuting with a physical sword those who do not agree with them and believe as they do, in accordance with their own minds and rational perceptions. They, however, reach for the sword under the pretense of extending, increasing and planting the kingdom of Christ thereby. But if someone tries to lay the cross and tribulation upon them, they strike it down and slough it off, utilizing all sorts of instruments of vengeance which have been created to take revenge. Such people take and use the sword to their own harm and ruin and, according to the words of the Lord, they must come to ruin and perish by the sword. <126> The guilt remains on their heads, since Christ's warning had no effect upon them.

---

250 *Margin*: Matthew 16, 24; Mark 8; Luke 9, 14
251 *Margin*: Luke 10[:10-11]
252 *Margin*: Mark 6[:11]

A Short, Simple Confession

We wanted to communicate this in writing, especially to those who in this day and age brag that they esteem the holy Gospel and the Christian name so highly and reverently, namely that the spiritual sword is fine and mighty—sharper than any two-edged steel sword,[253] yea, sharper than fire, the gallows, or cannon—which no steel or iron instrument can touch.

In addition we well know that those who do not have the spiritual sword must use and adapt what they have; otherwise they would have absolutely nothing to defend themselves with. But to what degree they will be judged for all this, they will certainly find out in His time.

Christ did not wish to judge in matters of capital punishment concerning the woman caught in adultery, as we know, although the law so decreed. Therefore a true and genuine Christian will also emulate the character and manner of his Lord and Master, for Christ says, "Just as my Father sent me into the world, so have I also sent you" [John 17:18] and to Pilate he said, "My kingdom is not of this world" [John 18:36] etc. Thus, neither is the kingdom of Christians of this world, for Christ says, "I have chosen you out of the world" [John 15:19], etc. The kingdom of the magistrates, however, is worldly, and they are the princes and rulers of this world.

Paul the apostle teaches Christians as follows:[254] "Do not repay anyone evil with evil," "do not be haughty, but <127> associate with the lowly," "never avenge yourselves, my most beloved, but leave room for the wrath of God, for it is written, 'Vengeance is mine, I will repay, says the Lord.'" Consequently the office of vengeance has never been commanded or permitted for the true Christian. And in 1 Corinthians 6[:7-8] he says, "In fact, to have lawsuits at all with one another is already a defeat for you. Why not rather be wronged? Why not rather be defrauded? But you yourselves wrong and defraud—and brothers at that." From this follows once again that to go to law and to judge is therefore not to be entered into in the church of Christ.

Believers, that is, Christians[255] are one body in Christ, and all are baptized into one body. Thus it would be unseemly for a body to use a sword against itself for its members, as just stated, comprise one body in Christ. Therefore the sword of vengeance shall be at rest among them.

---

253 *Margin*: Ephesians 6[:17]; Hebrews 4[:12]
254 *Margin*: Romans 12[:16-19]
255 *Margin*: Romans 12; 1 Corinthians 10, 12; Ephesians 4; Colossians 3

Love is patient and friendly;[256] the sword and its servants are quick on the draw, overly zealous, crude, and hostile. Love is not envious; the sword soon retaliates. Love is not belligerent or boastful; the sword and its servants, contradicting this, boast with great belligerence. Love does not insist on having its own way; the sword protects its self-interests. Love is not provoked to anger; the sword is nothing but anger, a vessel and instrument of anger. Love does not compete with malice and endures all things; the sword is vengeance and <128> requites all things. Therefore pure Christian love can in no way be joined to the worldly sword.

Every person is subject to the magistracy and the powers that be,[257] says Paul, for there is no authority except from God. Thus the apostles teach expressly that Christians are to be subject to the political authorities, but not that they themselves are to wield the worldly sword: "For what have I to do with judging those outside?"[258]

The sword of the Christians, however, as already noted, is the sword of the Spirit, Ephesians 6[:17], which they are to wield and apply within the church and fellowship of God, not according to their own opinions and perceptions, but according to the teaching of Christ and his holy apostles, Matthew 18[:15-18]; Romans 16[:17-20]; 1 Corinthians 5[:1-5; 11-13]; 2 Thessalonians 2[:3-12].

Christ appeared to the holy apostle John, Revelation 1[:16]; 19[:15], having a two-edged sword in his mouth. From this we, his believers, learn that the sword belongs not in our hands, but in our mouths, as noted above—the sword of the spirit, not the sword which draws blood. Consequently, it befits a Christian not at all to reach for the sword of the magistracy. On the other hand, it certainly would befit magistrates to glorify Christ of their own free will, lowering themselves with him, laying down the sword of vengeance, taking the cross upon themselves, and following him in humility. However, we still respectfully want to leave it up to them to do what they deem to lie in their best interests, before the Most High.

When Jesus noticed that the people were coming, wanting to lay hold of him <129> *to make him king, he escaped and fled, which he did to provide a precedent and example for us, that we are to follow in his footsteps. For*

---

256 *Margin*: 1 Corinthians 13
257 *Margin*: Romans 13; 1 Peter 2; Titus 3
258 *Margin*: 1 Corinthians 5[:12]

A Short, Simple Confession

"those whom God has called," says the apostle Paul, "the same he also chose to be conformed to the image of his Son."[259]

Since ancient times, the authority of the worldly sword has been given the distinctive name "the worldly magistracy" [*die Wältlich Oberkeitt*] the reason being that its office cannot be filled by those in the Christian church. For in Christ's church an absolutely different kingdom and rule has come into being, for which the old must come to an end and cease, as was prophesied by the patriarch Jacob that the scepter of Judah would not be taken until the hero, Christ, would come [Genesis 49:10]. Therefore the old kingdom ended in Christ, it ceased, and was destroyed. He began a new rule which is not like the old, and cannot be sustained by the worldly sword, etc.

The Jewish people were God's nation at that time,[260] but since Jewish rule ended and ceased in Christ and was taken from them, it is manifest that in Christ, [God's rule] is no longer to exist except solely among Christians, where Christ wishes to reign with his spiritual sword. Therefore God in Christ alone is King and Ruler of his people, as is written: God ordained the [worldly] magistrates over all nations, but over Israel he alone is Lord. In the same way that Christ is now a spiritual <130> King, so also does he have spiritual servants. He and all his servants wield a spiritual sword which pierces soul and spirit.

For indeed, the Son[261] was established by the Father, as is written: I established my King on my holy Mount Zion, given not in anger as the other kings, but for a blessing, with him alone becoming the source of our blessing, just as it was promised, that in him all peoples were to be blessed. Therefore, just as the others spill blood for blood, this one came to heal and preserve human souls. The others, to avenge evil; this one, however, to requite with goodness. The others, to hate their enemies; this one, established to love. All this has already been extensively explained and documented in the first article.

Thus[262] Christ initiated an absolutely different kind of kingdom and lordship, and desires that his servants be in accord therewith and become like him. This is why he said to them, as noted above, "the worldly princes

---

259 *Margin*: Romans 8[:29]
260 *Margin*: Hebrews 4; John 16; Romans 8
261 *Margin*: Matthew 28; Philippians 2; Psalm 2; Isaiah 13
262 *Margin*: Philippians 2[:6-11]; Matthew 10[:24-25]; Luke 14[:11]

are called gracious lords, and the powerful lord it over the nations, but for you it is not so, rather, whoever is the greatest among you is to be servant of you all."

Consequently the majesty of Christ and his servants *does not reside in outward things such as worldly splendor. The more one forgoes such splendor, the greater he will be in the kingdom of Christ, as the following words confirm: Whoever raises himself up will be humbled, and whoever humbles himself will be raised up.*[263] *Likewise, Whoever* <131> *does not renounce all that he has cannot be my disciple. Therefore it is crystal clear and plain, whoever still clings to created things* [den Creyaturen], *and will not renounce them for Christ's sake, cannot be his true disciple.*[264]

But our desire and point of view is not, as mentioned above, to do away with a worldly magistracy, or to be disobedient to it in good and justifiable things, for political authorities should and must exist in the world among human beings, as necessary as daily bread, and as necessary as a schoolmaster who must wield the rod with children. Since the multitudes of this world do not desire to receive or be ruled by God's Word, therefore the sword must compel and rule them, so that the rogues and rascals—the children of this world—*who do not desire to be ruled by the Spirit,*[265] *possess instead (based on a fear of the sword and gallows) a worldly devoutness among their own kind, in this manner being somewhat restrained by the bridle and controlled by the spurs. Otherwise, no one would be safe from anyone else, but instead the earth would be covered with blood and whoever from among the ungodly mob was best able to aggress, would do it.*

Therefore government[266] is ordained by God,[267] which we also with good reason should affirm and esteem,[268] *responding to them with love and good will, desiring to be subject to them in everything that is not against God, handing over to them their taxes and fees willingly and faithfully, such as tithes, interest, tribute and such like—these things a* <132> *Christian may do without compromising faith or conscience.*

---

263 *Margin*: Matthew 9[:9]; 1 Peter 5[:3-6]; Matthew 20[:25-27]; Luke 14[:10-11; 27; 33]
264 *Margin*: Matthew 19[:21; 27-30]; Luke 14[:26-27; 33]
265 Zurich Q3 adds: *nor want to demonstrate Christian devoutness*
266 Zurich Q3 adds (*Margin*): *Ecclesiasticus 17*
267 Zurich Q3 adds: *as it is written: Every people has an ordained ruler, but Israel is the Lord's part. Therefore...*
268 Zurich Q3 adds: *desiring to be subject and obedient*

A Short, Simple Confession

But a believer[269] *does not owe what is contrary to God, and what wounds the conscience. Neither did Peter and the apostles do this, for although Peter taught "Be subject to all human ordinances," when his own conscience was attacked, forbidding him to do what rightfully was good and just, and demanding what was improper, he said, "One owes greater allegiance to God than to human beings."*[270] Shadrach, Meshach, and Abednego also responded in a similar way before King Nebuchadnezzar [Daniel 3:18], as did also Maccabeus and his group at the time of King Antiochus [1 Maccabees 2:19-22]. The same for Eleasar [Leviticus 10:16-20], and the mother with the seven sons [2 Maccabees 7:20].

For one is to give to Caesar what is Caesar's and to God what is God's [Matthew 22:21], for which reason a Christian must decide between the two: rather than obey the magistracy in wrongful matters which are contrary to God and one's conscience, one must rather suffer death—as did the holy martyrs, the apostles, and those who followed them, who allowed their blood to flow rather than compromise their faith.[271]

But that magistrates do not belong in the church and community of God with their worldly sword, thereby conquering, afflicting, and persecuting consciences, is not something that we have just now substantiated and so interpreted from Holy Scripture. Rather, Martin Luther and other scholars before us also have written clearly about this, analyzing and <133> *substantiating this point with holy, godly Scripture, which we want to make known in summary fashion.*

Martin Luther wrote in the first part of his booklet of 1525 [sic],[272] *"Concerning the Worldly Magistracy, to what Extent one is Duty-Bound to Show them Allegiance," saying: "God the Almighty has driven our princes*

---

269 Zurich Q3 adds (*Margin*): *1 Peter 2[:19]*. The German reads "for the sake of conscience" whereas the English NRSV has: "while suffering unjustly."
270 *Margin*: Acts 5[:29]
271 Another authorial hand becomes evident at this point in the manuscript. Whereas the argument to this point has followed the common Anabaptist "topical concordance" approach of documenting specific topics with multiple scriptural citations, the writer of the following section surveys early writings by mainline reformers, culls citations from those writings that support the view that the "worldly sword" has no place in the church, and makes a pointed case for toleration in matters of faith.
272 Zurich Q3 has *1523*, the first date of publication of *Von weltlicher Obrigkeit, wie weit man ihr Gehorsam schuldig sei*. English translation: "Temporal Authority: to

mad, to the point that they think they have the power over their subjects to do and demand anything they desire; and their subjects also manifest their unbelief in thinking they are duty-bound to follow their princes in everything, so absolutely that the princes have now begun to command their subjects to carry out, believe in, and hold to what they, the magistrates, impose. They presume to sit on God's throne, thereby crushing consciences and faith, attempting to instruct the Holy Spirit[273] in accord with their own insane ideas."[274]

Martin Luther wrote further concerning this: "Therefore, Christ used no sword, nor established it in his kingdom,[275] for he is a King over Christians and rules solely through his Holy Spirit, without the law. And although he sanctioned the sword, he indeed did not use it; for it serves no purpose in his kingdom, where only the godly are found. Therefore David long ago was not permitted to build the temple since he had shed much blood and had wielded the sword—not that he had done wrongly by it, but rather that he could not prefigure Christ, who was to have a peaceful kingdom without the sword. <134> Instead, Solomon had to do it—whose name means "peaceful kingdom" or "peaceable" in German. He had a peaceable kingdom, so that the truly peaceable kingdom of Christ could be anticipated by true peaceableness, symbolized by Solomon. Likewise no tool of iron was heard in the temple while it was being built, says the text.[276] All this indicates, therefore, that Christ was to have a voluntary community, without coercion or duress, without law or sword. So thought the prophets, Psalm 109, Isaiah 2 and 11."[277]

And in the second part of the aforementioned booklet Luther also writes: "God cannot and will not allow anyone else to rule over the soul, only He Himself. Therefore whenever worldly authority presumes to enact decrees for souls, it encroaches upon the power of God and his rule, thereby only deceiving and corrupting souls. We want to make this so clear (says Luther)

---

what extent it should be obeyed," found in *Luther's Works*, vol. 45, ed. Walther I. Brandt (Philadelphia: Muhlenberg Press, 1962), 81-129.

273 *den h. geist zur schul füren*, or "sending the Holy Spirit back to school"
274 In the preceding, the codex reproduces a close paraphrase of the original. See LW, vol. 45, 83-4.
275 Zurich Q3 adds (*Margin*): *B, 2nd leaf*
276 *Margin*: 1 Kings 6[:7]
277 The preceding is found in LW, vol. 45, 93; it is a close paraphrase. Zurich Q3 adds (*Margin*): *D. on the 4th leaf*

A Short, Simple Confession

that our noblemen, the princes and bishops, see what kind of fools they really are when they try to coerce the people with their laws and statutes into believing this way or that way."[278]

In this same booklet Luther continues:[279] "A court must and ought to be absolutely certain when it is to render a judgment, and have everything out in the clear light. But one's inmost thoughts and feelings can be revealed to no one but to God. Therefore it is to no purpose, and impossible to command and coerce anyone into believing one way or another through force. Thoughts and feelings belong in another realm. Coercion does not work. <135> I am amazed at the great fools (writes Luther), for they all say, 'de ocultis non iudicat ecclesia' ('the church does not judge hidden things'). If then the church can apply its spiritual rule only to public things, how then can the irrational worldly authority (as Luther writes) hope to judge and rule over secret, spiritual, and hidden things such as faith?

"Consequently, how one believes poses a personal risk for each person, who must see for himself that he believes rightly. For just as nobody else can go to hell or heaven in my place, so is nobody else able to believe in my stead, or force me into unbelief.[280] Because it lies in everyone's own conscience as to how he believes or does not believe, and since no harm is done thereby to worldly authority, the magistracy should also be satisfied, look after its own affairs, and allow faith to take its course as the individual so desires and is able, coercing no one through force. For the matter of faith is a free work, to which no one can be coerced. Yes, it is a godly work in the spirit, not to speak of the fact that the magistracy is to carry and enforce its mandate through outward power. From this comes the common saying, which Augustine also used, 'no one can or dare try to coerce anyone into faith.'[281]

"Furthermore the blind, wretched people do not see (writes Luther) what a completely useless and impossible thing the magistrates are attempting to do. <136> For no matter how forcefully they command, and how often they rage, they can never coerce the people into following their commands any further than with the mouth and hands; indeed, they are not able to coerce the heart, even if they were to tear it apart (writes Luther), for the proverb is true, 'thoughts are tax-free.' How can it be that they wish to force the people

---

278 Preceding in LW, vol. 45, 105.
279 The following extended passage in LW, vol. 45, 107-109.
280 The Zurich Q3 copyist appears to have dropped a line or two at this place.
281 Zurich Q3 adds (*Margin*): *D. on the 4th leaf*

to believe in their hearts, yet at the same time see that this is impossible? In this manner they compel weak consciences to lie, renounce, and speak words that contradict what they know in their hearts, burdening themselves in this way with abominable and strange sins, although to be sure, all the lies and false confessions made by such weak consciences fall upon those who have extorted them."[282]

"If you then say (writes Luther) that Paul indeed said, Romans 13, that every person should be subject to the governing authorities, and that Peter said, we should be subject to all human government [1 Peter 2:13], *my answer is: You are right (writes Luther), for the saying illustrates my point. Saint Paul was speaking of the magistracy and worldly authority. Now you have just heard that no one but God has authority over the soul. Therefore Saint Paul could never have been speaking of obedience except where the authority corresponds. From this it follows that he was not speaking about faith, [to the effect that] the worldly authority is to govern over matters of faith, but rather [it is to govern] over outward things, overseeing and governing such things on earth. His own <137> words demonstrate this bright and clear when he sets the goal for both authority and obedience and says, 'Pay to all what is due them—taxes to whom taxes are due, revenue to whom revenue is due, respect to whom respect is due, honor to whom honor is due.' [Romans 13:7] This means that worldly obedience and authority extends only over taxes, revenue, respect, honor, and outer things. Likewise, where he says, 'Rulers are not a terror to good conduct, but to bad,' [Romans 13:3] he limits the magistrates, saying that their authority does not extend over faith or God's Word, but rather that they are to rule over evil deeds.*

"Saint Peter agrees when he speaks of human institutions [1 Peter 2:13]. *Now, human institutions truly cannot reach into heaven or rule over the soul, rather they rule only on earth and over the external relationships of human beings among one another, where human beings see, apprehend, hold court, pronounce judgment, punish and pardon. Christ himself made this distinction, stating it briefly when he said, Matthew 22[:21], 'Give to Caesar what is Caesar's, and to God what is God's.' If Caesar's authority extended into God's kingdom and authority, and were not an entity unto itself, Christ would not have made the distinction in this manner. For, as has been said,*

---

282 Zurich Q3 adds (*Margin*): *D. on the 4th leaf.* End of extended passage. After a short deleted portion, the copyist begins citing Luther again. The following passage is found in LW, vol. 45, 110.

A Short, Simple Confession

the soul is not subject to the authority of Caesar;[283] he can neither inform it nor guide it, neither kill it or revive it, neither bind nor loose it, neither judge nor pass sentence on it, neither restrain nor free it—all of which he would need to be able to do, if he had the authority to decree laws pertaining to the soul. Instead his authority pertains to body, possessions and honor, <138> for such things are under his authority.

"David also much earlier said the same thing in one of his short sentences, where he says in Psalm 115[:16], 'The heavens are the Lord's heavens, but the earth he has given to human beings.' That is, whatever exists on earth, belonging to the temporal, earthly kingdom, is where humanity has authority, granted by God. But whatever belongs to heaven and to the eternal kingdom, such authority belongs solely to the heavenly Lord."[284] Peter says 'We must obey God rather than any human authority,' [Acts 5:29] whereby he clearly states his conviction concerning worldly authority. For if a person were obliged to do everything the worldly authority demanded, it would have been stated in vain that 'we must obey God rather than any human authority.'"[285]

Furthermore, M. Luther states concerning Saint Peter's Epistle, in a booklet published in 1524 and printed at Basel,[286] as follows: "The Pope acted unjustly when he attempted to coerce and force the people with laws, for among Christian people there can and should be no coercion; and when one begins to bind consciences with outer laws, very quickly faith and the Christian life diminishes, for Christians must be guided and ruled by the Spirit alone."[287]

Luther continues, in the same booklet, "If an emperor or a prince were to ask me what <139> my faith is I would tell him, not because of

---

283 *Margin*: Matthew 10[:5-23]
284 Extended passage above, LW, vol. 45, 110-11. The copyist drops a few lines, and then continues, ibid., 111.
285 End of copying from Luther's *Temporal Authority*. Zurich Q3 adds: *All of this is found in M. Luther's aforementioned booklet, and is accurately copied here.*
286 Martin Luther, *Die erst Epistel Sanct Peters : Die ander epistel sanct Peters und eine sanct Judas / geprediget und nach rechtem Verstand ussgelegt durch Martinum Luther* (Basel: Cratander, 1524), accessed online: http://www.e-rara.ch/zuz/content/titleinfo/1301599, April 15, 2014. English translation of Luther's sermon on 1 Peter, in Jaroslav Pelikan, ed., LW, vol. 30, *The Catholic Epistles*, 3-145.
287 Citation in original, online: http://www.e-rara.ch/zuz/content/pageview/1301759 (page 159); translation in LW, 30, 77, commenting on 1 Peter 2:16.

his command, but rather since I am obliged to confess my faith publicly before everyone. If he, however, wanted to go further and command me that I ought to believe thus or so, I would say, 'Dear sir, attend to your worldly rule; you have no authority to interfere in the sphere of God and his kingdom.'"[288]

We have already heard above what Luther wrote *concerning the Psalter, that the true and properly established church is not protected with worldly power and arms, rather only the fictitious church, which may well carry the name of church, but denies its power.*[289]

Rudolf Walter also writes against coercion in matters of faith in the five sermons, which he wrote against the pope in Rome, called "The Antichrist," *published in Zurich in 1546:*[290] *"Christ coerced no one with force to follow him and his teaching, but rather taught and preached in a loving manner. But the Pope coerces all those who oppose him and his teaching with excommunication, fire, and sword, for which acts of tyranny*

---

288 Citation in original publication, online: http://www.e-rara.ch/zuz/content/pageview/1301767 (page 167); translation in LW, 30, 81, commenting on 1 Peter 2:17.

289 Zurich Q3 adds: *Psalm 17*. Although there are passing references to individual Psalms, there is no previous reference in this manuscript to Luther's writing on the Psalter as such. It appears that the copyist has a document in hand which has made reference to such a writing. The hint from the margin of Zurich Q3, that this is a reference to Luther's commentary on Psalm 17, leads to a publication by Martin Luther and others, *[Psalter wol verteutscht ausz der heyligen sprach]* : *[Verklerung des Psalters fast klar und nutzlich]* (Basel: Adam Petri, 1526). Accessed online: http://www.e-rara.ch/bau_1/ch16/content/titleinfo/197874, April 15, 2014. The published commentary on Psalm 17 speaks generally to the themes noted by the copyist, but does not coincide closely with the summary provided in the codex. See ibid., 25 verso (Ei verso) to 28 recto (Eiii recto) (pages 100-103 in the online version).

290 "Christus hat nieman mit gwalt gezwungen jm und siner leer anzuhangen/ sonder früntlich geleert und prediget. Der Papst aber zwingt mit dem ban/shür und schwaärt alle die/so jm und siner leer widersträbend...." Rudolf Walter, *Der Endtchrist: kurtze / klare und einfaltige Beweysung / in fünff Predigen begriffen / daß der Papst zu Rom / der rächt / war / groß und eigentlich Endtchrist sye* ... (Zurich: Froschauer, 1546). PDF copy online at: http://www.e-rara.ch/zuz/content/titleinfo/263000; citation on page 45, verso. Walter's conclusion, that the Pope would therefore be damned to hell, is a repeated theme throughout this third sermon.

A Short, Simple Confession

and persecution, he may consequently anticipate the fiery lake and eternal death, with which he will be punished and requited."[291]

In the first of his six sermons, *On the Incarnation of Christ*, published at Zurich in 1571,[292] Walter writes: "Christ Jesus, the Prince of Peace, is also authoritative concerning civil unity and the path our <140> life takes, for the sum total or main point of all the commands which he ordered for us is the love[293] which we are to have for one another in accordance with his example. Indeed, he demands this so rigorously that he even forbids every form of revenge, whereby we are to want the best for our enemies and pray for them [Matthew 5:44]. Furthermore, since he forms all those who believe in him as children of God into one body which is conducted and led by one Spirit, therefore it cannot be otherwise than that they persist in loving one another resolutely and truly, and refrain from acting in any manner which might destroy this love, or which might evoke conflict. In

---

291 At this point, Zurich Q3 adds the following (leaf 159): *Furthermore, in his book published at Zurich in 1578,* Concerning the True Bread of Life, *in his third sermon, and referring to John 6, R. Walter writes that there are those who ask, why does God tolerate such things? Why does not the Lord Christ coerce people to be obedient to him, since he is the powerful King of the earth, and holds human hearts in his hand? To this Walter answers, "The Lord anticipates all this, saying, 'All that my Father gives to me will come to me, and whoever comes to me I will not turn away.' He is thereby saying through this, 'nobody should be offended by your example, for if you already do not believe, and in your unbelief—as worthy as you indeed may be—die and perish, even then no diminution will befall my kingdom. Consequently it is not necessary that I apply eternal force or coercion,' and notes, among other things, that faith is a free gift of God. Walter says, further, in the volume just referred to, in the last sermon, that Christ gave those who forsook him no cause for their having fallen away, and that the Lord Christ with his kingdom is bound to no human, nor does Christ force anyone into his service with coercion."* Rudolf Walter, *Von dem waaren Brot dess Läbens, unserem Herren Jesu Christo, und wie der selbig genossen werde : zähen Predigen* über *das VI. Cap. dess heiligen Evangelisten Johannis* (Zurich: Froschauer, 1578). Located online at: www.e-rara.ch/zuz/content/titleinfo/864972. Lengthy citation from 40, verso; 41, recto; concluding citation, from the "last sermon," 169, recto.

292 Rudolf Walter, *Die Menschwerdung deß waarenn / ewigen und eingebornen Suns Gottes / unsers Herren Jesu Christi / erklärt und ußgelegt in sechs predigen* (Zurich: Froschauer, 1571). Located online at: www.e-rara.ch/zuz/content/pageview/1267996. Citation begins on print page 41, recto and runs to 42, verso, with some lines dropped from 42, recto-42 verso. Variations are minor.

293 *Margin*: John 13[:34], 15[:9]; Matthew [5:43]

support of this are the numerous prophesies of the prophets, all of which speak of such unity, of peaceful well-being among the faithful, and of the kingdom of Christ, as for example Isaiah, who says: 'They shall beat their swords into plowshares, and their spears into pruning hooks; nation shall not lift up sword against nation, neither shall they learn war any more.'[294]

"Then 'the wolf will live with the lamb, the leopard shall lie down with the kid, the calf and the lion and the fatling together, and a little child shall lead them. The cow and the bear shall graze, their young shall lie down together; and the lion shall eat straw like the ox. The nursing child shall play over the hold of the asp, and the weaned child shall put its hand <141> on the adder's den. They will not hurt or destroy on all my holy mountain; for the earth will be full of the knowledge of the Lord as the waters cover the sea.'[295]

"Zechariah, too, prophesies the same vision, that the Lord Christ 'will cut off the chariot from Ephraim and the war horse from Jerusalem; and the battle bow shall be cut off, and he shall command peace to the nations,' etc.[296] At this point, someone might want to ask (writes Walter), how these prophesies accord with what the Lord himself says in the Gospel: 'Do you think that I have come to bring peace to the earth? No, I tell you, but rather division! From now on five in one household will be divided, three against two and two against three; they will be divided: father against son and son against father, mother against daughter and daughter against mother, mother-in-law against her daughter-in-law and daughter-in-law against mother-in-law' [Luke 12:51-53].

"Here we also see that such conflict and division often accompanies the message of our Lord Jesus Christ. Civil insurrections and heinous wars spring up, in which no inhuman barbarity is considered off limits, etc. But to be noted here is the distinction contained in this prophecy. The holy prophets <142> are speaking about the faithful, and teaching what Christ with his words and Spirit would be creating and working among the same, namely, that the faithful, eliminating all the old enmity and conflict, would instead be dwelling together, showing affection and love to one another in such a manner that the above-mentioned lions, bears, snakes, and adders, as far as their grim, vengeful, vile hearts were concerned—before they had

---

294 *Margin*: Isaiah 2[:4], Micah 4[:3]
295 *Margin*: Isaiah 11[:6-9]
296 *Margin*: Zechariah 9[:10]

A Short, Simple Confession

experienced Christ and accepted him in true faith—would show love to humankind and would live in an entirely harmless way.

"The Lord, however, incorporates into his warning or prophecy both believers and unbelievers, the children of God and the children of the world, thereby pointing to what will take place between these two classes, namely, that his own believe the Gospel, separating themselves from the world and from all fellowship with its idolatrous, sinful being, which separation, however, the children of the world will not want to tolerate, out of which, then, will surface the conflict noted above."[297]

What appears above are Martin Luther's and R. Walter's own words, which we wanted to quote, verbatim, for the God-fearing reader to examine and consider, to see whether this does not agree with God's Word and our preceding introduction. But as to whether or not they then enacted this [teaching] with actual works, <143> however, this we want to document for devout hearts, concerning those who suffered from these authors for those exact same things against which they had written.

We also have come to understand, above, *what Ulrich Zwingli wrote against coercion* in his book, "Concerning Divine and Human Righteousness." Likewise *in his "Article Book," in the 36th article, he says to the Pope: Go away and bring sinful Sodom to repentance, not with guns and steel*[298] *but with the Word of God, and preach and shout like Jonah, like John, like Christ, "Mend your ways." And take no other sword into your hands except for the sword of the Spirit, which is the Word of God, and the other weapons which Paul forges in Ephesians 6, or you will perish. David could not wield these in steel armor. As long as you cry for weapons of steel, we will all see that you are not a disciple of Christ or Peter, but rather of the devil, and the true Antichrist.*[299]

Here Zwingli himself pronounced judgment on those who[300] *implore and incite a magistracy to attack the conscience of the inner person and to*

---

297 End of citation from R. Walter's *Die Menschwerdung deß waarenn / ewigen und eingebornen Suns Gottes....*
298 Zurich Q3 adds: *and do not travel hither and yon with the knights of the masked bishops.*
299 Close copying of "Auslegen und Begründen der Schlußreden," in *Zwingli, der Verteidiger des Glaubens*, II. Teil (Zurich: Zwingli-Verlag, 1952), commentary on the 36th Article, 95-96.
300 Zurich Q3 adds: *proceed to the temporal sphere concerning the sword of the Spirit ...*

coerce such a one into faith with worldly[301] *enforcement and sword.*[302] *For he clearly states above that the magistracy is to punish no part of what has to do solely with the conscience of the inner person, etc.*

Whoever wishes to read more from such scholars, how clearly they have written against the use of force and coercion <144> and worldly power in matters of judging and controlling faith, may read what Johann Brenz has to say in Sebastian Franck's *Chronica*, on pages 446-448. Likewise regarding Johann Odenbach and Philipp Melanchthon, on pages 449 and 460.[303]

As we have seen above, Rudolf Walter wrote that Christ had coerced no one with force to accept him and his teachings, but rather taught and preached lovingly. *Now how do the would-be Christians*[304] *justify utilizing a different means from that used by their Lord and Master, whom they honor so highly, and who taught all of his own that they were to learn from him, for he was gentle and humble of heart, and [in following his ways] they would find peace for their souls?*

Paul, too, says the same in Romans 8[:29], "For those whom he foreknew he also predestined to be conformed to the image of his Son," from which it is clearly understood that the bondsman and servant is not to be of any nature other than that of his Lord and Master; we could not be compared to the Lamb of God as lambs of Christ if we exhibit a wolfish, persecuting nature. For Paul says, "the child who was born according to the flesh persecuted the child who was born according to the Spirit, so it is now also," etc.[305] <145> Paul says, 2 Thessalonians 3[:2], "Having faith is not for everyone." *If now faith is not for everyone, then it is always a gift of God. Now if it is a gift, then it cannot be coerced with any worldly force or sword, rather must be attained through grace and strength from above, from the Father of Light.*[306]

---

301 Zurich Q3 adds: *coercion and*
302 *Margin*: In the booklet, Von göttlicher und menschlicher Gerechtigkeytt (Concerning Divine and Human Righteousness), F. on the 3rd leaf, and H. on the 3rd leaf
303 Following the 1536 Ulm edition of Franck's *Chronica*, the passages referred to are found in the third chronicle, "Chronica der Römischen Ketzer," ccv, verso, ff.
304 Zurich Q3 adds: *who, as the descendants of the above-mentioned authors, are leading and inciting the magistracy into such an intrusion*
305 *Margin*: Galatians 4[:29]
306 *Margin*: John 1[:1-9]

Christ himself spoke of this in a parable, Matthew 13[:24-30], that the householder did not want to gather the weeds until the time of harvest. For when the servant said to the lord, "Do you want us to go and gather them," he answered, "No, for in gathering the weeds you would uproot the wheat along with them. Let both of them grow together until the harvest." Here we see bright and clear that it is not the Lord's will[307] to uproot the weeds through physical means, even if our faith were likened to weeds, but rather the good will be separated from the evil only at the end of the world, and only then will the weeds be burned with fire.

And at another place he talks of those who disdain his Word, "On that day it will be more tolerable for Sodom and Gomorrah than for them" [Luke 10:12]. *The Lord, however, does not say to his disciples that they were to coerce people with force, but as noted above, they were to shake the dust from their shoes and go out from them,* Matthew 10[:14]; Mark 6[:11]; Luke 9[:5], 10[:11]. <146>

Therefore it is neither Christ's nor his apostles' command to defend the Gospel with the sword and with coercion and persecution in the manner of the law, for the Gospel of the heart demands righteousness, which can be compelled with no sword or act of violence such as is carried out in the name of civil fidelity and the decency of the law. For here, only a free Sarah is valid, but no Hagar [Genesis 21:8-14] in this free kingdom, for which reason Christians are called the free, voluntary bearers of gifts, Psalm 110[:3]; 2 Corinthians 9[:5]; Philippians 1. Therefore *no one who is coerced can do anything good or pleasing before God, for the Lord desires to have the heart, and a voluntary, joyous provider and worker rather than a forced service, servant and work.*

For in this free kingdom, where the pure freedom of the Spirit reigns, everything runs free, un-coerced and unforced, as noted above. Therefore one is to live in accordance with the command and teaching of Scripture, and in accordance with the example of Christ, the apostles, and the first church. Likewise in accordance with the right interpretation of the old and new teachers, spiritual things, faith, and the kingdom of God do not square with nor dare be confused with the worldly sword, and God thus does not reach for the sword and the courts when issuing his verdict, etc.

In this regard the above-mentioned teachers *have written much, and in great seriousness, since they perhaps were apprehensive that [the worldly*

---

307 Zurich Q3 adds: *as far as faith is concerned*

sword] might be applied to them. But now, since this freedom [in spiritual matters] seems to go against them, <147> they are again fleeing from the sun back into the shade,³⁰⁸ *contradicting their own above-mentioned teachings and writings concerning the worldly sword and the role of the magistracy, under the pretense of upholding the Gospel, as one may sufficiently hear and observe.*

In their teaching and preaching they are again goading, compelling, inciting, and stirring up people, as is happening to us, coercing and forcing people with duress and laws on account of matters of faith and the soul—such as going to church and similar issues—persecuting, executing, banishing, and afflicting those who do not obey them. To be sure, this happens in some places more ardently than in others. Through all this the teachers become participants in the shedding of innocent blood, thereby also leading the magistrates and other people as well into such sin.

*Some years ago in a synod held at Bern, according to the proceedings as published in a book in 1532,*³⁰⁹ *the preachers again established the worldly magistracy in the churches, for it to rule or reign over the outward teachings and life of the Gospel or faith, through which faith and conscience consequently are coerced with commands—bidding and forbidding—in outward things, permitting no dissent. Christian freedom was again suspended, and in its place a Mosaic coercion instituted, which again contradicts their above-noted teaching, and at the same time violates their own standards of scholarship, returning from the teaching of Christ back again to Moses, from a filial relationship again into slavery,* from the Promised Land back again into Egypt's <148> wilderness and Babylon.³¹⁰

---

308 Zurich Q3 adds: *again putting on the shoe which was trod upon*
309 The reference is to *Berner Synodus. Ordnung wie sich pfarrer und prediger zu Statt un Land Bern / in leer und leben/ verhalten söllen / mit wyterem bericht von Christo / unnd den Sacramenten ... am ix tag Januarii, AN. MDXXXII.* Facsimile edition: *Der Berner Synodus,* ed. Gottfried Locher (Neukirch: Neukircher Verlag, 1984). The introduction, written in the name of the mayor and the large and small councils, makes it clear that the published decrees of the synod were to be obeyed by all, on pain of civil punishment. Transgressors were to expect a punishment that would make visible "how much God's honor and disobedience to His Word means to us." Ibid., 26 (page 6 of original print).
310 The Bernese Ordinance of 1532 explicitly states that the authorities have power only over "outward things," and that no civil authority can coerce consciences in "spiritual and heavenly things." Ibid., 31 (page 8 of original print). The Anabaptist

A Short, Simple Confession

For how can one understand the coercing of faith otherwise than through outward bidding and forbidding, and on top of that, persecuting in matters of faith? *They also have, in the past, as already noted, labeled such coercion and persecution as tyranny.*[311] Consider them now, what they are now carrying out: this is in no way the preaching of God's pure Gospel, but rather much more its exact opposite, as already noted.

The Christian, Gospel-oriented people neither desire nor teach the forcing of anyone with coercion to attend their oral instruction, preaching, fellowship, or any other such thing, but rather indeed teach, as found above, the exact opposite, that one must never coerce another with force. For Paul, in Galatians 1[:9-10], declares as accursed that which is otherwise proclaimed, and continues saying: "If I were still pleasing people, I would not be a servant of Christ." But the current scholars and scribes of this world so remain— still pleasing people, to whom they show great honor, and are [in turn] well provided for with temporal goods, whereby one such person alone has more in way of salary, stipends and goods than had all the apostles together.

Rudolf Walter writes in his third sermon in "Concerning the Incarnation of Christ,"[312] *regarding the arrival of the Son of God into this world, and the first shelter <149> which he found in Bethlehem in the stable, in the crib, among the unknowing animals.*[313] *"We dare not be too surprised," he writes, "or blame those from Bethlehem or the Jews on account of their ignorance or aversion, since unfortunately this happens daily, and the majority of the people are so harsh and rude that when Christ comes to them in the form of His poor and thirsty members, the people even begrudge him the stable— not to speak of the tyranny and gruesome persecutions that drive the Lord Christ with His Word into the woods and caves whereby he often has to be completely on the run. For unfortunately it often comes to this," he writes,*

---

writer is not impressed by the argument, saying that by coercing obedience in the "outward things" of faith, consciences are being coerced as well. This argument is taken up again, in more detail, in an addendum to "Concerning Separation," copied in the codex beginning at page <401>.

311 Zurich Q3 concludes this paragraph: *learned scholars and [their] writings testify what their fathers judge concerning them.*

312 Rudolf Walter, *Die Menschwerdung deß waarenn / ewigen und eingebornen Suns Gottes*. Accessed online at: http://www.e-rara.ch/zuz/content/titleinfo/1267910, April 29, 2014. Citation below is found on print 130 verso to 131 recto (pages 263-64 on website location).

313 Zurich Q3 adds: *described on folio 1, leaf 2*

"that many prefer to tolerate all sorts of vicious and evil people, and hold in high esteem people who deceive and lead them into public idolatry and harmful unbelief. And they find sanctuary and protection with the princes and lords, who give them a high position in the great church cathedrals, along with expensive temples and palaces. Meanwhile, next to them the true believers in Christ, along with their Christ and his Gospel, are like beggars who may find a small corner in which they may be safe. Yes indeed, they would be truly satisfied if one allowed them to stay in the stable! But no one should be angry or mistaken about this, since it was no different for the Lord Christ at the beginning of His incarnation."[314] Indeed we would <150> truly be satisfied if the preachers would abide by their own writings, as has been noted numerous times above.

"But," Paul writes further in Galatians 4[:29], "just as at that time the child who was born according to the flesh persecuted the child who was born according to the Spirit, so it is now also," etc. This we wish to commit to the evaluation and judgment of the devout Christian God-fearing reader, on the basis of the pure, clear, and undeceiving Word of God and the writings and books of the highly learned secular scholars themselves [concerning] whether it is suitable for rulers to compel persons to believe through the use of force, sword, water, fire, incarceration, torture, tyranny, or persecution; whether they should, by such means, build up and expand the Church of Christ. Likewise what the nature of a magistrate's office is and what the office of a truly born-again Christian is, and to what extent the two are compatible and may be combined with one another. Likewise, under what circumstances a magistrate may wield a worldly scepter and not interfere in the affairs of Christendom to its detriment; also what the nature and characteristics of a true Christian are according to the prophets and the teachings of Christ and his holy apostles, as we have written above—what kind of a model they have prescribed for us and how we may prove and demonstrate it conclusively; and who would want to deny [the magistrate] his worldly scepter and magisterial office. Anyone who has truly received the Spirit of Christ will certainly be able to find an unequivocal judgment here. <151>

No doubt, the scribes of this world can tickle the ears of the magistrates and with flattering words convince them that they are

---

314 Zurich Q3 [*Margin*]: *Whoever so desires may read in the first sermon of this book: page 1, leaves 2-3*

Christians and Christian rulers and lords, even though, alas, they hardly lead a moral and Christian life. Sad to say, it is apparent to everyone with what fruits they prove their Christianity. The scribes know only too well why they praise the magistrates: namely, because they hold large and rich church livings from the rulers. They would not enjoy these if they did not say what the magistrates like to hear. For if they were to tell the magistrates that they are not Christians, the magistrates would not tolerate their wealthy incomes. These prophets know this only too well, and so they must tickle the magistrates' ears with praise and flattering words to their liking. In doing so, they defend and protect the magistrates, helping them hold the field. They affirm that they are Christian magistrates even though the latter have knowingly violated all of the good statutes introduced at the beginning of the Reformation and were the first to bring disorder into the movement. In spite of all this, the scribes still want to make Christian magistrates of them. But that cannot be, and is a vain consolation.

When a magistrate possesses the characteristics that a born-again Christian should have, as described above, then we do in fact believe that a magistrate can be a Christian, and a Christian a magistrate. <152> That is, if he truly lives and acts in accordance with the Gospel, as undoubtedly those Christians of the New Testament did who held such offices, such as the Centurion, Cornelius, Paul, Sergius, Erastus, the warden, all of whom were officials of the emperor—and also others. Where that happens, the Spirit, who is the ruler of consciences, will teach [magistrates] how to act, how to be guided much more by love than by anything contrary to it. Such a magistrate will not act in an unseemly manner; he will not be one who bends the law because of the person concerned, nor will he oppress the poor, but will avoid such actions.

Where this is not the case, we leave it to those who have been anointed with the Holy Spirit to judge whether such a person is a Christian ruler or a worldly magistrate. In short, we cannot, according to the teachings of the Gospel, consider a carnal, unregenerate person to be a Christian, even though he may be a king or an emperor. For the office does not make anyone Christian. This can only be done by the Holy Spirit who renews human hearts; the Holy Spirit will make and provide Christians. Consequently, those who are quick to make non-reborn [persons] into Christian magistrates will have great difficulty accounting for their actions.

Many a person <153> who has observed their life and their rule, and tried to assess it, has seen the extent to which such praise of their Christian and brotherly disposition is justified.

Therefore, it would be appropriate to instruct the magistrate, or others in his entourage who have ears to hear, how he could really become a Christian. Because of such a magistrate's virtue, others would then also realize what they are doing and change—if indeed they have ears to hear. For faith is not for everyone. The anointing and the Spirit of Christ will teach what should and should not be done. Therefore Christians cannot in good conscience agree with those who so easily make [magistrates] into gods and Christians, especially since the majority of them, as is lamentably obvious, live unchristian lives in lasciviousness of the flesh, pride, arrogance, ambition, drunkenness, gluttony, swearing, lying, and adultery that [their minds have become] darkened. It would be better for such rulers to be confronted with the wrath of God, following the teaching of Christ and the apostles, rather than be presented with such a false image of themselves. If this were done, magistrates might repent and be converted. This would be better for their souls than filling them with a vain hope, for true repentance is the proper noble plaster with which to cover the wounds of sin.

But even when such prophets confront the magistrate and his subjects with the letter of the law, giving the appearance that they are not flatterers in sheep's clothing, they still take care not to press them too hard for fear of being attacked. As a consequence, conditions never change. Therefore their sermons accomplish nothing, for the priests and prophets are just like their listeners, for they take it upon themselves to teach others while they themselves are unteachable. They preach that one is not to steal, but they do so themselves, even stealing from God what belongs to him. They preach that one is not to commit adultery, but are themselves adulterers.[315] Likewise, they preach against pride, greed, and ambition, but are themselves prideful, greedy, arrogant, and ambitious. They boast loudly and extravagantly of the Gospel with their mouths, but violate it with their life and deeds, as their own parishioners testify. If one just looks at what they say, they look as though they were the most pious people on earth, declaring they have meant it sincerely. They become like a pack of wild cats, raising a great hue and cry about

---

315 *Margin*: Romans 2[:1-11]

A Short, Simple Confession

Christ and God in heaven so that one would think and fear that one had made a mistake for not holding them to be the true prophets. But if one then sees and observes their life and conduct, one discovers the precise opposite of what they have been saying <155> and boasting about.

They give the appearance of a God-pleasing life but deny its power. They speak and sing much about God, Christ and his Gospel, praising virtue and piety, and write lengthy books about them. But if anyone so much as questions them about these things, they incite the magistrates against such a one and make sure that he receives the age-old recompense for such deeds, the same recompense that the prophets, Christ, and his apostles also received. But clearly they do not wish to be like the scribes and Jewish priests who opposed and in fact scolded and condemned the prophets, Christ, and his apostles. They openly declared before the entire world how terribly the [scribes] erred and sullied themselves with the blood of innocents, exactly as the Old Testament scribes did and said. Had we lived at the time of our fathers, they said, we would not have participated in spilling the blood of the prophets. Yet these were the very ones who delivered Christ and his apostles to be executed. In doing so, they filled the measure of their fathers.

The current prophets do the same: they exalt and highly praise the holy Gospel. But if one sincerely desires to live according to its precepts, bids the world farewell, gives oneself up to a truly repentant life, <156> sacrifices every temporal honor along with the good life, and despises what the world does and is able to do, concentrating solely on the kingdom of God, they soon regard him as mad and make sport of him. Even today these [so-called] prophets play with the members and disciples of Christ, inciting the magistrates to persecute them. God will deal with them in his own good time, however, and extend to them—measure for measure—what they have laid upon others. The judgment which they imposed upon the scribes of the Old Testament will fall upon their heads, and what they foretold and prophesied in that case will become true in theirs.

Paul says,[316] "Though I were to speak with the tongues of men and of angels, and do not have love, I am like a sounding brass, or a tinkling cymbal. And though I have the gift of prophecy, and understand all mysteries and have all knowledge, and though I had all faith so that I could

---

316 *Margin*: 1 Corinthians 13[:1-3]

remove mountains, and do not have love, I am nothing. And even though I give all my goods to the poor, and give my body to be burned, and I do not have love, it does me no good." Love fulfills the law and returns good for evil. Whether this true love is to be found, as it should be, with those who use their power ruthlessly and act in the manner mentioned above, those who have been persecuted and outlawed by them know only too well. <157> For they refuse to tolerate anyone who wishes to walk on the right path and separate himself from the sins and vices of this world in accordance with the [commands of] the Holy Scriptures: either he must do as they do or be banished from the land. By acting in such a manner, these prophets and shepherds demonstrate the kind of faith and love they have and whose spirit's children they are.

It has been amply proven, therefore, that such prophets are mere word mongers whose sermons are without fruit and consequence. For they have studied and learned their art and philosophy at the secular universities as one would any other craft, some of them without the Spirit and any life-giving power. Whoever has learned his craft well can expect to be rewarded with a generous living. Therefore a true faith and a pure, unfeigned love active in good deeds is far from such a person, as one truly sees and perceives from their fruit. But we will let devout readers reach their own conclusions as to whether we or our detractors are the ones who are muddying the pure, wholesome waters of grace, and uprooting and destroying the true peace of Christ and his members.

The Fourth Article

Whether or not a Christian may swear an oath, that is, use the name of God as a witness <158>

With regard to this article, we hope that we have distinguished at enough length between the old and the new person, the written law given on Mount Sinai and the law of the Spirit that came out of Zion and Jerusalem, as discussed in the first article [above]. And we hope that every God-understanding person will accept it.

A Short, Simple Confession

Since, as can be proven, oath swearing did not derive from the law that issued from Zion, but rather from the law that was received on Sinai, we will leave [oath swearing] to the old person, to those who are still under the written law. The new and born-again person will be content with yes and no, as he has been taught by his lord and master. Indeed, his yes and no is more to be trusted than the oath of the old man. For Christ said with emphasis: "You have heard that it was said to those of old, you shall not swear a false oath but shall fulfill your oaths to God." *Note that the Lord stresses that those of old were forbidden to swear a false oath, but the swearing and keeping of true oaths was allowed.* "But I say unto you," Jesus the highly lauded prince and king over all kings says, "that you shall not swear at all, neither by heaven for it is God's throne, nor by the earth for it is his footstool, neither by Jerusalem for it is the city of a great king. <159> Nor shall you swear by your head, for you are not able to make even one hair white or black. Instead, let your speech be yes, yes, no, no. Anything beyond that comes from evil" [Matthew 5:33-37]. Note well what the great king says—the one before whom we do well to bow and humble ourselves, obeying and following him with all our heart—whatever is beyond yes and no comes from evil. James says the same thing in chapter 5 [James 5:12], "But above all things, my brothers, swear not, neither by heaven nor by the earth, neither by any other oath. But let your yes be yes and your no be no, lest you fall into temptation." The apostle Paul says the same thing in Hebrews 6[:16], "Men swear by someone greater than they, and an oath of confirmation ends all strife."

Christians are not to dispute, quarrel, or swear, for an oath serves to confirm something that is either promised or in dispute. And in the law it is commanded that it be done in the name of God, only truthfully and not falsely. But Christ, who teaches the perfection of the law as we have heard, forbids his followers to swear at all, whether truly or falsely, neither by heaven nor by earth, neither by Jerusalem or one's own head for the reasons given above, for a person cannot make a single hair white or black. Therefore the Christian is forbidden to swear at all, <160> for we cannot make what was promised in the oath come to fruition if we cannot even change the smallest thing on our own person.

But some, who do not wish to believe the straightforward command of God, say: Yes, but did not God swear to Abraham in his own name when he promised that he wished him well and desired to be his God if he observed his commands? Why then should not I also swear when I promise someone something? The apostle Paul answers such people when he writes in Hebrews chapter 6[:17-18], "Since God wished more abundantly to show the heirs of promise the immutability of his counsel, He confirmed it by an oath, so that by two immutable things, in which it was impossible for God to lie, we might have a strong consolation." We should note as well that God has the power to do what he forbids us to do, for all things are possible with Him. God swore an oath to Abraham in order to prove that his counsel was immutable; that is, that no one may resist or hinder [the fulfillment of] his will. Therefore he can keep his oath. We, however, can do no such a thing, as Christ said above, and therefore we ought not to swear.

Others say that we have not been forbidden to swear by God in the New Testament, and in the Old Testament even commanded to do so. We have only been forbidden to swear by heaven, earth, Jerusalem, and our own heads. Christ responds to such people: <161> Whoever swears by heaven swears by the throne of God and by him who sits on it. One should note, therefore, that if one is forbidden to swear by heaven, which is the throne of God, how much more is it forbidden to swear by God himself. You blind and foolish people, says the Lord, what is greater, the throne or he who sits on it?

Still others say, if it is wrong for men to use God to confirm the truth, then the apostles Peter and Paul, who swore in this way, [did wrong]. We answer this by pointing out that Peter and Paul only witness to that which God promised Abraham through his oath; they themselves promise nothing, as the examples clearly indicate. Now witnessing and swearing are two different things, for in swearing one promises that something will take place in the future, as Christ was promised to Abraham. We received the fulfillment of that promise much later. But a witness testifies to whether something is good or bad in the present. They also spoke of that which the Holy Spirit had promised the elect in their hearts, which applied to some of the elect prophets and apostles of both the Old and New Testaments, but not to others. No human examples, however, may darken, overthrow or reverse the words that have come forth from the mouth of eternal truth, for [such examples] are all too weak, dull or powerless. For these words of truth will prevail in all eternity against all carnal reason, cleverness <162> and no sophistic glosses will be able to darken them.

Therefore only the old Adam, still under the written law that was given on Sinai, is obligated to confirm the truth through an oath. The new man, however, who has been freed from the constraints of the written law, is content simply to live by the spiritual law issued from Zion and Jerusalem by Christ Jesus, and confirms the truth with no and yes. That is what we, through the assistance and grace of God, want to adhere to in all simplicity. We do not wish to add to it or detract from it, for the Lord Christ says, "Whoever nullifies even the least of these commandments and teaches the people accordingly, will be the least in the kingdom of heaven. But whoever both teaches and fulfills them will be exalted in heaven." Saint John in Revelation 22[:18] agrees, saying, "If anyone takes away from the words of this book, God will remove his name from the book of life." May the Lord Jesus save us from this in all eternity. Amen.

The Fifth Article

Whether God the Father, God the Son and God the Holy Spirit constitute one eternal essence <163>

Because of the recognition that God the Father and his Son, Jesus Christ,[317] whom he has sent, is eternal life, this article concerning God the Father, God the Son, and God the Holy Spirit is unquestionably a necessary article. Nevertheless, the recognition of God's majesty does not only consist in being able to speak well and wisely about it. For there are probably many who believe and hold correct views [on the Trinity] and still do not possess the grace to speak convincingly about it. Furthermore, it is also probable that many speak correctly and convincingly about it out of custom [and tradition], imitation, and ability and still do not truly apprehend God the Father, God the Son, or God the Holy Spirit.

For it is true and incontrovertible that the person who says he knows God but does not obey his commandments is a liar, and that he who sins has not seen or known him, as Saint John says in his epistle [1 John 3:9-10]. Furthermore, Christ refused to concede to the Jews that they knew His father or had seen his form, for his word did not live in them, and their consuming desire was to stone and crucify him rather than to believe in

---

317 *Margin*: John 17

him. Therefore, whoever wishes to learn about the Trinity must devote himself to obeying it, allow it to cleanse his heart so that he does Christ's will above all else. Then the Trinity will reveal itself to him. <164> For those who have unclean hearts may never see, much less know [the Trinity], for it is a knowledge that cannot be passed from one person to another, nor can a person acquire it from another without the Trinity's consent. But where it discovers an abode prepared to receive it, there it enters in. That is why the Lord says: "No one knows the Son except the Father, and no one knows the Father except the Son. Therefore the Father must reveal and make known the Son and the Son the Father" [Matthew 11:27; Luke 10:22].

Likewise [he says that] no one can come to Him except the Father draws him [John 6:44]. To Peter he says: "Flesh and blood have not revealed this to you, but my Father who is in heaven" [Matthew 16:17]. Since, then, flesh and blood cannot impart such an understanding through its own power, nor receive it from anyone else, one should teach people to pray to the Father to reveal his Son, that the Son be revealed to them by the Father through the power of the Holy Spirit. One should not seek to instill a knowledge of the Trinity through subtle and clever words or demand that a person speak of him with subtle and clever words. For in doing so one only falls into greater quarreling and conflict, damning and accusing one another of heresy, before either party has received a proper fear or love of God. It is out of the latter—as out of a well—that these things flow <165> and from which alone one can draw and learn them.

In short, in regard to this article we are in agreement with those who believe as follows about the Holy Trinity, namely, that God the Father, God the Son, and God the Holy Spirit are one God; the Father in the Son, and the Son in the Father, the Holy Spirit, however, in both. But the Father is not the Son, nor the Son the Father, or the Holy Spirit the Father or the Son. Rather, that the Father is the same as the Son, and the Son the same as the Father, except with regard to their characteristics [*eigenschafft*] as we shall explain. And that the Holy Spirit is nothing that he has not received from the Father and the Son. The Father has life in and of himself; this life he has given to his Son so that he should have it from the Father.

But that God is one essential being, but that this one essential being is differentiated as three persons—namely, the Father, the Son, and the Holy Spirit—is not only proven by the fact that our Lord Christ commanded baptism in the name of the Father, the Son, and the Holy Spirit, but also the

Gospel of John testifies concerning the one God in three persons. There the heavenly master Jesus Christ teaches that the Godhead consists of one God, but that same one God is also divided into three persons. First he speaks of the Father who sent him and commanded him <166> to do the Father's will. Likewise, of himself he says that he is the Son, that he came to suffer and die, and that he will return to the Father. And of the Holy Spirit he says that after him will come the Comforter, the Spirit of Truth, whom his Father will send in his name. [This Spirit] will teach Christ's disciples all things and lead them into all truth, taking it away from his people and declaring it to us.

Here we clearly have one God, and three independent [*selbstendige*] persons in the one Godhead, namely the Father, and his Son Jesus Christ, and the Holy Spirit, who is the common Spirit of the Father and the Son. Though he issued from the Father and works in the hearts of the believers through the Son, he is inseparable from them. We confess this in the 12 Articles of the Christian faith which state: I believe in God the Father almighty, creator of heaven and earth, and in Jesus Christ his only begotten Son our Lord. Then follows: I believe in the Holy Spirit. Thus the Christian faith confesses one God in three persons. We wish first, however, to speak of the Father and the Son.

One of the characteristics of the Father is that he has an equally powerful Son, God of God, light of light, born of him <167> in all eternity before time began but who later, in [human] time, became man. Through him God created all things; through him he also sustains, administers, and rules all things. And rightly so, since the power to give birth to and create belongs properly to the Father; and the Father, who is of one being with the Son, is yet distinguished from him in his personhood.

In contrast, it is the characteristic or property of the Son that he is truly born of the Father, that he is the word, the power and the wisdom of the Father. Indeed, he is the very image of his Father's being[318] as Paul describes it in Hebrews chapter 1[:9-10]: That the Father, through him, as we have said, created all things. Likewise that he, in the fullness of time, became flesh or man, and as man suffered for us in the flesh, died, rose again, and ascended to heaven, and now sits at the right hand of his almighty Father, from whence he shall return. From this it is clear and apparent that the Son is born of the Father, that he was not, nor could he be, born of himself. For

---

318 *das ebenbild seines vätterlichen wesens ist ...*

nothing gives birth to itself and [anything born] must have the essence of its Father. Therefore, even though the Father and the Son have the same essential being and therefore are one God, they nevertheless constitute two separate and independent persons or names in God. From these comes the Holy Spirit as the third person or name, but even he is one essential being, indeed one God, with the Father and the Son.[319]

But that Christ says, I and the Father are one, <168> the Father in him and he in the Father, we take to be a figure of speech through which the Lord wished to teach us how intimate a fellowship he had with the Father, and the Father with him. In a similar speech he said: "I desire that they [the disciples] and I become one just as you and I are one" [John 17:21]. The disciples did not therefore become the Lord, or the Lord the disciples. In the same way the Father is not the Son, nor the Son the Father. What Christ said to Philip, "Whoever sees me sees the Father," is also a figure of speech [John 14:9]. Therefore we are to take careful note, for he expresses himself in like manner to his disciples when he says, "Whoever receives you also receives me" [John 13:20; Matthew 10:40; Mark 9:37]. Therefore the Lord is not himself the Father, nor the disciples the Lord. But the Father's power and characteristics are present in the Lord, just as the Lord's characteristics and power are present in the disciples. The Father does nothing without the Son, the Son nothing without the Father. The Lord, however, could do all things without his disciples. But he does not wish to do so. The disciples, however, even should they wish to do so, can do nothing without their Lord. Through him, though, they can do all things.

Concerning the Holy Spirit

As far as the third person of the Godhead is concerned, namely the Holy Spirit, we have already confessed that the Holy Spirit is God but is distinguished from the Father and the Son <169> by his office and personal characteristics. He is the Spirit of the Father, the Spirit of Christ, the Spirit of God, the Spirit of the Lord. He teaches us to understand Christ correctly and declares to us his great and mighty glory, his perfect Godhead and royal majesty. He takes from that which belongs to Christ and declares to his believers and elect that they love Christ—the truth of God—through him who is the Spirit of truth; that they honor, petition,

---

319 *Margin*: John 14

and acknowledge him. He fills them through Christ with many different gifts and graces.

The Holy Spirit also judges the world because of its sin, convinces it that it is lost, imprudent, and unbelieving when it comes to the things of God. He demonstrates that no vessel in our houses and carnal Adamic huts stands in the right place, in the place it ought to stand before God, as long as we do not make use of his power and remain unconverted[320] and unregenerate. He demonstrates that all our strength has been ruined and our hearts are dead in God's sight. In sum, that we are by nature poor, miserable sinners, and if we are not helped we must be eternally lost and damned.

But then [the Holy Spirit] also shows us the savior Jesus Christ and declares to us the grace-filled Gospel that is repentance and the forgiveness of sins in his name. He moves and compels us to confess our sins, to have remorse and be sorrowful over them, to weep over them, so that from our hearts we long to come to know Christ as healer and forgiver of sins. <170> He also teaches us to pray fervently, for in the prophets he is called a Spirit of grace and prayer. He ignites the believing heart with the fire of God's love, enlightens and strengthens what is dull and weak, warms and heats up what is cold and frozen before God, and consoles those who grieve over and regret their sins. He gathers believers together into a fellowship of saints, grants them one heart and mind, and unites them in Christ in an unfeigned brotherly love. He accepts people into God's family and makes them heirs in the kingdom of God. He grants his chosen servants a pure and genuine judgment in their hearts that can distinguish the clean from the unclean, the pure from the impure, the evil from the good.

[The Holy Spirit] is the only teacher of the Holy Scriptures, the true key of David. He alone has the ability to understand and interpret in accordance with the heart of God. He also wrote it through his servants. He is the one who explains the wonderful secrets of the kingdom of God and extends to believers the heavenly treasures of God's grace which Jesus Christ acquired for us through his bitter death. He is the one who refreshes and stills the hungry and thirsty hearts that long for Christ and his righteousness. He is the right pledge, seal and hope of all believers, Romans 8[:4-11]; Ephesians 1[:3-14]; 2 Corinthians 1[:21-22]. This is what the Holy Spirit is, in his office, work, power, characteristics and essential being. <171>

---

320 *nitt widergeboren*: 'un-reborn'

Now, one should not think that the Holy Spirit does all these things without Christ, as though he were separated from Christ in his office or actions because he is a person in his own right. Not at all. Rather, even though the illumination, sanctification, renewal, and completion of our salvation is the particular domain of the Holy Spirit, there is nonetheless no separation; it is one single unified operation, one strength, power, reality of all three persons in the Godhead. God does everything through Christ, Christ, however, the noble prince and ruling king of God, does it all in the Holy Spirit, who as a Spirit of the Father and Son is eternally praised.

Similarly, just as the Holy Spirit does not depart from the Father and the Son—even though he does not remain in the Father and the Son—in the same way Christ is not separated from the Holy Spirit in order that he, as well as the Father, can be present with us in and through the Holy Spirit. Indeed, Christ directs his kingdom and rule in the Holy Spirit, in and through whom Christ the Lord lives in all the hearts of the faithful. Through him He also plants eternal life within us, transforming us into new persons and children of God. Whoever loves me, says the Lord, will obey my word, and my Father will love him. We will come to him and erect our dwelling place near to him. I do not intend to leave you orphaned; for I will surely come to you in the Holy Spirit [John 14:15-21]. <172> Therefore there is no separation in the holy Trinity, only unity in all its actions. There is one strength and one operation of the Father, of the Son, and of the Holy Spirit, though without a submerging of the personal characteristics, as we have said. This must be recognized.

The office or work of the holy Trinity is the salvation of humankind. This is divided in such a manner that, originally, God the Father was to create the world, his son Jesus Christ our Lord was to save us, re-create us and make us fit for the future world, and the Holy Spirit was to renew us, make us spiritual and sanctify us, ignite us with spiritual power and light, to make our hearts steadfast and filled with grace in all eternity.

But now the Father has done nothing in creation without the Son and the Holy Spirit.[321] Rather, He created human beings and all things through the Son in the Holy Spirit. Just as the Son has not regenerated and saved us without the Father and the Holy Spirit,[322] so the Holy Spirit has not sanctified, renewed, made us spiritual or illuminated us apart from God

---

321 *Margin*: God the Father does nothing without the Son and the Holy Spirit
322 *Margin*: God the Son does nothing without the Father and the Holy Spirit

the Father and the Son.[323] Therefore one can recognize the unity of the Godhead through the actions of the various offices of the three persons of the Trinity, and that the Holy Spirit does nothing without Christ the Son of God, or without God the Father whose Spirit he is. Just as God the Father and Christ his Son do nothing without the Holy Spirit, <173> even so the Holy Spirit does nothing without Christ and God, who rule humankind through the Holy Spirit who dwells or lives in us. For where the Father is or dwells, there the Son and Holy Spirit also live, because all three are one unified Godhead now and in all eternity.

The response we have given to this article will have to suffice for the time being for reasons that will become apparent towards the end of the next article. We hope that it is not opposed to the Athanasian Creed which was accepted at Nicea. We omitted it here for the sake of brevity.

The Sixth Article

Whether or not Christ adopted the essence of his human body from the substance of the Virgin Mary or whether he took it from some other source

The Lord God spoke to the snake, Genesis 3[:15], "I will put enmity between you and the woman, and between your seed and her seed; and it shall trample on your head."

The holy evangelists and apostles describe the incarnation of the Son of God, our dear Lord Jesus Christ, in short and clear terms, thus: in Matthew 1[:20] the evangelist writes that the angel said to Joseph, do not be afraid to take Mary as your wife, for that which is to be born of her is from the Holy Spirit. <174> Luke writes in chapter 1 [Luke 1:35] that the angel said to Mary, the Holy Spirit will come upon you, and the power of the Most High will overshadow you. Therefore also that holy thing that shall be born of you shall be called the Son of God. And St. John says in chapter 1 [John 1:1-3; 14]: "In the beginning was the Word, and the Word was with God, and

---

323 *Margin*: God the Holy Spirit does nothing without the Father and the Son

the Word was God. The same was in the beginning with God. All things were made by him; and without him nothing was made that was made. . . . And the Word became flesh and dwelt among us, and we beheld his glory, the glory as of the only begotten of the Father, full of grace and truth." Later, in his first epistle chapter 1[1 John 1:1-2] he writes: "That which was from the beginning, which we have heard, which we have seen with our eyes, which we have looked upon, and our hands have handled, of the Word of life; for the life was made manifest and we have seen it, and bear witness and show you the life that is eternal, which was with the Father."

St. Paul says thus in Hebrews 2[:11-12], "For both he that sanctifies and they that are sanctified all come from one; because of this he is not ashamed to call them brothers saying, I will declare your name unto my brethren, and in the midst of the community I will sing praise to you." Likewise, [Hebrews 2:14-18] "Forasmuch then as the children are partakers of flesh and blood, he also himself <175> took part of the same, that through death he might destroy him that had power over death, that is, the devil. And he delivered them who through fear of death were subject to bondage all their lives. For he took to himself not the nature of angels, but of the seed of Abraham. Wherefore in all things it behooved him to be made like unto his brethren, that he might be a merciful and faithful high priest before God, to make reconciliation for the sins of the people. For in that he himself suffered and was tempted, he is able to help those who are tempted."

In Matthew 22[:42-45] Christ says to the Pharisees, "What do you think of Christ? Whose son is he? They said to him, the son of David. He said to them, how then does David in spirit call him Lord, saying, God said to my Lord, sit on my right hand till I make your enemies into your footstool. If David then calls him Lord, how can he be his son?" Furthermore, in John chapter 6 [John 6:50-51] Christ says, "I am the living bread that came down from heaven; whoever eats of this bread shall live forever; and the bread that I will give is my flesh, which I will give for the life of the world." And in [John] chapter 3 [John 3:31-33] he says concerning this, "He who comes from above is above all; he that is of the earth is earthly, and speaks of the earth; (but) he that comes from heaven is above all and testifies to what he has seen and heard <176> and no man accepts his testimony. But he who accepts it sets his seal to the fact that God is true." That is why Paul says, 1 Corinthians 15[:43-49] "The first man Adam was made into a natural life; the last Adam was made into a spiritual life. The spiritual body was not

A Short, Simple Confession

the first, rather the natural one was; the spiritual one came afterwards. The first man is of the earth and earthly; the second is from heaven and heavenly. As is the earthly, such also are they that are earthly; and as is the heavenly, such are also they that are heavenly."

In all simplicity, we wish to let the matter rest on Paul's confession and such holy writings of Christ and his holy apostles. This article has caused many quarrels and much tension, as well as much slander and reviling. People condemn and accuse one another of heresy because of it. One party wishes to determine, by means of human wisdom and cleverness, how much of his substance Christ received from the highly blessed Virgin Mary; the other denies it and wishes to prove that he received absolutely nothing, neither flesh nor blood of her substance. They have reached great flights of fancy in these matters which have nothing to do with our salvation, as we shall soon see; yet those <177> things which we should reasonably be expected to know, and for which we will be held accountable before the judgment seat of Christ, they have—with their debates and irrelevant scholastic quarreling—missed or stupidly ignored. They have thus allowed the wholesome period of God's grace to slip away, have not taken seriously the correct and true fear of God, nor allowed the true and living active life of Christ to work in them. Nor have they given themselves up to that obedience which is the beginning of godly wisdom.[324]

Therefore with a few brief words we confess our Lord Jesus Christ to be the holy, pure, and immaculate Lamb of God, and say with the holy apostle Paul in Romans 1[:3-4], a Son of God according to the Spirit, and a son of David according to the flesh. And as Peter calls him, a Son of the living God [Matthew 16:16].

In order, on our part, not to give any more cause for debate and quarreling about this article we will conclude here. For we hope that when we have to give an account of our life and deeds before the judgment seat of Christ on Judgment Day, we will not be held accountable in this matter— having to say that we have not paid enough attention to this question, or how much or how little Christ received with regard to his flesh and blood from the substance of the pure Virgin Mary. <178> That is why we do not wish to spend too much time treating matters we will not have to answer for on the Day of Judgment, for we do not want to allow ourselves to be diverted from those things of which we will most assuredly have to give an account.

---

324 *Margin*: Wisdom [Ecclesiasticus] 1; James 3

For as the wise teachers say, what does it profit you to speak and dispute on the profound matters relating to the Trinity if you do not have humility and are therefore displeasing to the Trinity, Psalm 119, James 4[:6-10], 1 Peter 5[:5-6]? Truly, exalted words produce neither holy nor righteous persons; rather, a moral life makes a person loved of God, Matthew 5, 25[:31-46]; 1 Corinthians 4[:20], 14[:11-12]. I long to experience it more than I wish to know how to interpret it. Matthew 3[:8-10], 7[:21?], 11; 1 Corinthians 4[:20], 11, 13. Had you memorized the entire Bible and knew all the wise sayings of the Ancients, what good would it do you if you did not possess the grace and love of God, 1 Corinthians 13? If I knew everything that is in the world but did not know the love of God, what good would it do me before God who will judge me on the basis of my deeds, Matthew 25[:31-46], Romans 2[:2-6], 2 Corinthians 5[:10], Acts 20[:18-24]? Truly, a simple peasant or a humble layman who serves God is better than a proud scholar who is schooled and excels in many arts but neglects himself, Psalm 34, 1 Corinthians 8[:1; 11-12], 13. For those who know much wish to be noticed and love it when they are praised for their wisdom, 1 Corinthians 8.[325] Many things are of little use or even unnecessary for the soul to know. And the person who pays more attention to things that are not useful to the soul, or do not do the soul any good, <179> is a very unwise person, Matthew 6, Luke 20[:45-47], 12[:4-5]. Many words do not satisfy the soul, but rather a good life strengthens the spirit, 1 Corinthians 4[:26-31], and a clean conscience produces a sound confidence toward God, 2 Corinthians 1[:12]. The greater and the better your knowledge, the more you will be judged; unless, of course, you have lived in holiness according to your knowledge, Luke 12[:47-48], 19[:26].

Of what use are high and learned discussions of heavenly and hidden things if we will not be punished at the judgment for not knowing them, Matthew 25[:31-46], 1 Corinthians 2[:1-5], 13? It is sheer folly to neglect useful and necessary things and in their place pursue clever and more detrimental things; to have eyes that see, yet be blind, Matthew 7[:1-5], 13[:11-17], 23. Oh, if men would demonstrate as much diligence in rooting out their sins as they devote to asking their many questions, there would not be as much evil and strife in the world as there is now, Matthew 3[:7-10], 7[:3-5], 12[:9-14].

---

325 *Margin*: To know this, read 1 Corinthians 8

The Seventh Article

Whether or not children have been conceived in and born with original sin, and are therefore by nature children of wrath and eternal damnation

We answer this article in such a way that, without a doubt, no one except those who have no understanding of the Scriptures, will contradict it. For the Lord himself says in Genesis 8[:21] that the imagination of man's heart is evil from his youth. And David says in Psalm 51[:5], I was conceived in iniquity and in sin did my mother conceive me. Paul develops this theme of God's anger <180> even further, writing that through Adam's fall, sin and death entered into the whole world, and that through this one sinner's single sin everything was ruined. He says that death reigned from Adam until the time of Moses, even over those who had not sinned with the same transgression as Adam. Christ says the same thing: What is born of the flesh is flesh. And the apostle Paul says that flesh and blood will not inherit the kingdom of God; but those who may not see the kingdom of God are children of wrath. This is undoubtedly to be understood as applying not only to those who lived prior to the birth of Christ, but also to those who came afterwards to the very end of the world. On the other hand, Christ the Son of God opposed natural human tendencies and was obedient to his heavenly Father, even unto death on the cross. And so the guiltless, holy, pure, immaculate one suffered—as if he were a guilty one—for the sins of the entire world, as Saint John testifies in his epistle. As Paul says, Christ suffered for us while we were yet sinners and unbelievers. [Romans 5:8] And again, just as through one man's disobedience many sinners were created, even so through one man's obedience many have become righteous. [Romans 5:19] And if he died for the sins of the entire world, he also died for the sins that the children have received from their parents. If children are sinners because of Adam's disobedience, then they are made righteous again because of the obedience of Christ Jesus. For if many have died because of the sins of one man, then many more have been granted grace by means of God's gift, through the grace of the one man, Jesus Christ.

Therefore, and because of this grace which has been made available to all men through the merits of Jesus Christ, the Lord says: Unless a person becomes like a child, he may not enter the kingdom of God [Matthew 18:3].[326] And in another place he says: Let the little children come to me, for of such is the kingdom of heaven, Matthew 19[:14], Mark 10[:14]. Therefore, since the kingdom of heaven belongs to them, they are—as long as they remain in their innocence—no longer in Adam, but rather in Christ Jesus. And if they are in Christ Jesus there is nothing condemnable about them. That is, as long as they do not walk in the flesh and transgress God's commands when they come to the age of understanding and are able to do so. For all souls belong to God, as he says through Ezekiel; they are the Father's as well as the Son's. And the soul that sins is the one that must die, for no one is able to take upon oneself the sins of another person, lest he too fall into sin.

Therefore, despite the fact that the children have fallen under the disfavor and wrath that has come upon Adam, nevertheless this does not count against them because of Christ's merits, as long as they do not themselves sin. Because they still cannot distinguish between good and evil, sin is not attributed to them. If we have been reconciled to God through the death of Christ while we were yet sinners, why should the children be regarded as unreconciled? <182>

---

326 *Margin*: How one should follow Christ will follow in 12 articles.

The Eighth Article

Whether the perfect obedience of Christ, grasped through true faith, is the one and only sufficient payment for our sins and reason for our salvation, or whether we are saved partially by grace through faith in Christ, and partially through the cross and good works

Answer: No good works, no matter how splendid, that do not come from faith and a pure love, are good and acceptable before God as we can see in the writings of the prophets. That is why Christ rejected the Pharisees' praying, fasting, and giving of alms, saying: They already have their reward, for they did these things in public in order to be seen, without true faith and pure love. There is no true faith without repentance or love of neighbor. Just as a tree without fruit is not a good tree, and a body without a soul is dead, in the same way a faith without good works is dead, as James the apostle testifies [James 2:26]. Therefore we wish to state this article plainly and simply in the manner of the apostles who refused to separate good works from faith.

Even though the tree is to be recognized by its fruit, one does not display that fruit ostentatiously, for the Lord looks at the heart and often praises the lowly person rather than the high and mighty, as he did the widow who contributed her two mites to God's treasury, and <183> Mary Magdalene, who washed his feet with her tears and dried them with her hair, [as well as] the public sinner in the temple. Repentance does not come from the righteous but from a former sinner; often it is nothing more than a profound inner sorrow. Likewise it is impossible to have a living faith without love; it is also impossible to do good without love. For love is stronger than death and hell; it manifests itself in a sincere desire to love one's neighbor and serve him willingly and wholeheartedly. For that reason we are happy to abide by the words of the holy apostle Peter, who states in the Acts of the Apostles that all the prophets testify how through the name of Jesus Christ, all those who believe in him shall receive forgiveness of sins. In Acts 5[:30-31] he says, "God our Father raised up Jesus, whom you have killed, hanging him on a tree. Him God has raised by his right hand to be a prince and a savior, to give repentance to Israel and forgiveness of sins."

From this it is clearly to be understood that He does not desire a faith without repentance, for to believe in Christ does not mean that we may do what we wish, but rather that we do the will of Him in whom we believe. He has saved us through his holy, pure and innocent blood and, as much as possible, we should let it work in us. For the Lord himself said, as did John also at the beginning of his ministry: change your ways and repent, for the kingdom of God has come near to you. <184> Likewise: If you love me, keep my commands. And again: Whoever hears my words and fulfills them, loves me. If then there is no love where one does not keep his commands, how can that be faith where one does not obey his commands, nor encourages their being obeyed? Therefore Christ says further, Why do you call me Lord if you refuse to do what I have commanded? If then the Lord ties faith, repentance, and love together, why should we separate them and say, as some do, that faith alone, without the addition of any good works, saves us?

We certainly know well that, from youth on, our [human] nature is too corrupt to believe correctly or act rightly, and that a true and living faith and the ability to do what is right must come into us only from God above through the power and co-working of his Holy Spirit. That is the only place where we should and must seek it, for God the Lord is the initiator and perfector both of faith and good works.

Those who wish to add the words "only and alone" to faith, while rejecting repentance and love (which empowers all that is good), deny God's mercy thereby. They do not realize that they diminish God's promised power and his oft-demonstrated grace, for they think that human beings are less able to do good works than to believe. Therefore, since [God] is gracious to us because of our struggling will, that is, because of faith, therefore this makes his mercy that much greater a gift, even though faith and good works are both God's work in us. And true faith is in fact more than truly good works, indeed it is impossible for human beings. For Christ states that faith, even if it is only the size of a mustard seed, can move mountains, raise the dead, cleanse the leprous, heal the sick, make the blind to see, the lame to walk, and drive out the evil spirits.

Through these little words, "only and alone," some—we do not wish to be understood as saying everyone—have come to separate not only the great works mentioned above from true faith, but also those good works which the Lord has commanded everyone (who call themselves by his name) to do at all times, lest they incur his wrath and disfavor. If we do not have these works he does not wish us to call him Lord, as we said above. I do not wish that we should boast of a faith that ignores these works, for to praise and justify a faith without works is nothing more than to praise a tree as being good, even if it does not bear fruit; or to call someone wise who hears God's Word, but does not act in accordance with it, or to call a person a fool who hears it and acts accordingly. Or to damn that part of the acre in which the good seed sprouted and brought forth much fruit, while praising and justifying the other three parts in which, first, the birds ate the seed, second, in which the seed dried up <186> because it had no ground in which to take root, and the last part in which the sprouting seeds were stifled and killed by weeds and thorns [Mark 4:3-8; Luke 8:5-8]. For the Lord praises the tree not just for bearing fruit, but for bearing good fruit; and he compares a man who not only hears his Word, but also fulfills it, to a wise man who builds his house upon a rock; and he also praises only that part of the acre where the seed fell onto good soil and produced much fruit.

To those, however, who say that we cannot do these good works, we reply: If we can come to faith through his grace—which is the much greater part—why should we not also be able to produce good works by his help, which is the lesser part? For by saying the above we do not testify to our own inability, but to the weakness of God. It is as if we were to say, God is a gardener who plants a large beautiful tree so that it will have no flowers and produce no fruit. In doing this we must, as must the gardener, assume that the flower has to be taken as fruit. To speak in this manner is to say nothing less than that a faith without good works will justify men [before God]. All God-fearing persons will recognize what this means.

Would to God that many a person would more diligently consider this article than has been the case until now so that we would not be <187> counted by the Holy Spirit among those who treat our God's grace wantonly and flippantly and thus deny God and Christ our savior, of whom St. Jude speaks in his epistle. For He who can make a tree grow and blossom can also make it bear much good fruit.

Paul is correct when he says *that we are saved without doing the works of the law*, for the works of the law were circumcision, the Passover lamb, and the different food and drink offerings, together with their festivals and holidays, as we explained above in the first article. Paul, like Christ, wishes to lay these aside and discontinue the trust the Jews placed in such works. And because Christ is the true Passover lamb, who has come to take upon himself the sins of the world, Paul desired to draw attention to Christ and his merits. But even though he often says that we have been saved freely without any merit of our own, so that no flesh may have anything to boast about, he does not mean to praise a faith without works; [he means] only a faith without our own works, not a faith without the works of faith. That is why [Paul] says in the same place to the Ephesians [Ephesians 2:8-10]—that we seek in vain to be saved, and yet are saved through faith without works, and immediately adds, *for we are His work created in Christ Jesus in order to do good works*.[327] That is, He and not we <188> do the good works that please God. We are the instruments; He, however, is the master craftsman; *we have been created that He might use us to do good works* and not lie idle, as we have amply demonstrated above.

Therefore it is inappropriate, according to both the prophets and the writings of the apostles, that we should say that we are saved through the cross or our own good works. *If we were to do some good works pleasing to God, they would not be ours but belong, as we said, to Jesus Christ. For of what can an instrument boast if the master craftsman does the work? That is why he teaches us to say that when we have done everything we ought and should have done, we are still useless servants.*[328] Even less are we entitled to say that we have been saved through faith without good works, since we are His work created in Christ Jesus to do good works, through whom we have not only been granted the forgiveness of sins, but also repentance, as is indicated in the Acts of the Apostles. The Lord himself compares His kingdom to a man who traveled to a far land, leaving the one servant one talent, the second two talents, and the third three talents [Matthew 25:14-30]. In due time he returned home and demanded an accounting of the monies entrusted to his servants. No one man who travels abroad leaves his servants empty-handed <189> and without money, for the Lord says,

---

327 *Margin*: Ephesians 2
328 These lines are paraphrased in Zurich Q3.

whoever loves me will obey my Word.³²⁹ And again: "I am the vine, you are the branches, he who remains in me and I in him will bring forth much fruit, for without me you can do nothing. Whoever does not remain in me will be cast away and wither, and be burned with fire" [John 15:1-6].

Therefore, whoever says that Christ saves us through faith without the doing of works denies that Christ has given us any gifts for serving our neighbors and building and improving his kingdom—something which he has indeed promised to all those who long for him with all their hearts—all of which are the appropriate ornaments and characteristics of an upright, true and living faith. *For James the apostle says [James 2:14; 26]: "What does it profit a man, my brothers, if he says he has faith but does not have works; for just as the body is dead without the spirit, even so is faith dead without works."*³³⁰

Therefore the highly educated scholars and scribes of this world lack the truth, and *treat us unjustly in this regard when they tell the magistrates that we wish to be saved through our own works and suffering, and so rendering the merits of Christ useless and of no account.* We categorically reject this [accusation], asserting that this is not our hope and faith, as we have amply demonstrated. For *we know only too well that there is no other remedy to be found for our sins, either in heaven or on earth, in all eternity, neither works nor merit, neither cross nor suffering,* neither <190> the innocent blood of the saints, nor angels or any other means *than alone the red, immaculate blood of Christ, the Passover lamb,*³³¹ which was shed once for the forgiveness of all sins out of pure grace, mercy and love, Isaiah 53; Matthew 26; Mark 14; Luke 22, 23; Romans 13; Colossians 2; 1 Peter 2; 1 John 2; Acts 1, 7.

---

329 *Margin:* John 14
330 Zurich Q3 adds: *for Christ produces a true, living faith in his own creatures, as noted above*
331 Zurich Q3 adds: *the eternal son of God*

The Ninth Article

Concerning divorce: Whether the ban and unbelief are reason for divorce

Christ our Lord and Savior, of whom Moses and the prophets, indeed even the great glory of God itself testify, says: "It has been said that whoever wants to divorce his wife shall give her a bill of divorce; but I say unto you, whoever divorces his wife, except for adultery, forces her to commit adultery; and whoever marries a divorced woman commits adultery." [Matthew 5:31-32] All God-fearing Christians will allow these words to suffice, nor will they add to or detract from them. Therefore, adultery alone is cause for divorce for Christ says: two will become one flesh. Whoever commits adultery sins against his own flesh, becoming one flesh with a whore, as Paul says in 1 Corinthians 6[:15-18]. Therefore he is now divided from his own flesh in that he has <191> attached himself to the foreign flesh of a whore. Thus is the marriage ended, for they are no longer one flesh, for the adulterer has become one flesh with the whore. Thus the divorced party may now marry anyone he or she desires, as long as it takes place in the Lord.[332]

In marriage we make a commitment to two unions: one with Christ the heavenly bridegroom[333] and another with our human spouse. It may come to pass that we must leave one spouse and be true to the other. We may have to choose: either do wrong in departing from our faith and the love and fellowship of God, or remain with our carnal partner and show more loyalty and obedience to him or her than we do to Christ, our spiritual spouse and bridegroom. In Matthew 10[:37], however, the infallible, pure and clear Word of God, coming from the mouth of eternal truth, tells us these very words: "Whoever loves father and mother more than me is not worthy of me." Likewise Luke 14[:25] says: "If anyone does not hate his wife and children, yes, even his own life—he cannot be my disciple."

At this point a battle begins with one's own flesh and blood, and it becomes apparent who God's elect are, namely those who leave everything and follow Christ, enduring suffering and the cross when tested in this

---

332 *Margin*: Hosea 2
333 *Margin*: Revelation 19[:6-8]

manner. In such instances, a brother or sister is no longer bound, for it is many thousand times better <192> and more beneficial to leave the fleshly spouse than to leave the spiritual and heavenly bridegroom. For Christ states clearly: "If anyone comes to me and does not hate his father and mother, his wife and children, his brothers and sisters—that is to say, whatever hinders and is detrimental to our love of God and our own salvation, as stated—he cannot be my disciple" [Luke 14:26; Matthew 10:37-38]. That is to say, if any person among you does not deny everything that he has (nothing is excluded here), he cannot be my disciple.

To be sure, marriage is a bond and an obligation, as Paul speaks of it,[334] for anyone who has entered into it is no longer master of his own body; the other person is. And no one is to deny him or herself to his or her spouse. But marriage is not so important to God that the believer, because of the bond of marriage, should or must do wrong such that the woman should obey her husband or the husband his wife more than [being obedient to] God, just so that the believer can remain one flesh with the unbeliever. In such a case our spiritual union with, and commitment to, Christ is more important than the earthly union, for no creature is to sever us from the love of Christ, our faith, love, and obedience to God, Romans 8[:38-39].

But our detractors accuse us of *carrying on promiscuous relationships in our midst under the appearance and pretense of doing and establishing the Father's will, saying: My spirit desires your body. Were we to do so we would indeed be doing the father's will; not the will of the heavenly Father, however, but the will of the devil, the father and ruler of all such abominations* <193> *and unclean spirits*. We rejoice, however, that such evil slander is false and unjustly accuses us, in accordance with the words of our Lord in Matthew 5[:11]. We say to you, furthermore, that *if we indeed indulged in such vices, we would be the most miserable people on the face of the earth. For we know only too well that, having already been robbed of the world's favor, love, peace, and friendship, we would also have to be rejected by God in all eternity because of this vice*, 1 Corinthians 6[:9-20]; Galatians 5[:16-21]; Acts 22.

Marriage is observed among us in the following manner: one man and one wife, in accordance with God's own ordering, Genesis 2[:18-24]; Matthew 19[:3-9]; 1 Corinthians 7; 1 Timothy 3[:2; 12]; Titus 1[:6], *and in accordance with what the apostle Paul says to the Hebrews 13[:4]: "Marriage*

---

334 *Margin*: 1 Corinthians 7[:25-40]

should be honored by all, and the marriage bed kept pure, for God will judge the adulterer and the sexually immoral." Therefore our detractors and the exalted scholars would do well to see that these words do not pierce their own hearts at the judgment seat of Christ.

For our part we do not wish—either here or there—to have any part or fellowship with such adulterers and scandalous persons when we celebrate the holy sacraments, when we have become aware of them. That is, unless they have produced the fruit of repentance. After we have excommunicated them in accordance with the Christian and apostolic ban, as related and described above, we commit them to God's judgment.

The Tenth Article

Concerning the community of goods: Whether or not Christians may purchase and possess their own goods and property without sacrificing Christian love

Our dear Lord and Savior Jesus Christ compares the kingdom of heaven <194> to a costly and precious pearl, and to a costly treasure hidden in a field, buried deep in the ground and hidden from the entire world and all carnal wisdom. However, he has revealed it by his grace to all his elect, but only on the condition that we sacrifice everything for it and exert all our powers to achieve it, nothing excepted. For he says quite clearly, as we have said in the foregoing article: "Whoever among you who does not deny everything he has cannot be my disciple." That is to say, if one does not submit oneself to him with one's whole heart, including body and possessions, but holds something back, such a one already has an idol and is not utterly devoted to Him. Therefore he himself admonishes us to deny ourselves, and free ourselves from all creaturely attachments such as father, mother, wife, child, fields, meadows, and so on. We are to treat these as though we did not have or possess them.[335] And insofar as they are a hindrance to our salvation we are to regard them all as so much dung and dirt, and not tie our hearts to them. For God desires a truly and completely submissive [*gelassen*] heart, Deuteronomy

---

335 *Margin*: 1 Corinthians 7

A Short, Simple Confession

6[:5], 10[:12], as both Moses and Christ teach:[336] You shall love the Lord your God with all your heart, soul and strength, and your neighbor as yourself.[337] In John 13[:34-35] the Lord says: "A new command I give you, that you love one another as I have loved you. By this all men will know that you are my disciples, if you love one another." "Greater love has no man than this, that he lay down his life for his friends. You are my friends, if you do what I command." [John 15:13-15][338] <195> And the apostle Paul says:[339] "Each of you should not look to your own interests, but also to the interests of others. Your attitude should be the same as that of Christ Jesus." [Philippians 2:4-5][340] And John says in 1 John 3[:16-19]: "This is how we know what love is: Jesus Christ laid down his life for us. And we ought to lay down our lives for our brothers. . . . Dear children, let us not love with words or tongue, but with actions and in truth. This is how we know we belong to the truth. . . ." Such things have to be honestly noted and understood if we wish to be Christ's disciples; that is, we are to love one another as he has commanded us, whatever it takes to do so—not only our possessions, which is the least of these things—but also to lay down our lives for others.

In Psalm 133[:1] David, the royal prophet, says: "How good and pleasant is it when brothers (and sisters) live together in unity." Therefore, where two, three, or more or less, agree to live together, sharing one household [one economy] and treasury among them, if they can do this lovingly and honestly without strife and hurting one another, it may—indeed should be—tolerated. On the other hand, those who do so are not to judge and condemn those who live upright lives and possess and use, in a correct and truly submissive [*gelassen*] manner, everything that God has entrusted to them. God himself does not judge them. For those who, in all submissiveness [*glassenheitt*], possess such temporal creaturely things, as wife, child, house, farm, fields, meadows, gold, money, and the like, and use them to come to the aid of their neighbors in an upright and loving manner, extending these things to them <196> at the right time—possessing [these things] as though they did not own them, as Paul writes in 1 Corinthians 7[:30]—such persons hold and possess them correctly. It

---

336 *Margin*: Deuteronomy 6, 10; Matthew 22[:36-39]
337 *Margin*: Leviticus 19; Matthew 22[:36-39]; Romans 13[:8]
338 *Margin*: John 15
339 *Margin*: Philippians 2
340 *Margin*: Christ gave his life in death; we should also have the same mind

matters not whether one dumps all these things together and holds them in common, or possesses them [personally] in all yieldedness [*glassenheitt*] in a correct, positively loving and active manner, as we reported of Christ and find it expressed in the apostolic epistles. They treated this matter in the same way in their day, nor did they take it to the extreme.

The Eleventh Article

Concerning the resurrection of the body: Whether the essence of this body will be resurrected on the Day of Judgment, or whether God will create a new body

Daniel states that the time will come[341] when those "who sleep in the dust of the earth will awake, some to everlasting life, others to shame and everlasting contempt." The Lord himself says in John 5[:28-29]: "Do not be amazed at this, for a time is coming when all who are in their graves will hear his voice and come out—those who have done good will rise to live, and those who have done evil will rise to be condemned. . . ." Paul confirms this in 1 Thessalonians 4[:16-17]: "For the Lord himself will come down from heaven with a loud command, with the voice of the archangel and with the trumpet call of God, and the dead in Christ will rise first. <197> After that, we who are still alive and are left will be caught up together with them in the clouds to meet the Lord in the air. And so we will all be with the Lord forever. Therefore encourage each other with these words." He says the same thing in 1 Corinthians 15[:20-23]: "But Christ has indeed been raised from the dead, the first fruits of those who have fallen asleep. For since death came through a man, the resurrection of the dead comes through a man. For as in Adam all die, so in Christ all will be made alive. But each in his own turn: Christ, the first fruits; then, when he comes, those who belong to him." But, Paul says, should someone ask: "'How are the dead raised? With what kind of body will they come?' You fool! What you sow does not come to life unless it dies. When you sow, you do not plant the body that will be, but just a seed, perhaps of wheat or something else. But

---

341 *Margin*: Daniel 12[:2]

God gives it a body as he has determined, and to each kind of seed he gives its own body. . . ." That is to say: "The body that is sown is perishable, and it is raised imperishable. It is sown in dishonor, it is raised in glory; it is sown in weakness, it is raised in power; it is sown a natural body, it is raised a spiritual body." [1 Corinthians 15:35-38; 42-44] St. John says the same thing in Revelation 20[:13-14]: "The sea gave up the dead that were in it, and death and Hades gave up the dead that were in them, <198> and each person was judged according to what he had done."

These Scriptures and articles of faith, which teach us the resurrection of the body, true believers will simply believe and let stand. They will not believe that the sea and hell will bring forth a different body than the one they received, except that in place of the perishable they will have received an imperishable, in place of the corruptible an incorruptible, and in place of the natural, a spiritual body.

The Twelfth Article

Whether or not children of Christians may be baptized

If only those are Christians who hear Christ's words and live in accordance with them, no longer living according to the written law but according to the law of the Spirit that has come from Zion and become a living reality in the born-again heart, then many children are being baptized who should not be baptized. For the situation has, sadly, become so bad [in Christendom] that one can hardly recognize a true Christian any more; [and if one is seen], such a one is called vicious names, and is scorned and persecuted. For if one no longer drinks or eats to excess, no longer swears and curses, or [no longer] lives in the lasciviousness and wantonness of the flesh, avoids frivolous luxury, when scolded does not scold in return, when beaten does not hit back, but lives in harmony with the law of Zion and the word of the Lord that has come from Jerusalem (of which we spoke at length in the first article), such a person will not be regarded a Christian <199> by the current unrepentant children of Adam, but will be denounced as an Anabaptist [*ein widertoüfer*], whether or not he is one. To call a person an Anabaptist in this current, so-called Christendom is much worse than if one were to accuse a Jew of being a Samaritan. Since this kind of blindness is a good indication of how many Christians are in existence, then one may well truthfully say that if only the children of [true] Christians were to be baptized, one would be amazed at how few, indeed how very, very few would be baptized.

Since the infant baptizers denounce us so ferociously because of this article and incite the magistrates against us, we will quote from the chronicles, decretals, councils and the old Fathers, likewise from Erasmus of Rotterdam, Martin Luther, Ulrich Zwingli, and others whom they hold in high esteem, namely what they said concerning the unfounded infant baptism, and what they wrote against it. We would like to commend these words to God-fearing readers for their consideration. For we shall prove from their own books and writings that they can give no clear and obvious reason for infant baptism, unless, of course, they wish to revoke their own books—books they themselves presented to be publicly printed—and concede that they wrote and taught incorrectly. And even though our detractors were to throw many cunning, lively, and ingenious questions and arguments in our face, they will not be able to circumvent <200> the clear and straightforward command of Christ in Matthew 28[:19-20], Mark 16[:15-16], and the manner in which the holy apostles applied it, Acts 2[:38], 8[:12-13; 35-38], 10[:44-48], 11[:16-18], 16[:14-15; 30-33], 19[:1-6]. Nevertheless, we shall answer their most essential arguments and articles in all simplicity from the teaching of Christ and his holy apostles so that devout hearts, who possess the Holy Spirit, will know and understand what the quarrel is all about.

First, from the Chronicles, Fathers and Decretals[342]

Ninety-one years after Christ's birth, Clement, the first bishop of that name and a disciple of the apostle Peter, proclaimed the following in 29 articles—among other places—that the baptism of heretics should neither

---

342 From this point in the codex up to codex page <211>, the manuscript copies large sections verbatim (with some editorial omissions and additions) from Balthasar Hubmaier's *Old and New Teachers on Believers Baptism* (printed in Nikolsburg in 1526). Of the two editions of Hubmaier's text, it was the second, longer edition that was copied in *Codex 628* and Zurich Q3. Critical edition in Westin and Bergsten, *Balthasar Hubmaier Schriften*, 227-55; translation in Pipkin and Yoder, *Hubmaier*, 245-74. The text has been re-translated here, following *Codex 628*.

be recognized or accepted. Whoever received baptism in accordance with the teachings of the church was not to be rebaptized, but those who refused to rebaptize persons who had been sullied with the baptism of heretics and the godless, should be deposed as persons who despised the cross of Christ and his death and did not distinguish between true and false priests.

In the year 137, Donatus, a learned bishop of Carthage, taught that no child should be baptized that did not confess the faith. These were all learned and experienced people.[343]

In the year 208 Tertullian, in his Libro de Corona Militis *[Book on the Garland of the Soldier]*, taught that those who wished to be baptized should confess beforehand and should be taught for a time, in the presence of a bishop in the congregation or church, that <201> they should renounce the devil, all pomp, and angels. Thereafter they should be immersed three times and baptized in the name of the Father, Son, and Holy Spirit.

In the year 230, the teacher Origen wrote that a person receives baptism for the forgiveness of sins. "Therefore I beseech you," he says, "that you come to baptism with care and a thorough preparation, that you demonstrate fruit worthy of the renewal of your lives." This he writes concerning John's sermon on repentance, Luke 3[:8]. Concerning Paul's words in Romans 6[:3], [Origen] states that with these words Paul tells [the people of Origen's time] that in the age of the apostles, the apostles did not baptize as they did in his own day. For at the time of the apostles only the understanding and instructed were baptized, and that into the death of Christ. For just as Christ rose from the dead through the glory of the Father, even so were the baptized to live in purity of life. In his fifth homily on Exodus, folio 48 E, [Origen] writes: "When we come to be baptized, we renounce all gods and other lords, and confess God the Father, Son and Holy Spirit alone."[344]

In the year 370, St. Jerome wrote: *When the bishop lays on hands he does so to those who are being baptized upon a true faith in the name of the Father, the Son and the Holy Spirit, upon those who believe in the names of the Godhead.* From Against the Sect of the Luciferians. *Further, concerning Matthew 28[:19] he writes: First of all, teach them—indeed all people—the Word [of God]; after they have been taught, baptize them in water. For it*

---

343 A paragraph on Theophylact is omitted here. Pipkin and Yoder, *Hubmaier*, 265.
344 Sections on Cyprian and Athanasius are omitted here. Pipkin and Yoder, *Hubmaier*, 266-67.

must not happen <202> that the body receive the sacrament of baptism unless the soul has first received the truth of the faith.³⁴⁵

In the year 371, the teacher Eusebius writes in Book 10, chapter 14, of his Ecclesiastical History³⁴⁶ that, at the time of Alexander, bishop of Alexandria, a large group of school children once went on an outing to the ocean. To amuse themselves [on the way] they re-read their lesson, for many of them had just learned of baptism in their catechism. As they interrogated one another [on the subject], one of them named Athanasius said: "We now know what baptism means and we all know the Christian faith well—how would it be if we were to baptize one another? In the church, we are embarrassed in front of the older people, but here it would be better." As a result, the children elected Athanasius as their servant and he proceeded to baptize all of them in the very manner they had observed it done in their church. Thereupon their rabbi (teacher) returned and noticed what they had done. He immediately informed the bishop, priests, deacons, and clerics what had happened. After a long discussion about the matter, the latter decided on the following course of action. Since [the youths] knew what baptism signified, and had observed how it was used, had sincerely desired it of one another, knew and confessed the faith, they should be brought before the congregation to be questioned, as is usually done. They were not to be rebaptized, however. Rather, they were to be accepted into the church and regarded as baptized members. This is the story, in summary. <203>

---

345 A section on Augustine is omitted here. Pipkin and Yoder, *Hubmaier*, 267.

346 This is a reference to Rufinus's Latin translation and continuation of Eusebius' *Church History*, which became a standard early church history text in the Latin West. The story is found in Book 10, chapter 15 in a contemporary English edition. See Philip R. Amidon, S.J., trans., *The Church History of Rufinus of Aquileia by Rufinus* (Oxford: Oxford University Press, 1997). There were sixteenth-century translations into German of Rufinus's expanded *Church History*. Reference to Caspar Hedio's German translation of the Eusebius/Rufinus *Church History* confirms the accuracy of the citation; in this translation edition the story is found in Book 10, chapter 14. See Caspar Hedio, *Chronica der Alten Christlichen Kirchen* (Strasbourg, 1545), das x. Buch, das xiiii Capittel, xciiii, recto and verso. I consulted the electronic book edition: https://play.google.com/books/reader?id=-ehEAAAAcAAJ&printsec=frontcover&output=reader&authuser=0&hl=en&pg=GBS.PA13 (pages 207-208 of the e-book).

A Short, Simple Confession

In the year 373, Cyril, a bishop in Basel, wrote: Those who are being instructed in the faith should not immediately be accepted for baptism. He wrote this concerning John, in Book 2, chapter 36. He also writes that the figures of water baptism in both the Old and New Testaments all point to believers' [baptism]. But this is too long to narrate here. Read Book 6, chapter 15, on John.[347]

In the year 420 Pope Boniface, the 44th in number, had a debate with Augustine, a person who often shifted his ground. The latter wished to have unknowing children baptized, and wished to establish godparents. The pope answered him that the godparents who brought a child to be baptized were, in truth, totally incapable of answering in the child's stead—that the child would renounce the devil, or that it believed—since they did not know whether the child would become chaste or not, become devout or a thief. To this [argument] Augustine gave him a silly answer, Contra Lib.

In the year 836[348] *Pope Leo I, the 48th in line, issued a decretal that baptism was to take place twice a year—at Easter and at Pentecost—unless there was a real emergency.*

In the year 490, Pope Basil the Great, number 22, in Book 3, folio 44 of his Contra Eunomium [Against Eunomius], *writes: Go forth, says Christ, baptizing in the name of the Father, the Son, and the Holy Spirit, for baptism is a seal of faith, and faith is an <204> affirmation of the Godhead. For one must believe first and then be marked with baptism. That is, where there is a ready will there is nothing to prevent [a person from] being baptized. He justifies this with the example of the Ethiopian eunuch. See also his* In Exhortatione ad Baptismum, *folio 142 following, and his tract* Quid Instruendi, ad Baptismum Venientes Lib. *He compares water baptism to the flood from which no one was saved except those who, by faith, entered the ark, as Peter also states. He makes the same observation when he writes on the 29th Psalm. [Psalm 29]*

In the year 863, Pope Nicholas I, the 90th in line, wrote his own catechism, describing how the teacher shall instruct the baptismal candidate and student in the faith and how (baptism) is to be practised. (Whoever wishes should look it up) Ex Baptismo fidei.

---

347 Sections on Pelagianus, Ambrose, and Pope Siricius omitted here. Pipkin and Yoder, *Hubmaier,* 268-69.

348 *Codex 628* has 435. Cf. Westin and Bergsten, *Hubmaier Schriften,* 247, where the date is given as 836 in the margin.

In the year 1315, Beatus Renanus[349] says that it was the custom of the Ancients to have the adults baptized and washed with the bath of rebirth;[350] this custom was maintained until the time of Charlemagne and Louis. They pointed to laws established and put in place by them in which priests were forbidden to baptize anyone—except with regard to the article dealing with imminent death—at times other than Easter and Pentecost.

Concerning Councils

In the year 315, the Council of Arles <205> was held in Gaul at the time of Emperor Constantine the Great and Pope Sylvester. That council determined that whoever returned to the church from a heretical group should be baptized in the name of the Trinity. In the year 323, it was decided at the Council of Nicea that heretics, or those baptized by them, should be rebaptized if they wished to return to the orthodox church.

In the year 368, the Council of Laodicea in Syria decided that catechumens who were to be baptized should be instructed in the faith, and, on Thursday [of the last week of instruction] should recite or narrate to the priest or bishop.

In the year 406, the Sixth Council of Carthage, held under the Emperor Honorius, decreed that those who desired to be baptized should, for a considerable time beforehand, be tested and examined, abstain from wine and the eating of meat for a time, then be diligently examined with the laying on of hands and baptized. It also designated a time when the catechumens were to be allowed to receive baptism, when they were to confess their faith, so that they would be able to answer the minister as to how they were to conduct themselves after baptism in order to avoid the ban.

In the year 438, it was decided at the Council of Laodicea that baptismal candidates should first be instructed in the faith and on Maundy Thursday give an accounting to the bishop regarding it.

---

349 *Codex 628* follows Hubmaier's text, which has misprinted "Romanus." Zurich Q3 has corrected this to "Renanus."

350 Following Hubmaier's text here; both *Codex 628* and Zurich Q3 have *dem brodt der widergeburt*, or "the bread of rebirth," clearly a copyist's mistake.

A Short, Simple Confession 333

THERE FOLLOWS NOW WHERE INFANT BAPTISM WAS FULLY FORMED AND WAS ESTABLISHED <206>

In the year 710, the Second Council of Braga met. Here it was declared that baptism is necessary for, and should be granted to, children.[351]

The testimony of Ulrich Zwingli that Infant Baptism was not as common or employed as often by the Ancients as we do in our day[352]

In Article 18 of his Artikelbuch Zwingli[353] writes the following concerning confirmation. "Because of the custom, and the fact that even today one is still investigating the term, I must conclude that confirmation first became customary at the time as when it began to be common practice to baptize children in infancy—indeed, as soon as they were born—in order that the faith of their father and mother—affirmed through the godparents—not be unknown to them. Although I know, as the Ancients indicate, that some children were baptized in ancient times, yet it was not as common then as it is today. For one taught them publicly as a group when they had reached the age of understanding. That is why they were called catechumens—because they had been taught the message of salvation. And when they had a firm faith in their hearts and they confessed it with their mouths they were baptized."

He writes further in the fifteenth Article against [John] Faber that all things are clearly and openly declared in God's Word.[354] And in the 24th thesis he states: No Christian is forced to do anything not commanded by God.[355] <207> In his booklet concerning the rebellious spirits, E page 2,

---

351 Excerpts from the section on Councils and Decrees found in "Old and New Teachers," Pipkin and Yoder, *Hubmaier*, 272-73.
352 The following in ibid, 257-58.
353 "Auslegung und Begründen der Schlußreden," in Oskar Frei, ed., *Zwingli, der Verteidiger des Glaubens*, 1. Teil (Zurich: Zwingli-Verlag, 1947), 158-59; English translation in E. J. Furcha, *Huldrych Zwingli Writings: The Defense of the Reformed Faith* (Allison Park, PA: Pickwick, 1984), 100.
354 This is an accurate paraphrase of Zwingli's words in this article, but not a literal citation. Frei, *Zwingli*, 1, 91-93; Furcha, *Huldrych Zwingli Writings*, 60-61.
355 "... ein ieder Christ zu den Wercken, die Got nit gebotten hat, verbunden ist." Frei, *Zwingli*, 10; Furcha, *Huldrych Zwingli Writings*, 197.

published in 1525, he declared: "Those who baptize children have no explicit command to do so."[356]

If then infant baptizers have no clear Word of God that commands them to baptize [children], and no Christian is bound to do anything not commanded by God, then the very own words and conclusions of *Ulrich Zwingli* (whom the infant baptizers hold in such high esteem), *quoted above, tell us that no Christian is forced to baptize children.*

Dear reader,[357] *these are Zwingli's very own clear words, published in print for all the world to see: all things are clearly and explicitly contained in the Word of God. No Christian is bound to do the works that God has not commanded. Likewise, those who baptize children have no clear and explicit command to do so. Now since this leaves everyone free and forces no one to baptize children, how do the learned students and highly honored scribes of this world hope to answer for this before God? Especially since they have long incited the secular rulers* to root out, with great severity and much spilling of blood, [those who desire the freedom not to baptize infants], and, instead, because of this persecute, kill, and expel them *when God, as they themselves confess, has not commanded infant baptism?*

To the contrary, those articles that are clearly and explicitly commanded by God in his Word are frivolously transgressed by them and their entire so-called Christendom <208> as we shall demonstrate in what follows.[358] Before we do that, however, we wish to hear what else these scribes have written and how well what they themselves have written and taught corresponds to infant baptism.

In his *Taufbuechlein* published in 1525, on P, page 4, Zwingli writes concerning young children as follows: I am unable to prove (or confirm) that they have faith even though some have attempted to do so; but they have done so in vain. Likewise on Q, page 1, he writes: Therefore one can see that Christ really only speaks of those who have heard the Gospel preached and believe it, or did not believe it. Now children of Christians who cannot

---

356 The section that follows, up to the short paragraph referring to Martin Luther (page <209> below) is a shared interpolation; it appears in both *Codex 628* and Zurich Q3, but is not taken from Hubmaier's booklet.
357 Zurich Q3 has *Dear lords, think on these things*
358 Zurich Q3, margin: *Colossians 6[?], Ephesians 5, Galatians 5. Pride, whoring, adultery, drunkenness, gluttony*

A Short, Simple Confession 335

as yet understand, do not hear the Gospel; therefore they neither believe nor disbelieve it.[359]

Furthermore, about 70 years ago[360] *Martin Luther delivered a sermon on the mass in which he declared, in article 17, that such signs as baptism and communion mean nothing without a preceding faith; they were like a sheath without a knife, like a case without a gem, or like a sign outside a tavern without wine.*[361]

Likewise the Strasbourg preachers Wolfgang Capito, [Caspar Hedio],[362] *Matthew Zell, Simphorianus Poll, Theobald Niger, John Latomus, Anthonius*

---

359 The text of the preceding paragraph is found in both *Codex 628* and Zurich Q3. It is copied from Hubmaier's *Dialogue with Zwingli's Baptism Book*, published in Nikolsburg in 1526. Critical edition in *Hubmaier Schriften*, 164-214; citations from 205; translation in Pipkin and Yoder, *Hubmaier*, 166-233; citations on 222.

360 *Codex 628* and Zurich Q3 return to copying from Hubmaier's *Old and New Teachers* at this point. Hubmaier's reference is clearly to *Eyn Sermon von dem newen Testament, das ist von der heyligen Messe (A Treatise on the New Testament, that is, the Holy Mass)*. WA 6, 353-378; translation in LW, vol. 35, 79-111.

361 Pipkin and Yoder, *Hubmaier*, 256, n. 43 observe that Hubmaier has incorrectly rendered the meaning of Luther's passage, found in LW, 35, 91. In the 17th article Luther writes "the best and greatest part of all sacraments and of the mass is the words and promise of God, without which the sacraments are dead and are nothing at all, like a body without a soul, a cask without wine ... etc." Hubmaier seems to have conflated "God's promise" and "faith," perhaps on the basis of Luther's words in article 14: "... if you would receive this sacrament and testament worthily, see to it that you give emphasis to these living words of Christ, rely on them with a strong faith, and desire what Christ has promised you in them; then it will be yours, then you will be worthy and well prepared." Ibid., 88-89. Luther notes later, "it is the nature of a sacrament or testament that it is not a work but only an exercise of faith." Ibid., 93. And again: "... it is not the priest alone who offers the sacrifice of the mass; it is this faith which each one has for himself. ... For faith must do everything. Faith alone is the true priestly office." Ibid., 100; 101, *passim*.

Hubmaier seems to have concluded that Luther was saying that without faith, there is no sacrament. Luther's mature understanding was that the promises of God, united to physical "signs," make a sacrament; the faith of an individual, while it has implications for that individual, does not "make" or "unmake" a sacrament as such. However, Luther's earlier statements were not without ambiguity and could easily have been interpreted in the way Hubmaier did. Later in *Codex 628* (on page <221> below) the copyist references a published sermon of 1522 by Luther that states that a sacrament without faith is "like a seal on a letter with no written words."

362 *Codex 628* omits Caspar Hedio.

Firm, Martin Hagk, Martin Bucer[363] *wrote in their booklet* Grund und Ursach[364] *how, in the beginning of the church <209> no one was baptized and accepted into the congregation except those who had totally committed themselves to the Word of Christ, K, folio 1. They drew the reasons for [such a statement] from the Scriptures, writing that a Christian life begins with the confession that everything we do is sinful. It was for this reason that John the Baptist, Christ, and the apostles all began with an exhortation to [their listeners] to repent, and in God's congregations the confession of sin had always come first: that is, it had always preceded baptism in the ancient church. For [in the ancient church] it had been common practice to baptize only those who had come to years of understanding, not children.*[365] *That is their unanimous conclusion presented openly in public print, K on pages 2 and 3. They write further in like manner that without the baptism of the Holy Spirit, water baptism is an act of delusion, M on page 2.*[366]

In the same manner Erasmus of Rotterdam, writing in his postil translated into German by Leo Jud and published in Zurich[367] *says the following about Matthew 28[:19]: After you have taught the people these things, and they have repented of their former lives and are prepared henceforth to walk in accordance with evangelical teachings, then immerse them in water in the name of the Father, of the Son, and of the Holy Spirit, so that by this important sign they may be initiated into [the Christian*

---

363 Zurich Q3 adds after Bucer: *who also was at the Bern disputation*
364 Martin Bucer, et al., *Grund und ursach auß gotlicher schrifft der neüwerungen an dem nachtmal des herren, so man dei mess nennet, Tauff, feyertagen, bildern...* (Strasbourg, 1524/1525), in R. Stupperich, ed., *Martin Bucers Deutsche Schriften*, Band 1 (Gütersloh: Mohn, 1969), 185-278.
365 "... bey den alten auch dem tauff vorgangen ist, dan man gemeinklich nur die verstendigen, nit kinder geteüfft hat." Bucer, *Grund und Ursach*, ibid., 247.
366 Referring to Paul's words, Acts 9:17-19, Bucer writes "hat er in nit zum wassertauff allein, sonder vil mer durch denselbigen zum tauff des geists gewisen..." Bucer, *Grund und Ursach*, ibid., 257. See Pipkin and Yoder, *Hubmaier*, 259 for the paragraph above, 255 for the following. The copyist freely changes Hubmaier's order in copying the material.
367 Desiderius Erasmus, *Paraphrasis oder postilla teütsch, das ist, Klare Ausslegung aller evangelischen und apostolischen Schrifften des Neüwen Testaments ...* , trans. Leo Jud (Zurich: Froschauer, ca. 1535). PDF copy read online from www.e-rara.ch/zuz/content/pageview/967556.

A Short, Simple Confession

life] and inscribed [in the church].[368] *Here Erasmus publicly points out that baptism was instituted by Christ for those instructed in the faith and not for young children. Furthermore, Erasmus writes regarding Acts 2[:38]* <210> *that Christ commanded the evangelical shepherds to go forth and teach all peoples, baptizing them, teaching them to observe everything I have commanded you, teaching those who are to be baptized the most important evangelical truths. If one does not believe these truths, he is baptized in vain.*[369] *Dear reader, see also what he has to say about chapter 8 in the Acts of the Apostles [Acts 8:12].*[370]

To this we answer: *If it is impossible to prove that children can believe, that they neither believe nor disbelieve as Zwingli related above,*[371] *and if baptism and communion are nothing without a preceding faith, as Luther confesses and in which Erasmus and the Strasbourg preachers concur, then small children are not to be baptized* and baptism without faith and the Holy Spirit is a delusion. We must not trivialize the sacraments nor turn them into child's play.

St. Jerome, the old teacher, agrees as demonstrated above, saying: It may not be nor should it happen that the body receives the sacrament of baptism if the soul has not first accepted the truth of the faith. But if we say these things today, we have to suffer imprisonment, torture, persecution, expulsion, and in some places even death. We therefore leave it up to all devout, God-loving hearts, to consider and judge what kind of Christians

---

368 Erasmus's text reads: "So jr diβ geleert haben/glauben sy euch den und nemmends an/haben sy am vorigen läben ein reüwen/sind sy bereit die Euangelische leer anzunemmen/so tauffen sy mit wasser in den nammen des vatters/des suns/und des heiligen geists: das sy mit disem bedeütlichen zeichen eyngezeichnet unnd eyngeschriben warden in die zal deren/die vertauwen das sy von jren sünden durch die gutthaet meines todts erloeβt und gewaeschen seyen/und zu kindern Gottes angenommen." Ibid., 212.
369 Erasmus's text reads: "Dann also befilcht Jesus seinen jüngeren: Gond hin und leerend alle völcker/und tauffen sy/und leeren sy halten alles das ich eüch gebotten hab. Leerend die die man tauffen sol die anfeng Euangelischer weyβheit: welcher den selben nit glaubt/der wirt vergäbens mit wasser getaufft. Wenn sy getaufft sind/so leeren sy daβ sy nach meiner leer läben/und yemerdar in volkommnerem zunemmen." Ibid., 698.
370 Here ends direct copying from Hubmaier's *Old and New Teachers*.
371 Zurich Q3 adds: *and one dunks them in water in vain, if one believes the well-grounded evangelical wisdom, as Erasmus reports here.*

they are who testify to the truth <211> with their mouths and in their writings, but then later deny it in word and deed. And they slander and harry out of the land those who sincerely desire to adhere [to these teachings]. We, for our part, will commit and leave this to the judgment of Him who knows the hearts of human beings and whose sentence is infallible. He also knows our hearts and the hearts of our detractors and what it is that both of us are concerned about.

For it was [God] who recognized Job's devotion and innocence (even though we do not regard ourselves equal to Job, except in that we would gladly, together with all the devout, do that which is right and just and, as much as God gives us grace, to abide by the clear and pure truth). We wish to flee all human laws and commands which the heavenly Father has not instituted (planted), *hoping that God will be merciful to us in our weakness but sincere good will. For even though his friends tried to undermine Job's innocent and upright words with many wise and clever speeches—which are held in high regard in wise and learned circles—when these speeches came before the impartial judge,*[372] *Job's friends were forced to recognize their folly. For the wisest of them missed the mark by the widest of margins and Job himself was forced to sacrifice, pray, and intercede for them.*

We fear the same will happen to those *who refuse to be satisfied with the simplicity of Christ and his holy apostles but instead, with many clever and intelligent human arguments that have no foundation in the bright and clear Scriptures* (as Zwingli himself confessed above), *seek to make white black* <212> *and black white, and to confirm and prove, with veiled words and twisted Scripture, the unscriptural and baseless infant baptism.*[373] *Indeed, they take the simple words of Christ and his apostles and paint them an entirely different color, making them mean something they never said or commanded.*[374] It is therefore to be feared that those few of the wise dissemblers, disputants, and learned scholars, *who take it upon themselves* to master the Scriptures, *trusting rather in their own wisdom and cleverness—as did Job's friends who repented of their folly—will come to*

---

372 Zurich Q3 adds: *whose judgment cannot deceive*
373 Zurich Q3 has *the scripture-less, unfounded infant baptism*
374 Zurich Q3 adds: *[contrary] to the Holy Spirit himself, who interprets [the word] in the hearts of the elect so that they understand*

regret and recognition too late, when no plaster or herb may cure it,³⁷⁵ when the sun of grace has set and the door to the royal chamber has been locked.

What follows deals with Christian and Apostolic Baptism, as well as Infant Baptism

Since young children are not born to faith and the new birth (which is brought about by the Holy Spirit) through the preached Word of God, and [also] cannot distinguish between good and evil, they cannot be baptized in a correct manner, for baptism is an acceptance into Christ's congregation. Now, just as all those born of the seed of Adam share in his [characteristics], even so must those who wish to be incorporated into Christ's congregation be born of Christ, in a Christian manner, if they wish to be accepted into his congregation correctly and in the way he has made it known.³⁷⁶ <213>

Being born of Christ takes place in the following manner: just as Mary the mother of our Lord believed the preached or announced word,³⁷⁷ and because of her faith received the Holy Spirit, who assisted her faith concerning Jesus who was to be born of her—so likewise, all who wish to be born in a Christian fashion must, like Mary, also first hear the Word and then believe it, so that when their faith is sealed with the Holy Spirit they may be accepted into the Church of Christ, in accordance with the truth. This was also the way the apostles treated the matter.

This is why there is no indication anywhere that the apostles baptized children; rather, they maintained the instructions and teachings of their master. In agreement with Philip they stated: *If you believe you may be baptized*. This is as though the apostle wished to say: *If you do not believe you may not be [baptized]*. Therefore we regard infant baptism to be wrong for the following reasons.

First, there is not a single word in the entire Holy Scriptures that can be cited that so much as touches on infant baptism, never mind commands it.

Secondly, one finds that the popes and councils, in their decrees, order that children who could recite the Lord's Prayer and the creed, as we saw above, should be baptized, which—if baptism had come first—they would not have had to do. Therefore [infant baptism] clearly appears to be a

---

375 Zurich Q3 has, in margin: *1 Corinthians 12*
376 *Margin*: 4 Esdras 3[:5-8; 20-22], 1 Peter 1[:22-23], Matthew 28[:19-20], Romans 16[:17-19]
377 Zurich Q3 : *of the angel*

human institution[378] which, in accordance with the Word of God, must be rooted out.[379]

Thirdly, because baptism is the covenant of a good conscience with God. <214>

Fourthly, because the covenant of grace[380] is a covenant of the knowledge and understanding of God, but children know neither good nor evil.

These should be reason enough—even if we had no others—to do away with infant baptism.

Zwingli writes in his Taufbuechlein: "Baptism is a sign of obligation that indicates that those who accept it have promised to reform their lives and wish to follow Christ." [381] Here Zwingli himself again freely confesses the truth. Now, if baptism is truly the sign of an obligation, a person must have already assumed the obligation before the sign is given him. That is to say, before one can fulfill the obligation, a person must have been informed in word or writing [what that obligation is], otherwise it is a blind obligation and amounts to nothing. At the same time, such a person must expressly have consented to the obligation; otherwise the sign would not have been properly conferred upon him.

In light of the above, we wish to ask the infant baptizers: What [child], or how can a suckling child in a crib accept such an obligation? You say,[382] their parents and godparents do this for the child. We answer: Did not Zwingli himself confess that baptism was the sign of an obligation, that the persons who accept it enter into, that [signifies that] they will reform their life and desire to follow Christ? It is not an obligation if someone else accepts on the child's behalf, for that would be an addition. Here Zwingli himself confesses the truth about infant baptism.

Judge for yourself, Christian reader, and <215> think about it, and *you will see how much of the [original] obligation and promise of this earliest Christian water baptism has remained—an obligation which for many years was mumbled in Latin to the child in the Catholic Church. And even*

---

378 Zurich Q3 : *which we heartily fear*
379 *Margin*: Matthew 15[:13], 1 Peter 4[:5]
380 *Margin*: Jeremiah 31[:31-34]
381 "Für das erst/ist der touff ein pflichtig zeichen das den der inn nimpt/anzeigt das er in leben beβren und Christo nachvolgen welle." Huldrych Zwingli, *Vom dem Touff, vom Widertouff unnd vom Kindertouff* (Zurich: Johann Hager, 1525), dii, recto. Accessed online at: http://www.e-rara.ch/zuz/content/titleinfo/987393.
382 Zurich Q3 : *Now your preachers say quite simply to us ...*

though one now mumbles the words in German, the child understands as little German as it did Latin, for the one language is as incomprehensible [to the infant] as the other. The baptismal priest asks: Credis in deum patrem omnipotentem creatorem coeli et terra *[Do you believe in God the Father, creator of heaven and earth]? [If you do], say: "I believe." Now, if the Word of God commands that the godparents shall answer for the child, prove it to us from Holy Scripture. If it does say this, why then does not the priest say to the godparents: "You godparents say: we believe." But truth cannot be hidden, for what they [the godparents] answer at this place, the child should answer for itself and say: "I believe in God the Father, etc., and in Jesus Christ, through whose death, burial and resurrection all my sins have been forgiven. Therefore I once more commend myself to him and obligate myself and promise that I will reform my life, renounce the devil and his minions, and [desire] henceforth to follow Christ to the extent that God the Father, Son and Holy Spirit grant me grace and strength."*

This is the correct baptismal pledge and obligation; there can be none higher than this one. And if this [pledge] had been observed in the church and correctly used in the past, then surely all the vows and obligations of monks, priests and nuns would not have been instituted. But since the correct Christian baptismal obligation (taken upon a personally confessed faith) was discarded, Satan insinuated himself [into the church] with his monastic vows. Without a doubt, many <216> *will take offense at what we have said here, but they will not be able to refute it in all eternity. For if the true baptismal pledge, taken upon a personally confessed faith, had remained [in place] it would have provided more than enough to do, and there would have been no need to devise any other.*

Look at and consider the words of Tertullian and Eusebius, about how one questioned children in their time. Likewise the words of Jerome and others, cited above, how the baptismal candidate was to be instructed and prepared before he was baptized. *If one asks infant baptizers what it really means or what is implied*—according to clear Holy Scripture—*to be baptized in the name of Jesus Christ, and on what basis one may or should baptize children, they present so many reasons concocted by man that no truly zealous heart can receive a satisfactory answer from them. Therefore papists, Lutherans and Zwinglians—since they have no sure foundation [for infant baptism]—have been unable to reach agreement [on the issue]. And one can prove this through [a study of] the books and writings which they* *have directed against one another.*³⁸³ *For some baptize their children upon an inner, hidden, faith to be revealed later, which at the moment is latent (asleep) and unknown to the child in the same way that a sleeping believer is unaware of his faith until* <217> *he awakens and comes to his senses, as Martin Luther wrote in a book concerning original sin against the pope in which he argued against [the papal] doctrine of original sin in children with many arguments.*³⁸⁴

*In the same way Zwingli writes against Martin Luther, denying and repudiating the hidden [or latent] faith of children, as described above.*³⁸⁵ Luther responded with a contrary opinion in his sermon, printed at Magdeburg in 1531, on the third Sunday after Epiphany, folio aa, page iiii: Baptism is useless, nor should it be given to anyone, unless the person believes for himself. Without such a personal faith no one is to be baptized, as St. Augustine himself says: *Non sacramentum iustificat, sed fides sacramenti.* The sacrament does not justify one, but rather faith justifies the sacrament.³⁸⁶

---

383 Zurich Q3, margin: *Luthero opinioni et doctrina de fide puerorum [Luther's opinion and doctrine concerning the faith of children].* The following section in the codex, with its reference to Luther and Zwingli on original sin and baptism, is copied from Pilgram Marpeck's "Vermanung [Admonition] of 1542," translation in Klaassen and Klassen, *Writings*, 159-302; copied references from 247. There are substantial additions to the Marpeck original made in the codex.

384 Klaassen and Klassen, *Writings*, note that Marpeck has misrepresented Luther here, since Luther always assumed the reality of original sin. Ibid., 247, n. 59. That error was reproduced by the copyist of *Codex 628*.

385 This was written by Marpeck, copied here. Klaassen and Klassen could locate "no precise references in this matter" (575, n. 60). The copyist, however, points back to Zwingli's *Vom dem Touff, vom Widertouff unnd vom Kindertouff* as documenting Zwingli's position (above at <214>), and proceeds to document Luther's view with reference to Luther's sermon for the third Sunday after Epiphany (on Matthew 8:1-13). A specific reference to a writing by Luther is not part of Marpeck's published pamphlet.

386 I was not able to consult the 1531 publication noted here, but reference to a translation of Luther's sermon for the third Sunday after Epiphany, on Matthew 8:1-13 (taken from Luther's Church Postil of 1525), confirms the accuracy of the copyist's words. For the citation above, see http://www.trinitylutheranms.org/MartinLuther/MLSermons/Matthew8_1_13.html, #26. The published source is *The Sermons of Martin Luther* (Grand Rapids, MI: Baker Book House, 1983). This eight-volume set is a reprint of John Nicholas Lenker's translation of Luther's Church Postil. Lenker's edition originally appeared in 1905 as "The Precious and

Luther writes further that these brothers[387] hold that everyone must believe for himself and receive baptism or the sacraments on the basis of their own faith. If this is not the case, baptism or the sacrament does them no good. Thus far (says Luther) they speak and have it right. But that they <218> continue to baptize young children whom they regard as not having any faith of their own amounts to a mockery of holy baptism. At the same time they sin greatly by disregarding that second commandment not to take God's Word and name in vain, making it of no account, using it frivolously rather than conscientiously. Nor does their excuse help them when they say that they baptize children upon their future faith, after they have reached the age of accountability (says Luther). Faith must be present before or in baptism, otherwise the child is not freed from sin and the devil.

Therefore, if they were correct in their assumption, then everything they do with the child in baptism would be bold lies and mockery. For at the ceremony the baptizer asks the child if it believes, and one answers yes, in its place. Then it is asked if it wishes to be baptized. Again, one answers yes, in its place. But no one is baptized in its place, for the child itself is baptized. Therefore it, too, must have faith (says Luther), or the godparents must lie when they answer "I believe," in the place of the child. Thereupon the baptizer boasts that the child has been born again, has had its sins forgiven, and been freed from the devil. He testifies that this [baptism] is a sign that he has become a new creature and that he is now dealing with a new and holy child of God, all of which must be false if the child does not possess a faith of its own. <219> And Luther continues: [If this were so], it would be better not to baptize any children than to juggle and make a fool of the sacrament and God's Word as though it were an idol.[388]

If we were to be allowed to answer the question—whether young children believe for themselves, possessing their own faith—with Luther's proof, the following would be our judgment and counsel: that one completely cease and desist from [baptizing infants], and the sooner the better. We should not baptize one more child. We should no longer mock

---

Sacred Writings of Martin Luther," volumes 1-14, published by Lutherans in all Lands. These sermons have since been scanned and edited by Dr. Richard Bucher and are in the public domain.
387 Luther refers to "the brethren called Waldensians" here. Ibid., #27.
388 The above is a close verbatim rendering of Luther's sermon. See ibid., #27 and 28.

and slander the exalted majesty of God with such chicanery and frivolous actions, actions that are utterly meaningless.

In another booklet published in Basel in 1523 containing some fourteen sermons, folio E, page iii, concerning the Gospel of Mark, chapter 16, Luther writes further: Baptism is meaningless without faith; it is like a letter having a seal but having nothing written in it. Therefore, whoever possesses the sign (signified by the sacrament) but has not faith, possesses only the seal and a letter without anything written on it.[389]

These are Martin Luther's own words <220> sent out in print for all to read, from which I have faithfully copied—without falsification—the foregoing passages. But what he wrote in his sermon on the mass, where he noted, in some 17 articles—as we remarked above—that signs like baptism and communion signified nothing without a preceding faith, for they were like a sheath without a knife, like a case without a gem, like a winepress without wine, etc., I have taken from a printed booklet that in turn took it from [Luther's] writings. That is why I have not been able to determine in which year it was printed or on what page it is to be found. But I have no doubt [of its veracity], for the person who made the booklet bore witness to his faith with his blood in Vienna, Austria.[390]

Take note also, my dear Christian reader, to what extent—from what I have cited above—Zwingli's opinions agree with those of Luther. Zwingli says he cannot verify that children have faith. That is to say, children cannot hear the Gospel since they cannot as yet understand or speak. Therefore they neither believe nor disbelieve the Gospel. In opposition to this Luther says: Baptism does no one any good, nor should it be extended to anyone, unless he first possesses a personal faith. For no one is to be baptized who does not possess a personal faith. Faith must be present before or during baptism, otherwise the entire transaction that takes place with a

---

389 "... baptism is worth nothing without faith, but is like seals affixed to a letter in which nothing is written. He that has the signs that we call sacraments, and has no faith, has only seals upon a letter of blank paper." Martin Luther, "Sermon for the day of Christ's Ascension; Mark 16:14-20," taken from Luther's "Church Postil, 1522" and accessed online April 4, 2014: http://www.orlutheran.com/html/mlsermmk1614-20-2.html, #26.

390 This is a clear reference to Balthasar Hubmaier, martyred in Vienna on March 10, 1528. It is from Hubmaier, *Old and New Teachers on Believers Baptism* that the copyist cited Luther's reported sayings a few pages before; the copyist was aware of Hubmaier's subsequent martyrdom. See above at <209>.

A Short, Simple Confession

child at baptism is a total lie and mockery. <221> Where a personal faith is absent it would be better not to baptize children at all rather than to play with and mock God's Word and sacraments. That is to say, if it cannot be demonstrated that young children believe for themselves and possess their own faith, it is his faithful advice and judgment that one cease and desist from baptizing children, and the sooner the better. [As well], we should no longer slander and mock the exalted majesty of God with such meaningless inherited nonsense.

May the God-enlightened reader judge whether we, or such learned teachers and doctors of the Scriptures, confuse the people. For we seek simply to abide by the Holy Scriptures in accordance with Christ's command as given in Matthew 28[:19-20], Mark 16[:15-16], and the apostolic practice, baptizing those who understand and have come to faith, Acts 2[:38], 8[:12-13; 35-38], 10[:44-48], 11[:16-18], 16[:14-15; 30-33], 19[:1-6], as Philip said to the eunuch: If you believe with all your heart, it [baptism] may take place.

In this fashion the rabbis [teachers] wish to maintain infant baptism, Luther even asserting that children have a personal faith. But Zwingli opposed him, asserting that it could not be demonstrated that children have faith. And so they slander each other, calling each other <222> persons who play foolishly with the holy sacraments, perpetrating lies [on the people], mocking and slandering the mighty majesty of God with such nonsense. If we were to do something similar they would declare us to be stupid idiots, sectarians and seducers, and call us heretics. But that they have [treated Scripture in this way] is plain for all to see. Such pastors have always pleased the world, because they give the world what it wants.

Note here, my God-fearing reader, who has inflicted greater wounds on infant baptism, or who has called it a greater abomination, and who has accused the infant baptizers (infants who cannot yet believe or disbelieve, as Zwingli himself confesses), of greater heresy and blasphemy than those who have directed [such things] against one another, as we have truthfully demonstrated from their own books and writings. Nevertheless, they seek to force us to observe an abomination they have themselves condemned [in one another]. [And when we refuse], they persecute, expel, imprison, and torture us because of it. Some tyrants (incited by their clerics) even turn us over to the executioner to be killed. They do all this in spite of their own confession, and that of the old church fathers, decretals, and councils. We can truly see quite clearly what follows from all these noble confessions <223> and judgments.

If infants have no faith,[391] *then baptizing infants would be the greatest blasphemy and idolatry that has ever arisen. For one would be taking the Word and the name of God in vain and dealing slanderously with it, wanting to prove and maintain [infant baptism]*[392] *with the same Scripture that says "Whoever does not believe will be condemned," and as Paul says, "it is impossible for anyone to please God without faith." Passages like these—and others—exclude neither children nor adults, says Luther.* Zwingli answers: It cannot be proven that children have faith, no matter how honestly one may try to do so, for it is impossible.

Thus Luther and Zwingli agree on baptism like white agrees with black, and fire with water. But in spite of this Luther, Zwingli, their successors, and the papists are all in agreement that any who do not practice infant baptism and *any who refuse to concede that they are right [about infant baptism] are to be persecuted under the guise of [defending] the truth.* And if one dares to confront them with the truth and testimony of Holy Scripture, they bring out the executioner to defend the matter. He is their best defense for retaining infant baptism.

The first argument of the Infant Baptizers

The infant baptizers concede that if one is dealing with unbelievers one should first preach and declare the Gospel to them. If they believe and accept it, they should be baptized upon the confession of their faith. <224> But the children of Christians are [already] certainly children of God, therefore they are to be baptized.

Answer: *We cannot attribute to a fleshly birth something that belongs only to the Spirit and the word of God, for to be a child of God is a work of God. But to be a child of sin derives from ourselves, for we inherit it from our fathers and mothers, whether or not they are Christians. For we are all conceived and born in sin, as was laid out and proven in Article Seven. Thus, everything born of flesh is flesh, as the Lord himself states. And regarding the godly, rather than the human actions which Christ performed, he said to*

---

391 Zurich Q3 : *no inward, hidden faith, known to God alone*
392 Zurich Q3 : *Luther*

his mother: Woman, what have I to do with you?[393] *And again: Who is my mother and who my brother? Whoever does the will of God is my brother, sister and mother.*[394] *And when a woman called out to him from among the people, saying: "Blessed is the womb that carried you and the breast that suckled you," he said to her, "Blessed are they who hear the Word of God and observe it."*[395] St. John confirms this when he states that he [Christ] gave the power to become children of God to those who believe in his name; not to those according to blood or the will of the flesh or the will of man, but to those who are born of God. *Therefore flesh and blood do not produce children of God; rather, [children of God are created] by renewal and the new birth through the Holy Spirit.* <225>

The entire world grew up with infant baptism and is nevertheless stuck in the most gruesome sins and vices, as is—sad to say—everywhere apparent. How then can infant baptism be a Christian baptism and covenant with God? Those who do the works of Abraham are the believing children of Abraham. The others, however, who wilfully indulge in sins and vices are not children of God because of their sins and misdeeds,[396] as Moses (himself) states. Christ says to Abraham's unbelieving descendants: Because they willfully indulge in sins and vices and sought to crucify rather than believe in him, [he said to them]: *"You are from your father the devil and you act according to his pleasure."*[397] *Therefore, since children are innocent and do not know the difference between good and evil, we should leave them to the Lord: in his eternal wisdom he knows everyone's coming and going. We, however, cannot know this, but only what we see, notice, and experience concretely with our own eyes. What presumption it would then be for us to baptize on the basis of this uncertainty, especially since we are unable to distinguish between Jacob and Esau, both of whom were born of the devout Isaac. But Esau was already hated in his mother's womb—to be sure not because he was in his mother's womb, for at that point he had not yet stretched out his hand to the forbidden tree*[398]—*but because God in his eternally unfathomable wisdom, which already saw through all things*

---

393 Zurich Q3 : John 2
394 Zurich Q3 : Mark 3
395 Zurich Q3 : Luke 11
396 Zurich Q3 : Deuteronomy 32
397 Zurich Q3 : John 8
398 Zurich Q3 : *that is, towards unrighteousness*

in eternity, <226> *knew in advance*³⁹⁹ that he would become an enemy of righteousness. Therefore it is impossible for any person on earth to bring Esau into God's eternal covenant, for God's eternal election remains in place and is immovable in all eternity. We must therefore wait, in the fear of God, to see who will and who will not honor God, who will prove to be an instrument of God's grace and who an instrument of his wrath and disfavor in order not to encroach on God's glory and heavenly counsel.

He has reserved these things for his own unfathomable and eternal wisdom and will reveal them to us through his grace and mercy at such a time as pleases him. Then the effects of his grace will be visible to our eyes and we will recognize [the elect] by their fruits. *Those children who die in childhood and innocence, however, we allow to die in the grace of Jesus Christ without baptism, for baptism does not save—only the pure grace of God and the precious and costly blood of Jesus Christ,*⁴⁰⁰ the holy, pure and spotless lamb of God, *saves. This blood is the sign of his grace. For the Lord accepts the children before they have consciously and knowingly stretched their hand out to the forbidden tree.*

But more is expected of those who grow up and reach the age of understanding and accountability. [This is true of all] those who give free reign to lascivious impurity, fornication, adultery, pride, arrogance, lying, deceiving, hatred, swearing, blasphemy, anger, discord, drunkenness, gluttony, etc., closing off their lives, and in such a condition <227> stretch out their hands to the forbidden tree and eat of its fruit, *refusing to follow Christ and enter into his obedience. These are the ones who belong to Esau's descendants, whom God hated in their mother's womb, Romans 9[:10-13]. Therefore it is not good to intervene in God's affairs in this instance and make light of his holy sacraments,* as Luther and the Strasbourg preachers themselves wrote, and as Leo Jud's translation of Erasmus's postil stated. For if someone does not first learn and come to believe evangelical wisdom, baptism will avail nothing. In making such assertions these highly learned scholars themselves attacked infant baptism, and we wish to leave it at that. *Nor should we try to determine the secret judgments of God concerning the manner in which he desires to use his creatures, in a partisan manner or on the basis of human descent, without a clear and unequivocal command; for his judgments are too profound to be fathomed. Romans 9, 10, 11.*

---

399 Zurich Q3 : *of what kind of metal he was forged*
400 Zurich Q3 : *which he shed on the cross for our sake*

The infant baptizers[401] concede to us that in dealing with unbelievers, one should first preach and declare the Gospel to them and then baptize those who accept it upon their confession of faith; but one is to baptize the children of Christians because they are surely already children of God. To this we say: We have answered this above and in doing so have laid a foundation that, we trust, will stand in eternity against all the gates of hell. *For how are children different from older persons who have not heard the Gospel, since young children also do not know anything about Christ and are therefore equally ignorant* <228> *and unknowing in matters relating to God and salvation as those mentioned above? Therefore it is only proper and necessary that children should, in like manner as older persons, first hear the Gospel proclaimed and only then be baptized.*[402] For they stand in the same ignorance as the others. If mature but ignorant persons must first hear the Gospel before baptism, why not much more so the children? Are they not much more ignorant, uninformed and irrational than the former? If not, prove—on the basis of the truth and Holy Scripture—that young children believe and know, recognize and understand, the Gospel. Even the apostles taught before baptizing. But neither men nor angels can provide such proof.[403] *Therefore children should not be baptized until one can deal with them in the manner in which the apostles always dealt with those who were to be baptized*, so that they may be baptized in accord with order of Christ. If the learned ones themselves tell us that the holy sacraments, administered without faith or a knowledge of God, are more harmful than beneficial,[404] why then is baptism administered not only without faith and understanding but also, in the case of young children, in the absence of reason and understanding?

The second argument
The clerics accuse us further, saying: Christ said, let the little children come unto me, for of such is <229> the kingdom of God. [Matthew 19:14; Mark 10:13; Luke 18:16] They argue that because Christ commanded that children be brought to him, this has to take place through baptism, for

---

401 Zurich Q3 : *preachers*
402 Zurich Q3 : *on the basis of their faith*
403 Zurich Q3 : *If it could be proven, we would give ourselves up to prison and admit defeat; but it can never be proven*
404 *Margin*: Martin Luther, Martin Bucer and other preachers, as noted above

Christ commanded that one was not to hinder them [from coming to him]. Whoever therefore refuses to baptize children sins against this passage of Scripture.

Answer: *We gladly concede that Christ scolded his disciples for not allowing parents to bring their children to him. But that it should follow from this that children are to be baptized is something we deny, for we note that Christ handled it differently. He neither baptized them himself nor did he tell his disciples to do so. Quite properly, therefore, they remained unbaptized until they reached the age of accountability, just as the Testament requires. And what does he do for them? He blesses them, embraces them, and lays hands on them. There, too, is where we wish to leave the matter, not concocting some other explanation out of thin air. And if they say, however, that Christ laid hands on them, and that this is also a sacrament and a sign of acceptance, therefore we should baptize them, we answer: If Christ wished to accept children through the laying on of hands, and therefore prescribed this as a sign for us by means of which we too are to accept persons into the congregation, then one should also properly leave it the way he has given it, that is, leave it with the laying on of hands and not make something else of it—like baptism—to suit ourselves. For if it should have been so, Christ would himself <230> have commanded the children brought to him to be baptized. But in no way did he do this. Therefore, even though their argument might be right—that Christ accepted children through the laying on of hands and that we should therefore not prevent them [from coming] but also accept them—this is not a proof drawn from Holy Scripture that we are to baptize them.*

But that Christ, with this action, did not introduce a sign through which people were to be accepted into the congregation is proven by the fact that he did not so much as mention baptism. For baptism is the first sign by which we are commanded to accept persons into the congregation and church of Christ, baptizing them upon their confession of faith, Matthew 28, Mark 16, Acts 8. Therefore the fact that Christ laid hands on the children absolutely does not prove the validity of infant baptism.

The infant baptizers[405] *say that Christ stated: The kingdom of God belongs to the children; therefore it is right to baptize them.*

---

405 Zurich Q3 : *the preachers*

A Short, Simple Confession

Answer: *We do not deny that Christ promised the kingdom of heaven to the children. However, we are not here dealing with the kingdom of heaven for children, but with baptism and who is to be baptized.* For not we, but only the Most High knows who—in their childhood—is a Jacob or an Esau. We have no desire, as stated above, to make mistakes, therefore *we must act in accordance with [Christ's] command and those passages of Scripture that teach us how we are to baptize* <231> *and not seek to take and teach this from passages that do not so much as mention baptism, as happens here.*

Therefore Christ has not commanded anyone to baptize those to whom the kingdom of God belongs while they are still children, especially since it is not known to us whether they belong to the descendants of Jacob or Esau. This knowledge is reserved exclusively to God's majesty, to his eternal election and unfathomable wisdom, which already knows all things from eternity, as we explained above in all simplicity and proved on the basis of Scripture. Rather, He—the great prince and king of heaven and earth—said to his disciples: Go forth and teach all peoples, baptizing them in the name of the Father, and of the Son, and of the Holy Spirit, and teach them to observe everything I have commanded you, Matthew 28[:19-20]. And again: He who believes and is baptized will be saved, but whoever does not believe will be condemned.[406]

Here one has a clear and unequivocal command concerning baptism given by the eternal Son of God himself; this command is to be kept. Nor should one devise another baptism out of carnal cleverness, sophistry, or ingenious arguments of human wisdom than the one He has commanded—an [infant] baptism that cannot be demonstrated or proven from Scripture as Zwingli himself confessed. For this is also the manner in which the holy apostles practiced it, Acts 2, 8, 10, 11, 16, 19; nor did they add glosses their own minds had concocted to these passages. <232>

Second, if it had been the custom at the time to baptize children, the apostles would, without doubt, have understood and considered why the children were being brought to Jesus—that is, to be baptized. Therefore they would not have gotten angry and grumbled at their being brought to Christ. But since they scolded and berated them, one must conclude that children were not being baptized at that time and that the apostles knew nothing about any infant baptism.

---

406 *Margin*: Mark 16[:15-16].

Thirdly, it follows that children were brought to Jesus solely in order for him to lay hands on them, which was a common practice at the time. For in the act of laying on of hands many good things were often spoken and a blessing given, as can be seen from Genesis 48. That is why Christ also laid hands on the sick. Now, it is in this fashion that one is also to bring children to Christ so that he may lay hands on them, that is, that he may bless them, and bestow good fortune, grace, and health upon them. This can no longer be done physically, nor through external baptism; rather, it must be done only through believing, Christian prayer and achieved through Christ.

Furthermore, Christ says in Matthew 21[:16]: "Have you never read, 'From the lips of children and infants you have received praise'?" Martin Luther writes concerning Psalm 8[:2][407] that the apostles <233> understood that those were true children who were childlike in spirit and sentiment. That is to say, all those who—in their faith and understanding of God as well as in all other things pertaining to salvation—are not firmly established or grounded, who are weak and imperfect, but who nonetheless hunger and thirst after righteousness and long to drink pure spiritual milk.

Such children one must not hinder, but rather allow to come to Christ. And woe to them who bar their access to Christ and his Word, and hinder them in their good and godly intention to come to Christ. They themselves desire to come to Christ in order to find peace and salvation for their souls. In Matthew 11[:16-17] the Lord also speaks of such children and not of infants in the cradle, for it is impossible to offend the latter; nor do they as yet take offense at anything. For offense takes place in the mind, in an understanding of good and evil. Infants, however, do not as yet possess these abilities; indeed, they are without all understanding.

This is to be understood in the following manner: that Christ uses the words "small children" to indicate those who are still young in their faith and understanding of God, in order to differentiate them from infants. For those who believe in him but are still spiritual children may well—and

---

407 See *Martin Luther's Complete Commentary on the First Twenty-Two Psalms*, trans. by Henry Cole, volume 1 (London: Simpkin and Marshall, 1826), 399-400. The copyist accurately paraphrases Luther's commentary on Psalm 8:2, "Out of the mouth of babes and sucklings hast thou ordained praise...." The theme in the codex is infant baptism. In his commentary on this verse, Luther argues that the "children" spoken of here should not be thought of as literal children, but refer figuratively to the lowly and humble who are instructed by the Holy Spirit. It is this point the copyist believes supports the Anabaptist position.

often—be offended in many different ways. And woe to those who offend such children in Christ. Therefore infant baptizers should <234> read this passage carefully so that they do not try to interpret it as referring to young human children whom they are to bring to Christ, for they possess no command to do so. But instead they hinder the true spiritual children who seek to come to Christ and his Word, barring their access so that they are unable, in truth and in any profound way, to come to Christ. For Satan is such a strange being that he can take a correct judgment of God and delude and blind the eyes and judgment of the worldly-wise and biblical scholars to such a degree that they act, with respect to godly matters, in a manner directly opposed to what God desires. They only offend, hinder, revile, and slander the believers, by which they think they are doing God a service and promoting the salvation of humankind.

Sadly, one is forced to experience and observe this throughout the entire world in that people attempt, with great diligence, pomp, and circumstance, to encourage and bring innocent but ignorant children to Christ by having them physically baptized, even though Christ has most certainly not commanded it and it cannot be defended with a single letter of Scripture. Nor does this bring the children any closer to Christ than they were before.

In contrast to this, as soon as children who are not only born of earthly flesh and blood <235> but also are born from above and become spiritual children of God, the world refuses to tolerate them. These, out of a zeal for the pure and clear Word of God, long for and demand to be awakened to, and grow in, faith in Christ and the knowledge of God through the power and influence of the Holy Spirit, becoming mature and attaining the measure of the fullness of Christ. Therefore we repeat that when God himself—and no longer flesh and blood—chooses and brings to birth children from above, the world no longer tolerates them. The infant baptizers, however, want to bring young and ignorant children to Christ through baptism when they are not to be brought to him in this fashion, as we have repeatedly said and intend to prove with even more passages from the Holy Scriptures. As soon as persons are driven by, and awakened through, God's power and Spirit, and desire—of their own accord—to come to Christ, however, these infant baptizers and their followers persecute and harry them out of the land, closing off every correct avenue of access to Christ. They do this to the very persons they earlier sought to keep under their control through confusion and force. Is that not a great blindness?

Therefore infant baptizers should consider with care what they are doing in God's sight with these young children whom they desire to bring to Christ through baptism, <236> but for which they have no command. To the contrary, they prevent the truly reborn spiritual children from coming to Christ, who—through a newly kindled zeal and love of God—are inwardly compelled to do so, compelled to commit themselves to Christ and grow up [spiritually] into a true dwelling place of God and temple of the Holy Spirit. These are the persons whom Christ has called to come to him and be baptized upon their confession of faith, as related above. Whether or not the infant baptizers do these things we leave to their own judgment and that of all understanding persons.

Truly, every time a person seeks to honor God without a direct command from Him, that person egregiously dishonors and insults God. This is certainly to be feared in the case of infant baptism. They attempt so assiduously to bring the children to him—even to the extent of using force—children whom Christ does not wish brought to him in this fashion, for he has not ordered or commanded it with even a single word. And yet those whom he desires to have come to him, and whom he has commanded to be baptized in accordance with the order he has established, these they turn away and hinder from coming to him.

For those who have become true children of God through the renewing of the Holy Spirit, and who through faith and a new birth desire to come to Christ and be baptized, should be allowed to <237> come to him. And woe to those who hinder them, who seek to suppress and extinguish the Word of God, His Spirit, and the knowledge [of God] in them. They will have much to answer for when they come before the face of God.

Nevertheless, it should be permitted and allowed, as stated above, to bring children to Christ if one so wishes. But it must be done in the correct manner, in the way Christ himself has determined, namely: *first, through prayer by means of which children may—and should—be brought to Christ, commended and dedicated to him, as we said earlier. Thereafter through godly teaching and a Christian upbringing in the fear of and obedience to the Lord. In this manner children are correctly prepared for baptism*

A Short, Simple Confession

and brought to Christ, brought into His body and offered up to Him.[408] In this manner we also become aware—to the extent that God allows—who belongs to the descendants of Esau or Jacob. *To baptize children without first recognizing this difference, however, at a time when they are as yet unable to know anything about Christ or understand his Word, is to exchange what is certain for what is uncertain and in doubt.*

The third argument

Some infant baptizers—against whom Zwingli wrote, as already noted—propose that children also believe and have the Holy Spirit, and therefore they too should be baptized.

Answer: As far as the Holy Spirit is concerned, the Holy Scriptures tell us <238> that John the Baptist, to whom Christ—above all other humans—gave a glowing testimony, received the Holy Spirit in his mother's womb. Jeremiah also was sanctified to become a prophet in his mother's womb.[409] And once the sun even stood still in the heavens for a whole day at Joshua's command,[410] and another time a dumb animal—namely Balaam's donkey—spoke when the angel of the Lord blocked his path. But does that mean that all such dumb animals before and after him spoke? Therefore not all persons are dealt with in the manner God dealt with Jeremiah, Romans 9, who was chosen to be a prophet already in his mother's womb, Jeremiah 1[:5], or as happened to John the Baptist, of whom Christ said: "I tell you the truth: Among those born of women there has not risen anyone greater

---

408 Prayer for and dedication of infants in an Anabaptist congregation was already practiced in Hubmaier's congregations in 1525. In a letter to Oecolampadius, Hubmaier writes, "I like to assemble the congregation in the place of baptism, bringing in the child. I exposit in the native tongue the gospel text: 'Children were brought...' (Matthew 19:13). As soon as his name has been given to him, the whole congregation on bended knee prays for the child, entrusting him to the hands of Christ, that he may be ever closer to the child and pray on his behalf." Pipkin and Yoder, *Hubmaier*, 72. Pilgram Marpeck described a similar ceremony for infant dedication (with more detailed elaboration) in his "Confession" to the Strasbourg city council, January, 1532. Marpeck includes a specific admonition to parents to raise the child "to the praise and glory of God." See Klaassen and Klassen, *Writings*, 147.
409 *Margin*: Jeremiah 1[:5]
410 *Margin*: Joshua 10

than John the Baptist," Matthew 11[:11], Luke 7[:28]. Nor does the sun stand still in the heavens every day as it did in Joshua's time. For the text states that there was no day like that one, not before and not after. Therefore, even though the example of John the Baptist may prove that he had the Holy Spirit even before his birth, his example does not apply to others, as Romans 9[:10-13] makes plain by using the examples of Jacob and Esau.

Even though some may say <239> that God can indeed impart faith and such [other] gifts to children—which we confess as well—experience teaches us the extent to which children can have faith and sense the presence of the Holy Spirit. Nonetheless, we too confess that God cannot only grant faith but also the understanding with which one must grasp faith, indeed even the ability to speak so that they can confess their faith. But what kind of faith children actually possess is demonstrated by their lives and the fruit which they bear.

Thus, even though God is all powerful and does what He wills, and what no man may oppose, he nevertheless keeps to a certain order, as it pleases him, in everything he does. Therefore we all should take heed not to try to master God, trying to make him act in accord with our opinions, for he has made everything well. To him be praise and honor in all eternity.

But the passages of Scripture which the infant baptizers cite to prove that young children have faith are no more understood by the children than those which state that he who does not work shall not eat.[411] For Scripture says: Unless a man is born again he cannot see the kingdom of God;[412] and unless you eat the flesh of the son of man . . . you have no life in you.[413] [Christ also says]: He who refuses to take up the cross and follow me is not worthy of me,[414] and many similar passages that are to be understood by mature persons rather than by children. The same is true of those passages that state: Whoever does not have the Spirit of Christ does not belong to Christ and without faith it is impossible to please God.[415] <240>

These statements, like the others, are all directed to understanding persons, not to young and ignorant children. For all Scripture has been given for the benefit of the mature and understanding persons, not the

---

411 *Margin*: 2 Thessalonians 3[:10]
412 *Margin*: John 3[:3]
413 *Margin*: John 6[:53]
414 *Margin*: Matthew 10[:38]; 16[:24]; Luke 14[:27]
415 *Margin*: Romans 8[:9]; Hebrews 11[:6]

children. And even if children possessed a hidden faith—a contention that cannot be proven with any biblical passage taken in its proper context and interpreted correctly, that is, in the sense that Christ and St. Paul wished it to be interpreted—no sure external sign may be granted on the basis of a hidden sense or an uncertain truth, without a special revelation that God might be pleased to give.

Now baptism signifies and is a declaration of faith in Christ for the forgiveness of sin, hence the apostles did not baptize upon a hidden faith or an unknown spirit, as the infant baptizers do and must do. For the apostles did not act upon an uncertainty, but only upon a previously understood and then confessed faith attested by the presence of the gifts of the Holy Spirit and confirmed and proven in actual fact by words and deeds. This and nothing else will one discover in the writings of the apostles. <241>

Now, children have not lived in unbelief, nor have unbelief; the deeds of unbelief are not or have not yet been revealed to them—that is, the sins that are the consequences of unbelief—nor also the deeds of faith. [Therefore], they cannot conceive of or receive the forgiveness of sins that is preached or taught regarding baptism in the name of Jesus. Nor can they believe any external teaching or give witness [to such a faith] upon which one may or should baptize externally with water as a sign of their faith.

Therefore children may not be given such an external sign of their faith. And if one nevertheless gives them this external sign on what is presumed to be a hidden or latent faith, then by the same token they should be given the bread and wine of communion upon their presumed hidden love in remembrance of the suffering and death of Christ. For the latter is as dependent upon the believer and his faith as is baptism: He who does not eat my flesh will not have eternal life. If the phrase, "he who does not believe," is to apply to uncomprehending children then, according to John 6, it must follow that the phrase, "he who does not eat," or "does not have love," must also apply to them.

If that is the case, what happens to Paul's words concerning communion? Namely, "One ought to examine oneself before the eating of the bread and drinking of the cup" [1 Corinthians 11:28]. How can ignorant children examine themselves? You say Christ is here speaking of the inner [spiritual] <242> eating in faith, and that is true. But if children are presumed to have a hidden faith they must also have a hidden love. Paul says, whoever has not love gains nothing, even if he has faith enough to move mountains

[1 Corinthians 13:2]. Therefore love is more important than faith. But [the clerics] do not differentiate between the two. Now, if [infants] have an inner and hidden faith and love, then it would be appropriate for them to have an inner baptism and communion. For they understand the one as little as the other.

How then do the infant baptizers intend to proceed, seeing that their case is so ill-founded and uncertain? For it does not do them any good to attempt to flee to the alien faith of the church, the parents or the godparents, since the church is built upon our own faith and commitment, as we have said, not the reverse. A living faith is the foundation, and the church is the structure. For if I did not believe the Gospel I would never believe the church, since the church is built upon the Gospel and not the Gospel upon the church. Thus St. Paul states: "For no one can lay any foundation other than the one already laid, which is Jesus Christ," 1 Corinthians 3[:11]. Christ says the same thing to Peter: "And I tell you that you are Peter, and on this rock (that is, upon the faith you have just confessed) I will build my congregation or church, <243> and the gates of Hades will not overcome it."[416]

It is for this reason that we must first be instructed in the Word of God, that Jesus is the Christ, the son of the living God, for faith comes from hearing, and hearing from the word of God, Romans 10[:17]. Then, secondly, on this foundation we are to build gold, silver, and precious stones—that is, faith and confession. Then, thirdly, the congregation or church is built upon our faith and confession; not our faith upon the church, but rather upon the preached Word of God, which is God himself who has become flesh. For Christ states: whoever believes and is baptized. He does not say: for whom father and mother or godparents believe.

Therefore, Christian reader, you can clearly see and understand from these powerful testimonies drawn from the Word of God, what kind of hidden inner faith children possess. For how can they believe if they have never not believed and are beings created by God in a state of innocence, good and pure creatures of God, totally perfect in their simplicity?[417] This condition is pleasing to God and continues to be until they stretch out their hand to the forbidden tree and sin is found in them, Ezekiel 28[:14-

---

416 *Margin*: Matthew 16[:18]
417 *Margin*: Ezekiel 28[:15]

A Short, Simple Confession

15]. God himself testifies against Jonah to this effect,[418] saying he will have mercy on those who cannot distinguish between right and left, for Jonah could not have called the people—as he did the king and the rest of the people—to repentance in such a way that they could have believed and acted upon their belief. <244> It was for the same reason that Moses said to the children of Israel: There are those among you today who do not know the difference between good and evil; they shall enter into the land of Canaan. God has mercy on the children because of their ignorance and true innocence; on the others, however, because of their faith and repentance. In this way the entire Word of God retains the order God has given it and confusion is avoided.

And even though parents may often be punished after the lesson has been preached, and their children in their innocence along with them (understood in a temporal sense), nevertheless the punishment does not occur because of the children—who are ignorant of good and evil—but because of the guilt of the parents. The same thing happened in the flood in Noah's time, and in Lot's day with Sodom and Gomorrah. In those instances the Scripture says nothing about the guilt of ignorant children, but addresses only the roguery, malice, wantonness and cunning of the adults, even though children were—and continue to be—punished along with the others. Nonetheless, no one may declare them ruined because of their own sins. The same is true today: those who know and understand good and evil repent and believe, but ignorant children are pardoned before [they do so]. Thus, also, parents are spared because of the innocence of their children, but children are not condemned because of the wickedness of their parents. Everyone in the world quarrels about the salvation of innocent children, paying no heed to their own damnation <245> even though everyone will be punished in accordance with their own cunning and wickedness.

Who then would be so presumptuous as to proceed with baptism in uncertainty, without a command from God, bending the Holy Scriptures, perverting and interpreting them as they deem right, even though it has been clearly laid before our eyes upon what [foundation] Christ wishes to build his church, how one is to baptize and what is required in Christian baptism? For every time the apostles baptized, they looked for a publicly confessed faith and knowledge of God, and wherever they noticed, saw and heard God's gifts and the external signs of the presence of the Holy

---

418 *Margin*: Jonah 4

Spirit, they also gave them the external sign of baptism, as the Acts of the Apostles clearly testify, Acts 2, 8, 10, 16.

When the queen's administrator requested to be baptized, Philip said to him: "If you believe with your whole heart, you may be baptized," as though Philip wished to say: only those may be baptized who have been granted true faith in Christ. No unbelievers, hypocrites or children [may be baptized]—that is, those who do not know good from evil or who do not understand. But if you believe with your whole heart, you may be baptized. Quite apparently it was not enough for Philip that the steward should receive baptism after having been taught and instructed thoroughly in the Scriptures, for he demanded a true, sincere, and self-confessed faith.

Therefore to defend infant baptism with facile sophistry, carnal wisdom, subtle and unfounded arguments is nothing less than to overturn and gloss into oblivion <246> the clearly and unequivocally expressed command of Christ, which all the apostles followed (of whom we read not a word about their having baptized ignorant young children; they baptized only those who understood and confessed a personal faith.). If one could see and perceive such signs and marks of faith and the Holy Spirit in infants as one saw, heard, and perceived in those who were baptized by the apostles, then we would concede that it would be possible to baptize children. However, since none of these things can be found in young children, one should wait until—through teaching and prayer—they have received it from God and have consciously confessed and demonstrated it in their actions. Then they may be powerfully baptized in the Spirit and in truth, just as the apostles did, but not before.

The infant baptizers put forward a further argument, saying that children participate in the greater, essential part of baptism and so they should justly be given the lesser part of baptism.[419] To this we answer directly, with reason and in truth: No. For baptism is not only a sign of the covenant of God's people, it is also an external sign which signifies the rebirth and renewal of the entire person who is receiving baptism. For Peter says very clearly that baptism <247> is not the removal of dirt from the body, but the pledge of a good conscience toward God, 1 Peter 3[:21]. *And the apostle Paul says to the Colossians 2[:11]: "In whom you were also*

---

[419] From the context, it appears that the argument being opposed here is that infants, as part of the covenant community, should receive the outward sign of baptism, marking them as belonging to that community.

circumcised in the putting off of the sinful nature, not with a circumcision done by the hands of men but with the circumcision done by Christ, having been buried with him in baptism and raised with him through your faith—mark well, through faith—*in the power of God."* Read Romans 6[:1-4], where you will find a clear account of what baptism means. Namely, nothing other than that those who let themselves be baptized confess, in accordance with the order established by Christ and his apostles—and with their actions testify—that they desire, with Christ, to die to sin and be buried; and just as he rose physically from the dead they wish to be spiritually resurrected from sin, no longer living in the old manner but serving God in a devout life while denying and rejecting the world, the devil and all godless living. [They promise] from henceforth to cling to Christ, to be obedient to him in true faith and upright love, in innocence of life, in joy and sorrow, in good and bad times, under the cross and in affliction, until death. That is the correct character and solid inner strength that baptism signifies and depicts externally. Therefore those who possess such a character, demonstrating [it with their actions], and who through true faith and a pure and undefiled love have been born again to a new life, <248> can and may be given the external sign of baptism to their advantage [*mit frucht und nutz*] in accordance with the command of Christ.

However, *wherever such essential nature of baptism is not present, the simple teaching and outward sign*[420] *is of no value. Worse, it is an abuse and mockery of God's order. For the soul cannot be cleansed by any element or external thing in this world; only faith and the illumination of the Holy Spirit,* who is the only true pledge and seal of a living faith, *can cleanse the human heart. It has to follow, then, that baptism cannot wash away sin; nevertheless it is instituted by God. Therefore it has to be an outward sign of an inner faith and as well as the outward sign of a pledge,* as Zwingli himself confessed above, *henceforth to live a new life,* in accordance with God's Word—to the extent that God grants us grace.

Let every understanding person therefore think about and consider whether young children have a character like the one signified by the act of baptism, whether or not they crucify the flesh, have rejected sin and unrighteousness, and have—with Christ—buried the old Adam and with him been raised to walk in newness of life. To this question everyone must

---

420 Zurich Q3 : *water*

answer: No. And if that is the case, how then can children have the meaning of baptism and the essence of baptism? <249>

Therefore, even though children may belong in God's covenant, it does not follow that they may and should be baptized. For baptism does not only symbolize membership in God's people, it is also the sign of a new birth and signifies the death and burial of the old person and the resurrection of a new one. This the young children neither possess nor can possess. Nor can we know when they will grow up and reach the age of accountability, whether or not they will become descendants of Jacob or Esau, as noted earlier. Therefore they are not to be baptized until one can tell and discern the difference in them—that is, not only when they can receive half of the sign, but when they also possess the entire essence and the full meaning of baptism. In this way they possess not merely a partial and incomplete [baptism], which amounts to an incorrect and useless baptism, but rather a right and proper Christian and apostolic baptism. Thus they are not left with an empty shell and a handful of straw, never getting to the kernel of grain inside.

Sadly, it is the former that takes place in the world, for everywhere one is only concerned with the external sign, quarreling over it and seeking to possess and retain it with great industry and violence, as though all salvation and happiness depended upon it. So much is this the case that Martin Luther himself confessed that baptism and the Lord's Supper should not be administered to persons who do not believe;[421] for [these sacraments without faith] are a sheath without a knife, like a sign outside a tavern with no wine inside, <250> or like a jewel case without a gem. The Strasbourg preachers confirm this, as we noted above.[422] Martin Bucer, present at the Bern Disputation, and others of his brothers, stated that without the baptism of the Holy Spirit, water baptism was nothing but an illusion. Zwingli himself, as noted above,[423] conceded in his booklet on baptism that he could not prove that infants could believe even though some persons attempted to do so, although in vain. Infants could neither believe the Gospel nor not believe it.

Yet in spite of all this, they seek to retain an empty symbol, as is clearly apparent on every hand. In order to do this they enlist the aid and assistance

---

421 *Margin*: M. Luther
422 *Margin*: Strasbourg preachers. M. Bucer
423 *Margin*: Zwingli

A Short, Simple Confession

of the secular rulers; and whoever refuses to go along with them has to suffer the consequences, being punished in person and in property. But no one quarrels about or spills any tears—never mind blood—over the true meaning of baptism, on which alone salvation depends, and without which the external sign is meaningless. And even though no one has the true meaning of baptism nor will ever receive true baptism, no one is expelled from city or country because of it. They all think they have acted correctly and are good believing Christians if they have given or received the bare sign in childhood, though it was given in total ignorance and without any understanding of the faith or knowledge of God. <251>

Oh God! Who can sufficiently lament and weep over such a miserable situation, a situation the whole world ignores, together with its learned scholars, a situation about which they are unconcerned. Consider, dear reader, the blindness of the world which expects to achieve in little children that which grown-ups neither can nor wish to do; this is everywhere apparent. For the adults refuse to renounce the devil, to bid the world farewell, crucify the flesh, kill the old Adam, die to sin and other similar things—unless, of course, they are born again from above through the Holy Spirit. Nevertheless, they want to achieve all this in the baptism of infants. Is that not a pitiful child's play, presuming that young children should be able to do what adults without the new birth cannot and will not do? Truly, if one is involved in such an important business, a business in which one is, together with other understanding and believing people, to undertake the renunciation of the most powerful of enemies, the devil, the world, sin and everything that is opposed to God, one does not need less, but rather more zeal and earnestness, and much grace if one wishes to accomplish and create something useful. That this cannot be achieved by young children all understanding persons know, as we have repeatedly heard above.

Since, according to the words of Peter, baptism is not the removal of dirt from the body <252> but a sure pledge of a good conscience toward God made by those who have come to know him, and that—as we have proven at length from the Word of God—this knowledge of God comes through hearing the Gospel proclaimed; therefore we teach that those who have heard the Word, and who know and believe it, are to be baptized upon their confession of faith as Christ commanded and the apostles practiced it. As we have repeatedly demonstrated, children are not to be baptized. For since those born of Adam's seed and in his manner inherit his characteristics, sharing his fellowship and partaking of his sinfulness; therefore also Christ, who was to take away sin, destroy its power, strength and force, has a very different beginning to his birth, as explained above. Therefore, those who inherit Christ's characteristics and become part of his fellowship, desiring to become members of his body, must be born of Christ, not in the Adamic but in the Christian manner. Such a birth is brought about through faith in God's Word and the illumination of the Holy Spirit. For whoever accepts the Word in faith becomes a child of God, as John declares: "Yet to all who receive him, to those who believed in his name, he gave the right to become children of God—children born not of natural descent, nor of human decision or a husband's will, but born of God."[424] That is why Paul also states: "it is not the natural children who are God's children, but it is the children of the promise who are regarded as offspring" [Galatians 4:28]. <253>

Therefore because we are to be born in a Christian, not in an Adamic, manner, we need to understand how Christ's birth occurs and takes place, which happens in faith through the working of the Holy Spirit. Whoever now desires to have Christ's essence, his characteristics and nature, must be born in like manner from God in order to become his child, with Christ, as Peter observes: "For you have been born again, not of perishable seed but of imperishable, through the word of truth" [1 Peter 1:23].

This birth takes place in the following way.[425] When the Word of God is heard and believed, this faith is sealed with the power of God by the Holy Spirit. Thereupon the person is renewed and made alive in Christ, after he had been dead in his transgressions, into a righteousness that counts before God. Thus man becomes a new creature,[426] a new person, created in God's own image or having that image renewed within. Now, anyone born in this manner may rightfully be baptized,[427] a washing of new birth, with which such a person is brought into and inscribed in the covenant of grace and the knowledge of God outwardly as well—a covenant with God and all his saints whom he joins and to whom he gives his pledge. From

---

424 *Margin*: John 1[:12-13]
425 *Margin*: Ephesians 4[:22-24]; Romans 12[:1-2]; Ephesians 2[:4-10]
426 *Margin*: Genesis 1
427 *Margin*: Ephesians 4[:22-24]; Colossians 3[:1-17]; Titus 3[:1-11]; Jeremiah 31[:31-34]

A Short, Simple Confession

henceforth such a person no longer serves himself but promises to obey God and his congregation, to the extent that God grants grace from above.

Concerning Circumcision[428]

We therefore teach[429]—*just as Abraham was commanded to circumcise his entire household—to baptize all those in the household of Christ,* <254> *as His words, which he spoke to John [the Baptist] prove: "Let it be so, for it becomes us to fulfill all God's righteousness." Now, since Abraham could not circumcise anyone in his house before the child had been born, nor any of his descendants after him, even so in the house of Christ no one may be baptized who has not first been born in a Christian manner through word and faith. But the person born in the above fashion will be baptized upon his publicly expressed faith. Abraham circumcised after he received a command from God the Lord to do so and not before, nor did he add anything to this command out of human cleverness or wisdom but, as remarked above, he simply and faithfully followed [the Lord's command]. Similarly, the believers of the New Testament must baptize, in accordance with the command of our mighty king and sovereign, Jesus Christ, God's Son (to whom the Father has given everything in heaven and on earth), Matthew 28[:19-20], Mark 16[:15-16], as a sure pledge with God, even as the apostles did, Acts 2[:38], 8[:12-13; 35-38], 10[:44-48], 11[:16-18], 16[:14-15; 30-33], 19[:1-6],* as we have proven above over and over again.

Infant Baptism may not be declared to take the place of Circumcision

Therefore infant baptism may in no way be proven and preserved through circumcision. For *the literal and external circumcision was reckoned to*

---

428 The argument on circumcision and baptism in this section closely follows the logic and argument of an anonymous early Swiss Brethren tract, *Wie die Gschrifft verstendigklich soll underschieden/und erklärt werden....* (n.p., n.d.), today found in Amsterdam. A photostatic copy of this tract resides at the Mennonite Historical Library, Goshen, Indiana. See the translation by J. C. Wenger, "An Early Anabaptist Tract on Hermeneutics," MQR 42 (January 1968), 26-44; and J. H. Yoder, *The Legacy of Michael Sattler* (Scottdale, PA: Herald Press, 1973), 150-77. There does not appear to be direct textual borrowing here, although the author does come close on occasion, as will be noted below. Later in the manuscript of *Codex 628*, the first part of *Wie die Gschrifft* ... will be copied verbatim.

429 *Margin*: Circumcision

the natural Jew to mean a [physical] circumcision. However, God no longer requires such a literal, external circumcision for [the people of His new covenant]. <255> Likewise, Christians do not regard the external, literal baptism to be a [true] baptism, as Paul testifies in many places.[430] Indeed, he observes that without faith, rebirth, and renewal, external baptism is useless. Everything depends upon the interior circumcision of the heart, Colossians 2[:11]. Therefore there is no equivalence between the old circumcision and Christian baptism.

In the second place, Christians are not tied to any specific time or day like those of old, especially since no command exists [in this regard].[431] That is why the Lord's Supper, likewise, is not tied to any specific day as was the crossing [of the Red Sea] for those of old. Instead, all believers are left free since nothing pertains any longer among the new people except what is done without a law [commandment] or coercion, and comes from a spontaneous spirit and flows from an unvarnished faith, as we have proven in the first article above many times over.

Should someone say, however: If baptism is not tied to any specific time, why may we not baptize children? We answer such a person by saying, because baptism is tied to faith, which children do not possess.

Third, circumcision had a clear and express command from God, Genesis 17[:10-14]; 21[:4]; Exodus 12[:48]. Infant baptism, on the contrary, has neither a scriptural command nor example in apostolic practice, as we have heard and as will yet be proven further.

In the fourth place, if one wished to treat baptism [in a manner] similar to the letter of the law concerning circumcision, <256> then one would have to baptize children only on the eighth day, as was done earlier with children who were to be circumcised.[432]

Fifth, one would not be able to baptize any girls, but only boys, for only the males, not the females, were circumcised.[433]

---

430 *Margin*: Romans 2[:25-29]; 1 Corinthians 2[:9-16]; Galatians 5[:3-6; 24-25], 6[:13-15]

431 *Margin*: Colossians 2[:8; 16-17; 20-23]; Galatians 2[:15-16]; Matthew 26[:26-29]; Exodus 12[:3]; Romans 12[:1]; 2 Corinthians 8, 9

432 A close paraphrase here of the printed pamphlet: "Die Beschneidung mag gar kain concordi sein auff die Tauff/sunst müst man eben den achten tag nemen...." So *Wie die Gschrifft verstendigklich soll underschiden/und erklärt werden ...*, C recto.

433 A close paraphrase: "So müst man auch die Mägdtlin nit tauffen/dann sy ja nit beschnitten wurden/ursach/sy haben kain gesetz als die Knaben." So *Wie die*

Sixthly, concerning the baptism of children, one would think that God, in his eternal providence, would have ordered his Son to be baptized in childhood had he wanted it to serve as a model for us; Christ would then not have allowed himself to be baptized only at the age of 30, Luke 3[:23].[434]

If someone should say, Christ was not subject to any law or any time, we agree, for it is true. But just as Christ observed the God-ordained time and order with regard to circumcision, so he was also doubtlessly careful to observe the correct and proper time for his baptism, a time that had been preordained in eternity.

Or who would wish to say that Christ held circumcision in higher regard than baptism, since the former was to be discontinued and the latter about to begin and come into use by the believers? Why, then, should Christ not also have as diligently recognized the right time at which it was to become customary to baptize as he did the time of circumcision? Especially since Christ acted and did all things for our example and instruction so that we might follow him. That is why his baptism should rightly be regarded as teaching and instruction for us. <257> This is not to say that one must postpone baptism until one is thirty years of age, but rather that one must not rush into it until one has reached the age of understanding and has received the true inner knowledge that is necessary for baptism, that is, that the outward baptism is merely a sign and a symbol, as St. Jerome, Martin Luther, and other preachers have described it, and Martin Bucer and his Strasbourg colleagues confessed in public print—that is to say, without the baptism of the Holy Spirit water baptism is an illusion.

Christ allowed himself to be baptized when he was about to enter his office and into the obedience of his heavenly Father; indeed, when he was about to enter into his challenges and temptations, into suffering and the cross, into his conflict and battles with the devil and the world, and about to accomplish those things necessary for the salvation of humankind. It was for that purpose that his Father had sent him into the world. That is why all these things began at, and followed upon, his baptism, Matthew 4.

In doing all the above-mentioned things, Christ intended to teach by his example; and this would have sufficed even if we possessed no other writing

---

Gschrifft ..., C recto.
434 A close paraphrase: "So müst sich Christus auch inn seiner kindthait Tauffen haben lassen/der doch wol gewißt hat/was der Tauff wer und bedeüt/den die andere kinder ye nit wissen...." So *Wie die Gschrifft ...,* C recto.

concerning baptism. *That is to say, whoever wishes sincerely to submit in all patience to the will of God and obedience to the Almighty in battle against the devil, world, flesh, and blood; who does not wish to depart from Christ until death, but instead persevere to the end in every kind of persecution and affliction by God's grace, such a person may—indeed should—join and unite with God and all believers through external baptism as a sure and certain sign.*[435] <258> This should then also encourage and compel all persons, who have truly submitted and signed themselves over to God, to total fear of God, piety, love, and patience in all adversity, as often as they recall to what they have so strongly bound themselves with the pledge that they made in baptism.

The fourth argument
The clerics also reproach us with the following [argument]: The apostles baptized entire households, and it must be assumed that children were present among them.

Answer: To this we answer, first, that with this counter-thrust they confess that they have no clear and sure passage from God's Word upon which to base infant baptism; therefore they seek to confirm their argument with an assumption.

Second, we answer that we may not seek to salve our consciences in such an important matter with an uncertain assumption, but must base it upon the clear and pure Word of God which is to be a light upon our path, Psalm 118[:27].

Third, we answer that the Scriptures speak of household servants: first with regard to the house of Cornelius, Acts 10, of Lydia the dealer in purple cloth, and the jailor, Acts 16, and that of the jailor in 1 Corinthians 1. The Scriptures state that the servants of these four households were baptized. But the Scriptures also clearly and expressly inform us that all these servants were believers, as were those of the house of Cornelius, the jailor's <259> house and the house of Stephanus, etc. Of the household of Stephanus[436] it is written that they had devoted themselves to the service of the saints. From that one may gather that the members of his household were not children, but understanding persons.

---

435 Zurich Q3 : *and commitment*
436 *Margin:* 1 Corinthians 16[:15]

Concerning Lydia or the dealer in purple cloth, even though the Scripture does not explicitly testify to it, the reader should know that it is not customary, either in the Scriptures or in the world, to call a household after the name of the woman as long as the man is still alive. But since Luke here names the house after the woman and not after the man, reason tells us that she was either a widow or an unmarried woman. That being the case, we will leave it up to the God-fearing reader to consider what kind of under-aged children were in her house. At the end of the chapter it states that Paul and Silas, when they were released from prison, returned to the home of Lydia, and when they had seen and consoled the brethren they departed. These "brethren" doubtlessly belonged to the servants of Lydia, for who would suggest that Paul and Silas consoled infant children? In Matthew 2[:3] it speaks of Herod being troubled and all Jerusalem with him. Who would dare to interpret this word "all" as referring to infant children? Were they also troubled and restless?

Fourthly, we answer that infant children were not included among those contained in the term "house" or "household," for Paul says that idle babblers misled whole households, but it is irrefutable that an ignorant child <260> cannot be misled by false teachings. Therefore one may not understand anything else under the term "house" than only those who have ears to hear and hearts to understand.

Fifthly, if it were the case—though it can never be proven to be—that the apostles baptized children for special reasons, even as Timothy[437] was circumcised because of a special circumstance, and certain persons were treated differently—as is reported of Jeremiah and John the Baptist—one cannot make a binding rule of such exceptions in order to baptize all children. Especially since we have never been commanded to do so and have no express Scriptural basis for doing so. It would be utter foolishness before God and all the saints for some of us in our time to allow ourselves to be baptized upon the graves of the dead in the hope that they would arise from the dead, as happened in the days of the apostles.

Certainly the community of goods among Christians can be supported with better arguments than can infant baptism, for there is an explicit apostolic example to support the former in Acts 2[:44-45], 4[:32]. This applied not only to two or three, but to many persons; indeed, to the entire apostolic and Christian church in and around Jerusalem. But in our time

---

437 *Margin*: Acts 16[:3]

it is argued that this single example does not constitute a rule, nor does it compel or bind anyone to this kind of a community. Therefore, since Holy Scripture nowhere expressly teaches or commands community of goods, the holy apostles <261> never treated it as a command or rule to be followed in the manner and form that Jerusalem implemented it. This can be clearly seen in many passages of Paul's epistles.

The same argument might be made and implications drawn if there were at least one or two examples of infant baptism in the Scriptures. But what is one now to say about it, since infant baptism has neither a command nor a single example in the entire Scriptures to commend it? If the apostles had baptized children, it would be a great and unbelievable wonder that the Holy Spirit would so completely have forgotten about it and not even mentioned it in a single passage of Scripture. For every time baptism is mentioned and treated in the Scriptures, not so much as a single word is used in reference to a child. In spite of this, the poor infant baptizers, with their biblically unsubstantiated infant baptism, defend such an outrage with obstinate force, as though they had been bidden and commanded to retain it on pain of eternal punishment and damnation.

Since therefore infant baptism has been invented by human cleverness, and Ulrich Zwingli—as noted above—himself wrote that those who baptize children have no explicit word that bids them to baptize, how dare the infant baptizers make it into such a strict command, using coercion to enforce it? And whoever wishes to exercise greater freedom in the matter must immediately be decried as a heretic and benighted human being, of which we wrote above. How can anyone be so wicked <262> as to make [infant baptism] compulsory when no clear word of God supports it and God himself has not commanded it? Woe to those who take it upon themselves to try to master the house of God in such a way that they command what God has not commanded, in order to do something that has not been spoken in the name of the Lord, nor has been commanded by Him, Ezekiel 13[:1-7]; Jeremiah 23[:16-17; 21-22; 32].

Christ said to his disciples: "Teach them to observe everything I have commanded you," when he sent them out to preach the Gospel. Here Christ bound his disciples' office to a specific command, namely to what he had commanded and specified, and not to what pleased them or to what they felt like doing. The devil, however, sadly, has turned this around so that one now nearly only commands and strictly enforces those things that

A Short, Simple Confession

Christ never commanded. In contrast, one leaves undone—or, at the very least, is not diligent or earnest—in doing what He has commanded. This is the case with all their human statutes, for these are much more diligently and conscientiously observed than God's commands. This is universally the case.

Example: To work six days is a command of God. But this is so seldom observed that everyone is free and allowed to be idle. In contrast, to fast on given days of a week is a human statute; but this is and must be most assiduously observed in papal lands. Decency, honesty, moderation and modesty in dress, eating and drinking, is universally mandated in the Holy Scriptures <263>, but these traits are universally despised while magnificence, intemperance, and superfluity are commended and honored in this perverted world and presumed Christendom. It does not matter that, in the beginning, pride was thrown from heaven into hell and condemned in the Holy Scriptures[438] just as drunkards and gluttons are denied entrance into the kingdom of God.

One can say the same thing of other sins and vices that are wickedly and with great horror and godlessness practiced in this presumed Christendom by rulers and subjects, learned and unlearned alike, even though they are thereby clearly denied entrance to the kingdom of God if they refuse to repent.[439] But at the present all of these vices are still in full swing, and everyone can see only too well with how much diligence and seriousness people seek to eliminate them. Indeed, those who should try to hinder [such vices]—the magistrates and the scholars—are most deeply enmeshed in them.

To raise a child well and in a godly manner, in the fear and admonition of the Lord, is another clear command that should be assiduously observed.[440] But this command is also generally transgressed in the world and this presumed Christendom that no evidence is necessary to prove it. By contrast, however, infant baptism, which is not commanded in the Scriptures but is a human statute, concocted and instituted by humans, is and must be more diligently observed in the world than anything else. And it is [now] more dangerous to refuse to baptize young children than to transgress God's commands or speak out and act in opposition to the

---

438 *Margin*: 1 Corinthians 6[:9-10]; Galatians 5[:19-21]; Ephesians 5[:3-5]
439 *Margin*: Revelation 21[:8; 27], 22[:3; 14-15]
440 *Margin*: Ecclesiasticus 7[:23-24]; 30[:1-13]; Ephesians 6[:4]; Colossians 3[:21]

proclaimed teachings of Christ and his apostles <264> with words and deeds, actions and transactions, as observed above.

One may therefore assume[441] that if Christ had, in unmistakable terms, commanded children to be baptized, and had commanded all those who denied and opposed it as a wicked teaching to be punished and uprooted, then, most assuredly, one would not place as much emphasis upon it as one now does. The same can be seen with respect to other of God's commands, commands that are most blatantly broken with impunity and the transgressors never punished; indeed, they are often even praised.

Adulterers, blasphemers, those who despise and dishonor father and mother, as well as usurers, drunkards, scolders, liars, and others like them should, according to the express command of Christ, be punished, banned and excommunicated from the Christian church and congregation, and be treated as heathen and publicans. These commands, however, are at best taken half as seriously as infant baptism, which has no command and no Scripture to support it, being a humanly devised statute concocted in direct opposition to Christ's true baptism.

If baptism were to be practiced as a free, non-compulsory ceremony without any coercion, and as a human arrangement, one could more easily defend its use among them. But since one makes it into such a compulsory thing and enforces it so strictly, placing such weight upon it, it has become an abomination in the eyes of God, as Christ himself testifies when he says: What humans hold in high esteem is an abomination before God, for they raise it up and hold it in higher regard than all of God's commands, <265> as we have heard.

Secondly, [infant baptism] also brings with it a very harmful carnal assurance that keeps the world in the most profound unbelief; for the moment the child is born people hurry with the greatest alacrity to baptize it as though baptism contains all salvation and holiness. Thus when the children come to the age of understanding they are considered Christians and are given communion. They themselves also believe themselves to be Christians because they were baptized, even though it was without any understanding in the complete ignorance of infancy, long before they possessed either faith in, or understanding of, God. Indeed, the vast majority remain obdurate and ignorant in the things of God, caring little about them; they are content with the observation of the bare externals.

---

441 The text has "abzunemmen" but the context indicates "anzunemmen."

A Short, Simple Confession

They never ask earnestly about those things that alone can make one a Christian and grant faith. [But] the external act of baptism does not make them Christians. Only a true and living faith in Christ can do that through conversion and the renewal of the whole person. But the world has convinced itself that its members have become Christians and believers through baptism; thus, throughout their lives, people place their trust in an empty husk and do not seek the real kernel on which all of salvation depends.

One can see how much weight people place upon baptism when parents bring their child to the priest to be baptized and ask, indeed beg, him if he would please make a Christian of the child. Thus the world believes that through baptism the child becomes a Christian; but this can only be accomplished through a living faith and knowledge of Christ, accompanied by a denial of self. <266> Thus one is much more eager to ask about and acquire the external baptism, on which so little depends, than the new birth and the renunciation of oneself upon which the soul's salvation alone depends, John 3[:3-5], Matthew 16[:24].

They think that, should such a child die without baptism, this would be detrimental and damaging to its salvation and entry into the kingdom of God; but should it die shortly after baptism it would be all the more certain to go to heaven. That is why today, one takes a child to be baptized so soon, especially if it is weak; that is also why the midwives very often pour water on such weak children already in the homes because they do not want to have to atone for these good children should they die unbaptized—indeed so that children who die at this early age not die as heathen, but as Christians. Thus they place [their trust] in external water baptism, something that should be placed only in the pure grace of God and in the innocent shed blood, suffering, and bitter death of the pure and undefiled lamb of God. For with such and similar things one clearly indicates that the entire essence, the complete significance of baptism, is placed solely and alone in the external, visible element of water baptism, even though it accomplishes nothing by itself without the true Christian and heavenly baptism that takes place with fire and the Holy Spirit.

Therefore, even though one has had water poured over oneself in childhood when no inner transformation has yet taken place or no power is present, these people nevertheless regard each other as Christians <267> because they have all been baptized in the same manner. As a consequence, they convince themselves that the external [action] has done it all, and they do not worry themselves overly much about the true inner essence of baptism even if they have never acquired it. This is clearly evident everywhere.

Because the entire world places such a great emphasis upon it, assumes that everything has been accomplished with it, indeed because infant baptism produces such a carnal and pernicious assurance in human beings that the entire world is kept in a state of the highest disbelief, it is impossible to defend infant baptism as simply a harmless external ceremony. People believe that if they have been baptized in the ignorance of childhood, they are already Christians even though they not only do not possess, but do not understand or desire those things that make one a believer and a Christian, such as: the new birth, the mortification of the flesh, denial of self, true faithfulness and love toward friends and enemies alike, patience in suffering and other similar things, about which we have talked at length above and which alone make people into believers and Christians. External baptism—which is satisfied with the empty shells and husks, never asking about the true kernel—does not, as the world believes, accomplish this. This is only too apparent. The world adheres only to the external husk, and never comes to Christ in the right manner and never experiences the true essence of baptism, which is the one necessary thing and makes a person a Christian. Behold, this is the most pernicious poison of infant baptism that remains hidden like a snake <268> in the grass.

Therefore one should not accept anyone into the Christian congregation on the basis of external baptism until that person has received those things from God that alone constitute a Christian and that are indicated by baptism, as we have stated often enough above. This would awaken in many an earnest zeal and desire to acquire that true, inner, and powerful aspect of baptism which they would otherwise never think about. This makes it apparent that all well-meaning (good-hearted) and believing persons are not simply concerned about mere ceremonies, but much more about the presumption and harmful trust people place in infant baptism, which produces such a carnal certainty in people that the godless and unscriptural infant baptism becomes an abomination and idol. It is this idol that the devil clings to so tenaciously, and not the mere and simple ceremony.

To be sure, neither the devil nor the world would take such a tyrannical and bloodthirsty attitude toward a merely external water baptism if such an abominable idol were not hidden in it. It is through this idol that the devil is served to his liking because virtually all trust and confidence is placed in the external transaction—even the learned ones seek to make the case through human argument, as anyone can clearly see. The true inner essence is so little considered that it is a miserable shame; indeed, in their own presumed Christendom they continue to live in incalculable sin and lasciviousness; <269> that is to say, they have dug cisterns that cannot hold any water. At the same time, they have forsaken the fountain of living water, as God complains through the prophet Jeremiah 2[:13].

The fifth argument

They also object further, arguing that Peter says: "To you and your children are these things promised, and to all that are afar off, even as many as the Lord our God shall call." [Acts 2:39] Here, the infant baptizers assert, baptism is promised to the children. Therefore it is right to baptize them.

Answer: *In the foregoing, using the example of Jacob and Esau, the servants of Abraham and Christ, the covenant of the letter of the law and of promise, and the covenant of grace, perception, knowledge, illumination, and achievement, together with Christ's teachings and the proofs provided by his holy apostles, we have, in our simplicity, explained what a snare infant baptism contains and how unfounded it is in the Word of God. We hope that all devout God-fearing persons will take pleasure in the fact that we have clearly and copiously proven from Holy Scripture that baptism should not be extended to the unknowing and the injudicious, but only to knowledgeable and understanding believers who have been illuminated by the Holy Spirit.*

In this passage we also see that the people had not gathered together because of baptism, but through the discussions which the disciples[442]*—being inspired and driven by the Holy Spirit—held among* <270> *themselves—discussions that moved and brought the people together, making them marvel and ask what this new phenomenon was all about. But when some began to poke fun at the disciples, saying their speech derived from too much wine, Peter stood up and said: "These are not drunk with wine as you*

---

442 *Margin*: Acts 2[:6-13]

suppose, since it is only nine in the morning. No, this is what was promised through the Prophet Joel:[443] *I will pour out my Spirit on all flesh and your sons and daughters shall prophesy."*

Because they [the disciples] testified that they had experienced such a gift and prophecy because it had been given them from God through Christ,[444] as a result of which they were now speaking (as to those to whom the gift had also been promised), the people were motivated to ask, out of enthusiasm and curiosity, what they had to do to receive such a gift. Then Peter said: "Repent and be baptized, every one of you, in the name of Jesus Christ for the forgiveness of sins. And you will receive the gift of the Holy Spirit. This promise is for you and your children."

Whoever wishes to see can see clearly enough here, what kind of promise Peter is speaking about, and also why the people were so enthusiastic—for it is incontrovertible that Peter here speaks of the outpouring of the Holy Spirit that had earlier been promised to them, and which had now been given them through Christ. When the people were moved to ask what they had to do <271> to receive this promised gift, Peter gave the questioning people an answer, namely, they were to repent and, living a repentant life, let themselves be baptized *in the name of Jesus Christ* for the forgiveness of their sins and they would receive the Holy Spirit. This is the correct understanding of this passage; whoever treats it differently deceives and misleads himself. For children, as long as they remain innocent, do not yet understand what repentance is and are not saved through baptism, but rather through the grace of God and the death of Jesus Christ who died for the sins of the entire world, as we have declared above and will explain further in article seven.

That the apostle here speaks of children[445] and says, for this has been promised to you and your children, is intended to indicate that he *is referring to the whole house of Israel; the entire seed of Abraham especially has been granted this promise.*[446] That is why[447] we are the children of the covenant and of the promise, as St. Paul says:[448] "Theirs is the adoption, the

---

443 *Margin*: Joel 2[:28-29]
444 *Margin*: John 4[:23-24], 16[:13-14]
445 *Margin*: Acts 2[:39]
446 *Margin*: Genesis 17[:4-7]; Acts 3[:25-26]; Romans 9[:6-8]
447 Zurich Q3 : *Acts 3 says that is why*
448 Zurich Q3 : Romans 9[:4]

glory, the covenant and the law; the service of God and the promises; whose are the fathers, and of whom as concerning the flesh Christ came." [Romans 9:4] However, it cannot be proven that he speaks even one word—as they claim—with respect to the promise of baptism for young children. If he had, he should also reasonably have said: therefore bring your children and let them be baptized. But he did not do this. Therefore this argument of theirs is without foundation. <272>

The sixth argument

The infant baptizers accuse us further, saying: Should your teaching on baptism be correct, it would follow that Christ, from the time of the apostles to the year 1522, was without a church, having completely abandoned it. This would flatly contradict his promise in Matthew 28[:20], where he states: "Lo, I am with you always, even to the end of the world." One can read in the histories, they say, that it is apparent that some people thought that persons baptized by heretics should be rebaptized. But that anyone directly attacked infant baptism until Nicholas Storch did in 1522, when he came out with his teaching, cannot be proven from these histories. Therefore they intend to defend their infant baptism as a truly Christian and apostolic baptism, and as much older than our usage and baptismal order which arose only a few years ago.

Answer: It is not true that infant baptism was not attacked before Nicholas Storch did so in 1522. As we have demonstrated above Pope Boniface, the 44th in line, attacked Augustine's defense of infant baptism in the year 420. Likewise, in the year 370 Jerome wrote: The body should not receive the sacrament of baptism unless the soul has first received the truth of faith. Does not <273> what Jerome and other Ancients wrote about baptism also oppose infant baptism? Or even what Martin Luther, Zwingli, and other preachers have written—notwithstanding the way our current great scholars use and abuse these passages to the contrary?

That the Lord promised that he would be with his followers until the end of the world and not withdraw his grace and Holy Spirit from them, leaving them orphans, we believe without a doubt.[449] Nor does the passage weaken [our argument], for his word is steadfast and true. Heaven and earth will sooner pass away before one jot or tittle of [his word] will fail,

---

449 *Margin*: Matthew 28[:20]; John 14[:18ff]

be broken, or falter. That is why [it is true] that ever since the time of the apostles believers and the elect seed have never ceased to exist on earth, even though the elect seed has been sparsely sown and has had to exist under this lascivious, adulterous, and sinful race, as happened in Israel also. There was no true public and external service of God in which the pure Word of God and Holy Gospel was preached and proclaimed. Nor was there any correct observance of Christian baptism, the ban, or communion because of the most gruesome persecution, tyranny, and destruction. The child of wickedness, the Antichrist, who has the appearance of an animal with seven heads and a mouth to speak great things that blaspheme God, along with his members, operates with the clever, sly, and subtle art of a university professor. This is amply apparent. They attack [God's] Word, glossing it with profound concepts in order to turn it to their <274> meaning and give it a different coloring. They blaspheme his holy name, his tents, and his anointed ones. They set themselves up in the middle of God's temple, abolish the daily sacrifice, and tear down the habitation of his sanctuary. They have attacked the holy ones of the Most High, strangled and slaughtered them.

In spite of this, the heavenly power and assistance, in the midst of such darkness, tyranny, and devastation of his holy temple, has kept a keen watch over his elect—even where these have been uprooted and beheaded—so that even under such circumstances the holy seed has survived; and though they already lay under the Babylonian captivity to such an extent that they could not receive the holy sacraments, they will nevertheless doubtlessly have been baptized with fire and the Holy Spirit, and have enjoyed the true, inner and spiritual essence in baptism and communion.

Sebastian Franck writes most clearly about this Antichrist and devastator of God's sanctuary in his *Kriegsbüchlein* (*War Booklet of Peace*).[450] [There he states that] the Antichrist, under the guise of being Christ, rules and strangles the holy ones as heretics. Mark this, he says, the Antichrist will now say that he is Christ. Thereupon the whole world

---

[450] The reference is to Sebastian Franck, *Krieg Büchlin des Friedes* (Frankfurt a. M., 1550; facsimile reprint, Hildesheim: Olms, 1975). From this point on page <275> through to page <286> of *Codex 628*, the author/editor copies, verbatim, from Franck's *Krieg Büchlin*. The copying spans pages 217a to 227b of Franck's 1550 edition, with only minor additions and deletions.

will bow down before him and honor, listen and pray to him as though he were Christ. Therefore he must have the appearance, name, and likeness of Christ. He will not appear openly as the Antichrist, the adversary of Christ for <275> if he did so, everyone would recognize him. Rather, he calls himself Christian, appeals to his Word but bends it to his meaning, and says and imitates everything Christ did. In sum, he constantly refers to Christ, has his name emblazoned on his shield, sings and speaks of nothing other than Christ, and begins and ends all things in his name. This will break him in the end, and be the means by which the saints recognize [the Antichrist].

In 2 Timothy 3[:1-9] and Titus 1[:16], St. Paul says that the Antichrist will deny Christ's power. And even though he and his members, vassals, and entourage will often assert that they acknowledge God, they will nevertheless deny him with their deeds. It will be just so much idle talk; it will have no force and will pass away as words with no meaning. They will, of course, put on and boast of a Christ-like and God-pleasing appearance, but in their life and deeds they will deny and reject the living Christ and his true followers.[451] Only in this manner will the Antichrist come out *against* Christ in both power and deed, but not in words and appearance, for he will talk like, and appear to be, Christ until the end. I say this against those who assert that the Antichrist will simply oppose Christ. Oh no, why would the world want to accept him, listen to him, and worship him, if he were so blatantly to expose who he is? Likewise, how could he claim to be Christ, and at the same time openly oppose him?

Oh God, lamentably the Antichrist will appear to be nothing other than Christ himself. <276> Otherwise how would he try to set himself up in God's temple, that is in our hearts, declaring himself to be God, if he did not creep into our hearts in the form of Christ, coming in his name, office, and person? One does not allow the devil to enter in all his wickedness. He must first transform himself into an angel of light and into Christ. Otherwise why should the whole world worship him?

It behooves us to be careful here, for he will present us with an appearance like no other: he will cite Scripture, call on God and God's Word, and want all of this to be noticed. For that reason the whole world will throng to him and become apostate so that virtually no one will remain consistently faithful. Should this last a long time and these days not be

---

451 The phrase "and his true followers" was added to Franck's text.

shortened, no human would be saved. Everyone would succumb [to him], for he will be so fortunate in all things that no one will be able to believe that God is not with him or on his side, indeed that it is not God and Christ himself. Then the entire world will regard those who refuse to agree or go along with this [so-called] holy one as the worst of heretics and take their anger out on them. They will come together to help accuse and burn them, destroying them from the face of the earth. For carnal man always assumes that where there is good fortune, victory, honor, and triumph, either God must be present or he must be on its side. Otherwise, the carnal man says, it would not prosper, just as Gamaliel argued in Acts 4 (sic) [Acts 5:39], saying: "If it is of God, it will succeed." Here, however, it will be the Antichrist and wickedness that will succeed, and shall have success for a long time, indeed until the end, when God brings his reign to its end. <277>

[Until then] there will be nothing but good fortune, victory, honor, money, world, and everything, as depicted in the book of Daniel 7, 8 and 9 and Revelation 13 and 14. The beast, by means of which the Scriptures portray and understand the Antichrist, speaks such great and magnificent things that Daniel himself was dumbfounded by the great things that came from the beast's horn that had a mouth with which to speak great things. With great amazement he listened to the great things the beast said. And behold, the horn did battle with God's anointed and defeated them. Toward the end Daniel speaks of a king who will arise first in the end times. He will destroy the foremost of God's saints and will take it upon himself to determine time and hold court. And he will do this for a time, two times and a half a time, until his power shall be taken away and given to the saints, Daniel 7.

Later, in chapter 8, he tells the same thing of another horn that grew up to the heavens, throwing some of the stars to the ground and trampling them underfoot. Indeed, says Daniel, the horn set itself up to be as great as the Prince of the hosts[452] and took away the daily sacrifice from him, destroying the place of sanctuary, as we observed above. By the daily sacrifice we are to understand our bodies, which we are daily to sacrifice in the service of God, Romans 12[:1]. Paul says we are to crucify the members of our body, Colossians 3[:5]; we are to crucify our flesh along with our desires and the passions of the flesh, not fulfil its lusts, Romans 13[:14], Galatians 5[:16-21]; and the daily fragrant sacrifice of our prayers and

---

452 *Margin*: Daniel 8

God-praising lips, are the true sheep, calves and oxen of the Scriptures, interpreted through the sacrifice of Isaac. <278>

The Antichrist dispenses with this daily sacrifice in that he paves another road to heaven for the conscience, and makes Christ into the savior of an unrepentant and godless world for which he shows no concern. [He does this] in spite of the fact that it is God's wrath, and not his grace through the Gospel, that is to be proclaimed to the godless, Romans 1[:18]. With this he loosens and frees consciences to perpetrate every form of vice, having abolished the daily sacrifice and buried and discharged Christ's power. Thus the Antichrist retains nothing but the mere name and appearance which he arrogates to himself and in which he falsely boasts.

And the angel Gabriel spoke further to Daniel: behold I am going to show you what will happen later, in the time of wrath, for the end has its appointed time. After this kingdom of the Medes and Persians, and of the Greeks—that is of Alexander the Great—when transgressions will have overrun the earth, a stern-faced Turkish king will arise who will be a master of intrigue. That is, he will be able to camouflage, color, veil, and mask all things. He will be very powerful, but not as powerful as the one who will overthrow him. He will cause astounding devastation and will succeed in everything that he attempts. He will destroy the mighty men and the holy people. He will cause deceit to prosper and have precedence over wisdom, and in his heart he will consider himself exalted. In his prosperity he will destroy many and he will rebel against the Prince of princes. Yet he himself will be destroyed without violence, 2 Thessalonians 2[:3-12]. <279>

It is in light of this that one must understand all of Daniel 11, where the prophet speaks of a king who will come from Turkey and conquer his kingdom with honied speech. He will do whatever his heart desires and no one will be allowed to oppose him. He will deal cunningly with his allies, exploiting their plunder and property; he will undertake many battles and be successful in all of them. He will abolish the daily sacrifice and appoint many powerful agents who will desecrate the sanctuary upon which his power rests. In its place they will erect the abomination of desolation. He will, with smooth words, dissemble before those who break their vows to God; but those who acknowledge and accept his god will be preferred [in his kingdom].

The truly understanding persons will stumble and fall from his sword, imprisonment and plunder, and many imposters will join his ranks, clinging to him because of his glib talk. But they will not prevail, for the king will do whatever he desires and will exalt and pit himself against everything that is of God or is called by His name. And he will succeed in this until the time of wrath has ended. He will have no regard either for God or the love of women, for he will desire to be sufficient in himself. He will trust only in his ability to dissemble, in his weapons and fortresses, and in his own god, Maosim—that is, his power and ability to bribe with gold, silver, jewels and other precious gems. This is a proper honor for such an avaricious god, for this is portrayed and modeled in the heart of Antichrist himself, a heart that is permeated with avarice. This will bring great honor to those who will help him exalt Maosim (that is, his captains, followers and apostles) and make them lords over vast estates which he will distribute among them as reward. <280>

You see in the above nothing but unadulterated destruction, tyranny, persecution, shouting, and victory for the kingdom of the Antichrist; on the other hand, nothing but defeat, lamentation, and oppression in life and property for God and His people. Consider well what kind of person you are and on which side you stand. [In the above] you do not hear that Christ went to war or conquered, but rather that he suffered and was defeated. How then have our eyes become so blinded that we must always assume that God is on the side of the victor?[453] The Antichrist will succeed, under the appearance of Christ which he has assumed in a carnal manner; he will be victorious and defeat the saints—for a time.

Nevertheless, Christ will succeed and be victorious in all his elect and believers after this suffering, and he will be eternally successful and victorious in the Spirit in the hereafter. No one will be able to tear this from his hands. Therefore, even though the Antichrist may defeat us in the flesh and kill us by water, fire, sword, or by other means, he has no means by which he can do harm to our souls. All he has accomplished is to free us from these decaying earthen vessels so that we may be crowned and clothed in the beautiful white wedding dresses with which the Lord Christ will reward his true witnesses.[454]

It is in this manner that the Antichrist with his tyrannical regime and following must—even against their will and thinking—be useful and beneficial to us for our sanctification. They do not do these things with the

---

453 A section of Franck's text is omitted here.
454 *Margin*: Revelation 6[:11], 7[:9; 13-17]; 4 Esdras 2[:39-40]

intention of serving us, especially when they curse us and commend us to the devil, but even under these circumstances they cannot proceed any further than the all-powerful God allows, and only so far as their tyranny is necessary to produce eternal life for us. <281> Therefore the persecutors of the saints, the mob of the Antichrist, are only slaves and servants—in the same way that Pharaoh was to the children of Israel—an instrument through which God the Almighty, the all-gracious Father, tests, tempts, and impels his elect so that people will be able to recognize them if they remain steadfast and constant in the Truth.[455] For it is through tribulation, suffering, and fear that they have to be purified, as gold in the refiner's fire.

At this point we should therefore note the distinction as to who makes war, [celebrates] victories, tyrannizes, robs, and destroys; which people persecute and which are persecuted. When this is done, one always finds that murder, robbery, persecution, the shedding of blood, together with victory always come down on the side of the Antichrist and Satan, for he must be successful and be fortunate in all things in this temporal realm. That is what Scripture says, as we have heard.

The Revelation of John—13, 14, 17, 18—is full of such matters; he makes the Antichrist's beast so beautiful that the whole world will bow down to worship it, and says: Who is like unto that beast and who may oppose him? [Revelation 13:4] He has been given a mouth to speak great, holy, and magnificent things—just as David describes his members in Psalm 12—and also to do battle with the saints and to overcome them. It is before this beast that every nation on earth prostrates itself in worship. For even though the dragon cruelly persecutes the seed of the woman and spews out fire against it, so that the woman with her offspring must fly with eagle's wings into the desert, Revelation 12[:1-6], it must have a powerful appearance in order for the entire world to kneel prostrate in worship before it. The beast also has two horns, that is two considerable kingdoms, <282> peoples, and testaments, just like the lamb. But it speaks like a dragon. It also performs great miracles, so that fire falls down from heaven upon the earth for all the people to see. It does this in order to deceive all those who live upon the earth. In this way it manages to drive virtually everyone—great and small, rich and poor, noble, prince, free and bondman—to put the stamp and mark of the beast on both hand and forehead in recognition of his power, so that no one may buy or sell without it, etc.

---

455 *Margin*: Wisdom of Solomon 3[:1-9]; Ecclesiasticus 2[:1-5]; 1 Peter 1[:6-7]

Under such circumstances, the patience of the saints who will not dissemble and refuse to accept the mark of the beast, will be severely tested until their faith will have been tried, purified, and proven itself, having overcome and been victorious in patience.

Here, too, is where the beautiful city of Babylon belongs, the beautiful red adulteress adorned with jewels and gold, [an exterior] that only has the appearance of virtue. Therefore all people on earth commit adultery with her. Her chalice of God's wrath is made of gold and reflects the pure gold of piety. But inside there is an abomination and the wine of God's wrath. Therefore one must be able to distinguish the appearance from the essence and the truth. Otherwise you cannot escape the Antichrist, and you will deny the truth of the Scriptures and not allow it to stand, the truth that always points in the direction of the Spirit and the inner truth—that is, points to how things are in God's presence.

But to those who understand all things in the Spirit, God will ascribe the triumph, the victory, riches, happiness, the good life and glory. The carnal world, however, which sees only the appearance of things with its human eye, believes all of this belongs to the Antichrist, who is called flesh and whose kingdom is of this world. <283> If you will take note of this, you will easily be able to recognize the Antichrist and where he rules today. [You will also be able to recognize] where Scripture speaks of him. If not, may God help you, the Scriptures and the prophets will long remain sealed, the book locked with seven seals. Indeed, both Christ and the Antichrist will remain unknown to you. Read Revelation 17 and 18.

To judge by the splendor of the honorable form and bearing of the Babylonian harlot, there is no one on earth more pious than she. Indeed, in appearance no one seeks God more sincerely than she, and she thinks that she, like Christ, fulfils every virtue represented by her precious clothing. This she arrogates to herself and trumpets abroad as something most lovely so that all peoples of the earth will commit adultery with her. And, indeed, before her lie all the kings of the earth, petitioning her and praying to her. The vast majority of the common people—Herr Omnes (Mr. Everyman)—do so as well, although this is not written in the Lamb's Book of Life.

John was amazed at the beauty of the beast and of the woman who was seated on it. Undoubtedly, this represents the false spiritual leaders and the dragon's religion, which is effeminate, nicely expressed by the donkey discovered in the Tiber River at Rome.[456] Both Peter, 2 Peter 2[:1-3; 12-22]: 3[:3-10] and Paul, 2 Timothy 3[:1-9] are in agreement with this, as is John's Revelation 17. This harlot captures a great city which rules over the kings of the earth; this is not opposed to the above interpretation. Other kings rule over this city. This city, however, which produces so many false prophets, rules over the kings of the earth. Many different people congregate in this city, which is why the dragon's apostle and chieftains are called one city and one harlot. This harlot, through the office of her apostle, rides and guides the beast how and where <284> she desires. That is to say, the false spiritual apostles persuade the kings of the earth as well as all nations of whatever they wish, and lead the poor beast—Herr Omnes—together with their captains around by the nose, how and wherever they desire.

Now, no matter how beautiful this woman may be, and however much John may have been astonished at her bearing and appearance—as the text says, he was so astonished that the angel had to speak to him about it and explain his astonishment to him with cogent reasoning—nevertheless she is drunk with the blood of the saints and satiated with the blood of Christian martyrs. The beast's seven heads and ten horns are nothing else than the kings, princes, and lords of this world. Its body consists of their members and followers, the world and its kingdoms—as John himself interprets it—which the false spiritual power—the Babylonian harlot—leads, directs, and rides with her sweet talk and magnificent jewelry and appearance.

The waters upon which the harlot sits are, according to John, the peoples and tongues of the earth, Revelation 17. Even though this beast has seven heads and is divided within itself—so that one kingdom and head is pitted against another—nevertheless, in their war against the Lamb they are all united. That is to say, when it comes to working against Christ, the

---

456 In 1496 a creature with the head of a donkey was said to have been found in the Tiber river; it was generally understood to be a divine portent. In 1523, Philipp Melanchthon and Martin Luther co-published a book of anti-papal propaganda featuring a woodcut by Lucas Cranach the elder depicting the "papal donkey." According to Luther and Melanchthon the appearance of the "papal donkey" in the Tiber indicated the corruption of the papal church and portended the nearness of the end times. See Philipp Melanchthon and Martin Luther, *Deuttung der czwo grewlichen Figuren, Bapstesels czu Rom und Munchkalbs zu Friberg ijnn Meijszen funden* (Wittenberg, 1523); Cranach's well-known illustration is on page 6.

Romans, Pilate, Herod, the Jews, and all others are united. All of them pipe the same tune against the Lamb, playing the same pitch with matching mouths. In this regard they are all of one heart and mind, the old as well as the new pope, being driven by the enemy of God, Revelation 13. <285>

Therefore Saint John admonishes us in Revelation 18[:4] to depart from this harlot in order not to be captivated by her beautiful appearance. We are to leave her be and not participate in her works, for her sins have risen up to the heavens. These sins are secret and hidden spiritual sins which the world cannot judge. Only the Holy Spirit has the power to judge them. For the righteousness of this world is sullied and filthy, and is an abomination before God. Such sins can only be punished by the Holy Spirit, John 16. However, since this mighty city of Babylon with its hordes of falsely pious hypocrites and frauds, who wish to instruct and ride the beast, has been uncovered, and since the wisdom of God, together with the joyous day of the elect, in which the latter will—triumphantly and with jubilation—celebrate the wedding feast of the Lamb, is finally about to dawn, the Antichrist and his followers will rue their beginning, and the kings and merchants of the earth who have been their clients will no longer want to buy anything from them because their kingdoms have become worthless. Then the people of this city who have grown rich and powerful will experience fear and trembling, and they will complain that their city has been miserably devastated.[457]

We have dealt at length with this matter in order that we might finally have our eyes opened and learn to know the Antichrist and his vermin, an Antichrist who has seated himself in God's temple, who has abolished the daily sacrifice, devastated the holy sacrament and sullied—to the extent that he was able—God's sanctuary and introduced innumerable other abominations through his man-made laws in opposition to <286> the command and institution of Christ, [giving to] baptism, the ban, and communion an altogether different interpretation. And now he wishes to maintain his abominations with many arguments, university learning and subtleties together with sly, snake-like questions.

Above we proved and successfully defended, on the basis of clear and explicit Holy Scripture, that our religion is not concocted from the speculations of men, the Fathers, or Councils, but that it is apostolic and based on Christ's teaching in Matthew 28 and Mark 16 as interpreted and

---

457 Here ends the copying of Franck's *Krieg Büchlin*.

A Short, Simple Confession

implemented by the apostles in Acts 2, 8, 11, 16, 19. But we were not able to confirm your infant baptism through clear and explicit passages drawn from Holy Scripture. Rather, [we discovered that] it was invented by man, with one pope patching this, another that, aspect of it until the Council at Braga which, without intending to do so, confirmed it and declared and recognized [baptism] as having to be administered to the child. This we demonstrated sufficiently above.

Therefore, because you have no passages of Scripture on which to base infant baptism, and have no proper continuity regarding it from the time of the apostles to the present; rather—as proven above—have forged it together from passages drawn from the Fathers, popes, and councils, your response, with which you attempt to overthrow the correct baptism commanded by Christ and practiced by the apostles, has been turned against you. That very argument will give your unfounded infant baptism itself the death blow.

However, if infant baptism is grounded in Holy Scripture and it can be conclusively proven that it was commanded and begun by Christ and his apostles, just like the true Christian <287> and apostolic baptism which we administer, we will not reject it, for one must not make fun of God's Word, even though our true baptism has been hindered and blocked from being implemented at every turn through the tyranny and cruel actions of the Antichrist. But because you have no passages from Holy Scripture on which to base infant baptism, and since it has not always been in use as you continually assert against us, and we have the eternal Son of God and the book of his apostles on our side with respect to the institution and practice of baptism, we will stop here, leaving it with the judgment that you have passed on yourselves.

For you know well enough that your own religion and the present reformation has not always been in place, but appeared and came to fruition at a certain point in time. The first efforts came from Wycliffe, John Hus, and Jerome of Prague and other enlightened hearts who were much more sincere than those of today. For John Hus and others acted upon their understanding with an undivided mind and heart; this they demonstrated by testifying to their faith with their blood. In Luther's and Zwingli's day this reformation broke out fully in our lands and was spread abroad through word of mouth, but in these latter times and days, all that is left on all sides is just words.

Should you not therefore concede that your religion and reformation is not from God, because it came through <288> the papacy and was—for a long time—hidden and obscured and not practiced in the open? For you will not win the day with such an argument, the same argument you accuse us of making, nor successfully defend your religion and infant baptism. Therefore, because you have not a single letter to support it, it falls of its own weight. We ask you to ponder and consider these matters, and we wish to challenge every Christ-believing reader with the question: from what spirit did such an argument flow?

Even though the infant baptizers throw even more arguments at us in order to prove and maintain infant baptism, they are all weak, null and void and obtuse, and have all been answered by our people long ago and overturned with passages from the Holy Scriptures. Whoever desires to do so should read our *Bundzeugnuss* (Covenant witness)[458] and Thoma Trucker's booklet,[459] a man who gave witness to his faith in Cologne with his blood.

Here, however, we want yet to present Balthasar Hubmaier's dialogue with Ulrich Zwingli's little booklet on baptism in order to hear what he has to say.[460] We will present the most essential articles in the briefest form

---

458 This is a clear reference to Pilgram Marpeck's *Vermanung* (Admonition) of 1542, which was also commonly called *"das Buch der Bundesbezeugung,"* or the book of witness to the covenant. The writer of these lines appears to stand within the Marpeck tradition, as the reference to "our *Bundzeugnuss*" makes clear. For more on this unique book, see Klaassen and Klassen, *Writings*, 159ff.

459 This is a reference to Thomas von Imbroich, also known as "Thomas Drucker," born in 1533 in the village of Imgenbroich, Germany. He was a printer by trade. He joined the Anabaptists in Cologne in 1554 and became a notable leader. He was arrested in 1557 and executed by beheading in March 1558. The confession of faith he wrote in prison was soon printed and circulated widely. The first edition of von Imbroich's confession has no date or place of publication. Historians believe it was published no earlier than 1560, most likely in Alsace. See *Mennonite Encyclopedia*, III, 12-13.

460 At the heading "Zwingli" below, *Codex 628* begins verbatim copying of significant portions of Hubmaier's *Ein Gespräch auf Zwinglis Taufbüchlein* (Nikolsburg, 1526). Critical edition in Westin and Bergsten, *Balthasar Hubmaier Schriften*, 164-214 (cited hereafter as *HS*); see 164-67 for details of composition and publication. English translation in Pipkin and Yoder, *Hubmaier*, 166-233. *Codex 628* keeps the dialogue form intact, although omitting sections here and there, and sometimes re-arranging sections of text in a new order. The copying of Hubmaier's

A Short, Simple Confession

possible. In doing so we wish to ask the Christian reader to consider and judge whether we or our detractors are making light of God's Word. The sections that are attributed to Zwingli below can be found in his book on baptism which he published in the year 1525.[461]

Zwingli
The way in which they now practice baptism is heresy; it is a sect and a faction.[462] <289>

Answer of Balthasar Hubmaier
Think about this carefully, my Zwingli, and consider well whom you are criticizing. For if to baptize those who are previously instructed [in the faith] and who believe is heretical, then you are criticizing not only us but also Christ Jesus, who commanded that it be so done; that is, that one should first preach and then believe, and only thirdly baptize: Matthew 28[:19-20], Mark 16[:15-16]. [If what you say is true], then the apostles, too, are heretics, for that is what they practiced, Acts 2[:38, 41], 8[:12-13, 35-38], 10[:44-48], 11[:13-18], 16[:14-15, 32-33], 19[:1-6], as we have copiously demonstrated and proven above.

Zwingli
You reject infant baptism in order to institute rebaptism.

Balthasar
Again and again you accuse us of rebaptism even though you have never, not even with one single word, proven that infant baptism is the right baptism. No matter how you twist and turn, squeeze and squirm, no clear Scripture will come forth. Remember what you said against [Johannes] Faber and published in your 15th Article, that all truth stands clear in the Word of God. If now infant baptism is truth, then point it out in the clear Word of

---

Dialogue runs from page <289> to page <316> of the codex. The text has been re-translated here, which accounts for minor variations in word choice and phrasing in comparison to the Pipkin and Yoder translation.

461 With only occasional exceptions, Hubmaier's "dialogue" was a literal engagement with Zwingli's *On Baptism, Rebaptism and Infant Baptism*, published in Zurich in May 1525. Hubmaier copied Zwingli's words, and set out to refute them.

462 Zwingli is referring to Anabaptist practice here; text in *Hubmaier Schriften*, 175.

God. Do it if you can, otherwise the vicar will complain that you have used a sword against him that you have now yourself discarded because you cannot suffer being stabbed with it. That will be a great disadvantage to you, your book, and the entire matter under discussion. In the end, you will have to overthrow your own *Theses [Schlussreden]*. <290>

I also beg this of you for God's sake,[463] give up your convoluted arguments regarding Old Testament circumcision. For you know well enough that circumcision is not a figure for water baptism. Nor do you have any Scripture to back up your argument. But Noah's Ark is [a figure of water baptism], 1 Peter 3[:20]. Look also at Cyril "Concerning John," book six, chapter 15.[464] Now just as none went into the ark unless they believed beforehand, likewise according to this figure, none should receive water baptism unless they have first confessed their faith with their mouth.

Zwingli
Since the rebaptizers were not been able to defeat us, they went out into the countryside and turned the hearts of the believers to nothing but quarreling over infant baptism.

Balthasar
He who teaches the truth does not quarrel, for love rejoices in truth. Rather, the one who quarrels is the one who contradicts the truth without any clear Scripture.

Zwingli
I know that they have been overcome through [our] teaching and that even today they stand defeated.

Balthasar
Tell me once, with which teaching? Or someone will say to you as someone at Zurich said to Faber: "Do not bring forth the sword by which the pastor of Fislispach was captured at Constance and killed." Similarly the pike with which you have overcome the baptizers does not want to come forth. <291> Answer

---

463 The copyist has inserted this phrase; Hubmaier had written: *for the sake of the last judgment*

464 The reference seems to be to "Cyril a bishop in Basel." The same reference to Book 6, chapter 15 of "Concerning John" is given above, page <204>.

A Short, Simple Confession

and fight with clear Scripture. Say: "There it stands written." A scholar should defend his cause with clear Scripture. At that time you demanded the same of Faber.[465]

Zwingli
I have a clear word that circumcision refers to baptism.

Balthasar
Where?

Zwingli
In Colossians 2[:11].

Balthasar
Oh, no. What Paul writes there concerning the circumcision which is done without hands and the baptism in which we are resurrected by faith, all refers to the inward baptism, not to the outward water baptism, as you say.[466] All devout God-fearing hearts will be able to understand whether young children also can be circumcised in this manner with a circumcision done without hands, through the renunciation of the sinful nature of the flesh, especially since they have not yet stretched out their hands to the forbidden tree and sinned of their own volition, and since original sin has been washed away by the blood of Christ.

Zwingli[467]
Whoever has been marked with baptism desires to hear what God says to him, learn his ordinances, and live in accordance with them.

Balthasar
Does a child who is one hour old possess such a will? You must confess: No. Then why do you baptize it? You say: The will only comes seven years later. Well said. Thus one should also postpone baptism until such a time

---

465 Codex 628 now jumps ahead in Hubmaier's text to *Hubmaier Schriften*, 179, bottom.
466 The following sentence appears to be an interpolation by the copyist. The phrasing parallels summaries found in other places in *Codex 628*.
467 The following from *Hubmaier Schriften*, 181.

as the will is present,[468] and Jacob and Esau can be <292> distinguished from one another. For he who is to be baptized should know and believe beforehand the will and ordinances that Christ taught and commanded, Matthew 28[:19-20], Mark 16[:15-16]—as you yourself have confessed—and promise to obey them in the act of baptism.

Zwingli
Christ has transformed circumcision and the Easter lamb into other, more gracious symbols.

Balthasar
Prove it with Holy Scripture. We know that Christ has instituted baptism and the Lord's Supper and abolished the ceremonies, figures, and shadows of the Old Testament with his coming, as the epistles to the Colossians and the Hebrews clearly prove, Colossians 2[:16ff.], Hebrews 8[:13].

Zwingli
Baptism is understood in four different ways in the Scriptures: first, for the dipping in water; second, for the inward illumination; third, for the outward teaching and for the dipping in outward water; finally, for the outward baptism and the internal faith.

Balthasar
How dark and obscure a division that is I will leave to the judgment of every Christian. In the first place, as concerns the dipping in water, and the third, as concerns the outward dipping in water, and the last, as concerns the outward water baptism; is this one, two, or is it three? Why do you not set the second, that is, the internal illumination before the first, namely before the dipping in water? For you also know full well that the bread on the Lord's table <293> is death without prior faith in the heart. Therefore the outward water baptism must also be nothing at all where the internal baptism of the Spirit has not preceded it. But it must be done that way, so that the error does not come to light.

Nevertheless, in summary: Baptism is sometimes taken for the internal baptism of the Spirit, John 3[:5-6], sometimes for the outward water

---

468 The author/editor of *Codex 628* interpolates his favorite "Jacob and Esau" reference here; it is not in Hubmaier.

baptism, Matthew 28[:19], and thirdly sometimes for the suffering that will follow, as when Christ says: "I must let myself be baptized beforehand with a baptism, and I am anxious until it has been completed," Luke 12[:50]. Because I place my faith in the Scriptures, whoever wishes to point out another baptism to me, [must] do it in light of the totality of Scripture, for I do not want to suffer patchwork.[469]

Zwingli
The disciples gave water baptism without teaching and without the Spirit, John 3[:22].

Balthasar
That goes too far. You cannot show me one person in all of Scripture who has been water-baptized without prior teaching. Or show us one with clear Scripture, and we are already defeated.

Zwingli
That one was baptized in water before one believed can be found in John 6[:66]. For undoubtedly, of the disciples who turned away from Christ, none was unbaptized. Nevertheless Christ pointed out their unbelief.

Balthasar
Oh, such perfidious treachery. Do you not fear God? Or do you think he does not know it, or that we do not understand it? Let me ask you something: did Peter, John, Andrew, et al. on Maundy Thursday believe the Supper or not? If you say yes, as you must, then Christ pointed out their unfaith to them on Easter day, Mark 16[:14].[470] <294>

Zwingli
With the word of Matthew 28[:19], where Christ says, "Go, teach all people, baptizing them in the name, etc. teaching them to observe all things I have commanded you," the opponents of baptism deceive themselves, but especially others. For they do not want to see that just after that stands, "teaching them to observe all things that I have commanded you."

---

469 The following text from *Hubmaier Schriften*, 184.
470 The following text from *Hubmaier Schriften*, 188ff.

Balthasar

Well then, Zwingli, let us make a pact with one another. I will allow you the teaching after water baptism and you allow me the teaching before water baptism. If you do that, we are already in agreement. But that preceding teaching will empty out your water baptism. If you will not make such a concession, it is nevertheless permitted by Christ. His Word, Matthew 28[:19-20], Mark 16[:15-16], stands as firm as a mighty fortress.[471] However, that teaching is commanded before and after water baptism by Christ in Matthew 28[:19-20] is the reason why it is not enough to drown Pharaoh in the Red Sea. There are still the Amalekites, Amorites, Jebusites, and other enemies at hand whom one must also resist and destroy with teaching, after water baptism.

Zwingli

It is true that you have "teaching all peoples and baptizing them," but you do not have what one should teach. But we have clearly, "teaching them to observe all things I have commanded you" and that stands after baptism. <295>

Balthasar

Christ did not neglect anything in this passage, nor does it disturb us that he commanded teaching before baptism but did not say what it was one was to teach all peoples. But might not a person respond to you with equal justice: You may well have "teaching them to observe all things I have commanded you," yes, after baptism. However, you do not have what those "all things" are. But if you do, we have it also, for to you and to us the Scripture has been equally given for teaching, comfort, and guidance.[472] But no God-fearing Christian will make fun of these words of Christ. For the moment he speaks of teaching he is talking about his Holy Gospel. But when he says, teach them to observe all things, this clearly encompasses the foregoing which is to be taught before and after baptism; it is nothing other than his Holy Gospel. Therefore the Lord did not neglect anything [in

---

471 Hubmaier writes: *ein Marpesische maur*, translated as "like Greek marble" in Pipkin and Yoder, 198.
472 The next four sentences are an interpolation by the author/editor of *Codex 628*.

A Short, Simple Confession

this passage]. Every devout Christian reader will recognize the argument you throw at us for what it really is.[473]

Zwingli

Since no person on earth achieves perfection of faith, you must admit that if a person is beginning to be taught, then one should baptize such a one in water.

Balthasar

Yes, we are well content with this speech. Still, "to begin to be taught" means that the person recognizes personal sin through the law and believes in the remission of sin through Jesus Christ. If you understand it otherwise, then you are purposely speaking obscurely in order not to be understood. <296>

Zwingli

The opponents of baptism cry out over the word in Matthew 3[:1, 6]: "Do you not see that John first preached and baptized after that?" We say quite frankly: Not only do we see it, we also act in accordance with it, for no one brings a child to be baptized unless the child is taught beforehand.

Balthasar

If you were blind, you would have no sin. But because you say that you see, therefore your sin will remain. For Matthew 3 says nothing about bringing a child. It says, "John preaches and whoever accepts his word; these he baptizes." Note: *these,* and not their children.

Zwingli

We confess firmly that John first taught and then baptized. No one can deny, however, that those who had first been taught later also let their untaught children be baptized.

Balthasar

Oh my Zwingli. How dare you say that John baptized young untaught children, in opposition to the clear text of Matthew 3[:6] which explicitly points out that those who were baptized by John confessed their sins? Oh, God, into what kind of difficulties does the truth force you? You would

---

473 The following text from *Hubmaier Schriften*, 191.

gladly flee, but do not know the way out. Oh reader, consider the text itself here and judge, for it is a notable error from which you know how to protect yourself.[474]

Zwingli

The opponents of baptism say, one should not baptize anyone unless such a one possesses <297> the Holy Spirit. Now who can tell us how God dwells in children?

Balthasar

We say that whoever is instructed in the Word of God, so that such a one confesses publicly the belief that Jesus Christ is the Son of the living God, [and desires henceforth to live in obedience to Him in accordance with the Gospel],[475] such a one is to be baptized. Such a confession is necessary before baptism, as Acts 8[:37] says regarding the [Ethiopian] treasurer. But how God dwells within little children, or whether they possess the Holy Spirit, or whether they belong to God,[476] we leave to the answer we have given above. God knows who is a Jacob or an Esau while they are yet children, and whom he has elected before time began. But the Scripture is written for the intelligent and the understanding, and not for the young non-understanding children, [at least not] until the old Adam and the image of God has been awakened in them, and they begin to understand and recognize the difference between good and evil.[477] But those who say: children belong to God, children belong to God, why then does one not want to baptize them? Such people intervene on God's secret judgment.[478] [For they have no way of knowing whether they will walk on the narrow or broad way, and the majority walk on the latter, in pride, cleverness, drunkenness, gluttony, jealousy, hatred, avarice, usury, lasciviousness, immorality, adultery, impurity, all of which lead to damnation. Such

---

474 Some of Hubmaier's text is omitted here; copying will continue further along on *Hubmaier Schriften*, 192.
475 Phrase in brackets added by the author/editor of *Codex 628*.
476 From here to "good and evil," interpolation by author/editor of *Codex 628*.
477 The following two sentences, up to "judgment," from *Hubmaier Schriften*, 193.
478 A lengthy interpolation by the author/editor of *Codex 628* begins here with the bracketed text.

conduct, sadly, is everywhere apparent and openly practiced. Therefore [it is clear] that more Esaus than Jacobs are being baptized.

From this it should be apparent to us whether or not infant baptism has been moistened by the dews of heaven <298> and blessed (by God), whether or not through the dawn the dew of its birth was made fruitful and watered. For we ourselves see—and this is much more astonishing—that it is most forcefully enforced and defended, [even though] we also see that those who practice it do not live Christian lives. And those who do live Christian lives, or desire sincerely to do so, are not acknowledged but are hated and persecuted. Indeed, these others[479] hate and condemn one another, calling each other heretics and most vigorously outlawing one another. In doing so they demonstrate well enough that they do not possess the true heavenly rain and divine blessing, nor are they enlightened and inspired from above.

Therefore we should have more than a little reason to fear [infant baptism], in the same way that Paul feared circumcision. True faith is a work of God and not of men. That is why fathers and mothers do not give birth to children of God, but rather to children of wrath, Ephesians 2[:3], Psalm 50[:16ff.], John 3[:3-6], Jeremiah 20[:14-18?].[480] For to be children of God does not derive from one's blood, or the will of the flesh, or the will of a man, but rather God has given all those who believe in His name the power to become His children. Faith is exclusively the work of God, and not of human beings.[481] That is why one must baptize the believer upon his confession of faith with water, and not because he has been born of Christian parents. Flesh and blood will not reveal this to us. Only our heavenly Father, not our earthly father, must bring about a rebirth <299> to which water baptism testifies.

Still you would like to say here [that] we are not speaking of the spiritual childhood on which salvation depends, we are speaking of the outward one. Thus the children of God are of such [a nature] that they can be counted among the children of God; therefore one should not withhold the outward sign from them. Answer: You can say what you want, but all your speeches are intended to demonstrate that all children of Christ-believers belong to God, have the Holy Spirit, and are saved. Christ called them to himself,

---

479 *Margin*: Papists; Lutherans; Zwinglians
480 Here ends the interpolation. The text following picks up at *Hubmaier Schriften*, 193.
481 *Codex 628* drops some material here.

etc.[482] [We will stop here and leave it with what we have stated above. As repeatedly observed above, we are unable to differentiate Jacob from Esau at birth. But when they have grown up and become enmeshed in all kinds of sin and unrighteousness, and persist in them without repentance or remorse, as is unfortunately the nature and custom of the vast majority [of people], they are the same kind of children of God as Esau was already in his childhood, whom God hated already in his mother's womb.][483] And some even want to make them believers through infused faith, [as we remarked above of Luther].[484] This has no basis in the Scriptures. [Even Zwingli opposed this, as stated above].[485]

To this they cry: One should not exclude the little children from the general salvation of Christians—"Who now wants to forbid water?"— according to the words of Peter, Acts 10[:47]. You write this in your book to the king of France, folio B, page 220.[486] The Jews had an explicit command from God to circumcise their boys on the eighth day and if they circumcised on the seventh day, they would have acted against God. In the same way we have a clear mandate to baptize people, whether <300> they be young or old. Yes, those who publicly testify to their faith orally before [God's congregation].[487] You say: "Yes, I confess that it is written that one should baptize believers. The children, however, are not excluded anywhere."

Answer: As soon as Christ commanded that believers be baptized in water, from that hour on all people were already excluded who were not yet instructed in the faith. We have a parable concerning this: As soon as God in the Old Testament commanded boys to be circumcised, from that hour on girls were already excluded. As soon as he designated and set the eighth day, from that hour on it was forbidden to circumcise on the fourth or seventh day, although God did not explicitly say or forbid it.

---

482 The author/editor of *Codex 628* interpolates the bracketed text.
483 *Codex 628* now returns to *Hubmaier Schriften*, 193.
484 Bracketed interpolation, *Codex 628*.
485 Bracketed interpolation, *Codex 628*.
486 The reference is to Zwingli's *Concerning True and False Religion*. See *Hubmaier Schriften*, 193, n. 145.
487 Hubmaier has *Kirche* (church); the codex has *gemeind Gottes* (God's congregation).

Zwingli
If this were to happen, then Christian children would be at a disadvantage compared to Jewish children, whom one registered among the people of God on the eighth day.

Balthasar
Zwingli, I have something to say to you. There was a rich man who had two debtors, both of whom were indebted to him for one hundred pounds. Since they did not have the money, he waited eight days for one and for the other eight years and even longer. I ask you, to which of these was he more gracious? You would have to answer: Without a doubt to the one for whom he waited eight years and longer. That would have been a correct judgment. So judge also to whom God is the more gracious, Jewish or Christian children <301>, then you will already have your answer.[488]

Zwingli
Now comes the strongest place which teaches us that water baptism is an initial sign by which we obligate ourselves to God to live a new life and also accept water baptism along with common Christians as a testimony. This is stated in Romans 6[:4].

Balthasar
That is precisely the strongest passage against you, which I will demonstrate with your own words and those of Paul. You yourself confess that baptism is a sign with which we obligate ourselves to God to live a new life. Note, you say: "We, We, We," not someone else on our behalf, and "We accept water baptism as a testimony." The crying child in the crib knows nothing at all about signs, obligation, baptism, new life, or testimony. Second, Paul describes the significance of outward baptism in that passage, namely it means that since the outwardly baptized person should inwardly have died with Christ to vices and be buried, so as Christ was resurrected from the dead by the glory of the Father, so also will the baptized person rise up from sin and walk in newness of life. Now whichever child knows the significance of water baptism and wants thereby to make a public commitment and testimony by affirmation of faith and requesting water baptism before

---

488 *Codex 628* omits some material here, and continues at *Hubmaier Schriften*, 194.

[God's congregation],[489] this same child one should baptize. If, however, it can neither desire nor request the same, <302> then wait with it until the child is drawn to it by God.

Here one should read the text of Paul in the above-mentioned passage and one will see whether Paul has written about babies in the cradle. From such a desire for water baptism before the church comes the custom to which water priests [i.e., priests who baptize infants] still adhere, when they question the little child in Latin: *"Vis baptizari?"* [Do you wish to be baptized?] Say, "I want it." Oh, the great foolishness whereby a child one, two, or three hours old, is asked in Latin and is expected to answer in German, just as if it had learned two languages in its mother's womb. Should not all Jews and heathen simply deride us for performing such a deceptive act? Even so, some masters want to force us with rope, fire, and water to [this unfounded, Scripture-less infant baptism].[490] But their coercion will bring them to shame before God and his angels.[491]

Zwingli

Concerning the origin of infant baptism: neither I nor anyone else can say anything from a clear word other than that there is no other baptism than the one true baptism in Christ. Just as many other things that are not distinguished by words, but are nevertheless still are not against God, but with God, etc.

Balthasar

Be still, be still, my Zwingli, so that Faber of Constance will not hear what you say. For that was also his opinion in Zurich at the disputation, but you would not let him have it. You demanded clear Scripture from him—and not without reason.[492]

Zwingli

Even though infant baptism is not described or <303> explicitly mentioned in words, it can be described from the testimonies of the divine Word, for

---

489 Hubmaier has *Kirche* (church); the Codex has *gemeind Gottes* (God's congregation).
490 Bracketed text from *Codex 628*; Hubmaier has "believe and obey their trickery," *Hubmaier Schriften*, 195.
491 The following is found in *Hubmaier Schriften*, 199.
492 The following is found in *Hubmaier Schriften*, 201.

the infants were no less baptized along with the common multitude who were baptized.

Balthasar
One time you say that infant baptism is written in the Word of God, but another time you say it is not written or expressed with words but that it is to be assumed. That is a real confusion and treachery in the Scripture. For it is not enough to assume, to be of the opinion, or to think; there must be knowing and believing.

Zwingli
The children and the women were also fed in the common multitude, but one did not count them, Matthew 14[:21].

Balthasar
The food was ordered by God for woman and child, also for the young ravens; but baptism was for the faithful and the Supper for those who had proven themselves. Baptized men and women were also reported in Acts 8[:12], but not young children.[493]

Zwingli
You say: One should not add to God's Word. Now I ask you: Does it stand anywhere that one should not baptize children? If you say "No," you thereby add something to the Word.

Balthasar
Oh, the perfidious treachery which you perpetrate on the simple. I am surprised, O Zwingli, that you are not afraid to give such a response. Or do you think that we do not understand? However, you have learned it from Faber, where he says, "Whoever is not against you is with you." <304> Now the customs and laws of the church which are created and instituted by man are not against God, etc. To this you answered: "Herr Vicar, prove that!" and you led him to the word of Christ in Matthew 15[:11] where he overthrows all human teaching and law which God the heavenly Father has not planted, and says that one serves him with these things in vain. If it does not say anywhere in Scripture that one should baptize children—

---

493 The following is found in *Hubmaier Schriften*, 178ff.

[as you yourself admit along with many other things that you have loosely spoken out of school]⁴⁹⁴—then one should not baptize them, for it is in vain. Now, however, one should not take the three high names of God the Father and the Son and the Holy Spirit into one's mouth in vain.

Note here, Zwingli, it is not necessary that we point out a prohibition. For Christ does not say: "All plants which my heavenly Father has forbidden should be uprooted." Rather he says, "All plants which my heavenly Father has not planted should be uprooted" [Matthew 15:13]. Here you must point out clearly the institution of infant baptism in the Scriptures, or it must be uprooted. [For God will not deviate from His Word].⁴⁹⁵ But because you want to practice infant baptism and cannot prove it as instituted by God, then you and not we are adding to the Word of God. For you make a water baptism where Christ has made none. Nor is the common legal rule unknown to you: *Affirmanto incumbit probation. Tu affirmas baptisma infanticum, ergo, etc.* [The burden of proof falls to the one affirming. You affirm infant baptism, therefore, etc.]

Listen here to <305> one more point. If the vicar had asked you at that time whether infant baptism was also clearly contained in the Word of God, what would you have answered? *Da demonstrandi* [Give proof]; show it. If you say no, then it does not bind us, as you also at that time wanted to be free in all points which were not clearly expressed in the Word of God, as you set forth in your twenty-fourth thesis where you write that "every Christian is free of the works which God has not commanded." You say yourself, "Not commanded." Therefore we beseech you for God's sake, let us remain by your own words.⁴⁹⁶

Zwingli

The opponents of infant baptism have sometimes wanted to deny that a person can be saved without water baptism.

Balthasar

You do us an injustice. We know well that salvation is bound neither to baptism nor to works. Being unbaptized does not condemn us, nor do evil works, but only unbelief. But whoever is a believer and wishes to be

---

494 Bracketed text, interpolation, *Codex 628*.
495 Bracketed text, interpolation, *Codex 628*.
496 The following is found in *Hubmaier Schriften*, 183.

a true servant of the Gospel, and a baptizer and water is present, such a one accepts baptism by power of the institution of Christ, and brings forth good fruit. If the person does not do so, condemnation comes not for lack of baptism, but for the unbelief that led to disobedience. Had such a person been truly believing, the sign of the Christian believer would have been accepted as Christ, with most excellent words, instituted it and the apostles practiced it. <306>

Zwingli
Baptism has also been accepted by those who have not believed beforehand. Like Simon Magus, Acts 8[:13], where it says: "Simon also believed." There faith must be taken for "he read," or for "he counted himself among the believers," as Augustine himself interprets the passage.

Balthasar
Whoever understands "faith" here differently when it explicitly states "he believed," destroys the Scripture and violates its own understanding of it, whether it be Zwingli or Augustine, for it does not only state there that he believed, but that he also practiced the works of faith. He joined Philip even though he sinned afterwards and tried to buy the Holy Spirit with money. This happens [to many amongst those who even today boast most extravagantly of the Christian name].[497] But when Peter admonished him, he confessed and desired that one pray for him so that his sins would be forgiven. But that is a deed of a believing person. If one were able to introduce foreign glosses over clear words, [oh, Zwingli],[498] the entire Bible would be overturned and confused and nothing upright or constant would remain in it. O God, protect us from such glossing! Until the present the old pope has also used the same glosses for such words as head, church, keys, rock, spiritual, etc., with which he has overturned all things. <307>

Zwingli
Even today there are unfortunately still some who allow themselves to be baptized and yet do not believe.

---

497 Hubmaier has "to us all." The bracketed text is substituted in *Codex 628*.
498 Zurich Q3 adds: *O Zwingli*

Balthasar

[This happens only where things do not proceed correctly, in a right and truthful manner,][499] namely when teaching and faith [do not] precede water baptism. Woe to those who practice hypocrisy in this matter.

Zwingli

The baptism of the Spirit is given without the baptism of water. Nicodemus, Joseph, and Gamaliel were believers, but in secret. Undoubtedly they were never baptized.

Balthasar

Believing secretly is something, but it is not enough. For, although one believes with the heart unto righteousness, one must still confess with the mouth unto salvation, Romans 10[:10]. That is why Nicodemus had to break out in words and works of faith afterwards, John 7[:50], 19[:39]; Joseph, in Matthew 27[:59ff.]; Gamaliel, in Acts 5[:34ff.]. I remember here several of those called Priscillians and Carpocratians. Gerson and Eusebius write of them. They thought it was enough to believe with the heart and thought it was unnecessary to confess [their faith] with the mouth and by fruits. But their opinion goes against Scripture, Romans 10[:10], Matthew 10[:32]: Whoever confesses me before the people, [him will I confess before my Father in heaven; whoever denies me before the people I will also deny before my Father in heaven].[500]

Zwingli

The thief on the cross believed and was on the same day with Christ <308> in Paradise, and absolutely not baptized with any outward baptism.

Balthasar

With this counter-argument you want completely to overthrow the water baptism of Christ. But I say to you: The person who has the excuse of the thief on the cross is wholly at peace with God although he has never had any water baptism. But wherever this excuse is lacking, there the person is deceiving himself. For the Word of God in its power states: "Whoever does not believe is condemned." The other passage next to it also remains as

---

499 *Codex 628* replaces some lines in Hubmaier with the bracketed text.
500 *Codex 628* completes the biblical text, within the brackets.

A Short, Simple Confession

powerful: "Whoever believes and is baptized will be saved," Mark 16[:16]. Here one must always leave faith and baptism together. Look at Theophilus; there you will find something on this text.[501]

Zwingli
Many years ago this error also misled me so that I thought it would be better if one baptized children only when they had come to a good age.

Balthasar
Yes, you have maintained this, written it, and preached it in the open pulpit; several hundred people have heard it from your own mouth. But now all those who say that of you must be liars. Yes, you speak outrageously when you say that such an opinion has never your life long entered your heart, and something else on which I will now remain silent. But I will ask you one more thing: How many years ago was this your opinion? Please remember <309> that you had Johann Faber, vicar at Constance, under your hand as you boasted that you had preached the Gospel purely, clearly, and brightly for five years in 1523. And after that in the same year, about Philip's and James's day,[502] I conferred with you personally on the Zurich Graben about the Scriptures concerning baptism. There you agreed with me that one should not baptize children before they had been instructed in the faith. That is the way it had been in prior times, and that was why they were called catechumens. In your *Articles* book you intended also to state that, as you then did in the eighteenth article on confirmation. Anyone who reads that will clearly discover your judgment. Sebastian Rugglisberger from St. Gallen, at that time prior at Sion in Klingau, was also there. You also publicly confessed the same thing in another book on the riotous spirits, published in 1525, on the second page, that those who baptize children have no clear word of Scripture that one is commanded to baptize them. Evaluate here, my Zwingli, how your word, writing, and preaching fit together. But may God illumine you and us all so that you abstain from your violent treatment of many righteous folk.[503]

---

501 The following is in *Hubmaier Schriften*, 186.
502 May 1, 1523. *Hubmaier Schriften*, 186, n. 109.
503 The following is in *Hubmaier Schriften*, 188.

Zwingli

Water baptism is an initiatory sign, ceremony, or *Teleta* (in Greek) just as when young people are pushed into the orders. The cowls are measured out for them, but they have not learned the law and the statutes; they only learn them in the cowls. <310>

Balthasar

Yes, Zwingli, just exactly as much as a child that is pushed (yes, well said: pushed) into the cloister is actually a monk or a nun, by the same amount is infant baptism a [true] baptism, and the little child an apparent Christian without knowledge of the law and without faith. Indeed, your example and infant baptism go well together.[504]

Zwingli

Paul admonishes the Corinthians in 1 Corinthians 7[:14] that where a spouse is a believer and the other an unbeliever, the believer should not dismiss the unbeliever for otherwise, he says, your children will be unclean. Now, however, they are holy. It is well known that "holy" was taken by Paul and the old Christians for a believer, for they called the servants of God "saints."

Balthasar

Here you want, Zwingli, that one should baptize the children of believers on the basis that they are holy. Now you write further that it is well-known that "holy" is taken for "believing." Thus it follows that young children are believers, which you have until now always denied. In the second place, since on the basis that Paul calls children of believers holy (assuming now that the word "holy" may be taken for "believing" or "pure") you want to prove that Paul calls children of believers holy, and you want to establish the foundation of infant baptism on that; but then you must also baptize the unbelieving husband of a believing woman, for Paul says that he is as holy as the child. <311> If now "holy" means "believing" here, then the unbelieving man is a believer. See here, dear reader, what happens when we spin glosses out of our own heads. For surely "holy" must not be taken here for "believing" as you contend.[505]

---

504 The following is in *Hubmaier Schriften*, 205.
505 The codex skips a few lines of Hubmaier's text here.

Zwingli

I cannot prove the faith of children. Although some have attempted to do so, it is in vain.

Balthasar

Have you not above, according to your own judgment, proven and said that Paul calls the children of Christians "holy," and since "holy" means "believing," therefore they are believers? Remember what you have said. Look at your book. I am not being unfair to you.

Zwingli

There one actually sees that Christ only speaks of those who hear the Gospel preached and thereafter believe or do not believe, Mark 16[:16]. Now, however, the children of Christians, who are still unable to speak, do not hear the Gospel. Therefore they are neither believing nor unbelieving. So the word does not apply to them.

Balthasar

Oh, you wonderful God, you testify to the truth and cry out even through those people who wish, along with Caiaphas, to kill you, and you stab them with the very words with which they seek to do away with you. Behold, we also say that the words of Mark 16[:16] are directed to those who hear the Gospel preached <312>, and not to young children. That, too, is the understanding of Saint Jerome on the word concerning water baptism in Matthew 28[:19]. [As regarding this passage] he writes: "In the first place, they teach all the people. After that they baptize[506] the taught ones in water. For the body should not receive the sacrament of baptism unless the soul has first received the truth of faith." So speaks Jerome, the teacher. If I also speak this way I am called a heretic. If these words [of Matthew] do not apply to young children, then the baptism of these words does not apply to them either. There must therefore be another baptism for children in the cradle; but of such a baptism there is no report either here or in Matthew 28, for there is a history here and there that no one can deny.

Therefore we beg you for God's sake to tell us, my Zwingli, where in Scripture water baptism was instituted by Christ for those who have not yet heard the Gospel, are not yet accountable and do not believe. If you

---

506 Hubmaier has *"tuncken"*: immerse or dip.

can point out this baptism with a clear word [from Holy Scripture][507] then, truly, truly we are rightly defeated. If, however, you are unable to do this we beg you for the sake of your soul's salvation, confess your error and [do not fight any longer against the truth].[508] Here I demand of you, [for the sake of your soul's salvation],[509] an account of your faith and of baptism, which is different from this one and to which the Word of Christ applies, Mark 16[:16] and Matthew 28[:19], as you yourself have confessed. <313> Give an answer, give an account, for God's sake. Show us where infant baptism is grounded in the bright and clear Word of God, since the word of Christ in Mark and Matthew does not apply to infant baptism. For the spirit of human being does not become peaceful except through a clear Word of God, without which there is neither faith nor peace.

This is what we desire from you, and this is what you are obligated to show us, 1 Peter 3[:15]. Otherwise we will not stop crying out over you: "Word, Word, Scripture, Scripture." But I counsel you faithfully: Surrender. You have caught and bound yourself with your own words where you say: The words of Mark 16 do not apply to young children. Look here, my Zwingli, how you had so much trouble above with the words "into the name" and "in the name," and with the [matter of the] preceding and following teaching, in order to make these words apply to young children. And now you confess openly: They do not apply to them. O truth, truth, you are immortal.

Zwingli

When one studies the nature of baptism, one sees that it is proper for children.

Balthasar

First of all, you said the opposite in Mark and Matthew. Then look also at the significance of water baptism in Romans 6[:3-4] and how the apostles practiced it in Acts. Also in Hebrews 10[:22] and 1 Peter 3[:21], and you will find that it is not suitable for them. The Holy Scriptures shall remain the judge.[510]

---

507 Interpolation in *Codex 628*, between brackets.
508 Interpolation in *Codex 628*, between brackets.
509 Interpolation in *Codex 628*, between brackets.
510 *Codex 628* drops some lines here from Hubmaier's text.

Zwingli

How can it be that a part of the Christian church should be baptized and another part should remain unbaptized? <314> For there is only one sheep's stall and one shepherd.

Balthasar

How does the one church come out of Cornelius and the thief, as well as Abraham and the jailor? Most certainly, when you find three kinds of baptism in the Scripture, through which the person testifies as a Christian.[511] Where the one cannot be had, in a time of need then there still is another to accompany faith.[512]

Zwingli

The reasons for godfathers and godmothers is as follows: If the father and mother have died, the godparents guarantee that the doctrine of salvation is taught to the child. Therefore one incorporates them in the presentation of the child and they are witnesses that the child has been baptized.

Balthasar

Baptism is a public testimony of faith which the baptized person makes before the church, not one made by godmother and godfather or godparents. Every believing person has three witnesses in heaven: Father, Son, and Holy Spirit, in whose name and power that person inwardly surrenders to God and outwardly has made an obligation to lead a new life according to the Rule of Christ. There also are three witnesses on earth: spirit, water, and blood. The Spirit leads, the water makes the breakthrough, the blood gains the advantage in the power of God and is finally victorious. Those who have ears to hear, let them hear. These are the true godfathers and godmothers.[513]

---

511 This is a reference to Hubmaier's teaching that baptism is three-fold: in Spirit, water, and blood. Cf. Hubmaier's catechism: *Ein Christennliche Leertafel...*, *Hubmaier Schriften*, 313: "Ein Tauff des geysts, Ein tauff des Wassers, Ein tauff des bluts." Pipkin and Yoder, *Hubmaier*, 349. As Hubmaier argues elsewhere, coming to faith is equivalent to the baptism of the Spirit.

512 The text that follows is in *Hubmaier Schriften*, 209.

513 The text that follows is in *Hubmaier Schriften*, 210.

Zwingli
Now follows the form of baptism as it is practiced at Zurich in the present time, and all additions not founded in God's Word <315> have been omitted.

Balthasar
Beware that no one asks you, Zwingli, where it is written that one should take godmothers and godfathers and ask them [about their faith] instead of asking the child whether it believes. And they answer in place of the child, "I believe," and yet the child neither believes nor disbelieves for itself, as you confessed above. Tell us one more thing. Where is the baptismal shirt based in the Word of God? For you did not allow Faber the smallest letter outside of the clear Word of God, and you were right and just. If you do the same for yourself, we will be at peace.[514]

Zwingli
They ridicule me and say that I stirred up the fire against them so that the city and countryside have been closed to them. There is no truth in that.

Balthasar
That does happen and it is true. How can you now deny that they punish them in body and goods? They capture them, incarcerate them, put them in dungeons, throw them into the heretic's tower where they can see neither sun nor moon, and [force them to] live only on bread and water. They send them forth into misery—men, women, widows, and maidens—and all on account of your teaching and outcries from the pulpit, where you say: "Punish, punish. You do not want to punish them. In accordance with Imperial law one should cut the heads off such heretics." I think that is stirring the coals enough.[515]

But how this corresponds with what Zwingli writes against the pope, as we described it above, and as long as you [Zwingli] <316> continue to call for the use of weapons of steel, everyone will be able to see that you are not a follower of Christ but of the devil and the true Antichrist. Every

---

514 *Codex 628* now jumps back to *Hubmaier Schriften*, 177ff.
515 At this point *Codex 628* concludes the copying of Hubmaier's *Dialogue with Zwingli's Baptism Book*.

A Short, Simple Confession

Christian should consider what kind of judgment Zwingli has passed upon himself.

Since we now hope to have answered and taken care of the foremost accusations against us, and answered with a good, clear, and godly foundations, we wish to indicate further:[516]

How the Holy Scriptures which speak of baptism may intelligently be differentiated and explained, how the Holy Spirit surrounds us with his gifts and guides his work through faith in teaching, Romans 10, for faith comes from hearing the Word preached.

1. Teaching
2. Hearing
3. Faith
4. Baptism: Acts 2, 8, 9, 10, 16, 18, 19
5. Spirit: Whoever comes to faith shall be baptized
6. Works[517]

---

516 *Codex 628* here begins a close copying of the anonymous Anabaptist pamphlet *How Scripture Should be Discerningly Exposited*: *Wie die Gschrifft verstendigklich soll underschiden/und erklärt werden* ... (n.p., n.d.), photostatic copy on file at the Mennonite Historical Library, Goshen, Indiana. English translations by J. C. Wenger, "An Early Anabaptist Tract on Hermeneutics," MQR 42 (January 1968), 26-44; and Yoder, *The Legacy of Michael Sattler*, "How Scripture should be Discerningly Exposited," 150-77. Older scholarship followed Ludwig Keller's attribution of authorship to Michael Sattler, as does also John H. Yoder (cf. *Legacy*, 150-51, and relevant notation), based on the initials "MS" on the title page. Werner Packull has presented convincing arguments that *Wie die Gschrifft* ... was a product of the Marpeck network, who composed the tract no earlier than the 1530s. Packull suggests that "MS" stands for "Marpeck/Scharnschlager." The earliest known print came from Ulhart's press in Augsburg in the 1540s. See Werner Packull, "Pilgram Marpeck: *Uncovering of the Babylonian Whore* and other Anonymous Anabaptist Tracts," 351-55. Contrary to Yoder's assertion that "there seems to be no record of sixteenth- or seventeenth-century awareness of this tract" (*Legacy*, 150), the appearance of this material in *Codex 628* argues for an active circulation and appropriation of the tract's contents, and even more, to the Marpeckite connection underlying both the tract and the codex. Pages <317-32> of *Codex 628* are taken up with copying *Wie die Gschrifft*.... The codex leaves off the concluding section on circumcision and the conclusion of the original tract, ending at Ci, recto of the original print.

517 *Codex 628* omits title page references to Matthew 15 and Colossians 2, as well as the greeting of the original.

So much division, error, and conflict has arisen, and continues to arise to this day, [in this presumed Christendom][518] because so many lazy, [unfaithful, ambitious, and greedy university scholars, who consider themselves most learned masters and scribes of the Scriptures, have, with their human wisdom, cleverness, and subtlety],[519] decided to take charge of the work in the Lord's vineyard. They have done so only because of the temporal honor attached to it. Nor are they much concerned[520] about the <317> ceremonies, [because of which they—as Christ has promised his followers—must expect to suffer the cross and affliction].[521] That is why they are so far removed from Christ and his apostles' commandments, indeed as far as heaven is removed from the earth, as far as God's Word is removed from man-made statutes.[522] [And even though they have made some changes from the papal church and given the old song a new tune, their church, unfortunately, still has man-made statutes and human spirits mixed up in it, as has been amply demonstrated above, especially in their infant baptism which is imposed with such great force and tyranny].[523]

For that reason we have completed this work, in the hope that, since we have the Scriptures clearly before our eyes, we might see where the errors are [if we are to adhere to the Holy Scriptures in all simplicity],[524] and so have no need to battle and dispute at length about what is, and what is not, commanded. If one looks to this guideline and order, [which has been sealed with the blood of saints],[525] one will find the foundation of the work. What is the point of much debate about chrism, salt, mud, the driving out of devils, godparents, and however many more things there are that have come to us from the Roman church and which, unfortunately, have never been abolished [in this presumed Christendom]?[526] If infant baptism and similar ceremonies are based upon the New Testament—something we have thoroughly exposed—then one should observe it

---

518 Interpolation, *Codex 628*.
519 Interpolation, *Codex 628*.
520 Some lines omitted here in *Codex 628*.
521 Interpolation, *Codex 628*.
522 *Codex 628* omits some lines from the printed text here, and interpolates the following.
523 Interpolation, *Codex 628*.
524 Interpolation, *Codex 628*.
525 Interpolation, *Codex 628*.
526 Interpolation, *Codex 628*.

A Short, Simple Confession 413

zealously in accordance with Christ's command together with everything that pertains to it. If it comes from the popes and human beings, then it must be abolished. The entire Scriptures speak of only one baptism. All true Christians, God be praised, know this well. Whoever seeks will find it. <318>

How the Scriptures that speak of Baptism must be intelligently interpreted and explained; How the Holy Spirit divides his gifts before and after and what effect they have.

The office of John the Baptist, Matthew 3, Mark 1, Luke 3, John 1; 3.
John taught and preached and admonished the people from the commands of God. First of all concerning repentance: [John] chastised them for their sins. Second, they were to repent [in righteous fear].[527] Third, [they were] to be baptized for their betterment. Fourth, [he] pointed converted persons toward the kingdom of God. Fifth, John pointed with his finger to the lamb of God.[528] Sixth,[529] he chastised the unrepentant Pharisees and others. Eighth, he trusted the wrath of God and his punishment.

John states: I baptize you with water to repentance.[530] But he who comes after me will baptize you with fire and the Holy Spirit, Matthew 3, Luke 3.[531]

Concerning water: John baptized with water, Acts 1.

Concerning the Holy Spirit: You, however, shall be baptized with the Holy Spirit.

Concerning teaching: John called out and said, Amend your ways

Concerning repentance: and repent.

Concerning the kingdom of God: The kingdom of God has come close to you.

Concerning hearing and faith: Then all the people came out to the Jordan to hear John, and the tax collectors praised God

Concerning water: and allowed themselves to be baptized

---

527 Interpolation, *Codex 628.*
528 A line was dropped in *Codex 628: Sixth: gave a rule to all according to their station.*
529 "Seventh" in the original print.
530 *Margin:* Water baptism
531 *Margin:* Baptism of the Holy Spirit

[*Confession:*]⁵³² and confessed their sins. <319>

Concerning the unconverted godless ones: But the Pharisees and scribes rejected the counsel of God against them and did not let themselves be baptized by him, Luke 7.

Jesus Christ the living Son of God first was baptized with water by John in the Jordan, Luke 3. After that the Holy Spirit descended from his heavenly Father, in order to fulfill all righteousness.

Christ says to Nicodemus, John 3: [*Teaching*]⁵³³ Truly, truly, I say to you that unless a man is born of water and the Spirit, he cannot enter into the kingdom of God.⁵³⁴

Concerning Christ's teaching: He taught and preached and imparted faith.

Concerning water: His disciples baptized the repentant, following instruction, [Acts 2, 9, 10, 16, 18, 19].⁵³⁵

Concerning the Holy Spirit: Christ baptized all those chosen by him and gifted them with the Holy Spirit, John 3 and 4.

What the apostles were to teach, Christ commanded them [in Luke 24].⁵³⁶ He explained the Scriptures to them with all understanding, saying: Thus must Christ suffer and be raised on the third day.

The teaching: and preaching was done in his name.

    First they taught repentance.

    Second, forgiveness of sins beginning at Jerusalem.

The last commandment of Christ, Matthew 28, Mark 16, and concerning the power of Christ. Christ spoke to his disciples: I have been given all power <320> in heaven and on earth, therefore go into all the world.

The teaching: Teach all people, and preach the Gospel of all creatures.⁵³⁷

Faith: He who believes

[*Baptism:*] and is baptized will be saved. Baptize them in the name of the Father, the Son, and the Holy Spirit.

---

532 Title omitted from *Codex 628.*

533 Title omitted from *Codex 628.*

534 *Codex 628* drops some lines here concerning water and Spirit baptism. Cf. *Wie die Gschrifft* ..., Aii, verso.

535 Scripture references interpolated in *Codex 628.*

536 Scripture reference missing in *Codex 628.*

537 Or: "the Gospel to all Creatures."

A Short, Simple Confession

Works: And teach them to observe all things I have commanded you. Behold, I am with you to the end of the world.

Unbelief: Whoever does not believe will be damned.

Whoever wants to know the teaching should read from the beginnings; it would take too long to repeat it at length here.[538]

All the Passages[539] from the Acts of the Apostles concerning Baptism.

Concerning repentance and faith, Acts 2.

Repentance: Peter said to the people, Repent

Water: and every one of you, let yourself be baptized in the name of Jesus Christ for the forgiveness of sins

The promise of the Holy Spirit: and you shall receive the Holy Spirit, for this has been promised to you and your children.

Concerning faith: Those who gladly accepted his word

Concerning water: let themselves be baptized and about three thousand souls were added to the church on that day.

Philip converted many people in Samaria, as recorded in chapter 8 of the Acts of the Apostles. <321>

Concerning teaching: Then the men and women heard Philip preach.

Concerning faith: Believe in the kingdom of God and in the name of Jesus Christ.

Concerning water: Then both men and women let themselves be baptized.

Concerning the Holy Spirit: Peter and John laid hands on them and they received the Holy Spirit.

Concerning the eunuch on the chariot, Acts 8.

Concerning teaching: Philip said to the treasurer from Egypt: Believe with all your heart and you may be baptized.

Concerning faith: He answered and said: I believe that Jesus Christ is God's Son.

---

538 Yoder, *Legacy*, 176, n. 20, suggests that "from the beginnings" means Jesus' teachings in the Gospels.

539 The print has "Alle Locos"; *Codex 628* has "Alle Örtter."

Concerning water: And he commanded the chariot to be halted and both he and Philip stepped down into the water and he [Philip] baptized him, Acts 8.

Concerning Paul's conversion. Acts 9.

Admonition: Ananias said, Dear brother Saul, the Lord, who appeared to you on the road to this place, has sent me so that you may receive your sight back and be filled with the Holy Spirit. Now why do you delay any longer. Acts 22.

Concerning baptism: Arise and let yourself be baptized

Concerning the Spirit: and wash away your sins

Concerning prayer: and call on the name of the Lord.

Concerning water: Then Paul again received his sight, got up and let himself be baptized. <322>

Peter converts Cornelius and many Gentiles to faith, Acts 10.

Concerning teaching: While Peter was still speaking these words to Cornelius and to the [other] men

Concerning the Holy Spirit: the Holy Spirit fell on those who heard the Word, and the believers who had come with Peter and were of the circumcision were astonished that the Holy Spirit was also being poured out on the Gentiles.

Concerning water: Then Peter said, Can anyone keep these people from being baptized with water? They have received the Holy Spirit just as we have.

Concerning baptism: So he ordered that they be baptized in the name of the Lord, Acts 10.

Concerning Lydia, the dealer in purple cloth, Acts 16.

Concerning hearing and faith: A devout[540] woman named Lydia, a dealer in purple cloth, listened to [the Word]. The Lord opened her heart to respond to Paul's message.

Concerning water: Then she and her house were baptized.

Concerning the works of love: She asked (the disciples) and said: If you consider me a believer in the Lord, come into my house and stay there. [Acts 16].[541]

---

540 Print has "God-fearing."
541 Added in *Codex 628.*

A Short, Simple Confession

Concerning the jailor, Acts 16.

His own request: The jailor said [to Paul and Silas],[542] Dear sirs, what must I do to be saved? <323>

Concerning teaching and faith: They said to him, believe on the Lord Jesus, and you and your house will be saved. They spoke the word of the Lord to him and to all who were in his house.

Works of faith: And he took them to himself in that late hour of the night and washed their wounds.

Concerning water: And he let himself and his entire household be baptized, Acts 16.

Crispus and his entire household along with many other Corinthians become believers, Acts 18.

Teaching and faith: Paul taught [in the house of Justus].[543] But Crispus, the ruler of the synagogue, believed on the Lord with his whole house, and many Corinthians who heard him also became believers.

Concerning water: And [they] let themselves be baptized, Acts 18.

Concerning the twelve men from Ephesus, Acts 19.

John's teaching concerning repentance and faith: [Paul came to Ephesus and found some disciples. He said to them: Did you receive the Holy Spirit when you became believers? They said to him: We have not even heard that a Holy Spirit exists. And he said: In what have you been baptized? They answered: In John's baptism.][544] But Paul said to them: John baptized with a baptism of repentance [or baptized the remorseful],[545] and told the people to believe in the one who was to come after him, that is in Jesus, who is the Christ. <324>

Knowledge of Christ and the Holy Spirit: When they heard that

Concerning water: they let themselves be baptized in the name of the Lord Jesus, Acts 19.

Concerning the Holy Spirit and the laying on of hands: And when Paul had laid hands on them the Holy Spirit came over them and they spoke in

---

542 Interpolation, *Codex 628*.
543 Interpolation, *Codex 628*.
544 Interpolation, *Codex 628*.
545 Interpolation, *Codex 628*.

tongues and prophesied. These twelve men had earlier been baptized by Apollos with John's baptism, Acts 18, and were rebaptized by Paul.

Testimonies concerning baptism from the Epistles, Romans 6.

Concerning water: Buried into death with water. Paul says: Do you not know that all those who have been baptized in Jesus Christ are baptized into his death. Thus we have been buried with him through baptism into death?

Resurrection in the Spirit: So that just as Jesus has been raised from the dead through the glory of the Father

New life: therefore we too must walk in newness of life.

Mortifying the old: If we have been planted with him like this in his death

Resurrection of the new: then we will also certainly be united with him in his resurrection. [From this we know that our old being has been crucified with Him, so that we not celebrate the sinful body but henceforth no longer serve sin. In the first epistle to the [1 Corinthians 1] Paul baptized the household of Stephanas which <325> dedicated itself, without being told to do so, to serve the saints.][546]

The Offices of Apostles and other servants, 1 Corinthians 3.

Who is Paul? Who is Apollos? They are servants through whom you became believers, to the extent that the Lord has granted this to each individual. I planted (that is, I have taught), Apollos watered (that is, he also baptized), but God gave the increase (that is, the Holy Spirit, whom God himself sends through Christ).

1 Corinthians 6.

Concerning Water: Paul teaches and says that we have all been washed clean.

Created by the Father's grace: You have been made holy.

Redeemed through Christ the Son: You have been justified through the name of the Lord Jesus Christ.

Illuminated by the Holy Spirit: And through the Spirit of our God.

---

546 Interpolation, *Codex 628.*

A Short, Simple Confession

Colossians 2.
Concerning water: Paul teaches, saying: Because you have been buried with Christ through baptism

Resurrection in the Spirit: in whom you have also been resurrected in the Spirit through faith created by God, whom he has awakened from the dead (that is Christ), Colossians 2.

Galatians 3.
Concerning water: Paul teaches, saying: However many have been baptized in Christ, have put on Christ.

Ephesians 4 [and 5].[547] Paul teaches, one faith, one baptism, one lord and Father of all.

Bath of water in the Word: Paul teaches, saying: And you have been cleaned through the baptism in the Word, Ephesians 5. <326>

Sanctified in the Spirit: That he may present to himself a glorious church without spot or wrinkle, or any such thing, but that it should be holy and without blemish, Ephesians 5.

Bath of water for rebirth: Paul taught, saying, Titus 3: Christ, according to his mercy, saves us through the baptism of regeneration.

Concerning the Holy Spirit: And renewal of the Holy Spirit which he has richly poured out over us, Titus 3.

Concerning water and the flood, 1 Peter 3: During the days of Noah when they were building the ark, in which few—that is eight—souls were saved through water. This is the figure of what also saves you.

Concerning baptism: Namely baptism, not the removal of dirt from the body

Resurrection in good conscience: but in the certain testimony of a good conscience toward God through the resurrection of Jesus Christ, 1 Peter 3.

Concerning the Spirit, 1 Corinthians 12 and 15: Paul teaches, saying: Through one Spirit we have all been

Concerning water: baptized into one body, 1 Corinthians 12.

---

547 Omitted from *Codex 628*.

Concerning water: What else do those do who have themselves baptized for the dead, 1 Corinthians 15.

Concerning the resurrection: if, indeed, the dead are not resurrected.

The danger of baptism: Why do they allow themselves to be baptized for the dead, and why do we constantly stand in danger <327> because of our boasting? Read the entire 15th chapter dealing with the resurrection.

Hebrews 10

The power of faith: Therefore let us come into his presence with an unfeigned heart and complete faith

The power of the Spirit: sprinkled in our hearts, and freed from a bad conscience

Water: and having the body washed with pure water.

The right way of life: And let us hold fast the confession of hope without wavering; for he who has promised it is [truthful],[548] Hebrews 10.

1 John 3

Three witnesses testify in heaven: 1. The Father (that is, God), 2. The Word (that is, humankind), and 3. The Holy Spirit (that is, Spirit).

Three witnesses testify on earth: 1. The Spirit (that is, spirit), 2. The water (that is, baptism), 3. And the blood (that is, the cross). And these three serve as one.

Paul says in Colossians 2: Do not let anyone, who walks in paths of his own devising, divert you from the goal.[549]

[God protect us, for it would be far better for us to die because of our witness for God than to be led astray by the glosses of strangers. Here we have listed for all to see the true, clear, bright, pure, and infallible texts about how one should baptize, presented and commanded by the eternal Son of God himself and implemented by his holy apostles. This foundation will remain in all eternity, and the gates of hell shall not prevail against it.] <328>

---

548 Print has *"getrew"*; Codex 628 *"warhafft."*
549 The following long section, in square brackets, appears in *Codex 628* but is not part of the printed pamphlet.

We have sought to point out these passages as briefly as possible. We have left the preliminary and bare words stand so that [the tract] would not become too long and so that only the most necessary aspects are included. Whoever wishes to read from the beginning, that is, how these teachings have developed, may do so. For the teaching concerning faith always precedes baptism and everything else. Paul says: Faith comes from hearing the Word preached.

The flood is a true figure of baptism, 1 Peter 3.

Peter says the following: For Christ suffered once for our sins, the just for the unjust, so that he might bring us to God. He was put to death according to the flesh, but quickened by the Spirit. In the Spirit he also went and preached to the spirits in prison, who long ago had been unbelievers at a time when once the longsuffering of God waited in the time of Noah when the ark was being built, in which the eight souls were saved through water. This is a figure of what also saves you, namely baptism, not by removing the dirt of the body, but through the sure witness of a good conscience with God through the resurrection of Jesus Christ, who has ascended to the heavens and now sits at the right hand of God.

Circumcision is an example and figure of the cleansing of the heart. Texts from the Old Testament. <329>

Deuteronomy 10: Moses spoke to the people of Israel at God's command: Therefore circumcise now the foreskin of your heart and be no longer stubborn. For the Lord your God is God of gods, and Lord of all lords.

Deuteronomy 30: And the Lord your God will circumcise your heart and the heart of your seed, to love the Lord your God with all your heart, and with all your soul, so that you may live.

Jeremiah 4: Thus spoke the Lord to those living in Judah and Jerusalem: Break up your fallow ground and do not sow among the thorns. Circumcise yourselves to the Lord and take away the foreskins of your heart, you men of Judah and you people of Jerusalem.

Jeremiah 6: Whom shall I warn that their ears are uncircumcised so that they may hear?

Jeremiah 9: Behold the day will come, says the Lord, that I will punish all the circumcised by the uncircumcised, namely Egypt, Judah, Edom, the children of Ammon, Moab, and all those who dwell in the various places of the wilderness. For all heathen have an uncircumcised foreskin, but the entire house of Israel has uncircumcised hearts.[550]

[*Ezekiel 44:* O house of Israel, you have taken your abominations to the limit, for you have brought into my sanctuary strangers, uncircumcised in heart and flesh, so that my sanctuary has become polluted. Therefore the Lord says: <330> No stranger, uncircumcised in heart and flesh, shall enter into my sanctuary. Indeed, not even those people who have departed from me.][551]

Circumcision is a symbol (figure) for the cleansing of the heart, which Paul call circumcision without hands. Witness of the New Testament.

Acts 6 and 7: Stephen accuses the hardened Jews that they slandered and persecuted God's Word, and said to them: You stubborn and uncircumcised in heart and ears, you continually oppose the Holy Spirit. As your fathers did, so you also do.

Romans 2: Paul says to the Romans, he is not a Jew who is one outwardly, nor is that a circumcision that is only performed externally on the flesh. Rather, he is a Jew who is one inwardly and in all secrecy; thus a circumcision of the heart is a circumcision that takes place in the Spirit and not according to the letter, whose praise is not of men but of God.

Philippians 3: Paul says to the Philippians, We are of the circumcision who serve God in spirit, and boast of Jesus Christ, and find no consolation in the flesh.

Colossians 2: Paul says to the Colossians: Beware that no one spoil you through philosophy and useless and vain deceits according to human and worldly traditions, which have nothing to do with Christ. For in him dwells all the fullness of the Godhead bodily. <331> And you are complete in him who is the head of all principalities and powers, in whom you are also circumcised with a circumcision made without hands, through the putting off of the sinful body of the flesh.

---

550 The following section, citing Ezekiel 44, is not found in the printed booklet. Was this an interpolation by the author/editor of *Codex 628*, or was the copying done from a currently unknown print or manuscript?
551 Interpolation, *Codex 628*.

Galatians 6:[552] In Christ Jesus neither circumcision nor un-circumcision avails anything, but a new creature.[553] And as many who walk according to this rule, may peace and mercy be upon them. From henceforth let no man trouble me, for I bear in my body the marks of the Lord Jesus. The grace of our Lord Jesus Christ be with your spirit, dear brothers. Amen.

The Thirteenth Article

Whether the Lord's Supper is a simple and empty symbol

With regard to this article we confess that the Lord's Supper is not simply a sign by which the Christians shall and may recognize one another. Rather, it is also a symbol [*ein zeichen*] through which Christ himself wishes to reveal and give us to understand his suffering and his death.[554] For since a true understanding of Christ and the Father who sent him is eternal life, and we are so slow of understanding that we cannot always grasp it, the Lord is concerned to lead his followers into an understanding [of these things] by all means possible, by means of clear words and analogies [*glychnis*].

That is why we believe that with the words of institution our Lord and Savior used to initiate his Supper, he did not desire or intend to teach us what makes up the bread and the wine, <332> for the natural and earthly man knows this already. Rather, with the bread and wine he sought to teach us what his body and blood are. With the breaking of bread and the pouring out and distribution of the wine, [Christ wishes to teach us what] his suffering, dying, and spilled blood means, which had not yet taken place, but was soon to take place. For the fact that he should and that he wished to suffer undoubtedly appeared to his disciples, as it would to all

---

552 The print omits the reference to Galatians 6; *Codex 628* has the reference. See Yoder, *Legacy*, 177, n. 30.
553 The copying of *Wie die Gschrifft* ... in *Codex 628* ends here. *Codex 628* completes the citation from Galatians; the print breaks it off at this point. The addition of the citation from Ezekiel 44 and the complete citation from Galatians 6 raise the possibility that the author/editor of *Codex 628* was copying from a more complete version of the text than the one print known to us.
554 *Margin*: John 17

natural humans, to be a childish and useless thing that did them no good and brought them no advantage.

But in order that his disciples, and we too, might better understand, he explains to them beforehand what his body is that is to be broken, and what his blood is that is to be shed. So he takes the bread, breaks it and says: Take and eat, this is my body. But what was it for which he gave thanks and commanded them to eat? It was bread. Thus he wishes to say: This, my body which is here present and tomorrow will be broken, is similar to this. It is also bread, a food, but it is not the food you see before you, which is just another loaf of bread meant for this temporal life. Rather, [my body] is meant for eternal life. In the same manner he took the wine and said: This is my blood. But what was this for which he also gave thanks? It was wine and a drink intended for this temporal life. He says that this is his blood, that is, that his blood that was to be shed on the morrow is also a wine, but not the present wine or drink. Rather his blood is a drink intended for the unending eternal life.

This is what we are to do, that is, break the bread with one another, and drink the wine with one another <333> and by doing so learn what His suffering, dying, and shedding of blood really is. Or, as he himself says, we are to proclaim his death until his return, and to teach this and inculcate this in our children down through the generations; [that is], that his body has become a true bread and his blood a true drink for all believers on the wood of the holy cross, of which we become participants by means of the diligent contemplation of this bread and wine, through faith.

But whoever eats worthily of this bread and drinks worthily of this cup acknowledges Christ as his Lord and Savior, as the Easter lamb who takes away the sin of the world, who has given his body as a true food, and his blood as a true drink, through which one's hunger for eternal life is stilled. In the same way such a person recognizes that he who refuses to eat of Christ's body or drink of his wine does not have life in him, and that Christ's flesh and blood became a sacrifice on the wood of the holy cross that is valid for all eternity, and that he now sits at the right hand of God and waits until all his enemies have been laid at his footstool. Whoever has a true hunger and thirst for such a sacrifice and follows our Lord Christ in upright and Christian obedience and believes that he truly eats this bread and drinks this wine, he is also partaking of the true body of Christ and his true blood through faith. Likewise, whoever acknowledges those as his brothers who partake of the Supper with him, who stand in the same faith as he does, against whom he carries no animosity <334> [also partakes of the body of Christ]—for Christ's Supper is a physical coming together of Christian believers in love. Without love it may be called a supper, but not a Christian [or Lord's] Supper, even though all other necessary things are present, as Paul testifies clearly and plainly enough. Therefore the Lord's Supper cannot be eaten without love, which is required in the Supper. But honest love comes only out of a true fear of God and an upright faith. That is why only truly believing Christians, and no one else, can hold such a loving gathering.

It is for these reasons that we believe and say that only the truly believing are to eat the bread and drink the cup in remembrance of our Lord. We do it for a communion [*gemeinschafft*] of his body and blood and as a demonstration of loving solidarity among Christian believers. This is also testified to clearly enough by the words of both Christ and Paul. Christ, after he had broken the bread with his disciples and offered it to them to eat, and had done the same with the wine, said: Do this in remembrance of me. From this it is apparent that the bread and wine in the Supper shall be given, eaten, and drunk in remembrance of Christ.

Paul speaks to the same effect: Is not the cup of blessing, with which we are blessed or give thanks, the fellowship of the blood of Christ; the bread that we break, is it not the fellowship of the body of Christ, for we who are many [are] one bread and body? [It is so] because we have shared and eaten of one bread [1 Corinthians 10:16-17].

These are clear and easily understood words of the holy Apostle Paul with which he shows that the bread that we break and the wine that we drink in the Supper is a communion of the body and blood of Christ in which the true children of God testify that they have communion with Christ, and that they have been united into one body through the one Spirit of love, in the same manner in which many kernels are made into one loaf of bread. And just as kernels that are ground together and mixed with one another become one bread, in the same manner those who eat of one bread and [drink of one] cup of the Lord in his Supper are to be one body of Christ, in the love and the obedience of faith, submitting to, and helping one another in all patience, not in the conflict of steel swords. Rather, they are to be ready and willing to do good to friend and foe alike, just as one member of the body is attached to another and depends on it. In this way we are, in love, to be members of one body.

It is upon this foundation that Paul introduces the Lord's Supper in 1 Corinthians 11[:23-29] and says: The Lord Jesus, in the night that he was betrayed, took the bread, gave thanks and broke it, saying: Take, eat, this is my body which is broken for you. Do this in remembrance of me. In the same manner he took the wine after the Supper, and said: This cup is the new testament in my blood; do this, as often as you drink it, in remembrance of me. For as often as you eat of this bread and drink of this cup you are to proclaim the Lord's death until he comes. <336> Whoever therefore eats of this bread and drinks of this cup of the Lord unworthily shall be guilty of the body and blood of the Lord. But let us examine and remind ourselves, and so let us eat of this bread and drink of this cup. For whoever eats and drinks unworthily, eats and drinks to judgment in that such a one does not discern the Lord's body.

Therefore we must wake up and make sure that we no longer are caught up in the vanity of the flesh, in fornication, lasciviousness, uncleanness, adultery, drunkenness, pride, ambition, greed, usury, jealousy, hatred, swearing, blaspheming God, and other vices. For such persons are denied entry to the kingdom of God, 1 Corinthians 6[:9-10], Galatians 5[:19-21], Ephesians 5[:3-6]; Revelation 21[:8] and 22[:3; 15]. [For if we do these things] we eat and drink, to our own condemnation, the sentence and judgment of God. Rather, we should be dressed in new wedding garments, clothes that have not been defiled with the above-mentioned vices, but rather decorated with Christian virtues which well become a believer, Romans 12[:6-21], 1 Corinthians 13[:1-13], 1 Peter 2[:11-24], 1 John 2[:4-11], 3[:6-18] and 4[:7-21].

Thus we should come to this meal with truthful hearts and a pure love, and consider with great thankfulness what Christ has accomplished for our sakes; that he gave his body and blood for the forgiveness of our sin. Such a remembrance makes a truly believing Christian rejoice not a little; it consoles, refreshes, and strengthens. Indeed, the bread and wine also feeds the body, for what can be more lovely and consoling to a believer than to remember the unspeakably great love because of which God the Father sent <337> his only begotten Son for us poor sinners, who gave his life for us in such an ignominious and bitter death, in order to win for us grace, mercy, and the forgiveness of our sins before his heavenly Father.

A Short, Simple Confession

Therefore Paul says in clearly expressed words: As often as you eat of this bread and drink of this drink, you shall proclaim the death of the Lord until he comes. As though he wished to say: This is why you eat of this bread and drink from this cup in fellowship; that is, in order to confess and proclaim the death of the Lord amongst yourselves, namely that Christ died for you, gave his body and shed his blood for you, and that you should place all your trust and life in the death of Christ. Also, with this we remember the works of Christ, which are love, patience, humility, etc., for these are required of every truly believing heart.

There is no other way in which one may observe and eat Christ's Supper. For even though an unbeliever thinks he may eat of this bread and drink from this cup, he nevertheless eats and drinks to his own eternal damnation. That is why Paul says that those who wish to eat of the bread and drink of the cup should examine themselves carefully, so that they do it with a pure heart, as they should.

Concerning the fact that the apostle says, Let a person examine oneself and then eat of the bread and drink of the cup, it is good to note that he does not say: Examine the bread and wine to see what it is. Rather, he says: Let one examine oneself; that is to say, each one for themselves. For the way the heart is inclined, so also is the bread <338> and the wine. Have you entered wholeheartedly into the love of Christ and your neighbor? Is your heart inclined to follow the example of Christ with regard to your brother—and not only your brother but also with regard to strangers and enemies—in accordance with the words of the Lord Jesus? Then the breaking of bread and the drinking from the cup is a true communion of the body and blood of Christ. But if your heart is a rogue, or if it is jealous or filled with ill-will, or embittered against your neighbor with some evil that you do not want to surrender to repentance in true remorse, then you eat and drink judgment in the bread and the wine. Therefore all the power depends upon the human heart[555] and not on the external elements of bread and wine.

Therefore, those who desire to partake of the Lord's Supper must examine themselves inwardly, and not concern themselves about the [composition] of the outward bread and wine. For, unfortunately, the contrary has been the case for a long time. Namely, [people] have racked their brains and tried, with great strife, to determine what the bread and

---

555 The phrase reads: *ligt die gantz macht an dem hertzen dess menschens*

the wine in the Lord's Supper are. One person makes it out to be this, another that.

Therefore, as the prophet Isaiah told the Jews when they placed too much reliance upon their earthly temple and thought that God could only be found there [Isaiah 66:1-2]: Heaven [he said], is my seat and the earth my footstool; what then is a house to me that you should build it? Or which is the place where I am to rest, for my hands have made everything? With this he wishes <339> to admonish them and lift them above all this, directing their hearts, minds, and thoughts to heaven.

It then stands to reason that we should, in the same way, point, lead, and direct the people away from this earthly, transitory bread to the immortal food and drink which flows from eternal life. For humans, unfortunately, depend altogether too much on outward things, indeed still cling to them most tenaciously, pretending that they are the very essence of the heavenly bread and drink, and praising them as such, even though they are only a figure [*gegenbild*] of the true essence, as Paul speaks of it in the epistle to the Hebrews, and not the essence itself [Hebrews 1:3].

However, some respond to our teaching by saying that one thereby changes Christ's Word and does not concede enough to his omniscience. To this we answer: No. One does not change Christ's Word with such a teaching. But those who make the creator out of the creature, who make something heavenly out of what is earthly, [they are the ones who] create the essence out of a shadow, truth out of vanity, and seek Christ—and direct others to seek him—in those things and places where he is not and where it is forbidden. These are the ones who change Christ's Word. And they do this even though [Christ] has forbidden them to do so, when he said: You are not to believe those who do such things.

With respect to the other thing that they say, namely, that one does not concede enough to God's omnipotence when we say and teach that we are to seek Christ in heaven and not on earth in the bread, we answer: The Lord Christ praised and boasted more of the Capernaum centurion's faith—whose servant lay sick and who said to the Lord: I am not worthy that you should come under my roof, but only speak a word and my servant will be healed <340>—than he did of the faith of the nobleman, who also was from Capernaum but thought that if Christ were not physically present his son would die. So Christ will doubtless value the faith more of one who seeks him in heaven at the right hand of the Father, and who believes that He feeds everything that lives with the finest food.

But that Paul says [1 Corinthians 10:16]: Is not the bread that we break the communion of the body of Christ, the cup that we drink, is it not communion in the blood of Christ—does he not wish to teach and say with these words that the bread is the body of Christ, and the wine of the cup is the blood of Christ? To be in communion with something does not mean to be the thing itself—but what does it mean to be in communion with the body or blood of Christ? We should better understand 1 Peter 5[:1-2] where the writer says: I exhort the elders who are among you as a co-elder and as a witness of Christ's sufferings, and also as a fellow recipient of the glory yet to be revealed. Therefore Christ's body and blood are filled with disgrace, suffering and dying. Peter was a witness to this and a participant in it. But [Christ's body and blood] are also full of grace, peace, power, strength, glory, and holiness, in which he also participated.

Therefore whoever eats of this bread and drinks of this cup in a correct way and worthy manner transports himself into the communion of the body and blood of Christ; that is, to suffer with him but also to inherit with him. Now, one wishes to be in communion with the Christ who rose up to <341> heaven to be seated at the right hand of the Father in order to share in his inheritance. But the unregenerate, unrenewed old Adam refuses to accept or have any communion with the Christ who humbled himself, who took on the form of a servant, served but did not allow himself be served, was slandered but did not slander in response, was crucified but crucified no one. Nevertheless, the two hang so closely together that you cannot have the one without the other.[556]

[Conclusion and Summary]

This is our simple understanding of the prescribed articles. We have presented and explained them out of our love for truth in the shortest and simplest way that we, in our simplicity, could do. We hope that this teaching is confirmed by the holy divine Scriptures and by the teachings of Christ and his apostles so that the gates of hell will not prevail against it,

---

556 Here ends the article on the Lord's Supper, and the direct responses to the specific articles taken up at the Frankenthal Disputation.

even though [many people] want to attack this simplicity with numerous veiled and sly questions of human cleverness, dexterity, and subtlety. The latter appear nicer and more beautiful to the cross-fleeing, carnally-inclined children of Squire [*Junckher*] Adam because they can pamper and caress their flesh with them and walk beside the cross at the same time. Nevertheless the immortal truth remains as taught by the eternal Son of God and practiced by the apostles until they testified to it with their deaths.

From this, devout, God-illuminated hearts will be able to note and understand that because we try, to the best of our ability and to the extent that God gives us grace, to hold to this teaching, we are not heretics, insurrectionists, or seducers. They accuse us of being rebels, <342> the same accusation the high priest Ananias and Tertullus brought against Paul. They found him to be dangerous, a person who incited to insurrection in the whole world, and a ringleader of the sect of the Nazarenes, Acts 24[:1-6]. Likewise, in Rome the Jews said to Paul: We know about this sect and that everyone everywhere opposes you [Acts 28:22]. All the slanderers of the truth should take stock of themselves, whether or not they do not act in the same manner, that is, slander Christ's teaching and the practice of the apostles as these did. On the other hand, that which they themselves have ordained and put in place, or which has been handed down to us by the pope, must be holy and right [they say], and be the Christian church. O God, guard and save us from all human statutes which you have not planted.

Here, now, my beloved reader in God, you have clearly and lucidly discovered what the Antichrist has brought about, and what kind of nice, wise, and learned teachers and masters of the Scriptures they are who believe and observe his decrees, statutes, and arrangements. Infant baptism was introduced, confirmed, and gradually put in place by the popes and councils until it became a seemingly original usage and tradition, as we sufficiently demonstrated and proved above. Through such an idolatry created by human dexterity and reason the true Christian baptism, as was commanded by Christ and practiced by the apostles, was hindered and this human institution was raised high above the command of God, so that today <343> the correct understanding of baptism is hidden to the vast majority of the world's people, not only among the common laymen, but also among the wisest people.

In this fashion they have all been deceived so that not even one among them considers and endeavors to do what is right. But we should know that God, through his Holy Spirit, does not neglect anything. Rather, all that is necessary for us to know and that serves the salvation of humankind has been more than adequately revealed to us in his Word and Holy Gospel. If it were pleasing to God to baptize young children who lack understanding then, surely, Christ would have revealed it to us and commanded and instituted it with clear and unmistakable words. That is why infant baptizers should beware, especially those who do not wish to be under the pope's jurisdiction. For, having separated themselves from him in several articles, they still cling to the Antichrist's main teachings on the sacraments and have diminished, set aside, and undone, Christ's command.

What thanks and reward can they receive, especially since they know that all power in heaven and on earth has been given him, and that he sent out his apostles into all the world with the command to preach the Gospel to all creatures so that whoever believes [in him] should be baptized—not young children who know nothing about faith? The holy apostles faithfully followed this teaching and the command of Christ to baptize upon a confessed faith. Nor is infant baptism remembered with even one word <344> in the entire Testament. One would have to wonder greatly at this: truly, if God held it in as high esteem as people do, how Christ, the faithful shepherd and teacher of humankind, could have omitted such an important point. For Zwingli himself confesses that those who baptize children have no clear Word which commands them to baptize, even though [Christ] faithfully taught and explained everything to us that we need to know to have eternal life. Paul writes the same thing to the Ephesians, saying that he had kept back nothing, but had declared the complete counsel of God to them.[557] And yet God did not so much as mention infant baptism with even one word. Now, if infant baptism is part of God's counsel, why has it been kept secret in the Holy Scriptures? Since it is not there, the infant baptizers have changed and diminished Christ's existing command, a command that united faith and baptism. In so doing, they have once again separated them so that they can baptize young children who neither believe nor disbelieve, as Zwingli himself confessed above. And whoever disagrees with them and would rather abide by the teaching of Christ and his apostles, because it has a foundation in the Holy Scriptures, must be robbed and persecuted.

---

557 *Margin*: Acts 20

In like manner the sacrament of Holy Communion has been obscured so that people in all this world no longer know its attributes and effects. The papist crowd has added to what Christ commanded and instituted, and cares little about what his command says. The Lutherans also observe the Supper <345> but do not distinguish the figurative sayings of the Lord. The Zwinglians know to distinguish the figurative sayings, but misuse them because they do not exercise the ban nor distinguish between the devout and the godless, mixing them together indiscriminately, even though it is known that this person is a public fornicator, the other a drunkard, the third a miser, and the fourth haughty. In this fashion they become part of one another and bind themselves together. Because of this the good observances become more and more obscured and polluted, being painted over with dirt and grime according to human opinion.

That the Church of Jesus Christ, from the time immediately following the apostles to this very day, has been ruled according to the application of the law drawn from Zion and the Word of God coming out of Jerusalem, and that the smaller portion of it is still so ruled, is clearly evident. In this manner Christ, at the very outset, equipped it well so that Satan, who had already broken into his heavenly Father's paradise in the beginning and brought about the fall of Adam—paradise's first gardener—through his cunning and lying, would not be able to celebrate [a second victory] by gaining entrance to his church and congregation and—once again through his cunning—bring about a great apostasy.

In order to expose Satan's cunning and malice and allow us to see it, he related the following parable in Matthew 13[:24-30]: The kingdom of God [he said] is like unto a man who sowed good seed on his land. When, however, all the people were asleep, there came an enemy who sowed weeds among the wheat and then left. When the wheat[558] had grown and began to bear fruit, the weeds also appeared. <346> Then the servants came to the master of the house and said: Sir, did you not sow good seed on your acre; where, then, do the weeds come from? The master answered: An enemy did that. But when the servants asked whether they should go and pull out the weeds, he gave them the following answer: No, so that you do not also pull out the wheat when you tear out the weeds. They were to let both grow together until the harvest. Then he would say to the (angels or)

---

558 The manuscript has *unkraut*, or *weeds*, a copyist's error; the Scripture text being cited has "wheat."

reapers that they should first gather all the weeds and tie them in bundles in preparation for burning; the wheat, however, they were to gather into his barn.

From this parable we are to learn that the statutes, ordinances, and ceremonies that have been in use in the church and in so-called Christendom already for a long time need not all have come out of the good seed. On top of that, even though they may not have grown out of the good seed, God nevertheless wishes—not only in the beginning, in the middle, but until the last days—patiently to tolerate them so that the wheat will not be uprooted. Therefore he tells his disciples to let the weeds grow.

This is the interpretation the Lord also wishes us to learn from John's Revelation 11[:1-2?], where he announces that the center part of the temple shall be given to the numberless heathen. <347> Thirdly, however, the time will come, in particular in the last days, when He will no longer tolerate these things but will send his angels to gather the tares, each according to its kind, and tie them in bundles—as we are also to learn from the above-cited chapter of Revelation where he speaks of measuring the rear part of the temple, that is the church existing in the last days, as well as the forward part, which was the church in the beginning.

Christ himself tells us quite clearly who the angels are and what the bundles will be in those last days when he says in Matthew 13[:37-42]: The Son of Man is the one who sows the good seed; the field is the world. The good seed are the children of the kingdom; the tares are the children of perdition, and the one who sows them is the devil. The harvest is the end of the world; the reapers are the angels. And just as one uproots the tares and burns them, even so will it be at the end of the world. The Son of Man will send his angels and they will remove every offence from his kingdom, and all who act unjustly will be gathered and thrown into the oven of fire; there will be wailing and gnashing of teeth.

It would therefore be a good thing if everyone, through the grace of God, would learn to know who they really are, what they consist of and what kind of plant they are: whether they belong to the good and noble seed that bears fruit a hundred-fold, sixty-fold or thirty-fold, and is gathered into the heavenly palace and the kingly hall to everlasting life; or whether they still belong to the tares <348> without any good or timely fruit, drowned in the lasciviousness of fleshly sins and vices, to be condemned, by God's righteous judgment, to the eternal fire.

Unfortunately, Christendom has, in these our last and dangerous times, acquired many breaches and tears, adding more to them the longer it lasts. And just as earth returns to earth, iron to iron, ore to ore, silver to silver, gold to gold when smelted in the fire, like every other metal according to its kind, in the same manner all persons join themselves to, and hang onto, those who are like themselves. And according to the matter of which they are made, and whether they have good or bad inclinations, they are attracted to and unite themselves with a sheaf that will either be gathered and brought into the Lord's barn or led into the fire. May the Lord grant each of us His grace so that we may learn to fear Him and enter into true obedience to Him, in order to come into that sheaf which will be taken into his barn and lead to eternal life where the righteous will shine like the sun in their Father's kingdom, for ever and ever.

In conclusion, however, we cannot omit noting that, through the preceding parable, the Lord predicted the accidental, though erroneous, development that would—from the very beginning to the very end—occur in his church due to the drowsy inattention of his followers. But through another parable, contained in the above-mentioned chapter of John's Revelation, he speaks of a considerable fruitfulness which also will become manifest in the last days, when the angel will command <349> the back and the front parts [of the temple] to be measured. He does the same in Matthew 24 and 25, where he speaks of the signs and harbingers that shall precede his coming.

Here [Matthew 25:1-12] he states in explicit terms that at the very time when these signs and harbingers will become visible, and his return therefore grows nigh, his kingdom will be like unto ten virgins, five of them wise and five foolish, who took up their lamps in order to go and meet the bridegroom. When his coming was delayed beyond what they had assumed, they all fell asleep. At midnight, however, the cry rang out saying that the bridegroom was coming; they should arise and go out to meet him. But when they arose and began to trim their lamps, the foolish virgins discovered that they had insufficient oil in their lamps. They therefore requested that the wise virgins give them some of their oil, for their lamps were going out. But the wise virgins answered: Not so, because there may not be enough for both of us. Rather, you go to the merchants who sell oil and buy for yourselves. While they were on their way, however, the bridegroom came; then those who were prepared entered with him into

A Short, Simple Confession 435

the wedding banquet, whereupon the doors were locked. Finally, the other virgins also arrived and cried: Sir, sir, open the door for us. But he answered them: Truly I say unto you, I do not know you.

In the above parable, the Lord enlightens us as to Satan's cunning and trickery, a cunning and trickery he will very soon attempt to use against Christ's church. He also shows us how patiently he has suffered such actions by Satan until the time of his appearing. <350> In the parable he has also in the same manner made us to understand the power of his blessing which he will demonstrate to us especially in these last days. Even though he will finally have to say that love has grown cold and unrighteousness overtaken the world, and will have to ask whether or not faith will be found at the time of his appearing [Luke 18:8], he nevertheless also wishes to inform us that the good seed will not be so choked out or overwhelmed by the weeds that a small remnant will not be found that has remained undefiled by the world and is ready to meet him at his appearing, wearing true wedding garments—that is, ready to meet him with an upright and truly converted heart, fired by an ardent love, just as one does when a mighty lord or emperor is about to ride into a great city. At such times the soldiers, who have been tested and proven in warfare, put on their armor and battle gear, and go out to welcome him dressed in their finest apparel. In the same way that the birds of the air begin to prepare for summer in the spring by growing their most beautiful feathers, some of the most watchful of the Lord's faithful will prepare for his coming. The Christian, too, should therefore prepare for Christ's return.

One should take seriously that these are the last days of which the Lord says: that in those last days his kingdom will be like unto ten virgins, because all the signs that may be detected here and there throughout the world are in place: the last cry of the rooster has already been heard, and the Lord's appearing is about to take place. <351> The eternal and omniscient God knows who these wise and foolish virgins are; he [also knows] his elect and believers, whose eyes he has anointed so that they may see; they are enveloped in the love of God. For we do not believe that those, who would very much like to add—whether justly or unjustly—one kingdom to another, one principality to another, one house and land to another so that they alone may be lords of the earth, are the wise and perspicacious virgins. Much less are [the wise virgins] those who with sword, weapons, and fire, attempt to pressure, force, and coerce everyone into their superstition, under the appearance and pretext of thereby building up and caring for the church of Christ.

Neither [do we believe that the wise virgins are] those who seek the world's honor and favor more than the honor and approbation of God. For Christ, who is lord of this kingdom, is not speaking of those who have soiled themselves with everything that is unclean, but he is speaking of those who have gone out in accordance with the law that comes out of Zion and the word of the Lord emanating from Jerusalem and who do [not] presume to praise themselves.

If half of those among the ones who have gone out to meet the bridegroom are carrying lamps low on oil, and are therefore seen to be unfit, what will happen to those who are not only indifferent to Christ's coming but who—not only with subtle and clever words, but also with the sword—actively hinder those who are preparing themselves for Christ's return? To be sure, Christ our Lord predicted <352> that the children of this world would—until the page has turned once more—to their own detriment and eternal damnation, treat us in such a wanton manner as to reenact the passion with us. The devout, however, will patiently battle their way through all affliction, and no one will tear them out of God's hand.

Therefore, since such a great danger lurks at our very door, and the time we have to suffer in this vale of tears is so very dangerous, though short; since it may so quickly change into eternal fear and sorrow if we do not take care and admonish one another; and since so few people adequately consider or take to heart the conclusion and ending of life in this vale of tears—[a life] which, like all things, must end either in eternal joy or eternal sorrow; and since we humans not only have a body but also possess a living soul, and that soul is a living immortal spirit; should this not encourage our hearts to seek our salvation with fear and trembling? It is therefore not only reasonable and right, but also necessary, that we should consider and care for our soul above all else. For the body must decay and return to dust; the soul, however, as we have already observed, is immortal and will continue to exist and live throughout eternity, either in eternal bliss and glory or in eternal sorrow, fear and damnation.

If, therefore, <353> human beings are concerned to take care of the temporal hunger and thirst of the body, how much more should they take into account the soul's hunger for eternity. Indeed, how much more should human beings be concerned not to end in eternal disgrace and shame, [in

A Short, Simple Confession

a place] where—in all eternity—there will be no alleviation, no hope for refreshment, comfort, or cooling. It were much better and more useful for us, therefore, to seek to assist our souls to achieve this eternal honor and rest than to concentrate solely on our body—this sack of dirt—which will remain here in the kingdom of this world.

Poor is the person who ends his life through theft, robbery, and other evil deeds; but more miserable is he who has so little concern for his soul before God that he would kill it through sin, evil deeds, and carnal pleasures, thereby robbing it eternally of God's presence. That is why the entire world, and all the so-called Christians, are in such a terrible condition; that is why they continue to live so securely in their pride, insolence, extravagant luxury, and evil transactions. They think that if they are currently living well, all is well, no matter what the future may hold. If only the body can eat and drink well, and possesses house and land. In this manner and through these things the whole world is deluded and deceived, and the death of all is assured. Everyone's heart, mind, and senses are placed on temporal things, on seeking and capturing the kingdom of heaven here on earth. Thus all neglect and miserably rob themselves of eternal life.

But the world neither knows nor believes this. Therefore it is impossible to either help or give it counsel. <354> In hell after death, however, it will have to acknowledge these things. For the Prophet Esdras says in chapter 9 of Book IV [2 Esdras 9:10-12]: Those who have received goodness in this life and have not acknowledged me; who were distressed about my laws when they were still free and the possibility of a reformation and a return [to me] was still possible; who did not understand but rather despised them; [these] will be forced to acknowledge [my laws] after death in pain. Likewise in chapter 7: From this—that is, from the striving for and preoccupation with strife which humans pursue here on earth—when a man is defeated, the angel says to Ezra, [only] then he will accept what you have said to him. But if he is victorious, he accepts what I say—that is, when the human soul has been defeated by the flesh and sin. Then fear and anguish overwhelms him, as we have said repeatedly. But when he is victorious, he accepts what the angel says, namely that the spirit and soul of man overcomes, retains the victory, and subdues the flesh and sin, suppressing them. [If he does so], he will enjoy victory joyously in all eternity. For the faces of those who have put an end to sin and unrighteousness will shine brighter than the stars, indeed like the sun in heaven itself, forever and ever, 4 Esdras [2 Esdras], 7[:55]; Daniel 12[:2-3]; Matthew 13[:40-43].

How circumspectly and wisely would a man look around himself if he were told how dangerous and poisonous the worms, snakes, dragons, and assorted vermin were that beset the road he was forced to travel. How careful and assiduous he would be to observe his surroundings. He would not allow himself to be annoyed <355> if he had to make a wide detour to avoid being stung, poisoned, or injured. If that is true in the above case, how much more should we flee and avoid sin in order not to be soiled or weakened by it, for the snakes, adders, and dragons are like a burning fire or a piercing sword. For it is indisputable that if a man injures his soul through sin and vice, and without true repentance falls into the hands of his judge, he will have to endure even more cruel suffering and anguish that will torture, punish, and martyr him throughout eternity. For God has prepared the punishing fire from the beginning—even for kings—and he has made it wide and deep. Theirs will be a bed of fire, and copious amounts of wood which the Lord will ignite like a river of sulfur with his breath. Likewise, Psalm 11[:6]: The Lord God will rain coals, fire, sulfur, and wind down upon them like a thunderstorm; all this will be theirs as recompense. And Matthew 22[:13]: Thereafter they will be thrown into the outermost darkness where there will be weeping and gnashing of teeth. Their worm will not die and their fire will not be put out. Cockroaches will be their mattress and worms their blanket. Throughout eternity these things will torture and gnaw at them. According to Matthew 13[:30], they will be thrown into the fiery furnace.

Therefore, since what Christ and his apostles have foretold is both true and most certain—that is, that we must either suffer here or there, as we have already stated and as will follow hereafter—why then would we not choose to suffer here for a short time, especially since this suffering will be followed by a time of eternal refreshment, <356> rather than pamper our flesh for a brief moment, bathing in carnal pleasures, concupiscence, lasciviousness, and wantonness? For the end result of this brief, transitory life is the frightful entry into the jaws of hell, the fiery pool, where there will be a never-ending boiling and roasting of the soul.

But the world cannot, will not, nor does it want to, believe that it finds itself in such a critical and dangerous state. Therefore it will continue on its chosen path until it will be forced to experience, to its sorrow, what we

A Short, Simple Confession

have already observed. Meanwhile, the devout will simply have to continue to suffer; they will be bound and thrown into prison until the [worldly persons], too, are bound and thrown into that eternal prison and into that outermost darkness in which they will—for all eternity—be forced to weep and gnash their teeth, Matthew 22[:13-14]; 25[:30-46]; Revelation 13. They will continue to harry the devout out of city and country, and make them tread the way of affliction, Matthew 10[:17-18]; 24[:10]; John 15[:6; 18-20]; 16[:2; 20-22]; 1 Corinthians 4[:11-13],[559] until the Lord Jesus himself will confront them with their merciless and unfaithful works, and drive them from the throne of his glory with the words: Depart, you cursed ones into the eternal flames which have been prepared for the devil and his angels, 4 Esdras 15 [2 Esdras 15:23]; Matthew 25[:41]. They will continue to kill the devout with the sword until they are themselves killed with the sword, Revelation 13. Because they spill the blood of the prophets and the Lord's anointed, God the Lord will give them blood a-plenty to drink, Revelation 16[:6]. The Lord God declares: The innocent blood of those who have wasted away cries out to me, and the souls of the righteous cry out to me without ceasing. Therefore I will surely <357> avenge it and bring back to me those who have had their blood innocently shed. In the very way that they today treat my elect, so will I treat them and repay them into their bosom, 4 Esdras 15 [2 Esdras 15:21].

Take heed, my people will be led—like a flock of sheep—to the slaughter and killed all the day long, Psalm 44[:11], Romans 8[:36]. The godless draw their sword and bend their bow in order to catch and destroy the suffering people who walk on the path of righteousness. But their sword will pierce their own heart and their bows will break; they will be drowned, and their destruction will overcome them like flooding water. [In this flood] they will have to drown in all eternity, for they will have to drink from the wine of God's fury which has been poured, full strength, into the cup of his wrath, Revelation 14[:10].

In 1 Corinthians 4[:9-13], St. Paul the apostle says: We are like men condemned to die and have become a spectacle to the whole universe, to angels as well as to men. We are fools for Christ, weak, despised, hungry, thirsty, naked, and are beaten with fists, we have no safe place to live, and we work and labor with our own hands. When we are cursed, we bless; when we are persecuted, we endure it; when we are slandered, we earnestly

---

559 *Margin*: Luke 21[:12].

pray [for our slanderers]; we are treated like the scum of the earth and have become everyone's refuse. But I pay all of this no heed, nor do I consider my life more precious than myself so that I might complete my course with joy. For Christ is my life and death is my gain. <358>

Moses, the beloved servant of the Lord, also chose to suffer scorn with the people of God rather than to enjoy the pleasures of sin for a season, esteeming the disgrace of Christ to be a greater treasure than all the riches of Egypt and all the pleasures of the royal court, for he considered the recompense. By faith he departed Egypt, not fearing the anger of the king, for he clung to the Invisible One as though he could see him, and remained strong. Therefore holy Job 1[:21] says: Naked I came from my mother's womb, and naked will I depart. The Lord gave and the Lord has taken away, blessed be the name of the Lord. If we have received every good and blessed thing from God, why should we not also, in contrast, suffer the unpleasant things? In this regard holy Job teaches us true patience [*glassenheitt*]. Where that is present, God himself is present; where it is absent, nothing but unrest is present.

All who have died in the faith acted in the same way, sacrificing the temporal for what was unseen, [sacrificing] life, possessions, blood itself, risking earthly home and fatherland in the process. The Ancients did likewise; see Hebrews 11. For that reason Paul writes in Romans 8[:17]: If we suffer with Christ we also will be glorified like him; but he who refuses to suffer with Christ will also be denied the joy of his presence. The whole world seeks to avoid and flee such suffering, nor are worldly persons worthy of the holy cross. Because they have scorned, derided, laughed at, and despised the cross of Christ <359> in the followers and members of Christ, their disobedient and sinful obstinacy with regard to the guilt of the cross will confront them through all eternity. St. Paul admonishes us, saying: Participate in the sufferings of Christ, for it is time that judgment begins in the house of the Lord. But if it is to begin with us, what kind of an outcome will it take with those who have rejected the Gospel? And if the righteous will hardly survive, what will happen to the godless and sinful person? Therefore those who suffer in accordance with God's will commend their souls by means of their good deeds to their faithful creator.

Therefore, after God has tested and cleansed his faithful sufficiently, has brought them home through affliction and the cross, and filled out the number of his elect, then he will no longer tolerate the godless but will gather them for punishment, damnation, and eternal crucifixion. What has ruined them now—their lasciviousness, their pride, fornication, adultery, impurity, usury, jealousy, hatred, ambition, and other evil habits which they nurse and for which they make room, caressing and pampering their bodies, so they will appear well-fatted for the slaughter—has been put in abeyance until such a time when the last elect will have been born into the world. Until such a time, they will continue to take advantage of the elect. But when that last elect will have been born, the hour will soon break through when the godless will be thrown into hell. Then God will treat them in the way that they have treated the devout, as we have abundantly proven above.

Therefore, beloved brothers and sisters, those who desire to enter through the heavenly gates into the New Jerusalem—that beautiful and beloved city of the eternal God—expect to find nothing less than that you must battle through to the end, fighting with patience under the cross and affliction. For that is the right path and way to life, <360> a way which Christ, our Lord and master, trod before us, which God originally ordained for us, and to which he has called us.

The same thing happened to Adam, Abel, Abraham, Isaac, Jacob, Joseph, Moses, Joshua, Job, Hezekiah, Jeremiah, Elijah, Micah, Amos, Daniel, Shadrach, Meshach, and Abednego, the mother with the seven sons, Christ the Son of God and his holy apostles, and all the elect martyrs, servants, and followers of God and Christ. Just as poor Lazarus's sores and boils were much more beneficial to him for entering the kingdom of God than the rich man's lavish life style and purple silk robes, even so is it better and more beneficial for us to suffer maltreatment with Moses and the people of God than to enjoy the pleasures of sin in this world. Being successful in this carnal Egypt and Babylon, falling in love with it and allowing it to numb us, will just rob us of our eternal inheritance. For even the carnal, wealthy voluptuary reached the point where he was unable to obtain, with all his money, a drop of water to cool his tongue.

On the other hand, the patient and suffering Christian's persecution, his hunger, thirst, cold, evil smell, martyrdom, bonds, prison, irons and chains will rather be more tolerable and more glorious before God than all the world's honor and wealth, indeed than all the gold and silver, golden chains, rings, and precious jewelry. For on the day of the Lord all these instruments [of torture] will, before the judgment seat of Christ, witness to the fact that he was a sincere follower of Christ, even unto death. Indeed, the believing person in particular must take Christ Jesus as an example and remember him continuously in all of his afflictions and sufferings. <361> This is also what happened to my Lord and Savior: he was persecuted, hated, despised, sold, imprisoned, bound, beaten, hit, derided, disdained, flogged, given a crown of thorns, tortured, and crucified outside, before the gates, with gruesome torments and torture, for my sake. Because I see Christ with his cross going on before me, I am on the right road to the homeland.

Therefore we are to go outside the camp, that is to sacrifice our own pleasures and desires, as well as those of the flesh and the world, and help to bear his disgrace. It is on this road we are steadfastly to remain, a road that he himself has designated, trodden, and that is sprinkled with his very blood. This is the road that leads to life, for whoever stays on this road to the end will undoubtedly be crowned by God, will be dressed in a white robe and will, together with the lamb, enter into that great Last Supper where Christ, the Lamb of God, will himself don an apron and serve at table. Then we, along with Paul and all the elect who have stayed the course, will eat of the tree of life that is to be found in the midst of paradise and we will live with Christ for ever and ever.

Therefore, together with all the elect, let us fight valiantly in these troubling times and do battle in this vale of tears, [entering] into the narrow, slippery path by way of the narrow gate. For whoever opposes and patiently overcomes his flesh and blood, overcomes sin and the devil, the world and all its pomp and splendor, and who does not <362> forsake the cross but perseveres to the end in sincere fear of God and with an unvarnished love, such a one will be gifted with incomparable treasures and crowned with an everlasting crown, a crown that is adorned with the kind of precious gems that find no comparison in all the earthly glories, whether they be silver, gold, jasper, jewels, or the riches of earthly kings and emperors. With such as these God will reward his elect; everything else is to be regarded as dirt and dung.

Therefore the greatest wisdom on earth consists of a true and sincere fear of God combined with an observation of his commands. These are more precious than pearls. Nothing that a person may dream of can compare with them. Their fruits are better than gold, even fine gold, and their reward better than choice silver. Such persons travel on the path of righteousness, on the streets of justice, bestowing wealth on those they love and filling full their own treasuries, Proverbs 8[:20-21]. Therefore, one cannot have both gold and this wisdom, nor pay for it with silver. The gold of Ophir may not be compared to it, nor may precious onyx and sapphires, crystal, diamonds, emeralds, rubies, and other of the finest gems. Nor will anyone confuse it with jewels of gold. It is more to be treasured than coral; topaz from Africa is not regarded as highly, and the purest gold cannot be compared to it, Job 28[:12-19].

The world neither knows nor understands this wisdom, nor does it travel on its pathway, Baruch 3[:20], 1 Corinthians 2[:6-8]. The true believer, however, treasures this <363> wisdom more highly than any kingdom or high worldly office. The translucent stone will never compare with it; gold will appear like sand next to it, and silver is filth in comparison. All illuminated persons have chosen it to light their way, for its glow and sparkle will never be extinguished. It is more beautiful than the sun and shines more brightly than the stars, nor is the day to be compared with it, Wisdom 7[:7-14]. Therefore—though we may be forced to present our backs to be beaten for righteousness sake, and turn our cheeks to the one who robs us, following our Lord Christ in suffering and affliction—this is nevertheless the right path upon which to enter the royal hall and New Jerusalem, that beautiful city whose streets are paved with pure gold and decorated with eternal, unspeakable heavenly treasures and jewels. By means of this heavenly wisdom all the elect gain the victory, for they are imbued with the pure love of God and incited, washed, purified, and sanctified by the precious blood of the Lamb of God. The godless, however, who despise the devout, will be punished according to the standards of their own counsel. It is a pleasure for the righteous person to do what is just; but for the evildoer there remains only fear, for the sinner has nothing else to look forward to. Thus will the light of the godless be snuffed out.

All of this, my God-beloved reader, we have brought to light so that, first and foremost, all believing and God-seeking persons, who long for the truth, may be able clearly to tell the difference; and we have put it into circulation that it might pay dividends and produce fruit to the honor of our Lord. <364> We have done this so that you might see a distinct and clear difference between us and our detractors. May our Lord Jesus Christ grant both the growth and the increase, and may he assist all those of good will in these dangerous times to heartily and sincerely pursue everything that is good, confessing his holy truth while remaining steadfast to the end.

Finally, my reader, beloved in God, you should know that this small work is not mine alone; for before I came to it, another God-enlightened person— as is my hope —put his talent to work in the fear of God and, through his industry and seriousness of purpose, extended his hand to me.[560] Thus, wherever it appeared to me that he had properly dealt with the matter, I allowed his work to remain unchanged, accepting his industry and work with thanks and placed it here as it was. Others also helped me in this work. But where I have shortened the material, and in some other instances extended it, I hope—that when his and my small work again falls into his hands—he and every God-fearing person will readily understand from the text why I was moved, and what caused me, to do this.

I would nevertheless sincerely desire that someone else with more understanding and wisdom would come to the aid of us both, especially in those places where we have been too simple for such an exalted work. Should anyone wonder why I wrote such a lengthy preface and conclusion, he should consider their purposes <365> and what is treated in the work. [Those who do this] will the more readily be able to understand the other articles.

Now I have intentionally not sought to write this book with the skill of the highly educated, worldly-wise university professors and scribes. Rather [I have sought to write] in accordance with simplicity and the clear and pure truth which has been sealed with the precious and innocent blood of Jesus Christ, and which has been testified to, even unto death, by his holy apostles and martyrs. May the merciful God lead me in simplicity, humility, and the true fear of God, and in a genuine, pure brotherly love, keeping me steadfast to the end. Amen.

And even though this booklet is issued without the name of any author—to make apparent that no carnal honor or praise is sought—I nevertheless feel more liberated and at peace in my heart for having excused myself and spoken of my assistant. For the Christian's glory is not vain honor. Therefore Paul himself says, Galatians 6[:14]: Far be it from me

---

560 For a discussion of the evidence concerning authorship of *Codex 628*, see above, page 156ff.

A Short, Simple Confession

that I should boast, except in the cross of our Lord Jesus Christ, through whom the world has been crucified to me, and I to the world.

End

Written and completed Monday, 29 January—new calendar—in the year 1590.[561]

<366>

---

[561] Following this conclusion, *Codex 628* continues with the copying of the anonymous tract *Concerning Separation* (pages <369> to <466> of *Codex 628*). This tract was hitherto known only through Heinrich Bullinger's having published it in 1561, as part of his *Der Widertöufferen ursprung, fürgang, Secten, wäsen* ...(Zurich: C. Froschauer, 1561), 214-30. It is not clear from what source this 1590 copying into *Codex 628* originates.

XIII
Concerning Separation. Why We do not Attend Preaching at the Papal, Lutheran and Zwinglian Churches[1]
[As found in Codex 628, 269-466]

INTRODUCTION

In 1560, Heinrich Bullinger published a lengthy and detailed book, *Der Widertöufferen ursprung / fürgang / Secten / wäsen / fürneme und gemeine irer leer Artickel*. As an appendix to this lengthy "history" and refutation of "Anabaptist errors," Bullinger printed an Anabaptist text that had come into his hands late in 1559. He reproduced this booklet, *Concerning Separation*, with the express aim of refuting its contents.[2] It appears that this Anabaptist text, like many of the manuscripts that made up the "Simple Confession," was never printed, but circulated in Anabaptist communities in handwritten form, beginning around 1546. It was written in the first person plural, in a Swiss dialect. Heinold Fast suggests that it originated in the Schaffhausen area. Its critique echoes Martin Weninger (Chapter I

---

1 *Codex 628*, 369-466.
2 Heinrich Bullinger, *Der Widertöufferen ursprung/fürgang/Secten... etc.* (Zurich: Christoffel Froschower, 1561; photo-reprint, Leipzig, 1975), 214r-231r. Critical edition in Heinold Fast, ed., QGTS, II, Ostschweiz, 141-65. Fast gives the composition date as ca. 1546, based on internal textual evidence. See ibid., 141, n. 1. The original manuscript and early copies are noted as "lost." Fast knew of the existence of the copy in *Codex 628* (identified as Codex 693 by Fast), and concluded that it was an expanded copy of Bullinger's print, ibid., 165, note. Based on internal differences between the two versions of the tract, it also seems possible that the version in *Codex 628* represents the copying and expansion of a manuscript tradition independent of Bullinger's print. An English translation of Bullinger's text was published as: "Answer of Some who are called (Ana)Baptists, why they do not attend the Churches," Shem Peachey and Paul Peachey, trans. and ed., MQR 45 (January 1971), 5-32.

above) and the criticisms of the clergy by Schaffhausen goldsmith Lorenz Rosenbom.[3]

Textual evidence suggests that the copyist/editor of *Codex 628* had in hand a version other than Bullinger's print. For instance, the title of the tract in *Codex 628* was written in first person plural; it clearly outlines the approach and the content of the tract, and most probably reflects the title of the original. It reads: *Concerning Separation, why we do not attend preaching at the papal, Lutheran and Zwinglian churches.* Bullinger's printed title, on the other hand, is in the third person, and probably comes from Bullinger's own pen: "Answer of some who are called (Ana)Baptists to the question of why they do not attend the churches." The copyist/editor of *Codex 628* certainly did not copy Bullinger's title, and it seems unlikely that he invented an alternate title for his copying of the tract—although this remains a possibility. Most likely he simply copied the title of the manuscript version he had in hand.

In comparison to Bullinger's printed version, the copyist/editor of the version of "Concerning Separation" found in *Codex 628* has produced a greatly expanded text—more than twice as long as Bullinger's printed version. It is possible that the original tract was much longer, and that Bullinger himself edited the original, although his own testimony would argue against this, since he claims to have printed the text just as it came into his hands.[4] Perhaps the manuscript grew by accretion and addition from Anabaptist copyists between 1546 and 1590, although internal evidence in the form of stylistic and thematic parallels found throughout *Codex 628* suggests that the 1590 copyist/editor was responsible for many of the additions to the tract *Concerning Separation*. But we cannot know for certain. Perhaps the *Codex 628* copyist was responsible for all the additions to the text reproduced by Bullinger, or perhaps not.

What we do know is that the *Codex 628* version of *Concerning Separation* both adds to and occasionally subtracts from the text that appears in Bullinger's book. Some of the lengthy portions of text found in the codex that are absent from Bullinger follow a pattern already seen in the foregoing pages of the codex. These addenda are marked by

---

3   As possible authors, Fast mentions Georg Sattler of Schaffhausen or Heinrich Weninger of Schleitheim. Fast, QGTS, II, 141, n. 1.
4   Bullinger notes that "wie es mir geschifftlich zukomen / hie zu disen minen Buchern getruckt worden ist." *Der Widertöufferen ursprung*, 213v.

references to the early writings of the Reformers, with calls for toleration and admonitions to contemporary preachers to be true to the principles articulated by the founding fathers of the Reformation.

The clearest early example of this tactic comes from Balthasar Hubmaier, who in his *Old and New Teachers on Believers Baptism* (1526) cited earlier writings by Luther, Oecolampadius, Zwingli, Leo Jud, Sebastian Hoffmeister, Wolfgang Capito, Martin Bucer, and others, in order to argue that they later contradicted their earlier positions on infant baptism. In material that appears to have been added to Bullinger's printed text, the 1590 codex argues very much along the lines taken by Hubmaier in 1526, with references to, and specific citations from, early Reformation writings. This time, however, the thematic focus is not baptism but rather the freedom for all believers to speak in worship services and opposition to coercion in matters of faith and conscience. On the basis of early writings by the Reformers, the 1590 copyist calls for openness and toleration in matters of faith, and admonishes contemporary preachers to be true to the principles originally articulated by the founding fathers of the Reformation.

One wonders about Hubmaier's long-range influence here. A tantalizing piece of evidence pointing back to Hubmaier is the appearance in this codex of substantially the same list of early church fathers that he had used in his 1526 publication *Old and New Teachers on Believers Baptism*, namely Cyprian, Ambrose, Eusebius, Chrysostom, and Cyril (see below at page <379> ff.). This material was not present in Bullinger's version of the pamphlet, suggesting a later addition by copyists with access to previously-composed material. The copyist of *Codex 628* references Hubmaier's writings throughout, and refers to him not by name but as dying a martyr's death at Vienna in 1528. Perhaps some unpublished manuscripts written by Hubmaier or inspired by him were preserved, copied, and circulated in Anabaptist circles in the decades following his demise.

The copyist/editor of *Codex 628* made a clear distinction between the *Simple Confession* and *Concerning Separation*; they are copied as separate works. But the copying is sequential in the codex, in the same hand, and there are internal references in the latter to the foregoing work (such as repeated advice to the reader of *Concerning Separation* to refer to a specific article found in the *Simple Confession*). The copyist/editor dates the copying of this expanded text of *Concerning Separation* as February 8, 1590, only nine days after the conclusion of the copying of

Concerning Separation

the *Simple Confession*, which had been concluded on January 29, 1590. Rather than simply attempting to incorporate the former into the latter, as he had done with several other works, the copyist/editor decided to treat *Concerning Separation* as a separate text, which was then expanded and contracted.

Since we have access to Bullinger's print, we can easily track additions and subtractions to that text. We know from internal evidence that the copyist of *Codex 628* had access to Bullinger's book because, in the midst of a lengthy interpolation criticizing the actions of the Bern Synod of 1532, the copyist makes a clear reference to Bullinger's *Der Widertöufferen ursprung* (although not by name), calling it Bullinger's "slanderous book" (*seins lesterbuch*), and countering specific and readily identifiable passages of it.[5] The author of the inserted material obviously had access to Bullinger's *Der Widertöufferen ursprung*, and thus also, by extension, to Bullinger's print of *Concerning Separation*. Given the manner in which manuscripts functioned among these Anabaptist groups, however, and the present state of the evidence, all we can know for certain is that large portions of Bullinger's text and *Codex 628* coincide verbally, that large portions of the codex are not found in Bullinger, and significant sections found in Bullinger are absent from the codex version of this tract.

In the absence of an "original" copy, it is impossible to piece together what elements Bullinger may have omitted from the copy he received, or to know whether the copy that came into his hands was indeed the "original." In fact, the notion of an "original" was better suited to the new world of print; the very concept of a textual "original" is problematic in the plastic milieu of manuscripts that circulate in communities and are being simultaneously copied and edited in various locations.

The version of *Concerning Separation* in *Codex 628* follows the same list of "Reasons," in the same order, as the Bullinger version, with the first three reasons showing the most additions to the text found in Bullinger, as the graph on the following page illustrates. The reasons listed are:

1. The state churches don't observe the "Christian order" concerning the freedom to speak in church (1 Corinthians 14:26ff). The appeal to this passage of Scripture has a venerable history in the Anabaptist movement. Here, the copyist/editor adds a contrast between early Reformation writings that insist upon the freedom to speak in church (as in Martin

---

5   See below at <412>.

Concerning Separation:
Why We Do not Attend Their Churches
(ca. 1546; expanded copy 1590)

1. 1 Cor 14:26-34 not followed in their churches (only preacher speaks)	368-73
Interpolation: Early Ref. writings, old and new teachers: 373-82	
2. They coerce people in matters of faith and conscience	383
Interpolation: They used to teach otherwise: 383-92	
Conclusion	393
3. Used to teach that Christians are a people of peace	393-94
Interpolation: 394-95	
Bern Synod allows authorities to rule on Gospel	395-96
Interpolation: Now they want the worldly sword 397-417	
Interpolation of separate writing: Bern Synod: 400-17	
4. Their actions testify to a lack of the Holy Spirit	417-21
Brief Interpolation: We are not Münsterites: 417-18	
5. The ban is not used in their churches	421-24
6. Their Supper is not the true celebration: no discipline	424-28
Interpolation: Won't let us admonish; they kill us: 428-29	
Body of Christ spiritual; separate	429-32
7. They don't follow "Christ's order" to first teach, then baptize	432-34
Brief Interpolation: previous book, Simple Confession: 433	
8. They abolish the cross of Christ (suffering) by not living rightly	434-35
Interpolation: R. Walter and others often taught the truth: 435	
Preachers do anything to not be called Anabaptists	435-37
[9.] Conclusion: Christians deal with world, but not in matters of faith	437-38
Interpolation: We are no better than anyone; Christ does the good: 439	
Bullinger dropped; copyist writes instead: 440-43	
Case of Judas	443-44
Interpolation: Judas; Christians born of Spirit; vs. hypocrites: 444-63	
Shared paragraph	463-65
Interpolation: 465-66	

Concerning Separation

Luther), and the current practice which forbids lay persons to speak or admonish, as the Spirit might lead. For this reason "we do not attend your churches."

2. The early Reformation leaders (Luther, Melanchthon, Capito, Bucer, Zwingli) all taught that there should be freedom of faith, and no coercion in matters of conscience. Their heirs, the present state pastors, by contrast, call for the authorities to persecute and even to kill those who disagree with them.

3. The early Reformation leaders taught that Christians should not bear the sword of violence. Current Protestant preachers say otherwise, and even invite and accept the civil sword into the church. As part of this argument, a long interpolation enters the tract elaborating on the necessary work of the Spirit and its manifestation in outer works (pages <397-418>).

4. Protestant pastors and congregations testify to a lack of the Holy Spirit. This is visible in their violent persecution of others, in their lies and slander of the Anabaptists, and in lives mired in sin. All these testify that they have no spiritual rebirth from God.

5. The Protestant churches do not practice discipline or the ban. They cannot do it because they lack the Holy Spirit. Since they have no access to the spiritual sword, they use the physical sword to punish matters of faith and conscience.

6. Since they lack the Holy Spirit, and the ban, they do not celebrate a true Lord's Supper which is ordained only for believers. Those who celebrate such a Supper cannot improve, since spiritual admonition is not included.

7. The Protestant churches do not follow the biblical order of first teaching, then baptizing, and insist on baptizing unknowing, unbelieving infants.

8. The Protestant churches do not insist that one must live a new life, avoiding sin. In fact, those in their midst who do live rightly are accused of being "Anabaptists." The preachers block the way of the cross and the way to the Kingdom of God.

[9.] In an unnumbered conclusion, the tract recapitulates the themes already broached, but especially emphasizes the necessity of spiritual rebirth for there to be a true church and for "good" works to follow. The good that is done, insists the copyist/editor, comes not from natural goodness or strength, but rather it comes "from Christ in us."

The writers and/or editors of this text were not skilled debaters or polished authors, and the insistent repetitions throughout bring to mind the circular and repetitive way points are hammered home in oral discourse, rather than the linear arguments of text or print. Although the temptation presented itself to edit the text by removing repetitions, it was decided to leave the text as it was written, to better reflect the style as well as the substance of communication in the manuscripts circulating among the Swiss Brethren in the last years of the sixteenth century.

In the interest of reflecting Swiss Anabaptist thought in the last decade of that century, this translation follows the expanded text of *Concerning Separation* as found in *Codex 628*. Where *Codex 628* follows Bullinger's text, our translation will follow closely the translation work of Shem and Paul Peachey, with some modifications;[6] in all cases the transcription of the manuscript is our own; a translation draft was prepared by the editor, then substantially improved and corrected by Walter Klaassen.

Our translation cannot provide a complete critical apparatus relating the two versions of "Concerning Separation," but it will indicate major textual variations, as follows:

Where Bullinger's earlier printed text coincides with the text found in *Codex 628*, it will be printed in regular type;

Text that is unique to *Codex 628*, and is not found in Bullinger's print, will be printed in italic;

Where Bullinger's text is not found in *Codex 628*, it will be printed in regular Arial font, and also bounded by square brackets and noted as omissions in the notes.

Minor linguistic variations will not be noted.

---

6 Peachey and Peachey, trans. and eds., "Answer of Some who are called (Ana) Baptists, why they do not attend the Churches," MQR 45 (January 1971), 5-32. Original document in German, QGTS II, #190, 141-65.

Concerning Separation: Why we do not attend preaching at the papal, Lutheran and Zwinglian churches.[7]

[We being those who are called baptizers (*töuffer*), who by the grace of God have no desire other than to believe and live according to the pure and holy Gospel, and who, should anyone show us otherwise, are willing to improve; we confess and make known to all: Since the worldly power and people with their preachers eagerly persecute us, saying or complaining that we refuse to come to their preaching, teaching and congregation; that we disdain (such gatherings) and God's Word, which especially alienates us from those who are so highly regarded by many for evangelical truth, that is those called Lutheran and Zwinglian, and also ask us repeatedly why we oppose the above-mentioned attendance at their meetings—we therefore feel impelled and constrained, of necessity, to answer and not be silent; indeed, to give the reasons why we do not go to their preaching, teaching, and congregation, nor have fellowship with them in their faith and worship. We wish to make known what is lacking and falls short, because of which we avoid them. In this way there will be light and no one may think that we are avoiding God's Word. It is our desire and prayer that this will be accepted, and not attack us or abuse us in things that have not been investigated, but will hear us fairly, as is legally appropriate, so that no one be judged or condemned without a hearing. For this reason the pious Nicodemus said, John 7[:51], "Does our law judge anyone before it hears and knows what has been done, etc.?" Even so not everyone may be able to hear, or may wish to hear our presentation of the truth according to Matthew 13[:14ff], John 12[:37ff], Acts 28[:26ff], Romans 11[:8], Isaiah 6[:9ff], having neither ears nor eyes, just as in other places our scriptural defence and presentation was neither heard nor received, but rather held in contempt. It may be asked whether they are not despising the Word of God—which is exactly what they accuse us of doing—and as Paul says in 2 Timothy 4[:3], will not endure sound doctrine but rather turn their ears

---

7 Bullinger's title is: "Answer of Some who are called Baptizers, why they do not attend the Churches." QGTS, II, 141. Codex 628 does not copy the following preface, in square brackets.

from it. Still, we cannot keep from replying, whether people listen or not, whether they obey or not, Ezekiel 2[:5-7], 3[:27], in the hope that some people and devout hearts will accept it and receive a right understanding and discernment of these things, to the further development and deepening of their lives. Amen.[8]

NOW FOLLOWS A SHORT SUMMARY OF THE ABOVE-NAMED REASONS WHY WE DO NOT ATTEND THEIR PREACHING.[9]

The First Reason is this one: that they do not observe a Christian order as it is taught in the Gospel or the Word of God, namely, if something that edifies is given or revealed to a listener, that listener is bound by the duty of Christian love to speak about it in the congregation, and in the meantime *the preacher* is bound to be silent according to the text, 1 Corinthians 14[:26, 29-34].[10] There we read: How is it now, dear brethren, when you gather together, one of you has a Psalm, another a teaching, another a tongue, another a revelation, another an interpretation. Let all be done for improvement, etc. And again: let prophets speak—that is, prophesying—first one, then a second or a third, and let others judge. If someone sitting there receives a revelation, let the first one keep silent. You are all to prophesy, one after the other, so that all may be instructed and comforted. The spirit of the prophets is subject to the prophets, for God is not a God of disorder, but of peace, as in all the churches of the saints. We find it clearly expressed that Paul spoke to the congregation of God, truly to all Christians, when at the beginning of the chapter he admonished all to seek the spiritual gifts, but above all, that they might prophesy—understand prophesying as sharing with others the meaning that they received from God—for improvement, instruction <369> and comfort. Yes [he spoke to] those whom he exhorted to instruct one another and build one another up and comfort one another,[11] and he says in Ephesians [5:19] speaking

---

8 As he will do repeatedly throughout the text, Bullinger here inserts a lengthy gloss, referring readers to different writings where these Anabaptist views are refuted. The glosses are not reproduced in Fast's critical edition, nor are they translated by Peachey and Peachey; they will also be omitted from our translation.
9 *Codex 628* parallels Bullinger beginning at this point.
10 *Codex 628* specifically states that preachers are to be silent; Bullinger does not.
11 Bullinger: 1 Thessalonians 5[:11]; 1 Corinthians 4 [or 14:3?].

Concerning Separation

with one another with Psalms, songs of praise and spiritual songs. As the apostle Peter also instructed,[12] serve one another, each with the gift that was received, as good stewards of the manifold grace of God. If anyone speaks, let such a one speak as God's word. Then all that is done will be done in the most seemly manner possible, so when the community [or congregation: *die gmeind*] gathers together, which communal body is the temple of the Holy Spirit,[13] where the gifts or inner workings of the Spirit in each one (note: in each one) serve the common good. Note: for the common good.[14] How could this be more suitably applied, offered or used for the common good than in the assembly, for the use and betterment of the same, just as the text above in 1 Corinthians 14[:32] says: When such believers gather together, every one—note, every one—has a Psalm, a teaching, a tongue, a revelation. And he enjoins them to allow all this to take place, that is to apply or to use, for the improvement of the community [congregation: *gmein*] which is gathered there, so that it may be a bright light, in spite of the presumptuous attacks of the adversaries.

And it is Paul's intention that if one is sitting there or listening and receives a revelation or a spiritual gift or a prophecy, then the first speaker should be still. And Paul says that all should prophesy, one after the other, and he desires that at all times the spirit of the first person prophesying, <370> teaching, or preaching should be silent when someone among those sitting or listening has something to prophesy. And those already speaking should not be contrary or unfriendly, as some are, especially among the preachers, who yield to no one, and especially not to us, in either being silent or speaking. For this reason sects and divisions result, which is contrary to the above-mentioned words of Paul, and even against themselves and the glosses they have placed at this point in several German Testaments.[15] So if Paul at the end of the chapter commands that speaking in tongues not

---

12 Bullinger: 1 Peter 4[:10ff].
13 Bullinger: 1 Corinthians 6[:19].
14 Bullinger: 1 Corinthians 12[:7[, Ephesians 4[:7].
15 Luther's translation of the New Testament of 1522 contains the following gloss on 1 Corinthians 14:32: "Some believe, because they have understanding and the gift of the spirit, they do not need to yield to anyone or be silent. Sects and divisions are the result of this." Luther's gloss on 1 Corinthians 14:2 contains the following explanation, repeated in the Anabaptist text: "To prophesy is to receive the meaning from God and being able to communicate it to another." See Fast, QGTS, II, 143, n 6.

be forbidden, while at the beginning of the chapter he says that speaking in (unintelligible) tongues does not build up the congregation, how much less authority can anyone claim to forbid prophesying, or teaching, or admonishing through which the congregation would be improved? When one comes into the congregation and hears only one person speaking and the listeners are all silent, neither speaking nor prophesying, who can or will judge this to be a spiritual congregation, or confess according to 1 Corinthians 14 that God is dwelling and working among them through his Spirit and gifts, when the above order of speaking and prophesying is not to be found among them?

And so, as mentioned above, they deny that we possess the evangelical order, nor do they permit us to exercise it when we go to their preaching, but they want to teach and admonish us that we should remain silent at their preaching, like the erring ones, regardless of what one might have to say for improvement, and regardless of whether <371> the preacher fails the truth or not, one must still be silent even though according to 1 Corinthians 14 one is to judge the preacher's teaching. All judgment and everything, indeed, all must accept the preacher and his teaching—be it good or evil—in their consciences, that they are bound to believe and do what he says, and are not bound to Christ and his teaching and the teaching of the Holy Spirit. And if a prophet or messenger of God came into their congregation, as happened in the time of the apostles, sent from God and not by men, such a person would have to be silent or would be persecuted by them.

In this way the holy Gospel and the Word of God is hindered under the appearance and pretext of the aforementioned order, and in the name of love they annul, transgress, and oppose, yes, they forbid those who follow their first teaching of evangelical liberty, and impede and stop up the flow of living waters to the faithful, which in John 7[:38] are called gifts of the Holy Spirit which should be received for the improvement of the congregation and the salvation of souls, so that one might recognize the congregation as spiritual. Otherwise each one has to bury one's talent through silence, and receive punishment from the Lord at the future coming of Christ, Matthew 25[:26ff]. This would be transgressing against rather than remaining in the Evangelical teaching of Christ and his apostles, and to have no God, 2 John 1[:9] and also not to be a true disciple of Christ or a Christian, John 8[:31].

Concerning Separation

This would be a significant and harmful error, and would not be God's Word or the voice of Christ, but would oppose it as the preaching of an alien voice. Therefore we rightly should not <372> listen to such a voice but rather flee according to the word of Christ, John 10[:5], so that we not be partakers of the impending punishment, or be cut off as unfruitful branches or members, John 15[:2, 6], or as trees that bear no good fruit, Matthew 7[:19], be cut down and thrown into the fire. They have long proclaimed that we are not to be allowed to speak openly or publicly, and forbid us this, as already mentioned. This is quenching the Spirit, despising prophecy and refusing to prove and test all things and hold to what is good, against God's Word, 1 Thessalonians 5[:21].

[For this reason we do not merely advise especially the weak, the uninformed, and those of limited experience not to listen to their preaching, nor to speak there, but much more warn them for the reasons mentioned, because through such listening one is soon worse off than before, and for one to speak before such persons leads more readily to blasphemy and malediction than to blessing, since the tendency there is more toward evil than good.][16]

According to their writings, their preachers first taught that they would allow no judge to stand over God's Word, that they knew of no such judge, and that there was no authority (*Oberkeitt*) over the Word other than God alone.[17] Therefore no one may forbid or allow, and if anyone did try to forbid it, such a one would be a servant of the Antichrist [and no magistrate][18] for he would be hindering the salvation of souls as much as he could. But they now transgress against this, their first teaching, as noted. You say yes, if someone has something to say concerning the sermon against the preacher's teaching, such a person should go to the preacher after the sermon and speak to him alone in accordance with Christ's teaching, Matthew 18[:15]: *If your brother sins against you, confront him in private.* Answer: This passage does not apply here at all, and saying such

---

16 Bracketed passage found in Bullinger; not found in *Codex 628*.
17 The tactic of pointing to the early Reformation writings, and the way later reformers went against earlier assertions, is used here in passing in the text Bullinger received in 1559. The elaboration of this theme, with chapter and verse, comes only with the 1590 additions.
18 In Bullinger; omitted from *Codex 628*.

a thing shows great ignorance in spiritual things and of stewardship in the true Christian congregation.

We say that if anything is revealed to a listener to the betterment of the congregation or to prophesy, as the text[19] above clearly indicates, even if it has nothing to do with an error by the preacher and has to do with <373> something else, but all the same, even if it has to do with the preacher, it must come publicly before the congregation who has heard it, and not dealt with privately with the preacher alone, for the sin is not against or for someone alone, but against the entire congregation. Such public matters may therefore not be done or decided outside the congregations. *Therefore the apostle says, bring no complaint against a Christian without two or three witnesses; if they have sinned, punish them in the presence of all, so that the others may fear. How much more reason one has, then, to reproach [a preacher], when the entire community has heard error from him.*[20] Certainly this opportunity is undermined in their congregations, since they allow no one to speak but the preacher, and in this way their congregations are deprived and robbed of all judgment in matters of the soul, bound as they are to the preachers and their personal understanding, contrary to the Word of God.[21]

Just how insultingly and dismissively the preachers cast aside our reasons and paint the apostles' words in an entirely different color is something we know well. For they have attacked us enough and used the word of the Lord blasphemously. Time will tell who has erred and stumbled most deplorably. Because of this article they bent their bows against the Pope at the beginning of the Reformation and armed it with arrows which may now rightly be shot against themselves. For Martin Luther wrote about the above-mentioned words of <374> Paul in 1 Corinthians 14, concerning one who listens and receives a revelation:[22] *What can you secret followers of the Pope say against*

---

19 Bullinger: 1 Corinthians 14[:26ff].
20 Italicized portions found in *Codex 628* only. Bullinger has in its place: "Therefore such public matters cannot be terminated or adjusted privately, apart from the congregation. And if the preacher otherwise sin against only one person in the congregation, and refuse to hear the first and then the second time, this then (according to the commandment of Christ) becomes a matter to bring to the congregation, that is, there to reveal the matter."
21 Here follows a lengthy interpolation found only in *Codex 628*, 375-383.
22 The reference is to Luther's *The Misuse of the Mass*, published in 1522. WA 8, 482-563; English translation in LW, vol. 36, ed. Abdel Ross Wentz, 133-235. The writer

this, when Paul said that all should prophesy, one after the other, so that if among those who are sitting and listening someone receives a revelation he should speak it, and the one who preached first should be silent and give way to him. And all who preach or read should be judged by the listeners, and be subject to them.

What are you now [Pope] Pelagius,[23] says Luther, with your prideful, shameless, blaspheming mouth, that you dare say with blown-up cheeks in your carnal law, that Christian authority has the right to give orders, and all others have simply to obey. Luther writes further, it is the Devil himself who has said this through your mouth against Christ which is in Paul's words. By his divine power, Christ has placed you and all that is yours below all people. He gave everyone the power and ability to judge, decide, read, and preach, and yet you dare to place all things under you on the basis of your own stolen power, and to set yourself over all things exactly like Lucifer, saying you alone may speak, and to presume this falsely against God and the Scriptures. Begone, you rascal, says Luther. All Christians have the full right to read and preach from the Holy Scriptures, even if you should burst into bits![24]

But we grant that even though all have the power to do so, not many today should preach, for when Paul spoke, <375> Barnabas was silent, just as when Peter spoke, the others were quiet, Acts 2 and 4. But this fact did not remove the office of preaching from the community; in fact that office was strengthened by this. For when all people are not allowed to preach, and only one has the power to preach, where is the need to establish and maintain a proper order? And just for this reason it is necessary to keep the rule that all have the power and opportunity to preach.

These are all Luther's own words as they are found in a booklet he published in Wittenberg in 1523 [sic] on the misuse of the Mass, in which he proves with a lengthy text how the office of preaching in Christ's church belongs not just to one person alone, but rather should be common and

---

of the codex closely paraphrases Luther. For the following two paragraphs, see LW, vol. 36, 149-50.

23   Earlier in this writing Luther noted that Pope Pelagius had decreed that "Whoever is the authority has the right to command; the rest should and must obey." LW, vol. 36, 148.

24   The following paragraph precedes the previous two in Luther's writing. See LW, vol. 36, 149.

allowed to all believers, since all believers are God's priests, taught by God himself and gifted with God's Spirit. He shows how Pope Pelagius acted so boldly and unashamedly that he appropriated this common office which belonged to all believers and Christians—yes, in fact he pilfered and stole it, with no command to do so, to the great harm and division of the Christian church—and handed this power over to the so-called clergy. Why have you priests, says Luther, stolen the name that belongs to all, and given it to yourselves alone? Are you not thieves and murderers and despoilers of Christ's church, who have forcefully taken and stolen the holy, common name from the other Christians, and scandalously abused it in the service of your own power, pride and avarice?[25]

Oh Luther, Luther, what have you done and written? If the Pope <376> *acted so illicitly, as is certainly true, when he stole the preaching office from the entire church of Christ, why did you not once again restore this common preaching office to all the believers, to whom it belongs, and which the Pope so willfully stole from them, as you yourself confessed? If the Pope appropriated and stole the common preaching office from the church, the so-called Evangelicals [i.e., Protestants] now possess it, and quite simply want to have the rights to this bold thievery and robbery against God's Word, never to give it up again. Even when they are admonished, they despise all admonition and consider admonition to be an insult, shamelessly twisting and bending the words of the Holy Apostle Paul in 1 Corinthians 14. Is that not willfully bantering and blaspheming God and His Word?*

They write and tell us that if we dare to exercise prophecy and preaching as Paul wrote to the Corinthians, we should demonstrate that we are trained in the languages as were those in Corinth. Otherwise we have no right to preach and they are not at fault in denying it to us.

To this we answer that we do not reject languages in and of themselves, be those languages Latin, Greek, or Hebrew, when they are used in a proper, godly way. Unfortunately what is demonstrated for the most part is the common saying that is applied to such learned rabbis, masters of the Scriptures <377> *and those learned in languages, that the more learned they are, the more perverted they are [je glerter, je verkerter].*[26] *This is plain*

---

25   The preceding found in LW, vol. 36, 140-41.
26   There is a strong connection between this saying and the emerging literature on toleration in the sixteenth century. See Carlos Gilly, "Das Sprichwort "Die Gelehrten, die Verkehrten" in der Toleranzliteratur des 16. Jahrhunderts," in J-G

as day and clearly visible, if only we actually see it and don't stumble over it. Therefore a humble, simple person, who loves and fears God from a pure heart, who humbles himself in order to find grace in God's eyes, and who is enlightened by the heavenly beams, stands far above any clever or learned ones who know many languages—who did not invest their talent better, as noted above. Where no pure love or pure fear of God can be found it is all in vain.

Even though they can prophesy and speak like the angels, and know all secrets and have all knowledge, yes, even if they had enough faith that they could move mountains, and gave all their possessions to the poor, 1 Corinthians 13, it would all be in vain without a pure, effective, active love.

But whoever has had the pure love of God poured out in his heart, and has been sealed with the power and enlightenment of the Holy Spirit, and has truly studied in Christ's school under the task-master of suffering, regardless of how insulted and rejected such a one may be by men and such learned persons—such a person is truly a priest of the living God. Yes, such a one esteems God's honor higher and dearer than the world's honor, pleasure and

---

Rott and S. L. Verheus, eds., *Anabaptistes et dissidentes au XVIe siècle* (Baden-Baden: Valentin Koerner, 1987), 159-72. Gilly states, 161, that beyond a reference by C. Entfelder, the saying doesn't appear in Anabaptist writing. This direct citation in *Codex 628* would be an exception, but the popular saying and theme also appears to have been alive and well in Marpeck circles. See Valentin Ickelsamer's poem by this name in Rempel, *Jörg Maler's* Kunstbuch, 37-60 and Martin Rothkegel's introduction to the poem in H. Fast and M. Rothkegel, eds., *Briefe und Schriften oberdeutscher Täufer 1527-1555. Das* Kunstbuch *des Jörg Probst Rotenfelder gen. Maler* (Gütersloh: Gütersloher Verlagshaus, 2007), 99-104, which also references Gilly's work.

The 1 Corinthians 14 text is discussed by Ickelsamer in stanzas 269-325, with the same conclusions drawn as in the codex. This poem, published before 1546 (the date of Ickelsamer's death) also notes how the "learned ones" changed their minds in their writings, a theme elaborated upon by Hubmaier, Marpeck, Scharnschlager, and at length in the present codex. Marpeck's colleague, Scharnschlager, in his "Congregational Order (ca. 1540) also refers to 1 Corinthians 14 and the exercise of various gifts "for the improvement of the members." See the *Kunstbuch* 406-407. See also the anonymous publication, but since identified with the Marpeck network, "A New Dialogue," trans. Werner Packull, in *Later Writings by Pilgram Marpeck and his Circle*, 49-65; reference to 1 Corinthians 14 on 56-57, given as a reason for not attending Protestant churches.

friendship, and therefore is ready to perfect his service to his Lord through cross and tribulation. But where such an attitude and character is not found, very little that is fruitful can come of it. No blessing or benediction <378> will follow from it, as one can clearly prove and see with open eyes, no matter how many languages someone has learned or how well one is able to prattle.

What do you Scripture experts say to this? Is it a matter of the languages and expert interpretation and glosses, or of the new birth, humility, and anointing from above? I trust you will not be able to avoid this, and Christ and Paul will not yield to you here. That being so, those who have the anointing from above and pure love, which is far superior to all human skill, will share in the greatness of all these words of Paul.

The Pope pilfered and stole the common preaching office from Christ's church, as Luther clearly wrote, but the so-called Evangelicals have appropriated and use this pilfered and stolen preaching office for themselves alone. They claim to have established the Church of Christ properly, but it is not as it ought to have been done. Therefore they have not straightened it out very well, for no matter how much they preach and teach, it goes in one ear of the hearers and right out the other, for the most part producing no fruit or improvement.

Now Martin Luther wrote further in the previously mentioned booklet—after he admonished at length that teaching and preaching should be common and free to all believers and to the Christian church, and that it should belong to no one person—he writes then that it must be concluded and taken as grounded in the Holy Scriptures that there is <379> only one office for preaching God's Word that belongs to all Christians together, that everyone may speak, preach, and judge, and the others are all duty-bound to listen; therefore, the Pope's office and priesthood has been established by the Devil in this world.[27]

But since today preachers and prophets will not acknowledge it and wish only to discard it, they are also dismissing the order of the ancient Christian church, concerning which old and new teachers have written.[28] *See Cyprian,*

---

27 An apparent paraphrase of LW, vol. 36, 154.
28 The phrase is striking, recalling as it does Balthasar Hubmaier's *The Opinion of the Ancient and New Teachers that One Should Not Baptize Young Children until They Have Been Instructed in the Faith,* published in Nikolsburg in 1526, in two editions. Translated as "Old and New Teachers on Believers Baptism," in

Concerning Separation 463

Ad Pomp. Contra Steph. Epist. Oportet Episcopum non solum.[29] *Item, Ambrosius, Tom. 4 in Epistolam ad Ephesios.*[30] *Item Euseb. Caesariensum,*

Pipkin and Yoder, *Hubmaier*, 245-74. Along with the noteworthy reappearance of Hubmaier's title in this tract is the fact that the "ancient writers" referred to here all appear in Hubmaier's baptism text—with the exception of Eleutherius, which was a pseudonym used by Sebastian Castellio in 1554 for Sebastian Franck (see note 34 below). The specific passages referenced in this tract are not cited in Hubmaier's earlier work as is to be expected, since the subject matter here is not baptism specifically, but the rather vague question of "proper church order."

29 Hubmaier's *Old and New Teachers* had included a reference to Cyprian's writing on heretics and baptism. See Pipkin and Yoder, *Hubmaier*, 266, note 72. See Epistle 73: "To Pompey, Against the Epistle of Stephen About the Baptism of Heretics," in *Ante-Nicene Fathers*, vol. 5, trans. Robert Ernest Wallis, ed. A. Roberts, J. Donaldson, and A. Cleveland Coxe (Buffalo, NY: Christian Literature Publishing Co., 1886). Accessed online March 7, 2014: http://www.newadvent.org/fathers/050639.htm. The subject matter of this letter fits with Hubmaier's concern with baptism but less with the question of speaking in churches. Nevertheless, Cyprian says things in this letter that the copyist may have found congenial, such as "there is no baptism where the Holy Spirit is not, because there cannot be baptism without the Spirit." Not everything Cyprian wrote supported the Anabaptist position. His Epistle 58 explicitly supports infant baptism, on the analogy of circumcision.

30 Possibly a reference to the letter by Ambrose of Milan to Irenaeus, regarding Paul's Letter to the Ephesians. In section 13, referring to Ephesians 4:16, Ambrose writes: "Herein I conceive we are to understand that not only holy men but all believers, and all the heavenly and reasonable hosts and powers are united in faith and spirit; that by a certain concord of powers and offices one body, composed of all spirits of a reasonable nature, may adhere to Christ their Head, being so united to the framework of the building, that in no single point of juncture the several members may seem to be severed from each other." *The Letters of S. Ambrose, Bishop of Milan* (Oxford: James Parker and Co., 1881), "Letter 76, Ambrose to Irenaeus," 448. Accessed online March 6, 2014.

l. Historia, Lib. 6, cap. 15.[31] *Item Chrysostum, in Gen. homil. 7 volo etc.*[32] *Cyril in Joh. Cap. 9, Hist. 6, cap. 20.*[33] *Eleutherius in Joan., Lib. 12, cap. 20.*[34]

---

31   In current English translations, book 6, chapter 15 of Eusebius' *Church History* has no bearing on the question at hand. A sixteenth-century German translation of Eusebius, however, has different numeration that confirms the accuracy and relevance of the citation in the codex. At the end of a long chapter on Origen (Book vi, chapter 15 in Hedio's German edition dated 1545), it is noted how Origen, who was not yet ordained, was assigned to "dispute" and teach Scripture in church by the bishop. In response to a letter criticizing a lay person teaching Scripture in the presence of a bishop, a letter from bishop Alexander is cited in which the bishop asserts: "Est ist aber keyn zweifel / dass an vil andern orten / die bischoff erbetten und ermanet haben zur leer / die jenigen so leerhafftig sind / und in göttlicher geschrifft erfaren." Caspar Hedio, *Chronica der Alten Christlichen Kirchen* (Strasbourg, 1545), lix, verso-lx, recto. Accessed online, July 16, 2014: https://play.google.com/books/reader?id=-ehEAAAAcAAJ&printsec=frontcover&output=reader&authuser=0&hl=en&pg=GBS.PA13, e-book pages 138-39.

32   In his seventh homily on Genesis, Chrysostom reproves Christians who live scandalous lives and counsels a visibly virtuous life as a witness to unbelievers. Accessed online March 6, 2014: http://www.docstoc.com/docs/19376312/Homilies-on-Genesis---Saint-John-Chrysostom, pages 91-104; citation, 103.

33   The references to 1 Corinthians 14 in Cyril's lengthy commentary on John do not relate to the general points made in the codex. See the Scripture index to the *Commentary on The Gospel According to S. John by S. Cyril, Archbishop of Alexandria*, 2 volumes (London: James Parker & Co., 1874 and 1885). Source accessed online March 6, 2014.

34   There are nine saints by this name in the Roman Catholic tradition, including one pope Eleutherius (178-189). No commentary on John by a writer of this name was located. More likely this is a reference to "Augustine Eleutherius," a pseudonym for Sebastian Franck. He was so identified in Sebastian Castellio's anonymous work of 1554, *Concerning Heretics. Whether they are to be persecuted and how they are to be treated. A collection of the opinions of learned men both ancient and modern*, in which Castellio cites parts of Franck's *Chonica* attributing the citations to "Eleutherius." The reference in *Codex 628* to a specific writing on John by "Eleutherius" remains unexplained. See Roland Bainton, *Concerning Heretics* (Columbia University Press, 1935; New York: Octagon Books, 1965), 183-97.

See also Zwingli[35] *and Melanchthon on 1 Corinthians 14.*[36] *How can it be then that they can so completely deny to us everything that they themselves confessed to be the truth, and say it is not valid for us? Or do you think that we are such simple and stupid people that we are unable to notice and understand their glosses and Scripture-twisting, that one time says something is one thing, the next time denies it, takes it back and paints it a completely different color?*[37]

Very well, since they will not be otherwise, the time will come when they will have to answer for it. The sheep of Christ hear the voice of their shepherd; they refuse to come for those who are hirelings and paid laborers, but rather <380> flee from them, since the sheep don't belong to them. With their spurious shepherd's staff they sneak into the sheepfold so they can strangle and devour with their false glosses. Like wolves they violently take

---

35 Zwingli published *On the Preaching Office* in 1524 and expounded 1 Corinthians 14 in this way: "So when the prophets explain, the whole church should judge, that is: all the others, whether he is doing it right or not." Hubmaier comments on the same passage in the same year in his *Theses Against Eck*. See Pipkin and Yoder, *Hubmaier*, 49-57, esp. 51, n. 6.

36 In the summer of 1521, Melanchthon lectured in Wittenberg on Paul's first letter to the Corinthians. Although Melanchthon was reluctant to publish his annotations, Martin Luther went ahead and had them published in 1522 in Nuremberg [*Annotationes in Epistolas Pauli ad Rhomanos et Corinthios*]. See Philipp Melanchthon, *Annotations on the First Epistle to the Corinthians*. Introduced, trans. and ed. John Patrick Donnelly, S.J. (Milwaukee, WI: Marquette University Press, 1995), 14-16. It appears that it is to an edition of these *Annotations* to which the author of the codex refers, for Melanchthon's comments fit the argument being made in the Anabaptist codex. Commenting on 1 Corinthians 14:29ff, Melanchthon writes "... by adding, 'You all can prophesy' [1 Corinthians 14:31] he establishes the right of each individual in the church to judge about doctrine and to teach, indeed he also commands teachers that if something should be revealed to a person seated, they should keep quiet and listen to the person seated." Ibid., 161. Melanchthon notes concerning 1 Thessalonians 5:19-21 ("Do not quench the Spirit ...") that its meaning is "all are free to teach, and all are to be heard and judged by all." Ibid., 161. He concludes, "Therefore the popes are acting very wickedly in usurping to themselves alone the power of judging about doctrine. Also much more wicked than this is that they have decreed that they are not to be asked to give the reason for their judgment." Ibid., 163.

37 Ickelsamer writes, in similar fashion: "they gloss it over nicely and lead us around by the nose. They even think they can make us blind while we see clearly with our eyes!" Rempel, *Kunstbuch*, 49.

possession of the sheepfold and separate the sheep from the Master Shepherd. They sully the pure water of the grace of God, with their domineering and disorder, as has been amply noted, destroying the ban, baptism, the Supper, and other Christian uses and orderings commanded by Christ and his Holy Apostles.

Therefore we cannot and may not, without harming our consciences, join them hypocritically in their church services, participate with them or be one community with them, but rather we must flee from them, since the Lord Christ and his apostles so truly warned us about them. Therefore all who carry out this preaching office by themselves in the church of God, even though the office belongs to all believers, are acting not on the basis of a Christian, apostolic order, but rather on the ordering and establishment of the Pope of the Antichrist and servant of the Devil. For it was neither Christ nor his apostles, but rather Pope Pelagius, as Luther wrote, who so ordered and established it with great impudence and arrogance.

What blessing or benediction can come from this may be recognized and demonstrated by their fruits. <381> God gives happiness, salvation, blessing, benediction, and good fruit. What he does not give but rather what these people give, who invent for themselves what the Pope offers them—[is] the spirit that got king Ahab, Jehoshaphat, the king of Israel and the king of Judah into the conflict at Ramoth in Gilead, or that entered the swine of the Gadarenes, or that in the beginning inhabited the lying snake in paradise. The opposite always results, as is clear as day: the abomination in Christendom that the unclean spirit produces and the destructive, unclean fruit that flows and originates therefrom.

So if one speaks of the order that the apostles and believers of the Christian church used, scorns and rejects it as foolish or idiotic, as fraudulent, confused, and unjust, as is done by those who have uncircumcised hearts and minds, one would also similarly reject and cast away the office and duty of Christian love, which requires that every Christian discipline and admonish his fellow members, as often as needed, when a failing or an error is seen or identified. For this is what God's Word teaches us, and what Christian love requires every believer to do with a fellow member. A Christian is even more duty-bound to warn fellow members in a brotherly way in their error, failing, or mistake and show them a better way, since

Concerning Separation

such errors do not affect only one person, but also other members—yes, they damage and affect the entire congregation. <382>

A preacher who truly has the love of God and neighbor will rejoice in the truth, if someone kindly corrects him before the congregation. He will not become impatient, obstinate or bitter, nor attribute the correction to evil intent, 1 Corinthians 13, and will shun the error as coming from evil, through the fear of God.[38] If otherwise, he lacks such love and fear and opposes the truth as long as he persists.[39]

So now when the highly-learned rabbis and highly-reasoned masters do not wish to let all this stand, they are not crying out and scorning only us, but rather the ordering of God and the use of the ancient apostolic, Christian church. Yes, they despise and reject the Holy Apostle Paul himself, who began this order and was the first to write about and to order its use in the Christian church. But whoever rejects Paul and his order must also be rejecting the work of Christ and the Holy Spirit, and is therefore laying another foundation other than the one that is laid, upon whom the curse will fall, as Paul prophesied in Galatians 1[:9]. Therefore we have no wish to attack such preachers and teachers, who reject and oppose the teaching of Christ and his Holy Apostles, but rather let us guard against such erring spirits as we would against a harmful poison, and thus avoid and flee from their teachings.[40] <383>

[Some preachers also interpret the words of Paul in 1 Corinthians 14: When you come together every one of you has a psalm, a doctrine, etc. Let all be done for edification, etc. And also: for you may all prophesy one by one, etc. They interpret these words as referring not to the entire church, but only to the elected ministers, when the preachers meet together (in their synods). Paul speaks to these in this passage. They infer the same meaning from other words in this chapter concerning the laity, where they apply the word "lay" to their hearers or sheep, whom they regard as laity, and they themselves as those to whom Paul spoke, even though Paul said "When you come together" not only to some, but to the whole Corinthian congregation of believing Christians. We cannot understand the word "lay" in this way, but rather as applying to those who are outside, who do not belong to the congregation of Christ, or who might come and listen,

---

38 Bullinger: Proverbs 16[:6].
39 Here begins another intepolation in *Codex 628*.
40 The following bracketed section is found only in Bullinger, not in *Codex 628*.

as the meaning of the word in the German text demonstrates. There the words "lay" and "unbeliever" mean nearly the same and say "and the lay or unbelievers come in," etc. Understand: into the Christian congregation as, according to our understanding, the Latin text concerning this word "lay" makes even more clear, that it cannot be applied to true believers or members of Christ.

Nevertheless, whoever thinks otherwise should bring proof, for we do not wish to oppose the truth. And even if Paul had meant the words "you will all prophesy" to apply only to those who spoke prophesies, prophesying would not be limited to one person alone in the congregation, but would be given by God to others, so they might also do as the words above indicate: You will all prophesy. And so the foregoing words, "When you come together, each one of you has, etc.; let all things be done for edification" undeniably apply to the entire congregation or all members of Christ.]

THE SECOND REASON

The second reason [we do not attend their churches] is that the *so-called* Evangelical preachers at first taught much from the Word of God, concerning freedom of faith and matters of faith, against the rulers and constrainers of faith, and that the authorities—pope, emperor, princes, and others in such places—had no power or were called to judge in matters concerning faith, the soul or the conscience.[41] *Therefore one is not obliged to obey them in such matters, as we have noted above in the third article of our confession*[42] *and also noted further from the writings of Martin Luther and*

---

41 Here begins a lengthy insertion that covers ten sequential pages of *Codex 628*. Text shared with Bullinger resumes on page <393> of the codex. Omitted from the codex is the following, found in this location in Bullinger: "Their earlier teaching concerning Christian freedom had its foundation and testimony in the following evangelical passages: Matthew 17[:26], John 8[:36], 1 Corinthians 6[:12], 10[:23ff], 2 Corinthians 3[:17], Galatians 2[:4], 3 [sic: 5:1; 13], 1 Timothy 1[:16?]."

42 This internal cross-reference to the third article of "our confession" makes it plain that the copyist considered the first writing to be a common Anabaptist "confession" and that the second writing was being copied as a further elaboration on points made in the first. This, and the nature and the length of the additions introduced, argues for the 1590 copyist also being a significant co-editor/author of *Codex 628*.

Concerning Separation

others, for Luther said more in his aforementioned booklet.[43] *But you say to the contrary concerning power, Luther says; truly, worldly power cannot coerce faith, but only functions outwardly to keep people from being misled. How can one defeat the heretics? Luther answers, the bishops, to whom this office belongs, should do it and not the princes, for heresy cannot be defeated with coercive power. Another method has to be used here, for it is another battle and issue that doesn't have to do with the sword. One must fight here with God's Word. If it cannot be done with the Word it will remain undone by worldly power, even if the world were to be filled with blood. Heresy is a spiritual thing that one cannot chop out with steel, cannot burn with fire, cannot drown with water. It is only God's Word that can remove it, as Saint Paul says in 2 Corinthians 10[:3-5]: our weapons are not fleshly, but mighty in God, to destroy all opposition <384> that resists the knowledge of God, and to take captive all thoughts to the service of Christ.*

There is no greater unbelief and heresy, says Luther, than to oppose it with naked power, without God's Word. For one can be certain that such power is unjustly used and is applied unjustly because it is applied without God's Word. They think that only brute force will help them, just as unreasoning animals do. Even in worldly matters one cannot simply use coercive power, unless justice is overcome by injustice. But it is impossible to proceed in these high spiritual matters with force, without justice and God's Word. Therefore look at what these clever lords do: they wish to root out heresy, says Luther. They use these methods which only strengthen them. They put themselves under suspicion and justify the heretics. My dear sir, if you truly want to root out heresy, you must reach deeper, and remove these things from the heart and change the will. You will not turn the heart and will by using force, but will only strengthen them. Of what help is it, then, if you strengthen heresy in people's hearts, and try to weaken and persuade heresy only with external words? It is God's Word that enlightens the heart, and when this happens, all heresy and error fall by themselves from the heart.

Isaiah 11[:4] speaks to such destruction of heresy, and says "He will strike the earth with the rod of his mouth, and kill the ungodly <385> with the spirit of his lips." Now you see, says Luther, that judgment is established

---

43 The book referred to here is *Temporal Authority: To what extent it should be obeyed*, found in LW, vol. 45, 81-129. The first three paragraphs cited below are found in ibid., 114-15.

through the mouth, to the punishment and conversion of the godless. Summa summarum, such princes and tyrants are not aware of the fact that in fighting heresy, they are fighting against the Devil, who possesses hearts with error, as Paul says in Ephesians 6[:12]: *For we are not fighting against flesh and blood, but against spiritual evil, against the authorities who rule this darkness.* Therefore, insofar as one does not get rid of the Devil and drive him from the heart, trying to destroy those he possesses is like fighting lightning with a straw. This is all richly attested to in Job 41[:27, 33], where he says that the Devil counts iron as straw, and fears no power on earth. It can be seen from experience: even if one were to burn all the Jews and heretics with force, still not a one of them would be defeated and converted because of it.[44]

Luther writes further, therefore stop your sacrilege and coercion, and realize that that is not the proper way to proceed. Let God's work have its way, which it must and should have, and you will not be able to prevent it. If heresy is present, it should be overcome with God's Word, as is fitting. But if you make much use of the sword, beware! Someone will come and order you to return it to its scabbard, and not in God's name.

Likewise Philipp Melanchthon writes in his Tractate, his *Instruction in the True Holy Scriptures of God, 1523*:[45] The worldly authorities have the legal right to no other office <386> than to punish and resist injuries, injustices, and harm. Therefore the laws are established in part to deal with contracts and their administration, and in part to deal with sentences and punishments of crimes. Officials are servants of God and executors of wrath against the evildoer, and a civil official has neither the justification nor the right nor the power to establish anything contrary to God's law. One should

---

44 The following paragraph found in ibid., 116-17.
45 This appears to be a reference to Melanchthon's *Loci communes rerum theologicarum*, first published in Wittenberg in 1521, with a second edition appearing soon after in Basel. The copyist seems to be paraphrasing Melanchthon's observations in the "Magistrates" section of the *Loci*, where Melanchthon writes: "Matters under the sword are civil rights, civil ordinances of public courts, and penalties for criminals. It is the obligation of the sword to enforce the laws against murder, vengeance, etc. ... On wielding the power of the sword, I have this to say. In the first place, if rulers command anything that is contrary to God, they must not be obeyed. Acts. 5:29: 'We must obey God rather than men.'" Wilhelm Pauck, ed., *Melanchthon and Bucer*, Library of Christian Classics, vol. 19 (Philadelphia, PA: Westminster, 1969), 148.

Concerning Separation

not render any obedience contrary to Godly law, as it states in the history of the twelve apostles [Acts 5:29]: One must be more obedient to God than to men. On the basis of this saying, a reasonable reader can easily judge to what extent we should be subject to human rights and laws.

Likewise Wolfgang Capito wrote against [Conrad] Treger,[46] *saying, wherever the church attempts to put its glory and authority into laws the situation is dangerous, for the church exists now in order to have faith in God, and to love the neighbor, and certainly not in order to establish laws against consciences that have been freed by Christ. And whenever the church does so, we should not allow ourselves to be silenced by the elements of this world, under the weak and pathetic laws, Galatians 4[:9-10].*

He writes further, Is it not true that the natural person hears nothing of God's Spirit? It is foolishness to him and he cannot accept it, for it must be judged in a spiritual way, 1 Corinthians 2. You dearly wish the clever rabbis would accept such a spiritual and common judgment. He says to Treger, I know of no judge <387> *over the Word of God; the spiritual person only makes the judgment to avoid false teaching, and not to make laws.*

Likewise Martin Bucer wrote in his booklet called "Answer to those from Weissenburg".[47] *There is no authority that stands over the Word of God, other than God himself. Therefore no one may forbid or allow it, and whoever wishes to forbid is a servant of the Anti-Christ and no lawful*

---

46 Conrad Treger, prior provincial of the Augustinian order and resident in Strasbourg, was a staunch opponent of the Reformed preachers Wolfgang Capito and Martin Bucer. The heated literary exchanges throughout 1524 led eventually to Treger's arrest and departure from the city in October of that year. See Martin Greschat, *Martin Bucer: A Reformer and his Times*, trans. Stephen E. Buckwalter (Louisville/London: Westminster John Knox Press, 2004), 61-62. The reference in the codex seems to be to *Antwurt D. Wolffgang Fab. Capitons auf Bruder Conrads Augustiner ordens Prouincials vermanung, so er an gemein Eidgnossenschafft jüngst geschrieben hat...*. Noted in Robert Stupperich et al., *Martin Bucers Deutsche Schriften*, vol. 2 (Gütersloh: Gerd Mohn, 1962), 18, n. 8. I was not able to consult this print. Editor.

47 Although a booklet by the given title was not located, the two page references copied in the codex correspond to those found in the 1524 print of Bucer's lengthy writing, refuting Treger point by point: *Ein kurtzer warhafftiger bericht von Disputationen und gantzem handel, so zwischen Cunrat Treger, Provincial der Augustiner, und den predigern des Evangelii zu Straßburg sich begeben hat...* (Straßburg: [Schott], 1524). Critical edition in Stupperich et al., *Martin Bucers Deutsche Schriften*, vol. 2, 37-173.

magistrate because he wishes to hinder the salvation of souls as much as he is able.[48] *Bucer wrote further concerning Conrad Treger's letter:* "Wherever princes and lords allow God's Word to be preached freely, and live according to it, and allow no one to act shamefully against it, one need have no fear of unrest. Therefore I wish to answer you, Treger, and your so-called divines, with Elijah's answer to King Ahab, when Ahab reproached him for upsetting Israel, no, you are the one who is upsetting and disturbing Israel, for you have abandoned the Lord's commandments and have set off after Baal, that is following your own willfulness, nor will you tolerate that the Lord's commandments are taught clearly and without deceit."[49] Likewise Section O, page 4, "Paul wrote, You have been dearly bought, don't become servants of man. Therefore in spiritual matters we recognize no one who gives us commands, for Scripture teaches us everything good and makes us fit for all good works."[50]

Bucer also wrote concerning Conrad Treger's letter, "Our Gospel teaches us not to seek our own, and also <388> not to resist evil, not to avenge ourselves, but rather to be ready to suffer. Furthermore, it proclaims to us that we have become children and heirs of God through Christ, and teaches us to seek treasure in heaven and not on earth, where we will not remain. Section B, page 3."[51]

Further, Martin Luther wrote in the first part of the already-cited booklet "Concerning Secular Authority," among other things: Now you see where Christ's Word is leading, that we have spoken about above from Matthew 5, that Christians should not judge or have the worldly sword in their midst. To be sure, he says all this only to his beloved Christians, who

---

48 I was not able to locate this exact sentence in Bucer's writing. The sentiment, however, is evident throughout, as in the following: "Vätter mögen yrren, Concilien mögen falsch sein, das du die kirch wilt machen, mag des teüffels synagog sein, die schrifft aber mussz Gottes wort sein, so wir die hören, so hören wir auch die wore Kirch, Vätter und Concilien, die greiff an und beweiß uns, des du uns schyltest." Stupperich, *Martin Bucers Deutsche Schrifften*, vol. 2, 69-70. Or the following: "Ist unser leere und predig wider die göttlich schrifft, so ist sye teüffelisch, und wenn wir schon alle Concilien für uns hetten. Ist sye uß der schrifft, so ist sye göttlich, und wenn sye alle wider uns weren. Darumb zur schrifft, Treger, zur schrifft." Ibid., 160.
49 Citation in ibid., 51, lines 4-14.
50 Citation in ibid., 158, lines 11-14.
51 Citation in ibid., 49, lines 17-22.

Concerning Separation

accept all things and act rightly, do not avenge themselves like the sophists, but rather have been so formed in their hearts by the Spirit that they do no evil to anyone, and willingly suffer evil done to them by anyone. And later, Isaiah 11[:9]: You shall not kill nor do any harm on all of my holy mountain, and Isaiah 2[:4]: They will turn their swords to ploughshares and their spears into hoes, and no one will lift up a sword against another, nor seek to fight any more.[52]

Likewise in the second part of said booklet, concerning the limits of secular authority, Luther says, Among Christians there should and can be no governmental authority, but rather everyone is equally subject to the other, as Paul says in Romans 12, each one should consider the other as superior, and 1 Peter 5[:3-5], all should be subject one to another. And later: There is no authority among Christians other than <389> Christ himself and only Christ. What kind of authority could there be, says Luther, since all are equal, and all have one law, power, possessions and honor. Furthermore, since no one wishes to be anyone else's superior, but rather all wish to be subject to the others, one could not establish an authority where there are such, even though one might wish to, because their manner and nature will not permit them to have superiors, since no one can or will be a superior. But where there are no such people, there are also no genuine Christians.[53] Now that is properly German.

Luther says further in the third part of this booklet "Concerning Secular Authority," Section F, page 3, You say: Should then a prince not go to war, or his subjects not follow him into battle? Answer: This is a large question, but in brief, in order to do the Christian thing here, I say that no prince may go to war against his overlord, such as king or emperor, or against his liege lord, but rather submit to be robbed. For no one should resist worldly authority with force, but only with the declaration of the truth. If the authority changes as a result, that is good; if not, you are not at fault and you suffer injustice for God's sake.[54]

---

52 Citation from *Temporal Authority: To what extent it should be obeyed*, in LW, vol. 45, 92-93.
53 Citation in ibid., 117.
54 Citation in ibid., 124-25.

Luther writes further in his "Sermon for Sunday after Christ's Ascension," on the Gospel of John, chapter 15[:26],[55] *When the comforter comes, etc.: [Christ] performed this word from the cross. Thus the confession must break through that God alone is the savior. This confession is costly, as he says later, you will be* <390> *rejected and banned by the entire congregation, etc. The cross cannot be painted in any other way than it is painted here, for this is its correct color. (Gloss: Notice how Christendom is thus opposed and not confirmed.) But lying at home ill in bed, he says, is nothing, although it is honored as suffering. Here is a genuine suffering: that we be persecuted and killed with dishonor; that those who persecute us receive the praise, and that glory, law, and honor be on their side, and shame, dishonor, and opprobrium be on our side against the world, and they believe to have extended God's honor by this; that all the world says that this has rightly happened to us, and that God, Scripture, and all the angels must be against us, and there must be no complaint, no legal right, but rather be dismissed with curses and insults. It happened this way also for Christ, that he was thrown into the most mocking and shameful death, and hung between two evildoers or murderers; he was mocked as the prize knave. And they said: He called himself God's son, let God help him now; God and all the angels must be against him. Christ also said, they will kill you, and not just simply, but with shame so that all the world will say that they have done God a service thereby. Now this is a difficult thing to endure, and to believe despite it that God is gracious to us and is a savior. It is hard* <391> *but has to be said.*[56]

And further on, says Luther, after Jesus had strengthened them he warned them about the suffering that was to come, so that they could suffer it courageously, because it is especially a good friend whom one warns, and evil can much more easily be borne if one has prepared for it beforehand. And they will treat you this way, and think they are doing the right thing, and will act as though God was against you, and will sing a Te Deum

---

55 Reference to a translation of Luther's sermon for the first Sunday after Christ's Ascension, on John 15:26–16:4 (taken from Luther's Church Postil of 1522), confirms the accuracy of the copyist's words. For the citations below, see http://www.trinitylutheranms.org/MartinLuther/MLSermons/John15_26.html, accessed April 16, 2014. This sermon is found in *The Sermons of Martin Luther*, volume III (Grand Rapids, MI: Baker Book House, 1983), 245-54, now in the public domain.

56 The citation above is found in ibid., sections 3 and 4.

Concerning Separation

Laudamus *(We Praise You, God)*.[57] Now he demands of them here that they be courageous when this happens and admonished them to be upright and keep God before them, even if no outward appearance were forthcoming. And he said: *They do this to you for they have not known the Father or me; therefore persevere, persist and be firm, taking care that you do not take offence at me, remembering that I have already told you, for they have known neither my Father nor me.*[58]

Likewise Zwingli wrote further in his Article Book *in [the] 32nd Article,* saying: "Christian faith is confirmed first in Christ's blood, after that it grows through suffering and the outpouring of the blood of the preachers; I believe this faith will now be cleansed again." He addressed the servants of the word and said: Teach all to have hope in God, and demonstrate your faith in the first place with patience unto death.[59]

These and still many more similar things they themselves taught <392> and wrote concerning patience and suffering, as will be clarified in the third article following (and also just how they act in the present). Likewise concerning evangelical freedom, that it is testified to and has its foundation in Holy Divine Scripture, as has been noted often above and will be noted further,[60] from which Christian teaching and word of God [concerning evangelical freedom] they have now fallen away again into this public and evident error, to the point that they now suppress and transgress (this teaching) under the appearance of the Gospel, in that—as everyone hears and sees—they again inflame, incite, and stir up the rulers, the civil sword, and others with their teaching and preaching (as happens to us). They coerce and compel matters of faith and the soul with force and laws, such as attending church and such things, and if one is not obedient to them, they then persecute, kill, exile, and afflict. With this they have become guilty of shedding innocent blood, and have led the authorities and others into the same sin *as will be seen further below*. Who would then wish to be with them, listen to them or be a part of the same congregation with them?

---

57 It had long been a practice in the church to sing the *Te Deum* after heresy had been successfully suppressed. Thanks to Walter Klaassen for this note.

58 The citation above is found in *The Sermons of Martin Luther*, volume III, sections 15 and 16.

59 "Auslegung und Begründen der Schlußreden," in Frei, ed., *Zwingli, der Verteidiger des Glaubens*, 2. Teil, 72; English translation in Furcha, *Huldrych Zwingli Writings*, 235.

60 *Codex 628* here rejoins the text found in Bullinger.

And how will those who are a part of them and in their community be pleasing to God? For according to Isaiah 33[:15ff], grace is promised only to those who stop up their ears to keep from hearing the plots of violence against the innocent, etc.[61]

[The preachers began this in the Bern Synod that was held, according to the booklet they themselves printed in 1532, in which they established the civil power again in the church to rule and reign over the outward teaching and life of the Gospel or faith.[62] With this, faith and conscience are coerced with commands and prohibitions of outward things without contradiction, Christian freedom is suspended and in its place a Mosaic compulsion is instituted which contradicts their first teaching. This is then teaching backwards, and erring back to Moses, yes, going back from the sun to the shadows. And how can one hope to coerce in matters of faith, other than through outward commands and prohibitions? Earlier they also decried such coercion and persecution as tyranny. Consider what they themselves are doing now. This cannot be called preaching God's evangelical word, but rather much more, a falling away from it, yes, falling away from the evangelical way and forcing those few who are on that way to fall from it. God complained in like manner about the priests of the Old Testament, Malachi 2[:8].][63]

The Christian, apostolic Gospel neither commands or teaches that anyone <393> be compelled by force to accept its teaching, preaching, fellowship, or any other such matters of the faith or the soul, but rather teaches the opposite, as already stated, that no one should be compelled in this with force, and accursed be, Galatians 1[:8ff], any teaching that is otherwise. Therefore because what is taught by the preachers and those who coerce (as above and in what follows) against evangelical and their own earlier teaching as noted, is accursed—and also because such teachers are no followers of the apostles, but rather deceptive and false, 2 Corinthians

---

61 The bracketed text that follows is in Bullinger, but not found in *Codex 628*.

62 See *Berner Synodus. Ordnung wie sich pfarrer and prediger zu Statt un Land Bern / in leer und leben/ verhalten söllen / mit wyterem bericht von Christo / unnd den Sacramenten ... am ix tag Januarii, AN. MDXXXII.* Facsimile edition: *Der Berner Synodus*, ed. Gottfried Locher (Neukirch: Neukircher Verlag, 1984). The information copied here closely parallels that found in the *Simple Confession*, page <148>; see notes 254 and 255. An extended treatment of the Bern Synod comes below, at page <401>.

63 *Codex 628* now begins paralleling the Bullinger text.

Concerning Separation 477

11[:13], it is fitting for us not to attend such teaching, nor to listen to them, but rather far better, to flee.

THE THIRD REASON

The third reason [we do not attend their churches] is, as we have heard in part, the *so-called evangelical* preachers at first taught Christian freedom [and then left it out. But they also taught this Christian evangelical teaching] that Christians were not to resist, protect or defend themselves with the worldly, fleshly sword, weapons or counter-force from those who hated and opposed them, the faith, or the Gospel. They were to do so using only the Word of God as the sword of the Spirit and the other weapons described in Ephesians 6[:11-17], in patience and suffering, not avenging or resisting evil, nor retaining among them the worldly or Mosaic sword; not going to law or conflict concerning their possessions or their honor but rather prepared for suffering and the cross. Otherwise one is no Christian, and the like. Christians' teaching and foundation is found in evangelical Scripture, such as Matthew 5[:38-48], Luke 6[:27-38], Romans 12[:14, 17ff], 1 Corinthians 6[:7], Ephesians 6[:13], Isaiah 2[:4], 11[:4ff]. These places thus confirm Christian patience in which it is fitting for all true Christians <394> to live, as in Hebrews 12[:1ff], James 1[:3ff], 5[:7ff], Romans 12[:14, 17ff], 2 Timothy 2[:8ff].

But the preachers have again fallen away from this Christian teaching, and also their own, have abandoned and transgressed the Holy Gospel and their own teaching under the appearance of the Gospel. This is evident since they use the external, worldly sword of steel to compel magistrates, cities and lands in faith and matters of faith, as well as to protect, shelter, counter-attack and defend their own interests, faith, and matters of faith. And they are prepared to attack, harm, and destroy their enemies, those who hate them or oppose them. Likewise they form alliances against towns, princes, and lords, and defend their own possessions and honor in the courts. They thus cast off the cross and the patience of Christ which, if they were to follow Christ's teaching, says that they should love and seek the welfare of their enemies, not return evil for evil, nor pursue vengeance—this according to the teaching of Christ, which they and the great crowd violate. It is generally rumored and we have plainly seen how the imperial cities have aligned themselves against the emperor and the papists.[64]

---

64 *Codex 628* begins an interpolation at this point in the text.

They indeed are not innocent in this, no matter that they wish to be clever about it. It can well be seen, among other such actions, in the Swiss War, where they urged, admonished and encouraged the authorities and subjects against their papal confederates in the five cantons, and promised them much success and victory (although not <395> from the Lord's mouth) and preached that the spears would turn around and piece their enemies. But what they won there gave them no room to boast afterwards. Their prophets were not unlike the 400 false prophets who advised kings Ahab and Jehoshaphat in the battle against Ramoth in Gilead.[1 Kings 22:6ff] In the same way, their prophesies of success led to disaster, and fell upon their own heads: they fell into the graves they had dug for others.[65] *This is what happens to all others who attempt to act under the appearance of the Gospel, and wish to impose the Gospel with force, coercion, and pressure. If they are punished in their own time here with the smaller and less severe sentence, in the fullness of time the heavier sentence will fall upon them, when the page turns upon itself again.*[66]

Likewise their preachers in the previously mentioned Synod of Bern, as the published booklet truly reports and shows, have asserted that the civil authorities are to maintain the outer teaching and life of the Gospel among their subjects, almost in the manner of Moses. This results, as the booklet demonstrates, in the mixing together of the Mosaic lordship and protection and Christ's name. And Christian love and patience (without which no one may be saved) against enemies and opponents is suspended, in contravention of Christ's teaching in Matthew 5[:38ff]. <396> These preachers and their flock reveal their apostasy from Christ's teachings in that when anyone offends them in word or deed, they seek legal recourse before the courts and magistrates to defend their honor and property, against their first teaching. Therefore it is not fitting for us to attend such communities or preaching, where people fall away from evangelical teaching, and especially because we and others must keep silent. What

---

65 The above is a pointed reference to the Second Kappel War of 1531, in which military forces from Zurich, including Ulrich Zwingli and other pastors, engaged military forces of the Catholic cantons. The Zurich forces were badly outnumbered, and around 500 Zurich citizens died. Among them was Zwingli himself and more than twenty pastors from the Zurich area.

66 End of interpolation.

would lead us to betterment? Or what good fruit, such as figs or grapes, can one gather from thorns and thistles, Matthew 7[:17ff]?[67]

[The Lutheran preachers say now (when someone reminds them of their earlier teaching) that such teaching is in error, contrary to the Gospel, and that earlier they had not understood it as well as they do now. Rather they say that they have learned from God's punishment (especially where the emperor has gotten the upper hand), lest they come to grief from the emperor or those whom he has won over. To this we answer: It depends on whether the Gospel is more in accord with their earlier teaching or their present teaching, or whether the Gospel testifies more to their earlier teaching than to their present teaching.][68]

But their preachers and learned masters say here, that it truly is proper for Christians to have such patience and love of enemies and the like in themselves and for themselves, but that love demands that one must come to the defense of others, or fight for others with swords of steel. To this we answer you: Unless it is true that you have adequately informed us on the foundation of evangelical Scripture, we cannot believe you, because with your words the simple Word of God is put to doubt, divided, ripped apart, and destroyed. We find the opposite in evangelical Scripture, that it is not allowed, as Christ made clear when he told Peter, when he attempted to protect him with his sword, to put his steel sword back in its place, and did not want to be protected by him, but rather pronounced the sentence:

---

67 At this place, *Codex 628* omits the concluding sentences to the third article, found in Bullinger. We include them here, within square brackets, as follows.

68 A lengthy interpolation is inserted here in *Codex 628*, in place of the omitted material found in Bullinger, bracketed above. The interpolation covers pages <397> to <418> of the codex. The interpolated section develops the theme of the necessary unity between the inner work of the Holy Spirit and the outer works of believers. The "spiritual" argument for nonresistance in this section is notable, standing in contrast to the logic of the sixth article of Schleitheim, which emphasized obedience to the biblical word and example of Christ, rather than spiritual rebirth. The coherent argumentation in this section, along with the personal notes at its conclusion, just before the Fourth Article, indicate a discrete piece of writing, interpolated into the larger work. The concluding autobiographical comments indicate that the copyist "received help" from others (suggesting that he was copying material composed by others), but also that he had composed some of the work himself—for which work he wished to remain anonymous, and to receive a reward only from God. The interpolation concludes with a request for God's benediction, and a resounding "Amen."

Whoever takes the sword will die by the sword, Matthew 26[:52]. And in John 18[:11] he said to Peter: Am I not to drink the cup <397> that my father has given me? Just as the Lord has spoken as the head, so also speak his members. Those who, as his members, wish to protect him as did Peter, have to be minded just as Christ was. As Paul says in Philippians 2[:5], let each of you be minded as Christ Jesus was. For those whom he foreknew he also fore-ordained to be conformed to the image of his Son, Romans 8[:29].

But when the worldly power exercises protection on his own account, without complaint from us, and does this solely in the name of his worldly office, with the desire to protect the common people and all the pious, and the desire to punish transgressors and evil people, he is ordained by God for this, Romans 13[:1-5]. In doing this he is not acting unjustly, but rather justly. But if he, out of a well-meaning heart and in a just manner, also comes into the Christian community, this outer justice should also be endured, as has been amply clarified and demonstrated above.

For Christ and those who are his are all of one mind, and not two, in matters concerning salvation, and so for us the words in Matthew 5[:39, 44] have one meaning, when he says: I also say, that you resist not evil, but I also say that you love your enemies, etc. With the words "you" and "your" he binds them all together into one body against the enemy and wishes to stand by these words. No one is to change the smallest point that he taught us, or to teach otherwise. Therefore we cannot tolerate your interpretation, <398> unless one were to twist God's Word and change it with glosses.

Luther taught those who wished to act in a Christian manner that no prince should go to war against his overlords, such as kings or emperor, or against his liege lord, but rather let himself be taken with no resistance, etc. Now if a prince is not to wage war, whose worldly office it is to protect his subjects, how much less may Christians use force on behalf of someone else, when the ordained princely worldly sword, office, or power is not even theirs?

Since we cannot find your interpretation or meaning anywhere in God's Word, in evangelical Scripture, in the entire New Testament, in the teaching of Christ or that of his apostles, namely that it is right for a Christian to go to war on behalf of another out of love, we are forced to ask where your understanding might come from. And we find no other reason than that it flows from the natural or fleshly understanding of this word LOVE, and not from a proper, spiritual understanding. For love according to the flesh and pure spiritual love must be distinguished from one another; truly they are as far separated as heaven is from earth, the natural from the supernatural, and spirit from flesh, and must be distinguished from one another.

Indeed, such masters of lofty thoughts demonstrate that they possess and teach a merely natural, fleshly, human love. <399> *For they teach that one must or may litigate, fight and use counter-force on behalf of another, against an enemy, using steel swords. So now it is possible to preserve and defend property, earthly possessions, wife, children, honor, body, life, yes even kingdoms of this world; this wins nothing for the soul, but rather takes and steals from it patience and salvation. Nevertheless, under the appearance of the Gospel they claim that in this way they may win and keep these things, coming to these views led and oriented by natural love. For they are not able to love enemies, and neither can natural law and justice forgive for injury received. Therefore they seek of themselves—but without God's evangelical word—such ways, means and teaching by which they can maintain and not lose their possessions and what is theirs by natural right, yes, even to save and preserve their very own lives. And so if, to the contrary, we teach the pure love of God, which strives against nature and nobly defeats flesh and blood, sin, the Devil, death, and hell, it is a repulsive abomination to them and they will neither allow nor tolerate this from us.*

And so we think of Paul's saying in 1 Corinthians, where he says that the natural person can perceive nothing of the Spirit of God; it is foolishness to such a person, and impossible to comprehend. This is exactly what we think, that natural persons, over whom natural love now hovers, know nothing of the supernatural, pure love which is the love of God which flows in the truly believing heart by God's Holy Spirit—as they ought to know. Rather, <400> *such love is also foolishness to them, for it teaches against natural love, as has been said, which divine love is against property, temporal goods, house, farm, wife, children, and other created things. Yes even against one's own self and one's own life, which must be lost, abandoned, and renounced to the gaining of eternal life, as is clear in God's word, which is love. Matthew 20[:26-28], 16[:24]; Mark 8[:34-38]; Luke 9[:23-26], 14[:26-27]; John 12[:24-26].*

To the contrary, natural love teaches the preservation of all such temporal things to such an extent that it leads to losing the eternal. In this way are these two loves, the spiritual and the temporal, so far removed from one another. For supernatural love teaches the love of enemies, that evil doers are not to be resisted, that blasphemers are to be blessed, that one should pray for persecutors and those who do one harm, that no one is to be taken to law, that evil is not to be returned for evil, and the like, Matthew 5, Luke 6. And there is such a power in this love that they who possess it, as already said, will nobly gain the victory in Christ over adversity and all elemental things. But natural love is not able to do this, which it sees as foolishness. Therefore natural love seeks to find ways and means in its naturally cohabiting knowledge to see whether it might be able to bypass all of this and nevertheless still be saved. In this way is humanity enmeshed and seduced. See 1 John 2[:9-11;15-28], Matthew 6, Luke 6[:20-49] and 14[:25-33], John 3[:6ff] and 12[:24-26] on the difference between spiritual and natural love, and see also 1 John 3.

CONCERNING THE BERN SYNOD:[69] ITS RESULT OF SEVERE PERSECUTION AND THE SPILLING OF MUCH BELIEVING CHRISTIAN BLOOD, WITH WHICH THE BERNESE HAVE BEEN STAINED, SULLIED, AND MARKED.[70]

And so we now come again to that part of your earlier <401> teaching concerning Christian freedom, against those who would rule and coerce the faith and matters of faith—which teaching we no longer find among you at this time for, as noted above, you have again fallen from it. Especially in the Synod of Bern poison was poured out and made public, when you accepted again the Mosaic and worldly authority and sword in the church. In our view, you did this at the instigation of an understanding and knowledge of natural love, with such subtlety that you have split into two parts the single work of the Holy Spirit, which works both inwardly and outwardly in believers. And you have taken the outward part and placed it under the worldly authority and rule, and left the inward part to the Holy Spirit—all of which was declared to be right and proper, but with no foundation in the

---

69 Reference is being made to *Berner Synodus. Ordnung wie sich pfarrer and prediger zu Statt un Land Bern / in leer und leben/ verhalten söllen / mit wyterem bericht von Christo / unnd den Sacramenten ... am ix tag Januarii, AN. MDXXXII.* Locher, *Der Berner Synodus.*

70 This is clearly a new section title of the manuscript. The contents may reflect an independent manuscript circulating among the Swiss Brethren as early as the 1530s and 1540s, or it may reflect the particular interests of the copyist of *Codex 628.*

Gospel and the clear Word of God.[71] *Now we want to consider the Synod of Bern and see how well it stands in comparison to the teaching of Christ and his Holy Apostles and your earlier teaching, as noted above.*

In this booklet, published in 1532, you manifestly fell away from your earlier, first evangelical teaching, since you again accepted worldly authority into the church of Christ, to judge the teaching and life of the Gospel, but only insofar, you say, as it pertains to and remains with outward things. Your understanding is that it is not possible to proceed and maintain (the outward things of the church) through the Word of God. With this you insult the power and activity of the almighty Word of God and the Holy Spirit, and also give witness to the fact that you do not have the use <402> of the spiritual power and sword. It was with this spiritual power that the apostles, and especially the apostle Paul, converted all of the unknowing, blind, unbelieving nations, and maintained and expanded the flock of Christ without the help, action, or support of human or worldly power.

Faith alone is not enough for salvation without the power, anointing, and working of the Holy Spirit. The papists believe or confess with their mouths that Christ is the Son of God who died for their sins, and such like things, which no pagan believed until they were converted through the apostles. Indeed without the enabling and birth of the Holy Spirit—in the power, manner and reality that he who is in us is stronger than is the one who is in the world—they still do not understand, no matter how sublimely they express their faith.

In the Synod, almost at the beginning, you say: It truly is not possible, my gracious lords, for common preachers and servants of the word of the eternal God, to initiate or maintain anything fruitful with outward ordinances, without the action and promotion of the temporal authority.[72] *Thus is the human mind disrupted and perverted to its own invented opinion, among both priests and common people, because there is so little Spirit and power*

---

71   In the article on civil authority, the Bernese Ordinance states that government has authority only over outward things and that "Christ Jesus our Lord ... is the only Lord of consciences." Locher, *Der Berner Synodus*, 31 (original page 8).

72   "Es ist nit wol moglichen/by gemeinen Pfarrern und dienern deß worts deß ewigen Gottes/Gnedigen lieben herrn/ettwas fruchtbars mit usserlichen ordnungen anzefachen und zuerhalten/on einer zytlichen Oberkeyt zuthun und fürderung." Ibid., 28 (original page 7).

of God in our hearts. Here the so-called spiritual ones (clergy) annul the ban of the Spirit and place it, along with all other forms of outward Christian life, into the hands and the coercive power of the magistrates, in opposition to Christian apostolic usage and your own above-mentioned first teaching, as one finds further in this Synod. <403> [You say:] *Now it is the obligation of the magistrates, who wish to be a Christian authority and godly rulers, to apply themselves diligently to see that their power is God's servant, and that they should establish the teaching and life of the Gospel, insofar as it is and remains outward, among their subjects. For this they will have to face the severe judgment with which God through Christ will judge and condemn the world, and will have to answer for their actions.*[73]

To this we say: If you thought about it, you would see that you have played a trick on yourselves in that you reveal in such an article that you have an utterly small spirit and power of God in your hearts, and you acknowledge the lack in you of which we have written above. This lack guided you to the opinion of this Synod, to establish the civil authority in the church and to turn against your proclaimed earlier teaching, for the reported Synod article is against your first teaching. It was Melanchthon in particular who did not wish to have the Gospel defended like the law, with the sword.

You say that you intend only the outer teaching and life of the Gospel. We answer that it all belongs under the name of Gospel, and we ask you: Is it not the case that this teaching and life of the Gospel that you call "outward," should actually be empowered, driven and ruled from the inner to the outer through faith, love, and the Holy Spirit? It is the same with all of the physical good works of Christians: teaching, speaking, words, baptism, disciplining for inclusion and exclusion, breaking of bread, all of which <404> should please God, all freely done, with no domineering, coercion, and pressure, as would fittingly follow from your proclaimed first teaching.

Therefore all that you call "inner" and "outer" Gospel or faith belongs in and serves only one, and is one undivided outworking of the Holy Spirit,

---

[73] "Nun gezumpt der Oberkeyt/die ein Christenlich regiment und Gottselige herrschafft syn wol/allen flyß anzukeren/uff das ir gwalt Gottes dienerin sye/unnd das sy deß Evangelions leer und leben (so verr es usserlich ist und blybt) by jren underthanen erhalte/Derenhalb sy vor dem strengen gericht/darinn Gott die welt durch Christum urteilen unnd verdammen wil/antwurt zugeben erfordert wirt." Ibid., 30 (original page 8).

Concerning Separation

carried out in the free love of God. This you are not able to deny with any foundation. And therefore in all eternity there cannot be a worldly, natural, fleshly, outer order and life named that may rule humankind.

Now see if you have not turned around your understanding of the Holy Spirit and his working, and tried to teach the Spirit lessons, all against Luther's teaching where he says that the true church does not know the secular or worldly arm, which the ungodly bishops above all use and call upon; and further (Luther says) that Christians should not have the worldly sword among them, for among Christians [in the church] there can be no magistrate. Now you establish it everywhere again, and use it and call upon it to rule over the outer teaching and life of the Gospel, for if the worldly sword is among Christians or in the Christian church, it will rule, lead, and control. You are thus acting against the above-mentioned writing by Zwingli, where he says that when you call for weapons of steel, we all see that you are not a follower of Christ or Peter, but rather of Satan and the true Antichrist—for what are you doing here, other than calling for worldly power in the form of weapons of steel?

Furthermore, it is against Luther's previously mentioned writing and teaching, <405> where he says that there should not and cannot be any coercion among a Christian people, and when one attempts to bind consciences with outer laws, the faith and the essence of Christianity are soon driven down. So you are establishing coercion again here in this Synod, when you ordain the magistracy over the outward teaching and life of the Gospel, for what are the magistrates to do other than coerce, rule, order, and also bind consciences?

It is also against Luther's aforementioned teaching, when he writes that all works that Christians do should proceed and flow without coercion and be free, out of willing and happy hearts, and that no law is given to the righteous. How then can Christian works stand outwardly, in their outward evangelical fruits, teaching, and life, as noted above, flowing outwardly from within, out of the flowing spring, pouring out freely and without coercion, when you establish the worldly sword over them? And how can they be a voluntary people, without coercion or pressure, without law or sword, as Luther says above, when you have again established the magistrates among them?

Likewise it is especially against Luther's first sermon, where he maintains that it does not belong to the magistrates to guard against someone seducing people with false teaching, but rather the bishops should do it with God's word. But now you once again establish the magistrates over the outward teaching of the Gospel to maintain it, from which it follows that they must act to maintain the same evangelical teaching <406> with their force and sword against the false teachers (the truly false teachers are against the Christians), and must strive against the heretics, as they are called. Therefore the office that is yours by right, if you were proper shepherds and caretakers of souls, is again removed from you and transferred to the magistrates, wrongfully and with great harm to their souls. And therefore it comes to pass, as Luther said above, that the bishops or pastors leave God's Word lie unused in the struggle against the heretics, and order the worldly power to manage or handle things that are spiritual.

Your practice also goes against Melanchthon's above-mentioned teaching where he says that the worldly authorities have legal rights and law and no other office than to punish and resist injuries, injustice and harm. It likewise goes against Zwingli's teaching where he writes in his booklet "Concerning Godly and Human Righteousness" regarding the office of the magistrates. He says in Section G, page 3: It is not their oath or obedient service to rule over the souls and consciences, for they are not able to do it, etc., as has already been amply noted.[74] Likewise in Section H, page 3 of this same booklet he says that no magistrate should punish anything that has to do solely with matters of conscience or things having to do with the inner person.[75] But now, in your Synod, you have placed the worldly authorities over spiritual things or matters of faith, when you try to rule the outer teaching and life of the Gospel, and coerce and force the thoughts and consciences of persons.

Furthermore, your previously mentioned article in the Synod is also against <407> Luther's teaching where he says that God can and will allow no one to rule over the soul, other than he himself. Therefore, wherever worldly power presumes to legislate for the soul it is trespassing on God's authority and harms and misleads souls.

---

[74] Ulrich Zwingli, "Divine and Human Righteousness," in Wayne Pipkin, trans., *Huldrych Zwingli Writings*, vol. 2 (Allison Park, PA: Pickwick, 1984), 25.

[75] Zwingli wrote: "For this reason, righteous magistrate, stay clear of punishing the little sheep of Christ. Where they do not act against God, you, too, must not act against God so you do not afflict and distress his innocent little sheep. For all authorities are unmistakably threatened in all Scripture when they burden or punish the innocent." Ibid., 28.

Now outward good works belong to Christians or the church, works such as love, mercy, baptism, the ban, discipline, teaching, breaking of bread and all of the Gospel: external teaching and life belongs to the soul. Christ also promised mercy, the soul's blessing and salvation for such outer works, Matthew 25[:31-46]. That is, as mentioned above, if they flow from a living faith, penetrated by the fire of pure, godly love, without which all external works are in vain, no matter how good and glowing they appear to be, Matthew 7, 1 Corinthians 13. But now you have arranged for the secular authority to rule over the external works and to give laws to the souls in these things. You have placed the external teaching and life above the Gospel.

Your practice also goes against Bucer's speech,[76] where he says to the papists: You are leading Israel astray and disturbing them, since you have abandoned the Lord's commandments and have followed after Baal. This is your own invention, and in addition you will not tolerate that the Lord's commandments are taught clearly, without the drivel of your laws, etc. Now, what are you doing, when you establish the worldly authority over the outer things of the Gospel, the Ban and other things, other than following after your own inventions, against your earlier <408> teaching, and thereby abandoning God's evangelical word and commandments? For the latter speak of the freedom of believers, and that such outer evangelical spiritual things, such as the Ban and other things, should be decided by the Christian congregation [gmein] itself, with its spiritual servants, together and face to face, through God's Word in the Holy Spirit and the love of God.

Considering the large amount of teaching of your own scribes in the previous booklet [the "Simple Confession"], in the third article concerning the office of the magistrate and here in this foregoing article (which we have shortened by the omission of some views), your Synod and these earlier writings fit as well together as do white and black, light and darkness. Indeed, they are as opposed to one another as are fire and water. According to the earlier teaching, you would not persecute; but now you persecute us. In this, your current and your earlier teaching are as unlike, and as far from one another, as the persecutor is from the persecuted. For whoever persecutes is of the flesh, but whoever is persecuted has been born of the Spirit, Galatians 4[:6-7; 29]. What else have you done at your Synod but invent many special articles against the teaching and practice of Christ and

---

76   M. Bucer, *Ein kurtzer warhafftiger bericht*, in Stupperich, *Martin Bucers Deutsche Schriften*, vol. 2, 51, lines 4-14.

his Holy Apostles, of which the first [invention] is to install the magistrates over outer evangelical teaching and practice, namely all the physical works and things of the church which [should be] an outworking of the Holy Spirit, to which now many are frightfully driven by coercion and pressure, etc.

Further, in your Synod <409> you say that insofar as the matter has to do with grace, the temporal authorities have to do only with those things pertaining to the outward person, but grace is established and proceeds inwardly, and cannot be brought about by human beings, and so does not belong to a worldly authority or human creature. For spiritual and heavenly things are too high, and far beyond all temporal power. Therefore no magistrates may get involved in matters of conscience, neither commanding or forbidding outwardly, through which good consciences would be burdened since their goal is set by the Holy Spirit. For Christ Jesus our Lord, to whom God gave all power and the promise of the Holy Spirit, is the sole Lord of consciences. Therefore, the Pope, bishops and priests and all their followers who hold to teachings of the Devil are against Christ since they all set out to master consciences. Thus states their booklet.[77]

To this we answer and say that you have again collided with yourselves and rendered a judgment against yourselves from your own mouths for, what do you do differently, with your aforementioned ordinance (as already noted above many times), than to obstruct and burden consciences and the inward progress of grace, and establish a goal for the Holy Spirit? For you ordain the authorities and establish them over consciences and outer matters of teaching and life of the Holy Spirit, which (the Holy Spirit) is free to bring about, working from the inward to the outward, how and when it pleases the Holy Spirit—and not when it pleases human beings.

How can it be, then, that the Holy Spirit and consciences are unburdened and undirected? For if one establishes the authorities over the Holy Spirit's outward things, which are things brought to outward expression from the inner person [von innen herauss gewirckten sachen], then the office, according to <410> Christ's words in Matthew 20[:24-28], has been established outwardly with force, rulings, commands, and prohibitions. How can it be then, that they do not invade consciences with commands and prohibitions, and rule outer things with coercion and pressure—things which flow from within, from the heart, conscience, and mind. Indeed with this you testify that, in the end, you yourselves don't know what you

---

77   The above citation is found in Locher, *Der Berner Synodus*, 31 (original page 8).

are writing. Further, concerning your Synod and this mixed-up thing, if a spiritual person anointed by the Holy Spirit were to read this confused, twisted thing, that person would find it arguing against itself out of fleshly wisdom, without spirit and evangelical knowledge.

Likewise when the Holy Spirit works from the inward to the outward, as in teaching and life, you call it "outward," yes, and an outward ordering, and in Section B on page 3 you say that your service and commanded office is spiritual, inward, and heavenly.[78] When we ask about this, whether outward teaching and preaching of the Gospel, breaking of bread, and other things are not a special case, you cannot deny it; here we see that you are speaking against yourselves. For now it is that your service is an outward one, and immediately following you call it spiritual, inward, and heavenly. So why do you not just call the Gospel, or believing outward teaching and living also spiritual, inward, and heavenly?

In the same way you speak and write in your Synod that the gracious, dear lords have <411> accepted the Gospel with such courage, by your grace, and brought it to your subjects and swore out a special municipal city law which was to function with you and yours in town and countryside. This law is to be respected just as is any other outer ordinance of your territory. Guided by your rabbis and masters of lofty intellects, you make the Holy Gospel into a municipal and city law, to be obeyed just like any other outer law and worldly authority. Such action must not be taken or proved with the Holy Gospel, and therefore is out of place and an insult to the Holy Gospel.

You also say, as noted above, that the magistrates will for that reason be called to give answer before God's judgment, and to the contrary in the Synod you say that if the magistrates act in this way, they have done well. In this way, following your teaching, you invest the magistrates with a conscience and by your law make them particularly responsible for the salvation of souls—which certainly cannot be found in evangelical Scripture and goes plainly counter to the teaching of Christ and his Holy Apostles. In this way you remove and mislead the magistrates out of their proper office and function, such as is established clearly by God in the Scriptures and also in your first teaching—that is, to rule over fleshly things—and you install them in the holy place which is the church, the house and temple of God, and give them authority over spiritual things, against your earlier teaching, and against the Holy Gospel, Matthew 24[:15]; cf. Daniel 11:31].

---

78 See Locher, *Der Berner Synodus*, 36 (original page 11).

Bullinger says <412> in his slanderous book [seins lesterbuch] that we unfairly attacked this Holy Council or Synod in which, as he says, nothing un-Christian was done that we should condemn and disparage.[79] *This is not surprising, for his book is chock-full of such clever, cunning, and fleshly arguments that are meant to turn the goods and the blood of Christians over to the hangman of the magistrates, just as the magistrates treat evildoers. If one compares the arguments, the practice and the council of the Jewish priests Ananias, Caiaphas, and their priestly and scribal conspiracy with those of the preachers and biblically learned ones of the Bern Synod, and the practice of the preachers—the rope, betrayal, and blows with which they judge those who believe in Christ, and the pits which they dig for them—see how wonderfully it all fits together. It is one spirit that works all of this, for someone who fears God and is enlightened and anointed by the Holy Spirit will truly discern and understand what spirit fathered such watchmen and soul-guardians. Note above in the third article in the foregoing booklet, at the beginning, to see how well these compare with the Scripture wizards of the Jewish people.*[80]

Indeed, we cannot, for the sake of God's honor, wave the fox tail over it[81] *in the manner of the false prophets, and call something sweet, when in fact it is bitterness and gall, yes, an evil and a deep darkness. We wish rather to leave them with the fox tail so that they can stroke one another with it and tickle each others' ears with it. But it will cost them later, when joking and etiquette <413> are no longer effective, and they will truly sorrow, but too late. For with your installation of the magistrates over the church you are strengthening both Emperor and Pope again in their former views, which situation you could not tolerate from the Pope and also considered it an abomination from the Emperor, as is clear in your often-mentioned first teachings which go directly against your installing the magistrates. Thus Luther clearly wrote, that there should be no magistrates among Christians, and that they should have no worldly sword among them, and that God will not permit human beings to displace him from his throne and set themselves up in his place; further that imperial authority does not*

---

79 See Bullinger, *Der Widertöufferen ursprung/fürgang/Secten ...etc.* 150 verso, ff. for Bullinger's comments regarding the Bern Synod.
80 This appears to be a reference to article 3 of the *Simple Confession.*
81 A medieval symbol of hypocrisy and deception.

extend into God's kingdom and power or touch what belongs to heaven and God's kingdom.

You also commit theft when you support the Authority in its wrongful seizure of office, for as you spoke in the Synod, the objection of some simple people should not divert your graces from such Christian intention; they say that Christianity is an inward thing, and must not be ruled by the sword, but rather must be governed by God's Word. Your graces, they charged, established a new papacy in which you wished to interfere in matters of faith. Now you yourselves know well that all your first teachings and writings made possible such objections, and that it was you yourselves who [earlier] used the same objections of these simple people against the Pope and Emperor, as noted. But now you have again fallen away from that and cast it away, as summarized above, and now hold the exact opposite <414>—which is something that you cannot truthfully deny—through which the magistrates have been encouraged to shed the blood of the innocent.

Likewise you say in your Synod, Section J, page 2: When the books and commentaries written in our time and in earlier times are placed together and compared to our present understanding, they may justly be read with understanding and for improvement.[82] Answer: We would wish that the books containing your earlier teaching, which were written on the basis of the Gospel, would similarly be compared and criticized as we have done here. But our experience is that the understanding or interpretation of your Synod, which we have overthrown above with the clear, living word of God, is in no way the same or can be compared, but rather stands completely against it, as we have amply demonstrated. And you cannot demonstrate with the Gospel word, teaching, and writing that your earlier teaching and writing is in fact false and that the understanding of your Synod is true—nor will you ever in all eternity be able to demonstrate such a thing. Thus you call this achievement by the Synod either simply a lack of understanding, or understanding, and you may yourselves judge whether you are not responsible—for your souls' salvation—to retract the mistaken view of this Synod and other previously mentioned errors, so that the magistrates and other persons may be warned and kept from further mistakes. <415>

But you certainly do not wish to do that. We truly fear you have sucked the wisdom of the lying serpent too deeply into yourselves and sunk it too deeply in your way of doing things. Thus we wish not to be made a part of

---

82 Locher, *Der Berner Synodus*, 147 (original page 66).

this, your great sin and grievous error against God and his anointed, but if you will not have it otherwise, we must let you bear the heavy burden that you have loaded upon yourselves. Finally you will fall, accompanied by a dirge and with great shame. Truly we do not envy you. But the word of the Lord will not give way to you; rather you will give way to him, or you will be put to shame by God and his holy angels.

As far as the rest of the articles and issues are concerned, we wish to abbreviate them and deal with them in shortened form, so that this book does not get too thick and large. We hope that the God-fearing reader, by the enlightenment of the Spirit of God, is able to differentiate—with an unpartisan, clear, and pure heart—between the cunning wisdom of the serpent and heavenly, godly wisdom, between fleshly, earthly natural love, and spiritual, heavenly, supernatural love. Such a reader truly will be able to note, on the basis of the reasons already presented, how useless against this godly truth are the fleshly, powerless, and groundless arguments of our opponents. If one holds them to the clear, godly light and the Holy Gospel, and puts them on the weigh scale of the Holy Spirit and righteousness, it turns out to be human wisdom, cleverness, and hair-splitting, an external, deceptive <416> fakery to which no one is able to give substance—not even if the high sorcerer, master, Satan and prince Lucifer were to take a seat beside them.

If God gives grace, we hope in time to write about the remaining articles at more length in a separate booklet; but now we will deal with these eight articles and reasons, with the help and grace of God and of those who have given direction to this my simple work and have helped in this task. For in and of myself, I am too weak and small, and I confess freely that were I to want to acquire any praise or honor I would be practicing the art of the false prophets who suck and steal their art from one another out of books, and then embellish that very thievery with their own names, as if they were themselves such wise, fine learned gentlemen. May my Lord and God protect me from such spiritual pride. My worthiness truly deserves ignominy and dishonor as befits a useless servant—albeit one who is hungry and thirsty for righteousness, if I may speak happily from the heart.

But all the glory, praise, and honor belongs to the Lord God. But to the enlightened, true servants of God, who in many places up to now have helped give guidance and several people who solved many a problem through the grace they received from God—for these I desire, from the heart, eternal joy

Concerning Separation 493

and honor; I hope that several have already won and received the crown, with God's help. <417> *Therefore I can report to you, my beloved reader, that I am truly free in my heart, for I know the cunning serpent rather well, how it can flatter the flesh at different places. That is how I set out to invest my small, limited gift. It would give me the greatest joy if, when my Lord Jesus takes souls into his kingdom, I could bring something on that day—with the Lord's help—and so return my little gift and pound with interest. To this end may dear God grant grace, blessing, and benediction. Amen.*

Now follows:

THE FOURTH REASON[83]

The fourth reason [we do not attend their churches]: Since they proceed, as indicated above, and set out to protect, uphold, and defend the teaching of Christ and the Gospel by means other than the sword of the Spirit, which is the word of God, and teach and counsel that it should be protected and defended (physically), they testify with this that they lack the sword of the Spirit. [And because they do not have it, it is clear that they also lack the Holy Spirit][84] as the one who should wield the sword in and through them. They also manifest this lack when they insult us and others like us [without distinction—which is the occasion of this booklet][85]—reproaching us in every way, accusing us of being part of the erring sects, with whom we neither share nor have communion. [But they do not speak the truth.][86]

Now they mix us in with the Münsterites, then with other rootless sects. *This one has, as they say, done such and such, and another that, in the name of the Father. But in fact the holy apostles,* <418> *who had more grace and power than we, were also not able to prevent the false apostles of their own time to go forth under their name, as noted above. They act against us with falsehood in that they speak evil of us everywhere, in order to create an evil reputation and name for us among the people, when in fact they have already caused a thousand times more destruction and abomination in their own name and among their own brothers. And in their midst they have*

---

83 At this point, parallels with the Bullinger text begin again.
84 Bracketed portion missing in *Codex 628*.
85 Bracketed portion missing in *Codex 628*.
86 Bracketed portion missing in *Codex 628*. The text following is found only in *Codex 628*.

executed many, not for the sake of the truth and testimony to Jesus Christ, but rather because of the vices and evil deeds they themselves have done.

We could have written an entire chronicle concerning what has taken place under the preachers, and how they slander, blame, condemn as heretics, damn, and consider each other to be more evil than the Turks. And yet we must continually be called the crazy, erring, perverted, stubborn, senseless Anabaptists, and they are called the Holy Christian Church. But just what kind of a holy church they are has been shown often enough above, with godly proof.[87] Therefore they act against the manner and nature of the Holy Spirit, who is the spirit of truth and not of untruth. And as they lack the Holy Spirit, so they also lack the love of God which is poured out by God's Spirit, Romans 5[:5]. This lack of love is seen also in their untruthful slander and accusation against us, as well as in their previously-mentioned resistance to the evil of their enemies, <419> or those who hate them, and in the coercion and persecution of persons on account of their faith, which also testifies to their lack of the Holy Spirit. They are not born of the Spirit, because in Galatians 4[:29] Paul states that persecutors are not born of the Spirit, but of the flesh.

They also manifest many other works of the flesh against us [such as enmity, anger, blasphemy, slander, and the like][88] with which they also demonstrate that they have not been born of the Holy Spirit and the love of God, which is given of God. [This they lack, being without the Holy Spirit and the love of the Spirit],[89] without which love they cannot know either God or his children, 1 John 3[:1]; 4[:8, 20ff]. Out of this ignorance they hate us and persecute us, according to John 15[:18, 20ff]; 16[:2ff].[90] Yes, since they do not know God nor do they come from him, they also do not hear our words as God's words, and do not know our speech, John 8[:47]; 1 John 4[:16].

This is also the reason they will not allow us to speak in their churches, fearing that we might deceive them. They do not realize that they are not yet delivered from deception, without the desired birth from God, still much more natural persons who know nothing from the Spirit of God, 1

---

87 Parallels with Bullinger begin again at this point.
88 Bracketed portion missing in *Codex 628*.
89 Bracketed portion missing in *Codex 628*.
90 Here Bullinger's text inserts a marginal note, missing from *Codex 628*. This may indicate that the copyist of the codex was not working from Bullinger's print.

Concerning Separation 495

Corinthians 2[:14]. Rather it is foolishness to them. [And since the Spirit and love of God are lacking, so they also cannot be baptized of Christ.]⁹¹ *For who can truthfully witness about them, that they possess the Holy Spirit and the pure, fervent love of God which can be seen in such public, visible work and fruit, and that they treat each other in a brotherly fashion, following the teaching of Christ and his apostles?*

[For such Spirit and love of God together constitute] the baptism with which Jesus Christ baptizes persons since his ascension, according to Matthew 3[:16], Mark 1[:10], Luke 3[:22], John 1[:32], Acts 1[:5, 8]. <420> [Without this same Spirit and love they also do not possess the living and saving faith, and also] lack the river of living water, John 7[:38] among and toward one another. Neither are they able, without the divine birth, to avoid sin or the assaults of the wicked, 1 John 3[:9ff]; 5[:18] [and therefore they remain in sin.]⁹² For without the Holy Spirit it is not possible to put to death the works of the flesh; one is not yet spiritual, but rather carnally minded, at enmity with God, not able to be subject to the law and commandment of God. Such a one is not the Lord's but rather lives according to the flesh and dies accordingly, Romans 8[:5ff]. For the wages of sin is death, Romans 6[:23].⁹³

Therefore we see with open eyes that they have sunk over their ears in arrogance, pride, avarice, seeking honors, drunkenness, gluttony, and other vices in lasciviousness of the flesh. In view of all this, who would recognize them and their preachers as a Christian, spiritual congregation, attend their preaching, and have fellowship in their faith? The Gospel regards and recognizes as the community or bride of Christ only those who follow after Christ, their bridegroom and spouse, and who live before him in obedience and unblamable holiness, Ephesians 5[:24ff]. But because, as indicated, they transgress the evangelical teaching and word of Christ, persist in their transgression, and oppose this teaching and word [thus having no God, not being true disciples of Christ, not being so regarded or held to be such by us, unless falsely or blasphemously so, nor yet (for that matter) regarding

---

91 Bracketed portion missing in *Codex 628*. Here begins an insertion, only in *Codex 628*.
92 Bracketed sections here and above in Bullinger only.
93 Italic portion following, only in *Codex 628*.

themselves or truthfully designating themselves as such.][94] Would to God we could truthfully say that <421> they were a Christian congregation, but if we said this untruthfully simply to please them, we would be like the false prophets about whom God complains, when they said "peace" and there was no peace.

THE FIFTH REASON

The fifth reason why we do not go to their preaching and church is this: because they do not maintain among themselves the Christian spiritual ban and punishment, nor separation from impurity, nor the Christian, apostolic authority, key, and power to exclude and include, to bind and loose on account of sin, to absolve and retain sin. Neither do they maintain a spiritual order and administration through the word of God, as the sword of the Spirit, for the establishment, preservation and improvement of a true, unblamable spouse, accepted by Christ, with the adornment, embellishment, and virtues with which Scripture portrays her. The [Scripture] references concerning the aforesaid ban, separation, authority, power, key, sword, inclusion and exclusion, binding, loosing and such administration and ordering are found written in Matthew 16[:19], 18[:15ff], Luke 17[:3ff], John 20[:22ff], 2 Corinthians 10[:8?], 13[:1ff], 1 Corinthians 5[:6ff], 6[:1-11], Ephesians 5[:11], 6[:4?], 2 Thessalonians 3[:6], 1 Timothy 1[:20], 3[?], 6[?], Acts 20[:28].

Yes, all this is impossible for them (as some of their preachers themselves admit, all the while using worldly power to this end). Why? Because, as indicated, they lack the Holy Spirit, and such discipline is commended and possible only for those who have the Holy Spirit, according to John 20[:22ff], and who alone <422> are the true hearers[95] of that which is to be taught and preached, John 14[:26], and who alone ordains and establishes bishops, Acts 20[:28]. For this reason Christ told his disciples to wait until they *were pregnant with this Spirit and until they were able to act with the power from on high*,[96] Luke 24[:49], Acts 1[:8].

---

94 Bracketed section not in *Codex 628*. The codex has instead: "Therefore we cannot consider them to be the Christian church or as disciples and followers of Christ." <421>.
95 *Codex 628* has "teachers" rather than "hearers."
96 Sentence added in *Codex 628*; Bullinger has "until they received this Spirit."

And therefore, however much they boast, cry out, and strut about, they still cannot possess or comprehend the church of God and Christ, about which Paul speaks in Ephesians 5[:26ff], which is cleansed by the washing of water in the word, that he might present it to himself as a holy church, without spot or wrinkle, or any such thing, but that it should be holy and faultless. The Christian ban is not a ban such as some have made of it, where Paul says in 1 Corinthians 5[:13]: Put away from yourselves whoever is evil. He means, away from the fellowship of the separated members of Christ, out into the world or among other evil persons living in the same city or country, to excommunicate them kindly, and not to expel them from city or countryside and to persecute them and even put them to death through the worldly magistrates, as these so-called churches and preachers now advocate. But this can never, into all eternity, be called a Christian ban.

Jesus makes the same point in the words "Let such a one be as a heathen to you [Matthew 18:17], and also Paul, "not as an enemy, but rather as a friend" [2 Thessalonians 3:15]. They do not say persecute, drive them from one city or territory <423> to another and torture them, or expel in a worldly manner, as it happens today when, under a Christian and spiritual pretense, instead of the sword and power of the Spirit, they apply, establish, and employ the worldly sword and power in matters of spirit and faith—against which practices the evangelical preachers wrote long ago, and condemned such practices as tyrannical.

If their preachers *and watchmen truly* had the Holy Spirit, they would have instituted the previously mentioned Christian ban, order, and manner among themselves, and would not have employed or appealed to the worldly power and sword. This [Christian ban] would have been possible for them without appeal to worldly power, as it was possible for the apostles, without calling upon or using worldly arms. For earlier, according to their original teaching concerning spiritual things, the preachers amply demonstrated that those who are of God do not resort to arms, which much more hinder, destroy, and persecute the spiritual matters of the Gospel, rather than furthering and serving them.[97]

---

97 *Codex 628* omits the following bracketed section, which refers to Zwingli and Luther's earlier writings, perhaps because the copyist has already employed these citations, above, in his own interpolations.

[So Zwingli says (as someone has written) in his 36th article to the preachers, saying: As long as you call for weapons of steel, we all see that you are not a follower of Christ or of Peter, but that you belong to the Devil and the Antichrist. And Luther writes, commenting on the Psalms: The true, righteous church is not to be defended with worldly arms and power, but rather (such is) the so-called church, which indeed claims the title "church" but denies her power." And again: The true church of Christ does know the *brachium seculare* (the temporal arm), which indeed the ungodly bishops employ above all and call upon.]

But they bring themselves under suspicion in that they seek to install again the worldly sword in the churches, and turn the matter in such a direction that, should one pursue it further, one would find a carnal arm and back. If anyone should point out their error with the sword of the Spirit, such a one is persecuted with the worldly sword, so that what is pure and clear does not come forth, Isaiah 59[:3; 7]. Yes, if they had the Holy Spirit <424> they would establish the ban and all that has been mentioned, as easily as the apostles did, through the teaching of the evangelical word of God. Those who allow themselves to be governed (by the word) would be Christian, and would not need the worldly sword at all; otherwise they would not be Christian and also would not be subject to this spiritual sword and administration, but rather would be outside, belonging under the worldly sword and administration. One suspects that they are afraid that this might bring them the cross and hatred because of excommunications *and might take away their benefices* and on this account it is impossible for them—*note above in the article concerning the temporal authority.*[98] And for this reason they establish the worldly sword (it is said) in the churches, to administer spiritual matters. With this they release the spiritual authority, sword and power, and abandon it.

The Sixth Reason

The sixth [reason we do not attend their churches] is because they (as they themselves may see and judge on the basis of the noted grounds and demonstrations) are no established, separated church of God, nor body of Christ (*not* baptized of Christ through the Holy Spirit as the spirit of love, yes, the Spirit and love of God, both of which they lack),[99] 1 Corinthians

---

98   Italicized portions in *Codex 628* only.
99   *Codex 628* adds the negative, not present in Bullinger: "not" baptized.

Concerning Separation

12[:13], Matthew 3[:11]. Furthermore, as indicated, they transgress the Gospel and also live in sin against godly love, and so we cannot consider their supper to be the Lord's Supper. For Christ has ordained [his Supper] only for his own followers and disciples, who are separated from the world, <425> that is, true Christians who love each other as he loved us, yes those who, Colossians 2[:11], are circumcised with the circumcision without hands through the putting off of the sinful body of the flesh. They alone are the body of Christ, his people and community. [Those outside] do not yet know this body of love; they hate it, let alone that they themselves should be it. And since they are not this body and do not know it, neither can they discern, and therefore they eat and drink to their condemnation, since they do not practice discernment according to Paul's intention.

Without the Spirit of God it is not the Lord's Supper according to 1 Corinthians 11[:17ff], but an abomination before God, even as it was also in the carnal, figurative Israel, and forbidden of God, and as it was an abomination to God when one who was uncircumcised in the foreskin of the flesh ate the Passover lamb, Exodus 22 [= Leviticus 22:10, 25]. How much more so today in the real, spiritual Israel must the partakers of the Lord's Supper be circumcised with the above-mentioned circumcision without hands, which is to be newly born, spiritual people who live in the obedience of faith, yes, in the Spirit and new life, and no longer walking according to the flesh, Romans 6[:12ff], 7[:5ff], 8[:9ff].

Yes, those who observe, 1 Corinthians 5[:6ff] this manner of Passover not in the leaven of malice and lusts, but with the unleavened bread of sincerity, love, and truth, wear the wedding garment of love and of the Spirit, Galatians 5[:22ff], Matthew 22[:11-13]. <426> For those who do not find themselves thus prepared are not circumcised without hands and can neither eat nor have fellowship in the Lord's Supper, being still dead in sin.

And therefore the aforementioned so-called churches can test themselves in this, that practically the entire Gospel, the strength, deed, and life of which they boast, is negated by their lives and that of their preachers. And they are a Christian church only in name and in the doing of certain things in speech and word (as also with the papists), and their eyes are so completely closed that those who show them the right way are accused and regarded as deceivers and heretics.

What should we then do concerning their preaching and Lord's Supper? We, especially the weak among us, would only be offended by their teaching and life, even as with their previously mentioned transgressions of the Gospel give offense to all people. Indeed, they are not light but rather darkness under the appearance of the Gospel [without its light and form], which is a grave offense, Matthew 18[:6ff], Luke 17[:1ff], 1 Corinthians 8[:9ff], Romans 14[:13ff]. They deliberately forget that Paul said: Give no offense to anyone, 2 Corinthians 6[:3]. In fact they themselves preached against such offence earlier.

Therefore, we are not improved, but rather made worse and more offensive, nor are we able to improve them, since they do not allow us <427> to speak. Yes, we would be made partakers with them of all the foregoing uncleanness, sin, and transgression. For this reason God calls us away from all offensive people and things, according to these references. See Revelation 18[:4ff]:[100] [Come out from her, my people, lest you take part in her sins . . . for her sins are heaped as high as heaven.] Also 2 Corinthians 6[:14-18]: [Be not unequally yoked together with unbelievers, for what fellowship does righteousness have with unrighteousness? And what communion does light have with darkness? And what does Christ have to do with Belial? Or what part does a believer have with an infidel? What agreement is there between the temple of God and idols? But you are the temple of the living God, as God has said, I will dwell in them and will walk in them, and I will be their God and they will be my people. Therefore come out from among them and be separate, says the Lord, and touch no unclean thing, and I will receive you and will be a Father to you, and you shall be my sons and daughters, etc. We read further in] Jeremiah 51[:6]: [Flee from the midst of Babylon, and let everyone deliver his soul; do not be cut off in her iniquity], *as was extensively reported in the foregoing booklet, in the first article concerning worldly authority.* Jesus ben Sirach also says Ecclesiasticus 13 [?]: He that touches resin will be stained, and he who has fellowship with the proud will become like them; and again: All flesh seeks its own kind and men quickly conform to their fellows. Likewise the wise king Solomon says in Proverbs 22[:5]: Thorns and snares are on the way of the perverted, but he that keeps his distance keeps his soul.

---

100 In the section that follows, *Codex 628* lists the Scripture references but does not reproduce the verses; these omissions are contained in square brackets.

Concerning Separation

For this reason God enjoined Israel in Exodus 24[=34:15]: Take heed that you make no covenant with the people of the lands into which you come, that they not become an offense to you. They did not take heed, however, as Psalm 106[:35ff] indicates, but mixed with the heathen, learned their ways and served their gods, as some today serve living idols, which led them to harm, etc. And of these David speaks in Psalm 26[:4ff, 8]: I have not sat with vain persons, neither will I go with dissemblers. I have hated the congregation of evildoers, and will not sit with the wicked. Lord, I have loved the habitation of your <428> house, and the place where you honor dwells. Yes, concerning this it is said: a man becomes ill from the company he keeps. Read also Numbers 16[:21], 26, 45, 2 Chronicles 20[:35ff].

Likewise Paul admonishes us, Romans 16[:17], to beware of those who cause divisions and offenses in opposition to the doctrine we have learned, and to avoid them. Since these preachers oppose the doctrine which they first preached from the Gospel, as indicated, thereby also instructing us, and since they now cause division and offense by now falling away, we withdraw from their preaching, according to the word of God spoken through Paul, to which word we are to be more obedient than to that of men, following the words of the apostles, Acts 4[:19], 5[:29].

And so the preachers have become apostate to their first evangelical teaching and have now turned themselves and their congregations into the same kind of rabble whose life and actions they themselves opposed in their first teaching. So Paul commands us in Titus 3[:10ff] to avoid those who are contrary and cause uproar, after the first and the second admonition— as we have often already admonished [them] with our writings and words, and still do.[101] *Yes, [admonished] by many true witnesses, who acted with the power from on high and were anointed with the Holy Spirit, who were willing to risk life, possessions and blood for the sake of God's truth and testimony to Jesus Christ, and gave <429> themselves over to the enemies of Christ and the stubborn worldly-wise. But in their slander books they treat such witnesses and servants of God as a mockery and foolishness. Since the Holy Spirit has not gripped them, we must point it out to them. Look at their slander book, when Bullinger shed his blood for the sake of witnessing to*

---

101 Here follows an insertion in *Codex 628*.

Jesus Christ—insofar as he understood it.[102] *We fear that we must take him to be a mockery before God, since he is so mistaken, as shown above, and yet he has not improved his understanding,* as reported above in some of the 13 articles (of the preceding copied book). If the preachers were the actual, true servants of God, they would hold firmly to the foundation of the apostles, and if we were the rabble that they blame us for being, then they would be acting against the teaching of Paul, since in contravention of that teaching, they wish above all to coerce us into joining them. Since, however, the label they unjustly wish to place on us belongs in truth with them, we intend to be obedient to the teaching of the holy apostles and to avoid [the preachers]. Such shepherds are strangers to us. In accordance with the words of Christ we flee from them, since we do not know their voice, John 10[:5].

Therefore we admonish them, if they have eyes and ears to see and hear, that they take the foregoing and following to heart, to their own good, and in the fear of God amend <430> their life and purpose, and set out to receive the Holy Spirit *in the right manner,* who alone is able to teach and remind them of what the body of Christ is, so that they might recognize it and become that body, along with *all true believers.*[103] It must be distinguished from the body of Satan as Paul distinguishes it, in accordance with the aforementioned words of 2 Corinthians 6[:15]. For the body of Christ is spiritually minded, as are those who in and by the Spirit walk and live in the new reality. And the body of the world is fleshly minded, lacks the Spirit of Christ, and is not Christ's, as seen in Romans 6, 7, and 8 and in Galatians 5[:17ff]. And again, the body of the world is born of the flesh [and persecutes the body of Christ which is born of the Spirit], Galatians 4[:29]. So also Christ says to his body: Because I have chosen you out of the world, the world hates you, John 15[:19].

From this it is evident that the world and the carnally minded is the body of Belial and Satan, and that Satan is (the world's) god and prince, 2 Corinthians 4[:4], John 12[:31], 14[:30]. Further, the body of Christ brings forth the fruit of the Spirit and of love; these are good fruits. The body of the world brings forth the fruit of the flesh; these are evil fruits.

---

102 Bullinger did not "shed his blood" as a witness; he died in 1575 of natural causes. The reference, including the comment "as he understood it," would fit Ulrich Zwingli, Bullinger's predecessor in Zurich, who died in 1531 on the field of battle, fighting the Catholic cantons.

103 Bullinger copy has "along with us." Italicized phrases only in *Codex 628.*

Concerning Separation

Concerning both kinds of fruit, in 1 Corinthians 13[4ff] and Galatians 5[:19ff] is written how one may recognize each kind. As the Lord says, Matthew 7[:16], 12[:33], Luke 6[:44]: By their fruits you shall know them. Likewise in 1 John 2[:29]: If you know that he is righteous, you know that every one that lives righteously is born of him. And also 1 John 3[:9ff]: Those born of God do not sin, for their seed remains in them, and they cannot sin, because <431> they are born of God.

In this the children of God are manifest and also the children of the Devil: whoever does not act rightly is not of God, neither is one who does not love his brother. The Lord says further, John 13[:34ff]: A new commandment I give to you, that you love one another; as I have loved you, you should also love one another. By this all will know that you are my disciples, if you love one another. This is how the body of Christ is to be recognized and separated from what is not that body, *as Christ and his apostles have taught us.*[104]

The Lord wishes to have such separation, especially in the Supper. Let all remember of which body they are a part, and whether they truly belong to the body of Christ as the body of God's love, and whether they love their fellow members. And then let them not eat and drink or have fellowship and be a part of those whom they know to belong to the body of the world, those who according to 1 Corinthians 5[:7] are to be purged as the old leaven and put out into the world. This must be done so that one may eat and drink the bread and drink of the Lord worthily and without blame. Thus we are to observe the Lord's Supper, or the Passover, not in the old leaven of malice and lust, but with the unleavened bread of sincerity and truth. For whoever eats or drinks unworthily, says Paul, eats and drinks to self-damnation, not discerning the body of the Lord, 1 Corinthians 11[:27ff].

In like manner God required a separation already under the law, as stated in Malachi 3[:18]: Then you shall return <432> and discern between the righteous and the wicked, between those who serve God and those who do not. So also Leviticus 10[:10]: Distinguish between the holy and unholy, and between pure and impure. And also Ezekiel 22[:26]: Your priests have violated my law, and have profaned my holy things; they have made no distinction between the holy and profane, neither between the pure and the impure.

---

104 Italic: *Codex 628.*

The Seventh Reason

The seventh reason [we do not attend their churches] is that in their office or service of preaching and baptizing, their preachers also do not maintain order commanded by the Lord Christ and practiced by the apostles, in order to establish, gather, and receive a Christian community. Rather they transgress this commandment or teaching of Christ and use of the apostles, which commands and teaches that instruction comes first (understand: of older people who are able to be taught) and only afterwards, baptism, Matthew 28[:19], Acts 2[:38]. And they have inverted the order and practice in that they first baptize the little children who are unable to speak, understand, or know, and they teach as though it were correct, something which is actually a perversion of the evangelical order, decree, and practice, and which has never been, nor can be, shown to be right by the pure, clear, indubitable word <433> of God,[105] *as the foregoing booklet in 13 articles clearly indicates, in which their leading arguments, regardless of whether they believe the old or the new Pope, are countered and defeated with the clear word of God.*

But we believe with no doubts what Christ Jesus taught and commanded and what the apostles also practiced. Zwingli himself confessed, as noted above, that the words that Christ spoke in Mark 16[:15-16] did not apply to young children. Hence, according to his words there must now always be a different baptism for children in the cradle of which Christ here makes no mention, nor in Matthew 28[:19-20]; in both places is found the history of why we do not wish to be sullied with the unfounded infant baptism.

But if perhaps the infant baptizers wish to come before the Lord Jesus Christ on his judgment seat, making their many arguments, so that he would grant them more validity than (Christ's) unmovable, clear word, then let them do it. But we do not believe that they will win anything by it; we would rather believe the word of God that does not shift or change—heaven and earth would break and pass away before the smallest part of God's word were to fall. So the apostle Paul says that no other foundation may be laid than the one that is already laid, which is Jesus Christ [1 Corinthians 3:11].

---

105 Material following inserted in *Codex 628*. Bullinger has "Concerning this we would have much to point out, also in answer to their refutations, but for the sake of brevity, we forbear."

And Paul condemns, Galatians 1[:8ff] anything that is preached contrary to what he and the other apostles preached. <434>

And so, as expressly recorded, we find in the apostles' preaching office only the preaching, teaching, and practice of baptizing mature persons and not the little children who are unable to speak or understand. And so since the infant baptizers do not have an authentic, separated church of Christ through and by their infant baptism, as indicated above, we believe they will not be able to establish (such a church) without the indicated evangelical order. And since they do not have that order, and we have objections and reasons against them on account of baptism and all the afore-mentioned reasons, we cannot have fellowship with them in faith and church matters. Therefore we cannot go to their preaching and churches, nor to any of their teaching which is not formed and shaped by the apostolic teaching [but rather, as stated above, is condemned by Paul].[106]

THE EIGHTH REASON

The eighth reason [we do not attend their churches] is because their preachers earlier also taught this Gospel, and to some extent still do, that one should avoid sin, lead a godly, Christian, irreproachable life, be newly born again of God, exercise Christian, fraternal love, follow after Christ and bear the cross, fear and love God above all things, stand by the evangelical truth and leave house, farm, wife, child, etc. rather than departing from it or renouncing it and the like—of which their first [evangelical] books, *written before the previously mentioned* <435> *Synod, are full*. And since then some have also fired at the mark, although with leaven mixed into the dough, as was noted above concerning Rudolf Walter.[107] One notes his sermons on the passion and suffering of Christ, how he describes the Christian life therein, and how the followers of Christ are to act and be born, over against how favorably he draws and paints the false priests and pastors, and the powers of darkness and the godless tyrants and authorities—yes, he and others often taught and wrote the truth. There is ample testimony everywhere in the New Testament.

---

106 Bracketed phrase omitted in *Codex 628*.
107 Rudolf Walter's theology and his writings were obviously valued by the copyist/editor. Walter's sermon notes on many biblical books, including the Gospels, were published after his death in 1586.

But now, if by the grace of God we take hold of such a way of life, faith and teaching as they first taught *and some since then (together with other confusing teachings and preaching which they also hold)*, they consider us to be an abomination, cannot bear us, slander and reproach us in our Christian faith, teaching and life, as if it were heresy and error. They cry out to the worldly powers and people against us, or incite and provoke them to persecute and kill us. Some of them advise us to forsake this way and life, so that we might keep house, farm, wife, and children. They call us fools because we endure persecution for the sake of such truth, *against Christ's teaching, Matthew 10, Luke 14.* Yes, even <436> if there are those in their own churches who undertake to do and live rightly, they give them our name, namely Anabaptists, thereby demonstrating that they hate those persons as they also hate us—*so odd do they find the true Christian life in their midst in fact, regardless of how highly they promote it in their speech and their writings.*

This demonstrates that the Gospel they preached earlier has been completely subverted, denied, and—under the appearance and cloak of that Gospel, is derided and trampled underfoot. They also abolish the holy cross of Christ. With this they identify themselves with those of whom the Lord spoke, Matthew 23[:13ff], Luke 11[:52], who do not enter the kingdom of God and oppose and shut it up to those who desire to enter it. And they oppose us in the aforementioned Christian faith, doctrine, and life, and cry out against us and scold us before or in their churches, as if it were heresy and error. Such people and the world believe that this is really the way things are, *and our way of life is as black as they proclaim it to be.*

The result is that this way into the kingdom of God is despised and mistrusted, and people are thus prevented and hindered from entering into the kingdom of God through observing the will of God, without which observance no one enters, Matthew 7[:21], 19[:16ff]. And from this it follows that they, the preachers, must often abstain from teaching the right Christian life, and say something else instead, something that does not bring them the cross, because the holy cross has become an abomination to them, lest they be called Anabaptists, <437> and have people hate and persecute them, as they do us.

But they say that they do not wish to be persecuted on account of the *baptizing sect. All the same they say that the true Christian faith and teaching of Christ and his apostles, in baptism, ban, Supper, and other* ordinances, which the holy apostles used, kept, and watched over, is a sect, as has been demonstrated above with the clear word of God. But giving the label of "sect" to the evangelical order is not something that just happened now, but rather it was given and applied long ago to the holy apostles by the scribes and priestly council. This is what Christ foretold, that people would say all kinds of evil things against us, as was amply described above in the first article of the foreword.

Those for whom the holy cross is a bitter drink the Holy Spirit calls the enemies of the cross of Christ, whose end is destruction, whose God is their belly, and whose glory is turned to shame, [who mind earthly things, Philippians 3[:18ff], Hebrews 6[:6?].] Therefore, in other words, they are earthly minded. See above in the foreword to the (article on the) authorities, and in the third article of the previous booklet.[108] [They may well take heed that the words of Peter: By reason of whom the way of truth shall be evil spoken of, do not apply to them, etc. And again: Which have forsaken the right way, and are gone astray, etc. And again: These are wells without water, clouds that are carried with a tempest, to whom the mist of darkness is reserved forever. For when they speak great swelling words of vanity they allure through the lusts of the flesh, through much wantonness, those that were clean escaped from them, who live in error. While they promise them liberty, they themselves are the servants of corruption, 2 Peter 2[:2, 15, 17-19]. And the words of Paul say: Ever learning, and never able to come to the knowledge of the truth, etc. They are people of corrupt minds, reprobate concerning the faith. But they will not succeed, for their folly will be manifest to all, as theirs also was, 2 Timothy 3[:7-9].]

[In conclusion, some refutations of their pretentious claims][109]

The Ninth Reason[110]

In the ninth place [and in conclusion], because of all the foregoing reasons, we find so little spiritual, and only carnal judgment and understanding advanced by such preachers and the churches led by them. This may be seen first in that they say to those of us who buy and sell from them, or

---

108 With this, *Codex 628* ends the section on the "eighth article." The Bullinger text continues.
109 This title in Bullinger only.
110 Title only in *Codex 628*.

have similar interaction with them, that we should therefore also attend their preaching and have fellowship with them in these matters also. To this we answer that it means mixing spiritual and earthly things together, or considering them to be one thing, without distinction. If they were spiritual *in the proper manner*,[111] <438> they would apprehend spiritual things, that is, the things of faith, spiritually, and would judge according to Paul's words in 1 Corinthians 2[:13].

Christians do have fellowship with the world, apart from its sins, in buying and selling and such temporal things for the sake of the body's nourishment. This kind of use is not forbidden to them by the Gospel, except that according to 1 Corinthians 7[:29-31] they are to use the world as if they did not belong to it. This, however, does not mean that we may have fellowship with them in matters of faith. For in these we make a distinction and say that in matters of faith we can have neither part nor fellowship with them or with others who live and act against the Gospel and the commandments of God. For the first apostolic Christians likewise associated with the world and used it, apart from matters of faith and sin, otherwise they would have had to go outside of the world. For us it is the same, as Paul says in 1 Corinthians 5[:10]. We could ask the Lutherans also, who in similar fashion buy and sell from the papists and have a similar interaction, why they then do not also have equal fellowship with them in matters of faith, doctrine, the mass, and such like things.

In the second place, they persuade the supposed evangelicals, in their carnal, unspiritual understanding, with their fleshly (carnal) words why, for the already mentioned reasons, we do not attend their preaching or fellowship with them in matters of faith. They accuse us of despising them or considering ourselves better than they are. They ignore the fact that we in turn could ask why <439> they consider themselves better than the papists? The papists also address the Lutherans in such a carnal manner. If they say that they do not consider themselves to be better, we ask them, then why censure them and avoid them in doctrine and faith? If they answer that of themselves they are not better, but only in faith, or on account of a better faith and life, well! Let them also grant us the same right.

We confess that our nature is definitely not better than that of all natural persons descended from Adam. Insofar as we are better than all godless children of the world, that comes not from us—certainly not from

---

111 Phrase added in *Codex 628*.

Concerning Separation

us—but rather is Christ in us, as is stated with good discernment above in the foreword and in the eighth article of the foregoing booklet [i.e., the Simple Confession]. *It is a matter of our salvation that we be converted in our hearts, and that we abandon and deny the ungodly nature* (wesen*), etc.* Therefore, insofar as by God's grace we seek to be obedient and to follow the Gospel and command of God more fervently than they, and insofar as they can report fewer such transgressions among us than among them, *to that extent we hope and believe that our case is better before God.*

We avoid their preaching and churches not out of carnal disdain, as they judge, but because we desire to obey the word of God which ordains such avoidance and separation for us [as described in the sixth reason, above]. This obedience to God's word, which is a spiritual thing, they regard or judge to be our carnal disdain. Yet we do not boast, for according to the words of Paul in 2 Corinthians 12[:1], boasting is worthless. <440> But if anyone ever causes us to boast, as they do here, we glory not in ourselves or in our flesh, but in the Lord Jesus Christ and in his cross, 1 Corinthians 11[:23ff], Galatians 6[:14].

Thirdly,[112] they reveal their carnal mind and ignorance in this, that when we say that they do not have the ban and other aspects of the order and discipline of the Holy Spirit among them, which we want to see done in their communities, some of their preachers say that we should help them establish such a ban, order, and cause. To this we answer that we are amazed (since there are so many of you preachers on earth, in fact, several hundred in the countryside and cities around here) that we find not even one, not to say several, who has established such a ban in his church—and this such a long time and years since Luther and Zwingli first rose up.

Thus we suspect, not unjustly, that the matter is neither serious nor important to them, indeed, that they lack the thing through which the apostles and apostolic bishops and pastors established it, namely the power of the Holy Spirit—as if the Spirit had lost his power, and were not as strong as in the time of the apostles. With this they make themselves suspect of not seeking the salvation of human souls, which is Jesus Christ, but rather that they seek themselves and their own interests. If they had the Holy Spirit, be they many or few, they would not need our help; there would be plenty enough for the task. The apostles were not nearly so many, and

---

112 *Codex 628* writes "thirdly" as well, but the content that follows in the codex is from the "fourth" point. The entire "third reason" is missing in the codex.

yet very soon in many places on earth they had gathered and established many true, spiritual, Christian congregations or churches, including the establishing of the ban, discipline and other spiritual ordinances.

But if the preachers do not have the Holy Spirit, which we cannot detect among them, given their fleshly speech, words, and works (which, as indicated above, they apply against the Gospel and us), then we cannot help them establish the things of the Holy Spirit. For they are not spiritual but carnal, and born according to the flesh, as indicated above in the fourth reason. Because of this nothing is more certain than that they, as persons born according to the flesh, would be totally opposed to the establishment of such spiritual things. But since they desire that we should help them establish such an order, they testify thereby that they regard us to be qualified, that is, that we have the Holy Spirit, without whom it cannot come to pass. In this manner they ignorantly pursue spiritual things.

How does this make sense, or what is their desire, when they ask for help, since at the same time they regard us as mistaken people, and censure and indeed, hate us particularly because of the Christian, apostolic order and usage by which we establish the true Christian church, ban, etc. through the Holy Spirit? That order is the proper apostolic baptism of mature persons, while they pursue the opposite with their invented baptism of infants, which is a hindrance and an inhibition to the establishment of such an order. Indeed, how are we to help them in this, since they are the ones who resist the Christian order and power in their churches and their preaching, as described above in the first reason, 1 Corinthians 14—preaching which would serve to promote improvement, gathering and establishment of a Christian congregation and order, as given by God.

Fourthly, it is also a great error and misunderstanding that some of their preachers say to those who do not want to attend their preaching—because they do not live according to the Gospel and the commandments of God—saying that even if they do not live according to it, nevertheless people are still obliged to attend their preaching, according to the words of Christ in Matthew 23[:2ff]: The scribes and Pharisees sit in Moses' seat. Therefore all that they ask you to observe, observe and do; but do not act according to their works, etc.[113]

---

[113] At this point *Codex 628* replaces a section of Bullinger's text with one of its own. We reproduce first the interpolation from *Codex 628*, in italic, followed by the text as it is found in Bullinger, in brackets below.

Concerning Separation

From this they conclude that just as the scribes and Pharisees sat on Moses's chair, and just as there was some bad leaven mixed in with the good leaven, of which the Lord warned the disciples when he said you should do everything that they tell you to observe, that now they sit on Christ's chair, even though their teaching and their actions are not upright and pure; and that in the same way one should listen to them as if they preached God's teaching, but we should not act according to their works, etc.

To this we answer, in the first place, by asking them whether they want to be considered one of the scribes and Pharisees or not. If they say yes, then they themselves must be judges and confederates of those who <441> crucified Christ, who stoned Stephen, who scourged the apostles, who persecuted the saints, and who are threatened so often with eternal woe. They may therefore rightly be terrified and fear the worst when they come before the Lord and his judgment. But if they say no, then they can prove nothing with this (Scripture) passage.

In the second place we say that to wish to apply this passage is almost an argument from similarity (argumentum a simili) *in that they observe that what it means to sit on Moses's seat is to preach and properly carry out Moses's law with his ceremonies. This is what the Pharisees and scribes did, when they left the law with its ceremonies complete and changed nothing concerning them. If, however, they added some superstitions as we read in Matthew 15[:3] and 23, they did change it and therefore they would not have been sitting in Moses's seat. In the same way now that the scribes and Pharisees sat on Moses's seat, today's (preachers) must also demonstrate that they preach and carry out Christ's Gospel, baptism, Supper, separation, and everything else properly; otherwise the argument from similarity* (argumentum a simili) *does not apply. But when this occurs one may seek the counsel of Scripture on how such human commandments are to be suffered and borne. However, we know full well that they will find nothing, etc.*

In the third place we say that as long as the scribes and Pharisees sat on Moses's seat and taught and used the law that pointed to Christ, with its legal ceremonies, as noted above, Christ at that time still directed the people and his disciples to them, <442> for the law had not yet been perfected, the perfect sacrifice that would bring an end to all figurative sacrifices had not yet been offered, the veil in the Temple had not yet been torn asunder, and the pictures and shadows had not yet been changed into the new and permanent substance. But when everything was established according to the

Scriptures and made new in Christ, he sent out his disciples with his own teaching, and not the scribes and Pharisees with the law of Moses, saying to his disciples: Go into all the world and preach the Gospel to all creatures, Mark 16, and teach them to observe all that I have commanded.

And so since there is now a new reality in and through Christ, and since Moses's people were instructed by Christ before his death, who taught them his proper law and ceremonies and sat on their seat, in the same way now, after the death of Christ, according to the New Testament, we are directed to those preachers who sit in Christ's seat to teach his word blamelessly and to use his sacraments as the Scripture teaches. But Scripture everywhere warns us about those who falsify Christ's teaching, misuse his sacraments, mislead the people, lead a wild and blameworthy life, (saying) that we should flee from them, avoid them, and separate from them, Matthew 7, John 10, Romans 16[:17-19], 2 Timothy 6 (sic), John 1. Since we have reported more than enough on how they have altered, changed, laid to waste <443> and perverted the holy sacraments and Christian and apostolic order, we wish to follow the words of the Lord Jesus Christ.[114]

[It is recorded further: They say and do not. For they bind heavy burdens that cannot be borne and lay them on people's necks, but they themselves will not move them with even one finger, etc. To this we answer: preachers who speak in this way demonstrate that they are not in Christ as the seat of grace, regarding which Romans 3[:25] and Hebrews 5 [= 4:16] speak, that they are not disciples and followers of Christ, but rather usurp the place of the Mosaic scribes and Pharisees before Christ's death, resurrection, and ascension, and the shedding abroad or sending of the Holy Spirit which had been promised; that they sit on the seat of Moses to preach the law and Mosaic compulsion and not the Gospel or evangelical freedom since Moses's seat is not a seat of evangelical preaching. Neither do those who sit upon it belong to Christ nor are they his disciples or followers. Christ gave them no commandment, nor did he send them to preach his Gospel. He did not give them his churchly power nor the Holy Spirit (who, according to John 7[:39] was not yet present), but rather commanded and gave all this to his disciples, Matthew 16[:19], 28[:19ff], Mark 16[:15], John 20[:2ff].

---

114 The text that follows, in square brackets, is found only in Bullinger's tract. It also is referring to the preachers' use of Christ's words in Matthew 23:2: Do as they say, not as they do.

Concerning Separation

Because they reveal themselves to be such Pharisees and scribes who have mounted Moses's preaching seat, being disobedient to God and not practicing what they preach, just as the seat of Moses may be ascribed to them, so also all the woe, judgment, and the rest belongs to them. They judge themselves, as the Lord pronounces upon the scribes and Pharisees in the next chapter [Matthew 23:13], saying that they are those who do not keep their own doctrine, but shut up the kingdom of heaven for others, nor do they enter themselves (which can come to pass only be keeping God's will, Matthew 7[:2]); and those who would enter, they hinder, as indicated above in the eighth reason.

Since they do all their works to be seen of people, and are denounced by the Lord himself as hypocrites, blind leaders of the blind, yes, fools, blind, serpents, beasts, full of thievery and uncleanness within, killing, crucifying, and persecuting the messengers of Christ, we do not find that Jesus anywhere commands us to attend their preaching or teaching, but said only: That which they say that you should do, etc. But we find that he commands that . . .][115] we should beware of the leaven of the Pharisees, that is, of their doctrine, Matthew 16[:6]. How can we then better beware than to not attend their preaching? And since they are blind, according to the words of the Lord, how can they as blind people show anyone the way? When one blind person leads another, they both fall into the ditch, says the Lord, and commands us to leave them alone, Matthew 15[:14], Luke 6[:39].[116]

[The Lord spoke the already cited beginning of Matthew 23 concerning Moses's seat, before his death, ascension, and the outpouring of his promised Holy Spirit. And he spoke not only to his disciples but also to all the people and the disciples without distinction, all of whom were still not redeemed and liberated from the law. In that case he did not speak to them as to Christians, or free children of God, for such a filial relationship and freedom did not yet exist, but only came to pass after his death and ascension through the holy and filial Spirit whom he sent, and through which one first is and becomes free, 2 Corinthians 3[:17].

The text says: All that they tell you to observe, observe and do that. This is to be understood as meaning "how persons were obliged to keep

---

115 At this point, Bullinger's text and *Codex 628* produce the same text again, for a few lines.
116 The following bracketed section is in Bullinger only.

the law of Moses," and not "what the Pharisees themselves commanded that was contrary to the law of God." For neither God nor Christ enjoins us to do what only human beings command us, and which God has not commanded, nor anything that is commanded that is contrary to his commandment, teaching, or law. But they preach neither the law of Moses nor the Gospel of Christ rightly. They sit neither in Moses's seat nor in the Christian seat properly, but rather mix and confuse the two—evangelical freedom and Mosaic compulsion—which cannot be done, nor can Moses and Christ be preached together. They not only mix them together, but also preach contrary to the Gospel, and suppress it, as indicated above in the first, second, and third reasons. Christians are not under the law but free from it, Romans 6[:15], 7[:4, 7], John 8[:5ff], 2 Corinthians 3[:16ff], Galatians 3[:13], 5[:18].

The Lord Christ is the end of the law to everyone who believes in him, Romans 10[:4]. For this reason Christians no longer listen to the preachers of the law who sit on Moses's seat, but rather are redirected by Paul from such preaching to the Gospel message of grace and freedom from law and sin, Colossians 2[:13ff], Galatians 3, 4, 5. For to preach the law and the things of the law to Christians is against evangelical freedom, and for this reason an action detrimental to the evangelical teaching which we have been taught. Paul bids us to avoid such destructive teaching, Romans 16[:17].

God the Father also bids us to hear his Son Jesus Christ and to obey him who proclaims only peace, grace, life and freedom from the law, death, and sin, Matthew 17[:5], Mark 9[:7], Luke 9[:35], while Moses teaches more concerning wrath, discord, judgment, death, captivity, and coercion through the law. Therefore those who sit on Moses's seat are shepherds who are strange to the lambs of Christ, to whom their voice is strange, and the lambs do not recognize (those voices) as the voice of Christ, which leads out of the legalistic, Mosaic prison, Romans 7[:6].

Therefore they do not listen to those voices but rather listen more to Christ and flee from such strange shepherds, according to the word of Christ, John 10[:5]. They are always hirelings in the employ of men, and shepherds of the sheep of Christ who were not sent by Christ, as noted above, and therefore the sheep of Christ pay them no heed. And because they do not live according to God's or Christ's commands, God has no pleasure in their teaching, as he has said: What right do you have to declare

Concerning Separation

my statutes, or take my covenant in your mouth? For you hate discipline and cast my words behind you. When you see a thief, you befriend him, and you keep company with adulterers. You give your mouth to evil and your tongue frames deceit, etc., Psalm 50[:16-19]. Such teachers are like those spoken of in Romans 2[:21], who teach others and do not teach themselves; and those who through their teaching undertake to pull a mote out of the eye of another (as becomes teachers), and they themselves have a beam in their own—for which reason Jesus calls them hypocrites, Matthew 7[:3ff].][117]

Some among such teachers, who do not obey the commandments of God and of Christ, who represent themselves as sitting in Moses's seat, also put themselves forward in another way to those who will not listen to their preaching or have no regard for it because of their manifest faults and transgressions of the Gospel. They say: But Judas Iscariot also preached as one sent of the Lord, Matthew 10[:4ff], Mark 6[:7], Luke 9[:1], even though he was a traitor, a thief, and such like.

This contention is best answered by the above answer against those who sit in Moses's seat. We believe that if Judas, at the time he preached, had shown by evil works that he was a thief or that he would betray Christ, or if his doctrine had erred from what he had been ordered to teach, as these (preachers) err regarding evangelical freedom and the like, the hearers would have paid little attention to his teaching and not amended their lives nor benefitted from it. We do not find that he erred in the preaching task assigned to him, as these preachers fail the Gospel, as noted. Furthermore, when Jesus sent him and the other apostles out to preach, he was not yet <444> a traitor; he became one only after that time. Nor is it certain that at that time he was already a thief, since they were sent out without gold, silver, or purse, and with no money to pay their way. He was called a thief only when John 12[:6], he was the keeper of the purse and in charge of what was given, when the Lord was approaching his passion, namely two days before the Passover, when he was to be betrayed and delivered to death, according to Matthew 26[:2], Mark 14[:1].[118]

---

117 *Codex 628* now begins to parallel the Bullinger text.
118 At this point, *Codex 628* no longer parallels the Bullinger text, and interpolates some eight manuscript pages unique to the codex. The bracketed section that follows concludes the discussion of Judas in Bullinger; the italicized section that will follow comes from the codex alone.

[Furthermore, at the time he was sent to preach he had not yet received the promised power of the Holy Spirit, nor had he received the apostolic commission which came only after Christ's ascension, at Pentecost. He did not wait for this commission but, devastated because of his misdeed, hanged himself before Pentecost [Acts1:15ff]. Thus if these preachers put themselves in his place, they admit that they, like that traitor, lack the Holy Spirit, the true teacher, who according to the words of Christ in John 14[:26], recalls the spoken words of Christ and guides into all truth,] *and promised by Christ to the true believers, namely when he says [John 14:16; 25-26]: I will ask the Father and he will send you another comforter who will abide with you into eternity, the Spirit of truth, which the world cannot receive, for they do not see or know the Spirit. But you, he said to his disciples and to all true Christians, do know the Spirit, and the Spirit abides with you and will be in you. I have told you this while I was with you, but the comforter, the Holy Spirit, which my Father will send* <445> *in my name, will teach you all things and remind you of what I have said.*

Likewise in John [15:26] he said: But when the comforter comes, which I will send you from the Father, the Spirit of truth which goes out from the Father, he will testify about me and you will also be witnesses. And in John 16[:7-14] he says: If I did not go away, the comforter would not come to you; but when I go away, I will send the comforter to you, and when the comforter comes, he will punish the world on account of its sin and on account of righteousness, and on account of judgment. About sin because they did not believe in me, about righteousness because I go to the Father and you will see me no more, about judgment because the prince of this world is judged. I still have much to tell you, but you are not yet able to bear it. But when that Spirit of truth comes, he will lead you into all truth, for he will not speak of himself, but will say what he has heard, and he will tell you about what is to come; he will praise me, for he will take from what is mine, and report it to you.

And after he had commanded the apostles this in Acts 1[:5-8], whom he had chosen through the Holy Spirit, as he was about to ascend into heaven and had gathered them together, he commanded them that they were not to leave Jerusalem, but rather were to await the promise of the Father which you have heard from me, for John baptized with water, but you will be baptized with the Holy Spirit not many days from now, which will come over you, and you will be my witnesses, in Jerusalem and in all the Jewish lands

Concerning Separation

and Samaria, and to the ends of the earth, etc. <446> And they received this Holy Spirit at Pentecost with full power; see Acts 2, the entire chapter, and also Acts 4, 8, 9, 10, 15, 19, and 20.

Likewise in Acts 1[:1-16], Peter told the brothers who were of the circumcision how he had proclaimed the Gospel to the gentiles and obeyed the revelation he had had from heaven concerning them, and after he had talked to them, he said, the Holy Spirit fell upon them just as it did upon us at the beginning. Here I thought of the word of the Lord, where he says: John truly baptized you with water, but you will be baptized with the Holy Spirit. But that they did not have this Holy Spirit before Christ's passion and death, the words of Christ testify, as already heard. Likewise in John 7[:37-39], where the Lord says: Whoever is thirsty, come to me and drink; for those who believe in me, as the Scripture says, living water will flow from their bodies—but this he said about the Spirit, as John the evangelist writes, whom they should receive who believed on Him, for the Holy Spirit was not yet present, he says, for Jesus had not yet been glorified, etc.

Here the lying pens of the scribal masters set forth against us, and wish to stuff such words of Christ back into our mouths, and turn them upside down, saying publicly in their slander books that we claim that no one had the Spirit of God before Pentecost. With this they do us a complete injustice; see the words and writings above, dear reader, and see if this is what we hold to and teach. We know very well that the ancients also had the Spirit of God in their measure, as <447> can be seen in the following chapters: Genesis 41, Exodus 28, Numbers 11, 24, Deuteronomy 4, 1 Kings 10, 16, 2 Kings 23, 4 Kings 2, Nehemiah 9, Psalm 50, Ezekiel 11, 37, Daniel 4, Micah 3, Haggai 2, Luke 2, 9, Acts (?—illegible), Romans 8, 1 Peter 1, 2 Peter 1, Hebrews 3.

But that they had the Spirit in the same manner, possession, power, and ability as the apostles received it, and to the same extent that the servants of the New Testament were to receive and be filled with the Spirit, is not possible, based on the words of the Lord cited above and also in the writings of the prophets. See Isaiah 32, 44, 49. And also in Ezekiel 11[:19] God spoke through the prophet: *I will put a new Spirit in your members*, etc. In the 36th chapter he says: *I will give you a new heart and spirit, and I will take the heart of stone from you.* [Ezekiel 36:26] Likewise in Ezekiel 39[:29] the Lord says: *In that time I will no longer hide my eyes from them, but will pour out my Spirit on the house of Israel.* Likewise in Isaiah 61[:1]:

The Spirit of the Lord God is with me, for the Lord has anointed me and sent me to proclaim good news to the poor, to bind up the hearts of the wounded. Likewise in Joel 2[:28]: And I will pour out my Spirit on all flesh, and your sons and daughters will prophesy, etc. And through the prophet Zechariah 12[:10] the Lord says: But I will pour out the Spirit of grace and mercy over the house of David and over the inhabitants of Jerusalem, who will mourn for me whom they had previously despised and slandered, etc.

Therefore, the children of God and believers of the New Testament must be filled and enabled with this new and gracious Spirit of Christ, of which the prophets prophesied <448> and Christ himself promised to all who believed in him. Thus Paul says in Romans 8[:9; 15-16]: *Whoever does not have the Spirit of Christ is not his*, etc. *For you have not received the spirit of slaves that you must live in fear, but rather you have received the spirit of children through which we cry out "Abba, dear Father." That same Spirit assures our spirits that we are God's children*, etc. See 1 Corinthians 2, 3, 6, 12; 2 Corinthians 1, 4, 5; Galatians 3, 4, 5; Ephesians 1, 4; Philippians 1; 2 Timothy 1; Titus 3; 1 Peter 1; 1 John 3, 4, 5; James 4; Hebrews 2, 6, 10 and still further, Matthew 10; Acts 5, 6, 7; 1 Corinthians 14; Galatians 6; Ephesians 3; 2 Corinthians 11; 1 Thessalonians 4, 5; 1 Peter 4; Revelation 5.

Therefore, these exalted masters and perverters of God's word must fight not against us, but against God the Father and with Christ Jesus his Son, who said such things through the prophets and promised the Spirit of grace to their own. Therefore we do not accept it when the worldly preachers say, as noted above, that the traitor Judas had received the gracious Spirit of Christ, and also preached and taught by that same Spirit. All of them together should not put themselves in his place and shout, but rather see whether they did not already stand there earlier, for their works, lives, and walk abundantly testify that they lack the gentle, peaceful, graceful Spirit of Christ, just as much as did Judas, and that they can truly be compared to him.

By their accusations and defamation they rob us of our honor and become responsible for our blood, for they incite worldly power <449> and people against us to persecute and kill us, Christ's innocent sheep, and so become guilty of our blood. Indeed the traitor was better than they are since he, according to Matthew 27[:3ff] felt remorse and confessed his wickedness, that he was guilty of the innocent blood of Christ. Such

Concerning Separation

remorse we do not find among these preachers, but rather they persist without shame.

We certainly know, and there are many public examples of this traitor Judas, that very few societies and assemblies here on earth can gather in such a holy fashion as to prevent Satan from sowing his seed and weeds in their midst, as the Lord Christ told us in Matthew 13[:24-30]. Therefore believers and the community of God must truly beware that Satan does not sow his seed and promote evil. There must be offence, so that the faithful may be revealed, writes Paul. We have an example in the case of Judas of how we should deal with such deceitful and hypocritical persons. For true believers and the community of God are enemies of all unrighteousness, hypocrisy, and all evil deception. Indeed, they zealously oppose these things out of love for their head (Christ), to whom they are betrothed, just as a pious husband opposes his unfaithful wife. They call upon the Almighty every day, that He protect their souls from pollution and purify and wash His community from all impurity with the water of His grace. They also train their souls to be patient and longsuffering, and keep watch over themselves not to judge in haste, not to judge leaves and flowers before their time,[119] out of suspicion, but rather they take care, following the teaching of Christ and his <450> holy apostles, to ban and exclude public sinners and miscreants from God's community.

Therefore the Lord's holy Supper is denied to them, and the body of the Lord is kept away from such godless, unclean transgressors and distinguished from their own, so that they would not be complicit in foreign sin, etc. When the community of God thus publicly punishes and keeps to God's word, it remains pure and unstained, without spot or wrinkle; but what is not perceptible is not reckoned against the community by the Lord, etc. Those who can put up a good front, and hide their sins as Judas did before the other disciples, we must leave alone until their time, and wait upon God with prayer and patience, until the

---

119 This exact theme and phrase is prominent in the first letter written by Pilgram Marpeck to the Swiss Brethren, in which he criticized their hasty judgments on the basis of only the flower, "prior to the fruit." See "Judgment and Decision" for numerous examples [Klaassen and Klassen, *Writings*, 309ff.; esp. 323, 325, 345ff]. That a "patient" Marpeckite approach to discipline (and Marpeck's own vocabulary) was circulating in Swiss Brethren manuscripts in 1590 is notable, given that six decades earlier, Marpeck had criticized the "hasty judgments" of the Swiss.

almighty brings the hidden into the light and makes it public. For it was the case with Judas that the other disciples did not know of his thievery when they sat down to Passover with him, for if they had known of his thievery at that time, they would not have patiently tolerated the person who would betray the Lord at the table.

But it was not hidden to the Lord, rather he saw in Judas' heart what he had done and what he was yet to do. Likewise today, no one can hide their sins from him, although they can hide their evil under the appearance of holiness among the children of God, but everything is exposed to God's eyes. It did no harm to the other disciples <451> that they accepted another with love in the things of God, as it indeed occurred that they had no suspicion of him (Judas) and so celebrated the Passover with him. In the same way today it does no harm to believers to share the Lord's Supper with those whose sins are hidden and unknown to them, and to partake in the outer covenant with them.

But that Christ patiently waited for this Judas, in spite of all his deceit, perfidy, evil and false heart, allowing the bloom to become fruit, does not affect the order (of discipline) of Christ and his apostles. Scripture fulfills this order with Judas, as the Lord Christ himself says in John 13[:18]: The one who ate the bread with me has lifted his heel against me. And he also saw with great longsuffering where it was going, whether Judas would reveal his sin and false heart to the community. He is the eternal wisdom, the Lord and Master over everything in heaven and on earth, who truly knows why he does everything.

But later, when he revealed such unclean members in his community, and when the community did not properly carry out the order of Christ and his apostles and punished the unrighteous, or expelled them from the community with the ban, the community was soiled by them and made unclean, and was no longer an honorable, blameless community as Paul says in Ephesians 5[:3-20; 26-27]: A community without spot or wrinkle, nor marked by anything of that sort, etc. But insofar as the matter stands only between God and such a <452> hypocrite, and the evil is hidden from the community of Christ, the community has not made itself a partaker of the sin of such a one. But if the community does not know of the sin, such persons should know without a doubt that, unless they convert with true repentance, they will not escape the judgment and sentence of God,

Concerning Separation

for Scripture must be fulfilled concerning such hypocrites, just as it was for Judas.

Therefore, someone who likens his position to that of the said traitor [or his like] *and who appeals to him* is in a sorry enough state. He has his appropriate honor and remorse; he deserves the same esteem as what is accorded to Judas, as well as all the gruesome things pronounced and prophesied upon him and his kind, according to Psalms 3[:8], 5[:6ff], 69[=70:3], 100[=101:5], Acts 1[:15ff]. Such persons can certainly not be considered successors to the apostles, since they neither live nor act as the apostles lived. *May God the heavenly Father through Jesus Christ protect and keep us from such false spirits and deceitful, incompetent workers who wish to hide and make acceptable their evil, stubborn, and godless fruit by appeal to Judas.*[120] [May God the heavenly Father through Jesus Christ keep all his true spiritual servants by the power of the Holy Spirit, that in doctrine and life they may walk in obedience to his commandments and will. May he guard them, that they not forsake the way of obedience to evangelical Christian truth through such evasive and repugnant speech, but rather by serving others as a light and an example by obedience to the Gospel, as befits their office, and that they become not darkness, offense, vexation, and derision. May God the Father grant this through Jesus Christ our Lord and Savior. Amen.][121]

There are also some preachers who, concerning all this, maintain with many arguments and with human cleverness, that even when the preacher is a godless, sinful person, who lives in the lusts of the flesh, as noted above, but yet maintains a proper teaching, then one is obliged to listen to him and to attend his preaching, for the teaching and not the life and manner of living is the fruit <453> *of which the Lord speaks in Matthew 7, etc. But just how well such an interpretation—that fruit is to be known only from the mouth—in fact corresponds with the words of Christ and the prophets any Christian with understanding can truly see where the shoe pinches such wise rabbis. Christ said: [Matthew 12:34-36] You brood of vipers, how can you speak good when you are evil? The mouth speaks of what is in the heart. A good person brings forth good out of a good treasure, and an evil person brings forth evil out of an evil treasure.*

---

120 The sentence in italics is the conclusion to this section in *Codex 628*; the bracketed sentences that follow are in Bullinger alone.

121 The following lengthy section is found in *Codex 628* alone.

This interpretation was made by the Lord Christ himself, interpreting the foregoing words he had spoken concerning fruit. Thus also Jesus ben Sirach says in [Ecclesiasticus 34:4]: Who hopes to be cleansed by someone who is unclean, or who hopes for the truth from a liar? Likewise God speaks through the prophet Jeremiah 13[:23]: Just as much as an Ethiopian can change his skin and a leopard his spots, so also may those who are accustomed to evil produce good.

Just how pure and clear your preaching is has been amply noted, and even if the truth were better presented in your preaching than it is now, yes, even if you could speak like the angels, had all faith, commanded mountains to be moved, and knew all secrets, prophesies, and predictions, yes, and gave all your possessions to the poor and your bodies to be burned, still, says Paul the apostle, it is all for naught and worth nothing, without love. But clearly he did not mean the fleshly, natural love, but rather the godly, heavenly, supernatural love which ignites a person through and through, so that the person proves the manner and presence of love <454> with good works and fruit. See 1 Corinthians 13 throughout the entire chapter, and how poorly the proposed argument of the preachers corresponds with it. For the kind of love they have and manifest, and who the father is that produces such persecuting, tyrannical goods and bloodthirsty love through them has been indicated and proven many times above, namely what spirit rules them and brings forth its work through them.

But the prophet Isaiah prophesied tellingly about such hypocrites, who completely reject the others and do not want to admit their worth. But (these others) struggle through cross and tribulation, fear God from the heart, and through the grace of God, stake their possessions and blood on the love of God. From the eyes of such people these hellcats want to remove a splinter, even though they themselves are full of evil, desolation, and uncleanness. Christ says through the prophet Isaiah [29:13]: This people comes close to me with their mouths, and honors me with their lips, but their hearts are far from me. But he says they serve him in vain, for what they teach is nothing more than human commandments. The one who is truthful, true, and is of God speaks only God's word, seeks only God's honor, a blessed increase and Christian building up of God's congregation, and the salvation of God's believers. But the one who is false and is here of his own account, seeks his own benefit, profit, and gain, along with vain honor. The one who is a

Concerning Separation

deceiver and of the world sets out eagerly to serve and please the world, and seeks the world's honor, praise, and fame, etc.

But to those whom he has himself called to his service, God the Lord himself is present. He gives them grace and Spirit as well as efficacy and power in their <455> service. For God is with them, and wishes to carry out the work of His grace through those who please Him, wait upon His calling, and are obedient to Him, etc. To the contrary, however, God the Lord is absolutely not with those whom He has not called, and does not recognize their calling. He did not elect them with grace or send them forth with Spirit and power. To their trouble and work He grants neither prosperity nor blessing, for they are not his workers and servants, since He did not call them to his work nor commanded them to do it. Rather, they set out on their own account, since God did not send them, and they speak what God did not command them to speak. Therefore such as these cannot accomplish anything in His service, since He is not with them, and He does not wish to have them in His service. What they do and attempt will come to nothing, since God does not give His blessing, prosperity, and growth to the work and the attempts of those who have not been sent.

Christ said: No one can serve two masters [Matthew 6:24; Luke 16:13]. He will either cling to one or despise the other. You cannot serve both God and mammon. Thus such prophets of the world set out to serve avarice, pride, temporal honor, their stomachs and fleshly lusts, and nevertheless wish to be called servants of Christ. But they are deceiving themselves and their listeners most foully, for no matter how much they sing and prattle about Christ, it is always the case that no one can serve two masters. And, as Paul says [Galatians 1:10], if I were pleasing to men, I would not be Christ's worker or servant. Likewise James says [James 4:4], the friendship of the world is enmity with God. Whoever wishes <456> to be a friend of the world will be God's enemy.

Note the clear distinction above, in the foreword to the preceding booklet, that depending on the part to which one subjects oneself, either the flesh or the Spirit, one becomes a servant to that part. As Paul also says, whoever wishes to be a member and servant of Christ cannot be stained with uncleanness and lust after the flesh and be a servant of sin [Romans 6]. Whoever wants the one must let the other one go. The word of the Lord stands fast: no one can serve two masters. Therefore the apostle says [1 Corinthians 6:15-16]: Should I now join the members of Christ to prostitutes? May that be far from me. Or do you not know, that whoever consorts with prostitutes is one body or member of whoredom; likewise whoever clings to images is a member of the image; whoever clings to avarice is a member of avarice.

The same applies to anger, strife, envy, hatred, swearing, blaspheming, etc. Whoever clings to arrogance is a member of arrogance, and has much in common with ambition, pride, and haughtiness, etc. Whoever clings to drunkenness is a member of the same, and the same with all the mortal sins. Here such watchmen and those who care for souls—who wish to use the seat of Moses, the traitor Judas and other evil arguments as a cover for their evil and prideful, fleshly, lustful lives and evil fruits out of season—must observe that if they are stained with these and similar vices and mortal sins, then they are not servants and members of Christ, but rather members of sin and vice in which they are found and entangled <457> and sunk into up over their ears. Neither Christ nor Paul will yield to them in this. No one can serve two masters. Whoever serves sin is a servant of sin, and a member and one body with sin.

However, it is to be feared that anyone mingling with these watchmen and those who care for souls would need a lot of candles to find one without a deadly sin, all of whom Paul excludes from the kingdom of God, 1 Corinthians 6[:9-10]; Galatians 5[:19-21]; Ephesians 5[:3-5]. See also Revelation 21[:7-8] and 22[:3-4]. The marked and stained are not allowed in, even if not all of them were involved in all mortal sins. They are a long way from measuring up to what Paul describes as the morals and properties of a true bishop and servant of God [1 Timothy 3:1ff], namely, a bishop and minister should be irreproachable, and be of upright mind, adorned with good moral conduct as a housekeeper and overseer of God, not self-willed and satisfied in himself, not given to anger, not a wine-bibber, not sharp-tongued, violent, or abusive, not a lover of shameful profit, but rather hospitable and welcoming, a lover of good things and good people, right-minded or with upright understanding, holy, pious, master of himself, eager and insistent to teach the faith. He should not only be strong in admonishing and comforting with healthy teaching, but also oppose those who contradict the faith, and expose and punish their falsity. He should be master of his own house, and have obedient, respectful and well-behaved children, courteous and with honorable manner, for whoever cannot manage his own house, how can he look after the community of God?

Concerning Separation

I fear that they lack more than a peasant's shoe[122] *to be able to measure up* <458> *to these requirements, for the entire world knows what their fruit and works are, and since they are now servants of sin, they will not be able to stand before God unless they produce the genuine fruits of repentance, etc. Christ said the servant is not above his lord and master. [John 13:16; John 15:20; Matthew 10:24; Acts 17:11] A disciple should be satisfied to be like his master, and the servant like his lord. As the world judged the master, so also will his workers be judged. They will slander and insult them, as happened also to him, etc.*

But now the situation and reality of the aforementioned prophets and guardians in the world is much better, honorable, and advantageous than it was for Christ and his apostles; the world regards them more highly and they are much better accepted than Christ, as cannot be denied. And so it follows that, either they are not Christ's servants or else Christ must have spoken poorly and untruthfully, and also Paul and James must not have written truthfully, as noted above. See Matthew 10[:24], Luke 6[:40], John 15[:20], Galatians 1[:10], James 4[:4]. But since Christ cannot lie, and also his holy apostles spoke and wrote the truth, which must endure for eternity, so it must certainly follow that the prophets who are beloved by the world, and rewarded with temporal goods and great benefices, and raised up high, and called by the world gracious, wise, and highly-learned gentlemen, are not Christ's workers and servants. There is no other possible conclusion, for the word <459> *of Christ and his apostles stands fast, and does not allow itself to be twisted and glossed.*

For Christ was poor, miserable, despised, and killed here on earth. But the noble and gracious lords are against him—these people who while their lives away in beautiful palaces, in expensive, beautiful, well-appointed houses, and who pass their time with carousing and debauchery, and speak and prattle about the cross and the poverty of Christ. Nevertheless they want to be considered servants and workers of Christ. Oh no! Christ does not allow such well-born, soft, delicate, lusty and smooth gracious lords in his court, people who go about in expensive furs, long robes and sheeps' clothing. Such servants are too expensive for him; they must seek and have another master than Christ, or put on another pelt and change into another skin. Indeed, they must accept another order and rule if they wish to serve him.

---

122 This appears to be a colloquial saying, its meaning now unclear: *es fäle mehr dann ein pawrenshuch.*

For truly, he does not recognize such people as his servants; they are better suited to serve the lords of this world, in their delicate, lusty beings, rather than the Lord Christ. Such libertines well please these same lords, who increase their weight so they will be fat enough for the day of slaughter. Even by natural human reasoning it is not fitting that the servant is better off than his lord. Note the situation and reality of the apostles, as has been noted in the foregoing booklet, in the preface. Likewise, one finds that all pious servants of God followed after their Lord through cross and suffering, <460> and fared no better than did their Lord and Master.

All who seek to secure their earthly living and possessions in the service of the church are not apostles of God, but rather preachers of their appetites and false apostles, as the highly learned themselves indicate and testify. The majority of them are such as have to do with their stomachs and worldly honor, as is well known and the whole world must accept as true. For were no church living involved, the majority of them would just as soon curse the little sheep and flock as preach to them and bless them—would to God this would cease. The majority of them—please God, not all—take more care to maintain their church livings cleanly and properly than to see that they themselves and their congregations live and conduct themselves properly.

Therefore numerous disputations and proofs are not necessary to demonstrate that they are not sent by God, but rather sent forth by themselves and the world. One needs to do no more than to note their own books and writings, especially those they published at the beginning, and contrast their present lives, actions and what they permit, for they go together as well as black goes with white. Indeed, they have already been judged by their own writings which witness to and overcome them as unfaithful guardians and prophets, as already noted sufficiently. No other judge is needed for those who are judged already by their own words, etc. In this same way the powerful fighter Goliath was killed with his own sword <461> and the evil, lazy and worthless servant was judged and sentenced by his own mouth, so that the saying of Christ would be fulfilled always, where he says: You will be judged by your own words and condemned by them. See, in this way lies betray themselves, and the godless judge themselves without realizing it, and are caught in their own cords and nets, etc.[123]

---

123 The following bracketed section does not appear in *Codex 628*. Its placement here is arbitrary, but it is part of the series of concluding paragraphs in Bullinger's text.

Concerning Separation

[And since such teachers lack the Holy Spirit, the Spirit of grace, of Christ himself, and because of this lack they find it impossible to observe God's will and commandment according to Romans 6[:12ff] and John 15[:10], they easily influence others to also walk in such disobedience, saying that no one is able to comply with the Gospel and the commandments of God, to obey them and keep them; nor in accordance with the ordinance and teaching, to believe in Christ and to die to sin. For this they especially hate us, seeing that we seek to live without sin, etc. These words we have already answered adequately in a special booklet.[124] Their speech and slander leads not to the amendment and salvation of persons and their souls but to their perdition, and is thus a grave and harmful error and deception. According to such reasoning no one would be saved, if it were to mean that no one is able to keep [the Gospel commandments]. For according to Mark 16[:16] one can be saved only by faith, and only by observing the will and the commandments of God can one enter the kingdom of heaven and eternal life, Matthew 7[:21], 19[:16ff], while those who transgress and do not abide in the teaching of Christ have no God, 2 John 1[:9].

And so their preaching and teaching is idle, vain, and futile, while the whole evangelical Scriptures, which testify that the apostles and others believed accordingly, Romans 5[:1ff], 6[:1ff], 2 Corinthians 4[:1ff], Galatians 2[:19ff], 3[:26ff], Colossians 2[:6ff], 1 Peter 1[:8], are thus made into lies. To say that they have kept God's commandments is to say that they have walked in his love, 2 Corinthians 12[:9ff], Colossians 1[:3ff], 2[:6ff], 1 Thessalonians 2[:10ff], 3[:6], Philemon 1[:5], 1 Peter 1[:13ff], 2 Thessalonians 1[:3ff], Ephesians 1[:3ff], 1 John 3[:18], 2 John 1[:4], Revelation 14[:13];[125] that they have died to sin or have put off the sinful body of the flesh or subjected it to the fire of judgment, Romans 6[:1ff], Colossians 2[:11]. Thereby they also accuse the Lord of falsehood, for he said that all things are possible to them who believe, Mark 9[:23], and to those who believe nothing will be impossible, Matthew 17[:20]. May almighty God keep us and all the devout to the very end from such preachers and teachers. Amen.][126]

---

124 This booklet is not extant.
125 This list of scriptural references follows Fast's critical edition, QGTS, II, 164, rather than the list found in the Peachey and Peachey translation.
126 The following in *Codex 628* only.

These [false] prophets reproach us and cry out about us publicly and often to their hearers that when the high priests asked him about his disciples and his teaching, Christ answered [John 18:20-21]: I have freely and publicly spoken before the world. I have always taught in the synagogue and in the temple where all the Jews gathered, and have taught nothing in secret.[127] *But we, on the other hand, sneak around in the hidden places, in the woods and barns. Why do we not stand up and move among the people, and preach openly, etc.?*

To this we answer that, in our simple understanding we know well and have no doubt whatsoever that the Lord Jesus did not answer properly and fully to the godless priest Annas, for concerning his disciples he gave little answer since they had left him, but concerning his teaching he answered, I spoke freely before the world, etc. and said nothing in private. Why do you ask me about it? Ask those who heard what I said to them; they certainly know what I said. And here the Lord was not willing to throw the kingdom and his pearls <462> before these dogs and swine, to testify much about his teaching, or to expound, explain and interpret for them the word of God and the prophecies of the patriarch Moses and the prophets who prophesied about him. Rather, they were simply to ask those who had heard him speak, what he had said to them, for he well knew that his pure and clear teaching could not be charged with any error by anyone.

And so when he taught by the shore of the sea, in the desert, on the mountain, or privately in houses and in other hidden places, he taught nothing that he dared not teach openly, and he was in no way ashamed of his teaching. For he himself was the fountain of truth and blessed, highly praised king, high priest, and Son of the living God. Through his teaching the figurative priesthood, shadows, ceremonies, and bloody sacrament of the law of the priests was to cease and the error and deception of the priests be revealed. He went into the temple publicly and taught and preached there, and also proved his teaching with Holy Scripture and divine miracles and signs, that he was the true Messiah and Savior of the world, in whom alone all might find salvation, and as true God he certainly knew that no hand would be laid on him until his time was fulfilled.

Thus also the apostles, in the beginning in Jerusalem, taught publicly and preached in the temple, in the name of Jesus healed the lame man at

---

127 *inn winckel*: in the corner. Anabaptists were often accused of being "Winkelprediger" or "corner preachers."

Concerning Separation

Solomon's gate, <463> publicly before the people, [Acts 3:1-10; 4:3] until the false priests and scribes became angry at them, arrested them, had them beaten with rods, stoned Saint Stephen, and also had Saint James executed and put to death by the sword under Herod, because of their envy and hate. The suffering became so great at that time that they no longer went publicly to the temple, since their public preaching and teaching about Christ would not be accepted.

They also protected themselves from their enemies and gathered here and there in houses where they taught and celebrated the Lord's Supper together, in memory of Christ, as can sufficiently be found in the Acts of the Apostles. Therefore they were accused as the Sect of the Nazarene by the scribes, and the scribes of this world see to it that this label is carried until this very day, even to the end of the world, by the disciples and followers of Christ, as noted. For the world will never lack for such scribes, until we all together receive our reward according to how well we have studied, and we prove our learning in the power and deeds through Christ, following the model of our forerunner who blazed for us the way to eternal life.[128]

[Likewise some of them say, according to their carnal understanding, that they are authorized to compel us to attend preaching by worldly, human force, according to the words of Christ where he says "Compel them to come in," Luke 14[:23]. We answer: the Lord indeed said to his servant in the Spirit "Compel them to come in," but he does not say that he should constrain them by worldly might or the sword, or that his armed officers should pursue those who do not heed the call. Rather he says rightly, "Compel them to come in." Thereby observe carefully: under no circumstances can this word be taken to mean worldly force or bodily coercion, for the statement "Compel them to come in" has various meanings. It means a beckoning or constraint without such force in the manner of Genesis 19[:4]: And he pressed upon them greatly; and they turned unto him. . . ." Thus also Luke 24[:29], "But they constrained him, saying, Abide with us. . . ." Again Acts 16[:15] concerning the seller of purple, "And she constrained us." This is constraint by good words, just as the apostles, according to their writings and epistles, brought the people to the obedience of the faith rather by good words, namely the words of God. Therefore the preachers cannot prove the opposite from the words of

---

128 The following bracketed paragraph is found in Bullinger only. Its placement in the text follows roughly the order of concluding ideas.

the ruler in Luke 14[:23] to mean constraint by the worldly sword, service or servants, for he speaks to the servant who holds a spiritual office, and cannot be taken as a worldly servant or coercer. Otherwise, what would become of the Scriptures that speak of free and voluntary service, that God is pleased only with such service, and not the service that is forced, 2 Corinthians 8[:3ff], 9[:7], 1 Peter 5[:2].]

The scripturally learned scribes of this world cry out, as noted above, to the true witnesses of God, Why they don't go openly into the temple, if they have a case that is honorable, clear, and grounded in God's word? To this we answer that truly the hearts of all pious servants of Christ desire the healing and salvation of many people, <464> *and are disposed to proclaim the truth to all hearts that are hungry, thirsty, and yearning for righteousness. Yes, not only to proclaim, but also where need be, to risk their lives for them, which is something no false prophet can manage. But wherever they do not want to hear or accept this clear, pure truth which cannot abide any planting by any human being, but rather persecute the same, then shake the dust from your shoes and depart from them, and don't impose this sacred thing on anyone by force, following the teaching of their master. Rather with prudence and humility they will guard themselves from their persecutors and enemies, as the Lord says, guard yourselves from men; when they persecute you in one city, flee to another, Matthew 10[:23].*[129]

We can easily figure out why such prophets challenge us this way, and it certainly is not out of love. For when we appear in their church or congregation and wish to speak of the salvation of souls, as has happened often to true witnesses who have allowed their blood to be shed because of it, they were the first to cry out against us, that we should be silent, and [then they] bring persecution and sorrow on us. The point is that they speak such words only to have reason to persecute us with force. How can they be in earnest when, as is shown in <465> the first reason above, they resist us in their congregation, not permitting us to speak openly according to the practice and custom of the Christian apostolic churches? But we will not fail to do so nonetheless, when it pleases God and when he moves through his Spirit. But not at the urging or request of the opponents, but

---

129 The paragraph that follows is the concluding paragraph in Bullinger's tract; it is matched closely in *Codex 628*, although the codex adds yet more material following.

rather only where and when the Holy Spirit calls and urges us to that end. Amen.[130]

In conclusion, we beg the Christian reader not to investigate whether this work is artfully done and how well it is written, as is the custom among the highly learned orators and on which the learned teachers place so much importance. It is to be feared that often they do not use their art and human wisdom enough, and they miss the truth, leaving the right, true, godly foundation behind. Rather look much more to the clear and simple godly truth which you will find established herein. And although the things necessary to our healing and salvation are often reported in this writing, don't be frustrated, for when we examine the Scriptures we find in many places that powerful and necessary things are often reported, and in many places not set forth artfully at all according to human wisdom, but rather artfully and truly set forth and ordered according to the Spirit of Christ and divine wisdom, mocking human wisdom with its simplicity. For God is more pleased with simplicity and the pure truth than with beautiful, well-crafted, human artful speaking.

Written and concluded on the 8th day of February, 1590. <466>

---

130 Here ends Bullinger's version.

XIV
Anabaptist Supplication to the Zurich Magistrates
(April 23, 1589)

Andreas Gut

Introduction

Andreas Gut was born acound 1530, probably in the parish of Ottenbach, located southwest of the city of Zurich.[1] The parish records show that in 1557 he married Margaretha Bär in Ottenbach. The records note that between 1558 and 1570 Andreas and Margaretha became parents to seven children. On the 26th of March 1570, the couple's seventh child, Jakob, was born. In a note next to the baptismal record it states that the father, Andreas Gut, "is a stubborn Anabaptist and did not desire the child to be baptized, but the child's mother, Margaretha Bär desired it."[2] By 1570, around which time Gut moved near Zwillikon in the neighboring parish of Affoltern am Albis, he had been an Anabaptist for at least seven years.

Andreas Gut first appears in the Zurich court records on November 20, 1563, when the authorities wrote to Hanns Ran, bailiff at Knonou, instructing him to place Gut under arrest.[3] It appears that this did take place and that Gut eventually was released on promises to obey the mandates.

---

1 Thanks to Dr. Hans Ulrich Pfister, archivist at the Staatsarchiv Zürich (STAZ), for providing biographical information from parish records, in a letter to the author dated November 10, 1993. See also useful information on the Gut family, including Andreas Gut and his descendants, in *Mennonite Family History* (January 1990), 27.
2 Dr. Pfister notes this information is found in the Kirchenbuch Ottenbach 1540-1623, STAZ E III 88.1.
3 STAZ EI-7-2, #108. The correspondence speaks of Andreas Gut of "Luneren." Lunneren is a valley west of Birmensdorf, in the Affoltern parish. Thanks to David Neufeld for this information.

However, in a letter dated May 8, 1564, Hanns Ran wrote to the Zurich authorities that since his arrest and release, Gut had not been obedient, nor had he been attending the local parish church. When confronted about it, Gut gave a "completely inappropriate reply" to the bailiff. Ran ends by saying that "I can conclude nothing else than that he will not comply with the promise he made."[4] Three months later, the bailiff had to report that Gut had left milords' territory, with costs unpaid. He requested instructions. In a letter to Zurich dated December 9, 1564, the bailiff noted an inventory of Gut's property, which included a house and barn, some acreage, and two cows. The question of unpaid costs was still pending, and Gut was still absent from the territory.[5]

A year and a half later the bailiff reported to Zurich on a conversation he had with Andreas Gut's wife. He had earnestly admonished her, he said, that since her husband insisted on staying with his "baptizing sect," she should no longer give him lodging or shelter and should obey milords' mandates and attend the local church. But, he reports, there had been disobedience all around on the part of both husband and wife. An archivist's note indicates that Gut was to be imprisoned again.[6] In April 1567, bailiff Ran refers to Gut's latest imprisonment in Zurich and that he was released on an oath that he would be obedient to the authorities and go to church. If he had not complied within fourteen days, he was to leave milords' territories; he was to sell his house and home (*sin huß und heim*) and if he was not able to sell it, to rent it and "leave my gracious lords' land with wife and children."[7]

With this the court records go silent for a time concerning Andreas Gut and his beleaguered family. He already had three children when his Anabaptist troubles began in 1563, and four more children had been born by 1570. Two more children were born to Gut after 1570 in the parish of Affoltern am Albis: a son Hans in 1573 and a daughter Anna in 1575 (the mother of these two children is unnamed). In 1569, Gut was spotted in Ottenbach, and it was reported that he had helped organize a large

---

4   STAZ EI-7-2, #109.
5   STAZ EI-7-2, #111.
6   STAZ EI-7-2, #116.
7   STAZ EI-7-2, #117.

Anabaptist gathering in the spring of 1572.[8] Apparently, he found a way of staying in Zurich territory and continued raising his family there, but the details are missing on how this was accomplished.

The years 1588 and 1589 brought about a crisis for the Zurich church and the magistracy.[9] In addition to the "Moravian problem," the year 1588 saw the emergence of an effort to promote religious toleration. First, a small circle of religious nonconformists was discovered in the city itself.[10] They had ceased attending Reformed church services, and instead gathered together for Bible study. This group believed religious beliefs should be tolerated, not coerced, and questioned the legitimacy of Christians bearing the sword and swearing oaths.

The first conclusion of the Zurich magistrates and preachers was that these people were Anabaptists, and they were so accused. It turned out that these nonconformists had no interest in adult baptism as such, and were inspired more by Schwenckfeldian spiritualism than by Anabaptist sectarianism: they supported an invisible "spiritual" communion, not a visible church of the baptized. Two members of this group of nonconformists, Samuel Heidegger and Balthasar Maler, wrote to the authorities appealing for religious toleration: how could the Zurich state and clergy justify coercing consciences in matters of faith, and labelling people "disobedient citizens," subjecting them to police action solely on account of their beliefs?[11]

---

8   Leu and Scheidegger, *Zürcher Täufer*, Chapter 3 [Christian Scheidegger], "Täufergemeinden, hutterische Missionare und schwenckfeldische Nonkonformisten bis 1600," 126, n. 35.

9   For the following, see Leu and Scheidegger, *Zürcher Täufer*, 117-64, esp. 144ff.

10 For details about this group, see Christian Scheidegger, "Wahrheit und Subjektivität. Warum schwenckfeldische Nonkonformisten in Zürich 1588 gegen Glaubenszwang protestierten," in MH 31 (2008), 91-111.

11 Scheidegger, "Wahrheit und Subjektivität," 97-98. Arguments for toleration in "inner" matters of faith had already been put to Leo Jud by Caspar Schwenckfeld in a letter dated September 10, 1533. See C. D. Hartranft, ed., *Letters Treatises Caspar Schwenckfeld von Ossig, vol. IV, December 1530-1533* (Leipzig: Breitkopf & Härtel, 1914), Document 143, 824-43. Schwenckfeld wrote, for example: "Des glaubens halben kan man ie niemands veriagenn. Es hett sust / Christus alle phariseier aussem Judisschen Lande Terra Sancta mussen aus triben." Ibid., 833.

Supplication to the Zurich Magistrates

Antistes Johann Rudolf Stumpf and his colleagues in the clergy were thus singled out to defend their policy of demanding civil punishment of religious dissenters. They immediately called on the mayor and the city council to imprison the dissidents and punish them severely, without delay. Not attending church services and guild meetings or refusing the oath could not be tolerated in a Christian society; such practices would destroy the social fabric, the preachers argued. Insulting the preachers amounted to harming God's honor and would surely earn God's wrath. So the Zurich clergy advised the Burgomaster and councillors to follow through energetically, to punish Anabaptists and nonconformists "without mercy" and so to protect pastors and Reformed teaching: "We seek to rescue our honor!" they concluded.[12]

Most of the small group of Schwenckfeldian nonconformists managed to escape the city and avoid arrest, but more problems soon surfaced. In the same year of 1588 a lengthy writing was submitted to the mayor and city council of Zurich. It carried the title "A Simple Confession," with the subtitle "To the mayor and council of the city of Zurich, concerning the reason for the great division and disagreement among all who boast of Christ and the Holy Gospel."[13] The "Simple Confession" was an apology for Anabaptist beliefs, edited and copied virtually verbatim from a larger writing whose content mirrored the *Short, Simple Confession* which forms the first part of *Codex 628*, translated above in chapter XII.[14] The composer or composers of the abridged *Simple Confession* submitted to the Zurich authorities remain unknown; Christian Scheidegger has established that Andreas Gut had nothing directly to do with the copying of this "Simple Confession."[15] In any case, one of the central themes of the "Simple Confession" was an appeal for toleration in matters of conscience

---

12 Ibid., 99.
13 STAZ EII, #443, 121-97. The seventeenth-century historian Ottius notes the submission of this "lengthy and abundantly elaborated writing" and places it under the year 1588. Joh. Heinrico Ottius, *Annales Anabaptistici* (Basel, 1672), 179 (anno 1588). A printed edition of the "Simple Confession" is found in Leu and Scheidegger, *Zürcher Täufer*, 335-402.
14 See Snyder, "The (not-so) 'Simple Confession' of the Later Swiss Brethren," MQR 73 (October 1999), 677-722 for more on the relationship between these two manuscripts. In this article I mistakenly link Andreas Gut to the "Simple Confession," a conclusion now corrected by Scheidegger.
15 See Leu and Scheidegger, *Zürcher Täufer*, 336.

and faith, another frontal attack on the policies of uniform religious observance mandated by the Zurich magistrates and strongly promoted by the Zurich clergy.

Shortly after the submission of the "Simple Confession," in April of 1589, Gut submitted a direct appeal to the Zurich authorities for acceptance and toleration of Anabaptists, namely the *"Supplication"* translated below.[16] It is apparent that he was attempting to drive a wedge between the city preachers and the magistrates, urging the magistrates not to interfere in matters of faith, and accusing the preachers of not abiding by the norms of Christ. His *Supplication* elicited a request from the mayor and council for a reply from the city's ministers and theologians. Gut had the nerve to sign the document and so identify himself by name. He was arrested in the fall of 1589, along with other Anabaptists in Horgen—including the future martyr Hans Landis. This group eventually managed to escape prison, to the apparent indifference of the authorities.[17]

I could find no more notices in the city or court records documenting Andreas Gut's fate. We do know, however, that his youngest son Hans Gut (born in 1573) was still identified as an Anabaptist living in Zwillikon in 1594.[18] And we also know, with historical hindsight, that Gut's attempt to elicit religious toleration for Anabaptists in Zurich territories would not bear the fruit he hoped it would. The archives contain notes in which the head of the Zurich church, Antistes Johann Rudolf Stumpf, sketched out a reply to Gut's "Supplication" and Anabaptist writings in general.[19] We have translated some excerpts from these informal notes below; they are placed following the text of the *Supplication*. The comments illustrate the frustration of the Zurich clergy with the stubborn, ongoing Anabaptist appeal for political space and religious toleration. The positions

---

16 I know of no reason to doubt that he is the same "Andreas Gut" who had been in and out of Zurich's prisons in the 1560s; he would have now been approximately 60 years old.

17 Leu and Scheidegger, *Zürcher Täufer*, 152. There was no effort to track down the escapees or to punish them further. They simply returned to their homes and their lives. The next arrests came a full 19 years later, in 1608. See Barbara Bötschi-Mauz, "Täufer, Tod und Toleranz. Der Umgang der Zürcher Obrigkeit mit dem Täuferlehrer Hans Landis," in Leu and Scheidegger, *Zürcher Täufer*, 171-72.

18 STAZ EIII 3.1: Affoltern ab Albis, Pfarrbuch, 1564-1624, new page 290.

19 Stumpf's authorship is identified by Christian Scheidegger, in Leu and Scheidegger, *Zürcher Täufer*, 153.

Supplication to the Zurich Magistrates 537

and arguments sketched out in these responses reflect positions already taken by Zwingli and Bullinger, and would continue to live on in official mandates and political policies. The implementation of those policies, in systematic imprisonment and property confiscation, eventually eliminated Anabaptists from Zurich territories by the last half of the seventeenth century.[20]

---

20 See Hans Ulrich Pfister: "Die Auswanderung der Zürcher Täufer in der mitte des 17. Jahrhunderts," in Leu and Scheidegger, *Zürcher Täufer*, 247-76.

The Anabaptist Supplication in the Knonou district to their overlord, written by Andreas Gut of Affholteren, sent by lord Burgomeister Thoman to the ministers of the church and theologians, for them to judge and answer it. Wednesday the 23rd of April, in the year 1589.[21]

To you, steadfast lord [*vester Jüncker*], we desire our friendly greeting and good-willed service in all that we are able to grasp through the godly Word. Further, steadfast lord, you have requested that we appear in Knonou, even though we have not been promised peace or safe passage. This we cannot agree to, since you have issued a mandate against us as disobedient people which will lead us to imprisonment.[22] For this we have been called despisers of Christian church attendance and Christian baptism, and also people disobedient to the magistrates. Steadfast lord, it is our friendly request that you learn more about this matter and see in fact who is obedient and who is not.

As far as obedience to the magistrates is concerned, we confess that there should be an honorable magistrate as God has ordained. For this we have the testimony of Scripture in the Old and New Testaments, as it is written in the 5th book of Moses in the 17th chapter (sic)[23] [Deuteronomy 16:18-20]: "You shall appoint judges and officials throughout your tribes, in all your towns that the Lord your God is giving you, and they shall render just decisions for the people. You must not distort justice; you must not

---

21 Found in STAZ, EII, #443, 110v-14.

22 This appears to be a reference to the Mandate issued in 1550: *Christenlich Ordnung unnd satzung eines Ersamen Rats der Statt* Zürich / den *gmeinen Kilchgang und predigen / die Widertöuffer / frömmde Religion / Verbotten aberglöubig künst / Kilchenrechnungen / fyrtagen / Gottslesteren / Spilen ... etc. Getruck worden / Anno 1550.*

23 Andreas Gut did not make a mistake in pointing to the 17th chapter of Deuteronomy. He is quoting the Froschauer Bible, published in Zurich. In the Froschauer edition of 1536, the verses he cites appear as the first verses of chapter 17. In the NRSV, the verses are found in Deuteronomy 16:18-20. Gut will cite the Froschauer version throughout; we will cite the NRSV.

show partiality; and you must not accept bribes, for a bribe blinds the eyes of the wise and subverts the cause of those who are in the right. Justice, and only justice you shall pursue, so that you may live and occupy the land that the Lord your God is giving you."

Likewise in Romans, the 13th chapter [Romans 13:1-6]: "Let every person be subject to the governing authorities; for there is no authority except from God, and those authorities that exist have been instituted by God. Therefore whoever resists authority resists what God has appointed, and those who resist will incur judgment. For rulers are not a terror to good conduct but to bad. Do you wish to have no fear of the authority? Then do what is good, and you will receive its approval; for it is God's servant for your good. But if you do what is wrong, you should be afraid, for the authority does not bear the sword in vain! It is the servant of God to execute wrath on the wrongdoer. Therefore one must be subject not only because of wrath but also because of conscience. For the same reason you pay taxes, for the authorities are God's servants, busy with this very thing."

We are not writing this to you as if you did not know it before, but rather so that you truly consider in what your office consists. For you and we and all people must come before Christ's judgment seat, where all will be considered in light of people's actions. Furthermore, Paul says [Romans 13:7-10]: "Pay to all what is due them—taxes to whom taxes are due, revenue to whom revenue is due, respect to whom respect is due, honor to whom honor is due. Owe no one anything, except to love one another; for the one who loves another has fulfilled the law. The commandments, 'You shall not commit adultery; You shall not murder; You shall not steal; You shall not covet'; and any other commandment, are summed up in this word, 'Love your neighbor as yourself.' Love does no wrong to a neighbor; therefore, love is the fulfilling of the law."

So we confess now that we owe the authorities taxes and levies, customs and tolls and all external duties. But in all matters that have to do with the faith, we confess that we are to look only to our teacher Christ, and learn from him. For he taught his disciples, Matthew 10[:14-15]: "If anyone will not welcome you or listen to your words, shake off the dust from your feet as you leave that house or town. Truly I tell you, it will be more tolerable for the land of Sodom and Gomorrah on the day of judgment than for that town."

Therefore you should truly note the difference between the word of Christ and that of the preachers, and see how the two correspond to each other. For Christ commanded his own that if they were persecuted in one city, they should flee to another. So we desire now to stay with the simple words of Christ, insofar as God gives us grace. Just as Christ gave the order to his own in Matthew 18[:15-17]: "If another member of the church sins against you, go and point out the fault when the two of you are alone. If the member listens to you, you have regained that one. But if you are not listened to, take one or two others along with you, so that every word may be confirmed by the evidence of two or three witnesses. If the member refuses to listen to them, tell it to the church; and if the offender refuses to listen even to the church, let such a one be to you as a Gentile and a tax collector."

Likewise in Luke 17[:1-4]: "Jesus said to his disciples, 'Occasions for stumbling are bound to come, but woe to anyone by whom they come! It would be better for you if a millstone were hung around your neck and you were thrown into the sea than for you to cause one of these little ones to stumble. Be on your guard! If another disciple sins, you must rebuke the offender, and if there is repentance, you must forgive. And of the same person sins against you seven times a day, and turns back to you seven times and says, 'I repent,' you must forgive." It also stands written in the *Index* to the Bible, believers should ban and exclude (*ußschliessen*) all who teach or live in an evil way.[24]

Likewise you may also read what Ulrich Zwingli writes concerning the ban in his "Article Book."[25] Paul writes to the Romans, chapter 16

---

24 Beginning in 1536, the Zurich printer Froschauer added a thematic concordance (*Zeyger*) to the prefatory material of the Bible. One of the topics treated in this index was the "Ban of the Faithful." An edited version of Froschauer's index was added in 1567 to the biblical *Concordance* published and used by the Swiss beginning around 1540. See Fast and Peters, trans., *Biblical Concordance of the Swiss Brethren, 1540*, especially the "Bibliographical Introduction" by Joe A. Springer, xxiii-xxxix, esp. xxix-xxxi, and ibid., 125. Andreas Gut presumably could have had easy access either to Froschauer's original Bible index or to the edited version in the Swiss Anabaptist *Concordance*.

25 This is a reference to Zwingli's *Auslegen und Begründen der Schlußreden*, published in 1523. Articles 31 and 32 deal with the ban. Zwingli does not cite Romans 16:17-18 in that place. Gut appears to have referenced Zwingli's book, and then continued with his scriptural collection on the theme of the ban. See

Supplication to the Zurich Magistrates

[Romans 16:17-18]: "I urge you brothers and sisters, to keep an eye on those who cause dissensions and offenses, in opposition to the teaching that you have learned; avoid them. For such people do not serve our Lord Christ, but their own appetites, and by smooth talk and flattery they deceive the hearts of the simple-minded." Likewise Paul writes to the Thessalonians in the third chapter [2 Thessalonians 3[:6]: "Now we command you, beloved, in the name of our Lord Jesus Christ, to keep away from believers who are living in idleness and not according to the tradition that they received from us." He also says in another place [1 Timothy 5:19-20] "Never accept any accusation against an elder except on the evidence of two or three witnesses. As for those who persist in sin, rebuke them in the presence of all, so that the rest also may stand in fear." Note, he says "before all," not in their own houses. Likewise in the prophet Isaiah in chapter 29 [Isaiah 29:13-14], see what the Lord trusts: "The Lord said: Because these people draw near with their mouths and honor me with their lips, while their hearts are far from me, and their worship of me is a human commandment learned by rote; so I will again do amazing things with this people, shocking and amazing. The wisdom of their wise shall perish, and the discernment of the discerning shall be hidden." Likewise read in the Gospel of Matthew in the fifteenth chapter, what the Lord says further concerning human laws.

On the basis of the foregoing and for other reasons, we cannot grasp that this is what concerns you. We beseech you, steadfast lord, that you fundamentally consider the matter and have pity on our people and include us in your mercy.

Thus we confess that there should be one Christian baptism following the specifications of Christ in Mark 16, Matthew 28, and the practice of the Apostles in Acts 2 and other places.

We also confess that in the [celebration of the] Lord's Supper with bread and wine, the bread indicates a remembrance of the broken body of Christ, and the wine is a remembrance of the shed blood of Christ.

We also confess that there should be one Christian marriage that should take place out of the desire of both parties.

Further, steadfast lord, please hear our friendly request that you truly take up your office and truly see the difference between us and those of your

---

Oskar Frei, ed., *Zwingli, der Verteidiger des Glaubens*, 2. Teil, 55-76. Translation by Furcha, *Huldrych Zwingli Writings*, 226-37.

subjects who go to church but nevertheless are disobedient to the mandate milords have published [which says] that one should not blaspheme God's name either with curses or swearing, also with unrestrained eating and drinking, also with miserliness and usury and overuse, lying, and deceiving.[26] Note how it goes with each of us concerning these things.

Therefore we would earnestly admonish you that you only punish those who do evil and protect and shelter the pious, as your office calls for. For we are ready, if an error can be shown to us on the basis of the Scriptures, and willing to be instructed just as children are bound to be instructed by their fathers when they sin. But if we are not able to come to the contrary opinion in light of the Gospel, we are disposed to persist in our simplicity, as long as God gives grace. For the Lord says, whoever is not willing to set aside all he has, such a one cannot be my disciple [Luke 14:26].

We wish therefore to do what our teacher Christ advised us to do, and we are also disposed to pray to God for you and for all magistrates, that God might protect you and not forget you, that we might lead a quiet, pious, God-pleasing life in all virtue under your governance. We beseech you that you consider our simple writings in the best light and that you not be angry with us. It is simple, but we hope that it is grounded in God's commandments.

---

26 This is another reference to the *Christenlich Ordnung unnd satzung eines Ersamen Rats der Statt Zürich* ... (1550), as in note 22 above, and is a partial listing of the topics taken up in that Mandate.

Concerning the Anabaptist Supplication, drawn up and written by Andreas Gut of Zwillikon in Affolteren parish concerning the Anabaptists in the Free Territories, to his grace Heinrich Meyer from Knonou, Bailiff at Knonou, [Johann Rudolf Stumpf][27]

[Notes sketched in reply to Gut's "Supplication"]

That one should earnestly oppose the Anabaptists:

1. That the office belongs to the church preachers and the authorities.

2. That the Anabaptist sect is much more evil and harmful than people wish to acknowledge.[28]

3. That the doctrine they teach and establish contains terrible, innumerable errors, blasphemies, and soul-damning things.

4. That they oppose all Christian obedience, virtue, and external worship; that they plant all disobedience and they misuse, as a cover, the name of God, Jesus Christ, Holy Scripture, Gospel, and Word of God.

5. That their sect and seduction is against the Word of God, against the teaching of the ancient fathers such as Augustine and others who wrote against the Donatists, whose damnable error the Anabaptists brought back, or the Devil through them.

6. That they are stubborn in standing over and against all reports, dialogues and disputations in which they have been amply and sufficiently

---

27 STAZ EII, #443, 199-206: "Ad Supplicationem Anabaptistarum, die gstellt und gmacht durch Andreß Guten von Zwilligkon in der pfarr Affholttren, von wägen der teüfferen im fryenampt, an den E.V.F. Heinrichen Meyer von Knonow Lantvogt zu Knonow." Scheidegger identifies the author as Johann Rudolf Stumpf, head of the Zurich church (Antistes) at the time. Leu and Scheidegger, *Zürcher Täufer*, 152-53.
28 Thanks to David Neufeld for his reading of this partly illegible sentence.

heard. Also their book and answer, with which they were not able to defend themselves, was printed here in the city of Zurich.[29] Together with the wide-ranging and copious answers and refutations of the entire enthusiasms of their manifold errors and sect.

7. That their stubborn disruption and conflict is manifestly against the reformation from God's Word undertaken by our church, against all commonly published confessions of faith of the Evangelical church and states of the Confederacy, and against our lords' well-established, divinely grounded laws and finally, against the decisions taken by the Evangelical states (cantons) in Aarau, as decided by civic and regional preachers, July 31, 1588.[30]

8. That the Anabaptists are not to be tolerated under any Christian magistrate, prince, or lord, especially not in an Evangelical, reformed church and government.

9. That without fail, the papists and Lutherans list us with the Anabaptists and cry out against us from the chancel, in writings and so forth, for no other reason than that not only have we allowed the Anabaptists to remain among us in peace up to now, and tolerated their gatherings and secret meetings, but also for a long time many hundreds of people, as if from a flowing spring and source, the Anabaptists have come from our land and territory and traveled to Moravia. In fact, the primary leaders were born in our fatherland and come from here. So truly, no other church leaders [than we Swiss] should more truly and earnestly oppose this sect with sermons, disputations and published writings.

10. . . . [The "publicly-known" articles of the Anabaptists threaten social order]: ". . . that one should swear no oath, nor allow oneself to be bound to obedience with the oath. That although one should and must have a magistrate, nevertheless no Christian may hold such an office, for

---

29 Having a book printed in Zurich would have been remarkable indeed. It is not clear to what printing this refers.
30 Ottius copies the conclusions from this meeting under the year 1588, with the title: "Supplication totius Ministerii urbis & agri ad Magistratum Tigur. in causa Anabaptistarum d. 31 Julii." The text is in German. See Ottius, *Annales*, 180-85.

a Christian person must not kill, should also not oppose evil persons; one should not oppose enemies with defense and weapons; one should have all things in common. A Christian should have no private property. One should not kill an evildoer, who should be saved by improvement and penitential works to become perfect; they want to come to perfection, and commit no more sins; what they appear to be, speak, and do is all spirit under which appearance they defend the greatest abominations.[31]

. . . .

Listing of Anabaptist articles

That one should coerce no one to the faith.

They take it to be a misuse of power to force anyone in matters of faith, against their conscience, for the Gospel does not allow this. For Christ said, whoever wishes to follow me, and not, whoever must follow me. Likewise Matthew 10: Whoever does not accept your teaching, shake the dust off of your feet. It does not say, force them to believe. Likewise 2 Thessalonians 2: Faith is not for everyone; a gift of God cannot be coerced with human power, but rather must be granted from above; the father of the house does not want the weeds to be rooted out, as if the Anabaptists were like weeds; this "uprooting" is the work of the angels and not the magistrates.

[The following is crossed out: The learned ones always use both Testaments to provoke the magistrates against the simple truth.][32]

Nota: the Anabaptists accurately describe themselves with the shaking off of the dust. So why do they not do that, since they see and hear that neither our magistrates, or communities, nor any of us have any need of them, neither cooked nor broiled [*weder gesotten noch gebraten*]. But nevertheless over and against all commands and prohibitions, against promises, oaths, and in the place of oaths their affirmations with "yes" and "no," against all commitments and assurances, they still work their way [tinker] into the community, church, state, and land. Why do they apply the apostolic command about shaking off the dust so unashamedly against

---

31 STAZ EII, #443, 199-200.
32 Ibid., 201.

the magistrates, and then not in the least in our proper apostolic and preaching offices?

Concerning the learned ones, they load suspicion and mistrust in the most malicious way on the necks of the true servants of the church, together with refusing all learning, skill, experience in speaking, and knowledge of the Scripture. To the contrary, what must be defended is all ignorance under the appearance of simple, bare truth, and that for this reason: the Anabaptists are unlearned, uneducated, ignorant numbskulls [*unkennende und unwüssende letzkopff*]. If the gift of speech were not needful and necessary, the Holy Spirit would not have been able, by means of this gift in the apostles, to work in such a remarkable way. If experience, study, practice, and diligent investigation of the Scriptures were not necessary, why did Christ say in Matthew 13[:52]: Every scribe [*geschriftgeleerter*] is like the master of a house, who brings forth from his treasure new and old things."[33] . . . .

The Anabaptists wish to be apostles and preachers, but they are idiots. They can't read three lines of German; they cackle and squawk like laying hens and cry out against the learned ones: "Everyone has a right to speak". . . .[34]

List of the most important points drawn from the Anabaptist writings that are to be answered.
    1. That the magistrates are enraged against them,
    2. against pious, blameless people,
    3. at the instigation of the preachers.
Concerning their false claim of obedience to the magistrates
    That one may compel no one to the faith.[35]
. . . .

---

33 Ibid., 201.
34 Ibid., 202.
35 Ibid., 203.

AGAINST THE ANABAPTISTS

Concerning coercion of faith. Anabaptist objections: One should coerce no one to faith. It is a gift of God.

Answer
Anabaptism is not a true daughter of faith, therefore, it is not a gift of God. That with this basic weapon they indicate that their understanding is not the true faith. For us it is the opposite: the true faith, since it is a free gift of God, may and should not be coerced, but does this mean, therefore, that false faith, lies, seduction, error, separation, blaspheming God and the truth should not be opposed or combatted or punished?

One should not create hypocrites by using coercion.

Answer
But it is nevertheless better that evil persons must cover themselves and disobedient people must fear that they not disturb good order; that evil does not break out or openly oppose the good, not encumbering good order and honorable people. When thieves and murderers do not break out in deeds because of the fear of punishment, they are also hypocrites; even if the pious deed is done because of fear, and the person is not truly pious inside, still other innocent people are safer for it. One coerces, ties up and locks up lions, bears, wolves, enraged people [words uncertain] in order to keep the sheep safe.[36]

[There follows a section against the "holy appearance" of the Anabaptists which is crossed out.] . . . .

Now, may God keep far from us what we can expect from all this. For we have seen visible, horrifying examples not long ago in Thomas Müntzer's activities, in the terrifying and bloody Peasants' War, in the Westphalian Münsterite revolt, in the English kingdom under king Edward the sixth in Suffolk.[37]

---

36 Ibid., 204.
37 This is perhaps a reference to the wide-spread rebellions "from below" that broke out in England in 1549, during the reign of Edward VI. See Barrett L. Beer,

These and many more pressing and important reasons, all of which are too long to recount here, should properly awake and motivate to daily vigilance not only all pastors, preachers and servants of the church, but also all proper and Christian magistrates, that such unrest be faced and controlled by the state.[38]

Rebellion and Riot: Popular Disorder in England During the Reign of Edward VI (Kent, OH: Kent State University Press, 1982).

38 STAZ EII, #443, 205.

XV
A Firm Answer from the Swiss Brethren, also Called the High Germans, to the Polish [Brethren], concerning the Issue of the Incarnation and Divinity of Jesus Christ, etc.
[1592]

INTRODUCTION

At the end of the year 1590, two Polish Brethren representatives traveled to Strasbourg, where they came in contact with a Swiss Brethren congregation in the city. As a result of this contact, the Swiss Brethren there composed a letter to the Polish Brethren congregation at Schmiegel, Poland (dated May 28, 1591), wishing to know more about Polish Brethren beliefs and practice. This letter eventually came into Christoph Ostorodt's hands, and he composed a reply to the Swiss Brethren in September of that year.[1] Ostorodt's letter laid out the fundamental beliefs of the Polish Brethren church and also was intended as a further exploration about possible agreement and union between Ostorodt's group and the Swiss Brethren.[2] The "Answer from the Swiss Brethren ... concerning the Issue of the

---

1 Christoph Ostorodt (d. 1611) was a minister in the Polish Brethren church (Polish Minor Church) who made several attempts to convince different Anabaptist groups to unite with his group. Son of a Lutheran minister, he united with the Socinian Polish Minor church in 1585, and after learning Polish became minister of a large Polish Brethren church. He carried out numerous attempts to unite with Anabaptist groups. See "Ostorodt, Christoph," in ME IV, 92-93.
2 See Theodor Wotschke, "Ein dogmatische Sendschreiben des Unitariers Ostorodt," ARG 12 (1915), 137-54. Thanks to Martin Rothkegel for his bibliographical help.

Incarnation and Divinity of Jesus Christ" (1592)[3] is the reply to Ostorodt's letter and "confession," written following a meeting of Swiss Brethren leaders in Strasbourg.

Socinianism as practiced by the Polish Brethren and represented in Ostorodt's writing had strong surface similarities to Anabaptist practice: the Polish Brethren practiced adult baptism; they refused to swear oaths and upheld nonresistance, including a refusal to serve in government offices. The fruit of conversion was to be a moral and Christ-like life.[4] Socinians also opposed predestination and upheld free will. The stumbling blocks for Anabaptist groups came not so much in the practice as in the theological foundations of Socinianism. At the heart of Socinian theology was a denial of the Trinity, a denial of the divinity of Christ (he was said to have been born a man, adopted by God at the ascension), and a denial of the "satisfaction" view of the atonement. Human beings were said to possess a free will and to be able to know God through reason and natural knowledge.[5]

---

3   "Copye ende Seecker Antwoordt van de Switser broeders ofte Hooghduytschen, alsoo genoemt; Over-gegeven aende Poolsche, betreffende het punct der Menschwordinghe ende der Godheydt Jesu Christi, in *Handelinghe der Vereenigde Vlaemse en Duytsche Doopsgesinde Gemeynten, gehouden tot Haerlem anno 1649 ... met de dry confessien aldaer geapprobeert* (Vlissinghe: Geleyn Jansz, 1666), 74-81.

4   The *Mennonite Encyclopedia* contains the following description of Socinian practice: "The church is a body of believers who are converted; in it strict discipline is to be exercised according to Matthew 18:15-17. Baptism and Communion are not mysteries with sacramental overtones, but merely acts of confession. Though infant baptism was not quite abolished in the Brethren church of Poland, it was not considered strictly necessary to their salvation and baptism (by immersion) was regularly administered to adults. The Socinians were opposed to taking oaths for the same reasons as the Mennonites. One of their principles was also nonresistance; the members of the Brethren church did not take military service and also refused to take government offices." "Much stress is laid upon Christ as a moral teacher; as such, men should be His disciples and followers." Socinianism, ME IV, 566.

5   Socinianism, ME IV, 565-69. As explained by George Williams, "Socinus sought to construct a complete Christian theology on the basis of Jesus as the Virgin-born Christ, otherwise totally human, dispensing with any received claims that presupposed Christ's essential deity. The very Word and Will of God appeared in flesh—in a human being. After his death and resurrection, Christ ascended to take a place at the right hand of God, in his transfigured glorified human nature,

Perhaps not surprisingly, in light of the many similarities in practice between the groups, the Polish Brethren were drawn to Anabaptist groups and pursued numerous talks in the interests of union with them. Polish Brethren representatives had already approached the Hutterites in Moravia around 1567,[6] and later had extended conversations with the Mennonites in the Netherlands and in Danzig and the Vistula Delta.[7] The 1592 Swiss Brethren "Answer" to Ostorodt's letter documents the one known attempt by the Polish Brethren to reach agreement with the Swiss Brethren. As is seen in the "Answer," however, the Swiss Brethren made short work of any talk of unity, making it clear that the dogmatic points of difference between the two would not be overcome.

The Hutterite *Chronicle* contains an account of several repeated visits to Moravia by Polish Brethren representatives beginning in 1569, based on what looked like promising similarities and an interest by the Polish Brethren in community of goods.[8] A visit from a second delegation in early 1570 led to dogmatic discussions, with the Trinity and Christology at the center. The *Chronicle* reports that

---

namely, as he on whom God Almighty bestowed co-regency, the governance of the world, in cosmic vindication of the righteousness of his Suffering Servant as his final Prophet. Socinus was thus able to assert that Christ, though wholly human, is nevertheless *verus Deus* because the Father shared his power with him at the Ascension (Acts 13:33), and, at this moment, assigned to Christ an adoptive deity as co-regent." George H. Williams, *The Radical Reformation*, third revised edition (Kirksville, MO: Sixteenth Century Journal Publishers, 1992), 985.

6   See Leonard Gross, *The Golden Years of the Hutterites*, revised edition (Kitchener, ON: Pandora Press, 1998), 157-71 for a good account of the Hutterite encounter with the Polish Brethren. Also Robert Friedmann, "The Encounter of Anabaptists and Mennonites with Anti-Trinitarianism," MQR 22 (July 1948), 139-62.

7   C. J. Dyck, "Hans de Ries en het Socinianisme," *Doopsgezinde Bijdragen* 8 (1982), 18-32. Thanks to Martin Rothkegel for this reference.

8   As described by Friedmann, "these Polish Brethren were rather strict, lived puritanically, practiced adult baptism and frequent communion services, accepted nonresistance, considered the introduction of community of goods...." Friedmann, "Encounter," 155. The Hutterite *Chronicle* notes the "fervent seeking for truth" that arose in Poland in 1569, in which "They gave up the unscriptural, ungodly baptism of infants ... teaching that baptism was for those who believed the Word of God." 410. The account describes a Hutterite delegation to Poland and the return of four young Polish Brethren who "stayed through the winter" with the Hutterites, but were described as "wordly wise" and not ready to submit "to serving the poor and crucified Christ." 411.

When we came to the article in which we confess to God the Father, the Son, and the Holy Spirit, they rejected our printed confession of faith because they were unable to grasp parts of it. A few of them wanted these passages revised, which we refused to do.... At this point God stopped us. He made us change our direction and put an end to further talks for the time being."[9]

The Polish Brethren sent another delegation to the Hutterites, but nothing came of this visit, following which Peter Walpot composed a long letter urging the Brethren to convert to the true way of the "life and discipline of the Lord's church."[10] In 1571 he wrote a further lengthy letter directly to Simon Ronemberg in Kraków, closing the door on any further talk of unity: "We cannot acknowledge you as a people of God or as brothers," he wrote.[11] Walpot did not revisit Trinitarian or Christological questions in his final letter; rather he focused on the refusal by the Polish Brethren to "submit" to the proper way of life.[12]

The Mennonite and Doopsgezind encounter with Anti-trinitarianism in the Netherlands and the Vistula Delta (particularly in Danzig) both pre-dated and extended well past the Hutterite and Swiss Brethren experiences. Already in 1547 Menno Simons had banned Adam Pastor for his anti-trinitarian convictions; these, however, were unrelated to Socinianism as such. In 1598 Christoph Ostorodt and a fellow Polish Brethren representative visited the Netherlands and held conversations with Mennonite leaders Pieter Jans Twisck and Jacques Outerman and the Waterlander Hans de Ries. These conversations yielded no fruit, and the Socinian representatives did not stay long, since they were banished from the land and left by 1599.[13] Socinian ideas, however, did make headway in

---

9 Hutterite *Chronicle*, 412.
10 Ibid., 414.
11 Ibid., 422. Walpot's letter is found on 415-26.
12 Ostorodt's letter to the Swiss Brethren notes that in the previous year (1590) two Polish Brethren visited two Hutterite settlements, but that there had been no answer to the confession of faith they had left with the Hutterites. Wotschke, "Sendschreiben," 153. A contact around 1608-9 was reported by John Amos Comenius of the Bohemian Brethren. "The outcome, writes Comenius, was the same as with all earlier visits. The Brethren kept strictly to the doctrine of the Trinity and called the Socinians 'heathen' with whom they did not wish to have anything in common." Friedmann, "Encounter," 159.
13 "Ostorodt, Christoph" in ME IV, 92.

the Netherlands in the seventeenth and eighteenth century among such groups as the Remonstrants and Collegiants. The conservative Mennonites rejected Socinianism out of hand, and held to "Trinitarianism and the deity and satisfaction of Christ"; the Waterlanders, the Flemish, and the Lamists were more open to some Socinian ideas. Historians conclude, however, that "as a whole, Socinianism was never accepted by the Mennonites."[14]

The bulk of the "Confession" that Ostorodt composed for the Swiss Brethren is taken up with biblical and rational arguments opposing a Trinitarian view and supporting the existence of only one true God, as well as explaining the person and the work of Christ, again with copious biblical references and interpretations. The personhood of the Holy Spirit is dispatched with in short order, by comparison, and the writing concludes with a brief discussion of baptism (which was practiced by immersion), the ban, the commemorative practice of the Lord's Supper, and the nature of the church, the latter of which sounds much like a description of a Swiss Brethren congregation.[15] In their reply, the Swiss Brethren do not take up questions of church practice, focusing instead on the dogmatic issues concerning the Trinity, the Incarnation, and the atonement.

Ostorodt makes some interesting references to the Mennonites in his letter, suggesting hypocritical practice on their part. He also suggests that the Swiss Brethren had joined with the Mennonites; perhaps he knew of the agreement reached in 1591 between High German and Frisian representatives, which led to the so-called "Concept of Cologne."[16] Ostorodt was not impressed. The Mennonites, he says, "with whom you

---

14   "Socinianism," ME IV, 567. See this article for more details about the Mennonites and Socinians in the Vistula Delta and the Netherlands in the 17th and 18th centuries. Noting that Ostorodt's attempts ended in failure, Friedmann states that "It was not until the late 17th century, when the Polish Brethren were expelled from their home country and were thereupon kindly received in the Netherlands, that closer ties developed between them and Mennonites." Ibid., 569.

15   Ostorodt wrote: "In die Gesellschaft nemen wir niemands auf, er müsse dann vor getauffet sein, ablassen vom Bösen vnd das Gutte thun, nicht nach dem Fleische, sondern nach dem Geiste leben, nicht allein die Brueder, sondern auch die Feinde lieben, dulden, leiden Gewalt vnd Unrecht, Krieg, Haderschafft faren lassen, ja nicht allein nicht thuen, sondern auch kein Ursach oder Hilff darzuthuen." Wotschke, "Sendschreiben," 152.

16   English translation of the "Concept of Cologne" in Karl Koop, ed., *Confessions of Faith in the Anabaptist Tradition, 1527-1660* (Kitchener, ON: Pandora Press: 2006), 115-22.

have united," do not want to be prideful people themselves, but they have no problem making prideful clothing for others, painting works of art for others, making guns and other things that enable others to sin.[17] Along with the reprehensible Mennonite tendency to encourage pride, miserliness, and usury, Ostorodt hoped that the Swiss Brethren would also take care to avoid the "amazing disorder" of banning and separating that characterized the Mennonites. Ostorodt apparently had some first-hand experience with Mennonites and had already formed some negative opinions about their practice.[18] By 1598 he would be in the Netherlands, in conversation with Mennonite leaders.

The "Answer from the Swiss Brethren" reproduced here exists only in a Dutch translation from an original high German autograph. The Swiss Brethren Answer is found in the third edition of a collection of documents that originally contained the minutes ("Proceedings" or *Handelinge*) of meetings of Mennonite congregations in Haarlem, in June 1649.[19] The 1666 edition of these proceedings, published by Geleyn Jansz, adds several documents to the collection and reproduces, as its fifth discrete document, the "copy" of the Swiss Brethren Answer translated below.[20] Perhaps encounters of the Dutch Mennonites with Socinianism in the

---

17 "... nicht wenig irren die Mennoniten, mitt welchen ir euch vereiniget habt, die selbst nicht wollen hoffertig gehen, vnd machen doch, anderen hoffertige Kleider, malen die Bilder, machen Büchsen vnd dergleichen Dinge mehr, die die Welt zur Wollust vnd Hoffart ires Lebens haben wil." Wotschke, "Sendschreiben," 152.

18 "Wolt Gott, daß ir vnd sie auch weret so fürsichtig gewesen in dem, eh ir euch zu den Mennoniten geschlagen habet, bei welchen noch viel grober Mengel sein (es sei denn, daß sie es ytzo wollen abstehen) als Hülff zur Hoffart, Geitz, Wucher, ein wunderliche Verwirrung des vilen Bannens vnd Scheidens vndt daß sie auch getruncken haben vom Geist des Antichrists, daß, so bald man ettwas so nicht verstehet wie ire Lehrer, so muß er gebannen sein, wie daß denn etzliche vnserer lieben Brueder, die zuvor bei inen sein gewesen, wol sein inne geworden." Ibid., 154.

19 The "Proceedings of the Baptism-Minded [*Doopsgesinde*] called the United Flemish and German communities, held at Haarlem, June, 1649" (*Handelinghe der Doopsgesinde, ghenaemt de Vereenigde Vlaamsche en Duytsche Gemeynte, gehouden tot Haerlem anno 1649 met de dry confessien aldaer geapprobeert*) were published in three editions: n.p., 1649; Amsterdam, 1664; and Vlissingen, 1666.

20 See Nanne van der Zijp, "Handelinghe der Doopsgesinde." Global Anabaptist Mennonite Encyclopedia Online, 1956. Accessed November 11, 2016: http://gameo.org/index.php?title=Handelinghe_der_Doopsgesinde&oldid=107875.

seventeenth century gave a contemporary relevance to this earlier Swiss Brethren Answer to the Polish Brethren that led to its being printed. No other version of this document is known to exist.

At the end of the Swiss Brethren Answer we read: "Written in the gathering of elders and ministers from many lands in the year one thousand, five hundred, and ninety-two, in Strasbourg." And further, "signed by hand and translated from Rauf-bits's [Bisch's] own handwritten copy from high German to low German." As it happens, Rauff Bisch is known to us as one of the primary spokesmen for the Swiss Brethren Anabaptist group that debated the Reformed at Frankenthal in the Palatinate in 1571.[21] The fact that the Swiss Brethren Answer of 1592 was written in Bisch's hand points to his involvement in this dogmatic discussion two decades later, and also permits us to look back to Rauff Bisch's documented answers in 1571 for precedents in the biblical argument. The text below will note some of these precedents at the appropriate places.

---

21 A 1571 report from Ulrich Cubicularius, superintendent at Pfaffenhofen, states that Bisch had worked as a scribe in the Heidelberg chancery. QGT IV, 192, line 13.

A Firm Answer from the Swiss Brethren, also called the High Germans, to the Polish [Brethren], concerning the Issue of the Incarnation and Divinity of Jesus Christ, etc. [1592]

All the many beloved men who are concerned about these articles: we have read and understand your written confession,[22] but it does not agree with ours, nor [does it], which is much more troubling, agree with our understanding of Scripture. Nevertheless, we do not wish to quarrel with your understanding, but simply to set out the biblical foundation of our Confession and pray you will consider the following in the fear of God, without reliance on human wisdom, but with reference to the Wisdom of Solomon 9[:13ff] where it says: "For what man can learn the counsel of God? Or who can discern what the Lord wills? ... We can barely understand what happens on earth, and what is at hand we find with labor. Who then can trace out what is in the heavens?" etc.[23]

In the first place we believe and confess: That the Word was in the beginning, and did not "become" in Mary; that through the Word heaven and what is in it, the earth and what is upon it, and also human beings were created and made.[24] We teach and believe that without the Word

---

22 This is Christoph Ostorodt's letter "To the Elders and Servants and the entire community in Strasbourg, Alsace, who are called High Germans or Swiss Brethren," 1591. The letter is found in Wotschke, "Sendschreiben," 137-54.

23 The appeal to leave such "high matters" to God recalls the earlier Swiss Brethren approach to incarnational matters in discussions with the Reformed and the Mennonites, namely that the issue was "too high" for human capacities, and that believers were better served by being good disciples rather than speculating about such things. See Chapter V, above. The text from the Wisdom of Solomon is being recycled. At the Frankenthal Disputation in 1571, Rauff Bisch refused to go beyond Scripture in discussing the Trinity, citing chapter 9 of the Wisdom of Solomon. See Frankenthal *Protocol*, 123, under "Rauff. 33."

24 Here the Brethren reject a central Polish Brethren dogma. Ostorodt begins by confessing God, maker of heaven and earth, father of Jesus Christ, God who is greater than all and above all "ja auch grösser denn sein Son, der H. Jesus ..." (truly greater than his son, the blessed Jesus). After spending many pages arguing the point biblically, he concludes: "By these points (arguments) it is

Answer from the Swiss Brethren to the Polish Brethren

nothing was made that has been made, as the Scriptures say, John 1[:1-3] and Hebrews 11[:3]: "By faith we understand that the world and all that is in it was created from nothing through God's Word."[25] This Word is not a spoken Word, as when God said 'Let there be light, and it was light.' We confess, rather, that he was the Word that in the beginning was with God and was God himself. That same Word which is above all human understanding, ingenuity, or philosophy, and above all human arguments, thanks to eternal providence became flesh in Mary through the Holy Spirit and illumination of the Most High. It had not been flesh before, as is abundantly clear in the message of the angels and the birth of Christ spoken of in your Confession.[26] We are satisfied with this [biblical account] with respect to the birth out of the Virgin Mary.[27] It is thus unnecessary to write extensively about that.

We therefore confess and teach with the witness of Scripture: that this Jesus Christ, visible and invisible, moved and unmoved, is God's first-born and only Son, the first-born of all creatures.[28] Yes, he is before everything, and everything exists in him,[29] which the Scriptures unreservedly,

---

strongly proven, that Christ the Lord is not the same as the Father, namely the creator of heaven and earth." ("Aus disen Puncten wirt auch krefftiglich bewiesen, daß Christus der Herr nicht derselbige sey, der der Vater ist, nemlich der Schöpfer Himmels vnd der Erden.") Wotschke, "Sendschreiben," 145.

25 Ostorodt argued that God alone created heaven and earth, but through Christ the "new creation" was accomplished. "Denn Gott hatt Himmel vnd Erden allein one alle Gehülffen geschaffen, aber die newe Welt durch Christum." Ibid., 147. The Swiss Brethren rejected this interpretation.

26 The text has "Vleysch geworden ende niet gheweest," that is, become flesh which it had not been before.

27 "der Jonck-vrouwe Maria." Elsewhere the Dutch copy uses the word "Maghet" for "virgin." See *Handelinge*, 75; 76. At the Frankenthal Disputation, Rauff Bisch denied the implication that Jesus had a beginning in Mary, "Sonder wie Paulus zun Ebreern meldet / Daß Christus gestern / heut / und inn ewigkeit sey." This seems to be a reference to Hebrews 11:3, repeated in the 1592 "Answer." Frankenthal *Protocol*, 127.

28 The text says "Eerste gheboren ende Eygen gheboren Soon." "Eygen" appears to be a misprint for "einig."

29 Here the Swiss Brethren argue the orthodox understanding of the pre-existence of the Word, John 1. Ostorodt argued the Socinian position that Christ did not pre-exist before his conception through the Holy Spirit in Mary. In spite of that miraculous conception and birth, Ostorodt says, Scripture says nowhere that Jesus was born out of God's substance or essence. Wotschke, "Sendschreiben," 142.

conceivably and inconceivably, confesses with us. We thus read in 1 John 1[:1] where he writes, "We declare to you what was from the beginning, what we have heard, what we have seen with our eyes, what we have looked at and touched with our hands, concerning the word of life," etc. He writes further, "therefore we confess and proclaim that this eternal life, which was with the Father has appeared," etc.

This is the irrefutable witness of the Holy Spirit that will bring to shame all masters of high human understanding. Here human reason must become quiet, remove the shoes of its understanding, and proceed barefoot by faith. For the place is holy and above human understanding, since a human being cannot taste of the Spirit of God.[30]

The fact that Scripture makes it appear as if it speaks only of the Word, and only secondarily of Christ's humanity, should not lead you to believe that Scripture confesses two Sons. This thought is not drawn from the faith of Scripture but from human understanding. What can be concluded by human understanding is not faith but a kind of natural knowledge which we must evaluate by faith, in the realization that divine things and wonders are too high for human understanding. As he [Christ] says: "Before Abraham was, I am" [John 8:57-58]. Abraham saw him and rejoiced, though he was not yet fifty years old, and Abraham is long dead. Paul said in Romans 1[:1-4]: "Who is born of the seed of David, according to the flesh, etc." yet not as Solomon, but from Mary according to the promise to Abraham and David that descendants would be given to them. This [text] strongly confirms a single Son of God after the Spirit. These are not two sons.

But we confess and witness to the one Son of God, which is also called Mary's son and the Son of man, and that therefore he was conceived, born and nurtured of Mary, but not that he was her natural son in the same way as other children are conceived and born. She remained a pure virgin [or maiden], Isaiah 7[:14].[31] We have no scripture that she did not remain a virgin. Surely it was not impossible for him, who created heaven and earth without material from which to make it, to keep his promise that a virgin

---

30 Here again the rationalistic approach of the Polish Brethren is explicitly rejected, in favor of simple "faith."

31 "een onverfwackte Maget gebleven." The Biestkens Bible translates Isaiah 7:14 as "Siet, Een *maecht* is beurucht, ende sal eenen Soon baren, dien sal sy Immanuel noemen." The Greek text has "a virgin"; the Vulgate "virgo"; the Froschauer Bible (1536) has "ein magdt"; Luther's Bible has "die Jungfrau."

would bear [a child]. That is why it is called, correctly, a sign and not a work of nature, Isaiah 7[:14]. That is why they are wrong, who assert that Christ was born from the natural seed of Mary and received his flesh and blood from her.[32] That is why Mary wondered how she could conceive without knowing a man since she, as stated, remained a pure virgin.[33] Hence the Lord himself (John 6) clearly gave us to understand from whence he came, etc. and your own confession also states this.[34]

Mary was impregnated surrounded by the power of the Most High and the Holy Spirit. That is why we do not assert, as some unwisely do through natural investigation, that there are two sons in or out of Christ. But we understand in this the mystery of God who nurtured him with the flesh of his mother and, as you write in accordance with Scripture, increased in age, wisdom and understanding, Isaiah 7[:15?], discarding evil and choosing the good. In short, that he was like other human beings in all things, except sin. And this occurred out of the eternal providence of God so that human frailty could bear it.

Nevertheless, it was not promised that he would be born of angels, revealed to the human race as a terrifying spirit, but was promised to be born of the seed of Abraham according to the flesh. How else could the sacrifice that is prefigured in many places by the priesthood be recognized

---

32 This statement is directed against the Socinian assertion of the purely human birth of Christ, not yet divine until his adoption at the ascension. The Melchiorite doctrine of a "celestial flesh" makes no appearance in this Swiss Brethren writing. At Frankenthal in 1571, when confronted with Menno's celestial flesh Christology, Rauff Bisch stated in no uncertain terms that he did not agree with it and repeated the Apostles' Creed that Jesus took flesh and blood from Mary; further, he made it clear that he did not consider Menno to be part of his group. See Frankenthal *Protocol*, 141; 145-47; 150. "Daß wir aber darumb sagen wolten / daß Christus wie ein wasser durch ein Rohr passirt / gestehen wir nit." Ibid., 164. Pressed to answer questions concerning Menno's writing, Rauff said they did not know how to answer "dieweil er mit uns nit einig ist / auch nie gewesen ist." Ibid., 171; also 175.
33 "een Reyne Maghet ghebleven is." *Handelinge*, 76.
34 Ostorodt does claim a miraculous birth for Christ through Mary, by the Holy Spirit: "Christus ... ist aus dem heyligen Geiste vnd der Krafft des Höchsten in der Jungfrawen Leibe entfangen. Darum er denn auch ein Son Gottes genennet worden, wie der Engel zuvorgesagt...." Wotschke, "Sendschreiben," 142.

as an eternal Spirit? For it had to be purified by flesh and blood, and a Spirit has neither the flesh nor the blood that Christ showed his disciples.[35]

Nevertheless, even though Christ was born of Abraham's seed according to the flesh, he was not conceived from natural seed since, as mentioned above, he had to be equal to his brothers in all things. According to the witness of Paul, Hebrews 2[:14-17], it had to be this way. Since God was not satisfied by the sacrifice of cattle, he prepared a body meet for sacrifice in this Lord Jesus, since he needed a sacrifice, Hebrews 10[:4-22]. Also, people need to remember that the Word became flesh, and that in the beginning the flesh did not exist, but the Word did.

We therefore confess that the Word became flesh, the body of Christ, prepared by God in cooperation with the Holy Spirit, which [mystery] is above all bold wisdom and understanding, which in any case is too small to discern the ways and judgments of God, as can be seen in 4 Esdras [2 Esdras 4:3ff].[36] Therefore true faith consists of this: that everything (destiny) is ascribed to almighty God, and we can say with Mary, "Let it be with me according to your Word." No thing is too wondrous for God to do, Genesis 18, Job 26 [Luke1:38].

Therefore, the Word that became flesh is Christ Jesus our Lord, who has delivered the people from their sins, the visible and invisible Son of God, Isaiah 7[:14], God with us, called Emmanuel. Therefore his people, who were created by him, are also redeemed by him but [in another world], through the temple curtain where their sins are not imputed to them, 2 Corinthians. 5[:19-21].

For this [conclusion] we have abundant scriptural evidence that we present here. First, John the Baptist testifies, John 1[:16; 30], "After me will come someone who preceded me for he existed before me . . . and from his fullness we have all received. . ." etc. "No one has ever seen God, the only

---

35 Ostorodt's confession denied the sacrificial atonement of Christ, arguing that God is not vengeful and did not need such a sacrifice. Rather, Christ overcame sin by love: "Nicht glauben wir, wie der Antichrist euch etwa betrogen hat, daß Christus, der Herr, seinen Vater als ein zornigen Richter solte mit seinem Blut versünet haben vnd zufrieden gestellet oder genug gethan. Denn das war nicht von nöten, weil es aus Gnaden alles vnd aus Liebe Gottesgeschehen ist...." Wotschke, "Sendschreiben," 153. The Swiss Brethren go on to offer scriptural counter-arguments.

36 Original has 4 Esdras, corresponding to 2 Esdras in modern Bible versions of the Apocrypha.

Answer from the Swiss Brethren to the Polish Brethren 561

begotten Son, who is in the bosom of the Father has revealed this to us" [John 1:18]. "He stood in your midst, the one that you do not know, the one who would come after me, the one who preceded me, since he existed before I did and I did not know him." Also, Christ himself, John 3[:31-35]: "No one ascends to heaven than the one who came from heaven," etc. Keep reading until the end of the chapter.

Also you have from the first epistle of John [1 John 1[:1]: "What was from the beginning, what we have seen with our eyes, what we have looked at and touched with our hands, containing the Word of life." These are the words of Christ's truth when he said to Philip, "Do you not believe that I am in the Father and the Father in me?" [John 14:10]. Also John says, 1 John 1, "This is the true God" [1 John 5:20]. Here he does not name an authority or ruler of a people, but he adds, "and eternal life." For he adds in 1 John 4[:2-3], "Every Spirit that does not confess that Jesus Christ came in the flesh is not from God."

You also wrote that in the law those who held office or had authority over others were also called gods. We confess this as well, but not if Christ has the testimony that all angels, Hebrews 1[:6], and also his disciples upon his ascension worshipped him [Luke 24:51-52].[37] That is why Thomas confesses the whole Christ for his Lord and God [John 20:28]. That is why Paul compares him to Melchizedek, Hebrews 7[:17; 28], since he had no beginning of days nor end of life, etc. There are many more scriptures like this that can be pointed out, such as David saying in Psalm 110[:1] "The Lord said to my Lord . . ." etc. And Christ himself in Matthew 22[:41ff.],

---

37 This difficult sentence reads: "Dat bekennen wy ooch, maer nitt als Christus een getuygenisse heeft." *Handelinge*, 79. Ostorodt made the argument that the name "God" was used in two ways in Scripture: to indicate the one Creator God, and to point to those who were given a divine office or power by God. According to Ostorodt, Christ is the prime example of this second use of the name "God." Therefore, Christ is God (as he is sometimes called), but not the Creator God; he is named God because the only Creator God gave him this office: "So bekennen wir nu, daß Christus Gott sei (aber nicht der einige Gott, welches sein Vatter ist), ja ein Gott, der ein Gott über sich habe, wie denn klerlich gelesen wird Joh. 20,17 vnd oben mehr Zeugnus sind angezogen." Wotschke, "Sendschreiben," 149. Ostorodt thus argues that Christ is a God (and Savior) who has a God over him. The Swiss Brethren seem to be arguing that although some are called gods in Scripture, this does not apply to the special case of Christ, since Scripture witnesses to his divine pre-existence.

"How then is he his Son if he calls him Lord?" etc. To add to this testimony we can also cite the texts in Isaiah 9[:6-7] and Hebrews 13[:8?] as well as others, which we consider unnecessary to cite since you have the Scriptures. However, search them diligently, believe God and his Word without trying to rationalize them. Remember that Paul said in Hebrews 5[:11], that he had many things to say [about Melchizedek] that were difficult to explain. Also, that this mystery of God must be understood through faith and not through human understanding [Colossians 1:26].

Further, consider that Paul was taken up into the third heaven, where he heard inexpressible words, 1 Corinthians 12 [2 Corinthians 12:1-4] that no human being is allowed to speak,[38] and about which there is less to say than about a Divine Majesty and Creator who created and made all things. This in order for us to better understand that the Word was made flesh, John 1[:14], and appeared to us in the flesh, so that we humans could bear [the sight of God]. Yet God remains one, even though he reveals himself in many ways,[39] such as to Moses at the bush, to Israel in the fiery pillar in the clouds, to Jacob and many more. Even so he was not a special person in every appearance. And to understand this more fully through faith, you have similar scriptures, the irrefutable witness of the Holy Spirit, and the appearances of the Holy Spirit.

Thus you know that God himself is a Spirit, John 4[:24], etc. and that we should not impute two persons, that of the Father and Spirit, when we see God's almighty power. That is to say that the Holy Spirit, as John the Baptist testified, appeared or was revealed in the form of a dove [Luke 3:22]. Now, despite all argument to the contrary, the Holy Spirit was not that dove, but was clothed in that form in order to become visible to human beings, Acts 2[:33]: "And appeared above each one of them [as a tongue of fire]," etc. Since no one can see God and live [Exodus 33:20], so you should not judge why the eternal Word became flesh, why God through the Holy Spirit, sacrificed through such a veil, redeemed us so as to fulfill the words of Paul in 2 Corinthians 5[:19], "God was in Christ reconciling the world to himself." That is to say, through this prepared body, etc.

---

38 At the Frankenthal Disputation, Rauff Bisch also appealed to Paul's unspeakable experience to make the point that certain truths must be believed, and cannot be arrived at by reason. Frankenthal *Protocoll*, 123.

39 The original has "blijft God doch eenigh," or "God remains undivided."

Answer from the Swiss Brethren to the Polish Brethren

Here you have, in brief, our Confession of Faith concerning Jesus Christ the Son of God, according to the scriptures and the measure of our faith. We hope that you will reflect on this matter, without questioning God's omnipotence, and agree with the truth. For faith is not a clever human judgment or discernment, but goes completely beyond human understanding and ingenuity. Those who fear and trust God's Word as much as those who crossed the Red Sea, as Shadrach, Meshach, and Abednego in the fiery furnace, as Daniel in the lion's den, as Abraham sacrificing Isaac (in whom, after all, he had the promise that his seed would multiply) can see from these examples that they transcend human reason. Therefore beloved, fear God and pray to him for understanding, so that the hope of our joy may be fulfilled. This we wish for you through him who is and was and always shall be. Amen.

Transacted in the general meeting of elders and ministers from many regions in the year one thousand, five hundred, and ninety-two, in Strasbourg. (And after all the necessary articles had been explained to them, they signed them. But those who cannot agree with us in these examined articles cannot be received among us nor fraternally greeted by us.)

Signed by hand and translated from Rauf-bits's [Bisch's] own handwritten copy from high German into Dutch.

Appendix

Authors and Works Cited and Copied in Codex 628

AUTHORS AND WORKS IN THE SIMPLE CONFESSION, CODEX 628, MS. PP. <1-366>

The background publication to which the "Simple Confession" is a response, is the official *Protocol* of the Frankenthal Disputation: *Protocoll. Das ist / Alle Handlung des Gesprechs zu Franckenthal inn der Churfürstlichen Pfaltz / mit denen so man Widertäuffer nennet / Auff den 28. May angefangen / und den 19 Junij dises 1571 jars geendet.*

Bern: *Berner Synodus. Ordnung wie sich pfarrer and prediger zu Statt un Land Bern / in leer und leben/ verhalten söllen / mit wyterem bericht von Christo / unnd den Sacramenten . . . am ix tag Januarii, AN. MDXXXII.* Facsimile edition: *Der Berner Synodus*, ed. Gottfried Locher (Neukirch: Neukircher Verlag, 1984).
    Noted in passing, <147>.

Martin Bucer, Wolfgang Capito, et al., *Grund und ursach auß gotlicher schrifft der neüwerungen an dem nachtmal des herren, so man dei mess nennet, Tauff, feyertagen, bildern. . .* (Strasbourg, 1524/1525), in R. Stupperich, ed., *Martin Bucers Deutsche Schriften*, Band 1, 185-278.
    Cited <208-209>, part of Balthasar Hubmaier's *Old and New Teachers*. Passing references to Bucer at <250>, <257>.

Epiphanius, *De Vitis Prophetarum* written by Pseudo-Epiphanius (*Patrologia Latina*, XLIII).
    Some paraphrasing of this writing, <25-26>.

Desiderius Erasmus, *Paraphrasis oder postilla teütsch, das ist, Klare Ausslegung aller evangelischen und apostolischen Schrifften des Neüwen Testaments . . .*, trans. Leo Jud (Zürich: Froschauer, ca. 1552).
    Direct citation, <70>; mentioned in passing, <199>. Citation via Hubmaier's *Old and New Teachers*, <209-10>. In passing, <210>; <227>.

Appendix   565

Sebastian Franck, *Chronica, Zeitbuch unnd Geschichtsbibel* (Strasbourg, 1531). References were checked in the edition published in Ulm, 1536 (photo-reprint, Darmstadt: Wissenschafliche Buchgesellschaft, 1969).
  Cited for information concerning the persecution of apostles, beginning with St. Peter, <27-34>; Brenz, Odenbach and Melanchthon, <144>.

Sebastian Franck, *Krieg Büchlin des Friedes* (Frankfurt a. M., 1550; facsimile reprint, Hildesheim: Olms, 1975).
  Lengthy verbatim citation, <275-86>.

Balthasar Hubmaier, *Old and New Teachers on Believers Baptism* (printed in Nikolsburg in 1526). Critical edition in Gunnar Westin and Torsten Bergsten, eds. *Balthasar Hubmaier Schriften* (Gütersloh: Gerd Mohn, 1962), 227-55; translation in H. Wayne Pipkin and John H. Yoder, trans. and eds. *Balthasar Hubmaier, Theologian of Anabaptism* (Scottdale, PA: Herald Press, 1989), 245-74.
  Verbatim copying, <200-210>.

Balthasar Hubmaier, *Dialogue with Zwingli's Baptism Book*, published in Nikolsburg in 1526. Critical edition in *Hubmaier Schriften*, 164-214; translation in Pipkin and Yoder, *Hubmaier*, 166-233.
  One paragraph from *Dialogue* inserted into a copying of Hubmaier, *Old and New Teachers*, on <208>; lengthy verbatim copying, <288-316>.

Martin Luther, *Temporal Authority: to what extent it should be obeyed*, LW, vol. 45, 81-129.
  Referenced, <76>; extended verbatim citation, <133-38>.

Martin Luther, *Die erst Epistel Sanct Peters : Die ander epistel sanct Peters und eine sanct Judas / geprediget und nach rechtem Verstand ussgelegt durch Martinum Luther* (Basel: Cratander, 1524), accessed online: http://www.e-rara.ch/zuz/content/titleinfo/1301599. Translation of Luther's sermon on 1 Peter, LW, vol. 30 (*The Catholic Epistles*), 3-145.
  Citation, <138-39>.

Martin Luther, on the Psalter (Zurich Q3 has Psalm 17).
  Cited, <140>. Source not found.

Martin Luther, *Eyn Sermon von dem newen Testament, das ist von der heyligen Messe*. Weimar Ausgabe 6, 353-378. Translation: *A Treatise on the New Testament, that is, concerning the Holy Mass* in LW, vol. 35, 79-111.
   Cited, <208>, part of Hubmaier, *Old and New Teachers*.

Martin Luther, book concerning original sin against the pope.
   Cited, <217>, part of copying from Pilgram Marpeck, *Vermanung of 1542*. (See Marpeck entry below.)

Martin Luther, "Sermon on the third Sunday after Epiphany, Matthew 8:1-13"; taken from Luther's Church Postil of 1525. [printed at Magdeburg in 1531]; accessed in English translation, online.
   Cited, <217-19>; reference inserted into material copied from Marpeck's *Vermanung*, strengthening Marpeck's argument.

Martin Luther, "Sermon for the day of Christ's Ascension, Mark 16:14-20," taken from Luther's Church Postil of 1522; accessed in English translation, online.
   Cited, <219>; reference inserted into material copied from Marpeck's *Vermanung* to strengthen the argument.

Martin Luther, "Commentary on Psalm 8," in *Martin Luther's Complete Commentary on the First Twenty-Two Psalms*, trans. Henry Cole, volume 1 (London: Simpkin and Marshall, 1826), 388ff.
   Luther's commentary on Psalm 8:2, paraphrased, <232-33>.

References to Martin Luther, in passing: <210>; <220>; <221>; <223>; <227>; <249>; <257>.

Pilgram Marpeck, "*Vermanung* (Admonition) *of 1542*," in Klaassen and Klassen, *Writings*, 159-302.
   Cited, <217>, expands text found in the *Vermanung*, 247 with references to Luther's published sermons that support the content of the paragraph in Marpeck.

Appendix

Pilgram Marpeck's *Vermanung* (Admonition) of 1542, also commonly called *"das Buch der Bundesbezeugung,"* or the book of witness to the covenant. Klaassen and Klassen, *Writings*, 159ff.
Reference to "our *Bundzeugnuss*," <289>.

Philipp Melanchthon, general reference in passing, <144>.

Tertullian cited as historical source, reporting on John the Evangelist, <31>. The account matches Franck, *Chronica* closely, but Franck does not mention Tertullian as source. [No such reference is found in Rhenanus's edition of Tertullian's *Opera Omnia*. (Basel: Froben, 1521)].

Rudolf Walter (or Walther/Gwalther), *Der Endtchrist: kurtze / klare und einfaltige Beweysung / in fünff Predigen begriffen / daß der Papst zu Rom / der rächt / war / groß und eigentlich Endtchrist sye...* (Zürich: Froschauer, 1546). Accessed online at: http://www.e-rara.ch/zuz/content/titleinfo/263000
Cited, <140>.

Rudolf Walter, *Die Menschwerdung deß waarenn / ewigen und eingebornen Suns Gottes / unsers Herren Jesu Christi / erklärt und ußgelegt in sechs predigen* (Zurich: Froschauer, 1571). Accessed online at: http://www.e-rara.ch/zuz/content/pageview/1267996
Cited, <139-42>; <148-49>.

Rudolf Walter, *Von dem waaren Brot dess Läbens, unserem Herren Jesu Christo, und wie der selbig genossen werde : zähen Predigen* über *das VI. Cap. dess heiligen Evangelisten Johannis* (Zurich: Froschauer, 1578). Accessed online at: http://www.e-rara.ch/zuz/content/titleinfo/864972
This reference in Zurich Q3 edition only, at <140>.

Rudolf Walter, in passing, <144>. Copyist mentions Walter appreciatively.

Ulrich Zwingli, mentioned in passing (common locution: "as Zwingli himself noted . . .")., <143>; <210>; <211>; <214> (twice); Zwingli vs Luther: <220>; <221>; more: <222>; <223>; <231>; another ref. to Zwingli vs Luther, <237>; <248>; <250>; <261>; <273>; <315-16>; <344> (twice).

Ulrich Zwingli, "Auslegen und Begründen der Schlußreden" ["Article Book"], in *Zwingli, der Verteidiger des Glaubens*, II. Teil (Zürich: Zwingli-Verlag, 1952).
    Cited, <76-77>; <143>; cited by Hubmaier, <206>.

Ulrich Zwingli, "Concerning Divine and Human Righteousness," trans. E. J. Furcha, *Huldrych Zwingli Writings, Vol. 1: The Defense of the Reformed Faith* (Allison Park, PA: Pickwick, 1984).
    Cited, <77-78>.

Ulrich Zwingli, ["*Concerning the Rebellious Spirits*"] refers to Zwingli's *Welche Ursach gebind ze Ufruoren*... (Zurich: Froschauer, 1525). Accessed online: http://dx.doi.org/10.3931/e-rara-1021.
    Cited, <208>; via copying of Hubmaier, *Old and New Teachers*.

Ulrich Zwingli, *Taufbuechlein: Vom dem Touff, vom Widertouff unnd vom Kindertouff* (Zürich: Johann Hager, 1525), dii, recto. Accessed online at: http://www.e-rara.ch/zuz/content/titleinfo/987393
    Cited, <208>, via Hubmaier's "Dialogue with Zwingli's Baptism Book." Cited directly, <214>; Zwingli vs Luther on latent faith, pointing back to the *Taufbuechlein* (inserted into copying of Marpeck's *Vermanung*, <217>; via Hubmaier, in long copying of the "dialogue" in Hubmaier's book, <288-315>.

Ulrich Zwingli, *Concerning True and False Religion*.
    Cited, <300-301>; via Hubmaier, "Dialogue with Zwingli's Baptism Book."

Thomas von Imbroich (also known as "Thomas Drucker"), "Confession of Faith," ca. 1560.
    Referenced, <289>.

Appendix

Ancient Authors Cited via Copying of Hubmaier

Donatus, *a learned bishop of Carthage*, 137 AD.
Reference, <200> [source intended by Hubmaier has not been found].

Tertullian, *Libro de Corona militis* [Book on the Garland of the Soldier], 208 AD.
Reference, <200>; and again, <216>.

Origen, 230 AD; writing on Luke 3[:8]; Romans 6[:3]; fifth homily on Exodus, fol. 48 E.
Reference, <201>.

St. Jerome, 370 AD, "Against the Sect of the Luciferians." On *Matthew* 28[:19].
Cited, <201-202>; cited, <216>; referenced as part of Hubmaier, *Dialogue*, <272-73>; <312>.

Eusebius, *Ecclesiastical History*, 371 AD, [Book 10, chapter 14] (story of children baptizing one another). The book and chapter reference correspond with contemporary German editions. See Caspar Hedio, *Chronica der Alten Christlichen Kirchen* (Strasbourg, 1545), das x. Buch, das xiiii Capittel, xciiii, recto and verso.
Copied from *Old and New Teachers*, <202>; return references, <216>; <307>.

Cyril, bishop in Basel, 373 AD; writing on John, book 2, chapter 36; also John, book 6, chapter 15.
Cited, <204>; referenced as part of Hubmaier, *Dialogue*, <290>.

Pope Boniface, 420 AD, vs. Augustine on infant baptism. In *Corpus Iuris canonici* I:1402 (canon 129).
Cited, <203>, part of copying Hubmaier, *Old and New Teachers*; referenced as part of Hubmaier, *Dialogue*, <272>.

Pope Leo I, 836 AD, In *Corpus Iuris canonici* I: 1365 (canon 12).
Cited, <203>, part of copying Hubmaier, *Old and New Teachers*.

Basil the Great, *Book 3, folio 44 of his Contra Eunomium* [Against Eunomius], 490 AD. *In Exhortatione ad Baptismum,* folio 142 following, and his tract *Quid Instruendi, ad Baptismum Venientes Lib.*

Cited, <203-204> as part of copying Hubmaier, *Old and New Teachers.*

Pope Nicholas I, 863 AD, *Ex Baptismo fidei.*
Cited, <204>, as part of copying Hubmaier, *Old and New Teachers.*

Beatus Renanus, 1315 AD [d. 1547].
Cited, <204>, as part of copying Hubmaier, *Old and New Teachers.*

Ancient Councils Cited via Copying of Hubmaier

Council of Arles, 315 AD [314 in fact]; CIC I:1396 (canon111).
Cited, <204-205>, as part of copying Hubmaier, *Old and New Teachers.*

Council of Nicea, 323 AD [325 in fact]; CIC I:378 (canon 52).
Cited <205>, as part of copying Hubmaier, *Old and New Teachers.*

Council of Laodicea in Syria, 368 AD; CIC I:1383 (canon 58).
Cited, <205>, as part of copying Hubmaier, *Old and New Teachers.*

Sixth Council of Carthage, 406 AD; [actually the fourth Aurelian synod of Carthage, 398; Pipkin/Yoder, 273, n. 96].
Cited, <205>, as part of copying Hubmaier, *Old and New Teachers.*

Council of Braga, 710 AD [actually 572]; CIC I:1382 (canon 55); CIC I:1383 (canon 58).
Cited, <206>, as part of copying Hubmaier, *Old and New Teachers*; mentioned in passing, <286>.

Appendix 571

AUTHORS AND WORKS IN CONCERNING SEPARATION,
CODEX 628, MS. <369-466>

Bern, *Berner Synodus. Ordnung wie sich pfarrer and prediger zu Statt und Land Bern / in leer und leben/ verhalten söllen / mit wyterem bericht von Christo / unnd den Sacramenten . . . am ix tag Januarii, AN. MDXXXII.*
Facsimilie edition: *Der Berner Synodus*, ed. Gottfried Locher (Neukirch: Neukircher Verlag, 1984).
Referenced, <395>; extended citations, <400-17>.

Martin Bucer, *Ein kurtzer warhafftiger bericht von Disputationen und gantzem handel, so zwischen Cunrat Treger, Provincial der Augustiner, und den predigern des Evangelii zu Straßburg sich begeben hat* . . . (Straßburg: [Schott], 1524). Critical edition in Robert Stupperich et al., *Martin Bucers Deutsche Schriften*, Vol. 2, 37-173.
Verbatim citing of text, <387-88>; return reference, <407>.

Heinrich Bullinger, *Der Widertöufferen ursprung/fürgang/Secten . . . etc.* (Zurich: Christoffel Froschower, 1561; photoreprint, Leipzig, 1975), 150 verso, ff. for Bullinger's comments regarding the Bern Synod.
Referenced as "Bullinger's slanderous book," <412-13>.

[Marpeck/Scharnschlager]: *Wie die Gschrifft verstendigklich soll underschiden/und erklärt werden...* (n.p., n.d.), today found in Amsterdam. A photostatic copy of this tract is held at the Mennonite Historical Library, Goshen, Indiana. See the translation by J. C. Wenger, "An Early Anabaptist Tract on Hermeneutics," MQR 42 (January 1968), 26-44; and J. H. Yoder, *The Legacy of Michael Sattler* (Scottdale, PA: Herald Press, 1973), 150-77.
Lengthy verbatim copying, <317-32>.

Wolfgang Capito, *Antwurt D. Wolffgang Fab. Capitons auf Bruder Conrads Augustiner ordens Prouincials vermanung, so er an gemein Eidgnossenschafft jüngst geschriben hat* . . . Book noted in Robert Stupperich et al., *Martin Bucers Deutsche Schriften*, Vol. 2 (Gütersloh: Gerd Mohn, 1962), 18, n. 8.
Appears to be a direct copying from text; not able to verify, <386>.

Martin Luther, *The Misuse of the Mass*, published in 1522. *Weimar Ausgabe* 8, 482-563; English translation in LW, 133-235.
 Citation, <373-75>.

Martin Luther, *Temporal Authority: To what extent it should be obeyed*, found in LW, vol. 45, 81-129.
 Citation, <383-85>; again, <388-89>.

Martin Luther, "Sermon for the first Sunday after Christ's Ascension, John 15:26-16:4," taken from Luther's Church Postil of 1522. Accessed online: http://www.trinitylutheranms.org/MartinLuther/MLSermons/John15_26.html
 Cited, <389-91>.

References to Luther, in passing: <398>; <404>; <405>; <406>; <413>; <440>.

Philipp Melanchthon, [*Tractate*, his *Instruction in the True Holy Scriptures of God*, 1523], apparently *Loci communes rerum theologicarum*, first published in Wittenberg in 1521, with a second edition appearing soon after in Basel. [Wilhelm Pauck, ed., *Melanchthon and Bucer*, Library of Christian Classics, vol. 19 (Philadelphia, PA: Westminster, 1969), 148.]
 Cited, <385-86>.

Philipp Melanchthon, *Annotations on the First Epistle to the Corinthians*. Introduced, trans. and ed. John Patrick Donnelly, S.J. (Milwaukee, WI: Marquette University Press, 1995), 161.
 Cited, <379>.

Philipp Melanchthon, mentioned in passing, <403>; <406>.

Rudolf Walter, mentioned appreciatively, <435>

Ulrich Zwingli, referenced: <404>; <433>. [There are about 110 references to Zwingli (not all of them significant) in *Codex 628*, many of them in the manner of "as Zwingli himself confessed...."]

Appendix

Ulrich Zwingli, his "commentary on 1 Corinthians 14" seems to point back to Zwingli, *On the Preaching Office* (1524).
Cited, <379>.

Ulrich Zwingli, ["Article Book"] "Auslegen und Begründen der Schlußreden," in *Zwingli, der Verteidiger des Glaubens*, II. Teil (Zürich: Zwingli-Verlag, 1952).
Cited, <391>.

Ulrich Zwingli, "Concerning Divine and Human Righteousness," trans. E. J. Furcha, *Huldrych Zwingli Writings, vol. 1: The Defense of the Reformed Faith* (Allison Park, PA: Pickwick, 1984).
Cited, <406>.

Ancient Authors Cited with No Source

Cyprian, *Ad Pomp. Contra Steph. Epist. Oportet Episcopum non solum*, <380>.

Ambrosius, *Tom. 4 in Epistolam ad Ephesios*, <380>.

Euseb. Caesariensum, *Eccl. Historia, Lib. 6, cap. 15*. CSep, <380>. Modern editions of Eusebius have different book and chapter numbers. Reference to a contemporary German edition confirms the accuracy and relevance of this citation. See Caspar Hedio, *Chronica der Alten Christlichen Kirchen* (Strasbourg, 1545), lix, verso-lx, recto. Accessed online: https://play.google.com/books/reader?id=-ehEAAAAcAAJ&printsec=frontcover&output=reader&authuser=0&hl=en&pg=GBS.PA13 (e-book pages 138-39).

Chrysostom, *in Gen. homil. 7 volo etc.*, <380>.

Cyril *in Joh. Cap. 9, Hist. 6, cap. 20*, <380>.

Eleutherius *in Joan., Lib. 12, cap. 20*, <380>. Reference uncertain, but "Eleutherius" was a pseudonym for Sebastian Franck.

No systematic study was undertaken exploring the use of *The Concordance of the Swiss Brethren* by the author/copyist/editor of *Codex 628*. For the Concordance, see G. Fast and G. A. Peters, trans., *Biblical Concordance of the Swiss Brethren, 1540* (Kitchener, ON: Pandora Press, 2001). A systematic comparison of the Marpeck network's *Testamentserlauterung* with Scripture usage in *Codex 628* also would have been instructive, but remains to be done. The 800-page biblical concordance exists in two extant copies. The copy in the Stadtbibliothek, Zurich can be found in microfilm at the Mennonite Historical Library, Goshen, Indiana. The preface to the *Testamentserlauterung* in English translation is published in Klaassen and Klassen, *Writings*, 555-66.

Scripture Index

The Old Testament

Genesis
Genesis 1 364
Genesis 2 150
Genesis 2[:18-24] 323
Genesis 3[:15] 311
Genesis 3 81
Genesis 8[:21] 315
Genesis 17[:4-7] 376
Genesis 17[:10-14] 366
Genesis 18 560
Genesis 19[:4] 529
Genesis 21[:4] 366
Genesis 21:8-14 295
Genesis 22 81
Genesis 25[:29-34] 133
Genesis 34 108, 110
Genesis 38 232
Genesis 41 517
Genesis 48 352
Genesis 49:10 277, 283

Exodus
Exodus 2:12 260
Exodus 12[:3] 366
Exodus 12[:48] 366
Exodus 15 130
Exodus 20:5 256
Exodus 21:24-32 264
Exodus 23 111
Exodus 23[:4-5] 264, 265
Exodus 24[= 34:15] 501
Exodus 28 517
Exodus 33:20 562

Leviticus
Leviticus 10[:1-2] 274
Leviticus 10:1-3 257
Leviticus 10[:10] 503
Leviticus 10:16-20 285
Leviticus 16 110
Leviticus 18 111
Leviticus 18[:28-29] 266

Leviticus 19 265, 325
Leviticus 19[:17-18] 265
Leviticus 20[:14] 266
Leviticus 22:10 499
Leviticus 25 499
Leviticus 34 108

Numbers
Numbers 11 517
Numbers 15 111
Numbers 16[:21] 501
Numbers 24 517
Numbers 26 501
Numbers 45 501

Deuteronomy
Deuteronomy 4 82, 517
Deuteronomy 4[:2-4] 82
Deuteronomy 6[:5] 324
Deuteronomy 6 325
Deuteronomy 7[:1-2] 264
Deuteronomy 7[:1-5] 268
Deuteronomy 10 325, 421
Deuteronomy 10[:12] 324
Deuteronomy 12 111
Deuteronomy 13 105, 108, 114, 115, 222, 224
Deuteronomy 13[:6-11] 114
Deuteronomy 13; 19; 21 105, 108, 113, 115
Deuteronomy 16:18-20 538
Deuteronomy 18 266
Deuteronomy 18[:15-22] 81
Deuteronomy 18, 22[Note: probably Deut 13:10, 21:21] 266
Deuteronomy 19:19-20 105
Deuteronomy 21:21 105
Deuteronomy 25[:1-2] 266

Deuteronomy 30 421
Deuteronomy 32 232, 347
Deuteronomy 32[:15ff] 232

Joshua
Joshua 2 109
Joshua 7 108
Joshua 7 109
Joshua 10 355
Joshua 22:20 109

Judges
Judges 8:23-9:18 277

1 Samuel
1 Samuel 3-4 109
1 Samuel 15 109
1 Samuel 15:33 260
1 Samuel 34 108

2 Samuel
2 Samuel 7[:12-17] 81

1 Kings
1 Kings 6[:7] 286
1 Kings 10 517
1 Kings 16 517
1 Kings 19:1 215, 260
1 Kings 22 236
1 Kings 22:6ff 478

2 Kings
2 Kings 1:10 261
2 Kings 12 261
2 Kings 23 517
4 Kings 2 (sic) 517

2 Chronicles
2 Chronicles 18[:12ff] 215
2 Chronicles 19:6-7 143
2 Chronicles 20[:35ff] 501
2 Chronicles 24[:20-21] 148, 215

2 Chronicles 32[:8] 227

Nehemiah
Nehemiah 9 517

Job
Job 1 233
Job 1[:21] 440
Job 12 233
Job 12:4-6? 214
Job 21 233
Job 26 560
Job 28[:12-19] 443
Job 41[:27, 33] 470

Psalms
Psalm 1[:5] 22
Psalm 2 233, 283
Psalm 2[:11] 233
Psalm 5[:5-7] 22
Psalm 5[:6ff] 521
Psalm 8:2 352
Psalm 11[:6] 438
Psalm 12 383
Psalm 17 290
Psalm 26[:4ff] 24
Psalm 26[:4ff, 8] 501
Psalm 27 233
Psalm 34 314
Psalm 37[:2, 9, 20, 28] 22
Psalm 37[:14-15] 226
Psalm 44[:11] 228, 439
Psalm 46 279
Psalm 46[:1-3] 227
Psalm 46[:8-9] 257
Psalm 46[:9]; 76 254
Psalm 49 233
Psalm 50 23, 73, 397, 515, 517
Psalm 50[:7] 73
Psalm 50[:16-19] 515
Psalm 50[:16-21] 23
Psalm 50[:16ff.] 397
Psalm 51[:5] 315
Psalm 59[:13] 20
Psalm 69[=70:3] 521
Psalm 76 279
Psalm 76[:2-3] 257

Psalm 83[:4] 214
Psalm 83:4-5 149
Psalm 97 130
Psalm 106[:35ff] 501
Psalm 109 286
Psalm 110[:1] 561
Psalm 110[:3] 295
Psalm 115[:16] 289
Psalm 115[116:15] 149
Psalm 116[:15] 245
Psalm 118[:27] 368
Psalm 119 313
Psalm 124[:2ff] 26
Psalm 124[:7] 22
Psalm 126[:6] 228
Psalm 129 26
Psalm 131 81
Psalm 132:11-12 81
Psalm 133[:1] 325
Psalm 139 [140:5-6] 132
Psalm 144 26
Psalm 150[:6] 130
Psalm 3[:8] 521
Psalm 100[=101:5] 521

Proverbs
Proverbs 13[:19] 214
Proverbs 16[:6] 467
Proverbs 17[:15] 110
Proverbs 21[:15] 111
Proverbs 22[:5] 500
Proverbs 25[:21-22] 265
Proverbs 29[:27] 110
Proverbs 30[:6] 82

Ecclesiastes
Ecclesiastes 2 22

Isaiah
Isaiah 2 251, 254, 276, 286
Isaiah 2[:1-4] 254
Isaiah 2:2-4 251
Isaiah 2[:4] 273, 279, 292, 473, 477
Isaiah 3 108
Isaiah 3:13 108
Isaiah 5 236
Isaiah 5[:20] 242

Isaiah 6[:9ff] 453
Isaiah 7[:14] 558, 559, 560
Isaiah 7[:15?] 559
Isaiah 8:14-15 260
Isaiah 9[:6] 82
Isaiah 9[:6-7] 562
Isaiah 10[:5] 136
Isaiah 11 81, 286
Isaiah 11[:4ff] 477
Isaiah 11:6-7 276
Isaiah 11[:6-9] 292
Isaiah 11[:9] 473
Isaiah 13 283
Isaiah 25[:8-9] 228
Isaiah 28[:7-8] 237
Isaiah [29:13] 522
Isaiah 29:13-14 541
Isaiah 32 517
Isaiah 33[:15ff] 476
Isaiah 42:3 260
Isaiah 43:1-2 227
Isaiah 44 517
Isaiah 49 517
Isaiah 51:12-13 226
Isaiah 52:11 234
Isaiah 52 108
Isaiah 53 151, 321
Isaiah 55:13 277
Isaiah 56[:10-12] 237
Isaiah 59[:3; 7] 498
Isaiah 59[:15] 149
Isaiah 60 108
Isaiah 61 108
Isaiah 61[:1] 517
Isaiah 66:1-2 428
Isaiah 66[:1-3] 252

Jeremiah
Jeremiah 1[:5] 355
Jeremiah 2 108
Jeremiah 2[:8] 108
Jeremiah 2[:13] 375
Jeremiah 4 149, 421
Jeremiah 4[:12] 149
Jeremiah 5[:24] 133
Jeremiah 5[:31] 242
Jeremiah 6 237, 421
Jeremiah 6[:13] 237

Scripture Index

Jeremiah 6[:14] 20
Jeremiah 7[:4] 253
Jeremiah 8 236
Jeremiah 8[:11] 20
Jeremiah 9 237, 421
Jeremiah 9[:3] 237
Jeremiah 11[:16] 210
Jeremiah 11:19 215
Jeremiah 11:21 215
Jeremiah 13[:23] 522
Jeremiah 14 222, 236
Jeremiah 18[:18] 148, 214
Jeremiah 20[:14-18?] 397
Jeremiah 23 236
Jeremiah 23[:1ff] 20, 21
Jeremiah 23[:16-17; 21-22; 32] 370
Jeremiah 23[:38] 24
Jeremiah 25:9 136
eremiah 28 236
Jeremiah 31[:31-34] 258, 340, 364
Jeremiah 51[:6] 234, 500

Lamentations
Lamentations 2[:21] 224
Lamentations 4:5-11 224
Lamentations 4[:12-14] 224

Ezekiel
Ezekiel 2[:5-7] 454
Ezekiel 2[:8-10] 208
Ezekiel 3[:27] 454
Ezekiel 11[:19] 517
Ezekiel 11 517
Ezekiel 13[:1-7] 370
Ezekiel 13[:3ff] 20, 21
Ezekiel 13:18-19 242
Ezekiel 13[:18-19] 242
Ezekiel 13[:18ff?] 237
Ezekiel 13 236
Ezekiel 15 242
Ezekiel 18 21, 25
Ezekiel 18 21
Ezekiel 22 236, 242
Ezekiel 22[:26ff] 237, 503
Ezekiel 28[:14-15] 358
Ezekiel 28[:15] 358
Ezekiel 32[:20ff] 221
Ezekiel 32:23. 221
Ezekiel 33[:12ff] 21
Ezekiel 34 242
Ezekiel 36 23, 24
Ezekiel 36:26 23, 517
Ezekiel 37 517
Ezekiel 43[:7-8] 252
Ezekiel 43:7-9 275
Ezekiel 44 422, 423
Ezekiel 44[:7] 252

Daniel
Daniel 3:18 285
Daniel 4 517
Daniel 6 216
Daniel 7 232, 380
Daniel 8 232, 380
Daniel 9 24, 380
Daniel 11 278, 381
Daniel 11[:33-35] 278
Daniel 12 216
Daniel 12[:2] 326

Hosea
Hosea 2 322
Hosea 4[:4-9] 238
Hosea 4[:9ff] 23
Hosea 6[:9] 238
Hosea 9[:7] 148, 214, 238
Hosea 13[:11] 277

Joel
Joel 2[:28] 518
Joel 2[:28-29] 376

Amos
Amos 7[:10] 148
Amos 7[:10-11] 215

Jonah
Jonah 4 359
Jonah 4:5 134

Micah
Micah 3 236, 238, 242, 517
Micah 3[:5; 11] 238
Micah 4 251, 254, 273, 276
Micah 4:1-3 251
Micah 4[:1-4] 254
Micah 4[:3] 273, 279, 292
Micah 5[:2-4] 82

Haggai
Haggai 2 517

Zechariah
Zechariah 2[:8] 149, 245
Zechariah 9 254, 257, 279
Zechariah 9[:9-10] 257
Zechariah 9[:10] 292
Zechariah 12[:10] 518
Zechariah 13 222

Malachi
Malachi 1[:13] 136
Malachi 2[:8] 476
Malachi 3[:18] 503

THE APOCRYPHAL BOOKS

Wisdom of Solomon
Wisdom of Solomon 1:1 144
Wisdom of Solomon 2[:12-20] 214
Wisdom of Solomon 3[:1-4] 226
Wisdom of Solomon 3[:1-9] 383
Wisdom of Solomon 4 144
Wisdom of Solomon 5[:4] 202
Wisdom of Solomon 5[:4-13] 221
Wisdom of Solomon 7[:7-14] 443
Wisdom of Solomon 9[:13ff] 556

Wisdom of Solomon 15[:3] 82
Wisdom of Solomon 18[:4] 201

Ecclesiasticus [The Wisdom of Jesus ben Sirach]
Ecclesiasticus 1 225, 313
Ecclesiasticus 2[:1-5] 383
Ecclesiasticus 3[:21-23] 82
Ecclesiasticus 4:27-28 226
Ecclesiasticus 5[:7] 116
Ecclesiasticus 7[:23-24] 371
Ecclesiasticus 13 [?] 500
Ecclesiasticus 15[:9] 131
Ecclesiasticus 17 279, 284
Ecclesiasticus 17[:17] 279
Ecclesiasticus 30[:1-13] 371
Ecclesiasticus 34:4 522
Ecclesiasticus 39[:13-14] 130

Baruch
Baruch 3[:20] 443
Baruch 3[:35-37] 82
Baruch 4:25-26 228

1 Maccabees
1 Maccabees 2:19-22 285

2 Maccabees
2 Maccabees 6[:18-20] 216
2 Maccabees 7[:1-41] 216
2 Maccabees 7:20 285

3 Esdras
3 Esd 3:1-4:63 249

4 Esdras
4 Esdras 2[:36-38, 42-47] 227
4 Esdras 2[:39-40] 382
4 Esdras 3[:5-8; 20-22] 339
4 Esdras 4:3ff 560
4 Esdras 5[:11-12] 132
4 Esdras 7[:6-9; 18] 229
4 Esdras 7[:55] 438
4 Esdras 8:1-3 231
4 Esdras 9:10-12 437
4 Esdras 15[:21] 225, 439
4 Esdras 15:23 439
4 Esdras 16[:70-73] 214
4 Esdras 16[:71-73] 149
4 Esdras 16[:78] 22

The New Testament

Matthew
Matthew 1[:20] 311
Matthew 2[:3] 369
Matthew 3 210, 314, 395, 413
Matthew 3[:1, 6] 395
Matthew 3[:6] 395
Matthew 3[:7-10] 314
Matthew 3[:8-10] 314
Matthew 3[:10] 210
Matthew 3[:11] 499
Matthew 3[:16] 495
Matthew 4 236, 367
Matthew 4:8-10 236
Matthew 5 24, 113, 145, 150, 193, 229, 255, 256, 263, 264, 265, 266, 280, 291, 303, 314, 322, 323, 472, 477, 478, 480, 482
Matthew 5[:1-48] 263
Matthew 5[:11] 323
Matthew 5[:20?] 24
Matthew 5[:29-30] 113
Matthew 5:31-32 322
Matthew 5:33-37 303
Matthew 5[:38] 256
Matthew 5[:38-48] 477
Matthew 5[:38ff] 478
Matthew 5:39 145
Matthew 5[:39-40, 44] 264
Matthew 5[:39, 44] 480
Matthew 5:43 264, 291
Matthew 5 [:43-44] 145, 265
Matthew 5[:43-45] 265
Matthew. 5[:43-48] 272
Matthew 5[:44] 229, 291
Matthew 6 314, 482
Matthew 6:24 523
Matthew 7 23, 111, 149, 151, 229, 231, 240, 314, 457, 479, 487, 503, 506, 512, 513, 515, 521
Matthew 7[:1-5] 314
Matthew 7[:2] 513
Matthew 7[:3-5] 240, 314
Matthew 7[:3ff] 515
Matthew 7[:6] 111
Matthew 7:12 149
Matthew 7:13-14 229
Matthew 7[:15-20] 240
Matthew 7[:16], 12[:33] 503
Matthew 7[:17ff] 479
Matthew 7[:19] 22, 210, 457
Matthew 7[:21] 314, 506
Matthew 7[:22ff] 23
Matthew 8:1-13 342
Matthew 9[:9] 284
Matthew 9[:17] 209
Matthew 10 25, 71, 147, 205, 213, 222, 226, 230, 233, 235, 261, 266, 278, 280, 283, 289, 295, 308, 322, 323, 356, 404, 439, 506, 515, 518, 525, 530, 539, 545
Matthew 10[:4ff] 515
Matthew 10[:5-23] 289
Matthew 10[:8] 71
Matthew 10[:14] 54, 147, 266, 295
Matthew 10[:14-15] 539
Matthew 10[:16] 147, 159, 213
Matthew 10[:16-39] 280

Scripture Index

Matthew 10[:17-18] 439
Matthew 10[:18-19] 278
Matthew 10[:22] 25
Matthew 10[:23] 530
Matthew 10[:24] 213, 525
Matthew 10[:24-25] 213, 283
Matthew. 10[:26] 245
Matthew 10[:32] 404
Matthew 10[:32-33] 226
Matthew 10[:37] 322
Matthew 10:37-38 323
Matthew 10[:38] 261, 356
Matthew 10:40 308
Matthew 11 314
Matthew 11[:11] 356
Matthew 11:13 256
Matthew 11[:16-17] 352
Matthew 11:27 306
Matthew 11:29-30 144
Matthew 11[:30] 24
Matthew 12 205
Matthew 12[:9-14] 314
Matthew 12:34-36 521
Matthew 12:50 23
Matthew 13 115, 147, 192
Matthew 13[:9] 202
Matthew 13[:11-17] 314
Matthew 13[:14ff] 453
Matthew 13[:24-30] 115, 294, 432, 519
Matthew 13[:29-30] 147
Matthew 13[:30] 438
Matthew 13[:37-42] 433
Matthew 13[:40-43] 438
Matthew 13[:40-43, 49ff] 22
Matthew 13[:52] 546
Matthew 14[:21] 401
Matthew 15 26, 108, 340, 401, 402, 411
Matthew 15[:3] 511
Matthew 15[:11] 401
Matthew 15[:13] 26, 340, 402
Matthew 15[:14] 108, 513
Matthew 16 20, 106, 147, 229, 269, 280

Matthew 16[:6] 20, 513
Matthew 16[:16] 82, 313
Matthew 16:17 306
Matthew 16[:18] 358
Matthew 16[:19] 106, 496, 512
Matthew 16[:24] 147, 356, 373, 481
Matthew 16[:24-25] 229
Matthew 16[:27] 269
Matthew 17[:5] 514
Matthew 17[:26] 468
Matthew 18 82, 100, 101, 102, 105, 106, 107, 110, 113, 114, 150
Matthew 18[:1-6] 265
Matthew 18[:3] 230, 316
Matthew 18[:6ff] 500
Matthew 18[:8-9] 113
Matthew 18[:15] 457
Matthew 18[:15-17] 244, 266, 540
Matthew 18[:15-18] 106, 282
Matthew 18[:15-20] 110
Matthew 18[:15-35] 114
Matthew 18:15ff 101, 496
Matthew 18[:17] 107, 497
Matthew 18:18 106
Matthew 19 73, 150
Matthew 19[:3-9] 323
Matthew 19[:12] 202
Matthew 19:13 355
Matthew 19[:14] 73, 316, 349
Matthew 19[:16ff] 506
Matthew 19[:21; 27-30] 284
Matthew 19:[28] 272
Matthew 20 231, 278
Matthew. 20:1-16 271
Matthew 20[:14-15?] 231
Matthew 20[:24-28] 488
Matthew 20[:25-26] 278
Matthew 20[:25-27] 284
Matthew 20[:26-28] 481
Matthew 21[:16] 352
Matthew 21 229

Matthew 21:31 256
Matthew 22 229
Matthew 22[:11-13] 499
Matthew 22[:13] 209, 438
Matthew 22[:13-14]; 25[:30-46] 439
Matthew 22[:14] 231
Matthew 22[:15-21] 279
Matthew 22[:21] 285, 288
Matthew 22[:36-39] 325
Matthew 22[:41ff.] 561
Matthew 22[:42-45] 312
Matthew 23 148, 223, 314, 506, 510, 512, 513
Matthew 23:2 512
Matthew 23[:2ff] 510
Matthew 23:13 513
Matthew 23[:13ff] 506
Matthew 23[:29-38] 223
Matthew 23[:35] 148
Matthew 24 24, 25, 26, 132, 213, 222, 235, 280
Matthew 24[:3ff] 132
Matthew 24[:4] 24
Matthew 24[:4ff] 25
Matthew 24[:9] 213, 278
Matthew 24[:10] 439
Matthew 24[:12] 26
Matthew 24[:15] 489
Matthew 24[:36] 245
Matthew 25 145
Matthew 25:1-12 434
Matthew 25:1-13 233
Matthew 25:14-30 320
Matthew 25[:26ff] 456
Matthew 25[:31-46] 314, 487
Matthew 25[:41] 439
Matthew 26 150, 151, 278, 321
Matthew 26[:2] 515
Matthew 26[:26-29] 366
Matthew 26[:52] 278, 480
Matthew 27[:3ff] 518
Matthew 27[:59ff.] 404
Matthew 28 42, 43, 73, 149, 150, 230, 265, 283, 328, 329, 336, 339, 345,

350, 351, 365, 377, 386, 389, 392, 393, 394, 407, 408, 414, 504, 541
Matthew 28[:18] 149
Matthew 28[:19] 43, 73, 265, 329, 336, 393, 407, 408, 504
Matthew 28[:19-20] 42, 328, 339, 345, 351, 365, 389, 392, 394, 504
Matthew 28[:19ff] 512
Matthew 28[:20] 377

Mark
Mark 1 413
Mark 1[:10] 495
Mark 3 205, 347
Mark 4:3-8 319
Mark 6 222
Mark 6[:7] 515
Mark 6[:11] 280, 295
Mark 8 147, 229, 233, 280
Mark 8[:34-35] 229
Mark 8[:34-38] 481
Mark 8[:35-37] 233
Mark 9 113, 114
Mark 9[:7] 514
Mark 9:37 308
Mark 9[:43-48] 113
Mark 10 278
Mark 10:13 349
Mark 10[:14] 316
Mark 13 213
Mark 13[:9] 213, 278
Mark 13[:32] 245
Mark 13[:37] 278
Mark 14 150, 321
Mark 14[:1] 515
Mark 16 43, 62, 72, 150, 328, 344, 345, 350, 351, 365, 386, 389, 392, 393, 394, 405, 407, 408, 414, 504, 512, 541
Mark 16[:14] 393
Mark 16:14-20 344
Mark 16[:15] 512
Mark 16[:15-16] 62, 328, 345, 351, 365, 389, 392, 394, 504
Mark 16[:16] 43, 72, 405, 407, 408

Luke
Luke 1:35 311
Luke 1:38 560
Luke 2 517
Luke 3 210, 329, 367, 413, 414, 562
Luke 3[:8] 329
Luke 3[:9] 210
Luke 3[:22] 495, 562
Luke 3[:23] 367
Luke 6 23, 236, 264, 265, 280, 477, 482
Luke 6[:20-38] 280
Luke 6[:20-49] and 14[:25-33] 482
Luke 6[:26] 236
Luke 6[:27-31] 265
Luke 6[:27-38] 477
Luke 6[:29] 264
Luke 6[:39] 513
Luke 6[:40] 525
Luke 6[:44] 503
Luke 6[:46ff] 23
Luke 7 356, 414
Luke 7[:28] 356
Luke 8:5-8 319
Luke 9 115, 146, 147, 222, 280, 517
Luke 9[:1] 515
Luke 9[:5] 295
Luke 9[:23-26] 481
Luke 9[:35] 514
Luke 9:51-56 115
Luke 9[:52-55] 265
Luke 9[:52-56] 146
Luke 9:54 261
Luke. 9[:54-55] 268
Luke 9:56 268
Luke 9[:58-62] 229
Luke 10 222
Luke 10[:3] 280
Luke 10:7 71
Luke 10[:10-11] 266, 280
Luke 10[:11] 295
Luke 10:12 295
Luke 10:22 306
Luke 11 205, 347
Luke 11 205
Luke 11[:52] 506
Luke 12 205
Luke 12[:4-5] 314
Luke 12[:47-48] 314
Luke 12[:50] 393
Luke 12:51-53 292
Luke 13[:5] 22
Luke 14 230, 280, 283, 284, 322, 323, 356, 506
Luke 14[:10-11; 27; 33] 284
Luke 14[:11] 283
Luke 14[:23] 529, 530
Luke 14[:25] 322
Luke 14:26 323, 542
Luke 14[:26-27] 229, 481
Luke 14[:27] 356
Luke 15[:11ff] 133
Luke 16[:13] 22, 523
Luke 17[:1-4] 540
Luke 17[:1ff] 500
Luke 17[:3-4] 244
Luke 17[:3ff] 496
Luke 17:26-30 26
Luke 18:8 435
Luke 18:16 349
Luke 19[:10] 115
Luke 19:11] 136
Luke 19[:26] 314
Luke 19:41-44 223
Luke 20[:45-47] 314
Luke 21 213, 245, 278
Luke 21[:12] 213, 278, 439
Luke 21[:12-19] 280
Luke 22 150, 151
Luke 22 321
Luke 23 321
Luke 23[:34] 261, 265
Luke 24 414, 561
Luke 24[:29] 529
Luke 24[:49] 496
Luke 24:51-52 561

Scripture Index

John
John 1 22, 81, 82, 206, 208, 311, 364, 413, 495, 512, 557, 560, 561, 562
John 1[:1-3] 557
John 1:1-3; 14 311
John 1[:1-5] 208
John1[:1-9] 294
John 1[:1-14] 82
John 1[:12-13] 364
John 1[:12ff] 22
John 1[:14] 81, 82, 206, 562
John 1[:14] 81
John 1[:16; 30] 560
John 1:18 561
John 1[:32] 495
John 2 347
John 3 22, 23, 73, 74, 115, 208, 230, 312, 356, 373, 392, 393, 397, 413, 414, 561
John 3[:3] 230, 265, 356
John 3[:3-5] 373
John 3[:3-6] 397
John 3[:3ff] 22
John 3[:5] 73, 74, 208
John 3[:5-6] 392
John 3[:6ff] 482
John 3[:13, 31] 81
John. 3[:17] 115, 269
John 3[:19ff] 23
John 3[:22] 393
John 3:31-33 312
John 3[:31-35] 561
John 3 414
John 4 414
John 4[:23-24] 376
John 4[:24] 562
John 5[:18] 22
John 5[:22] 269
John 5[:28-29] 210, 326
John 6 81, 291, 306, 312, 356, 357, 559
John 6:44 306
John 6:50-51 312
John 6[:53] 356
John 6[:66] 393

John 7[:1] 26
John 7[:7] 23
John 7[:29] 81
John 7[:37-39] 517
John 7[:38] 456, 495
John 7[:39] 512
John 7[:50] 404
John 7[:51] 453
John 8 21, 23, 208, 232, 269, 347, 558
John 8[:5ff] 514
John 8:11 269
John 8[:12?] 23
John 8[:31] 456
John 8[:34] 21
John 8[:36] 468
John 8[:42] 81
John 8[:42, 44] 232
John 8[:47] 23, 494
John 8:57-58 558
John 9[:41] 223
John 10 21, 24, 206, 457, 502, 512
John 10:1-16 206
John 10:3] 21
John 10[:4] 24
John 10[:5] 457, 502, 514
John 10[:8] 206
John 10[:12] 21
John10:16 270
John 11[:27] 82
John 12[:6] 515
John 12[:24-26] 481, 482
John12:26 261
John 12[:31] 21, 502
John 12[:37ff] 453
John 12:47 115
John 13 82, 207
John13:16 525
John 13[:18] 520
John 13:20 308
John13[:34] 291
John 13[:34-35] 207, 325
John 13[:34ff] 503
John 14 81, 82, 146, 206, 207, 209, 232, 308, 310, 321, 561
John 14[:1-11] 82

John 14:9 308
John 14:10 561
John 14[:12] 209
John 14:15-21 310
John 14:16; 25-26 516
John14[:18ff] 377
John 14[:23ff] 232
John 14[:26] 496, 516
John 14[:27] 146, 206
John 14[:30] 21, 502
John 15 22, 25, 82, 146, 151, 202, 207, 208, 210, 211, 212, 213, 235, 280, 325
John 15:1-2 207
John15:1-6 321
John 15[:2, 6] 457
John 15:3-6 207
John 15[:4-5] 211
John 15:5 208
John 15[:6] 22, 210
John 15[:6; 18-20] 439
John 15:9-10 207
John 15[:10] 527
John 15:13-15 325
John 15[:18-19] 146, 202
John 15[:18-20] 280
John 15[:18, 20ff] 494
John 15[:18ff] 25
John 15[:19] 235, 281, 291, 502
John 15[:20] 525
John [15:26] 474, 516
John 15:26-16:4 474
John 16 146, 213, 235, 245, 269, 278, 280, 283, 386
John 16:1 213
John16[:2] 278
John 16[:2-4] 213
John 16[:2; 20-22] 439
John 16[:2; 33] 280
John 16[:2ff] 494
John 16[:7-14] 516
John 16[:8-11] 280
John 16[:13-14] 376
John 16[:28] 81
John 16[:33] 146

John 17 82, 281, 305, 308, 423
John 17[:3] 82
John 17[:18] 81, 281
John 17:21 308
John18 263
John 18:10 261
John 18[:11] 279, 480
John 18[:36] 146, 235, 263, 281
John 18[:37] 23
John 19[:39] 404
John 20[:2ff] 512
John 20[:22ff] 496
John 20[:28] 82, 561
John 21[:18-19] 217

Acts
Acts 1 321, 413
Acts 1[:1-16] 517
Acts 1[:5-8] 516
Acts 1[:5, 8] 495
Acts 1[:8] 496
Acts 1[:15ff] 516, 521
Acts 2 81, 150, 328, 337, 345, 351, 360, 365, 369, 375, 376, 387, 389, 411, 414, 415, 459, 504, 517, 541, 562
Acts 2[:6-13] 375
Acts 2[:29-30] 81
Acts 2[:33] 562
Acts 2[:38] 43, 328, 337, 345, 365, 504
Acts 2[:38, 41] 389
Acts 2[:39] 375, 376
Acts 2[:44-45] 369
Acts 3 206, 376
Acts 3:1-10; 4:3 529
Acts 3:[23] 206
Acts 3[:25-26] 376
Acts 4 459, 517
Acts 4:[12] 206
Acts 4[:19] 501 Acts 5[:29] 501
Acts 4[:32] 369
Acts 5 518
Acts 5[:29] 136, 285, 289, 471, 501
Acts 5[:30-31] 317
Acts 5[:34ff.] 404
Acts 5[:38ff] 26
Acts 5:39 380
Acts 5[:40-41] 272
Acts 6 422, 518
Acts 7 224, 268, 321, 422, 518
Acts 7: 51-52 224
Acts 8 82, 150, 337, 350, 351, 360, 387, 396, 401, 403, 411, 415, 416, 517
Acts 8[:12] 337, 401
Acts 8[:12-13; 35-38] 328, 345, 365, 389
Acts 8[:12f.] 43
Acts 8[:13] 403
Acts 8[:27-39] 82
Acts 8[:37] 396
Acts 9 220, 245, 411, 414, 416, 517
Acts 9[:4] 245
Acts 9[:18f.] 43
Acts 10 26, 150, 351, 360, 368, 387, 398, 411, 414, 416, 517
Acts 10[:35] 26
Acts 10[:44-48] 328, 345, 365, 389
Acts 10[:47] 43, 398
Acts 11 351, 387
Acts 11[:13-18] 389
Acts 11[:16-18] 328, 345, 365, 389
Acts 13 220
Acts 14 220
Acts 14[:22] 214, 229
Acts 15 517
Acts 16 148, 220, 351, 360, 368, 369, 387, 411, 414, 416, 417
Acts 16[:3] 43, 369
Acts 16[:14-15; 30-33] 328, 345, 365, 389
Acts 16[:15] 529
Acts 17 148, 220
Acts 17:11 525
Acts 17:18 220
Acts 17[:28?] 211
Acts 18 220, 411, 414, 417, 418
Acts 18[:8] 43
Acts 19 25, 73, 150, 220, 351, 387, 411, 414, 417, 517
Acts 19[:1-6] 73, 328, 345, 365, 389
Acts 19[:2ff.] 43
Acts 19[:9] 25
Acts 20 238, 244, 314, 431, 517
Acts 20[:18-24] 314
Acts 20[:22ff] 244
Acts 20[:28] 496
Acts 20[:29] 238
Acts 21 220
Acts 22 323, 416
Acts 22[:12ff.] 43
Acts 23 220
Acts 24 205, 220
Acts 24[:1-6] 430
Acts 24[:5, 14] 145
Acts24[:14] 25
Acts 25 220
Acts 26[:14] 245
Acts 27 220
Acts 28 205, 220
Acts 28[:22] 25, 430
Acts 28[:26ff] 453

Romans
Romans 1 81, 232
Romans 1[:1-4] 558
Romans 1[:2-4] 81
Romans 1[:3-4] 313
Romans 1[:18] 381
Romans 2 23, 300, 314, 366, 422
Romans 2[:1-11] 300
Romans 2[:2-6] 314
Romans 2[:13, 21ff] 23
Romans 2[:21] 515
Romans 2[:25-29] 366
Romans 3 73, 151

Scripture Index

Romans 3[:21-31] 263
Romans 3:23 73
Romans 3[:25] 512
Romans 5[:5] 494
Romans 5:8 315
Romans 5:12 74
Romans 5:19 315
Romans 5:20 210
Romans 6 21, 22, 23, 43, 62, 210, 232, 329, 361, 399, 408, 418, 495, 499, 502, 514, 523
Romans 6:1-2, 16-23 210
Romans 6[:1-4] 361
Romans 6[:1ff] 22
Romans 6[:3] 329
Romans 6[:3-4] 62, 408
Romans 6[:3ff.] 43
Romans 6[:4] 399
Romans 6 502
Romans 6[:12] 23
Romans 6[:12ff] 499, 527
Romans 6[:15] 514
Romans 6[:16ff] 21
Romans 6[:23] 495
Romans 7 502
Romans 7[:4, 7] 514
Romans 7[:5ff] 499
Romans 7[:6] 514
Romans 8 23, 212, 228, 230, 232, 283, 294, 323, 356, 439, 440, 480, 495, 502, 517
Romans 8[:1-27] 230
Romans 8[:4-11] 309
Romans 8[:5ff] 495
Romans 8[:6, 13] 232
Romans 8[:9] 23, 356
Romans 8[:9; 15-16] 518
Romans 8[:9ff] 499
Romans 8[:10] 23
Romans 8[:17] 440
Romans 8[:29] 283, 294, 480
Romans 8[:36] 439
Romans 8[:36-37] 228
Romans 8[:38-39] 323

Romans 9 82, 265, 348, 355
Romans 9[:4] 376, 377
Romans 9[:6-8] 376
Romans 9[:10-13] 348, 356
Romans 9[:22-26] 265
Romans 10 136, 262, 348, 358, 404, 411
Romans 10[:4] 514
Romans 10[:5] 262
Romans 10[:10] 404
Romans 10[:17] 358
Romans 11 348
Romans 11[:8] 453
Romans 12 230, 264, 272, 280, 281, 364, 366, 380, 426, 473
Romans 12[:1] 366, 380
Romans 12[:1-2] 364
Romans 12[:6-21] 426
Romans 12[:9-21] 280
Romans 12[:14, 17ff] 477
Romans 12[:14-21] 272
Romans 12[:16-19] 281
Romans 12[:17, 19] 264
Romans 13 127, 136, 147, 279, 282, 288, 321
Romans 13[:1-5] 480
Romans 13:1-6 539
Romans 13[:1-7] 279
Romans 13:3 288
Romans 13:7 288
Romans 13:7-10 539
Romans 13[:8] 325
Romans 13[:14] 380
Romans 14[:13ff] 500
Romans 14[:17] 263
Romans 16 24, 105, 237
Romans 16[:17] 24, 501, 514
Romans 16:17-18 540
Romans 16[:17-19] 339, 512
Romans 16[:17-20] 244, 282

1 Corinthians
1 Corinthians 1 202, 368, 418
1 Corinthians 1[:26-27] 202
1 Corinthians 2 26, 143, 203, 314, 366, 443, 471, 518
1 Corinthians 2[:1-5] 314
1 Corinthians 2[:6-8] 203, 443
1 Corinthians 2[:9-16] 366
1 Corinthians 2[:12] 26
1 Corinthians 2[:13] 508
1 Corinthians 3 143, 211, 235, 246, 248, 358, 418, 518
1 Corinthians 3[:11] 358, 504
1 Corinthians 3[:16-17] 211, 235, 248
1 Corinthians 3[:18ff] 246
1 Corinthians 4 [or 14:3?] 454
1 Corinthians 4[:1] 263
1 Corinthians 4[:9-13] 439
1 Corinthians 4[:11-13] 439
1 Corinthians 4[:13] 235
1 Corinthians 4[:20] 314
1 Corinthians 4[:26-31] 314
1 Corinthians 5 25, 105, 106, 107, 108, 110, 111, 114, 150, 209
1 Corinthians 5[:1-5; 11-13] 282
1 Corinthians 5[:1-13] 244, 266
1 Corinthians 5[:5] 108
1 Corinthians 5[:6] 111, 114
1 Corinthians 5[:6ff] 496, 499
1 Corinthians 5[:7] 503
1 Corinthians 5[:7-8] 209
1 Corinthians 5[:10] 25, 508

1 Corinthians 5[:12] 282
1 Corinthians 5:13 106
1 Corinthians 5[:13] 108, 497
1 Corinthians 6 22, 23, 106, 211, 232, 252, 275, 322, 323, 371, 418, 518
1 Corinthians 6[:1-11] 496
1 Corinthians 6[:7] 477
1 Corinthians 6[:7-8] 281
1 Corinthians 6[:9-10] 106, 110, 252, 371, 426, 524
1 Corinthians 6[:9-11] 275
1 Corinthians 6[:9-20] 323
1 Corinthians 6[:9ff] 22
1 Corinthians 6[:12] 468
1 Corinthians 6[:14, 17?] 23
1 Corinthians 6:15-16 523
1 Corinthians 6[:15-18] 322
1 Corinthians 6[:19] 211
1 Corinthians 6[:19-20] 246
1 Corinthians 7 150, 323, 324
1 Corinthians 7[:14] 406
1 Corinthians 7[:25-40] 323
1 Corinthians 7[:29-31] 508
1 Corinthians 7[:30] 325
1 Corinthians 8 314
1 Corinthians 8[:1; 11-12] 314
1 Corinthians 8[:9ff] 500
1 Corinthians 9:13 71
1 Corinthians 10 233, 281
1 Corinthians 10:16 425, 429
1 Corinthians 10:16-17 425
1 Corinthians 10[:20] 23
1 Corinthians, 10[:23ff] 468
1 Corinthians 10[:31?] 20

1 Corinthians 11 112, 150, 314
1 Corinthians 11[:17ff] 499
1 Corinthians 11[:23-29] 426
1 Corinthians 11[:23ff] 509
1 Corinthians 11[:27-34] 112
1 Corinthians 11[:27ff] 503
1 Corinthians 11:28 357
1 Corinthians 12 281, 339, 419, 518
1 Corinthians 12[:13] 498
1 Corinthians 13 282, 301, 314, 358, 426, 461, 467, 487, 522
1 Corinthians 13[:1-3] 301
1 Corinthians 13[:1-13] 426
1 Corinthians 13:2 358
1 Corinthians 13[4ff] 503
1 Corinthians 14 61, 449, 454, 455, 456, 458, 460, 461, 464, 465, 467, 510, 518
1 Corinthians 14:2 455
1 Corinthians 14[:11-12] 314
1 Corinthians 14[:26, 29-34] 454
1 Corinthians 14:26-33 61
1 Corinthians 14[:26ff] 449, 458
1 Corinthians 14:29ff 465
1 Corinthians 14[:32] 455
1 Corinthians 15 81, 326, 327, 419, 420
1 Corinthians 15[:20-23] 326
1 Corinthians 15:35-38; 42-44 327
1 Corinthians 15[38-49] 81
1 Corinthians. 15[:43-49] 312

1 Corinthians 16[:15] 368

2 Corinthians
2 Corinthians 1 518
2 Corinthians 1[:12] 314
2 Corinthians 2[:6-8] 114
2 Corinthians 3[:5] 24
2 Corinthians 3[:16ff] 514
2 Corinthians 3[:17] 23, 468, 513
2 Corinthians 4 518
2 Corinthians 4[:3ff] 21
2 Corinthians 4[:4] 502
2 Corinthians 4[:7] 24
2 Corinthians 5 518
2 Corinthians 5[:5, 18] 24
2 Corinthians 5[:10] 314
2 Corinthians 5[:15] 23
2 Corinthians 5[:18-21] 82
2 Corinthians. 5[:19] 562
2 Corinthians. 5[:19-21] 560
2 Corinthians 6 23, 25, 105, 110, 111, 211, 230, 248
2 Corinthians 6[:3] 500
2 Corinthians 6[:14] 23
2 Corinthians 6[:14-18] 110, 234, 500
2 Corinthians 6[:14ff] 25
2 Corinthians 6[:15] 111, 502
2 Corinthians 6[:16] 211, 246
2 Corinthians 6[:16-18] 235
2 Corinthians 6[:19-20] 235
2 Corinthians 7 109
2 Corinthians 8 366
2 Corinthians 8[:3ff] 530
2 Corinthians 9 366
2 Corinthians 9[:5] 295
2 Corinthians 9[:7] 530
2 Corinthians 10 [sic] 110
2 Corinthians 10[:3-5] 469
2 Corinthians 10[:3-6] 264
2 Corinthians 10:4-5 279

Scripture Index

2 Corinthians 10[:8?] 496
2 Corinthians 11 21, 220, 238, 244, 476, 518
2 Corinthians 11[:12-15] 238
2 Corinthians 11[:13] 476
2 Corinthians 11[:13-15] 244
2 Corinthians 11[:15] 21
2 Corinthians 11[:23-27] 220
2 Corinthians 12[:1] 509
2 Corinthians 12:1-4 562
2 Corinthians 13[:1ff] 496

Galatians
Galatians 1[:1] 24
Galatians 1[:8ff] 476, 505
Galatians 1[:9] 467
Galatians 1[:9-10] 297
Galatians 1[:10] 202, 523, 525
Galatians 1:20 236
Galatians 2[:4], 3 [sic: 5:1; 13] 468
Galatians 2[:15-16] 366
Galatians 2[:17] 22
Galatians 2[:17-20] 210
Galatians 3 419, 514, 518
Galatians 3[:13], 5[:18] 514
Galatians 4 147, 221, 245, 250, 514, 518
Galatians 4[:6-7; 29] 487
Galatians 4[:9-10] 471
Galatians 4:28 364
Galatians 4[:29] 147, 221, 265, 278, 294, 298, 494, 502
Galatians 5 22, 23, 106, 110, 114, 230, 232, 252, 275, 323, 334, 514, 518
Galatians 5[:1] 22
Galatians 5[:3-6; 24-25] 366
Galatians 5[:9] 111, 114
Galatians 5[:16-21] 323, 380
Galatians 5[:16ff] 230
Galatians 5[:17ff] 502
Galatians 5:19-21 106
Galatians 5[:19-21] 110, 252, 275, 371, 426, 524
Galatians 5[:19ff] 503
Galatians 5[:22ff] 499
Galatians 5[:24] 23
Galatians 6 160, 423, 444, 509, 518
Galatians 6[:13-15] 366
Galatians 6[:14] 160, 444, 509

Ephesians
Ephesians 1 518
Ephesians 1[:3-14] 309
Ephesians 1[:22] 263
Ephesians 2 21, 24, 209, 211, 225, 320
Ephesians 2:1-2 225
Ephesians 2[:2ff] 21
Ephesians 2[:3] 397
Ephesians 2[:4-10] 364
Ephesians 2[:10] 24, 211, 209
Ephesians 3 518
Ephesians 4 22, 23, 25, 230, 281, 419, 518
Ephesians 4[:4;17-32] 230
Ephesians 4[:8] 22
Ephesians 4:16 463
Ephesians 4[:17ff] 25
Ephesians 4[:22] 23
Ephesians 4[:22-24] 364
Ephesians 5 25, 105, 108, 112, 130, 232, 252, 275, 334, 371, 419
Ephesians 5[:3-5] 275, 371, 524
Ephesians 5[:3-6] 426
Ephesians 5[:3-13] 252
Ephesians 5[:3-20; 26-27] 520
Ephesians 5[:8ff] 25
Ephesians 5[:11] 25, 496
Ephesians [5:19] 454
Ephesians 5[:19-20] 130
Ephesians 5[:24ff] 495
Ephesians 5[:26ff] 497
Ephesians 5[:27] 112
Ephesians 6 263, 264, 279, 281, 282, 293
Ephesians 6[:4] 371, 496
Ephesians 6:11 264
Ephesians 6[:11-17] 279, 477
Ephesians 6[:12] 470
Ephesians 6[:13] 477
Ephesians 6[:17] 263, 281, 282

Philippians
Philippians 1 20, 295, 518
Philippians 1[:29ff?] 20
Philippians 2 24, 81, 230, 283, 325
Philippians 2:4-5 325
Philippians 2[:5] 480
Philippians 2:6-8 230
Philippians 2[:6-11] 283
Philippians 2[:7-8] 81
Philippians, 2:[9-11] 206
Philippians 2[:13] 24
Philippians 3 137, 262, 263, 422
Philippians 3[:5-14] 20
Philippians 3[:7-21] 263
Philippians 3[:9] 262
Philippians 3[:17] 137
Philippians 3[:18ff] 507

Colossians
Colossians 1 42, 108, 112, 151
Colossians 1[:18] 42, 112
Colossians 1[:20] 206
Colossians 1:26 562
Colossians 2 279, 321, 366, 391, 392, 411, 419, 420, 422
Colossians 2[:8; 16-17; 20-23] 366
Colossians 2[:11] 360, 366, 391, 499
Colossians 2[:13ff] 514

Colossians 2[:16-17?] 279
Colossians 2[:16ff.] 392
Colossians 3 20, 230, 281
Colossians 3[:1-17] 230, 364
Colossians 3[:5] 380
Colossians 3[:16ff] 20
Colossians 3[:21] 371
Colossians 6[?] 334

1 Thessalonians
1 Thessalonians 1 151
1 Thessalonians 4 518
1 Thessalonians 4[:5] 20
1 Thessalonians 4[:16-17] 326
1 Thessalonians 5 23, 25, 230, 518
1 Thessalonians 5[:9ff] 23
1 Thessalonians 5[:11] 454
1 Thessalonians 5:19-21 465
1 Thessalonians 5[:21] 457

2 Thessalonians
2 Thessalonians 2 150, 236, 282, 381, 545
2 Thessalonians 2[:3-12] 282, 381
2 Thessalonians 2[:8] 236
2 Thessalonians 3 105
2 Thessalonians 3[:2] 147, 294
2 Thessalonians 3[:6] 496, 541
2 Thessalonians 3[:6-15] 110
2 Thessalonians 3[:6; 14-15] 244, 266
2 Thessalonians 3[:10] 356
2 Thessalonians 3[:13] 266
2 Thessalonians 3:15 497

1 Timothy
1 Timothy 1 20, 105
1 Timothy 1[:7] 20
1 Timothy 1[:8-10] 279
1 Timothy 1[:16?] 468

1 Timothy 1[:20] 496
1 Timothy 3 75, 150, 496
1 Timothy 3:1ff 524
1 Timothy [3:1-13] 63
1 Timothy 3:2 75
1 Timothy 3[:2; 12] 323
1 Timothy 3[:2ff] 24
1 Timothy 4[:1-3] 244
1 Timothy 4[:12] 24
1 Timothy 5 111
1 Timothy 5:19-20 541
1 Timothy 6[?] 496
1 Timothy 6[:3-5] 24

2 Timothy
2 Timothy 1 24, 518
2 Timothy 1[:13] 24
2 Timothy 2[:8ff] 477
2 Timothy 2[:17] 24
2 Timothy 2[:19] 26
2 Timothy 2[:19ff] 25
2 Timothy 2[:20-26] 166, 263
2 Timothy 2[:21] 23
2 Timothy 2[:26] 22
2 Timothy 3 25, 82
2 Timothy 3[:1-9] 238, 379, 385
2 Timothy 3[:4ff] 25
2 Timothy 3[:7-9] 507
2 Timothy 3:8 239
2 Timothy 3[:12] 214, 229, 266
2 Timothy 3[:13] 25
2 Timothy 4[:3] 236, 453
2 Timothy 4[:3-4] 242
2 Tomothy 4[:3ff] 25
2 Timothy 6 (sic) 512

Titus
Titus 1 20, 25, 150
Titus 1[:6] 323
Titus [1:6-9] 63
Titus 1[:11ff] 20
Titus 1[:16] 25, 379
Titus 2[:7] 24
Titus 2[:14] 22
Titus 3 20, 112, 282, 364,

419, 501, 518
Titus 3[:1-11] 364
Titus 3[:10-11] 112
Titus 3[:10ff] 501

Hebrews
Hebrews 1[:3] 81, 428
Hebrews 1[:6] 561
Hebrews 1[:9-10] 307
Hebrews 2 518
Hebrews 2[:9-18] 81
Hebrews 2[:11-12] 312
Hebrews 2[:14-17] 560
Hebrews 2:14-18 312
Hebrews 2[:14ff] 22
Hebrews 3 25, 116, 517
Hebrews 3[:12-15]; 13 116
Hebrews 3:13 116
Hebrews 3[:14] 25
Hebrews 3:15 116
Hebrews 4 263, 279, 281, 283
Hebrews 4[:12] 263, 279, 281
Hebrews 5 25
Hebrews 5 [= 4:16] 512
Hebrews 5[:11] 562
Hebrews 6 518
Hebrews 6[:6?] 507
Hebrews 6[:16] 303
Hebrews 6[:17-18] 303
Hebrews 7[:15-17] 81
Hebrews 7[:17; 28] 561
Hebrews 7[:26-28] 253
Hebrews 8[:1-2] 253
Hebrews 8[:6-7] 267
Hebrews 8:6-8 259
Hebrews 8[:7] 266
Hebrews 8[:13] 258, 392
Hebrews 9[:1-10] 262
Hebrews 9:11-14 258
Hebrews 9[:24] 253
Hebrews 10 22, 267, 408, 420, 518, 560
Hebrews 10[:1-4] 267
Hebrews 10[:4-22] 560
Hebrews 10[:22] 408
Hebrews 10[:35] 22

Scripture Index

Hebrews 11 20, 137, 201, 356, 440, 557
Hebrews 11:1 137
Hebrews 11[:1ff] 20
Hebrews 11[:3] 557
Hebrews 11[:6] 356
Hebrews 11[:38] 201
Hebrews 12[:1ff] 477
Hebrews 12[:16-17] 133
Hebrews 12[:28] 23
Hebrews 13 81, 150
Hebrews 13[:4] 323
Hebrews 13[:8?] 562

James
James 1 147
James 1[:3ff] 477
James 2 20, 21, 25, 72, 151
James 2[:14, 17] 151
James 2:14; 26 321
James 2[:14ff] 21
James 2[:21, 27] 25
James 2[:22] 20
James 2:26 317
James 3 144, 313
James 3[:17] 144
James 4 24, 202, 235, 313, 518
James 4[:4] 202, 235, 523, 525
James 4[:6-10] 313
James 4[:7] 24
James 5[:7ff] 477
James 5:12 303

1 Peter
1 Peter 1 20, 49, 225, 230, 339, 364, 383, 517, 518
1 Peter 1[:6-7] 383
1 Peter 1[:14] 20
1 Peter 1[:22-23] 339
1 Peter 1:23 364
1 Peter 2 22, 26, 147, 230, 260, 282, 285, 288, 289, 321
1 Peter 2[:1] 26
1 Peter 2:8 260
1 Peter 2[:11-24] 426
1 Peter 2:13 288
1 Peter 2:16 22, 289
1 Peter 2[:19] 285
1 Peter 2[:24] 22
1 Peter 3 20, 112, 360, 390, 408, 419, 421
1 Peter 3[:15] 20, 408
1 Peter 3[:18] 22
1 Peter 3[:20] 390
1 Peter 3[:21] 360, 408
1 Peter 4 25, 230, 260, 272, 340, 518
1 Peter 4:1 260, 272
1 Peter 4[:2ff] 20
1 Peter 4[:4] 25
1 Peter 4[:5] 340
1 Peter 5 230
1 Peter 5[:1-2] 429
1 Peter 5[:2] 530
1 Peter 5[:3] 24
1 Peter 5[:3-5] 473
1 Peter 5[:3-6] 284
1 Peter 5[:5-6] 314
1 Peter 5[:8ff] 23

2 Peter
2 Peter 1 25, 211, 517
2 Peter 1: 4 25, 211
2 Peter 2 20, 21, 22, 239
2 Peter 2[:1-3] 244
2 Peter 2[:1-3; 12-22] 385
2 Peter 2[:1ff] 20
2 Peter 2[:2, 15, 17-19] 507
2 Peter 2[:3ff] 22
2 Peter 2[:12-19] 239
2 Peter 2[:14] 21
2 Peter 2[:18ff] 21
2 Peter 3[:3-10] 385
2 Peter 3[:17] 24

1 John
1 John 21, 23, 24, 25, 73, 82, 151
1 John 1[:1] 557, 561
1 John 1:1-2 311
1 John 1[:6] 21, 25
1 John 1[:6ff] 25
1 John 1:8 73
1 John 2 82, 244, 321
1 John 2[:4] 25
1 John 2[:4-5] 82
1 John 2[:4-11] 426
1 John 2[:9-11;15-28] 482
1 John 2[:18-26], 4[:1] 244
1 John 2[:29] 503
1 John 3 21, 24, 210, 235, 305, 325, 420, 482, 518
1 John 3[:1] 235, 494
1 John 3[:3ff], 3[:6ff], 5[:18ff?] 21
1 John 3[:6-18] 426
1 John 3[:8-9] 210
1 John 3:9-10 305
1 John 3[:9ff] 495, 503
1 John 3[:16-19] 325
1 John 3[:33] 24
1 John 4 518
1 John 4[:2-3] 211, 561
1 John 4[:3] 211
1 John 4[:5] 24
1 John 4[:6] 23
1 John 4[:7-21] 426
1 John 4[:8, 20ff] 494
1 John 4[:16] 494
1 John 5 23, 24, 82, 518
1 John 5[:3] 24
1 John 5[:18] 495
1 John 5:20 561

2 John
2 John 1[:7-10] 212
2 John 1[:7-11] 244
2 John 1[:9] 21, 456
2 John 1[:10ff] 24
2 John 1:11 212

3 John
3 John 1[:10] 21

Jude
Jude 1[:2?] 22
Jude 1[:4] 239
Jude 1[:12ff] 239
Jude 1[:17-19] 244

Revelation
Revelation 1 81, 130
Revelation 1:5-6 130
Revelation 1 151
Revelation 1[:16] 282
Revelation 2 22, 225
Revelation 2[:2] 22
Revelation 2[:7] 226
Revelation 2:10 225
Revelation 3:5 226
Revelation 4:8-11 270
Revelation 5 81, 518
Revelation 6[:11] 382
Revelation 7 151
Revelation 7[:9; 13-17] 382
Revelation 7:9-17; 21:4 228
Revelation 10[:9-10] 208
Revelation 11[:1-2?] 433
Revelation 12[:1-6] 383
Revelation 13 225, 232, 233, 234, 380, 383, 386, 439
Revelation 13:4 383
Revelation 13:10 225
Revelation 13[:15-18] 234
Revelation 13[:16] 233
Revelation 14 232, 380, 383
Revelation 14[:1-5] 131
Revelation 14[:9-11] 234
Revelation 14[:10] 439
Revelation 14[:11] 133
Revelation 14[:12] 266
Revelation 15[:2] 250
Revelation 15:4 270
Revelation 15:5 252
Revelation 16:5-6 225
Revelation 16[:6] 439
Revelation 16:15 133]
Revelation 17 383, 384, 385
Revelation 18 383, 384
Revelation 18[:4] 25, 234, 386
Revelation 18[:4-8] 110
Revelation 18[:4ff] 500
Revelation 18[:8] 133
Revelation 19[:5] 130
Revelation 19[:6-8] 322
Revelation 19[:11-16] 245
Revelation 19[:15] 282
Revelation 20[:13-14] 327
Revelation 21 232
Revelation 21[:7] 226
Revelation 21[:7-8] 52
Revelation 21[:8] 426
Revelation 21[:8-9] 252
Revelation 21[:8, 27] 371
Revelation 22 82, 202, 232, 252
Revelation 22[:3-4] 524
Revelation 22[:3; 14-15] 371
Revelation 22[:3; 15] 426
Revelation 22[:7] 82
Revelation 22[:14] 253
Revelation 22[:15] 252
Revelation 22[:17] 202
Revelation 22[:18] 305

Name and Subject Index

A

Aarau 140, 544
Aarburg 141, 152
Aargau 7, 21
Aaron 257, 274
abandonment
  See: *Gelassenheit*
Abbot Diethelm 70
Abednego 216, 285, 441, 563
Abel 223, 251, 265, 441
Abimelech 277
abominations 42, 151, 215, 234, 240, 244, 275, 323, 386, 422, 545
Abraham 10, 13, 74, 84, 232, 256, 267, 272, 303, 304, 312, 347, 365, 375, 376, 409, 441, 558, 559, 560, 563
Achaia 217
Adam 45, 74, 101, 133, 230, 231, 274, 290, 304, 312, 315, 316, 326, 327, 339, 361, 363, 364, 396, 429, 430, 432, 441, 508, 552
Adelheit, wife of Wilhelm Reublin 31
Adelheit Kin from Embrach 66
Adelheit Spilman from Tellikon 66
admonition 11, 39, 46, 88, 89, 100, 101, 102, 103, 127, 204, 249, 251, 257, 266, 355, 371, 451, 456, 460, 464, 501, 524
adult baptism 29, 37, 38, 58, 69, 102, 534, 550, 551
  See also: baptism
adulterers/adultery 23, 63, 140, 150, 202, 216, 225, 232, 235, 236, 239, 244, 275, 281, 300, 322, 324, 334, 348, 384, 396, 426, 441, 515, 539
Affoltern am Albis 183, 532, 533
Agag the king 260
Agricola, Theophilus 192
Alexander, bishop of Alexandria 330
Alexander the Great 381
Alsace 84, 90, 92, 388, 556
Amalekites 109, 394
Amaziah 148, 215, 216

Ambrose of Milan 331, 448, 463
Amish 11, 92, 119
Amorites 264, 394
Amos 128, 148, 215, 216, 441, 552
Amsterdam 10, 11, 83, 84, 120, 365, 554
Anabaptist/Anabaptists/Anabaptism 1-18, 26, 30-42, 57, 58-73, 76-80, 84-87, 92, 100- 105, 117-124, 126, 128-129, 139-143, 147, 153, 155, 157-165, 167-168, 170-173, 179, 181, 183, 185, 186-187, 190- 200, 285, 296, 327, 352, 355, 365, 388-389, 411, 446-452, 454-455, 461, 463, 465, 468, 494, 506, 528, 532-540, 543-547, 549, 550-551, 554, 555
Ananias 35, 220, 416, 430, 490
Andrew the apostle 217
Angel Gabriel 381
angels 147, 226, 234, 254, 269, 301, 312, 321, 329, 349, 400, 432, 433, 439, 461, 474, 492, 522, 545, 557, 559, 561
anger 179, 224, 232, 234, 249, 277, 282, 283, 315, 348, 380, 440, 494, 524
Antichrist 61, 147, 222, 235, 240, 247, 290, 293, 378, 379, 380, 381, 382, 383, 384, 386, 387, 410, 430, 431, 498, 560
Anti-trinitarianism 552
apocalyptic 77, 78
  See also: End Times
Apollos 418
Apostles' Creed 126, 144, 307, 311, 559
Apostle Thomas 218
apparel
  See: clothing
Appenzell 3
armor 257, 293, 435
  armor of God 264
Arndt, Johann 198
arrogance 140, 221, 225, 230-232, 236, 246, 252, 275, 300, 348, 466, 495, 524
Asia 217, 219
Athanasius 329, 330
Athens 220
atonement 121, 133, 550, 553, 560

Attilus, governor of Judah 219
Auerbacher, Kilian 34
Augsburg 36, 77, 163, 191, 192, 411
Augustine 191, 287, 330, 331, 342, 377, 403, 464, 543
Ausbund 2, 11, 12, 118, 119, 120, 121, 122, 123, 124, 125, 126, 127, 128, 135, 163, 164, 167, 179, 190
Auspitz, Moravia 34, 55, 56
Austerlitz, Moravia 8, 33, 34, 35, 39, 42, 48, 49, 50, 51, 53, 54, 55, 59
Austerlitz Brethren 8, 42
authorities, political 13, 14, 16, 17, 31, 33, 36, 37, 38, 61, 64, 65, 67, 70, 76, 98, 100, 127, 136, 140, 147, 155, 156, 164, 167, 168, 170, 171, 172, 173, 181, 182, 183, 185, 186, 187, 189, 194, 195, 198, 243, 247, 256, 282, 284, 288, 296, 451, 468, 470, 475, 478, 486, 488, 505, 507, 532, 533, 534, 535, 536, 539, 543
See also: government; magistracy/magistrates
avarice 382, 396, 460, 495, 523, 524
avoidance 84, 509

B

Baal 260, 472, 487
Balaam's donkey 355
Babel 82
Babylon 234, 296, 384, 386, 441, 500
Baden 18, 37, 65, 66, 68, 163, 461, 555
Baecher, Claude 121, 125, 128
Bär, Margaretha 532
Balaam 132, 239
ban 5, 9-11, 23, 32-33, 38, 39, 46, 51, 58, 63, 79, 80, 84-87, 89, 94, 100-109, 112-117, 127, 137, 144, 150, 162, 193, 204, 213, 231, 244, 246, 250, 290, 296, 322, 324, 332, 372, 378, 386, 432, 451, 466, 474, 484, 487, 496, 497, 498, 506, 509, 510, 519-520, 540-541, 552-554
banishment 18, 76, 139
baptism 6, 8, 16, 28, 29, 30, 31, 32, 37, 38, 41, 42, 43, 46, 47, 52, 53, 58, 62, 66, 69, 72, 73, 74, 75, 77, 88, 93, 101, 102, 141, 144, 150, 158, 162, 164, 165, 181, 182, 246, 306, 328, 329, 330, 331, 332, 333, 334, 335, 336, 337, 338, 339, 340, 341, 342, 343, 344, 345, 346, 347, 348, 349, 350, 351, 352, 353, 354, 355, 357, 358, 359, 360, 361, 362, 363, 365, 366, 367, 368, 369, 370, 371, 372, 373, 374, 375, 376, 377, 378, 386, 387, 388, 389, 390, 391, 392, 393, 394, 395, 396, 397, 399, 400, 401, 402, 403, 404, 405, 406, 407, 408, 409, 410, 411, 412, 413, 414, 416, 417, 418, 419, 420, 421, 430, 431, 448, 463, 466, 484, 487, 495, 504, 505, 506, 510, 511, 534, 538, 541, 550, 551, 553
See also: adult baptism; infant baptism; rebaptism
Bär, Margaretha 532
Barnabas 459
Barteli from Baden 66
Bartholomew the apostle 218
Basel 1, 3, 6, 12, 17, 26, 27, 36, 140, 155, 172, 179, 183, 289, 290, 331, 344, 470, 535
Beatus Renanus 332
Bechi, Hans 57, 58, 60, 65, 66
Belial 111, 205, 234, 500, 502
Bender, Harold S. 2, 10, 92, 94, 97
Bergmann, Cornelius 1, 14
Bern 3, 6, 7, 12, 13, 17, 58, 59, 66, 90, 139, 140, 141, 143, 147, 148, 153, 162, 163, 164, 171, 173, 179, 185, 186, 187, 193, 194, 199, 296, 336, 362, 449, 476, 478, 482, 483, 490
Bern Disputation 58, 59, 66, 362
Bethlehem 218, 252, 297
Bichel, Hans 126, 163, 179, 190
Bisch, Rauff 79, 555, 556, 557, 559, 562
bishops 27, 75, 92, 93, 95-97, 240, 287, 293, 328-332, 464, 469, 485, 486, 488, 496, 498, 509, 524
Blanke, Fritz 29
blasphemy 218, 231, 240, 345, 346, 348, 426, 457, 459-460, 494, 524, 547
Blaurock, George 16, 29
Blonde Hans from Tschipfen 66
Body of Christ 110, 111, 112, 424, 425, 429, 498, 499, 502, 503, 541, 560
Bohemian Brethren 126, 552

Name and Subject Index

Boll, Hans Jakob 179, 180, 186, 188, 193-199
Bonn 90
born again
born from above
born of Christ
See: rebirth, spiritual
Bosch, Sigmund 126
Bouwens, Leenaert 10, 79, 85-87
breaking of bread
See: Lord's Supper
Breisgau 16, 84, 90
Bremgarten 57, 58, 61, 65
Brennwald, Carli 58
Brenz, Johannes 191, 192, 193, 294
brothers and sisters 21, 23, 48, 52, 54, 62, 76, 81, 88, 89, 90, 91, 97, 98, 111, 133, 151, 220, 281, 303, 312, 321, 323, 325, 343, 362, 423, 425, 441, 493, 517, 541, 552, 560
Brötli, Johannes 28, 29, 30
Bucer, Martin 78, 103, 116, 182, 336, 349, 362, 367, 448, 451, 470, 471, 472, 487
Buchman, M. Joder 61
Bülach 57, 66
Bülach woods 66
Bullinger, Heinrich 13-14, 35-36, 57, 61, 155, 165, 222, 445-449, 452-455, 457-458, 467-468, 475-476, 479, 490, 493-496, 498, 501-502, 504, 507, 510, 512-513, 515, 521, 526, 529-531, 537
Bünderlin, Hans 33, 77
Burckhart von Offen 51
Bürg 117

C

Caesarea 220
Caiaphas 255, 407, 490
Cain 251, 265
Calvin, John 104, 191
Canaan 254, 359
Capernaum 428
capital punishment 76, 103, 277, 281
Capito, Wolfgang 31, 181, 335, 448, 451, 471
Castellio, Sebastian 191, 192, 193, 463, 464

catechumens 332, 333, 405
celestial flesh 79, 559
Centurion, the 299, 428
ceremonies 132, 258, 261, 262, 374, 392, 412, 433, 511, 512, 528
Charlemagne 332
children 16, 20, 21, 28, 43, 52, 53, 54, 62, 73, 74, 90, 93, 95, 107, 126, 130, 133, 137, 146, 159, 166, 177, 201, 204, 208, 209, 210, 213, 221, 223, 224, 228, 230, 231, 232, 235, 239, 242, 249, 250, 265, 266, 268, 272, 273, 274, 275, 276, 279, 284, 291, 293, 302, 310, 312, 315, 316, 322, 323, 325, 327, 328, 330, 331, 333, 334, 336, 337, 339, 340, 341, 342, 343, 344, 345, 346, 347, 348, 349, 350, 351, 352, 353, 354, 355, 356, 357, 358, 359, 360, 361, 362, 363, 364, 366, 367, 368, 369, 370, 371, 372, 373, 375, 376, 377, 383, 391, 395, 396, 397, 398, 399, 401, 405, 406, 407, 408, 415, 422, 424, 425, 430, 431, 433, 436, 472, 481, 494, 503, 504, 505, 506, 508, 513, 518, 520, 524, 532, 533, 542, 558
children of Korah 273
Christendom 11, 240, 249, 275, 298, 327, 334, 371, 375, 412, 433, 434, 466, 474
Christology 94, 551, 559
Christ's sacrifice 151
Chrysostom 191, 448, 464
church attendance 7, 16, 20
church discipline 1, 80, 84, 85, 100, 106, 166
church, true 18, 38, 39, 168, 451, 485, 498
circumcision 6, 74, 257, 262, 267, 320, 361, 365, 366, 367, 390, 391, 392, 397, 411, 416, 422, 423, 463, 499, 517
Clasen, Claus-Peter 4, 165
Clement the 7th 159, 328
clergy/ state church pastors 8, 37, 162, 168, 179, 181, 330, 345, 349, 358, 368
See also: preachers and priests
Clock, Leenaerdt 80
Clothing 98, 435, 554
Mortal clothing 228, 384
Sheeps' clothing 240, 241, 300, 525
coercion 46, 126, 127, 135, 136, 145, 147, 149-150, 163, 165-166, 187, 190, 192,

201, 205, 212, 225, 235, 250, 255, 262, 270, 273, 276, 277, 278, 279, 280, 286-287, 289, 290-297, 366, 370, 372, 400, 435, 448, 451, 469-470, 475-476, 478, 482, 484-486, 488, 494, 502, 514, 529, 534, 545, 547
Collegiants 553
Cologne 12, 80, 85, 87, 121, 123, 388
Comenius, John Amos 552
command, divine 41, 42, 43, 50, 53-54, 61-63, 74, 89, 106, 109, 136, 148, 150, 164, 215, 222, 224-225, 246, 257, 260, 264, 276, 278, 286-287, 290, 292, 295, 303, 325-326, 328, 334, 345, 348, 351, 353-355, 359-361, 365-366, 370-372, 386, 398, 413, 421, 430-432, 434, 459-460, 470, 509, 514, 523, 541, 545
commandments 22, 24, 51, 72, 82, 88, 116, 144, 205, 211, 215, 253, 305, 412, 472, 487, 508, 510, 511, 515, 521, 522, 527, 539, 542
Communion
See: Lord's Supper
community 10, 18, 34, 35, 38, 39, 43, 47, 48, 50, 51, 52, 54, 56, 58, 62, 69, 95, 96, 98, 107, 118, 151, 156, 157, 158, 187, 199, 203, 204, 243, 256, 257, 264, 266, 270, 285, 286, 312, 324, 360, 369, 370, 455, 458, 459, 466, 476, 480, 495, 499, 504, 519, 520, 524, 545, 551, 556
Concept of Cologne 80
concordance, biblical 105, 122, 130, 285, 540
Confederate states, Swiss 4
confessionalization 4, 5, 104, 162, 189
congregation 22, 26, 28, 31, 32, 34, 35, 38, 48, 49, 52, 53, 62, 64, 66, 79, 84, 85, 89, 91-95, 97, 102-103, 105-106, 108-109, 110-115, 161, 218, 329, 330, 336, 339, 350, 355, 358, 365, 372, 374, 398, 400, 432, 451, 453, 454, 455, 456, 458, 467, 468, 474, 475, 487, 495, 496, 501, 510, 522, 526, 530, 549, 553-554
conscience(s) 6, 58, 62, 82, 85, 96, 106, 132-134, 142-143, 145-146, 149, 165-166, 186-187, 189, 190, 192, 205, 235, 246-247, 248, 262, 284, 285-289, 293, 294, 296, 299, 300, 314, 340, 360, 363, 368,

381, 419, 420, 421, 448, 451, 456, 464, 466, 468, 471, 476, 483, 485-486, 488, 489, 534-535, 539, 545
Constance 58, 100, 117, 390, 400, 405
Constantine, Emperor 332
conversion 44, 55, 57-59, 103, 115-116, 126, 131, 217, 300, 373, 413, 415-416, 435, 470, 483, 509, 550
Cornelius the Centurion 299, 368, 409, 416
Council at Braga 387
Council of Arles 332
Council of Laodicea 332
Count Joachim von Zollern of Hohenberg 31
covenant 6, 42, 62, 74, 135, 148, 161, 258, 259, 261, 262, 264, 267, 340, 347, 348, 360, 362, 364, 366, 375, 376, 377, 388, 501, 515, 520
Covenanters 8, 59, 60, 122, 126, 128, 155, 161, 176-177, 182, 189-190, 196-198, 255
creatures 62, 122, 321, 348, 358, 414, 431, 512, 557
Crispus 417
cursing 225, 231
Cyprian 329, 448, 462, 463
Cyril of Alexandria 331, 390, 448, 464

D

Danzig 551, 552
darkness 21, 23, 25, 41, 42, 88, 136, 201, 205, 209, 234, 238, 241, 242, 249, 253, 378, 438, 439, 470, 487, 490, 500, 505, 507, 521
David the Psalmist 20, 24, 149, 214, 226-228, 245-246, 257, 260, 286, 289, 293, 315, 325, 383, 501, 558, 561
David a Bohemian brother 51-53
David, house of 517
David, key of 309
David, seed of 558
David, son of 94, 96, 312-313
deacons 33, 330
de Bakker, Willem 10
deeds and misdeeds 48, 101, 214, 221, 288, 300-302, 313, 314, 347, 357, 372, 379, 437, 440, 494, 529, 547

Name and Subject Index

Denck, Hans 77, 122, 168
denial of self 276, 373, 374
 See also: *Gelassenheit*
Deppermann, Klaus 2, 31, 77
Devil 21, 22, 23, 42, 51, 130, 168, 210, 212, 213, 225, 232, 236, 237, 238, 239, 244, 247, 262, 264, 273, 293, 312, 323, 329, 331, 341, 343, 347, 361, 363, 367, 368, 370, 374, 375, 379, 383, 410, 433, 439, 442, 459, 462, 466, 470, 481, 488, 498, 503, 543
 See also: Satan and Lucifer
Dietikon 66
disciple(s) 62, 146, 207, 208, 213, 216, 219, 222, 230-231, 235, 238, 260, 268, 272, 278, 279, 280, 284, 293, 295, 301, 307, 308, 322-325, 328, 350, 351, 370, 375, 376, 393, 414, 416, 417, 423, 424, 425, 433, 456, 495, 496, 499, 503, 511, 512, 513, 516, 519, 520, 525, 528, 529, 539, 540, 542, 550, 556, 560, 561
discipline 1, 5, 23, 64, 79, 80, 84, 85, 90, 93, 94, 100, 101, 102, 103, 107, 115, 166, 193, 244, 276, 451, 466, 487, 496, 509, 510, 515, 519, 520, 550, 552
divinity of Christ 550
divorce 204, 260, 322
Donatists 543
Donatus 329
Doopsgezind 552
Dordrecht Confession 3
drunkenness 23, 63, 111, 113, 140, 179, 225, 232, 236, 237, 241, 244, 275, 300, 334, 348, 371-372, 396, 426, 432, 495, 524
Dyck, Cornelius J. 10, 84, 86, 90, 102, 551

E

ecclesiology 11, 16, 18, 63, 100
Edessa 219
Edom 221, 421
Egypt 219, 249, 250, 258, 296, 415, 421, 440, 441
Eifel 90
elders 48, 49, 50, 51, 52, 76, 79, 81, 84, 85, 88, 90, 91, 92, 95, 220, 228, 429, 555, 563
Eleazar 216

election/the elect 24, 28, 131, 132, 149, 211, 214, 225, 271, 279, 304, 308, 322, 324, 338, 348, 351, 378, 382, 383, 386, 435, 439, 440, 441, 442, 443, 523
 See also: predestination
Eli the priest 109
Elier 285
Elijah 146, 215, 260, 268, 441, 472
Embrach 65, 66
Emden 85
Emmental 92
emperor 246-247, 289, 299, 435, 442, 468, 473, 477, 479-480, 490-491
Emperor Constantine 332
Emperor Ferdinand I 36
Emperor Domitian 219
Emperor Honorius 332
Emperor Nero 220
End Times 132, 154, 178-179, 184, 251-252, 254, 257-258, 380, 385, 433-435
 mark of the beast 383-384
Entfelder, Christian 77, 461
envy 166, 225, 231, 251, 492, 524, 529
Ephraim 257, 292
Epiphanius 159, 182, 215, 216
Erasmus, Desiderius 159, 182, 191, 243, 328, 336, 337, 348
Erastus 299
Esau 43, 133, 265, 347, 348, 351, 355, 356, 362, 375, 392, 396, 398
Eschlperger, Hans 55
Esslingen 30, 32, 33, 35, 38
eternal life 192, 204, 207, 208, 210, 211, 226, 232, 262, 305, 310, 357, 383, 423, 424, 428, 431, 434, 437, 481, 527, 529, 558, 561
Ethiopian eunuch 82, 331
Etliche schöne Christliche Geseng (Some Beautiful Christian Songs) 11, 118, 120-125, 127, 130-133, 135, 227, 239, 455
Eusebius 330, 341, 404, 448, 464
Eve 74
exclusion 43, 62-63, 97, 99, 102, 103, 105-108, 110, 113, 114, 115, 137, 190, 255, 323, 346, 398, 484, 496, 519, 540
excommunication 79, 85, 102, 290
 See also: Ban

execution 4, 69, 103, 139, 165, 191, 193, 227
expulsion 27, 34, 35, 49-51, 103, 137, 141, 149, 215, 221, 224, 231, 235, 249, 264, 334, 345, 363, 475, 497, 520, 553

F

Faber, John 333, 389, 390, 391, 400, 401, 405, 410
faith 1, 8, 20, 22, 24-27, 33, 38-39, 41-43, 46, 53, 55, 60, 62-63, 74, 81, 85, 88, 90-91, 93, 101, 104, 110, 118, 126-127, 132, 135, 136-137, 142, 144-147, 149-151, 158, 162, 165, 170, 186-187, 189-190, 192, 194, 196, 201, 204-206, 208, 211, 217, 222, 225, 232, 234, 241, 243, 245, 261-262, 266, 272, 280, 284-291, 293-297, 300-302, 307, 317-323, 327, 329-335, 337, 339, 341-346, 349-350, 352-354, 356-366, 372-373, 377, 384, 387, 388-393, 395, 397-399, 403-411, 413-417, 419-421, 424-425, 428-429, 431, 435, 440, 448, 451, 453, 461, 463, 468-469, 471, 475-477, 482-487, 491, 494-495, 497, 499, 505-508, 522, 524, 527, 529, 534, 536, 539, 544-547, 552, 557-558, 560, 562-563
false prophets 121, 132, 160, 164, 193, 215, 222, 224, 225, 236, 239, 240, 241, 242, 244, 385, 478, 490, 492, 496
false teachers 52, 486
Fast, Heinold 13, 17, 26, 59, 70, 83, 105, 155, 165, 172, 446, 447, 454, 455, 461, 527, 540
fasting 27, 317
fear of God 26, 81, 88, 96, 107, 156, 160, 233, 234, 253, 313, 348, 368, 425, 442, 444, 461, 467, 502, 556
Fedminger, H. 152
Felix, governor 220
fellowship 21, 23, 24, 25, 96, 106, 107, 108, 110, 111, 112, 114, 116, 212, 234, 244, 264, 279, 282, 293, 297, 308, 309, 322, 324, 364, 425, 427, 453, 476, 495, 497, 499, 500, 503, 505, 508
Ferdinand I. 36
figurative interpretation of Scripture 37, 172, 177, 261, 263, 264, 270, 273-274, 279, 308, 390, 419, 421-422, 428, 432, 499, 511, 528, 530
Firm, Anthonius 336,
Fischer, Hans 8-9, 57-67
Flam, Hans 66
flattery 236-237, 541
flesh 9, 23, 44, 76, 79, 81, 90, 94, 96, 108, 117, 135, 147, 161-162, 202, 204, 206, 211-212, 217, 221, 227, 229-233, 236, 239, 245, 250, 252, 260, 265, 272, 275-276, 278, 294, 298, 300, 306-307, 311-313, 315-316, 320, 322-323, 327, 346-347, 353, 356-358, 361, 363, 368, 374, 376-377, 380, 382, 384, 391, 397, 421-422, 424, 426, 430, 437-438, 442, 470, 480-481, 487, 493-495, 499-500, 502, 507, 509-510, 518, 521, 523, 527, 550, 557-562
Fluri, Adolf 185
follow Christ 24, 51, 75, 146, 222, 231, 290, 367, 473
force 72, 137, 146,-47, 163, 176, 201, 205, 212, 222, 225, 235, 255-256, 270, 287, 289, 290-291, 294-295, 297-298, 345, 354, 364, 370, 379, 395, 400, 410, 412, 435, 469-470, 473, 475-478, 480-481, 486, 488, 529-530, 545
forgiveness of sins 309, 317, 318, 320, 329, 357, 376, 414, 415
fornication 150, 225, 232, 236, 244, 252, 275, 348, 426, 432, 441
Francis, druggist 41
Franck, Sebastian 77, 126, 159, 182, 191, 193, 217, 218, 219, 220, 222, 294, 378, 379, 382, 386, 463, 464
Franeker 84
Frankenthal 13, 79, 102, 120, 121, 150, 153, 155, 156, 157, 158, 163, 165, 166, 167, 171, 172, 173, 174, 175, 176, 177, 179, 181, 185, 186, 197, 198, 199, 201, 249, 255, 264, 429, 555, 557, 559, 562
Fraternal admonition
See: Ban
freedom of conscience 6, 165, 186
free will 282, 550
Freisleben, Christoph 32, 35
Freundschaft 5

Name and Subject Index

Fridli, a blacksmith's helper 66
Friedmann, Robert 2, 3, 163, 171, 551, 552, 553
Friesen, Abraham 13
Froschauer, printer 105, 243, 290, 291, 336, 445, 538, 540, 558
Froschauer Bible 3, 538, 558
fruit 29, 37, 45, 52, 64, 114, 127, 136, 151, 166, 206-212, 215, 240, 302, 317, 319, 321, 324, 329, 348, 356, 403, 432-433, 443, 457, 462, 466, 479, 495, 502-503, 519-522, 525, 536, 550, 552
Furner, Mark 173, 185

G

Gadarenes 466
galley slaves 147
Gamaliel 380, 404
Gelassenheit [Abandonment, Renunciation, Yieldedness, Surrender] 31, 42, 63, 80, 82, 116, 122, 208, 210, 324-326, 373, 377, 408, 427, 440, 472, 477, 481, 487, 552
Gentiles 46, 220, 245, 260, 264, 265, 266, 270, 416
gentleness 144, 277, 294, 518
Gerson, Jean 404
Gideon 277
Glattfelden 66
gluttony 140, 179, 225, 236, 244, 275, 300, 334, 348, 371, 396, 495
godparents 331, 333, 340, 341, 343, 358, 409, 412
God's Word 23, 87, 143, 144, 176, 201, 242, 243, 248, 249, 284, 288, 293, 319, 333, 343, 345, 361, 364, 368, 379, 387, 389, 401, 410, 412, 422, 453, 457, 460, 462, 466, 469, 470, 472, 480, 486, 487, 491, 544, 557, 563
Goertz, Hans-Jürgen 2
Goliath 526
Gomorrah 280, 295, 359, 539
good works 24, 25, 72, 204, 211, 317, 318, 319, 320, 472, 484, 487, 522
Gordon, Bruce 141
Goshen College 10, 13, 84, 170
government 30, 36, 94, 99, 102, 167-168, 181, 189, 246, 274, 284, 288, 483, 544, 550
  See also: authorities, political; magistracy/magistrates
grace 22-23, 42, 49, 50, 52-54, 56, 70, 74, 81-82, 88-89, 91, 101, 109, 115-116, 144-145, 147, 150-152, 160-161, 176, 187, 204-205, 208, 210-211, 239, 244, 249, 251-252, 263, 268-270, 276-277, 294, 302, 305, 309-311, 313-319, 321, 324, 338-341, 348, 352, 361, 363-365, 368, 373, 375-377, 381, 418, 423, 426, 429-430, 433-434, 453, 455, 461, 466, 476, 488-489, 492-493, 506, 509, 512, 514, 518-519, 522-523, 527, 540, 542-543
Graubünden 3, 7
Grebel, Conrad 2, 8, 16, 28, 29, 37
greed 231, 239, 275, 300, 412, 426
Griessen parish 27
Gross, Leonard 13, 551
Groβ, Jakob 77
guard oneself 20, 114, 209, 430, 467, 485, 521, 530, 540
guard duty 32, 98, 249
Guengerich, Christian 99
Guntelmeiger, Hans 65
Gut, Andreas 14, 164, 183, 185, 532, 533, 534, 535, 536, 538, 540, 543
Gwalter, see Walter, Rudolf

H

Haas, Martin 2, 6, 147
Hafner, Galle 20, 23
Hagar 295
Hagi, Friedrich 99
Hagk, Martin 336
Hallau 28, 29, 30, 37, 38
Hamor the ruler 109
Hans de Ries 551, 552
Harlingen 85
hate 24, 41, 145, 148, 166, 214, 225, 229, 231, 232, 235, 251, 264-266, 283, 322, 323, 348, 396-397, 426, 441, 477, 494, 498-499, 506, 510, 515, 524, 527, 529
Hätzer, Ludwig 77
haughtiness 225, 231, 524
heart(s) 20-21, 43-46, 48-49, 53-55, 82,

88-89, 91, 96-97, 106, 116, 122, 126, 130-133, 135-136, 140, 144-145, 147, 149-152, 160-161, 166, 174, 194, 205-206, 208, 210, 214, 224, 226, 235, 237, 239-240, 243, 247, 249, 252-253, 258, 262-263, 267, 269, 272-273, 275, 288, 291-295, 299, 303-307, 309-310, 315, 317, 321, 324-325, 327-328, 333, 337-338, 341, 345, 360-361, 366, 369, 374, 379, 381-382, 386-387, 390-392, 404-405, 415-416, 420-422, 426-428, 430, 435-437, 439, 444, 454, 461, 466, 469-470, 472, 480-481, 484, 488, 492-493, 502, 508, 517, 519-522, 529, 541
circumcision of the heart 224, 252, 275, 366, 421-422, 466
covenant in the heart 42
heathens 42
heaven 48, 73, 81, 106, 111, 114, 133, 146, 149, 151, 194, 206, 207-208, 218, 220, 226, 230-231, 234, 245-247, 249, 252-253, 257, 265-266, 268, 272, 287-289, 300, 303-307, 312, 316, 321, 324, 326, 341, 351, 365, 371, 373, 381, 383, 397, 404, 409, 412, 414, 420, 428, 429, 431, 437-438, 472, 481, 491, 500, 504, 513, 516-517, 520, 527, 556-558, 561-562
Hedio, Caspar 191, 330, 335, 464
Heidegger, Samuel 534
hell 53, 114, 121, 221-223, 226, 262, 264, 287, 290, 317, 327, 349, 371, 420, 429, 437, 438, 441, 481
heresy/heretic(s) 36, 165, 186, 193, 205, 216, 220, 255, 306, 313, 329, 332, 345, 370, 377-378, 380, 389, 397, 407, 410, 430, 463, 469-470, 475, 486, 494, 499, 506
hermeneutics 118, 157, 182
Herod, King 216, 369, 386, 529
Herodias 216
Hesse 92
Hieropolis 217
High German 79, 80, 83, 84, 85, 86, 89
High Germans 78, 79, 80, 86, 87, 549, 556
High Priest 203, 251, 252, 254
Hillerbrand, Hans J. 2, 173, 174
Hittites 264
Hoffaman, lord 70, 71
Hoffingen 98

Hoffman, Melchior 9, 31, 77, 78, 79
Hoffmeister, Sebastian 448
Hofmanites 81
holy/holiness 4, 41-42, 48, 53, 55, 61-62, 74-75, 108, 111-112, 149, 160, 205, 207-208, 211, 214, 216-217, 219-222, 224, 227, 230, 234, 236, 237-241, 244, 246, 252-254, 257, 262, 267-269, 271, 273-276, 279-283, 285, 292, 298, 301, 306, 310-311, 313-315, 317-318, 324, 328, 338, 343, 345, 348-349, 351, 370, 372, 375, 378, 380-381, 383, 386, 406-407, 418, 419, 420, 424, 425, 429, 430, 431, 440, 441, 444, 453, 456, 460, 463, 473, 489, 492-495, 497, 502-503, 506-507, 512-513, 519-520, 524-525, 547, 558
holy of holies 273
Holy Spirit 48-50, 52-53, 73-74, 88, 103, 127, 137, 143-144, 154, 204-205, 209, 211, 217-218, 224, 239, 256, 259, 262-263, 267-275, 280, 286, 299, 304-311, 318-319, 328-329, 331, 336-339, 341, 347, 351-357, 360-364, 367, 370, 373, 375-378, 386, 396-397, 402-403, 409, 411, 413-420, 422, 431, 450-451, 455-456, 461, 463, 467, 479, 481-485, 487-490, 492-498, 501-502, 506, 509-510, 515-517, 521, 526, 530, 546, 552-553, 557-559
See also: Spirit, Divine (of God, of Christ)
Hoover, Amos 128
Horb 31, 32, 35
Horgen 536
Hottinger, Margret 16
Hotz, Hans 18, 58
household of Stephanas 418
Hubmaier, Balthasar 3, 8, 29, 30, 37-39, 77, 101-103, 158, 164, 181-182, 187, 199-200, 328-337, 344, 355, 388-392, 394, 396, 398, 400, 403-404, 406-410, 448, 461-463, 465
humility 91, 96, 160, 243, 277, 282, 313, 427, 444, 462, 530
Hüninghausen 99
Hürliman, Jagli 117
Hus, John 387
Hut, Hans 32, 77, 122

Name and Subject Index

Hutter, Jacob 38, 49
Hutterite(s) 29, 32, 34-37, 39-40, 48-50, 52, 54, 59, 78, 118, 120, 140, 163, 187, 551-552
Hutterite *Chronicle* 34, 35, 49, 50, 54, 551
Hymeneus 24
hymn(s) 3, 11-12, 118-119, 121-128, 163, 167, 179, 190

I

Ickelsamer, Valentin 461, 465
idols/idolatry 217, 240, 298, 324, 343, 346, 374, 375, 430
Iglau 34
Illikhoven 85
images 28, 61, 103, 222, 232, 524
immorality 244, 396
impartiality 205, 338
impurity 210, 225, 232, 237, 238, 348, 396, 441, 496, 519
Incarnation of Christ 9-10, 79, 81, 94, 96, 291, 297-298, 311, 549, 553, 556
India 218
Indiana 13, 92, 170, 173, 365, 411
infant baptism 28-29, 38, 43, 47, 58, 72, 75, 150, 328, 334, 338-341, 345-348, 350-352, 354, 360, 365, 368-372, 374-375, 377, 387-390, 397, 400-402, 406, 408, 412, 431, 448, 463, 504-505, 550
    See also: dedication of infants 355
interest, charging of 33, 133, 161, 176, 284, 452, 493, 534, 551
inwardness 46, 240, 274, 346, 354, 391-392, 399, 409, 422, 427, 482, 488-489, 491
Iowa 92, 99
Isaac 265, 347, 381, 441, 563
Isaiah 108, 149, 214-215, 226, 228, 234, 237, 251-252, 257, 260, 273, 276-277, 279, 283, 286, 292, 321, 428, 453, 469, 473, 476-477, 498, 517, 522, 541, 558-560, 562
Isidorus 215
Israel 74, 102-103, 105, 130, 148, 215, 249-250, 258, 260, 265, 272, 275, 277, 283-284, 318, 359, 376, 378, 383, 421-422, 466, 472, 487, 499, 501, 517, 562

J

Jacob 43, 251, 255, 260, 265, 277, 283, 347, 351, 355-356, 362, 375, 392, 396-398, 441, 562
James the Apostle 217
James the greater 219
James the Lesser 218
Jannes and Jambres 239
jealousy 232, 396, 426, 441
Jebusites 394
Jecker, Hanspeter 6, 139-140, 155, 172-173, 193-197
Jehoshaphat 215, 466, 478
Jeremiah 136, 148-149, 214, 224, 234, 242, 258, 355, 369-370, 375, 397, 421, 441, 500, 522
Jerome 181, 191, 329, 337, 341, 367, 377, 387, 407
Jerome of Prague 387
Jerusalem 148-149, 175-176, 214, 218-220, 222-225, 249, 251, 253-254, 257, 271, 273, 292, 302-304, 327, 369-370, 414, 421, 432, 436, 441, 443, 516, 518, 528
Jews/Jewish people 26, 46, 54, 107, 151, 218, 220, 235, 259, 260, 264, 265, 270, 283, 297, 305, 320, 386, 398, 400, 422, 428, 430, 470, 490, 528
    See also: Israel
Jezebel 215
Job 214, 338, 440-441, 443, 470
John the Baptist 216, 256, 336, 355, 356, 365, 369, 413, 560, 562
John the Evangelist 217, 219
Jonah 133, 293, 359
Joshua 102, 109, 355-356, 441
Jotham 277
Jud, Leo 243, 336, 348, 448, 534
Judah 148, 214-215, 218-219, 258, 277, 283, 421, 466
Judas 63, 219, 244, 289, 515, 518-521, 524
Judas Thaddaeus 219
judges 143, 162, 238, 245-246, 256, 269, 308, 511, 538
    See also: magistrates
Jura 92

K

Kaiserstul 65, 66
Kautz, Jacob 8, 27, 33-34, 37-39, 41-42, 45-47, 78
Kimenhof 57
Kin, Adelheit 66
king 136, 146, 148, 175-176, 207, 215-216, 219, 226, 231, 246, 249, 253-254, 257, 260, 277, 282, 299, 303, 310, 351, 359, 365, 380-382, 398, 440, 466, 473, 500, 528, 547
King Abgarus 219
King Ahab 215, 466, 472
King Antiochus 285
King Darius 176
King Jeroboam 148
King Manasseh 215
King Nebuchadnezzar 216, 285
kings (monarchs) 141, 148-149, 213, 221-222, 224, 230, 245, 252-253, 260, 275, 283, 303, 384-386, 438, 442, 478, 480
King Saul 109
King Solomon 221, 265
Klaassen, Walter 12-13, 77- 78, 89, 143, 161, 164, 187, 342, 355, 388, 452, 475, 519
Klettgau 65, 66
Klingau 405
kneeling 93, 96
Knonou 532, 538, 543
Koop, Karl 80
Krahn, Cornelius 3, 79, 85, 86, 87
Kreuznach 84
Krufft, Heinrich 85
Kußenburg 66
Kutal 66

L

Landis, Hans 194, 536
lasciviousness 22, 300, 327, 375, 396, 426, 433, 438, 441, 495
Latomus 335
Lavater, Hans Rudolf 6, 139, 148
law 30, 48, 52, 64, 71, 107, 108, 145, 147-149, 168, 177, 201, 210, 214, 222, 238, 253-259, 261-263, 265-270, 273, 279, 281, 286, 292, 295, 299-300, 302-304, 320, 327, 366, 367, 375, 377, 395, 401, 406, 410, 432, 436, 453, 459, 471, 473-474, 477, 481-482, 484-486, 489, 495, 503, 511-514, 528, 539, 561
laying on of hands 93, 95, 332, 350, 352, 417
Lazarus 441
leader(s) 3, 8-10, 17, 29-30, 32, 34, 37-38, 48-49, 58, 65, 68-69, 71, 77-78, 84-86, 90, 93, 127, 136, 139, 140, 162, 167, 172, 179, 183, 190, 197, 199, 216, 220, 255, 384, 388, 451, 513, 544, 550, 552, 554
learned ones 20, 62, 107, 148, 159, 168, 187, 349, 375, 461, 490, 545, 546
See also: scholars
Lemke Cramer 10, 79, 84-86, 88, 90-91, 94
Leopolden, Martin 56
Leu, Urs B. 5, 6, 13, 14, 57, 170, 173, 183, 193, 198, 534, 535,-537, 543
Leupold, Hans 32
Levites 256
Lichtensteig 70
light 5, 8-10, 21, 23-24, 34-35, 41-43, 53, 93, 120, 144, 177, 197, 201, 205, 212, 214, 221, 234, 238, 241-242, 248-249, 251, 254-255, 261-262, 287, 294, 307, 310, 340, 348, 368, 379, 381, 389, 392-393, 443, 453, 455, 487, 492, 500, 520-521, 539, 542, 551, 557
Lindner, Thomas 50
lords 26, 41, 43-44, 61, 65, 67, 143-151, 205, 207, 216, 245-246, 278, 284, 298-299, 329, 334, 382, 385, 421, 435, 469, 472, 477, 483, 489, 525-526, 533, 544
Lord's Prayer 49, 53, 278, 339
Lord's Supper 32, 38-39, 43, 46, 62-63, 77, 93, 96, 99, 102, 110-112, 141, 150, 158, 162, 175, 204, 208-209, 235, 246, 335, 337, 344, 357-358, 362, 366, 372, 378, 386, 392-393, 401, 423, 425-429, 432, 442, 451, 466, 484, 487, 489, 493, 499-500, 503, 506, 511, 519-520, 529, 534, 541, 550-551, 553
Lot 26, 359
Lourens van Mundelsz 83

Name and Subject Index

love 24-25, 42, 48, 51, 54, 56, 64, 88-89, 91, 95, 132-133, 145-146, 149-151, 160, 165-166, 176, 193-194, 202, 204, 207-209, 211-213, 231-232, 235, 237, 239, 241, 246, 249, 251, 262, 264, 265-266, 282-284, 291-293, 299, 301-302, 306, 308-310, 314, 317-318, 321-325, 354, 357-358, 361, 368, 374, 382, 390, 416, 421, 425-427, 429, 435, 441-444, 454, 456, 461-462, 466-467, 471, 477-482, 484-485, 487, 492, 494-495, 498-499, 502-503, 505, 519-520, 522, 527, 530, 539, 560
 divine love 48, 262, 481
 natural love 481-482, 492, 522
Lucerne 68, 75
Lucifer 459, 492
Luneren 532
Luther, Martin 103, 116, 150, 158, 164-165, 167, 181-182, 186-187, 189-192, 195, 247-248, 254, 285-290, 293, 328, 334-335, 337, 342-346, 348-349, 352, 362, 367, 377, 385, 387, 398, 448, 451, 455, 458-460, 462, 465-466, 468-470, 472-474, 480, 485-486, 490, 497-498, 509, 558
Lutheran(s) 13, 126, 153, 163-165, 189-190, 240, 341, 343, 397, 432, 446-447, 453, 479, 508, 544, 549
Lütisberg 70
luxury 327, 437
Lydia 368, 369, 416
lying 35, 71, 203, 224, 229, 237, 241, 244, 251, 300, 348, 432, 466, 474, 491, 517, 542

M

Maccabeus 285
magic 232, 242
magistracy/magistrates 1, 4, 12, 14, 59, 64, 127, 136-137, 139, 141-143, 147-148, 162-164, 167-168, 181, 185, 194, 201, 203-205, 247-248, 273-275, 278, 281-288, 293-294, 296, 299-301, 321, 328, 371, 477-478, 484-486, 488-491, 497, 534, 536, 538, 542, 545-546, 548

See also: authorities, political; government
Maler, Balthasar 534
Maler, Jakob 9, 68-70, 73, 75
Maler, Jörg 59, 161, 196, 461, 465,
Mantz, Felix 8, 16, 29, 37
Marpeck, Pilgram 1, 8, 27, 33-34, 37, 39, 42, 48, 59-60, 77-78, 122, 126, 128, 161, 164, 166, 168, 176-177, 182, 186-187, 189-190, 192, 196-198, 342, 355, 388, 411, 461, 519
marriage 53, 57-58, 66, 85-86, 89, 93-94, 96, 99, 150, 322-324, 541
Martha 82
Martijn Snyder 83
Martinscreek, Ohio 99
martyr(s)/martyrdom 17, 31, 49, 126, 158-160, 182, 212, 219, 221, 227, 285, 344, 385, 438, 441, 444, 448, 536
Martyrs Mirror 200
Mary, Mother of Jesus 79, 81, 204, 311, 313, 339, 556-560
Mary Magdalene 317
mass, the 28, 68, 71, 158, 335, 344, 508
Matthew 11, 61, 106, 193, 218, 222, 231, 240, 244, 255, 264, 288, 294, 311-312, 314, 316, 321-323, 328-329, 335-336, 342, 345, 350-352, 356, 365, 367, 369, 373, 377, 386, 389, 392-395, 401-402, 404, 407-408, 411, 413-414, 432-434, 438-439, 453, 456-457, 468, 472, 477-482, 487-489, 495-497, 499-500, 503-504, 506, 510, 512-515, 518-519, 521, 525, 527, 530, 539-541, 545-546, 561
meetings 9, 10, 57, 79, 94, 141, 453, 535, 544, 554
Melanchthon, Philipp 163, 294, 385, 451, 465, 470, 484, 486
Melchizedek 561, 562
Mengeringhausen 99
Menno Simons 9-10, 78-79, 84-87, 90-91, 94, 102-103, 197, 552, 559
Mennonite(s) 2-4, 7-9, 11, 13, 27, 32, 79, 85, 92, 94, 120, 170, 173, 365, 388, 411, 532, 549, 550-554, 556
mercy 42, 48, 52, 54, 88-89, 91, 116, 135, 144-145, 151-152, 205, 208, 212, 224, 261, 268, 318, 321, 348, 359, 419, 423,

426, 487, 518, 535, 541
Meshach 216, 285, 441
Mesopotamia 219
Meyer, Thomas 100, 102-104, 116-117, 200
Meyer, Heinrich 543
Meyger, Fridolin 33
Micah 215, 251, 252, 257, 441, 517
Michel, J. David 152
minister(s) 32, 51, 84, 90-93, 95-97, 99, 192, 253, 332, 467, 524, 536, 538, 549, 555, 563
miserliness 140, 232, 432, 542, 554
Moab 422
monks 240, 341
Montfort, Basil 192
Moravia 8, 11, 34, 39, 55-57, 59, 65, 84, 90, 120, 140, 161, 544, 551
Moses 6, 166, 177, 206, 232, 239, 250-251, 254, 256, 260, 263-265, 267-268, 270, 296, 315, 322, 324, 347, 359, 421, 440-441, 476, 478, 510-515, 524, 528, 538, 562
Mount Horeb 252
Mount of Olives 279, 280
Müller, Hans 6
Müller, Heinsi 66
Müller's wife from Glattfelden 66
Mumprat of Constance 58
Münster 76, 78
Münsterites 145, 243, 493, 547
Müntzer, Thomas 547

N

Nadab and Abihu 274
Nesper, Henß 66
Netherlands 3, 78, 81, 87, 89, 91, 102, 124, 200, 551-554
New Jerusalem 253, 441, 443
Nicea 311, 332
Nicodemus 404, 414, 453
Niger, Theobald 335
Nikolsburg 39, 49, 51, 164, 181, 199, 328, 335, 388, 462
Noah 26, 273, 359, 390, 419, 421
nonresistance 1, 26, 38, 93, 205, 479, 550, 551

North Germany 78, 84, 87
nuns 341

O

oath(s) 6, 16-18, 20, 32-33, 38, 59, 64, 68, 69, 75, 141, 162, 203, 247, 253, 266, 302-304, 486, 533-535, 544-545, 550
obedience 16-17, 20, 23, 25, 42, 45, 58-59, 82, 136, 141, 143, 145, 166, 189, 204, 207, 208, 210, 247, 250, 267, 285, 288-289, 296, 303, 305, 310, 313, 315, 317-318, 321-323, 348, 354, 365, 367, 368, 392, 396, 400, 424, 425, 434, 454, 459, 468, 470-471, 479, 495, 499, 509, 514-515, 517, 521, 527, 529, 532-533, 538, 543, 544, 546
Oberhallow 65
Odenbach 294
Oecolampadius, Johannes 103, 116, 355, 448
Ohio 92, 99, 104, 117, 119
Old and New Testaments 5, 150, 165, 205, 221, 250, 255, 260, 268-270, 277, 304, 331, 538
Old Testament 1, 64, 101-102, 105, 164-165, 166, 193, 203, 222, 225, 255, 258-270, 276, 301, 304, 390, 392, 398, 421, 476
Olmütz 34
order 4, 17, 20, 32, 46, 61, 72, 82, 89, 93, 96, 97, 101, 103, 105, 108-109, 112, 115, 125, 127, 136, 140, 148, 164-165, 167, 187, 208, 212, 226, 233, 235, 269, 271, 274, 278, 304, 310, 313, 317, 320, 332-333, 336, 339, 348-349, 352, 354, 356, 359, 361-362, 364, 367, 369-370, 377-378, 383, 386, 388-389, 395, 408, 412, 414, 424, 426-427, 429, 432, 434, 438-439, 448-449, 451, 454, 456, 459, 461-463, 466-467, 470-471, 473, 485-486, 493, 496-497, 504-505, 507, 509-510, 512, 520, 525, 529, 540, 544, 547, 553, 562
order of Christ 101, 349, 520
Origen 181, 329, 464
original sin 73, 74, 84, 90, 204, 315, 342, 391

Name and Subject Index

orphans 64, 93, 95, 377
Ostorodt, Christoph 10, 549-561
Ottenbach 532, 533
Outerman, Jacques 552
Oyer, John 9, 32, 76-77, 163

P

Packull, Werner 2, 29, 32, 36-37, 40, 49, 52, 78, 120-121, 182, 187, 411, 461
pagans 107
Palatinate, the 13, 78, 92, 122, 171, 173, 201, 555
papist(s) 135, 341, 346, 397, 432, 477, 483, 487, 499, 508, 544
Passau 11, 120-122, 124-125, 132, 167
Passover lamb 320-321
pastor(s) 20-30, 36, 38, 58, 61, 68-70, 84, 148, 172, 197, 222, 240, 345, 390, 451, 478, 486, 505, 509, 535, 548
patience 26, 91, 96, 143, 145, 149, 152, 204, 208, 222, 233, 243, 245, 263, 266, 273, 368, 374, 384, 425, 427, 440-441, 475, 477-479, 481, 520
Patmos 219
peace 4, 20, 48-50, 55, 64, 81, 88-91, 134, 136, 146, 160, 206-208, 212, 223, 226, 238, 244, 251, 254, 257, 263, 268, 277, 292, 294, 302, 323, 352, 404, 408, 410, 423, 429, 444-454, 496, 514, 538, 544
Peachey, Shem and Paul 13, 446, 452, 454, 527
Peasants' War of 1525 28, 30, 547
Pelagianus 331
Penner, Sydney 8-9, 11, 57, 68, 105, 112
Pennsylvania 92
persecution 4, 26, 36, 90, 93, 96, 127-128, 137-139, 141, 145, 147-148, 159, 162-163, 181, 187, 189, 191-192, 194, 205-206, 214-215, 222-225, 227, 229, 231, 235, 244-245, 248, 250, 265-266, 277-280, 285, 291, 294-296, 297-298, 301-302, 327, 334, 337, 345-346, 353, 368, 378, 382-383, 397, 422, 431, 439, 441-442, 451, 453, 456, 464, 474-475, 476, 482, 487, 494, 497-498, 506, 511, 513, 518, 522, 530, 540

perseverance 88, 90, 91, 133, 207, 368, 442, 475
Persia 219
Peter, Apostle 22, 43, 49, 82, 96, 106, 147, 159, 206, 211, 217, 239, 247, 260, 271, 278-280, 285, 288-289, 293, 304, 306, 313, 317, 328, 331, 358, 360, 363-364, 375-376, 385, 393, 398, 403, 415-416, 421, 426, 429, 455, 459, 479-480, 485, 498, 507, 516
Peter and Wolffen von Landaw 56
Pfeddersheim 163
Pfister, Hans Ulrich 532, 537
Pfungen 61, 65
Pharaoh 130, 249, 250-251, 383, 394
Pharisees 20, 218, 223, 256, 265, 312, 317, 413-414, 510-514
Philetus 24
Philippi 148, 220
Philippians 3 237, 262, 422, 507
Philippites 11, 120-121, 124, 126, 167
Philips, Dirk 10, 78, 85-87, 102
Philips van Dankelsz 83
Philip the apostle 217
Pilate 136, 146, 164, 216, 281, 386
Polish Brethren 10, 549-553, 555-556, 558
Poll, Simphorianus 335
Pope, the/papacy/papal 13, 21, 43, 44, 47, 61, 135, 147, 153, 222, 240, 247, 249, 251, 254, 255, 289, 290, 293, 331, 332, 339, 342, 371, 377, 385-388, 403, 410, 412-413, 430-431, 446-447, 453, 458-460, 462, 464-466, 478, 488, 490, 491, 504
Pope Basil the Great 331
Pope Boniface 331, 377
Pope Leo I 331
Pope Nicholas I 331
Pope Pelagius 459, 460, 466
Pope Siricius 331
Pope Sylvester 332
possessions 89, 143, 149, 204, 229, 233, 250, 266, 272, 276, 289, 324-325, 440, 461, 473, 477, 481, 501, 522, 526
prayer 56, 74, 89, 91, 96, 145, 152, 218, 277-278, 291, 306, 309, 317, 338, 352, 354-355, 360, 379, 384, 403, 416, 440, 453, 482, 520, 542, 556, 563
preachers 8, 16, 21-22, 31, 33-34, 37-39,

41, 43-44, 46, 52, 58, 62-64, 69, 71, 75-76, 100, 121, 127, 136, 140-141, 147, 150, 162-163, 189, 238, 240, 296, 298, 335, 337, 340, 348-350, 362, 367, 377, 448, 451, 453-455, 457-458, 462, 467-468, 471, 475-479, 483, 490, 494-499, 501-502, 504-507, 509-512, 514-516, 518-519, 521-522, 526-529, 534-536, 540, 543-544, 546, 548
See also: clerics and priests
preaching 13, 18, 24-25, 28, 32, 37, 39, 46, 49, 61-62, 70-71, 121, 140, 153, 215, 219, 236, 238-239, 293, 296, 297, 300, 346, 349, 370, 389, 405, 414-415, 431, 446, 447, 453-457, 459-460, 462, 466, 475, 476, 478, 489, 495, 496, 500-501, 504, 505, 506, 508, 509, 510-516, 521, 522, 526-529, 546
predestination 550
prejudice 143, 243
Prentl, George 50
pretention 275, 507
pride 20, 89, 97, 98, 135, 136, 159, 161, 231, 236, 275, 300, 348, 371, 396, 426, 437, 441, 460, 492, 495, 523, 524, 554
priests/priesthood 20, 27-28, 70-71, 109, 127, 148-149, 214-216, 218, 220, 224, 237-238, 240, 242, 253-255, 256, 259-261, 263, 273, 276, 278, 300, 301, 312, 329, 330, 332, 335, 341, 373, 400, 430, 460-462, 476, 483, 488, 490, 503, 505, 528-529, 559
princes 164, 205, 213, 221, 230, 246, 252, 260, 281, 283, 285-287, 298, 381, 385, 468-470, 472, 477
prison 8, 11, 16, 32, 95, 120, 124-125, 127, 135-136, 201, 212, 215, 217, 225, 227, 349, 369, 388, 421, 439, 441, 514, 536
prophets 36, 52, 54, 121, 132, 141, 148, 149, 159-160, 164, 193, 206, 215-216, 222-226, 236, 238-242, 244, 252, 256-257, 259-260, 279, 286, 292, 298-302, 304, 309, 317, 320, 322, 384-385, 439, 454, 462, 465, 478, 490, 492, 496, 517-518, 521, 523, 525-526, 528, 530
proto-Pietist 193, 197, 198
Pseudo-Epiphanius 159, 215
purity 24, 54, 63, 82, 89, 102, 108, 110-112, 122, 144, 151, 160, 205, 207, 209, 212-213, 218, 233, 235, 237, 246, 273, 282, 295, 297-298, 302, 309, 313, 315, 317, 318, 321-322, 324, 329, 338, 348, 352-353, 358, 361, 368, 373, 378, 384, 406, 420, 426-427, 443-444, 453, 461-462, 466, 481, 487, 492, 495, 498, 503-504, 511, 519, 522, 528, 530-531, 558-559

Q

quarreling 232, 254, 275, 277, 306, 313, 362, 390
Quirijn van Nachalden 83

R

Ramoth in Gilead 466, 478
Ran, Hanns 532-533
Rätterschen 100, 117
reading 2, 5-6, 18, 25, 34, 39, 43, 58, 68, 71, 73, 80, 86, 97, 104, 107, 117, 119, 131, 141-143, 150, 152, 157, 159, 160, 166, 173, 175, 177, 194, 195, 198, 200, 226, 243, 249, 259, 294, 298, 314, 330, 336, 344, 352-353, 360, 377, 388, 400, 403, 415, 421, 454, 459, 489, 491, 500, 511, 540-541, 546, 555-557, 561
reader(s) 68-69, 115, 132, 135, 138, 156, 161, 177, 181, 193, 233, 269, 293, 298, 330, 334, 337, 340, 344-345, 358, 363, 369, 388-389, 395-396, 406, 430, 443-444, 448, 464, 471, 492-493, 517, 531
rebaptism 41, 65, 389
rebirth, spiritual 21, 38, 73, 122, 137, 148, 166-167, 177, 194, 198, 208-209, 211-213, 230-231, 236, 243, 262-263, 265, 267, 272, 298-299, 303, 309-310, 327, 332, 339, 343, 347, 353-354, 356, 360-364, 366, 373-375, 397, 419, 429, 451, 462, 479, 494, 505
regeneration 122, 419
new person 207, 267, 302, 343, 364, 423
new life 62, 103, 122, 166, 198, 199, 329, 361, 399, 409, 451, 499
spiritual children 268, 352, 353, 354
See also: spirit
recantation 17, 18, 32, 44, 57, 60, 67-68, 194

Red Sea 250, 366, 394, 563
Reformation 1, 3-5, 18, 31, 36, 77, 102-103, 141, 158-159, 187, 192, 246, 299, 448-449, 451, 457-458, 551
Reformed Church 5-6, 20, 36, 58, 61, 71, 102, 104, 120, 141, 155, 164-165, 167, 171-172, 195, 197-198, 222, 243, 247, 264, 333, 471, 475, 534-535, 541, 555-556
Regio, provincial ruler 217
remembrance 150, 357, 425-426, 541
Remonstrants 553
repentance 10, 21, 36, 43, 62, 87, 89, 93, 97, 105, 114-116, 121, 194, 207, 252, 256, 269, 275, 293, 300, 309, 317, 318, 320, 324, 329, 336, 359, 371, 376, 398, 413-415, 417, 427, 438, 520, 525, 540
respect of persons 52, 143, 176, 246
Reublin, Wilhelm 8, 27-39, 41-42, 45-49, 77-78
Rhegius, Urbanus 191
Rhine river 76, 78, 80, 85
righteousness 20, 21, 22, 37, 51, 53, 55, 64, 75, 82, 88, 108, 110, 111, 112, 120, 132-133, 149, 161, 162, 210, 218, 223-224, 226, 229-230, 234, 237, 239, 245, 257, 262, 263, 266, 268, 277, 295, 309, 314-315, 317, 348, 352, 364, 365, 386, 404-405, 413-414, 433-434, 439-440, 443, 485-486, 492, 498, 500, 503, 516, 530, 551
Roman Catholic 3-5, 20-21, 27, 36, 70-71, 126, 164, 193, 289, 340, 412, 464, 478, 502
Roman Empire 148, 220
Rome 219, 254, 290, 385, 430
Ronemberg, Simon 552
Rosenstock, Erhard 56
Roth, John 1, 2, 5, 10, 27, 32, 34, 84, 104, 117, 198
Rothkegel, Martin 12, 33-36, 39, 42, 121, 123, 161, 461, 551
Rottenburg on the Neckar 27, 31-32, 36
Rugglisberger, Sebastian 405
Rule of Christ 61, 63, 106, 114, 244, 409
ruler(s) 24, 70, 110, 143, 168, 176, 217, 222, 226, 278, 281, 284, 298-300, 323, 334, 363, 371, 417, 468, 470, 475, 484, 530, 539, 561

S

Sabbath 256, 258, 262
sacrament(s) 45, 111, 244, 246, 262, 275, 324, 330, 335, 337, 342, 343-345, 348-350, 362, 377-378, 386, 407, 431-432, 512, 528
sacrifice 151, 253, 257-258, 267, 301, 324, 335, 338, 378, 380, 381, 386, 424, 442, 511, 559, 560
Salem 257
Samaritans 146, 268
Samuel 256, 260
Sarah 295
Satan 106-108, 110, 159, 168, 212-213, 264, 341, 353, 383, 432, 435, 485, 492, 502, 519
Sattler, Georg 65, 447
Sattler, Margaretha 17, 31, 36-37
Sattler, Michael 7-8, 16-18, 29-32, 36-38, 58, 77, 90, 182, 191, 365, 411, 447
Saul 109, 245, 273, 416
Schaffhausen 3, 7, 16-18, 27, 29-30, 37, 57, 66, 140, 446, 447
Scharnschlager, Leupold 126, 164, 182, 186-190, 192, 197, 411, 461
Scheidegger, Christian 5-6, 13-14, 36, 57, 170, 173, 183, 193, 198, 534-537, 543
Schiemer, Leonhard 122
schism 232
Schlaffer, Hans 122
Schleitheim Articles 2-3, 14, 16-18, 30-32, 38, 66, 90, 93, 119, 121, 167-169, 177, 197, 447, 479
Schmalkaldic League 36
Schmalkaldic war 36
Schmiegel, Poland 549
Schnabel, Georg 78
scholars 85, 145, 147-148, 205, 246, 248, 253, 271, 285, 294, 297-298, 321, 324, 338, 348, 353, 363, 371, 377, 412
Schueler, Caspar 48
Schwarzendruber, Jacob 99
Schwenckfeld, Caspar 77, 534
Schwenckfeldian(s) 128, 187, 191-193, 534-535
scribes 107, 160, 172, 216, 218, 222-223, 225, 236, 242-243, 269, 297, 299, 301,

321, 334, 412, 414, 444, 487, 507, 510-513, 529, 530
Second Council of Braga 333
Second Kappel War 3, 21, 478
sect/sectarians 25, 141, 145, 164, 185-186, 205, 220, 345, 389, 430, 506, 507, 533, 543, 544
sect of Nazarenes 220
Senn, Roland 194-197
separation 7, 11, 13-14, 16-19, 25, 30, 38, 58-59, 78, 87, 89, 93-94, 100-101, 103, 106-109, 111-114, 121, 140, 190, 197, 198, 205, 234, 240-241, 244, 253, 266, 274, 278, 293, 295, 302, 431, 445, 450, 466,ff. 481, 496-500, 503-504, 509, 511-512, 547
Sergius 299
Shadrach 216, 285, 441
Shechem 109
shepherd(s) 21, 39, 46, 108, 206-207, 238-239, 270, 302, 337, 409, 431, 465, 486, 502, 514
shunning 9-10, 79, 84, 86-87, 89, 94, 96. 112
Siglistorf 65
Siglistorfer woods 65
Simon Magus 403
Simon the Apostle 219
sin(s) 20-25, 62-64, 72-74, 84, 88-90, 93, 98, 101, 105-110, 112-116, 121, 133, 135, 144, 148-149, 151, 166, 179, 204, 208-211, 214-215, 223-224, 231-232, 234-236, 238-239, 252-253, 256, 258, 263-264, 267-269, 275, 280, 288, 296, 300, 302, 305, 308-309, 312, 314-318, 320-322, 329, 336, 341-343, 346-347, 350, 357-359, 361, 363-364, 371, 375-376, 386, 391, 395, 398-399, 403, 413-416, 418, 421, 424, 426, 433, 437-438, 440-442, 451, 457-458, 463, 475, 481, 483, 492, 495-496, 499-500, 503, 505, 508, 514, 516, 519-520, 523-525, 527, 533, 540-542, 545, 554, 559-560
Sinai 177, 252, 254, 273, 302, 304
sisters 23, 51, 53-55, 89-91, 98, 111, 220, 260, 323, 325, 441, 541
Sixth Council of Carthage 332
Snyder, C. A. 1-2, 6, 8-9, 11-14, 16-18, 27-33, 57, 66, 68, 76, 83, 84, 128, 143, 153, 157, 166, 167, 191, 196, 255, 535
Socinianism 79, 550, 552, 553, 554
Sodom 224, 280, 293, 295, 359, 539
Solomon 144, 201-202, 214, 221, 226, 260, 265, 273, 286, 383, 500, 529, 556, 558
Solothurn 4, 7, 17, 18
Some Beautiful Christian Songs
 See Etlicher schöner Christlicher Geseng
sons of Aaron 257, 274
sons of Zebedee 278
soul 90, 106, 115, 192, 208, 214, 226, 233, 247, 261, 268, 273, 283, 286, 288-289, 296, 314, 316-317, 325, 330, 335, 337, 361, 373, 377, 407-408, 421, 436-438, 458, 468, 475-476, 481, 486-487, 490, 500, 543
Spilman, Adelheit 66
spirit 20-21, 26, 42, 46, 55, 90-91, 116, 121-122, 127, 146, 151, 161, 164, 167, 189, 193, 205, 209, 211-212, 214, 217-218, 238, 241, 247, 250, 252, 254, 261-262-264, 268, 269-270, 275-277, 279, 281-283, 287, 295-296, 302, 304, 310, 312, 314, 321-323, 327, 352-354, 357, 361, 366, 378, 388, 397, 408-409, 420-423, 436-437, 451, 454, 455, 457, 463, 466-467, 469-472, 480-484, 486-490, 492, 494-499, 502, 507, 509-510, 517-518, 522, 529, 545, 559
Spirit, Divine (of God; of Christ) 21, 23, 26, 46, 54-55, 90, 94, 96, 103, 109, 122, 127, 135-137, 143, 147, 159, 164, 207, 209, 211-212, 221, 230, 231, 245, 251, 257, 263, 265-266, 269, 278, 282, 284, 286, 289, 291-295, 298-299, 300, 302, 309, 310, 313, 327, 346, 353-354, 356, 360, 376, 382, 384, 392-393, 397, 404, 409, 411, 416, 418-422, 425, 451, 456-457, 460, 463, 465, 467, 471-473, 477, 481, 483-484, 485, 487-488, 492-499, 502, 513, 516-518, 521-523, 527, 529-530, 531, 558, 560, 562
See also: Holy Spirit
spiritual law of Zion 177, 302, 327
spiritual songs 122-124, 126, 130-131, 133, 177, 454

Name and Subject Index

spiritualism 8, 33, 38-39, 46, 77-78, 126, 128, 534
stand watch 94, 98
Starlitz 35, 55
Stayer, James 1-2, 27-28, 30, 34
Stefan from Heglingen 66
Stein am Rhein 194, 195
Stephanus, household of 368
Stephen, Saint 148, 217, 223, 422, 511, 528
St. Gallen 3, 7, 9, 68, 70, 405
Stössel, Jakob 68, 70, 72-75
St. Peters of the Black Forest 17
Strasbourg 8-10, 17, 30-31, 33-34, 37-39, 41-42, 45, 47, 55, 76-79, 81, 84-86, 88, 90, 92-95, 159, 164, 186, 189, 191, 217, 330, 335-337, 348, 355, 362, 367, 464, 471, 549-550, 555-556, 563
Strasbourg preachers 39, 335, 337, 348, 362
Strübind, Andrea 1-2
Studer, Andli 66
Stumpf, Johann Rudolf 14, 162, 535-536, 543
Sturm, Johann 41
Sudermann, Daniel 128
suffering 25, 45, 53, 55, 98, 114, 126, 133, 151-152, 159, 208, 219-220, 226, 229, 243-244, 266, 278, 285, 321-322, 357, 367, 373-374, 382-383, 393, 423-424, 429, 438-441, 443, 461, 474-475, 477, 505, 526, 529
Swabia 35, 84, 90
Swaen Rutgers 85
swearing 6, 16, 17, 32-33, 38, 64, 75, 140, 300, 302-304, 348, 426, 524, 534, 542
See also: Oaths
Swiss Brethren 1-2, 7-12, 14, 19, 58-60, 69, 78-79, 92, 94, 98, 101-102, 104-105, 117-124, 126, 128-129, 153, 156, 159, 165-167, 169, 171-172, 176, 186-187, 190, 194, 196, 198, 200, 255, 365, 452, 482, 519, 535, 540, 549-557, 559-561
Swiss Confederation 2-3
Swiss Reformation 1, 3-4, 141
Switzerland 1-4, 6, 9, 14, 17, 32, 35, 57, 84, 90, 92, 98, 100, 104, 122, 128, 150, 171, 179, 197, 254

sword, physical 30, 38, 64, 102, 115, 127, 135-136, 146-147, 154, 162, 165, 178, 180, 184, 186-187, 189, 190, 193, 203, 205, 216-218, 220-222, 224-227, 250, 254, 256-257, 263-264, 271-272, 273, 275-276, 277-286, 290, 292-296, 298, 381-382, 390, 425, 435-436, 438-439, 450-451, 469-470, 472-473, 475, 477, 479-482, 486, 490-491, 493, 496-498, 526, 528-529, 534, 539
sword of our consciences 133
sword, two-edged (Word of God) 164, 282, 293, 390, 469
swords, two (worldly and spiritual) 167, 188-190, 192-193, 197, 222, 226, 251, 254, 263-264, 271-285, 292, 451, 473, 479, 483, 493, 496-498
swords into plowshares 251, 254, 292, 473
Synod of Bern 478, 482-483

T

Tasch, Peter 78
taxes 36, 64, 136, 284, 288, 539
teacher(s) 20, 24-25, 35, 52, 58, 65, 68, 71, 78, 90, 114, 127, 136-137, 192, 196, 218, 242-243, 295-296, 309, 313, 329, 330, 331, 337, 345, 407, 430-431, 462, 465, 467, 476, 486, 496, 515-516, 527, 531, 539, 542, 550
Teck, Ulrich 17
temple 24, 112, 148, 175-176, 203, 209, 211-212, 218, 223, 228, 234-235, 246, 248-249, 251-254, 257, 259, 273, 286, 317, 354, 378-379, 386, 428, 433-434, 455, 489, 500, 511, 528-530, 560
Temple of God 235
Ten Commandments 70, 255
ten virgins 434-435
Tertullian 219, 329, 341
Tertullus 220, 430
Thaurer, Sebastian 55
Thayngen 17
theocracy 4, 6
Theophilus 191-192, 405
Theophylact 329
Thessalonica 148, 220
Thurgau 21, 68

Timothy 63, 369
tithes 27, 28, 30, 64, 284
Toggenburg 9, 68, 70, 71
toleration 12, 14, 101, 103, 127-128, 141-142, 162, 164-165, 167-168, 179, 181, 183, 185-186, 189-194, 196-197, 285, 448, 460, 534-537
torture 17, 90, 141, 212, 214-216, 218-219, 221, 227, 231, 235, 245, 298, 337, 345, 438, 441, 442, 497
Träffer, Georg 58
Treger, Conrad 471-472
Trinity 10, 305-306, 310, 313, 332, 550-553, 556
truth 20, 25-26, 34, 37, 41, 43-45, 49-54, 64-65, 82, 87, 96, 132, 148-149, 160, 176, 201, 209, 212-214, 221, 226, 237, 239, 241-244, 246, 249, 251, 268, 270, 304-305, 307-308, 311, 321-322, 325, 330-331, 337-341, 346, 349, 353, 355, 357, 360, 364, 377, 384, 389, 390, 395, 407-408, 410, 428-430, 443-444, 453, 456, 464-465, 467-468, 473, 492-494, 499, 501-503, 505-507, 516, 521-522, 525, 528, 530-531, 545-547, 551, 561, 563
Tübingen 27, 191
Turks 274, 494
Turkey 381
Twisck 552

U

Ulm 31, 32, 36, 193, 217, 294
unity 5, 42, 63-64, 81, 89-91, 96, 291-292, 310, 325, 479, 551-552
University of Freiburg 27
unregenerate 299, 309, 429
unrighteousness 22, 26, 42, 110, 113, 116, 128, 132, 136, 148, 209, 214, 225, 231, 237, 238, 239, 268, 347, 361, 398, 435, 437, 500, 519-520
Usa 274
usurers 23, 110, 275, 372
usury 140, 225, 396, 426, 441, 542, 554

V

Veh, Cornelius 59
Veltijn van Bethen 83

vengeance 193, 216, 221, 230-231, 265, 268, 272-273, 277-278, 280-282, 470, 477
vice 89, 106, 108, 111, 208, 236, 244, 269, 323, 381, 438, 524
Vienna 49, 158, 182, 344, 448
Virgin Mary See: Mary, Mother of Jesus
Vistula Delta 551-553
Volckhamer, Kilian 49

W

Waldeck 99
Waldshut 27, 29, 30, 57, 77
Walpot, Peter 552
Walpurga von Pappenheim 126
Walter (Gwalter; Walther), Rudolf 61, 147, 182, 187, 190, 195, 222, 290-294, 297, 450, 505
wantonness 20, 225, 275, 327, 359, 438, 507
war 3, 21, 30, 36, 53, 151, 194-196, 238, 252, 254, 257, 264, 290, 292, 382-383, 385, 473, 478, 480, 560
Waterlanders 80, 553
Wattenwyl 152
weapons 30, 32, 93, 98, 250, 252, 254, 257, 263, 272, 279, 293, 382, 410, 435, 469, 477, 485, 498, 545
Weiningen 34, 65, 66
Wenger, J. C. 4, 7-8, 16, 20, 23, 26-27, 365, 411
Weninger, Martin 7, 16-20, 32, 58, 66, 446-447
Werdmüller, M. Otto 61
Wick, Konrad 70, 75
wickedness 22, 89, 221, 240, 269, 276, 359, 378-380, 518
Widertoüfer 327
widows 64, 96, 410
Wiedemann, Jacob, elder at Austerlitz 34, 48-52
Wil 68, 70, 75
Winckler, Conrad 58
Winter, Diebold 163
Winterthur 57, 61, 65
Wiser, Mathis 57-60, 66
Witikon 27, 28
Wittenberg 254, 385, 459, 465, 470

Name and Subject Index

wives in common 243
Wolkan, Rudolf 12, 118, 123-126
Word of God 37, 45, 49, 50-51, 61, 62, 65, 70, 107, 109, 111, 143, 145, 164, 206, 208, 245, 263, 275, 293, 298, 322, 334, 339, 340-341, 346-347, 353-354, 358-359, 363, 364, 368, 370, 375, 378, 389, 390, 396, 401, 402, 404, 408, 410, 432, 453, 454, 456, 458, 468, 471, 475, 477, 479, 483, 491, 493, 496, 498, 501, 504, 507, 509, 528, 543, 551
works 1, 20-21, 23-25, 49, 61, 72, 88, 118, 120, 130, 137, 145, 151, 157, 181, 195, 200, 204, 209, 211, 232, 237, 257, 262, 269, 293, 307, 317-321, 334, 347, 386, 402-404, 416, 427, 439, 448-449, 451, 472, 479, 482, 484-485, 487-490, 494-495, 510-511, 513, 515, 518, 522, 525, 545, 554
Worms 33, 45, 84, 90, 163
worship 11, 20, 61, 216, 228, 232-234, 248, 257, 261-262, 270, 379, 383, 448, 453, 541, 543
Wotschke, Theodor 10, 549, 552-554, 556-561
Wülflingen 65
Württemberg 84, 90, 122
Wüstenfeld 85
Wycliffe 387

Y

yieldedness *See*: *Gelassenheit*
Yoder, Jesse 155, 171-173, 264
Yoder, John H. 17-18, 30, 101, 164-165, 181-182, 199, 328, 329-331, 333, 335-336, 355, 365, 388-389, 394, 409, 411, 415, 423, 462-463, 465
young woman from Utlikon near Würenloß 66

Z

Zaunriden (Zaunridt), George 50, 51
Zechariah 148, 149, 215, 223, 245, 257, 292, 518
Zedekiah 215
Zell, Matthew 335
Zerubbabel 175-176, 249, 251
Zion 177, 222, 227, 251, 254, 257, 261, 267, 273, 283, 302, 304, 327, 432, 436
Znaim 35, 36
Zobeli, Hans 66
Zofingen 18, 165, 194
Zollikon 29
Zorzin, Alejandro 3
Zuck, Hans 55
Zurich 1-3, 6-9, 12-14, 16-17, 26-31, 34-36, 56-57, 59, 61, 117, 119, 140, 147, 162, 164, 170-173, 175, 177, 179, 182-183, 185-186, 193-195, 198-201, 205-208, 212-213, 222, 226-227, 229-231, 243, 247-248, 250-251, 257, 264-266, 268-269, 271, 273-276, 284-291, 293-298, 320-321, 332, 334-340, 342, 346-350, 361, 368, 376, 389-390, 400, 405, 410, 445, 478, 502, 534-537, 543
Zwillikon 532, 536, 543
Zwingli 2-3, 21, 29, 31, 61, 103, 116, 150, 165, 181-182, 186-187, 189-190, 195, 222, 247, 254, 293, 328, 333-335, 337-338, 340, 342, 344-346, 351, 355, 361, 362, 370, 377, 387-396, 398-411, 431, 448, 451, 465, 475, 478, 485-486, 497-498, 502, 504, 509, 537, 540-541
Zwinglian(s) 13, 21, 153, 189-190, 240, 341, 397, 432, 446, 447, 453
Zylis Jacobs 10, 79, 84-86, 88, 90-91, 94

Translators

Harold S. Bender (d. 1962) is perhaps best known as the author of "The Anabaptist Vision" (1944). He oversaw the publication of the *Mennonite Encyclopedia* (four volumes), was founder and editor of the *Mennonite Quarterly Review*, and the author of several books and numerous articles. He served as Dean of Goshen College, Goshen, Indiana (1931-1944), and Dean of Goshen College Biblical Seminary (1944-1962), as well as serving on many church-wide committees.

C. J. Dyck (d. 2014) was professor of historical theology at Associated Mennonite Biblical Seminary from 1959 until his retirement in 1989. He authored many scholarly articles and several books, including the widely-read *Introduction to Mennonite History*, and edited many more; he was co-editor with Dennis Martin of the fifth volume of the *Mennonite Encyclopedia*. He was executive secretary of the Mennonite World Conference (1961-1973), and served on numerous local and international committees and organizations.

Abraham Friesen is professor emeritus of History at the University of California, Santa Barbara, where he specialized in Renaissance and Reformation History and taught from 1967 until his retirement in 2004. He has authored many scholarly articles as well as seven books, including *Erasmus, the Anabaptists, and the Great Commission*. He has continued active research, writing and publication in retirement.

Leonard Gross attended the University of Hamburg and (as Fulbright Scholar) the University of Basel. He taught at Western Michigan University (1968-1970) and subsequently served as Executive Secretary of the Historical Committee of the Mennonite Church, and director of the Mennonite denominational archives and historical research program located at Goshen, Indiana (1970-1990). He has authored/co-authored five books and published numerous articles on Anabaptism, the Amish, Hutterites, and Mennonites. He currently serves on the executive of the (Goshen) Mennonite Historical Society.

Walter Klaassen, professor emeritus in Religious Studies and History, University of Waterloo, taught at Conrad Grebel University College from 1964 until his retirement in 1986. Author of several books and many scholarly articles, his translations of sixteenth-century texts remain in use in the popular anthology *Anabaptism in Outline* and the co-translation (with William Klassen) of *Writings of Pilgram Marpeck*. He has published a biography of Pilgram Marpeck, co-authored with William Klassen (2008).

Sydney Penner received a doctorate in philosophy from Cornell University, and subsequently completed a postdoctoral fellowship at Merton College, University of Oxford. Currently he teaches philosophy at Asbury University in Wilmore, Kentucky. Penner now focuses on sixteenth- and seventeenth-century scholastics, especially Francisco Suárez. He maintains a website of Suárez translations and resources.

C. Arnold Snyder is professor emeritus of History, University of Waterloo. He taught at Conrad Grebel University College from 1985 until his retirement in 2011. His research continues to focus on sixteenth-century Anabaptism. He has written several books on this topic, including *Anabaptist History and Theology: An Introduction*, and has also published numerous articles.

J. C. Wenger (d. 1995) was a long-time professor of history and theology, first at Goshen College and then at Goshen Biblical Seminary, where he worked closely with Harold S. Bender. He was an active church leader and a prolific author, publishing some twenty books and many articles and pamphlets.

www.ingramcontent.com/pod-product-compliance
Lightning Source LLC
Chambersburg PA
CBHW052132010526
44113CB00035B/1928